INTERNATIONAL MONETARY AND FINANCIAL ECONOMICS

Joseph P. Daniels

Department of Economics
Marquette University

David D. VanHoose

Department of Economics
University of Alabama

South-Western College Publishing

an International Thomson Publishing company I(T)P®

Cincinnati • Albany • Boston • Detroit • Johannesburg • London • Madrid • Melbourne • Mexico City
New York • Pacific Grove • San Francisco • Scottsdale • Singapore • Tokyo • Toronto

Team Director: Jack Calhoun
Acquiring Editor: Keri Witman
Developmental Editor: Jan Lamar
Production Editor: Deanna Quinn
Production House: Shepherd, Inc.
Cover Designer: Jennifer Lynne Martin
Cover Photograph: Bill Frymire/Masterfile
Marketing Manager: Lisa L. Lysne
Manufacturing Coordinator: Georgina Calderon

Library of Congress Cataloging-in-Publication Data
Daniels, Joseph
    International monetary and financial economics / Joseph Daniels,
David VanHoose.
        p.   cm.
    Includes index.
    ISBN 0-538-87533-X (alk. paper)
    1. International finance.   I. VanHoose, David
II. Title.
HG3881.D3264   1999
332.1′5–dc21   98-28157
                                                           CIP

BRIEF CONTENTS

UNIT THREE: CENTRAL BANKS, EXCHANGE RATES, AND BALANCE-OF-PAYMENTS DETERMINATION 233

UNIT FOUR: OPEN ECONOMY MACROECONOMICS AND POLICY ANALYSIS 333

CONTENTS

UNIT TWO: INTERNATIONAL FINANCIAL INSTRUMENTS, MARKETS, AND INSTITUTIONS 101

UNIT THREE: CENTRAL BANKS, EXCHANGE RATES, AND BALANCE-OF-PAYMENTS DETERMINATION 233

Chapter 9: Traditional Approaches to Exchange-Rate and Balance-of-Payments Determination 280

Chapter 12: Economic Policy with Fixed Exchange Rates 373

PREFACE

TO THE INSTRUCTOR

Instructors we know typically spend considerable time and effort trying to find accessible textbooks that cover the full range of topics they wish to discuss in a course in international money and finance. There are a number of texts that concentrate on international finance, and there are several good books on open-economy macroeconomics. Our key objective in writing *International Monetary and Financial Economics* was to develop a book that encompasses these broad areas, as well as important topics in international money and banking, thereby simplifying the instructor's efforts to cover all relevant topics in international monetary and financial economics. This led us to write a book that accomplishes the following:

- The economics of spot and forward exchange markets, spatial and triangular arbitrage, purchasing power parity, and interest parity are clearly presented.
- Markets for international financial instruments, including derivative securities, receive considerable attention, as do such topics as the Eurocurrency markets, vehicle currencies, and international financial market linkages.
- Considerable attention is devoted to issues in international banking, including topics in payment systems, bank regulation, and the role of central banks.
- Traditional, monetary, and portfolio approaches to the balance of payments are covered in depth.
- The implications of varying degrees of capital mobility, international interdependence, and aggregate price flexibility for monetary and fiscal policies under fixed and floating exchange rates are examined both in a basic small-open-economy setting and in the context of pedagogically straightforward two-country frameworks.

FEATURES THAT TEACH AND REINFORCE

Our belief is that a text in international monetary and financial economics should include discussions of real-world applications. To motivate student learning, we have included examples drawn from nations throughout the world. In addition, two features are incorporated throughout the text.

Policy Notebooks

International monetary and financial policy issues dominate the news. Hence, features covering a wide range of important policy issues appear at appropriate locations. Topics covered include the following:

- Too Many Zaires in Zaire
- Are European Payment System Policies on "TARGET"?
- Central Bank Profit Sharing–An Impediment to European Monetary Union?
- Bank Reserve Requirements–On the Way Out, or In?
- The United States and Canada–"J-Curves" or "S-Curves?"
- Inducing Russians to Pay Their Taxes
- Thailand's Penalty for Sticking to Its Guns
- Fiscal Stimulus by Trading Partners–Good News or Bad News?

Management Notebooks

Businesspeople can no longer ignore international developments, which continually present both opportunities and challenges. To acquaint students with the variety of international financial issues faced by managers, we have included features on topics such as the following:

- Why a Country Is Not Like a Corporation
- Trends and Trade-Offs in Currency Hedging
- Are Credit Derivatives the Wave of the Future?
- Would You Like Fries with that PPP? The Big Mac Index
- The "Japan Premium"
- Changes in the Value of the U.S. Dollar and the Price of Luxury German Autos
- Profit Sharing–Is the Market Working?
- All in a Day's Work–Depending on Where You Live

Critical-Thinking Exercises

Critical thinking is an important aspect of every college student's education. We make sure that students are introduced to critical-thinking activities by ending each *Policy Notebook* and *Management Notebook* with critical-thinking questions called "For Critical Analysis."

GLOBAL ACCESS TO THE INTERNET: THE WORLD WIDE WEB

Today, students around the world know how to use the Internet. We provide two very useful features for them:

1. **Margin URLs:** A feature entitled "On the Web" appears in the left-hand margin throughout the text. At appropriate locations relative to text discussions, a URL is presented.
2. **Chapter-Ending On-Line Applications:** Each chapter concludes with an extensive Internet exercise, which guides the student to a particular URL and provides a set of application questions.

SPECIAL NOTE ON THE GRAPHS

We have spent considerable effort in developing over 175 graphs for this textbook. All schedules are shaded in a consistent manner to assist students in understanding the relationships between the various schedules. In addition, we have provided full explanations in captions that appear below or alongside each graph or set of graphs.

KEY PEDAGOGY

Student learning must be an active process. We have included an ample number of pedagogical devices to help students master the material.

Fundamental Issues and Answers Within the Text of Each Chapter

A unique feature of *International Monetary and Financial Economics* is the inclusion of five to seven fundamental issues at the opening of each chapter. At appropriate locations within the chapter, these fundamental issues are repeated and appropriate answers are provided. This allows the student to immediately see the relationship between the text materials and the fundamental issues while reading the chapter.

Vocabulary Is Emphasized

Vocabulary is often a stumbling block in economics courses, and this can be a particular difficulty for students in a course in international economics. Consequently, we have **boldfaced** all important vocabulary terms within the text. These boldfaced terms are defined both in the margin and in the end-of-text glossary.

Chapter Summary

The chapter summary follows a numbered point-by-point format that corresponds to the chapter-opening fundamental issues, further reinforcing the full circular nature of the learning process for each chapter.

Questions and Problems

Each chapter ends with several questions and problems. Suggested answers are provided in the *Instructor's Manual.*

References and Recommended Readings

Appropriate references for materials in the chapter are given in this section.

INSTRUCTOR'S MANUAL/TEST BANK

The *Instructor's Manual/Text Bank,* which was written by Peter Pedroni, is designed to simplify the teaching tasks faced by instructors of courses in international money and finance. It provides chapter learning objectives, chapter outlines, summaries of in-text pedagogy, answers to end-of-chapter questions and problems, and multiple-choice test questions.

ACKNOWLEDGMENTS

We benefited from an extremely active and conscientious group of reviewers of the manuscript for this first edition of *International Monetary and Financial Economics.* Several of the reviewers went above and beyond the call of duty, and our rewrites of the manuscript improved accordingly. To the following reviewers, we extend our sincere appreciation for the critical nature of your comments, which we feel helped make this a better text.

Moshen Bahmani
University of Wisconsin, Milwaukee

Charles Britton
University of Arkansas

Jay H. Bryson
*International Finance Division
Federal Reserve System*

Tom Grennes
North Carolina State University

Alan G. Issac
American University

Bruce Mizrach
Rutgers University, New Brunswick

Robert G. Murphy
Boston College

Robert Schlack
Carthage College

Cynthia Royal Tori
*University of North Carolina
at Charlotte*

William Walsh
University of St. Thomas

Roy VanTil
University of Maine, Farmington

Of course, no textbook project is done by the authors alone. We wish to
thank our development editor, Jan Lamar, and the economics editor, Keri Witman, for their assistance. Our production editor, Deanna Quinn, put together
an excellent design and provided consistent guidance throughout the project.
The copy editor, Cheryl L. Ferguson, masterfully rearranged our manuscript to
make the book read more smoothly.

We anticipate revising this text for years to come and therefore welcome all
comments and criticism from students and instructors alike.

J.P.D.
D.D.V.

INTERNATIONAL PAYMENTS AND EXCHANGE

KEEPING UP WITH A CHANGING WORLD—GROSS DOMESTIC PRODUCT, PRICE INDEXES, AND THE BALANCE OF PAYMENTS

FUNDAMENTAL ISSUES

1. What is gross domestic product?

2. What is the difference between nominal GDP and real GDP?

3. What are the consumer price index and the producer price index?

4. What is a country's balance of payments, and what does this measure?

5. What does it mean for a country to be a net debtor or net creditor?

During the middle-eighteenth century, a group of French economists, known as the Physiocrats, developed the basics of a national income accounting system. An early founder of this school of economic thought was François Quesnay. Quesnay was a scholar of medical science who, early in the seventeenth century, had researched the circulatory system of the human body. During his career, Quesnay served the royal household as the physician of the king. Quesnay and his colleagues borrowed from their studies of physical science to make great technical contributions to economics.

One significant contribution was a circular flow model of the economy, not unlike the circulatory system of the human body. Quesnay called this model of national income the tableau économique. *Agriculture was at the core of this model. It assumed that one dollar of farm cost generated one dollar of farm revenue and one dollar of farm product, or* produit net. *Successive rounds of expenditures, therefore, eventually generated the national income of the economy for that year.*

Today we devote considerable resources to measuring the overall performance of national economies. Various agencies within national governments and international organizations undertake this monumental task. Nonetheless, the approach to national income accounting used today still has the tableau économique *at its heart.*

With this chapter we embark upon our study of international monetary and financial markets. We begin by considering why it is important to understand international money and finance. We then examine some of the most important economic measures needed to study international money and finance: a nation's output, its price level, and its trade with other nations.

WHY IT IS IMPORTANT TO UNDERSTAND INTERNATIONAL MONEY AND FINANCE

We begin a new century on the heels of a series of fascinating events in the global monetary and financial markets. These include the continuing variability in the value of the dollar, a collapse in the value of the Mexican peso, the failure of Barings Bank, struggles to achieve European monetary unification, the growth of foreign direct investment in the United States, the developing financial and monetary systems of Central and Eastern Europe and of China, and the financial crises of the nations of Southeast Asia.

Firms and individuals have expanded their business and investment activities internationally, making these events increasingly important to all of us. As a result, student interest in international economics has grown considerably. In particular, international financial and monetary economics is a topic of increasing interest because it examines how the world monetary and financial system works. This knowledge, in turn, helps us in understanding the significant global economic events of our age.

Before we begin our examination of international monetary and financial economics, we must understand how to measure the economic activity of a nation. In this chapter, we will examine the key measures that economists and statisticians have developed to track the output, prices, and trade of nations. We begin with a conceptual model of a nation's economy, the circular flow model of income and product.

THE CIRCULAR FLOW OF INCOME AND PRODUCT

To track the overall performances of national economies and the transactions between economies, we require aggregate, or *macroeconomic,* performance measures. These measures include gross domestic product and national income, price indexes, and the balance of payments. We begin with the most important of these macroeconomic variables, *gross domestic product (GDP).*

Gross Domestic Product

GROSS DOMESTIC PRODUCT (GDP) The market value of all final goods and services produced within a nation's borders during a given period.

Economists cannot simply add together the quantities of very different items such as annual oil production, the provision of educational services, and the production of stereo equipment, because their units of measurement are different. We therefore total the *market values* of all final goods and services, measured in terms of prices and expressed in units of a nation's currency. Hence, **gross domestic product (GDP)** is the total of all *final* goods and services produced *domestically* during a given interval (such as a year) and valued at market prices.

Economists include only the final goods and services that individuals, businesses, and governments exchange in *markets.* They multiply market prices of goods and services by the quantities of these goods and services produced and sold during a given interval, such as a year. For this reason, GDP excludes non-market transactions such as house-cleaning services, yard work, or fence painting provided by roommates or family members. This activity does not take place in a formal market in which the spouse or roommate receives payment for providing such services. In addition, because GDP measures a nation's production, it includes only the values of *goods and services.* GDP does not include the exchange of stocks, bonds, or other such financial assets, which do not involve the production of new output.

Finally, GDP counts only the production of goods and services in their *final form* during a specific interval. If a computer manufacturer purchases microchips from various suppliers and uses them in the production of laptop computers and sells the assembled computers within the same year, then only the final price of the *computer* counts in tabulating that year's GDP. The market value of the microchips is not separately included in GDP because their market value is reflected in the sale price of the laptop computers.

Nevertheless, if the computer manufacturer stores some microchips or perhaps some partially assembled laptop computers at its assembling facility, then we count the market values of these microchips—as well as all partially assembled and unsold assembled computers—as *inventory investment* for that year. Inventory investment includes all of the production during the year that firms did not sell for final consumption. The tabulation of GDP always includes such inventory investment, which ensures that GDP measures all production during a given year.

GDP also includes the value of *depreciation,* which is the value of *capital goods* such as machines or tools that are repaired or replaced if businesses are to maintain their existing amount of capital. Depreciation expenses reflect the consumption of or wear and tear on physical capital that occurs during the current-year production of goods and services. The term *gross* means that GDP does not adjust for depreciation. Economists subtract depreciation from GDP to *obtain net domestic product.*

The Equality of Income and the Value of Product

To visualize the components of GDP, consider Figure 1–1. This figure displays a basic *circular flow diagram,* which is an illustration of the total flows of income and product in the economy. Business firms use factor services such as labor, service flows from capital goods, service flows from land, and entrepreneurial skills to produce goods and services, which they sell in *product markets.* Individuals and families, called *households,* buy these goods and services with the income they earn by providing factor services to firms. Households receive this income as wages and salaries, interest, rents, and profits. *Factor markets* are the markets for labor, service flows from capital and land, and entrepreneurial skills. Factor markets determine the values of the factor services that households provide.

In short, the circular flow diagram shows that households use the income that they earn from providing factor services to purchase the product of firms. The total value of the circular flow in Figure 1–1, therefore, is always equal to GDP. Thus, we may conclude the following:

GDP serves both as a measure of a national economy's total output of goods and services *and* as a measure of the total income of all individuals in that economy.

FIGURE 1-1   THE CIRCULAR FLOW OF INCOME AND PRODUCT

Business firms make factor payments to households in return for the use of households' factor services. The total value of these factor payments constitutes total household income, which households spend on the goods and services that firms produce. The aggregate value of these goods and services is gross domestic product (GDP).

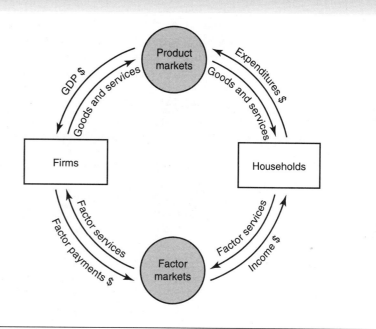

This is so because the production of output generates the total income of households.

Hence, we can refer to GDP both as a measure of total national output and as an overall measure of a nation's income. Although many nations make slight accounting distinctions between GDP and national income, on a purely conceptual level the two are equivalent.

ESSENTIALS OF NATIONAL INCOME ACCOUNTING

The circular flow diagram illustrates that economists can tabulate GDP in two ways. One way to compute GDP is to add together all expenditures on goods and services produced and sold or counted as inventory investment. The other is to sum all income earnings of households. Figure 1–1 indicates that either approach should yield the same value for GDP. Indeed, *national income accounts,* which are the formal tabulations of aggregate incomes and levels of GDP for countries around the world, incorporate both of these approaches to calculating GDP.

The Product Approach to GDP

The product approach to GDP tabulation determines the magnitude of the upper flow, through the product markets, that Figure 1–1 depicts. Hence, the product approach for a nation's income and product focuses on GDP as a measure of a nation's total output of goods and services. Under the product approach, economists simply sum the total expenditures on final goods and services produced during a given year.

Table 1–1 uses the U.S. national income accounts to illustrate the product approach to GDP computation. The product approach tabulates four fundamental forms of expenditures on final goods and services:

1. *Consumption spending* is household expenditures on domestically produced goods and services.
2. *Investment spending* includes business spending on capital goods and inventories as well as household and firm investment in residential and business construction.
3. *Government spending* is the total amount of expenditures on goods and services by state, local, and federal governments.
4. *Net export spending* is equal to total expenditures on domestically produced goods and services by residents of other nations, less spending on foreign-produced goods and services by domestic residents.

Table 1–1 shows that in 1997, net export spending in the United States was negative. This indicates that, in dollar terms, spending by U.S. residents on foreign goods and services exceeded foreign spending on U.S.-produced goods and services. The sum of all four types of spending on domestically produced final goods and services during a year is that year's GDP.

TABLE 1–1	THE PRODUCT APPROACH TO CALCULATING GROSS DOMESTIC PRODUCT			
	1981	**1986**	**1991**	**1997**
Consumption spending	1,941.3	2,892.7	3,975.1	5,485.8
Investment spending	556.2	722.5	736.2	1,242.5
Government spending	633.4	938.5	1,225.9	1,452.7
Net export spending	–15.0	–131.5	–20.5	–101.1
Gross domestic product	3,115.9	4,422.2	5,916.7	8,079.9

SOURCE: 1998 *Economic Report of the President* and *Economic Indicators* (various issues).
NOTE: Amounts are in billions of dollars.

The Income Approach to GDP

Table 1–2 displays the *income approach* to computing GDP. This approach measures the lower flow (through the factor markets) in the circular flow diagram in Figure 1–1. Economists follow a four-step process in the income approach to GDP calculations.

1. Sum all wages and salaries, interest income, rental income, and profits to obtain national income, which is the total of all factor earnings in the economy.
2. Add indirect taxes, which are sales and excise taxes that artificially reduce reported income flows to national income, to obtain *net national product* (NNP).
3. Add depreciation to obtain *gross national product* (GNP).
4. Subtract *net factor income from abroad*—income earned by domestic factors from production that occurs abroad, less income earned by foreign factors from production that takes place in the domestic economy—from gross national product, GNP.

GNP and GDP, as shown in Table 1–2, are different measures of a nation's output. GNP measures the market value of newly produced final goods and services using a nation's factors of production, regardless of where those factors are located in the world. GDP, on the other hand, measures the market value of final goods and services newly produced within the nation's borders, regardless of the ownership of the factors used to produce it.

TABLE 1–2 THE INCOME APPROACH TO CALCULATING GROSS DOMESTIC PRODUCT

	1981	1986	1991	1997
Wages and salaries	1,827.8	2,572.4	3,457.9	4,703.6
Interest income	234.5	363.1	448.0	448.7
Rental income	45.7	42.3	68.4	147.9
Business profits	362.2	538.7	745.4	1,349.5
National income	2,470.2	3,516.5	4,719.7	6,649.7
Indirect taxes and transfers	260.5	365.7	489.6	654.9
Net national product	2,730.7	3,882.2	5,209.3	7,304.6
Depreciation	419.9	552.9	723.1	868.0
Gross national product	3,150.6	4,435.1	5,932.4	8,172.6
Net income payments abroad	–34.7	–12.9	–15.7	–92.7
Gross domestic product	3,115.9	4,422.2	5,916.7	8,079.9

SOURCE: 1998 *Economic Report of the President; Economic Indicators.*
NOTE: Amounts are in billions of dollars.

The Limitations of GDP

Although economists have found GDP to be invaluable in measuring the absolute and relative economic performances of the world's nations, GDP is not a perfect measure. For one thing, including only market transactions in GDP is problematic if countries have different definitions of legal versus illegal activities. For instance, a nation in which currency exchange is legal includes the income of currency traders in GDP, because traders report their trading income as a legal activity. In a country in which governments declare possession of other nations' currencies to be illegal, however, currency traders do not report their incomes from such endeavors. Hence, that country's reported GDP does not count those incomes. In addition, GDP includes only the value of goods and services traded in markets. It excludes nonmarket production, such as the home-maintenance services of family members discussed earlier. This can complicate efforts to compare the GDP of a highly developed, industrialized nation with the GDP of a less-developed, mostly agrarian country, because nonmarket production typically is more important in less-developed nations.

Furthermore, GDP is not necessarily a good measure of the overall well being of a nation's residents. The production of some goods, such as paper or electrical power, can create negative spillovers for the environment. For instance, paper mills require trees, and poor timber management can destroy forests, and the particulate emissions in the production of electrical power can cause air and soil pollution. Consequently, it is important to recognize that GDP is only a measure of production and an indicator of economic activity. It is not necessarily a measure of welfare.

FUNDAMENTAL ISSUE #1

What is gross domestic product? Gross domestic product (GDP) is the value, at market prices, of all final goods and services produced within a nation's borders during a given period. According to the product approach, GDP is the total of consumption spending, investment spending, government expenditures, and net export spending. According to the income approach, GDP is the total of all wages and salaries, net interest, rental income, profits, indirect taxes, and depreciation generated from the production of output that occurs within the nation's borders.

FIGURE 1-2   NOMINAL GDP OF SELECTED NATIONS

Nominal GDP has increased each year in the United States, Germany, Mexico, and South Korea because actual production has risen and because the price level has increased.

SOURCE: Data from International Monetary Fund, *International Financial Statistics.*

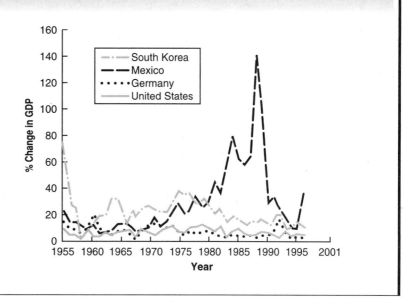

ACCOUNTING FOR INFLATION: PRICE DEFLATORS AND REAL GDP

Figure 1–2 shows that GDP for the United States, Germany, Mexico, and South Korea has risen each year since 1955. There are two reasons for these increases. One is that in most years the nation's production of goods and services has actually increased. During this period, businesses in these countries expanded their resources and developed innovative ways to increase their production.

This does not mean that these nations' actual production increased in every year, however. Aggregate production actually declined in some years, even though GDP for those years increased. The reason that measured GDP still rose in such years is that the prices of goods and services increased in almost every year. Because economists compute GDP using market prices to value the production of firms, general price increases, or inflation, raise the *measured value* of output. Thus, we cannot conclude from Figure 1–2 that total production of goods and services actually increased every year. At least a part of the overall rise in the annual GDP data in the figure occurred because of inflation.

Nominal GDP, Real GDP, and the GDP Price Deflator

It follows that relying on GDP data that are unadjusted for inflation would, during periods when inflation is prevalent, result in persistent *overstatements* of the true amount of aggregate production. Making reliable comparisons of an economy's year-to-year level of aggregate production thereby requires adjusting GDP figures to account for inflation.

Real versus Nominal GDP   Consider a situation in which it is clear why we need to adjust for inflation. Suppose that your employer were to promise you a 10 percent annual wage increase. If the prices of all goods and services remained unchanged, then the purchasing power of your labor income would rise by 10 percent. If the prices of the goods and services you consume were to increase by 10 percent during the coming year, however, then the pay raise would do nothing more than maintain your purchasing power. As a result, your *real* income, or income adjusted for price changes, would be no higher than it was before the wage increase.

Likewise, if GDP were to rise by 10 percent from one year to the next only because the prices of goods and services rose at that rate, then the aggregate production of goods and services actually would not have changed. The year-to-year change in GDP, then, would be a very poor measure of the *real* annual change in aggregate production.

Economists have addressed this problem by developing an inflation-adjusted measure of GDP, known as **real gross domestic product,** or *real GDP.* This measure of aggregate output takes price changes into account. As a result, real GDP better gauges the economy's true volume of productive activity.

To keep real GDP and the unadjusted GDP measures separate, economists classify the unadjusted GDP measure as **nominal gross domestic product,** or *nominal GDP.* This means that nominal GDP is computed in current dollar terms without any adjustment for inflation.

The GDP Price Deflator   Real GDP is intended to gauge a nation's actual production volume. Thus, multiplying real GDP by a measure of the overall price level for all goods and services should render the value of real GDP in terms of current prices, which, by definition, is nominal GDP. Let's denote real GDP as y and the overall price level as P. Then it follows that nominal GDP, which we shall denote as Y, must be

$$Y \equiv y \times P.$$

Hence, nominal GDP is equal to real GDP times the overall price level.

Economists call the factor P the **GDP price deflator,** or simply the *GDP deflator.* We call P a *deflator* because if we rearrange the previous equation to solve for y, we obtain

$$y \equiv \frac{Y}{P}.$$

Thus, real GDP (y) is equal to nominal GDP (Y) adjusted by dividing, or "deflating," by the factor P. For example, suppose that South Korean nominal GDP measured in current prices, Y, is equal to 351.3 trillion won (KW 351.3 trillion) but the value of the GDP deflator, P, is equal to 1.36. Computing real GDP, then, entails dividing the KW 351.3 trillion nominal GDP by 1.36, to get KW 257.5 trillion for South Korean real GDP.

REAL GROSS DOMESTIC PRODUCT A price-adjusted measure of aggregate output, or nominal GDP divided by the GDP price deflator.

NOMINAL GROSS DOMESTIC PRODUCT The current market value of all final goods and services produced by a nation during a given period with no adjustment for prices.

GDP PRICE DEFLATOR A measure of the overall price level; equal to nominal gross domestic product divided by real gross domestic product.

BASE YEAR A reference year for price-level comparisons, which is a year in which nominal GDP is equal to real GDP, so that the GDP deflator's value is equal to one.

Denoting a Base Year A value of 1.36 for the GDP deflator P gives us little useful information unless we also have a point of reference for judging what this value means. Economists provide such a reference point by defining a **base year** for the GDP deflator. A base year is a year in which nominal GDP is equal to real GDP ($Y = y$), so that the value of the GDP deflator by definition is equal to one ($P = 1$). Therefore, if the base year were, say, 1975, and the value of P in 2000 were equal to 2, then this would indicate that between 1975 and 2000 the overall level of prices would have doubled.

The International Monetary Fund (IMF), an international organization that maintains and provides data for many countries, currently uses 1990 as the base year for the GDP deflator. Figure 1–3a shows the values of the South Korean GDP deflator since 1955. As you can see, the overall level of prices increased by almost a factor of 150, from 0.009 to 1.36 between 1955 and 1995. This means that an item that required KW1 to purchase in 1955 would have required nearly KW150 to purchase in 1995.

Figure 1–3b plots South Korea's real and nominal GDP figures since 1955. Note that in 1990, nominal and real GDP are equal because 1990 is the base year in which $P = 1$, so that $Y = y$. Clearly, adjusting for price changes has a significant effect on our interpretation of GDP data. This is why it is so important for us to convert nominal GDP into real GDP using the GDP price deflator. Thus:

> **Only real GDP data can provide useful information about true year-to-year changes in an economy's productive performance.**

FUNDAMENTAL ISSUE #2

What is the difference between nominal GDP and real GDP?
Nominal GDP is the total value of newly produced goods and services computed using the prices at which they sold during the year they were produced. In contrast, real GDP is the value of final goods and services after adjusting for the effects of year-to-year price changes. The basic approach to calculating real GDP is to divide nominal GDP by the GDP deflator, which is a measure of the level of prices relative to prices for a base year.

Fixed- and Flexible-Weight Price Measures

The GDP deflator is an example of a *price index*. A price index is a measure of the general price level calculated by tracking the prices of a specific set of goods and services from period to period (usually month to month). As in the

Figure 1–3   The GDP Deflator and Real and Nominal GDP

Panel (*a*) shows annual values of the GDP deflator for South Korea. Panel (*b*) displays South Korean nominal GDP and real GDP. As panel (*b*) shows, because real GDP accounts for changes in prices, it exhibits less growth each year.

SOURCE: Data from International Monetary Fund, *International Financial Statistics.*

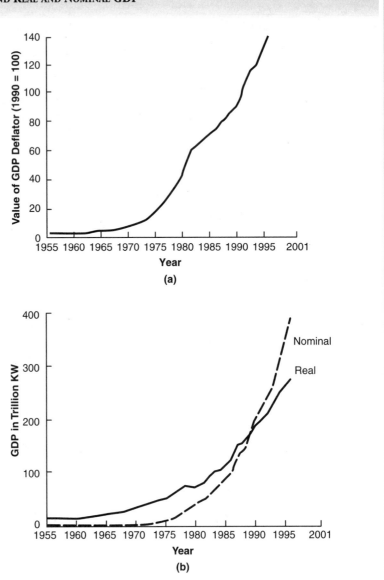

case of the GDP deflator, economists must select a base year for any alternative price index. In addition, economists must also determine the types of goods and services and their significance in the index. Weighting the goods in the index usually follows two types of approaches: a flexible-weight basis or a fixed-weight basis.

ON THE WEB
To obtain various GDP measurements on a wide variety of countries, visit the Penn World Tables at:
http://datacentre.epas. utoronto.ca:5680/pwt

CONSUMER PRICE INDEX (CPI) A weighted sum of prices of goods and services that the government determines a typical consumer purchases each year.

PRODUCER PRICE INDEX (PPI) A weighted average of the prices of goods and services that the government determines a typical business purchases from other businesses during a given period.

The GDP Price Deflator: A Flexible-Weight Price Index The GDP price deflator employed in the previous section to convert nominal GDP to real GDP is an example of a flexible-weight price index. A flexible-weight price index is a price index in which weights on various goods and services change automatically as the output of goods and services varies over time.

Fixed-Weight Price Indexes Alternative measures of the overall price level are fixed-weight price indexes. Economists calculate the measures of the economy-wide price level by selecting a fixed set of goods and services and then tracking the prices of these specific goods and services from year to year.

As a simple example of such a fixed-weight price index, let's construct one of our own. Let's call it the "college consumer price index." Suppose that the "typical" college student spends one-fourth of his or her available resources on tuition, one-fourth on housing, one-fourth on food and clothing, and one-fourth on supplies and other expenses. We could then go out and collect information on the average prices of each of these components of the typical college student's expenses. Then we could multiply each one by one-fourth. Summing the results would then yield a numerical value for our college consumer price index.

The Consumer and Producer Price Indexes The agencies of national governments compute actual, overall **consumer price indexes (CPIs)** in the same basic manner as in our fictitious example. CPIs, however, are weighted sums of prices of a full set of goods and services that governments determine typical domestic consumers purchase. Various categories of expenditures that governments incorporate into their weighting scheme for CPIs are a typical consumer's annual purchases of food and beverages, shelter, fuel and other utilities, transportation, and medical care. In the United States, the Bureau of Labor Statistics (BLS) is the government agency that collects the price data to compute the CPI. The BLS samples prices on about 95,000 different items. In addition, the BLS calculates a number of alternative consumer price indexes, such as CPIs for urban consumers, for rural consumers, and so on.

Another fixed-weight price index that many governments calculate is the **producer price index (PPI).** This is a weighted average of prices of goods that a typical business firm purchases from other businesses and then uses in its own production process. Like the CPI, most governments compute several versions of the PPI. The basic categories used in various PPI weighting schemes are finished goods; intermediate materials, supplies, and components; crude materials that require extensive additional processing by a business firm; and food materials.

For reasons discussed shortly, economists often prefer to use the GDP deflator as a basic measure of the overall, or economy-wide, price level. Nevertheless, as you know from your own experience, the media most commonly report inflation rates using annual percentage changes in the CPI. Further, the United States and many other countries use the CPI to adjust certain government benefits, such as government pensions and welfare payments, to account for price changes.

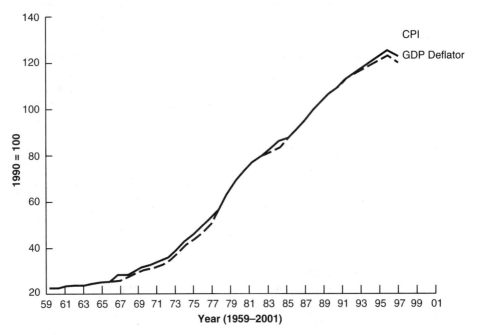

FIGURE 1–4   U.S. GDP DEFLATOR AND CONSUMER PRICE INDEX

Although the U.S. GDP deflator and the U.S. CPI are computed differently, they tend to move closely together over time.

SOURCE: Data from International Monetary Fund, *International Financial Statistics,* and other estimates.

We should note, however, that the GDP price deflator and the CPI generally give us the same basic indications about the overall price level. Figure 1–4 shows annual values of the GDP price deflator and the CPI for the United States from 1959 through 1998. As you can see, both follow roughly the same path. From a broad perspective, therefore, both price measures provide similar information.

ON THE WEB
To obtain monthly consumer price and producer price information, visit the United States Bureau of Labor Statistics at:
http://stats.bls.gov

FUNDAMENTAL ISSUE #3

What are the consumer price index and the producer price index?
The CPI and PPI are weighted-average measures of the overall price level, in which the weights of different goods are invariant over time. The consumer price index is a weighted average of the prices of goods and services purchased by a representative consumer, and the producer price index is a weighted average of the prices that businesses pay for goods that they buy from other firms.

THE BALANCE OF PAYMENTS

BALANCE OF PAYMENTS SYSTEM
A system of accounts that measures transactions of goods, services, income, and financial assets between domestic residents, businesses, and governments and the rest of the world during a specific time period.

The **balance of payments** is a complete tabulation of the total market value of goods, services, and financial assets that domestic residents, firms, and governments exchange with residents of other nations during a given period. Like gross domestic product, a nation's *balance of payments* is a system that accounts for flows of income and expenditures. Unlike gross domestic product, however, the balance of payments includes the flow of financial assets. Figure 1–5 provides a summary statement of the U.S. balance of payments system that we shall refer to throughout the next several sections of this chapter. The statement is provided every quarter by the U.S. Commerce Department in the *Survey of Current Business.*

Balance of Payments as a Double-Entry Bookkeeping System

A *double-entry bookkeeping system* records both sides of any two-party transaction with two separate and offsetting entries: a debit entry and a credit entry. The result is that the sum of all the debit entries, in absolute value, is equal to the sum of all the credit entries. The balance of payments system is like a typical double-entry accounting system in that every transaction results in two entries being made in the balance of payments accounts. A **debit entry** records a transaction that results in a domestic resident making a payment abroad. A debit entry has a negative value in the balance of payment account. A **credit entry** records a transaction that results in a domestic resident receiving a payment from abroad. A credit entry has a positive value in the balance of payment account.

DEBIT ENTRY A negative entry in the balance of payments that records a transaction resulting in a payment abroad by a domestic resident.

CREDIT ENTRY A positive entry in the balance of payments that records a transaction resulting in a payment from abroad to a domestic resident.

In the balance of payments accounts, an international transaction that results in a credit entry would also generate an offsetting debit entry, and an international transaction that results in a debit entry would also generate an offsetting credit entry. In the balance of payments accounts, therefore, the sum of all the credit entries is equal to, in absolute value, the sum of all the debit entries.

To illustrate the double-entry nature of the balance of payments system, consider the following example. Suppose a U.S. manufacturer exports a computer to a Canadian firm in exchange for a payment of $2,000. Table 1–3 (page 19) shows the transaction's effects on the U.S. balance of payments. The export of the computer is a $2,000 credit, because it results in a $2,000 payment being made to the U.S. firm from the Canadian firm. Because of the double-entry nature of the system, there is an offsetting $2,000 debit entry made. Note that the sum of the debits in absolute value, $2,000, is equal to the sum of the credits, $2,000.

Balance of Payments Accounts

Countries exchange a vast array of goods, services, and financial assets. Economists group these transactions by type. There are different categories for each

FIGURE 1–5 SUMMARY STATEMENT OF THE U.S. BALANCE OF PAYMENTS FROM THE *SURVEY OF CURRENT BUSINESS*

LINE	(CREDITS +: DEBITS −)[1]	1996	1997
1	**Exports of goods, services, and income**	**1,055,233**	**1,167,610**
2	Goods, adjusted, excluding military[2]	612,069	678,348
3	Services[3]	236,764	253,220
4	Transfers under U.S. military agency sales contracts[4]	14,647	15,175
5	Travel	69,908	74,407
6	Passenger fares	20,567	21,710
7	Other transportation	27,216	28,194
8	Royalties and license fees[5]	29,974	30,269
9	Other private services[5]	73,569	82,681
10	U.S. Government miscellaneous services	893	784
11	Income receipts on U.S. assets abroad	206,400	236,043
12	Direct investment receipts	98,890	109,227
13	Other private receipts	102,866	123,278
14	U.S. Government receipts	4,644	3,538
15	**Imports of goods, services, and income**	**−1,163,450**	**−1,295,530**
16	Goods, adjusted, excluding military[2]	−803,239	−877,282
17	Services[3]	−156,634	−167,929
18	Direct defense expenditures	−10,861	−11,345
19	Travel	−48,739	−52,029
20	Passenger fares	−15,776	−16,927
21	Other transportation	−28,453	−29,771
22	Royalties and license fees[5]	−7,322	−7,512
23	Other private services[5]	−42,796	−47,548
24	U.S. Government miscellaneous services	−2,768	−2,796
25	Income payments on foreign assets in the United States	−203,577	−250,320
26	Direct investment payments	−32,132	−41,527
27	Other private payments	−100,103	−117,712
28	U.S. Government payments	−71,342	−91,081
29	**Unilateral transfers, net**	**−39,968**	**−38,526**
30	U.S. Government grants[4]	−14,933	−11,688
31	U.S. Government pensions and other transfers	−4,331	−4,075
32	Private remittances and other transfers[6]	−20,704	−22,763
33	**U.S. assets abroad, not (increase/capital outflow (-))**	**−562,444**	**−426,938**
34	U.S. official reserve assets, net[7]	6,668	−1,010
35	Gold		
36	Special drawing rights	370	−350
37	Reserve position in the international Monetary Fund	−1,260	−3,575
38	Foreign currencies	7,578	2,915
39	U.S. Government assets, other than official reserve assets, net	−690	177
40	U.S. credits and other long-term assets	−4,930	−5,237
41	Repayments on U.S. credits and other long-term assets[8]	4,134	5,439
42	U.S. foreign currency holdings and U.S. short-term assets, net	106	−25
43	U.S. private assets, net	−358,422	−426,105
44	Direct investment	−87,813	−119,444
45	Foreign securities	−108,189	−79,287
46	U.S. claims on unaffiliated foreigners reported by U.S. nonbanking concerns	−64,234	−76,298
47	U.S. claims reported by U.S. banks, not included elsewhere	−96,186	−151,076
48	**Foreign assets in the United States, net (increase/capital inflow (+))**	**547,555**	**690,497**
49	Foreign official assets in the United States, net	122,354	18,157
50	U.S. Government securities	115,634	−2,971
51	U.S. Treasury securities[9]	111,253	−7,019
52	Other[10]	4,381	4,048
53	Other U.S. Government liabilities[11]	720	539
54	U.S. liabilities reported by U.S. banks, not included elsewhere	4,722	21,274
55	Other foreign official assets[12]	1,278	−685
56	Other foreign assets in the United States, net	425,201	672,340
57	Direct investment	76,956	107,928
58	U.S. Treasury securities and U.S. currency flows	172,878	187,854
59	U.S. securities other than U.S. Treasury securities	133,798	189,273
60	U.S. liabilities to unaffiliated foreigners reported by U.S. nonbanking concerns	31,786	44,740
61	U.S. liabilities reported by U.S. banks, not included elsewhere	9,784	142,545
62	**Allocations of special drawing rights**		
63	**Statistical discrepancy (sum of above items with sign reversed)**	**−48,927**	**−97,113**
63a	Of which seasonal adjustment discrepancy		
	Memoranda:		
64	Balance on goods (lines 2 and 16)	−191,170	−198,934
65	Balance on services (lines 3 and 17)	80,130	85,291
66	Balance on goods and services (lines 64 and 65)	−111,040	−113,643
67	Balance on investment income (lines 11 and 25)	2,824	−14,277
68	Balance on goods, services, and income (lines 1 and 15 or lines 66 and 67)[13]	−108,216	−127,920
69	Unilateral transfers, net (line 29)	−39,968	−38,526
70	Balance on current account (lines 1, 15, and 29 or lines 68 and 69)[13]	−148,184	−166,446

NOTE: Amounts in $ million.

SOURCE: Data from the *Survey of Current Business*, October, 1997, U.S. Bureau of Economic Analysis, U.S. Department of Commerce.

1. Credits, +: Exports of goods, services, and income; unilateral transfers to United States; capital inflows (increase in foreign assets (U.S. liabilities) or decrease in U.S. assets); decrease in U.S. official reserve assets; increase in foreign official assets in the United States.

Debits, −: Imports of goods, services, and income; unilateral transfers to foreigners; capital outflows (decrease in foreign assets (U.S. liabilities) or increase in U.S. assets); increase in U.S. official reserve assets; decrease in foreign official assets in the United States.

2. Excludes exports of goods under U.S. military agency sales contracts identified in Census export documents, excludes imports of goods under direct defense expenditures identified in Census import documents, and reflects various other adjustments (for valuation, coverage, and timing) of Census statistics to balance of payments basis; see table 2.

3. Includes some goods: Mainly military equipment in line 4; major equipment, other materials, supplies, and petroleum products purchased abroad by U.S. military agencies in line 18; and fuels purchased by airline and steamship operators in lines 7 and 21.

4. Includes transfers of goods and services under U.S. military grant programs.

5. Beginning in 1982, these lines are presented on a gross basis. The definition of exports is revised to exclude U.S. parents' payments to foreign affiliates and to include U.S. affiliates' receipts from foreign parents. The definition of imports is revised to include U.S. parents' payments to foreign affiliates and to exclude U.S. affiliates' receipts from foreign parents.

6. Beginning in 1982, the "other transfers" component includes taxes paid by U.S. private residents to foreign governments and taxes paid by private nonresidents to the U.S. Government.

7. For all areas, amounts outstanding December 31, 1997, were as follows in millions of dollars: Line 34, 69,995; line 35, 11,047; line 36, 10,027; line 37, 18,071; line 38, 30,809. Data are preliminary.

8. Includes sales of foreign obligations to foreigners.

9. Consists of bills, certificates, marketable bonds and notes, and nonmarketable convertible and nonconvertible bonds and notes.

10. Consists of U.S. Treasury and Export–Import Bank obligations, not included elsewhere, and of debt securities of U.S. Government corporations and agencies.

11. Includes, primarily, U.S. Government liabilities associated with military agency sales contracts and other transactions arranged with or through foreign official agencies; see table 4.

12. Consists of investments in U.S. corporate stocks and in debt securities of private corporations and State and local governments.

13. Conceptually, the sum of lines 70 and 62 is equal to "net foreign investment" in the national income and product accounts (NIPA's). However, the foreign transactions account in the NIPA's (a) includes adjustments to the international transactions accounts for the treatment of gold, (b) includes adjustments for the different geographical treatment of transactions with U.S. territories and Puerto Rico, and (c) includes services furnished without payment by financial pension plans except life insurance carriers and private noninsured pension plans. A reconciliation of the balance on goods and services from the international accounts and the NIPA net exports appears in the "Reconciliation and Other Special Tables" section in this issue of the SURVEY OF CURRENT BUSINESS. A reconciliation of the other foreign transactions in the two sets of accounts appears in table 4.5 of the full set of NIPA tables (published annually in the August issue of the SURVEY).

TABLE 1–3	RECORDING A U.S. FIRM'S EXPORT IN THE BALANCE OF PAYMENTS ACCOUNTS		
TRANSACTION	**OFFSETTING ENTRIES**	**CREDIT**	**DEBIT**
Computer export	$2,000 computer exported by the U.S.	$2,000	
	$2,000 payment received by the U.S.		–$2,000

type of transaction, with various categories combined to form accounts. Therefore, the balance of payments system consists of a number of different accounts. Most nations have many accounts. We can understand the balance of payments system, however, by focusing on just three accounts; the current account, the private capital account, and the official settlements balance.

The Current Account   The **current account** measures the flow of goods, services, and income across national borders. It also includes transfers or gifts from the domestic government and residents to foreign residents and governments, as well as foreign transfers to the domestic country. The four basic categories within the current account are goods, services, income, and unilateral transfers. Figure 1–5 shows the exports and imports of goods, services, and income for the United States on lines 1 through 28. Lines 29 through 32 are for the unilateral transfers category. Let's examine each of these four categories of the current account.

Goods   The goods category measures the imports and exports of tangible goods. This category includes trade in foods, industrial materials, capital goods (such as machinery), autos, and consumer goods. An export of any of these items is a credit in the goods category, because this would result in a payment from abroad. An import of any of these items is a debit in the goods category, as this would result in a payment made abroad.

Most economists consider the goods category to be the most accurately measured balance of payments category, because this category measures the trade of tangible items that, in many countries, must be registered with customs agents.

Services   The services category measures the imports and exports of services, tourism and travel, and military transactions. Payments, royalties, or fees received from abroad for providing consulting, insurance, banking, or accounting services, for example, are recorded as credits in the service category. Likewise, payments, royalties, or fees sent abroad for the import of these services are debits in the services category. The services category also includes the import and export of military equipment, services, and aid.

CURRENT ACCOUNT Measures the flow of goods, services, income, and transfers or gifts between domestic residents, businesses, and governments and the rest of the world.

To understand how travel and tourism services appear in the balance of payments, consider a domestic college student who traveled abroad during a semester break. Expenditures by this student on items such as a rail pass and hotel accommodations are imports, or debits, in the services category because these services are, in a sense, imported by the student.

The imports and exports of services are much more difficult to measure than exports and imports of goods. Because a tangible item is not registered at a customs point, it can be very difficult to estimate the amount of services provided internationally. Hence, economists refer to services as *invisibles*.

Income   The income category tabulates interest and dividend payments to foreign residents and governments who hold domestic financial assets. It also includes payments received by domestic residents and governments who hold financial assets abroad.

To illustrate how investment income appears in the balance of payments, suppose a U.K. resident receives an interest payment on a German treasury bill that she holds. The interest payment is an export, or credit, in the income category of the U.K. balance of payments. The interest payment is a credit, because the U.K. resident received payment from abroad. Therefore, income payments received by domestic residents who hold financial assets abroad are credits, or exports, whereas income payments made to foreign residents who hold domestic financial assets are debits, or imports.

It is important to note that economists do not record the *purchase* of a financial asset in the services category. Only the income earned on the financial asset is included in the current account, as income earned on assets can be used for current consumption.

Unilateral Transfers   The unilateral transfers category measures international transfers, or gifts, between individuals and governments. This category, therefore, records the offsetting entries of exports or imports for which nothing except "goodwill" is expected in return. To illustrate how a gift appears in the unilateral transfers category, suppose the U.S. government sends $500,000 worth of rice as humanitarian aid to a country that had just experienced a flood. The export of the rice appears in the goods category as a credit. However, the U.S. government expects no payment for this export. A debit entry appears in the unilateral transfers category the United States effectively has imported a $500,000 payment of goodwill from the foreign country.

CAPITAL ACCOUNT A tabulation of the flows of financial assets between domestic private residents and foreign private residents.

The Capital Account   The private **capital account** measures the outflow of domestic assets abroad and the inflow of foreign assets into the domestic country that result from transactions involving private (nongovernmental) individuals and companies. The private capital account includes three categories of financial assets: financial assets of the domestic government, private domestic financial assets, and foreign financial assets. These financial assets include physical assets and financial assets such as bonds, bills, stocks, deposits, and currencies.

The private capital account tabulates two types of asset *flows:* investment flows, and changes in banks' and brokers' cash deposits that arise from foreign transactions. Investment flows include:

- Purchases of foreign securities by domestic residents and purchases of domestic securities by foreign residents;
- Lending to foreign residents by domestic residents and borrowing by domestic residents from foreign residents;
- Investment by domestic firms in their foreign affiliates and investment by foreign firms in their domestic affiliates.

PORTFOLIO INVESTMENT The acquisition of foreign financial assets that results in less than a 10 percent ownership share in the entity.

DIRECT FOREIGN INVESTMENT The acquisition of foreign financial assets that results in an ownership share in the foreign entity of 10 percent or greater.

To better understand the potential impact of capital inflows from abroad, economists distinguish between *portfolio investment* and *direct foreign investment.* **Portfolio investment** refers to an individual or business's purchase of stocks, bonds, or other financial assets, and deposits. **Direct foreign investment** is the purchase of assets to establish financial control of a foreign entity. Direct foreign investment is the way in which multinational firms expand their operations in other countries.

It may be difficult to determine whether the purchase of a foreign asset was intended to earn income or establish financial control. To help distinguish between portfolio and direct foreign investment, economists consider the foreign acquisition of less than 10 percent of the entity's outstanding stock as portfolio investment, and the acquisition of 10 percent or more of the entity's outstanding stock as direct foreign investment. Figure 1–5 shows direct foreign investment by U.S. residents and firms on line 44, and direct foreign investment in the United States by foreign firms on line 57.

A debit entry in the capital account, for example, records the purchase of a foreign financial asset by a domestic private resident, because this transaction results in a payment made abroad. Likewise, a credit entry records the purchase of a domestic financial asset by a foreign private resident, as this transaction generates a payment from abroad.

Table 1–4 shows, using the data from Figure 1–5, the categories of the capital account for 1997. These three categories tabulate transactions of domestic government assets, domestic private assets, and foreign assets. Changes in private U.S. assets abroad reflect an increase or decrease in private ownership of foreign assets. A net capital outflow means that the net purchases of foreign assets by domestic residents exceeds the net purchases of domestic assets by foreign residents. Changes in foreign assets in the United States reflect an increase or decrease in foreign ownership of domestic assets. A net capital inflow means that the net purchases of domestic assets by foreign residents exceed the net purchases of foreign assets by domestic residents.

TABLE I–4	CATEGORIES OF THE BALANCE OF PAYMENTS SUMMARY STATEMENT THAT ARE INCLUDED IN THE CAPITAL ACCOUNT	
		1997
Private U.S. assets abroad		−426,105
Foreign assets in the United States		+672,340
Official settlements balance		+ 17,324

SOURCE: Economic Indicators.
NOTE: $ millions

OFFICIAL SETTLEMENTS BALANCE A balance of payments account that tabulates transactions of reserve assets by official government agencies.

The Official Settlements Balance   The third and final account, the **official settlements balance,** measures the transactions of financial assets and deposits by official government agencies. Typically, the central banks and finance ministries or treasuries of national governments conduct these types of official transactions.

It is common for foreign central banks and government agencies to keep deposit accounts with other central banks. If, for example, the U.S. Treasury or Federal Reserve were to make a deposit with the Bank of England, the deposit appears as a capital outflow, or debit, in the U.S. balance of payments. If, on the other hand, the Bank of England were to make a deposit with the Federal Reserve, the deposit is a capital inflow, or credit, in the U.S. balance of payments. In Figure 1–5, lines 34 through 38 show the U.S. official assets that include gold and foreign currencies. U.S. official assets also include assets, such as Special Drawing Rights at the International Monetary Fund. These assets will be explained in Chapter 2. Foreign official assets in the United States are shown on lines 49 through 55 of Figure 1–5. The official settlements balance is the sum of lines 34 and 49.

Deficits and Surpluses in the Balance of Payments

If we sum all of the debits and credits that appear in the current account, private capital account, and official settlements balance, the total should be zero. However, this seldom happens in practice. A number of transactions are missed in the accounting process or hidden from the process intentionally. For example, illegal transactions are hidden from government agencies, and some legal transactions may be hidden from government agencies, such as customs officials, to avoid taxes. Furthermore, government statisticians make errors in their tabulation of credits and debits.

If the sum of the credits and debits in the current account, private capital account, and official settlements is not zero, then an offsetting entry appears in the balance of payments. Economists call this offsetting entry the *statistical discrepancy*. The statistical discrepancy can be very large. Line 63 of Figure 1–5 shows that the statistical discrepancy for the United States in 1997 was $97.1 billion!

The *overall balance of payments* is the sum of the credits and debits in the current account, capital account, official settlements, and the statistical discrepancy. Because debit entries offset each and every credit entry, and the statistical discrepancy offsets any errors, the overall balance of payments necessarily is equal to zero.

It is common, and somewhat confusing, when economists and the media refer to balance of payments deficits or surpluses. As just explained, ignoring the statistical discrepancy, the overall balance of payments must sum to zero. Therefore, what economists and the media refer to is something other than the *overall* balance of payments.

A balance of payments deficit refers to a situation in which the official settlements balance is positive. Ignoring a statistical discrepancy, if the sum of the credits and debits in the current account and the private capital account is negative, private payments made to foreigners exceed private payments received from foreigners. In this case, the official settlements balance must be positive. This is called a *balance of payments deficit.* A situation where the sum of the debits and credits in the current and private capital account is positive means that private payments received from foreigners exceed private payments made to foreigners. In this case, the official settlements balance is negative, and there is a *balance of payments surplus.* A *balance of payments equilibrium* refers to a situation where the sum of the debits and credits in the current account and the private capital account is zero, and thus the official settlements balance is zero. Therefore, we can conclude that:

> **A balance of payments equilibrium, ignoring a statistical discrepancy, arises when the sum of the debits and credits in the current account and the private capital account equal zero, so that the official settlements balance is zero. A balance of payments deficit corresponds to a positive official settlements balance, and a balance of payments surplus corresponds to a negative official settlements balance.**

Other Deficit and Surplus Measures

Economists use other deficit and surplus measures that are part of the balance of payments system. The *balance on merchandise trade* is the sum of the debit and credit entries in the merchandise or goods category. If the sum of the debit entries in this category exceeds the sum of the credit entries, then the balance on merchandise trade is negative, and there is a deficit in merchandise trade. If the sum of the debit entries is less than the sum of the credit entries, then the balance on merchandise trade is positive, and there is a merchandise trade surplus. Figure 1–5 on page 18 lists merchandise credits on line 2 and debits on line 16. The sum of the two amounts is the balance on merchandise

MANAGEMENT NOTEBOOK

Why a Country Is Not Like a Corporation

Though a nation's balance of payments system is much like an accounting system for a company, deficit or surplus measures in the balance of payments are quite unlike the bottom line, or the net of expenditures and receipts, for a corporation. Paul Krugman of Stanford University provides four examples of why the balance of payments of a nation is unlike the balance sheet for a corporation:

1. The bottom line for a corporation is truly its bottom line. If a corporation cannot afford to pay its workers, suppliers, and bondholders, it will go out of business. Countries, on the other hand, do not go out of business.
2. The bottom line for a country, perhaps the trade balance, does not necessarily reflect weakness or strength. A deficit is not necessarily "good" or "bad."
3. An economy such as the United States produces approximately 90 percent of its goods and services for its own consumption. As Professor Krugman points out, even the largest corporation sells hardly

any of its output to its own workers; the exports of General Motors—its sales to people who do not work there—are virtually all of its sales.

4. Countries do not compete the same way that companies do. Only a negligible fraction of Coca-Cola's sales goes to Pepsi. The major industrialized economies, on the other hand, export and import most of their goods and services among one another.

Even though our description of a nation's balance of payments system may appear similar to an accounting system of a company, we must be careful about drawing conclusions about the meaning of a deficit or surplus measure. The assertion that a surplus country is stronger or more competitive than a deficit country may be completely untrue.

FOR CRITICAL ANALYSIS:

Why might a nation find a trade deficit to be beneficial? What difficulties might a nation face in the future if the deficit persists for a lengthy period?

trade, and this balance appears on line 64 of Figure 1–5. Because the debits, or merchandise imports, exceed the credits, or merchandise exports, the total is a negative amount representing a merchandise deficit on line 64.

The balance on goods, services, and income is the sum of the debit and credit entries that appear in the merchandise, service, and income categories. If the total of the debit entries, or imports, exceeds the sum of the credit entries, or exports, then there is a deficit in goods, services, and income. If the total of the debit entries, or imports, is less than the sum of the credit entries, or exports, then there is a surplus in goods, services, and income. Figure 1–5 provides the balance on goods, services, and income on line 68. This amount is negative, indicating that the United States experienced a negative balance, or *deficit,* on goods, services, and income in 1997.

As explained earlier, the current account includes the categories of goods, services, income, and unilateral transfers. Thus the balance on the current account is the sum of all the debit and credit entries in these categories. The current account balance is the most reported balance of payments measure. If the sum of the debit entries exceeds the sum of the credit entries, then there is a current account deficit. If the sum of the debit entries is less than the sum of the credit entries, then there is a current account surplus. Figure 1–5 provides the balance on the current account on line 70. This balance is also negative, indicating that the United States experienced a negative balance, or deficit, on the current account in 1997.

The balance on the capital account reflects the net flow of financial assets purchased by private individuals. As explained earlier, purchases of foreign financial assets by private domestic residents represent a capital outflow, and appear as a debit. Purchases of domestic financial assets by private foreign residents represent a capital inflow and appear as a credit. The balance on the capital account reflects the net inflow or outflow of capital. If the debit entries exceed the credit entries, there is a net capital outflow. If the debit entries are less than the credit entries, there is a net capital inflow. This balance does not appear in Figure 1–5 but is provided in Table 1–4. In Table 1–4, the sum of the debit and credit entries is a positive balance. This positive balance indicates that the United States experienced a surplus on the capital account in 1997.

EXAMPLES OF INTERNATIONAL TRANSACTIONS
AND HOW THEY AFFECT THE BALANCE OF PAYMENTS

Now that we have overviewed each category of the balance of payments, let's consider how typical international transactions result in both credit and debit entries and how they affect the various deficit and surplus measures. We shall look at five examples, summarized in Table 1–5.

Each of the examples presents a transaction as it affects the balance of payments for the United States. None of the examples involves any tabulation error or transaction of financial assets by an official government agency. As a result, there is no statistical discrepancy, and the official settlements is equal to zero in each example. Thus, the sum of debit and credit entries in current account and capital account will be zero.

Example 1: Import of an Automobile

An automobile dealer in the United States imports a Swedish automobile and pays the Swedish auto manufacturer $20,000. The automobile manufacturer deposits the $20,000 in its U.S. bank account.

The value of the imported automobile is a debit in the merchandise category because the transaction results in the outflow of currency. The payment is a credit, or capital inflow, in the foreign assets in the United States category,

	EXAMPLE 1	EXAMPLE 2	EXAMPLE 3	EXAMPLE 4	EXAMPLE 5
Merchandise	−$20,000				$200,000
Services		−$1,000			
Income				−$500	
Unilateral transfers					−$200,000
Home assets abroad			−$ 10,000		
Foreign assets in the home country	$20,000	$1,000	$ 10,000	$500	
Balance on merchandise			$180,000		
Balance on goods, services, and income			$178,500		
Balance on current account			−$ 21,500		
Balance on capital account			$ 21,500		

TABLE 1–5   BALANCE OF PAYMENTS EXAMPLES

because the Swedish auto manufacturer now owns a U.S. financial asset, the deposit. The fact that the funds were deposited in a bank in the United States is irrelevant. As long as the payment is made and the foreign entity receives the funds, it is a credit from the standpoint of U.S. balance of payments accounting.

Example 2: A College Student Travels Abroad

A college student travels abroad during a break from school, spending $1,000 on hotels and food.

The value of services consumed as a tourist—food, lodging and transportation— is a debit in the services category, as the consumption of these services results in a payment abroad. The amount of funds the student spends abroad is a credit, or capital inflow, in the foreign assets in the United States category.

Example 3: A Foreign Resident Purchases a Domestic Treasury Bill

A foreign resident purchases a $10,000 U.S. treasury bill from a U.S. brokerage firm.

The payment for the treasury bill is a credit, or a capital inflow, in the foreign assets in the United States category, because the foreign resident now owns a U.S. financial asset. The payment received by the brokerage firm is a debit, or capital outflow, in the U.S. assets abroad category, because the brokerage firm acquires a foreign deposit.

Example 4: The United States Pays Interest on a Foreign-Held Asset

The U.S. Treasury makes a $500 interest payment to a foreign resident that holds a previously purchased U.S. treasury bill.

The $500 payment made to the foreign resident is a debit in the income category. The payment also is a credit, or capital inflow, in the foreign assets in the U.S. category, because the foreign resident receives $500 of the domestic currency, which also is a domestic financial asset.

Example 5: A Charitable Organization in the United States Provides Humanitarian Aid Abroad

A U.S. charitable organization, as a humanitarian gesture, donates $200,000 of wheat to a country that recently experienced a flood.

The value of the wheat is a credit in the merchandise category because it is an export of a tangible good. The wheat is a donation, with only goodwill expected in return, so the offsetting entry is a debit in the unilateral transfers category. In theory, there is an import of $200,000 of goodwill from the foreign country.

Examples Combined

If these transactions represent all the international transactions of the United States for the period, then we can determine the balance on merchandise trade, balance on goods, services, and income, the current account balance, and capital account balance in Table 1–5. Summing across the row for the merchandise category, we see that the sum of debit and credit entries is $180,000, yielding a surplus on merchandise trade of $180,000. Combining debit and credit entries in the rows for merchandise, services, and income yields the balance on goods, services, and income, which is a surplus of $178,500. Adding the debit and credit entries in the row for unilateral transfers to the entries for merchandise, services, and income yields the current account balance, which is a deficit of $21,500. Combining the entries in the rows for U.S. assets abroad and foreign assets in the United States provides the balance on the capital account. This yields a surplus, or positive balance of $21,500. The sum of the debit and credit entries in the current account and the capital account equals zero, for the reason already discussed.

The U.S. Current Account Balance in 1991

When was the last time the United States ran a surplus in the current account? The 1950s? The 60s? The 70s? Figure 1–6 provides the answer. The United States ran a current account surplus in the first two quarters of 1991. Viewing the graph, this event appears to be somewhat of an anomaly. Indeed, the surpluses were not due to economic forces. Instead, the most notable event of this period was the Persian Gulf War. The current account surplus resulted from cash contributions to the United States from coalition partners in Operation Desert Storm and amounted to $22.7 billion in the first quarter of 1991 and $11.6 billion in the second quarter of 1991.

The payments to the United States represented an outflow of capital as the United States acquired foreign financial assets. As a result, debit entries appear in the capital account for the first two quarters of 1991. Due to the double-entry nature of the balance of payments system, there must be offsetting entries. The offsetting entries are debits to the unilateral transfers category. This is why the two-quarter surplus occurred in that year.

FOR CRITICAL ANALYSIS:
Construct a table similar to Table 1–5. Record the payments made to the United States from the perspective of a country that made the payment. How would the payment affect the other country's current account balance?

FIGURE 1–6   THE U.S. CURRENT ACCOUNT BALANCE

SOURCE: Data from International Monetary Fund, *International Financial Statistics*.

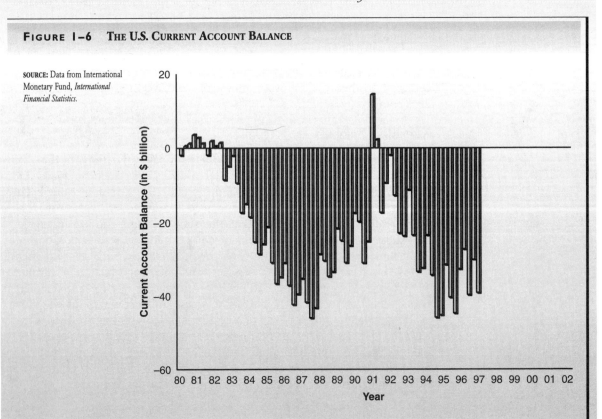

FUNDAMENTAL ISSUE #4

What is a country's balance of payments and what does this measure? The balance of payments is an accounting system used to tabulate a nation's international transactions. The balance of payments system measures trade in goods, services, income, unilateral transfers, private transactions of financial assets, and official reserves.

THE CAPITAL ACCOUNT AND THE INTERNATIONAL FLOW OF ASSETS

The capital account measures the flow of financial assets, and the current account measures the flow of goods, services, income, and unilateral transfers. Therefore, a starting point for thinking about capital account transactions is to view these transactions as necessary to finance current account transactions.

Consider the following example. If a country runs a current account deficit, the country consumes more goods and services than it produces, and it must import this excess from abroad. Because the country spends more than it earns, it must borrow from abroad to finance purchases of the goods and services. This means that, on net, capital must flow into the economy, thereby yielding a capital account surplus. Viewed from this perspective, a current account deficit is undesirable because a deficit country must borrow from abroad to finance its current consumption. This is a very narrow perspective, however.

A broader way to view a capital account surplus is to recognize that capital may flow into a nation because foreign residents may consider the nation an attractive and promising location for investment. In other words, foreign residents may consider the nation healthy and poised for economic growth that yields sufficiently high returns on their investment. Foreign investment, in turn, expands the capital stock of the nation. An increase in the capital stock can yield a higher future standard of living for the nation's residents. Viewed from this perspective, the capital account surplus, which by definition implies a current account deficit, can be good for a nation.

Example: A College Student

Let's put this discussion in the context of college students. While in college, the students typically spend more than they earn. They pay rent, purchase food, books, and entertainment, and pay tuition. Their earnings usually arise from a part-time job. Often, they borrow from parents, a bank, the university, or from the state or federal government.

Suppose that a student arranges a guaranteed student loan from the federal government. This loan must be paid back, with interest, over a maximum of ten years beginning upon graduation. What is the student's motivation for borrowing? It is likely that the student is making an investment in the *student,* acquiring *human capital,* which is the knowledge and abilities an individual possesses. If the increase in human capital yields greater increased future earnings that exceed the cost of paying the loan back, then the investment is wise. If the student instead spends all the borrowed funds on current consumption, fails to finish college, and forgoes the higher earnings stream that an education would have provided, then the cost of repaying the loan actually reduces the student's future standard of living.

Clearly what is important is not that the student borrowed, but how the student used the borrowed funds. The key question is this: Did the student invest the funds in education so as to increase future earnings, or were the funds spent on current consumption?

A Capital Account Surplus

A capital account surplus should be viewed in much of the same way, if funds borrowed from abroad add to the capital stock of the nation, and if the resulting increase in future potential output exceeds the cost of borrowing, then the residents of the nation may enjoy an increased ability to consume goods and services in the future. If the borrowed funds finance current period consumption, however, then the burden of repaying the borrowed funds may reduce the nation's future prosperity.

The capital *flows* are the lending and borrowing of a nation's residents over a specific period. These capital flows, on net, add to or reduce the stock of foreign assets held by domestic residents and the *stock* of domestic financial assets held by foreign residents. Economists call a nation that has a stock of foreign financial assets that exceeds the stock of foreign-owned domestic financial assets a **net creditor.** In contrast, a **net debtor** is a nation that has a stock of foreign financial assets that is less than its stock of foreign-owned domestic financial assets. As we have noted, it is not necessarily "good" or "bad" for a nation to be a net debtor or net creditor.

NET CREDITOR A nation whose total claims on foreigners exceed the total claims of foreigners on the nation.

NET DEBTOR A nation whose total claims on foreigners are less than the total claims of foreigners on the nation.

The United States as a Net Debtor

Consider the case of the United States. In the course of its history, it has experienced periods when it was a net creditor and periods when it was a net debtor. The original colonies of the United States began as a net debtor, borrowing from France and the Netherlands to finance Revolutionary War expenditures. As shown in Figure 1–7, the late 1800s was a period of significant net indebtedness. This was also a period of high investment for the United States. The growth potential of the United States attracted considerable foreign capital inflows, resulting in a net debtor position. This investment financed increases in railroads and other physical capital and led to an increase in manufacturing output of approximately 10 percent per year in the latter part of the nineteenth century.

FIGURE I–7 U.S. CREDIT POSITION 1800–1900

The United States has been a net debtor nation at various times in its history. In particular, the United States was a net debtor in the late 1800s. During this period the United States experienced considerable capital inflows. The investment spurred a dramatic increase in manufacturing output.

SOURCE: Data from *Economic Review of the Federal Reserve Bank of Kansas City*.

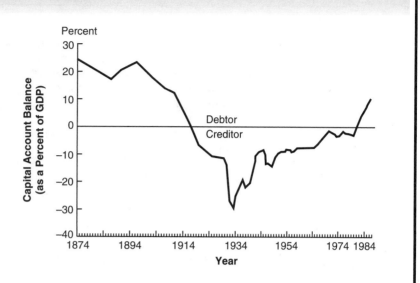

In the 1980s, the United States experienced sizable capital inflows and current account deficits. As a result of these inflows, the United States became a net debtor (see Figure 1–7). The popular press characterized the United States as being the world's largest debtor nation and claimed that foreigners were "buying up" U.S. businesses and properties. This situation is not necessarily good or bad for the United States. What is important is whether the inflow of capital into the United States is financing current consumption or productive investment.

FUNDAMENTAL ISSUE #5

What does it mean for a country to be a net debtor or net creditor? A net debtor nation is one whose stock of foreign financial assets held by domestic residents is less than the stock of domestic financial assets held by foreign residents. A net creditor nation is one whose stock of foreign financial assets held by domestic residents is greater than the stock of domestic financial assets held by foreign residents. Being a net debtor or net creditor is not necessarily "good" or "bad." Capital inflows may add to a nation's capital stock and increase an average resident's ability to purchase goods and services in the future.

CHAPTER SUMMARY

1. **Gross Domestic Product:** Gross domestic product, or GDP, is a comprehensive measure of production that occurs, during a given time period, within a country regardless of the ownership of resources. GDP includes personal consumption expenditures, gross private domestic investment, net exports of goods and services, and government purchases of goods and services.

2. **Difference between Nominal GDP and Real GDP:** GDP can be measured in nominal terms, or not adjusted for price changes, or in real terms, with price changes eliminated by using a deflator or price index. The GDP price deflator is a flexible-weight price index, whose weights on various goods and services change automatically as the output of goods and services varies over time. Uncompensated or nominal GDP reflects real output of goods and services and any changes in prices, or inflation. During periods of significant inflation, nominal GDP overstates the real production of an economy. Real GDP measures output in constant dollar (constant prices) and therefore more accurately reflects the actual output of goods and services.

3. **The Consumer Price Index and the Producer Price Index:** The consumer price index (CPI) is a measure of the change in the prices of a fixed basket of goods and services purchased by the average or typical consumer. Comparisons of price levels over time using the CPI are often used as a measure of inflation. The producer price index (PPI) is a measure of the prices of the output of domestic producers.

4. **What the Balance of Payments Measures:** The balance of payments is a system of accounts used to record the international transactions of a nation. This system measures trade in goods, services, income, unilateral transfers, private transactions of financial assets, and official reserves. The current account comprises the goods, services, income, and unilateral transfers categories.

5. **Net Debtor and Net Creditor Nations:** A net debtor nation is one whose total claims abroad are less than the total foreign claims on the nation. A net creditor nation is one whose stock of foreign financial assets is greater than the stock of foreign-held domestic financial assets. Being a net debtor is not necessarily "good" or "bad" for an economy. Foreign investment that adds to a nation's capital stock may improve its prospects for prosperity.

QUESTIONS AND PROBLEMS

1. Using the following data (in billions of dollars) for a given year, compute GDP.

Consumption spending	2500	Rental income	600
Net export spending	100	Investment spending	1000
Wages and salaries	2000	Government spending	500
Net factor income from abroad	50	Depreciation	150
Interest income	900	Indirect taxes	200
Profits	300		

2. Explain, in your own words, the difference between GDP and GNP.

3. Using the data in Question 1, compute GNP, net national product, and national income.

4. Explain, in your own words, the difference between real and nominal GDP.

5. Suppose that real GDP for the period is $3280. Using your answer from Question 1, what is the GDP implicit deflator for the period? What was the percentage change in overall prices in the economy since the base year?

6. Using the following data (billions of dollars) for a given year, calculate the balance on merchandise trade; balance on goods, services, and income; and the current account balance. Indicate whether these balances are deficits or surpluses.

Exports of merchandise	106	Imports of services	28
Exports of services	34	Capital inflow	6
Net unilateral transfers	+8	Imports of merchandise	119
Statistical discrepancy	0	Capital outflow	29
Official settlements balance	−22		

7. Using the data in Question 4, calculate the capital account balance. Is the capital account balance a surplus or deficit?

8. What is a balance of payments equilibrium? Considering your answers to Questions 6 and 7, is this country experiencing a balance of payments deficit or surplus?

ON-LINE APPLICATION

This chapter presented concepts and measurements of national income accounting and balance of payments systems. Often economists desire to estimate the *openness* of an economy. That is, how great are international trade flows for a particular nation? The most common method of measuring the openness of a nation is to divide the sum of the nation's exports and imports by its nominal GDP. This measure yields total trade flows as a percent of the nation's total economic activity, as measured by nominal GDP.

Internet URL: http://www.nber.org/pwt56.html

Title: The Penn World Tables

Navigation: Begin with the data query interface provided at this site. Under *variable,* scan down and highlight *OPEN.* Next, under *country,* select *U.S.A.* Under, *date,* select the most recent year available. Record the number provided after the search is completed. Repeat the exercise for *Belgium.*

Application: Based on the openness measures your query generated, answer the following questions:

1. Write a brief statement as to what these measures mean, using the United States and Belgium as examples in your answer.

2. Which country is more open? What explanation can you provide for the large difference between the openness of the two nations?

REFERENCES AND RECOMMENDED READINGS

Clayton, Gary, and Martin Gerhard Giesbrecht. *A Guide to Everyday Economic Statistics, Third Edition.* New York: McGraw-Hill Inc., 1995.

Faust, Jon. "U.S. Foreign Indebtedness: Are We Investing What We Borrow?" *Federal Reserve Bank of Kansas City Economic Review* (July/August, 1989): 3–20.

Grayboyes, Robert F. "International Trade and Payments Data: An Introduction." *Federal Reserve Bank of Richmond Economic Review* (September/October 1991): 20–31.

Kemp, Donald. "Balance-of-Payments Concepts: What Do They Really Mean?" *Federal Reserve Bank of St. Louis Economic Review* (July 1975): 14–23.

Krugman, Paul. *Pop Internationalism.* Cambridge, MA: MIT Press, 1996.

Spiegel, Henry William. *The Growth of Economic Thought.* Durham, NC: Duke University Press, 1991.

THE MARKET
FOR FOREIGN EXCHANGE

FUNDAMENTAL ISSUES

1. What is the foreign exchange market?

2. What does it mean when a currency has appreciated or depreciated?

3. How is the general value of a currency measured?

4. What is foreign exchange arbitrage?

5. What determines the value of a currency?

6. What is purchasing power parity, and is it useful as a guide to movements in exchange rates?

In May 1997, many currency traders believed that the value of the baht, the currency of Thailand, was too high. They questioned whether Thailand's Central Bank, the Bank of Thailand, would be able to maintain the value of the baht, because the government's policies had led to double-digit interest rates and a declining stock market. Some of these currency traders had previously profited on the currencies of nations facing similar economic situations. By purchasing financial instruments that generate a profit when a currency declines in value, these traders benefited from the currencies' plunge. George Soros, a famous big-league currency speculator, had received considerable media attention for profits he enjoyed from the collapse of the British pound in 1992 and the Mexican peso in 1994. So began the "battle of the baht."

Typically traders exchange a billion dollars' worth of baht each day. Individual contracts on the baht may range up to $30 million. By launching tens of billions of dollars of sell contracts on the baht within a couple of days, currency traders made a serious challenge to the central bank. By acting in concert with other Asian central banks, however, and by preventing the baht to be loaned abroad, the Thai central bank won the early round of the battle. Traders reported in press articles that one casualty of the battle was Mr. Soros's organization, which exited the market amid mounting losses.

By the end of June 1997, however, pressure on the baht became too great, and on July 2, 1997, the baht was allowed to float. On July 29, the governor of the Bank of Thailand was sacked amidst the resulting financial crises. The collapse of the Thai baht sparked financial crises across Southeast Asia. By the end of 1997, the exchange values of the currencies of Thailand, Indonesia, and South Korea had fallen by more than 40 percent against the U.S. dollar.

In this chapter we begin our study of the $1.25 trillion-per-day foreign exchange market. We shall examine foreign exchange and various types of exchange rates. We shall explore the forces that determine the value of a currency and investigate how arbitrage generates profits. We shall also consider one of the most popular theories of exchange rate determination.

EXCHANGE RATES AND THE MARKET FOR FOREIGN EXCHANGE

Often, economists speak of foreign trade and capital flows, as if the goods, services, and assets are like water flowing from one country to another. Pushing this analogy a little further, we might say that the *foreign exchange market* is the international plumbing. The foreign exchange market is a system of private banks, foreign exchange dealers and brokers, and central banks through which households, firms, and governments buy and sell *foreign exchange,* or another nation's currency. By providing an arrangement for valuing transactions and delivering payments, the foreign exchange system promotes the flows of goods, services, and assets from one nation to another. *Exchange rates,* which are the market prices of foreign exchange, are a critical element of this system.

As an example of the role of exchange rates, suppose you decide to purchase a new stereo. After shopping the local appliance store, you select a receiver and speakers made by a Japanese company that have a dollar price of $300. Your decision to purchase this particular stereo partially depends on the price. Conveniently, the price is denominated in your own currency, the currency you have in your wallet or handbag and in your bank account. Your payment to the appliance store for the Japanese stereo is therefore a simple, straightforward transaction. After receiving your $300 payment, the appliance store can purchase new stereos from the Japanese company.

The Japanese residents who own the Japanese electronics company, however, must pay the company's workers and suppliers in Japanese yen. They do not want to receive dollars in Japan. Therefore, they deposit the payment with their bank and have the proceeds converted into yen. They can now make their payments from a yen-denominated bank account. How many yen is each dollar worth? In other words, what is the value of the dollar relative to the yen? This is what an exchange rate tells us. An exchange rate expresses the value of one currency relative to another and, therefore, converts the value of this transaction into the local currency terms of each party involved.

The Role of the Foreign Exchange Market

What function does the foreign exchange market perform in the previous example? The notion of a foreign exchange market may invoke the image of frantic traders in shirt sleeves and visors hustling money on a cluttered trading floor, with their actions determining the quotations for currencies we see in daily newspapers such as the *Wall Street Journal* and the *Financial Times*. In our example, however, a foreign exchange market was not prominent. The Japanese company used the services of its bank, not the foreign exchange market. Further, the currencies involved, the dollar and the yen, never crossed international borders. Only the stereo did.

Indeed, the actual flow of currencies from one nation to another is an insignificant element of the foreign exchange market. Such flows usually arise only as a result of such activities as tourism or illegal transactions. The financial assets that people typically trade in foreign exchange markets are foreign-currency-denominated financial instruments, such as bonds, stocks, and especially bank deposits.

Spot Market A market for contracts requiring the immediate sale or purchase of an asset.

There are many different foreign exchange instruments and, therefore, many foreign exchange markets. The market in our example is the spot market for foreign exchange. A **spot market** is a market for immediate purchase and delivery of an asset. In the foreign exchange market, delivery usually occurs within two or three days. The daily media publish spot rates that pertain to the trading of foreign-currency-denominated deposits among major banks for $1 million or more. We shall examine other important markets for foreign exchange in Chapters 4 and 5.

Spot exchange rates are the market prices of foreign exchange in the spot market. Table 2–1 displays spot exchange rates published in the *Wall Street Journal*. The spot rates in Table 2–1 are for foreign exchange transactions undertaken in the New York market, and represent the rate that a currency sold for at 3:00 P.M. Eastern time. Notice in the text at the top of Table 2–1 that the rates "apply to trading among banks in amounts of $1 million and more," and that "retail transactions provide fewer units of foreign currency per dollar." This means that the spot rates quoted here pertain to very large transactions. Smaller spot transactions, such as those of individuals and small- to medium-sized businesses, would

---

TABLE 2–1 SPOT RATES FOR CURRENCY EXCHANGE

CURRENCY TRADING

EXCHANGE RATES

The New York foreign exchange selling rates below apply to trading among banks in amounts of $1 million and more, as quoted at 4 p.m. Eastern time by Dow Jones and other sources. Retail transactions provide fewer units of foreign currency per dollar.

Country	U.S. $ equiv. Thu	U.S. $ equiv. Wed	Currency per U.S. $ Thu	Currency per U.S. $ Wed
Argentine (Peso)	1.0001	1.0001	.9999	.9999
Australia (Dollar)	.6543	.6520	1.5283	1.5337
Austria (Schilling)	.07893	.07937	12.669	12.599
Bahrain (Dinar)	2.6518	2.6518	.3771	.3771
Belgium (Franc)	.02690	.02703	37.170	36.993
Brazil (Real)	.8749	.8754	1.1430	1.1424
Britain (Pound)	1.6650	1.6717	.6006	.5982
1-month forward	1.6626	1.6693	.6015	.5991
3-months forward	1.6580	1.6645	.6032	.6008
6-months forward	1.6516	1.6578	.6055	.6032
Canada (Dollar)	.6963	.6983	1.4362	1.4321
1-month forward	.6968	.6988	1.4352	1.4311
3-months forward	.6974	.6995	1.4338	1.4296
6-months forward	.6985	.7006	1.4316	1.4273
Chile (Peso)	.002210	.002214	452.45	451.65
China (Renminbi)	.1208	.1208	8.2789	8.2790
Colombia (Peso)	.0007375	.0007366	1355.94	1357.51
Czech. Rep. (Koruna)				
Commercial rate	.03006	.02990	33.264	33.450
Denmark (Krone)	.1458	.1462	6.8580	6.8400
Ecuador (Sucre)				
Floating rate	.0002002	.0002002	4995.00	4995.00
Finland (Markka)	.1830	.1840	5.4630	5.4340
France (Franc)	.1658	.1663	6.0300	6.0135
1-month forward	.1661	.1666	6.0195	6.0023
3-months forward	.1667	.1671	5.9992	5.9828
6-months forward	.1675	.1680	5.9699	5.9535
Germany (Mark)	.5561	.5576	1.7981	1.7935
1-month forward	.5571	.5585	1.7951	1.7905
3-months forward	.5589	.5604	1.7892	1.7845
6-months forward	.5616	.5631	1.7805	1.7760
Greece (Drachma)	.003199	.003217	312.58	310.82
Hong Kong (Dollar)	.1290	.1290	7.7496	7.7500
Hungary (Forint)	.004761	.004759	210.04	210.11
India (Rupee)	.02519	.02517	39.693	39.725
Indonesia (Rupiah)	.0001242	.0001252	8050.00	7987.00
Ireland (Punt)	1.4043	1.4051	.7121	.7117
Israel (Shekel)	.2674	.2664	3.7403	3.7536
Italy (Lira)	.0005627	.0005640	1777.00	1773.00
Japan (Yen)	.007683	.007667	130.16	130.43
1-month forward	.007715	.007699	129.61	129.89
3-months forward	.007783	.007766	128.49	128.76
6-months forward	.007886	.007869	126.80	127.08

Country	U.S. $ equiv. Thu	U.S. $ equiv. Wed	Currency per U.S. $ Thu	Currency per U.S. $ Wed
Jordan (Dinar)	1.4134	1.4134	.7075	.7075
Kuwait (Dinar)	3.2765	3.2755	.3052	.3053
Lebanon (Pound)	.0006577	.0006577	1520.50	1520.50
Malaysia (Ringgit)	.2644	.2655	3.7825	3.7663
Malta (Lira)	2.5575	2.5575	.3910	.3910
Mexico (Peso)				
Floating rate	.1181	.1184	8.4670	8.4490
Netherland (Guilder)	.4942	.4951	2.0234	2.0197
New Zealand (Dollar)	.5615	.5609	1.7809	1.7828
Norway (Krone)	.1337	.1344	7.4778	7.4393
Pakistan (Rupee)	.02289	.02285	43.680	43.760
Peru (new Sol)	.3556	.3560	2.8119	2.8089
Philippines (Peso)	.02620	.02608	38.425	38.340
Poland (Zloty)	.2936	.2935	3.4064	3.4075
Portugal (Escudo)	.005428	.005439	184.24	183.87
Russia (Ruble) (a)	.1631	.1631	6.1300	6.1300
Saudi Arabia (Riyal)	.2666	.2666	3.7505	3.7506
Singapore (Dollar)	.6289	.6303	1.5900	1.5865
Slovak Rep. (Koruna)	.02881	.02891	34.708	34.591
South Africa (Rand)	.1975	.1981	5.0635	5.0470
South Korea (Won)	.0007313	.0007278	1367.50	1374.00
Spain (Peseta)	.006549	.006563	152.70	152.37
Sweden (Krona)	.1293	.1303	7.7313	7.6733
Switzerland (Franc)	.6713	.6729	1.4897	1.4860
1-month forward	.6737	.6755	1.4844	1.4803
3-months forward	.6785	.6801	1.4739	1.4703
6-months forward	.6855	.6873	1.4588	1.4549
Taiwan (Dollar)	.03031	.03030	32.991	32.999
Thailand (Baht)	.02545	.02545	39.300	39.300
Turkey (Lira)	.00000406	.00000406	246535.00	246535.00
United Arab (Dirham)	.2723	.2722	3.6730	3.6731
Uruguay (New Peso)				
Financial	.09704	.09713	10.305	10.295
Venezuela (Bolivar)	.001869	.001873	535.00	533.87
SDR	1.3497	1.3508	.7409	.7403
ECU	1.0997	1.1031		

Special Drawing Rights (SDR) are based on exchange rates for the U.S., German, British, French, and Japanese currencies. Source: International Monetary Fund.

European Currency Unit (ECU) is based on a basket of community currencies.

a-fixing, Moscow Interbank Currency Exchange. Ruble newly-denominated Jan. 1998.

The Wall Street Journal daily foreign exchange data for 1996 and 1997 may be purchased through the Readers' Reference Service (413) 592–3600.

---

receive less favorable selling and buying rates. Table 2–1 displays two versions of the spot rate, *U.S. dollar equivalent* and *currency per U.S. dollar*. In the next section we shall explain these two versions of the spot rate. We will refer to Table 2–1 often for the examples that appear in this chapter.

ON THE WEB
To obtain daily exchange rates for 164 currencies, visit Olsen and Associates Currency Converter at:
http://www.oanda.com/ cgi-bin/ncc

FUNDAMENTAL ISSUE #1

What is the foreign exchange market? The foreign exchange "market" is the system through which people exchange one nation's currency for the currency of another nation. A large portion of the transactions in this market consists of exchanges of foreign-currency-denominated deposits of $1 million or more among large commercial banks. The actual movement of a currency from one country to another is a relatively insignificant feature of activity in the foreign exchange market.

Exchange Rates as Relative Prices

As we indicated in the previous section, the role of the exchange rate is to measure the value of one currency relative to another. An exchange rate, therefore, is a *relative price* that indicates the price of one currency in terms of another currency.

Because an exchange rate relates two currencies, economists commonly call an exchange rate a *bilateral exchange rate,* because *bilateral* means "two sides." In Table 2–1, there are two columns for spot exchange rates on Wednesday and Thursday. The first is the *U.S. dollar equivalent,* or how many U.S. dollars it takes to purchase one unit of a foreign currency. For example, in Table 2–1, the exchange rate for the U.S. dollar relative to the British pound (£) is 1.6650 $/£, meaning that one must give 1.6650 U.S. dollars in exchange for 1.0 British pound.

The exchange rate also expresses how many foreign currency units it takes to purchase one dollar, or *currency per U.S. dollar.* This is simply the reciprocal of the U.S.-dollar-equivalent rate. Hence, the rate of exchange of the British pound for the U.S. dollar is 1/(1.6650 $/£), or 0.6006 £/$. This means that one must give 0.6006 pounds in exchange for 1.0 U.S. dollar. Because there are two different ways to express an exchange rate, it is very important that you determine whether an exchange rate is a U.S.-dollar-equivalent rate or a currency-per-U.S.-dollar rate.

Currency Appreciation and Depreciation Looking at the U.S.-dollar-equivalent rate for the British pound in Table 2–1, we see that the rate changed from 1.6717 $/£ to 1.6650 $/£ between Wednesday and Thursday.

This means that the dollar *appreciated* against the pound from Wednesday to Thursday, because the number of dollars required to purchase one pound decreased. In other words, the dollar price of the pound fell. At the same time, the pound *depreciated* relative to the dollar. The currency-per-U.S.-dollar rate changed from 0.5982 £/$ to 0.6006 £/$, indicating that the number of pounds required to purchase one dollar increased, or the pound price of the dollar rose.

We can determine the rate of appreciation or depreciation by calculating the percentage change in the exchange rate. We calculate the percentage change of an exchange rate by subtracting the old value of the exchange rate from the new value, dividing this difference by the old value, and multiplying by 100. Using the U.S.-dollar-equivalent rates from Table 2–1, the percentage change is

$$[(1.6650 - 1.6717)/1.6717] \times 100 \approx -0.40\%.$$

The dollar has appreciated relative to the pound by 0.40 percent. Using the currency-per-U.S.-dollar rate, the percentage change is

$$[(0.6006 - 0.5982)/0.5982] \times 100 \approx 0.40\%.$$

The first percentage change calculation is negative because the number of dollars required to purchase a pound decreased. The second percentage change calculation is positive because the number of pounds required to purchase a dollar has increased. As you can see, in order to determine whether a positive change or a negative change indicates an appreciation or depreciation, one must know how the exchange rate is expressed.

FUNDAMENTAL ISSUE #2

What does it mean when a currency has appreciated or depreciated? When an exchange rate changes, one currency either gains or loses value relative to another currency. When a currency appreciates, it gains value relative to another currency. When a currency depreciates, it loses value relative to another currency. The percentage change in the exchange rate measures the amount of the currency's appreciation or depreciation.

Cross Rates   Table 2–1 indicates that, for this particular day, the U.S.-dollar-equivalent and currency-per-U.S.-dollar exchange rates for the deutsche mark (DM) were equal to 0.5561 $/DM and 1.7981 DM/$, respectively. Suppose, however, that our interest is in the exchange rate between the British pound and the German deutsche mark, not the dollar and the deutsche mark. To determine this rate, we can compute a **cross rate,** which is a third exchange rate that we calculate from two bilateral exchange rates.

CROSS RATE A bilateral exchange rate calculated from two other bilateral exchange rates.

In Table 2–1, the U.S.-dollar-equivalent rate for the British pound is 1.6650 $/£, and the U.S.-dollar-equivalent rate for the deutsche mark is 0.5561 $/DM. From these two bilateral rates, it is straightforward to calculate either the British-pound-equivalent rate for the deutsche mark or the deutsche-mark-per-British-pound rate.

To calculate the British-pound-per-deutsche-mark cross rate, we divide the dollar rate for the deutsche mark by the dollar rate for the British pound. Thus, we can calculate the pound–mark cross rate in the following manner:

$$\frac{0.5561 \ \$/DM}{1.6650 \ \$/£}.$$

Division by a fraction is the same as multiplying by the reciprocal of the fraction. Therefore, we can express the problem as

$$\frac{0.5561}{1.6650} \times \frac{\$}{DM} \times \frac{£}{\$}.$$

Notice in this calculation, the dollar cancels out because it appears in the numerator of one fraction and the denominator of another. This yields the British-pound-equivalent exchange rate for the deutsche mark, 0.3340 £/DM.

If we wish to determine the deutsche-mark-per-British-pound rate, we invert the British-pound-equivalent rate, which yields

$$\frac{1}{0.3340 \ £/DM} = 2.9940 \ DM/£ \ .$$

By using the U.S.-dollar-equivalent rate for the British pound and the deutsche mark, we have calculated a cross rate of exchange between the British pound and the deutsche mark.

The foreign exchange sections of major newspapers provide cross rates for many high-volume currencies in a cross-rate table. Table 2–2 is an example of a cross-rate table. The table lists the currencies across the top row and the left-hand column. The rates in Table 2–2 are the exchange rates between the currencies of the countries listed on the corresponding row and column. When

TABLE 2–2   CROSS-RATE TABLE BASED ON RATES IN TABLE 2–1

	UNITED STATES	CANADA	GERMANY	BRITAIN
United States	–	1.4362	1.7982	0.6006
Canada	0.6963	–	1.2521	0.4182
Germany	0.5561	0.7987	–	0.3340
Britain	1.6650	2.3913	2.9940	–

the same country appears on both the row and the column, the entry is either blank or 1. The first column provides the U.S.-dollar-equivalent rate for each currency listed on the corresponding row. Therefore, the first row provides the foreign-currency-per-U.S.-dollar exchange rates.

Bid–Ask Spreads and Trading Margins

If you live in a large metropolitan area, your bank is likely to have a foreign exchange service. Try calling your bank for a quote on a currency. The person you speak with likely will either quote two rates or will ask whether you are buying or selling. The rate at which the bank is willing to buy the currency from you is the *bid price*. The rate at which the bank is willing to sell the currency to you is the *ask price,* or *offer.*

The Bid–Ask Spread As an example, suppose you are going to London, England, to study economics for a semester. Prior to your trip, you want to exchange dollars for British pounds. From Table 2–1, we see that the British-pound-per-U.S.-dollar rate is 1.6650 $/£. Suppose that when you call your local bank and ask for a quote on the British pound, the reply is "647 and 653." Because bankers want to economize on everything, including words, the banker is quoting only the last three decimal points of the spot rate. What was meant then, is 1.6647 $/£ and 1.6653 $/£. The lower rate, the *bid price* or *buying price,* is the number of U.S. dollars the bank is willing to give you in exchange for one British pound. The higher rate, the *ask price* or *selling price,* is the number of U.S. dollars you would have to give the bank in exchange for one British pound. The difference between the bid price and the ask price is the **bid–ask spread.**

The Bid–Ask Margin Typically, banks do not charge fees for foreign exchange transactions. The **bid–ask margin,** or *trading margin,* expresses the bid–ask spread as a percentage, and represents the cost and risk associated with the foreign exchange transaction. We calculate the bid–ask margin as the difference between the ask price and the bid price, divided by the ask price, and multiplied by 100:

$$\text{Bid-ask margin} = \frac{\text{ask price} - \text{bid price}}{\text{ask price}} \times 100.$$

In this example, the bid–ask margin is

$$\frac{1.6653 - 1.6647}{1.6653} \times 100 = 0.036\%.$$

This bid–ask margin is very small at 0.036%. Currencies with a high trading volume and low exchange variability typically have lower bid–ask margins, indicating the relatively low cost and risk associated with a foreign exchange.

Table 2–3 displays trading margins for spot exchange rates of four selected currencies. The table presents two high-volume and low-variability currencies,

BID–ASK SPREAD The difference between the *bid price,* or price offered for the purchase of a currency, and the *ask price,* or price at which the currency is offered for sale.

BID–ASK MARGIN The difference between the *ask price,* or price at which a currency is offered for sale, and the *bid price,* or price offered for the purchase of the currency, expressed as a percent of the *ask price.*

TABLE 2-3   BID–OFFER AND MARGIN CALCULATIONS

	BID	ASK	MARGIN (%)
Switzerland (SFr)	1.4905	1.4915	0.0670
Japan (¥)	129.300	129.360	0.0464
South Korea (Won)	1391.00	1395.00	0.2867
Israel (Shk)	3.7207	3.7309	0.2734

ON THE WEB

Obtain spot rates and bid price–ask price spreads from the Financial Times. *Register for free at:* **http://www.ft.com**

the Swiss franc and the Japanese yen, and two low-volume and high-variability currencies, the South Korean won and Israeli shekel. The bid–ask margins of the South Korean won (0.29%) and the Israeli shekel (0.273%) are about four times those of the Swiss franc (0.067%) and the Japanese yen (0.065%).

Real Exchange Rates

NOMINAL EXCHANGE RATE
A bilateral exchange rate that is unadjusted for changes in the two nations' price levels.

REAL EXCHANGE RATE
A bilateral exchange rate that has been adjusted for price changes that occurred in the two nations.

So far we have discussed **nominal exchange rates.** These are exchange rates that do not reflect changes in price levels in the two nations. The nominal exchange rate tells us the purchasing power of our own currency in exchange for a foreign currency. What if we are interested in the amount of foreign *goods and services* that our currency will buy, however? In other words, what if we really care about the *purchasing power* of our currency in terms of foreign goods and services? The **real exchange rate** adjusts the nominal exchange rate for changes in nations' price levels and thereby measures the purchasing power of domestic goods and services in exchange for foreign goods and services. Hence, if we want to know how much of another country's goods and services that a unit of our own nation's goods and services can buy, we need to know the value of the real exchange rate.

As an example, take the case of Canada and Mexico from 1990 through 1995. This period provides an excellent example because of the significant change in the value of the Mexican peso during that time. Chapter 13 details the events that led to a significant depreciation of the Mexican peso.

The spot exchange rate for the Canadian dollar ($C) per U.S. dollar was 1.1603 $C/$ in 1990 and 1.3652 $C/$ in 1995. The spot exchange rate for the Mexican new peso (peso) per U.S. dollar was 2.9454 peso/$ in 1990 and 7.6425 peso/$ in 1995. We can calculate the peso/$C cross rates, which are

$$\frac{2.9454 \text{ peso/\$}}{1.1603 \text{ \$C/\$}} = 2.5385 \text{ peso/\$C,}$$

and

$$\frac{7.6425 \text{ peso/\$}}{1.3652 \text{ \$C/\$}} = 5.5981 \text{ peso/\$C,}$$

respectively.

Hence, the rate at which the Canadian dollar appreciated relative to the Mexican peso was equal to

$$\frac{5.5981 - 2.5385}{2.5385} \times 100 = 120.5\%.$$

The value of each Canadian dollar relative to the Mexican peso increased, as each Canadian dollar could buy 2.5385 Mexican pesos in 1990 and 5.5981 pesos in 1995.

The Effect of Price Changes

Now consider the effect that price changes had on the purchasing power available to a "typical" Canadian consumer of Mexican goods and services. To determine this effect, we need to use a price index. Let's use the Consumer Price Index (CPI), because, as explained in Chapter 1, the CPI measures the change in prices of a basket of goods and services consumed by a hypothetical "typical" consumer.

The CPI for Canada was equal to 100 in 1990 and was equal to 111.8 in 1995. In Mexico the CPI was equal to 100 in 1990 and was equal to 224.5 in 1995. Economists often use the percentage change in the CPI over a given interval as a measure of consumer price inflation during the period. Therefore, for Canada, inflation from 1990 through 1995 was 11.8 percent. That means that the domestic purchasing power of each Canadian dollar decreased over this period as the domestic price level rose. For Mexico, inflation over this period was 124.5 percent. Thus, during the same period each Mexican peso lost considerably more domestic purchasing power. One can see that although the Canadian dollar appreciated relative to the Mexican peso, at the same time each peso could buy fewer Mexican goods and services.

For Canadian consumers that means that the price inflation in Mexico offset some of the currency gain brought about by the appreciation of the Canadian dollar. To see why this is so, we calculate the real exchange rate by dividing the nominal Mexican-peso-per-Canadian-dollar exchange rate by the ratio of Mexican prices to Canadian prices. This adjusts the nominal value of the Mexican peso relative to the Canadian dollar by price changes in Mexico relative to price changes in Canada.

Let S_t denote the nominal Mexican-peso-per-Canadian-dollar exchange rate, peso/$C, at time period t. We shall also let P_t^{Cn} denote the Canadian CPI at time period t, and P_t^M denote the Mexican CPI at time period t. Using this notation, the real Mexican-peso-per-Canadian-dollar exchange rate at time period t, s_t, is

$$s_t = \frac{S_t}{(P_t^M / P_t^{Cn})}.$$

Once again, we have a ratio in the denominator of an expression. We can, therefore, rewrite the expression by multiplying by the reciprocal of the ratio in the denominator. The expression then becomes

$$s_t = S_t \times (P_t^{Cn}/P_t^{M}).$$

From this expression we see that the real Mexican-peso-per Canadian-dollar exchange rate is the nominal Mexican-peso-per-Canadian-dollar exchange rate multiplied by the ratio of Canadian prices to Mexican prices. Using this expression, the Mexican-peso-per-Canadian-dollar real exchange rate for 1990, s_{1990}, is

$$s_{1990} = 2.5385 \times (100/100) = 2.5385.$$

Because 1990 is the base year for the CPI, and therefore the base year for our real exchange rate, the nominal exchange rate is equal to the real exchange rate. Similarly, the Mexican-peso-per-Canadian-dollar real exchange rate for 1995, s_{1995}, is

$$s_{1995} = 5.5981 \times (111.8/224.5) = 2.7878.$$

Thus, between 1990 and 1995, the real exchange rate increased in value. This indicates that there was a real appreciation of the Canadian dollar relative to the Mexican peso. The real appreciation was much smaller, however, than the nominal appreciation. The percentage change in the real exchange rate was only 9.8 percent, whereas the nominal appreciation was 120.5 percent. Since the Mexican CPI rose at a rate of 112.7 percent more than that of the Canadian CPI, this inflation differential offset most of the 120.5 percent currency appreciation.

MEASURING THE OVERALL STRENGTH OR WEAKNESS
OF A CURRENCY: EFFECTIVE EXCHANGE RATES

EFFECTIVE EXCHANGE RATE A measure of the weighted-average value of a currency relative to a selected group of currencies.

As explained earlier in this chapter, the exchange rates we have discussed so far are bilateral exchange rates, which measure the value of one currency relative to *one* other currency. On any given day, a currency will strengthen, or appreciate, against some currencies and weaken, or depreciate, against others. On a given day, the dollar's value may have fallen against the German mark, Japanese yen, and Canadian dollar. Its value may have risen, however, against the French franc, Swiss franc, and Mexican peso. So, some bilateral rates would have fallen and some would have risen. But overall, or in general, is the dollar "stronger" or "weaker"? To answer this question, economists use an **effective exchange rate,** which is a measure of the average value of a currency relative to two or more other currencies.

Constructing an Effective Exchange Rate

To construct an effective exchange rate, economists must make a number of choices. The first is the basket of currencies in which to measure the effective exchange rate. It is not practical to measure the value of a currency against every other currency in the world. Thus, economists include only the currencies that they judge to be most important. What constitutes "important" currencies depends on the particular application. If a businessperson wanted to know how changes in the value of the dollar affect U.S. imports and exports, then the individual would want to include the bilateral exchange rates of the largest trading partners of the United States. If a portfolio manager wanted to know how changes in the value of the dollar would affect the return on a portfolio of international assets, then that individual would want to include the bilateral exchange rates of the currencies that represent the largest shares of the portfolio. The currencies that one eventually selects compose what economists call the currency basket.

Next one must select a base year. As we discussed in Chapter 1, a base year serves as a reference point in time. The base year value is equal to 100. Economists then measure changes from this base year. For example, if 1998 were the base year, then the value of the effective exchange rate for 1998 would be 100. If the effective exchange rate were 125 for 1999, then we know there was a 25 percent increase in the effective exchange rate.

Finally, because an effective exchange rate is a weighted average of bilateral exchange rates, economists must select *weights*. The weights are a means of placing greater emphasis on the more important currencies in the currency basket and less emphasis on the least important currencies in the currency basket. Typically, economists construct weights on either a bilateral or multilateral basis. Bilateral weights reflect the trade flow of an individual country with the United States relative to the total trade of the United States with all of the countries included in the index. Multilateral weights reflect the trade flow of the *individual* country with all countries included in the index relative to the *total* trade volume among all of the countries included in the index. If we consider the value of a single currency (say, the U.S. dollar), a bilateral weighting scheme typically is fine. If we want to compare the performance of the U.S. dollar with the currencies of other countries over the same period, we should use a multilateral weighting scheme.

A Two-Country Example of an Effective Exchange Rate

To illustrate these points, let's use 1998 as the base year and construct a simple effective exchange rate for the United States between 1998 and 1999. For illustrative purposes, we shall use only two of the top trading partners of the United States, Canada and Japan.

Constructing Bilateral Weights   Because we will consider an effective exchange rate for only one country, we shall use bilateral weights. Let X represent exports and M represent imports. Further, let W^b denote the bilateral weight. We calculate the weight placed on the Canadian dollar as the exports of the United States to Canada, X_{Cn}, plus the imports of the United States from Canada, M_{Cn}. This sum of X_{Cn} and M_{Cn} is the total trade of United States with Canada. Likewise, the sum of X_J and M_J is the total trade of the United States with Japan.

To calculate the weight assigned to the Canadian dollar, we divide the total trade of the United States with Canada, $X_{Cn} + M_{Cn}$, by the total trade of the United States with Canada and Japan, $(X_{Cn} + M_{Cn}) + (X_J + M_J)$. We can write the formula for the weight of the Canadian dollar as

$$W^b_{Cn} = (X_{Cn} + M_{Cn})/[(X_{Cn} + M_{Cn}) + (X_J + M_J)].$$

This weight represents the trade of the United States with Canada as a fraction of the total trade of the United States with Japan and Canada.

Suppose during the base year, 1998, U.S. exports to Canada were $114,869 million and imports were $131,115 million. U.S. exports to Japan were $51,517 million and imports were $119,135 million. We calculate W^b_{Cn} as

$$W^b_{Cn} = (\$114{,}869 + \$131{,}115)/[(\$114{,}869 + \$131{,}115) + (\$51{,}517 + \$119{,}135)] = 0.59.$$

This weight indicates that of the total trade of the United States with Canada and Japan, 59 percent was with Canada. Likewise, the weight to be placed on the Japanese yen, W^b_J, is equal to

$$W^b_J = (\$51{,}517 + \$119{,}135)/[(\$114{,}869 + \$131{,}115) + (\$51{,}517 + \$119{,}135)] = 0.41.$$

This weight indicates that of the total trade of the United States with Canada and Japan, 41 percent was with Japan. Note that the weights, $W_{Cn}{}^b$ and $W_J{}^b$ sum to one. This fact, that the weights sum to one, is always true regardless of the number of currencies in the basket.

Determining Relative Exchange Rates   The next step in constructing the effective exchange rate is to calculate each of the bilateral exchange rates relative to the base-year exchange rate. This means that we should divide each exchange rate by the base year value. For the example here, suppose the Canadian-dollar-per-U.S.-dollar exchange rate for 1998 was 1.4000 $C/$, and for 1999, 1.3652 $C/$. Further suppose that the Japanese-yen (¥)-per-U.S.-dollar exchange rate for 1998 was 130.1600 ¥/$, and for 1999, 134.1950 ¥/$. Because 1998 is our base year in this example, we divide the Canadian dollar exchange rate by the 1998 Canadian dollar exchange rate, yielding 1 for 1998 and 0.9751 for 1999.

The intuition of this step is as follows. Dividing the current rate by the base-year value yields the value of the currency relative to its value during the base year. Therefore, the value 1 for 1998 means that the 1998 value is 100 percent of the 1998 value. The value 0.9751 for 1999 means that the 1999 exchange value is 97.51 percent of the 1998 exchange value. Completing the same calculations for the Japanese yen yields the value 1 for 1998 and 1.0310 for 1999, meaning that the 1998 value is 100 percent of the 1998 value and the 1999 value is 103.1 percent of the 1998 value. We then multiply these relative exchange values by the appropriate weight. Then we sum the weighted relative exchange values for a given year and multiply by 100. This process yields the effective exchange rate for that year.

If we follow this procedure, we can calculate the effective exchange rate for the base year, 1998, EER_{1998} as

$$EER_{1998} = [(0.59)(1) + (0.41)(1)] \times 100 = 100.$$

This effective exchange rate indicates the average exchange value of the U.S. dollar against the Canadian dollar and the Japanese yen relative to the average exchange value of the U.S. dollar against the Canadian dollar and the Japanese yen during the base year. In our example, 1998 is the base year, so the value of the effective exchange rate for 1998 is 100. The effective exchange rate for 1999 was

$$EER_{1999} = [(0.59)(0.9751) + (0.41)(1.0310)] \times 100 = 99.80.$$

This value indicates that the average value of the U.S. dollar against the Canadian dollar and the Japanese yen for 1999 was 99.8 percent of the value for 1998.

What an Effective Exchange Rate Tells Us   Now that we have calculated an effective exchange rate, what does it tell us? In the example here, note that the U.S. dollar depreciated relative to the Canadian dollar from 1998 to 1999. Nevertheless, the U.S. dollar appreciated relative to the Japanese yen from 1998 to 1999. So relative to both currencies, did the dollar appreciate or depreciate? In our example, the value of the effective exchange rate was 100 in 1998 (the base year), and 99.80 in 1999. Because the value of the effective exchange rate declined, the dollar *depreciated,* on average, relative to both currencies during this period. Using the percentage change formula, the amount of depreciation was $[(99.80 - 100)/100] \times 100 = -0.2\%$.

A number of effective exchange rates are available in leading exchange rate sources. The International Monetary Fund publishes multilateral-weighted effective exchange rates on a nominal and real basis in its monthly bulletin, *International Financial Statistics.* The Federal Reserve board publishes a nominal multilateral-weighted effective exchange rate for the U.S. dollar in the *Federal Reserve Bulletin.* *The Financial Times* and the *Wall Street Journal* report the J. P. Morgan nominal index. Figure 2–1 displays the multilateral-weighted nominal effective exchange rates for the U.S. dollar, the U.K. pound, the German mark, and the Japanese yen, since 1980.

Figure 2–1 shows that there was a dramatic increase in the average value of the dollar from 1980 through 1985 and a subsequent decline from 1985 through 1988. Following 1988, there was a steady, general decline in the average value of the dollar until 1995, when the dollar began to gain in value again. The figure shows that for the British pound, there was a decline in the average value over the period until 1995. The effective exchange rate for the British pound began the period at a value of about 125 and finished at a value

---

Between 1985 and 1995, the average value of the U.S. dollar and the British pound declined, while the average value of the deutsche mark and the Japanese yen increased. This trend reversed in 1995.

SOURCE: Data from International Monetary Fund, *International Financial Statistics*.

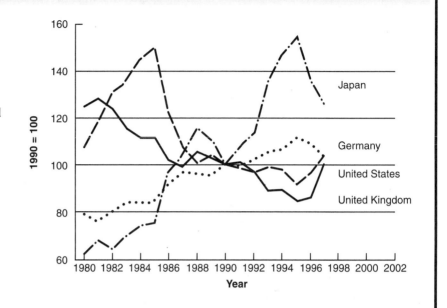

of around 90 in 1994, indicating a 28 percent decline in average value. For the German mark and Japanese yen, the figure shows a general increase in value from 1980 until 1995. This is particularly evident for the yen, which began at 60 and ended at 150 in 1994, constituting a 150 percent appreciation over the period. Between 1995 and 1996, however, the yen lost more than 13 percent in general value.

Real Effective Exchange Rates   Earlier in this chapter, we explained that it is the real exchange rate that indicates changes in international purchasing power. Therefore, it may be desirable to construct a *real effective exchange rate,* which is an effective exchange rate based on real exchange rates as opposed to nominal exchange rates. A real effective exchange rate is calculated in much the same way as a nominal effective exchange rate. In contrast to calculating effective nominal exchange rates, however, we use real exchange rates in computing the real effective exchange rate. Thus, to construct a real exchange rate, we need, in addition to the information already given, CPI data for all countries in the index, as well as for the United States. Then, we would need to convert each nominal exchange rate to a real rate. We then would complete the remaining calculations as described earlier. Problem 4 at the end of the chapter asks you to construct a real effective exchange rate.

ON THE WEB
To obtain data on the Federal Reserve Board's ten-currency U.S. dollar effective exchange rate, visit the Federal Reserve Bank of St. Louis at:
http://www.stls.frb.org/publ/usfd

FUNDAMENTAL ISSUE #3

How is the general value of a currency measured? An effective exchange rate tracks the movement of a currency against a number of currencies. Because an effective exchange rate is a weighted average of a set of bilateral exchange rates, effective exchange rates are very useful as a general guide for changes in a currency's value. A real effective exchange rate is based on real bilateral exchange rates, whereas a nominal effective exchange rate is based on nominal bilateral exchange rates.

COMPOSITE CURRENCIES

COMPOSITE CURRENCY
A currency unit in which the value is expressed as a weighted average of a selected basket of currencies.

Sometimes it is useful to denominate transactions and value single currencies relative to composite currencies. A **composite currency,** or *artificial currency unit,* is a currency unit formed from a standardized currency basket composed of a weighted average of several currencies. The two most common composite currencies are the *Special Drawing Right (SDR),* established and maintained by the International Monetary Fund, and the *European Currency Unit (ECU),* established and maintained by the European Monetary System of the European Union. Economists typically express the values of these composite currencies relative to the dollar and/or pound, like any other individual currency. You can find the daily values of these composite currencies listed at the end of the currency tables of the *Wall Street Journal,* as shown in Table 2–1, or *Financial Times.* Now that we understand the construction of effective exchange rates, understanding a composite currency is straightforward.

Special Drawing Right (SDR)

SPECIAL DRAWING RIGHT (SDR)
A composite currency of the International Monetary Fund in which the value is based on a weighted average value of the currencies of five member nations.

The **Special Drawing Right (SDR)** is a composite currency first proposed in 1968 and eventually allocated in 1970 by the International Monetary Fund (IMF). The IMF and sponsoring industrialized nations developed the SDR. Policymakers at the IMF and in the sponsoring nations believed that there would not be sufficient gold reserves to provide the liquidity needed for international transactions. They intended for the SDR to serve as a *reserve currency,* or the currency that central banks would use to settle transactions.

The expected liquidity crises did not occur, so the SDR did not become the primary reserve currency. Nonetheless, the SDR does fulfill some limited functions. It is a means for some countries to finance short-term liquidity shortages, and for some nations it serves as a currency basket for pegging national currencies. (We shall discuss fixed or pegged exchange rate systems and the use of a currency basket in this regard in Chapter 3.)

The IMF defines the SDR in a manner analogous to an effective exchange rate, basing it on a basket of selected currencies. Since 1991, the countries whose currencies constitute the basket are the five members of the International Monetary Fund that experienced the greatest exports of goods and services during the period 1985 through 1989. These countries are the United States, Germany, France, Japan, and the United Kingdom. Multilateral weights, which reflect relative export volumes of the five countries, as well as the relative balances of these five currencies held by all member countries of the IMF, are used in the construction of the SDR.

To derive the daily SDR value, we begin with the basket as of its last revision in 1991. The basket consists of 0.5720 U.S. dollars, 0.4530 German marks, 0.8000 French francs, 31.8000 Japanese yen, and .0812 British pounds. We then convert these currency amounts to their U.S. dollar equivalents using daily market exchange rates. Then we sum the dollar equivalents of the five currency amounts to yield the U.S.-dollar-equivalent rate for the SDR.

We can use the information in Table 2–1 to construct an SDR calculation. Table 2–4 provides SDR currency amounts and the current U.S.-dollar equivalent rates for the five currencies. We multiply the currency amount, in the second column, by the U.S.-dollar-equivalent rate in the third column, to yield the U.S.-dollar-equivalent amount of each currency in the SDR, given in the fourth column. Then we add the U.S.-dollar-equivalent amounts in the fourth column together to give the dollar equivalent exchange rate of the SDR, 1.3366 SDR/$, which approximates the value in Table 2–1.

We can calculate the SDR rate of any currency other than the dollar as a cross rate using the U.S.-dollar-equivalent exchange rate of the SDR and the individual currency's U.S.-dollar-equivalent exchange rate. For example, in Table 2–1, the U.S.-dollar-equivalent rate of the Belgium franc is 0.03282 $/BF and the U.S.-dollar-equivalent rate of SDR is 1.4557 $/SDR. Dividing the second rate, $/SDR, by the first rate, $/BF, yields the Belgium franc–SDR cross rate, 41.2431 BF/SDR.

TABLE 2–4   CALCULATION OF THE SDR

CURRENCY	CURRENCY AMOUNT IN SDR	$ EQUIVALENT RATE	$ EQUIVALENT AMOUNT IN SDR
U.S. dollar	0.5720	1.0000	0.5720
German mark	0.4530	0.5561	0.2519
French franc	0.8000	0.1658	0.1326
Japanese yen	31.8000	0.0077	0.2449
British pound	0.0812	1.6650	0.1352
			1.3366

European Currency Unit (ECU)

The **European Currency Unit (ECU)** is a composite currency created and maintained by the European Union. The ECU serves as a unit of account in the European Monetary System for determining currency values and claims between members' central banks.

Currently the European Union uses twelve member-nation currencies to compute the ECU. The number and weights used in the calculation of the ECU changed periodically from 1979 until 1991. The Maastricht Treaty, signed in 1991 by twelve European leaders in the city of Maastricht, in the Netherlands, froze the number and amount of each currency used to determine the ECU. Economists calculate the ECU dollar-equivalent rate using the same procedure that they utilize to compute the SDR-dollar-equivalent rate. Again we can use the U.S.-dollar-equivalent rates from Table 2–1 as an example to how to calculate the U.S.-dollar-equivalent rate of the ECU. Table 2–5 provides the twelve currencies and their amounts in the ECU, the U.S.-dollar-equivalent rates, and U.S.-dollar-equivalent value of the ECU.

Comparing Tables 2–4 and 2–5, we see that the U.S.-dollar-equivalent exchange rate of the ECU is calculated in the same way as the U.S.-dollar-equivalent rate of the SDR. We first multiply the amount of each currency by its U.S.-dollar-equivalent exchange rate to yield the U.S.-dollar-equivalent amount. The sum of the U.S.-dollar-equivalent amounts is the U.S.-dollar-equivalent exchange rate of the ECU.

TABLE 2–5   CALCULATION OF THE ECU

CURRENCY	CURRENCY AMOUNT IN ECU	$ EQUIVALENT RATE	$ EQUIVALENT AMOUNT OF ECU
Dutch guilder	0.2198	0.4942	0.1086
German mark	0.6242	0.5561	0.3471
French franc	1.3320	0.1658	0.2208
Irish pound	0.0086	1.4043	0.0121
British pound	0.0878	1.6650	0.1462
Spanish peseta	6.8850	0.0065	0.0448
Belgian/Lux franc	3.4310	0.0269	0.0923
Greek drachma	1.4400	0.0032	0.0046
Danish krone	0.1976	0.1458	0.0288
Italian lira	151.8000	0.0006	0.0911
Portuguese escudo	1.3930	0.0054	0.0075
			1.1039

FOREIGN EXCHANGE ARBITRAGE

Many people envision foreign exchange dealers buying and selling currencies at a furious pace and generating magnificent profits. Indeed, some traders have reputations for earning enormous profits in the foreign exchange market. We must understand, however, that an activity known as *arbitrage* leads to these profits. Arbitrage, in its simplest terms, means "buy low–sell high," and is an activity through which individuals seek immediate profits based on price differentials. Individuals can also profit on currencies across time, through currency speculation or hedging. We shall discuss these latter types of activity in Chapters 4 and 5.

SPATIAL ARBITRAGE The act of profiting from exchange rate differences that prevail in different markets.

Spatial arbitrage refers to arbitrage transactions conducted across space, such as across two different geographical markets. For spatial arbitrage opportunities to exist, a currency's exchange rate in one market must be different from the exchange rate in another market.

Suppose you happen to have $1 million handy. (Recall that the spot market for foreign exchange is for transactions of $1 million or more.) You notice that the Finnish-markka (Fmk)-per-U.S.-dollar rate in New York is 4.5370–4.5375 Fmk/$, and the currency-per-U.S.-dollar rate in London is 4.4458–4.4533 Fmk/$. (Recall that the first number represents the bid price and the second the ask price on the markka.) Suppose both markets are open and there are no restrictions against buying and selling currencies in either market. Ignoring any brokerage fees, the difference in rates indicates that there is an arbitrage opportunity. In New York, the $1 million would purchase Fmk4,537,000, while in London it would purchase Fmk4,445,800. Therefore, you could buy Fmk4,537,000 for $1 million in New York, and then sell the Fmk4,537,000 for $1,018,795 in London. Thus, if you bought the markka in New York with dollars and sold it in London for dollars you would make a profit of $18,795! Note that this arbitrage activity would take place across space (in two different markets), hence the term *spatial arbitrage*.

If an arbitrage opportunity exists, foreign exchange traders engage in transactions that reduce or eliminate the arbitrage opportunity. Consider the spatial arbitrage example just given. If foreign exchange traders were to buy the markka in New York and sell it in London, the New York markka per-U.S.-dollar rate would fall and the London markka per-U.S.-dollar rate would rise, eliminating the difference in rates. Thus, the opportunity is "arbitraged away."

TRIANGULAR ARBITRAGE Three transactions undertaken in three different markets and/or in three different currencies in order to profit from differences in prices.

Triangular arbitrage (or three-way arbitrage), is slightly more complex and involves three or more currencies and/or markets. Again, for triangular arbitrage opportunities to exist, a currency's exchange value must differ across markets. In the previous example, the currency-per-U.S.-dollar exchange rate in one market had to be different from the currency-per-U.S.-dollar exchange rate in another market. For a triangular arbitrage opportunity to exist, one of three exchange rates must not be equal spatially.

For ease of exposition, we will consider only the mid-point of the U.S.-dollar-equivalent rates (in other words, the average of the bid and ask rates). Suppose the Finnish markka currency-per-U.S.-dollar rate in New York is 4.5373 Fmk/$, and the British pound currency-per-U.S.-dollar rate is 0.6454 £/$, while in London the Finnish markka currency per pound rate is 6.9845 Fmk/£. The two rates in the New York market imply a cross-rate between the markka and the pound of 7.0302 Fmk/£ (4.5373 Fmk/$ ÷ 0.6454 £/$). Note that the implied cross rate in New York is different from that in the London market. Therefore, an arbitrage opportunity exists. (Again, we are ignoring any transaction costs.)

Because the markka per British pound rate in London is less than that in New York, as savvy traders we would wish to purchase the pound in London, using the markka. We first must obtain the markka, however. Therefore, using the $1 million that we happen to have handy, we purchase Fmk4,537,300 in New York.

We then use the Fmk4,537,300 to purchase £649,624 in London (Fmk4,537,300 ÷ 6.9845 Fmk/£ = £649,624). Then we use £649,624 to purchase $1,006,545 in New York (£649,624 ÷ 0.6454 £/$ = $1,006,545). This arbitrage activity netted a profit of $6,545. Note that we would have traded *three* currencies in this example, the dollar, pound, and markka, hence the term *triangular arbitrage.*

FUNDAMENTAL ISSUE #4

What is foreign exchange arbitrage? Foreign exchange arbitrage is the act of buying a currency at one price and immediately selling it at a different price. Spatial arbitrage refers to arbitrage activities that span separate markets. Triangular arbitrage refers to arbitrage activities in which the foreign exchange transaction involves more than two currencies.

THE DEMAND FOR AND SUPPLY OF CURRENCIES

So far our discussion has focused on descriptions and calculations. Now let's consider an *analytical model* of the foreign exchange market. We shall use this simple supply and demand model in several of the following chapters. In this framework, we shall assume that there are no obstructions or controls on foreign exchange transactions. In addition, we shall assume that governments do not buy or sell currencies in order to manipulate their values. Under these assumptions, market forces of supply and demand determine the value of a currency.

The Demand for a Currency

The primary function of a currency is to facilitate transactions. Thus, the demand for a currency is a *derived demand*. That is, we derive the demand for a currency from the demand for the goods, services, and assets that people use the currency to purchase. Consider two countries, Germany and the United States. The demand for the deutsche mark stems from the U.S. residents' demand for German goods, services, and deutsche-mark-denominated assets. If U.S. consumers' demand for German goods were to increase, then, indirectly, there would be a rise in the demand for the deutsche mark to purchase the German goods. The price the U.S. consumer would have to pay for the deutsche mark would be the prevailing U.S.-dollar-per-deutsche-mark exchange rate.

Illustrating the Demand Relationship: The Demand Curve   Figure 2–2 illustrates this demand relationship. An appreciation of the dollar relative to the deutsche mark is a decrease in the U.S.-dollar-per-deutsche-mark exchange rate, as it takes fewer dollars to purchase each deutsche mark. The intuition of the downward-sloping demand curve is that as the dollar appreciates relative to the deutsche mark, German goods become relatively cheaper to U.S. consumers. As a result, U.S. consumers desire to purchase more German goods and require a greater amount of German deutsche marks to facilitate these additional transactions. There is, therefore, a negative relationship between the price of the currency and the quantity demanded. We may conclude that a change in the exchange rate results in a movement down and along the demand curve for the deutsche mark, as depicted by the movement on the demand curve from point *A* to point *B*. This is a *change in the quantity of deutsche marks demanded*.

FIGURE 2–2   THE DEMAND FOR THE DEUTSCHE MARK

The demand curve illustrates the relationship between quantity demanded and the exchange rate. A decrease in the exchange rate from S_A to S_B indicates that the U.S. dollar has appreciated relative to the deutsche mark. This would make German goods and services relatively cheaper to U.S. consumers. As a result, U.S. consumers would increase their quantity demanded of the deutsche mark in order to buy more German goods and services.

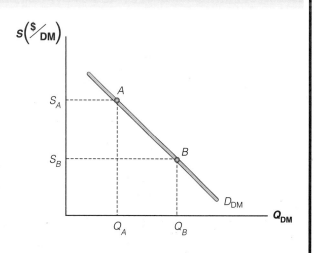

FIGURE 2–3   AN INCREASE IN THE DEMAND FOR THE DEUTSCHE MARK

An increase in U.S. consumers' demand for German goods, services, and deutsche-mark-denominated assets would lead to an increase in the demand for the deutsche mark. The increase in demand is illustrated by a rightward shift of the demand curve from D_{DM} to D'_{DM}.

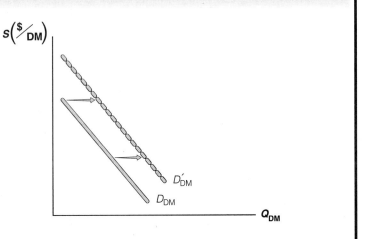

A Change in Demand   Let's suppose that, at a given exchange rate, U.S. consumers' demand for German goods, services, or deutsche-mark-denominated-assets increases at every exchange rate. Then, as just described, there is an increase in the quantity of deutsche marks demanded at the given exchange rate. This is a *change in the demand* for the deutsche mark. Figure 2–3 illustrates the change in demand as a *shift* of the demand curve. A rightward shift of the demand curve illustrates an increase in the demand for the deutsche mark, and a leftward shift illustrates a decrease in the demand for the deutsche mark.

Because the demand for a currency is a derived demand, the various factors that cause a change in the demand for a currency are all of the factors that cause a change in the foreign demand for that country's goods, services, and assets. We shall discuss these factors in more detail in Chapters 9 and 10.

The Supply of a Currency

To understand the supply of a currency, consider a German consumer's demand for the U.S. dollar, which we may derive from the German consumer's demand for U.S. goods, services, and assets. When the German consumer purchases U.S. dollars in order to buy more U.S. goods, the German consumer exchanges marks for dollars. As a result, there is an increase in the supply of marks in the foreign exchange market. Thus the German demand for the dollar also represents the supply of deutsche marks.

Illustrating the Supply Relationship: The Supply Curve   Figure 2–4 depicts the relationship between the German demand for the dollar and the supply of the mark. The main difference between Panel *a* and Panel *b* is the labeling of

FIGURE 2–4   THE SUPPLY OF THE DEUTSCHE MARK

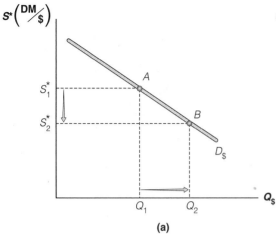

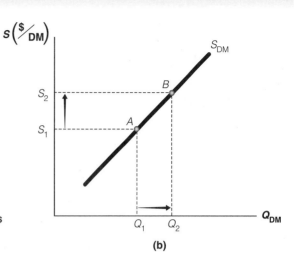

(a)   (b)

Panel *a* depicts the demand for the U.S. dollar. The exchange rate in this diagram is the deutsche mark per U.S. dollar rate. A decrease in the deutsche mark per U.S. dollar rate leads to an increase in the quantity demanded of the U.S. dollar. As more U.S. dollars are purchased with the deutsche mark, the quantity of deutsche marks supplied in the foreign exchange market increases. Panel *b* illustrates the relationship between

the exchange rate and the quantity supplied of the deutsche mark. This exchange rate in panel *b* is the U.S. dollar equivalent rate. As this rate rises, which is equivalent to the deutsche mark per U.S. dollar rate declining, the quantity supplied of the deutsche mark increases. The supply curve, S_{DM}, illustrates the positive relationship between the exchange rate and the quantity supplied.

the axes. The vertical axis in panel *b* inverts the mark-per-U.S.-dollar exchange rate, yielding the U.S.-dollar-per-mark exchange rate. On the horizontal axis, the quantity of deutsche marks replaces the quantity of U.S. dollars in panel *b*.

Viewing panel *a*, when the mark appreciates (a decrease in the DM/$ exchange rate), U.S. goods are relatively cheaper to German consumers. As a result, German consumers wish to buy more U.S. goods. To do so, they must purchase more U.S. dollars. In other words, there is an increase in the quantity of U.S. dollars demanded, shown by the movement from point *A* to point *B*.

Panel *b* shows an equivalent way to express this relationship. When the mark appreciates, the $/DM exchange rate rises. As German consumers purchase more U.S. dollars, they exchange their deutsche marks for the dollar, so there is an increase in the quantity of deutsche marks supplied. Thus, there is a positive relationship between the $/DM exchange rate and the supply of marks, illustrated by the upward-sloping supply curve in panel *b*. A movement along the supply curve represents a *change in the quantity of deutsche marks supplied*.

FIGURE 2–5   A SHIFT IN THE SUPPLY OF DEUTSCHE MARKS

An increase in the demand for the U.S. dollar by German consumers leads to an increase in the supply of deutsche marks. The increase in the supply of deutsche marks is illustrated by a rightward shift of the supply curve.

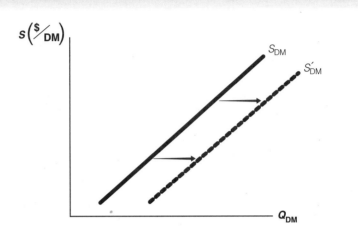

A Change in Supply   If, at a given exchange rate, there is an increase in the demand for U.S. goods by German consumers, there is an increased demand for the dollar. As German consumers purchase dollars to facilitate the additional transactions, they exchange deutsche marks for dollars, increasing the quantity supplied of deutsche marks in the foreign exchange market at the given rate. This is a *change in the supply of deutsche marks,* shown by a rightward shift of the supply curve in Figure 2–5. As shown, we depict an increase in the supply by a rightward shift of the supply schedule. The various factors that cause a change in the supply of a currency are the factors that cause a change in a country's demand for a foreign country's goods, services, and assets, which we shall examine in detail in Chapters 8 and 9.

The Equilibrium Exchange Rate

The forces of demand and supply determine the equilibrium, or market clearing, exchange rate of a currency. The equilibrium exchange rate is the rate at which the quantity of a currency demanded is equal to the quantity supplied. At the equilibrium exchange rate, the market *clears,* meaning that the quantity demanded is exactly equal to the quantity supplied.

Illustrating the Market Equilibrium   Figure 2–6 combines the demand and supply schedules in the same diagram and depicts the point of equilibrium for the foreign exchange market as point E, at which the equilibrium exchange rate is S_e, and the equilibrium quantity is Q_e. At exchange rate S_b, there is an excess quantity of deutsche marks supplied in the market. The quantity supplied at this rate, Q_2, exceeds the quantity demanded, Q_1. Because there is an excess quantity of the currency supplied, S_b is a *disequilibrium rate.* Hence, the

---

FIGURE 2–6 MARKET EQUILIBRIUM

At exchange rate S_b, the quantity supplied of deutsche marks is greater than the quantity demanded and there is downward pressure on the exchange rate. At exchange rate S_c, the quantity demanded of deutsche marks is greater than the quantity supplied and there is pressure for the exchange rate to rise. At exchange rate S_e, the market for deutsche marks is in equilibrium: the quantity demanded is equal to the quantity supplied.

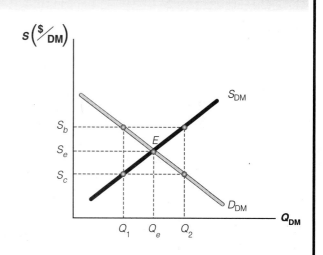

---

deutsche mark will depreciate to the point at which there is no excess quantity supplied. This occurs at point E.

Similarly, but in the opposite situation, at exchange rate S_c there is an excess quantity of deutsche marks demanded, as the quantity demanded at this rate, Q_2, exceeds the quantity supplied, Q_1. As a result, the deutsche mark will appreciate until there is no excess quantity demanded. Again, this takes place at point E. This adjustment process continues until the market clears, meaning that the quantity supplied equals the quantity demanded, which is a point of equilibrium. The market remains at this point until something causes one or both of the schedules to shift.

Example: A Change in Demand Figure 2–7 again shows the market equilibrium at point E, with the equilibrium exchange rate labeled S_e, and the equilibrium quantity denoted as Q_e. Now consider what happens if there is an increase in the demand for German goods by U.S. consumers. As explained earlier, there is a corresponding increase in the demand for German deutsche marks by U.S. consumers. This causes the rightward shift of the demand schedule in Figure 2–7. At the initial equilibrium exchange rate, S_e, there is an excess amount of German marks demanded, because the quantity demanded at this rate is Q_d' and the quantity supplied is still Q_e. This puts upward pressure on the dollar price of the mark, $/DM. The appreciation of the deutsche mark relative to the dollar makes U.S. goods relatively cheaper to German consumers. Consequently, German consumers increase their purchases of U.S. goods, exchanging deutsche marks for dollars. This increases the quantity of deutsche marks supplied, which induces a movement up and along the supply curve, from point E to point E'.

The depreciation of the dollar relative to the deutsche mark also makes German goods relatively more expensive to U.S. consumers. U.S. consumers reduce

FIGURE 2–7 **A CHANGE IN THE DEMAND FOR THE DEUTSCHE MARK**

Initially the market for deutsche marks is in equilibrium at point A. An increase in U.S. consumers' demand for German goods increases the demand for deutsche marks. The increase in the demand for deutsche marks is illustrated by a rightward shift of the demand curve. At the initial equilibrium exchange rate S_e, the new quantity demanded exceeds the quantity supplied, as shown by the distance between Q'_d and Q_e. The deutsche mark appreciates to S', where the market clears.

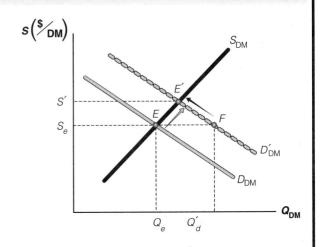

their purchases of German goods due to this change in the exchange rate. As a result, the quantity of deutsche marks demanded declines, as shown by the movement up and along the demand curve from point F to point E'. (Note carefully the difference between a change in the demand for the deutsche mark, which is a *shift of the demand schedule,* and a change in quantity of deutsche marks demanded, which is a *movement along the demand schedule.)* This market adjustment process continues until the quantity demanded equals the quantity supplied, so that the market clears. A new equilibrium occurs at E' and spot exchange rate S', indicating that the deutsche mark has appreciated relative to the dollar.

We shall use this supply and demand framework often throughout the text. We have not yet explained all of the non-exchange-rate factors of currency supply and demand, however. Let's turn our attention now to one fundamental non-exchange-rate factor that determines currency demand, which is the level of prices of goods and services.

FUNDAMENTAL ISSUE #5

What determines the value of a currency? The interaction between the demand for a currency and the supply of the currency determines the currency's market value. If the exchange rate is free to change, then a currency's value adjusts to its market equilibrium through a market-clearing process. The equilibrium market exchange rate is the value that eliminates any excess quantity of the currency that is demanded or supplied in the market.

POLICY NOTEBOOK
Too Many Zaires in Zaire

In 1993, the government of the African nation of Zaire, now the Congo, introduced a new currency, appropriately named the *zaire*. At that time, it took three zaires to purchase one U.S. dollar. By 1997, however, most residents of Zaire had no interest in holding zaires. The reason: The most common currency note, the 10,000-zaire note, had dropped in value to about 6 cents. As a result, obtaining a dollar required more than 160,000 zaires.

What happened between 1993 and 1997? The answer is that the government of Zaire fell into a pattern as old as governmental involvement with the production of money. It began to print money to purchase goods and services, and it got "hooked." By early 1997, the government had become so dependent on new money creation to finance its spending that it introduced currency notes denominated in 500,000 and 1 million zaires so that it could pay back wages owed to civil servants based in the nation's capital of Kinshasa.

In Kinshasa itself, people did not wish to hold these large-denomination notes. Indeed, they began to run short of the smaller, 10,000-zaire notes, which they desired for small transactions and for making change. Therefore, most Kinshasa residents exchanged their 1-million-zaire notes either for 10,000-zaire notes or dollars immediately upon receipt, until they could find a way to exchange the dollars for 10,000-zaire notes later on. This currency-trading activity drove the exchange rate for the 1-million-zaire notes to 340,000 zaires per U.S. dollar in Kinshasa.

In the nation's Shaba province, located some distance from Kinshasa, few residents used any zaires to purchase goods and services and, consequently, had little use for small-denomination notes. Some people in Shaba, however, were willing to hold some of their wealth in large-denomination notes, so in Shaba the exchange rate for 1-million-zaire notes was about 300,000 zaires per U.S. dollar. The divergence between exchange rates on the large-denomination notes in Kinshasa and Shaba created arbitrage opportunities for those willing to fly large-denomination notes from Kinshasa to Shaba and exchange them for small-denomination notes that they would take back to Kinshasa to exchange for dollars. There are not too many flights between these locales, however, and so the differential in the dollar exchange rate for large-denomination notes in Kinshasa and Shaba never fell to zero. Another factor kept arbitrage from fully eliminating the differential: The Zairean government kept printing more 1-million-zaire notes for distribution in Kinshasa, and the arbitrageurs simply could not keep up!

FOR CRITICAL ANALYSIS:
Illustrate the supply and demand conditions described here for the large-denominated zaire notes in Kinshasa and Shaba. What type of arbitrage activity was taking place between Kinshasa and Shaba? Illustrate in the supply and demand diagrams how this type of arbitrage activity would affect the market for the large denominated zaire notes.

PURCHASING POWER PARITY

OVERVALUED CURRENCY A currency in which the current market-determined value is higher than the value predicted by an economic theory or model.

We often hear that a currency is "undervalued" or "overvalued." What does that mean? A currency will be viewed as over- or undervalued if the current market-determined rate is not consistent with a rate implied by a formal or informal economic model. Therefore, economists would predict that some adjustment is likely to occur in the market. An **overvalued currency** is one in which the current market value is stronger than that predicted by a theory or model. This currency is likely to experience a market adjustment that brings about a depreciation in the value of the currency. An **undervalued currency** is one in which the current market value is weaker than the value predicted by a theory or model. This currency is likely to experience a market adjustment that brings about an appreciation in the value of the currency.

UNDERVALUED CURRENCY
A currency in which the current market-determined value is lower than that predicted by an economic theory or model.

The first, and oldest, exchange rate theory used to determine if a currency might be over- or undervalued is known as *purchasing power parity*. Sixteenth-century Spanish scholars first formalized this simple and straightforward theory. Because of its simplicity, economists have given considerable attention to purchasing power parity and its application to a variety of policy and practical issues.

Absolute Purchasing Power Parity

PURCHASING POWER PARITY
A condition that states that if international arbitrage is unhindered, the price of a good or service in one nation should be the same as the exchange-rate-adjusted price of the same good or service in another nation.

Purchasing Power Parity (PPP) states that, ignoring transportation costs, tax differentials, and trade restrictions, traded homogeneous goods and services should have the same price in two countries after converting their prices into a common currency. Thus, purchasing power parity is often called the *law of one price*.

To illustrate this, suppose that the market price of a trench coat is $450 in New York. The market price of the same trench coat in London, however is £300. Thus, PPP would imply that the dollar equivalent exchange rate of the pound should be 1.5 $/£. Using this rate, we can convert the pound price of the trench coat in London to a dollar price of $450 (£300 × 1.5 $/£ = $450). Therefore, the trench coat has the same price in London as it does in New York after adjusting for the exchange rate.

Arbitrage and PPP If, in this example, the market exchange rate is not 1.5 $/£, then an arbitrage opportunity exists. Suppose the exchange rate is equal to 1.6 $/£. Then the dollar price of the trench coat in London is £300 × 1.6 $/£ = $480. The astute arbitrager would be able to buy a trench coat in new York for $450, take it to London and sell it for £300, exchange the £300 for $480 on the foreign exchange market, and earn a profit of $30, ignoring transaction and transportation costs.

The arbitrage activity just described would cause a flow of trench coats from New York to London. The exchange of the British for the U.S. dollar on the foreign exchange market would generate an increase in the demand for dollars relative to pounds. The three markets (New York trench coat market, London trench coat market, and foreign exchange market) would experience adjustments. The increased demand for trench coats in New York would cause an increase in the price of trench coats in New York. The increased supply of trench coats in London would cause a decrease in price of trench coats in London.

If a number of goods and services were being traded, then there would be an increase in the demand for the dollar relative to the British pound. The increased demand for the dollar relative to the pound would cause the dollar to appreciate relative to the pound. All of these adjustments, which result from the arbitrage activity, would tend to equalize the (same currency) prices of traded goods and services, and thus eliminate the arbitrage opportunity.

At this point we can see that price differences between the two economies can lead to changes in the demand for a currency. In our example, the lower price of trench coats in New York would lead to an eventual increase in the demand for the dollar relative to the pound. Therefore, we would expect an outward shift in the demand curve for the dollar. We may conclude that price differences could be considered a factor of currency demand because relatively lower prices in a nation causes the demand for that nation's currency to increase.

Absolute PPP   This theory of the relationship between prices and exchange rates is absolute purchasing power parity, because it deals with absolute price levels. We can formalize and express absolute PPP as follows. Let S denote the U.S.-dollar-equivalent exchange rate of the pound, $/£. Let P denote the price level in the United States and P^* denote the price level in the United Kingdom. Then we can express absolute PPP as

$$P = S \times P^*.$$

In words, the domestic price level should be equal to the foreign price level times the spot exchange rate. Note that the spot rate converts the foreign price level so that it is expressed in terms of the domestic currency. We could say, therefore, that the domestic price level expressed in the domestic currency should equal the foreign price level expressed in the domestic currency. This is the law of one price.

The absolute PPP theory applies to all internationally traded and identical goods and services of the two economies. Consequently, P represents the price level of this *range* of goods, not a single good, as in our previous example. This would imply that arbitrage activity would ensure equality of the same-currency price level of these goods and services across the two economies.

Practical Problems and Shortcomings of Absolute PPP   What is the practical application of absolute PPP? As discussed earlier in the chapter, economists use price indexes to measure the price level of a basket of goods within an economy. Therefore, we would use a common price index, such as the CPI, to represent the price level in the United States and in the United Kingdom. Substituting the CPI for the price level in the previous equation yields:

$$CPI = S \times CPI^*.$$

We can rearrange this equation as

$$S = CPI / CPI^*.$$

This equation expresses the spot exchange rate as the ratio of the CPIs in the two economies. This would lead one to believe that the ratio of the CPIs could be used to determine the equilibrium exchange rate level, and, therefore, to predict exchange rate movements.

Although absolute PPP is intuitively appealing, it is not worth much as a predictor of exchange rate movements. There are several obvious reasons why this form of PPP may not perform well. First, we know that our initial assumptions of no transportation costs, no tax differentials, and no trade restrictions do not apply to the real world. Even in light of these assumptions we would still expect a strong relationship between relative price levels and the exchange rate.

Another problem we encounter in applying absolute PPP is in the nature of the price index itself. The U.S. CPI attempts to measure the price of goods and services purchased by a typical U.S. consumer. The U.K. CPI attempts to measure the price of goods and services purchased by a typical U.K. consumer. The typical U.S. consumption basket is likely to be different from the typical U.K. consumption basket. The types and amounts of goods and services that a typical U.K. consumer might purchase is likely to be different from that of a U.S. consumer. Further, many goods and services included in a CPI, such as housing and medical care, are not traded internationally. Therefore, there are no arbitrage in goods and services only. It does not address international flows of financial assets, a very important feature of the international economy, as explained in Chapter 1.

For these reasons, absolute PPP typically fails to hold. Short-run deviations from PPP are significant. As a result, economists discount this form of PPP as a short-run guide. As a long-run theory, it performs only slightly better, with deviations from PPP being eliminated very slowly over time. Nonetheless, this version of PPP continues to be used in a number of different applications. One of the most popular applications is the "Big Mac Index," published by the *Economist* magazine, as described in the following Management Notebook.

ON THE WEB

For weekly articles on the global economy, visit the Economist *magazine at:* **http://www.economist.com**

Relative Purchasing Power Parity

The version of PPP discussed in the previous section was *absolute* PPP, because it deals with absolute price levels. *Relative* purchasing power parity is a weaker version of purchasing power parity, as it addresses price changes as opposed to absolute price levels. Relative PPP, as an exchange rate theory, relates exchange rate changes to the differences in price changes across countries.

We can use the earlier expression for absolute PPP to derive the relative version of PPP. Let's denote the percentage change of a variable by placing the characters "%Δ" in front of the variable. Then, for example, %ΔP would represent the change in the price level over a given period. By calculating the change of each variable in the expression for absolute PPP, we can express relative PPP as

$$\%\Delta S = \%\Delta P - \%\Delta P^*.$$

Relative PPP, as a guide to exchange rate changes, implies that the change in an exchange rate is equal to the difference in price changes between the two economies. As we discussed in Chapter 1, economists refer to the change in an exchange rate as an appreciation or the currency of depreciation, and they use the percentage change in a price index as a measure of inflation. Let π denote the rate of inflation over a given period. In keeping with our earlier example, let π^* be the rate of inflation in Britain as measured by the percentage change in the CPI. Let π denote the rate of inflation in the United States as measured by the percentage change in the CPI, and let $\%\Delta S$ denote the rate of appreciation or depreciation of the U.S. dollar relative to the British pound as measured by the percentage change in the U.S.-dollar-equivalent exchange rate. Then we can rewrite relative PPP as:

$$\%\Delta S = \pi - \pi^*.$$

In words, the appreciation or depreciation of a currency is given by the difference between the two nations' inflation rates.

To show how this version of relative PPP is used as a guide for exchange rate determination, consider the following example. In 1995, the CPI for the United States was 116.7, and it was 119.9 in 1996. For the United Kingdom, the CPI was 118.8 in 1995, and it was 121.3 in 1996. The U.S.-dollar-equivalent exchange rate of the pound was 1.603 in 1995, and it was 1.558 in 1996. Using these numbers, we can calculate the rates of inflation and currency appreciation or depreciation.

Using the percentage change formula, the rate of inflation in the United States between 1995 and 1996 was 2.74 percent [(119.9 − 116.7)/116.7 × 100 = 2.74]. For the United Kingdom, the rate of inflation over this period was 2.10 percent [(121.3 − 118.8)/118.8 × 100 = 2.10]. The rate of appreciation of the dollar was 2.807 percent [(1.558 − 1.603)/1.603 × 100 = −2.807]. Substituting the percentage changes into the equation for relative PPP yields the implied rate of depreciation (if positive) or appreciation (if negative) of the dollar,

$$\%\Delta S = 2.74\% - 2.10\% = 0.64\%.$$

Thus, relative PPP suggests that the percentage change in the U.S.-dollar-equivalent exchange rate should have been 0.64 percent, or a depreciation of the dollar relative to the pound of 0.64 percent. It was already shown, however, that over this period the dollar *appreciated* relative to the pound by 2.807 percent. Because the dollar appreciated as opposed to depreciating, relative PPP suggests that the dollar is *overvalued* against the pound. Provided the dollar was neither overvalued nor undervalued relative to the pound in 1995, the market determined exchange value of the dollar relative to the pound should decrease, or the U.S. rate of inflation should decline further below that of the United Kingdom.

Did this adjustment occur in 1997? In 1997 the U.S. CPI was 122.7. Using the percentage change formula once again, the rate of inflation in the United States between 1996 and 1997 was 2.34 percent [(122.7 − 119.9)/119.9 × 100 = 2.34]. The U.K. CPI was 124.9 in 1997. The rate of inflation in the United Kingdom between 1996 and 1997 was 2.97 percent [(124.9 − 121.3)/121.3 × 100 = 2.97]. The U.S.-dollar-equivalent exchange rate of the pound was 1.663 in 1997, so, using the percentage change formula, between 1996 and 1997, the

MANAGEMENT NOTEBOOK

Would You Like Fries with that PPP? The Big Mac Index

Undoubtedly the most popular version of PPP is the Big Mac Index. First published in 1986 as a satirical approach to exchange rate prediction, the Big Mac Index has become an annual feature of the *Economist* magazine. Because a Big Mac is pretty much the same basket of goods around the world (two all-beef patties, special sauce, . . .), and its price information in various locations is easily obtained, the Big Mac is a tasty little price guide to use in the PPP equation. The 1997 version of the Big Mac Index is provided in Table 2–6.

Table 2–6 shows the price of a Big Mac in the United States as $2.36, whereas the price of a Big Mac in Britain is £1.79. Using the earlier equation for PPP, dividing the U.S. price of the Big Mac by the British price yields an exchange rate value as implied by PPP of 1.32 $/£. We then compare the implied value and the actual (market-determined) value of 1.51 $/£. The actual, or market-determined, value of the dollar relative to the pound is lower than that implied by PPP. Therefore, the Big Mac Index indicates that the local currency, the pound, is overvalued against the dollar. We can express this over-valuation in percentage terms as the percentage difference between the implied value and the actual value,

which works out to be 14 percent in this example. The "burgernomics" of this is that because the pound is overvalued relative to the dollar, we would expect the pound to depreciate relative to the dollar.

How does the Big Mac perform as a guide to exchange rate movements? A number of studies investigating this very question have emerged in recent years. The general conclusions are mixed. In the short run, the index does not predict exchange rate changes well. It performs better in the long run, but most of the adjustment to PPP is in the form of price changes. Therefore, the Big Mac Index is not a good predictor on a systematic basis.

FOR CRITICAL ANALYSIS:

Using any issue of the Economist *magazine, locate the Italian lira price of the magazine from the bottom of the front cover and compare it with the U.S. price. Now turn to the financial indicators at the very back of the magazine and find the lira-per-U.S.-dollar exchange rate. Using the expression for absolute PPP, did PPP hold? If not, what type of adjustment in the Italian-lira-per-U.S.-dollar exchange rate would you expect?*

dollar depreciated relative to the pound by 6.739 percent [(1.663 − 1.558)/1.558 × 100 = 6.739]. Thus, some adjustment, as suggested by relative PPP, did occur: The dollar depreciated relative to the pound, and the United States experienced a lower rate of inflation than did the United Kingdom.

How does relative PPP perform under empirical examination? The evidence shows that relative PPP performs better than absolute PPP. Nonetheless, it is still a poor short-run guide to exchange rate changes in the major economies

TABLE 2-6 **THE HAMBURGER STANDARD**

	BIG MAC PRICES		IMPLIED PPP* OF THE DOLLAR	ACTUAL $ EXCHANGE RATE 7/4/97	LOCAL CURRENCY UNDER(−)/OVER(+) VALUATION,† %
	IN LOCAL CURRENCY	IN DOLLARS			
United States‡	$2.42	2.42	–	–	–
Argentina	Peso2.50	2.50	1.03	1.0	+3
Australia	A$2.50	1.94	1.03	1.29	−20
Austria	Sch34.00	2.82	14.0	12.0	+17
Belgium	BFr109	3.09	45.0	35.3	+28
Brazil	Real2.97	2.81	1.23	1.06	+16
Britain	£ 1.81	2.95	1.34††	1.63††	+22
Canada	C$2.88	2.07	1.19	1.39	−14
Chile	Peso1,200	2.88	496	417	+19
China	Yuan9.70	1.16	4.01	8.33	−52
Czech Republic	CKr53.0	1.81	21.9	29.2	−25
Denmark	DKr25.75	3.95	10.6	6.52	+63
France	FFr17.5	3.04	7.23	5.76	+26
Germany	DM4.90	2.86	2.02	1.71	+18
Hong Kong	HK$9.90	1.28	4.09	7.75	−47
Hungary	Forint271	1.52	112	178	−37
Israel	Shekel11.5	3.40	4.75	3.38	+40
Italy	Lire4,600	2.73	1,901	1,683	+13
Japan	¥294	2.34	121	126	−3
Malaysia	M$3.87	1.55	1.60	2.50	−36
Mexico	Peso14.9	1.89	6.16	7.90	−22
Netherlands	F15.45	2.83	2.25	1.92	+17
New Zealand	NZ$3.25	2.24	1.34	1.45	−7
Poland	Zloty4.30	1.39	1.78	3.10	−43
Russia	Rouble11,000	1.92	4,545	5,739	−21
Singapore	S$3.00	2.08	1.24	1.44	−14
South Africa	Rand7.80	1.76	3.22	4.43	−27
South Korea	Won2,300	2.57	950	894	+6
Spain	Pta375	2.60	155	144	+7
Sweden	SKr26.0	3.37	10.7	7.72	+39
Switzerland	SFr5.90	4.02	2.44	1.47	+66
Taiwan	NT$68.0	2.47	28.1	27.6	+2
Thailand	Baht46.7	1.79	19.3	26.1	−26

*Purchasing-power parity; local price divided by price in the United States. †Against dollar
‡Average of New York, Chicago, San Francisco and Atlanta ††Dollars per pound
From *The Economist*, April 12, 1997. © 1997 The Economist Newspaper Group, Inc. Reprinted with permission. Further reproduction prohibited.

and is only slightly better as a long-run guide. Relative PPP does perform well during periods of very high inflation, because during these periods price changes are the dominant influence on the value of a currency.

In conclusion, absolute PPP and relative PPP are common, but perhaps ill-advised, guides to exchange rate movements. One of their principal short-comings is that they provide theories based only on the international exchange of goods and services and do not consider financial flows and money stocks.

FUNDAMENTAL ISSUE #6

What is purchasing power parity, and is it useful as a guide to movements in exchange rates? Purchasing power parity is a theory of the relationship between the prices of traded goods and services and the exchange rate. There are two versions of PPP. Absolute PPP relates price levels and the exchange rate level. Relative PPP relates price changes and changes in the exchange rate. Although both versions are commonly used guides to exchange rates and their movements, generally neither are very useful, particularly in the short run.

Chapter Summary

1. **The Foreign Exchange Market:** The foreign exchange market is a system of private banks, foreign exchange dealers, and central banks through which individuals, businesses, and governments trade foreign exchange, or other nation's currencies. The foreign exchange rate is the rate at which one currency exchanges for another in the foreign exchange market.

2. **Currency Appreciation or Depreciation:** When the domestic currency appreciates relative to a foreign currency, it gains in value relative to the foreign currency. This means people can trade fewer domestic currency units in exchange for each foreign currency unit. When the domestic currency depreciates relative to a foreign currency, it has lost value against the foreign currency. This means people must give more domestic currency units in exchange for each foreign currency unit. When the exchange rate rises, the domestic currency may have appreciated or depreciated, depending on how we express the exchange rate.

3. **How Economists Measure the Overall Value of a Currency:** In the course of a typical trading day, a currency may appreciate against some currencies and depreciate against others. An effective exchange rate is an index that measures the weighted average value of a currency relative to a basket of currencies. An effective exchange rate, therefore, is a useful measure of general changes in a currency's value.

4. **Foreign Exchange Market Arbitrage:** Foreign exchange arbitrage is the act of profiting from differences between the exchange rates of foreign exchange. Spatial arbitrage refers to an arbitrage transaction that is conducted in two different markets, or separated by space. Triangular arbitrage involves more than two currencies and/or markets.

5. **Determining the Value of a Currency:** The interaction of the forces of supply and demand in the foreign exchange market determines the value of a currency. A currency is over- or undervalued if the market-determined exchange rate is inconsistent with the value predicted by a formal or informal model.

6. **Purchasing Power Parity and Its Usefulness for Predicting Exchange Rates:** Purchasing power parity is a theory of the relationship between the prices of traded goods and services and the exchange rate. There are two versions of purchasing power parity. Absolute PPP relates the price levels of two countries and the level of the exchange rate. Relative PPP relates two nations' inflation rates and the rate of change in the exchange rate. Although both versions are commonly used guides to exchange rates movements, neither is particularly useful as a short-run guide to exchange rate movements.

QUESTIONS AND PROBLEMS

1. Suppose the U.S.-dollar-equivalent exchange rate of the French franc was 0.1715 on Thursday and 0.1718 on Friday. Did the French franc appreciate or depreciate relative to the U.S. dollar? How much was the appreciation/depreciation (in percentage change terms)?

2. Complete the following cross-rate table.

NUMERATOR	NORWAY NKr	GERMANY DM	FRANCE FFR	BELGIUM BFR
Denominator				
Belgium BFR	20.170			
France FFR	12.360			
Germany DM	4.162			
Norway NKr	—			

3. Suppose in New York the French franc and British pound trade at the following exchange rates: FFr/\$ = 5.7480, and \$/£ = 1.6386. In London, the French-franc-equivalent rate of the pound is 9.4184 FFr/£. Is there an arbitrage opportunity? Why or why not? Calculate the profit to be made on \$1,000,000. (Show your work to four decimal points.)

4. Suppose we observe the following information for France, Canada, and the United States.

	S(1990)	S(1997)	CPI(1990)	CPI(1997)	1990 U.S. EXPORTS	1990 U.S. IMPORTS
France	\$0.198/ff	\$0.179/ff	100	114.3	8,652	11,634
Canada	\$0.867/\$c	\$0.741/\$c	100	117.4	75,243	80,621
U.S.			100	121.0		

Calculate the 1990 and 1997 *bilateral weighted effective exchange value* for the U.S. dollar using 1990 as the base year. Does your answer indicate an *appreciation* or *depreciation* of the U.S. dollar from 1990 to 1997? What were the rates of change? Next, construct a real effective exchange value. Does your answer indicate an *appreciation* or *depreciation* of the U.S. dollar from 1990 to 1997? What were the rates of change?

5. Using the data provided in problem 4, construct the 1990 and 1997 *real exchange rates* between the U.S. dollar and the French franc. Was there a real appreciation or depreciation of the dollar relative to the franc? What were the rates of change?

6. Suppose the German mark price of a dollar was 1.5545 DM/$ in 1990 and 1.6522 DM/$ in 1999. The price index for Germany (1990 = 100) was 111.11 in 1999 and the price index for the United States (1990 = 100) was 117.86 in 1999. According to absolute PPP, is the dollar overvalued or undervalued in 1999? Considering this information, would you expect the dollar to appreciate or depreciate? By what percentage?

7. Using the data provided in problem 6, was the dollar overvalued or undervalued in 1999 according to relative PPP? Considering this information, would you expect the dollar to appreciate or depreciate, and by how much (in percentage terms)?

ON-LINE APPLICATION

This chapter presented numerous exchange rate concepts including that of the trading margin. The trading margin reflects, among other things, the risk associated with holding the currency.

Internet URL: http://www.ft.com

Title: The Financial Times

Navigation: Begin with the registration page at this site. If this is the first time you have visited the site, you will have to register. After registering, go to *index.* Select *Currencies: Pound and Dollar spot.* Next select *South Korea* in the query window and click on *get spot rates.* Calculate today's trading margin and the trading margin of six months earlier.

Application: Based on the trading margin you calculated, answer the following questions.

1. Write a brief statement as to how the currency risk affects the trading margin

2. How did the trading margin change? How much did it change in percentage terms?

3. Write a brief statement explaining why the trading margin changed as it did.

REFERENCES AND RECOMMENDED READINGS

Clayton, Gary, and Martin Giesbrecht. *A Guide to Everday Economic Statistics, Third Edition.* New York: McGraw-Hill, Inc., 1995.

Cumby, Robert. "Forecasting Exchange Rates and Relative Prices with the Hamburger Standard: Is What You Want What You Get with McParity?" *NBER Working Paper, 5675* (July 1996).

Eichengreen, Barry. *International Monetary Arrangements for the 21st Century.* Washington D.C.: The Brookings Institution, 1994.

Kim, Taeho. *International Money and Banking.* New York: Routledge, 1993.

"McCurrencies: Where is the Beef?" *Economist.* (April 27, 1996): 82.

Pakko, Michael, and Patricia Pollard. "For Here or To Go? Purchasing Power Parity and the Big Mac." *Federal Reserve Bank of St. Louis Review, 78*(1) (1996): 3–22.

Rogoff, Kenneth. "The Purchasing Power Parity Puzzle." *Journal of Economic Literature, XXXIV* (June 1995): 647–668.

Taylor, Mark. "The Economics of Exchange Rates." *Journal of Economic Literature, XXXIII* (March 1995): 13–47.

Wallich, Henry C. "The Evolution of the International Monetary System." In Michael B. Connolly, ed., *The International Monetary System: Choices for the Future.* New York: Praeger Publishers, 1982, pp. 280–292.

3

EXCHANGE RATE ARRANGEMENTS AND SYSTEMS, PAST TO PRESENT

FUNDAMENTAL ISSUES

1. What is an exchange rate arrangement or exchange rate system?

2. How does a gold standard constitute an exchange rate arrangement or system?

3. What was the Bretton Woods system of "pegged" exchange rates?

4. What post–Bretton Woods system of "flexible" exchange rates prevails today?

5. What are crawling peg and basket-peg exchange rate arrangements?

6. What is a currency board or an independent currency authority?

7. Which is best, a fixed or flexible exchange rate arrangement?

The Czech Republic began a transitional process from a centrally planned economy to a market-based economy in the early 1990s. The early economic performance of the Czech Republic—relatively low inflation, low unemployment, positive growth and investment, and most notably, a stable currency—distinguished it from the other transitional economies. The Czech National Bank, the central bank of the Czech Republic, fixed the exchange value of the Czech currency, the koruna, to a weighted average of the exchange values of the U.S. dollar and the deutsche mark. The objective of this policy was to promote price stability of imported and exported goods.

In late 1995, a rising current account deficit led some economists to believe that the Czech National Bank would have to adjust its pegged exchange rate. Michael Friedlander and Richard Morawetz, economists with Nomura, a Japanese investment bank, speculated in a bank report titled "Devaluation likely after June Elections" that the Czech National Bank would have to adjust the rate as much as 20 percent. Outraged that such a report would emerge before national elections, Czech Prime Minister Vaclav Klaus demanded and received a letter of apology from Hitoshi Tonomura, the chairman of Nomura's European management committee. At the time, Nomura was bidding on the right to issue a $70–$100 million international share offering for a bank believed to have close ties with the Czech Prime Minister's political party.

Speculative pressure on the koruna mounted, and on February 28, 1996, the Czech National Bank widened the range in which it allowed the value of the koruna to fluctuate. On May 26, 1997, Prime Minister Klaus stated that "foreign capital is losing faith in us," and the Czech National Bank abandoned its peg against the U.S. dollar and the deutsche mark, ending 75 months of a stable currency for the Czech Republic.

The determination of the international value of a nation's currency is a very important issue. This issue, combined with the way in which a nation conducts its macroeconomic policies, may result in a stable economic environment that promotes trade and investment, or an unstable environment that puts its industries at a competitive disadvantage. The history of exchange rate management shows us that, though entered with the best intentions, few exchange rate arrangements can avoid speculative and political pressures forever.

EXCHANGE RATE ARRANGEMENTS AND SYSTEMS

MONETARY ORDER A set of laws and regulations that establishes the framework within which individuals conduct and settle transactions.

Before we can begin to understand the institutional framework that governs the value of a nation's currency, we must first understand a nation's monetary order. A **monetary order** is a set of laws and regulations that establishes the framework within which individuals conduct and settle transactions.

One decision a nation must make is whether its national money will be a commodity money, a commodity-backed money, or fiat money. A *commodity money* is a tangible good that individuals use as means of payment, or a medium of exchange, such as gold or silver coins. *Commodity-backed money* is a monetary unit whose value relates to a specific commodity or commodities, such as silver or gold, and that national authorities will accept in exchange for the commodity. *Fiat money,* which is our money today, is a monetary unit not backed by any commodity. Its value is determined solely by the worth that people attach to it as a medium of exchange.

EXCHANGE RATE ARRANGEMENT OR EXCHANGE RATE SYSTEM A set of rules that determine the international value of a currency.

A nation's monetary order also sets forth the rules that form the nation's exchange rate arrangement, and, either formally or informally, the nation's participation in an exchange rate system. An **exchange rate arrangement** or **exchange rate system** is the set of rules governing the value of an individual nation's currency relative to other foreign currencies. *Exchange rate arrangement* or *exchange rate system* will be used interchangeably throughout this chapter.

To better understand the relationships among a monetary order and an exchange rate arrangement or exchange rate system, we will examine the history of three important exchange rate systems: the gold standard, the Bretton Woods System, and the Post–Bretton Woods floating-rate system.

FUNDAMENTAL ISSUE #I

What is an exchange rate arrangement or exchange rate system? An exchange rate arrangement or system is the set of rules established by a nation to govern the value of its currency relative to foreign currencies. The exchange rate arrangement or exchange rate system evolves from the nation's monetary order, which is the set of laws and rules that establishes the monetary framework within which transactions are conducted.

THE GOLD STANDARD

By the mid–1870s, the major economies of the world had adopted a commodity-backed monetary order for their national currencies. Gold served as the underlying commodity, and the period until 1914 became known as the

CONVERTIBILITY The ability to freely exchange a currency for a reserve commodity or reserve currency.

gold standard era. Under this framework, a nation would fix an official price of gold in terms of the national currency, known as the *mint parity,* and establish convertibility at that rate. **Convertibility** is the ability to freely exchange a currency for a commodity or another currency at a given rate of exchange. For example, between 1837 to 1933 (except for the suspension of convertibility during the Civil War), the U.S. mint parity of one fine ounce of gold was $20.646, with the dollar convertible at that rate. To maintain the mint parity, or the exchange value between gold and the national currency, a nation must condition its money stock on the level of its gold reserves.

The Gold Standard as an Exchange Rate Arrangement

Other industrialized nations had adopted a commodity-backed order before or shortly after the same time that the United States reinstated convertibility following the Civil War, which ended in 1865. These decisions, though adopted unilaterally, also established each nations' exchange rate arrangement and informally led to an exchange rate system among the nations. The gold standard established an exchange rate arrangement because it meant that people could exchange the dollar both domestically and internationally, at the mint parity rate. Thus, the exchange value between gold and the dollar determined the international value of the dollar.

This also established an exchange rate arrangement among the countries that had adopted a gold standard. Because each country valued its currency relative to gold, this indirectly established an exchange value between the domestic currency and the currencies of all other countries on a gold standard.

As an example, under the gold standard, Britain's gold parity rate was, as shown in Figure 3-1, £4.252 per fine ounce. Using the gold parity rates of the U.S. dollar and the British pound, we can determine the rate of exchange that existed between the two currencies. The mint parity rate of the United States was $20.646 and the mint parity rate of the British pound was £4.252. As shown in Figure 3-1, the U.S.-dollar-equivalent rate of the British pound, $/£, was therefore $20.646/£4.252, or 4.856 $/£.

If the exchange rate deviated from this amount, ignoring transportation costs of gold, then an arbitrage opportunity would have existed. For example, suppose that, at the mint parity rates just given, the exchange rate between the U.S. dollar and the British pound was 5 $/£. One would have been able to take $20.646 and exchange it for one ounce of gold. The gold could then have been exported to Britain and exchanged for £4.252. The £4.252 would have exchanged on the foreign exchange market for £4.252 × 5 $/£, or $21.26, earning a profit of $0.614. If we consider the transportation costs of gold, the exchange rate between two currencies would remain in a range or band centered on the ratio of the mint parity values. These transportation and transaction costs of gold determine the width of the range, because they affect the profitability of exporting or importing gold.

Under the gold standard, all of the currencies of the nations adopting a gold standard were linked together, with their exchange values determined in

---

FIGURE 3–1   THE GOLD STANDARD AS AN EXCHANGE RATE SYSTEM

Countries adopting a gold standard valued their currencies relative to gold. The gold parity rate for the British pound was £4.252 per troy ounce of gold and for the U.S. dollar $20.646 per troy ounce. The gold parity rates determined the exchange rate between the two currencies.

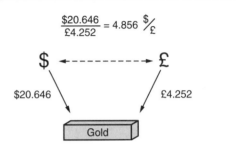

$$\frac{\$20.646}{£4.252} = 4.856\ \$/£$$

---

the manner just described. Just as the mint parities established the exchange rate between the dollar and the pound, they also established the exchange values among the dollar, the French franc, and the deutsche mark.

For example, under the gold standard the mint parity of the French franc was Ffr107.008 and the deutsche mark mint parity was DM86.672. The exchange rate between the dollar and the French franc, therefore, was 5.183 Ffr/$ (Ffr107.008/$20.646). The exchange rate between the dollar and the deutsche mark was 4.198 DM/$ (DM86.672/$20.646). The link to gold determined all of the cross rates between the various currencies, as well. It is in this manner that the adoption of a commodity-backed monetary order by individual nations established the basis of an exchange rate system.

FUNDAMENTAL ISSUE #2

How does a gold standard constitute an exchange rate arrangement or system? A gold standard constitutes an exchange rate arrangement for an adopting nation because it establishes a domestic and international rate of exchange between the domestic currency and gold. A gold standard also links the exchange rate arrangements between all of the nations adopting a gold standard. The exchange value between gold and a nation's currency indirectly establishes rates of exchange among all of the currencies.

Performance of the Gold Standard

Because the gold standard resulted from the decisions of individual nations made at different times, there is no single starting date for the system. Generally, however, economists consider the gold standard era to have existed from the 1870s onward. Though the system was temporarily suspended during World War I, and eventually collapsed in the early 1930s, some individuals still argue for a return to a gold standard. In the 1996 U.S. presidential election, conservatives such as Steve Forbes and Jack Kemp recommended that a new president should stabilize the dollar value of the nation's gold reserves as a critical first step toward restoring "sound money" to the United States. What is the record of the gold standard, and why do individuals such as Mr. Forbes and Mr. Kemp long for its return?

Positive and Negative Aspects of a Gold Standard As indicated earlier, an important element of a commodity-backed monetary order is that a nation's quantity of money, or its *money stock*, depends directly on the amount of commodity reserves the nation's monetary authority has. A given amount of commodity reserves may support a multiple number of units of money. As an example, between 1879 and 1913 the U.S. money stock was 8.5 times the amount of the monetary gold stock. Thus, *changes* in a nation's money stock depend only on *changes* in the mining and production of monetary gold.

If the supply of gold is rather constant, this particular aspect of a gold standard, therefore, promotes long-run stability of the nation's money stock and long-run stability of real output, prices, and the exchange rate. Another important aspect of a commodity-backed monetary order is that it does not require a central bank. An official authority can maintain the ratio of money stock to gold reserves. Canada and the United States, for example, did not have a central bank during the late 1800s and early 1900s.

A commodity-backed monetary order has some negative aspects, as well. For example, a gold standard has very significant resource costs, such as minting and transportation costs. It can be quite costly for a nation to maintain and exchange a tangible commodity such as gold.

The Economic Environment of the Gold Standard Era Now that we understand these important aspects of a gold standard, lets consider both the conditions that existed and were specific to the 1870–1913 period, and the contributions of the gold standard to the world economic environment. First, this period represents a very peaceful period, with no major wars among the participating nations. Second, there was virtually free capital mobility among nations. Finally, London was the center of the world's money and capital markets.

These latter two characteristics enabled the efficient and smooth functioning of the gold standard. Further, the Bank of England, at the center of the world's financial markets, maintained its gold parity values and established the credibility of the system. The apparent concentration of influence in the London market was so significant that economist J. M. Keynes stated that the Bank of England could almost have claimed to be the "conductor of the international orchestra." We can conclude, therefore, that the early gold standard period had some unique characteristics, at least two of which are not prevalent today.

During this period, most nations did indeed experience stable long-run real economic output, prices, and exchange rates. It is this long-run stability that proponents of a return to a gold standard praise. Because there were short-run random changes in the demand and supply of gold, however, there were also short-run random changes in the money stock and in the prices of goods and services. The short-run volatility of the money stock, in part, led to periodic financial and banking instability. Further, the short-run volatility of prices was greater under the gold standard than the exchange rate systems that followed.

The Collapse of the Gold Standard

In 1914, after the beginning of World War I, many European nations suspended convertibility of their currencies into gold. For all practical purposes, the gold standard was no longer in effect, and exchange values between currencies did fluctuate. Many nations, therefore, restricted the types and amounts of international payments that their residents could make in hopes of maintaining the prewar values of their currencies.

World War I formally ended with the signing of the Versailles treaty in 1919. There was a general desire among the leading nations to return to a gold standard at the prewar parities. In 1925, the United Kingdom returned to a gold standard at the prewar parity, but other countries, such as France, returned at much lower values. As a result, many believed that the prewar parity rate would result in an overvalued pound. To maintain the parity value, the United Kingdom had to endure high interest rates and high unemployment. The political costs of maintaining the value of the pound became too great, and the United Kingdom abandoned the gold standard in 1931 by suspending the convertibility of the pound to gold. The United States followed suit in 1933. By 1936, most of the industrialized nations had left the gold standard.

What brought about the demise of the gold standard was a return to parity values that led to overvalued currencies, such as the case with the United Kingdom, or undervalued currencies, such as the case with the French franc. In addition, nations facing a worldwide depression decided to pursue objectives such as higher employment levels and real growth rates, rather than to maintain the exchange value of their currencies.

The collapse of the gold standard, combined with the passage of protectionist trade policies such as the Smoot–Hawley Act in the United States, wreaked havoc on international trade flows. As a result, the volume of international trade in 1933 was less than one-third of its 1929 amount. This, in addition to other prevailing economic factors, contributed to the Great Depression, which began with an industrial depression in the United Kingdom in 1926 and the crash of the stock market in the United States in 1929. The Great Depression continued until the outbreak of World War II.

THE BRETTON WOODS SYSTEM

During World War II, the leaders of the United Kingdom and the United States recognized the importance of having a sound monetary order in place when the war ended. The economies of Europe and Japan would be in great need of rebuilding, and therefore would need imports from nations with intact industrial bases, such as the United States. The nations' leaders pressed for negotiations on an exchange rate system that would facilitate international trade and payments.

Although forty-four nations participated in the conference that led to the postwar exchange rate system, the primary architects of the system were Harry White of the U.S. Treasury and the renowned British economist John Maynard Keynes. Negotiations concluded with the ratification of a new system in 1944 at a small resort in Bretton Woods, New Hampshire. The conference, though officially called the International Monetary and Financial Conference of the United and Associated Nations, became known as the Bretton Woods Conference; hence, the agreement reached there became known as the Bretton Woods Agreement.

ON THE WEB
Learn more about the International Monetary Fund and its functions at the IMF web site: **http://www.imf.org**

The Bretton Woods Agreement

One significant outcome of the Bretton Woods Agreement was the creation of the **International Monetary Fund,** or IMF. The IMF's principle function was to lend to member nations experiencing a shortage of foreign exchange reserves. Nations could become members of the IMF by subscribing, or paying a quota or fee. The size and economic resources of a nation determined the initial quota, with 25 percent of the quota paid in gold and 75 percent in the nation's currency. Two other important institutions that arose at the end of the war were the International Bank for Reconstruction and Development (IBRD), known as the *World Bank,* and the *General Agreement on Tariffs and Trade, (GATT).* The World Bank financed postwar reconstruction and GATT promoted the reduction of trade barriers and settled trade disputes.

INTERNATIONAL MONETARY FUND A supranational organization whose major responsibility is to lend reserves to member nations experiencing a shortage.

The exchange rate system that emerged from the agreement was one of pegged, but adjustable, exchange rates. Under a **pegged exchange rate system,** nations fix the value of their currencies to something other than a commodity, such as another nation's currency. As under a gold standard, each nation pegged its exchange rate. In contrast to a gold standard, the U.S. dollar was the anchor of the system. The Bretton Woods system, therefore, was a **dollar-standard exchange rate system,** which is a system in which nations peg the value of their currencies to the dollar and freely convert their currencies for the dollar at the pegged value.

PEGGED EXCHANGE RATE SYSTEM An exchange rate arrangement in which a country pegs the international value of the domestic currency to the currency of another nation.

DOLLAR-STANDARD EXCHANGE RATE SYSTEM An exchange rate arrangement in which a country pegs its currency to the U.S. dollar and freely exchanges the domestic currency for the dollar at the pegged rate.

Under the Bretton Woods Agreement, each country could choose to state the par value of its currency in terms of gold, or establish a par value for its currency relative to the U.S. dollar. All but the United States chose the dollar, making the dollar the common unit of value in the system. Each country would then stand ready to buy and sell U.S. dollars in the foreign exchange market to maintain the exchange value of its currency within 1 percent, on either side, of the par value, commonly referred to as the *parity band*.

The United States, by way of contrast, fixed the value of the U.S. dollar to gold at a mint parity of $35 per troy ounce. The United States agreed to buy and sell gold with other official monetary agencies in settlement of transactions. Because each country pegged its currency to the U.S. dollar, and the U.S. maintained the value of the dollar relative to gold, this indirectly linked each nondollar currency to gold.

Figure 3–2 illustrates the system and the relationships among gold, the U.S. dollar, the British pound, and the German deutsche mark. The figure shows the dollar with a mint parity value of $35 per troy ounce of gold. The British pound is pegged to the dollar at an exchange rate of 2.80 $/£ and the deutsche mark is pegged to the dollar at an exchange rate of 4.20 DM/$. This system established the link among the British pound and gold, the British pound and the deutsche mark, and the deutsche mark and gold.

Although each country pegged its currency, under the Bretton Woods Agreement it could change the par value with the approval of the IMF. A nation **devalues** its currency when it raises the mint parity value or par value, meaning that a person must offer more units of the currency to purchase a unit of the commodity or foreign currency. A nation **revalues** its currency when it lowers the mint parity value or par value, meaning that one may offer fewer units of the currency to purchase a unit of the commodity or foreign

DEVALUE A situation in which a nation with a pegged exchange rate arrangement changes the pegged, or parity, value of its currency so that it takes a *greater* number of domestic currency units to purchase one unit of the foreign currency to which the nation's currency value is pegged.

REVALUE A situation in which a nation with a pegged exchange rate arrangement changes the pegged, or parity, value of its currency so that it takes a *smaller* number of domestic currency units to purchase one unit of the foreign currency to which the nation's currency value is pegged.

FIGURE 3–2 THE BRETTON WOODS EXCHANGE RATE SYSTEM

In practice, the Bretton Woods system linked all currencies, other than the U.S. dollar, to gold and to each other, through the U.S. dollar. The United States pegged the dollar to gold at a parity rate of $35 per troy ounce. Other nations, such as the United Kingdom and West Germany, pegged their currencies to the dollar. This indirectly established exchange values among the British pound and the deutsche mark, and among the pound and the deutsche mark and gold.

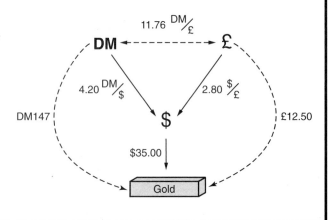

currency. Thus, the Bretton Woods system was an adjustable peg system, rather than a system of fixed exchange rates.

Under the Bretton Woods system, nations used the U.S. dollar to settle international transactions. This made the dollar the primary **reserve currency** of the system, or the currency accepted as a means of settling international debts. Typically, only the United States settled international debts with gold under this system.

One problem encountered during the late 1940s and 1950s was that participating nations did not have sufficient U.S. dollar reserves. The Marshall Plan and the European Payments Union alleviated this dollar shortage problem. The purpose of the *Marshall Plan,* officially titled the European Recovery Program, was to help rebuild the European economies by supplying financial capital. The inflow of capital funds yielded dollars that the nations could use to conduct current account transactions.

The *European Payments Union* was an arrangement among European nations to help settle deficits and surpluses with each other. Under this arrangement, member nations would track their net monthly deficit or surplus balances with one another. At the end of the month, the nations would settle, in U.S. dollars, only the net balance they had with each other.

RESERVE CURRENCY The currency commonly used to settle international debts and to express the exchange value of other nations' currencies.

FUNDAMENTAL ISSUE #3

What was the Bretton Woods system of "pegged" exchange rates? The Bretton Woods system was a system of adjustable pegged exchange rates whose parity values could be changed when warranted. Each country established and maintained a parity value of its currency, or peg, relative to gold or the U.S. dollar. All chose the U.S. dollar, making the system a dollar-standard system. Nations could change their parity values, either revaluing or devaluing, with approval of the IMF.

Performance of the Bretton Woods System

Because the United States stated the par value of the dollar in terms of gold while all other participating countries stated their par values in terms of the U.S. dollar, the system had two sets of rules: one for the United States and one for all other countries. Accordingly, the United States had to follow an independent and anti-inflationary monetary policy while standing ready to exchange the dollar for gold at the par value. All other nations had to buy or sell U.S. dollar reserves to keep their domestic currency exchange values against the dollar within the 1-percent parity band.

For most of the period 1945 to 1968, the world economy experienced growth in output and a rapid increase in world trade. Nations did not experience the type of liquidity crises that were prevalent during the gold standard. Consequently, short-run prices were more stable as well. The Bretton Woods system was not without its shortcomings, however.

Because the United States was the only country committed to converting its domestic currency for gold, the system had an inadvertent weakness. Even if the United States followed an anti-inflationary monetary policy, the possibility of a *run on the dollar,* in which traders and official foreign agencies seek to convert the dollar for gold *en masse,* existed. Because there was a limit to the U.S. gold stock, the dollar would not increase in value relative to gold, but it could always decrease in value. This situation made the dollar the target of foreign exchange speculators, as well as nationalistic politicians who opposed the dollar as the standard of the world's exchange rate system. (See "Policy Notebook: de Gaulle Attacks the Dollar!")

The Gold Pool   In 1960, the United States and many of the European economies collectively began to intervene in the gold market. The purpose of these interventions was to maintain the dollar price of gold and to ensure the stability of the foreign exchange system. This coordinated arrangement became known as the *gold pool.*

Beginning in 1964, the U.S. government increased federal spending under heightened military involvement in Vietnam and the social programs termed the *Great Society.* The United States experienced a considerable economic expansion accompanied by rising inflation. The United States ran sizable balance of payments deficits with Germany and Japan in particular, and as a result, there was a considerable increase in the amount of dollars abroad. What had once been a dollar shortage on the world market was now a dollar glut.

The increase in the volume of dollars on the world market led many traders to believe that the United States would devalue the dollar relative to gold. That is, they anticipated that the dollar's parity value would increase, meaning that they would have to offer more dollars in exchange for a troy ounce of gold. If the parity value of the dollar increased, any individual or government holding dollar reserves would experience a capital loss on those dollar holdings.

In 1967, a devaluation of the British pound, which caused individuals and monetary agencies holding the pound to experience a 14.3 percent capital loss, increased speculation that the United States would devalue the dollar. Because of the speculation that a dollar devaluation was imminent, the demand for gold increased in the London commodities market. To meet the increase in demand and maintain the dollar parity value, the United States had to increase the supply of gold to the market. At one point, U.S. gold sales were so great that the weight of an emergency air shipment from Fort Knox to London collapsed the weighing room floor of the Bank of England.

The participating nations eventually abandoned the gold pool in 1968. Following the end of the gold pool, there was considerable pressure on the central banks of France and Germany to maintain their par values. Eventually, the

POLICY NOTEBOOK

de Gaulle Attacks the Dollar!

During World War II, French President Charles de Gaulle had a clear vision of France as the leader of a postwar united Europe. The postwar reality was a U.S.-designed rearmament of Germany, NATO as a U.S.-dominated military alliance, and the Bretton Woods system.

The Bretton Woods system, which was negotiated primarily by British and U.S. officials, allowed nations to peg their currencies against either gold or the U.S. dollar. Most nations, excluding the United States, pegged to the dollar and settled their international debts with the dollar. The Bretton Woods system was, therefore, a dollar-standard system, and in President de Gaulle's view, an Anglo-Saxon dominated exchange rate system.

During a relatively calm period of the Bretton Woods system, when France was not borrowing reserves from the IMF, President de Gaulle became both vocal and active in his opposition to the dollar as the international reserve currency. During a press conference on February 4, 1965, President de Gaulle announced that the Bretton Woods system should be

. . . on an unquestionable monetary basis that does not bear the stamp of any one country in particular, On what basis? Truly it is hard to imagine that it could be any

standard other than gold, yes gold, whose nature does not alter, which may be formed equally well in ingots, bars, or coins, which has no nationality, and which has, eternally and universally, been regarded as the unalterable currency par excellence. . . .

The U.S. Treasury issued a statement the same day rejecting a return to a gold standard and asserting that the U.S. Treasury would maintain the parity value of gold. A week later, the French stepped up their purchases of gold from the U.S. Treasury, increasing gold flows from the United States.

Within the next three years, gold flows from the United States became acute, and in March 1968 President de Gaulle took aim at the dollar again, calling the existing system "unworkable." Six weeks later, France experienced a currency crisis of its own and borrowed reserves from the United States, temporarily cooling the French assault on the dollar.

FOR CRITICAL ANALYSIS:
Why was it in the interest of France for de Gaulle to "take aim at the dollar"?

crisis forced France to devalue the franc relative to the dollar by more than 11 percent. The day after the German elections of September 28, 1969, the German central bank, the *Bundesbank*, sought to maintain the parity value by purchasing $245 million in dollar reserves in the first hour and a half that the market was open. Eventually the deutsche mark was revalued by more than 9 percent. Although these two nations did change their parity values, other European nations did not, so pressure on the system continued.

In early 1971, the U.S. balance on goods and services, illustrated in Figure 3–3, swung from a small surplus to a surprisingly large deficit, further confirming speculation of an overvalued dollar. In May 1971, as the U.S. trade deficit continued to expand, pressure to maintain the parity values

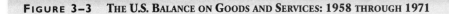

FIGURE 3–3   THE U.S. BALANCE ON GOODS AND SERVICES: 1958 THROUGH 1971

The U.S. balance on goods and services changed from a small surplus in 1970 to a surprisingly large deficit in 1971. The deficits that emerged early in 1971 reinforced speculations that the dollar was overvalued relative to the other major currencies.

SOURCE: Data from International Monetary Fund, *International Financial Statistics.*

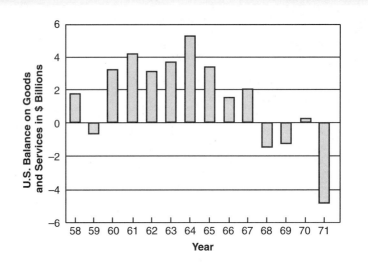

between the European currencies, particularly the German mark, and the U.S. dollar climaxed. On May 4, 1971, in order to prevent an appreciation of the deutsche mark relative to the dollar, the Bundesbank bought $1 billion on the exchange market. During the first hour of trading on the following day, the Bundesbank bought more than $1 billion. The Bundesbank then announced that it was abandoning official exchange operations to maintain the parity value. Austria, Belgium, the Netherlands, and Switzerland followed suit.

President Nixon Closes the Gold Window   On August 8, 1971, newspapers reported that the French were about to present $191 million of reserves to the United States in exchange for gold so that the French government could make a loan repayment to the IMF. This amount was far short of being a major concern to the United States. In this regard, economist Peter Kenen said, that "No one country was large enough to blackmail Washington by demanding gold for dollars, but each was large enough to fear its actions could undermine the monetary system." Nonetheless, speculation against the dollar further increased and the media reported gold outflows on a daily basis. Eventually, on August 15, 1971, during a televised address, U.S. President Richard Nixon announced that the United States would "suspend temporarily the convertibility of the dollar into gold or other reserve assets, except in amounts and conditions determined to be in the interest of monetary stability and in the best interest of the United States."

By abandoning the convertibility of the U.S. dollar into gold to foreign central banks, the United States eliminated the anchor of the Bretton Woods system. The incompatibility of U.S. and European macroeconomic policies and the unwillingness of the U.S. government to devalue the dollar or of European governments to revalue their currencies brought about the end of the system. Once again, the world's exchange system was in disarray: consequently, international trade between nations also fell into a more chaotic state.

The Smithsonian Agreement and the Snake in the Tunnel

In an effort to restore order to the exchange rate system, the ten nations with the largest share of reserves of the IMF met on December 16 and 17, 1971, at the Smithsonian Institution in Washington, D.C. These ten nations—West Germany, France, Japan, the United Kingdom, the United States, Italy, Canada, Belgium, the Netherlands, and Sweden—which together compose the **Group of Ten (G10)**, negotiated the Smithsonian Agreement. This established a new exchange rate system that was similar in many respects to the Bretton Woods system. The agreement established new par values, most representing a revaluation of European currencies relative to the dollar, but with a wider band of 2.25 percent on either side of the parity value. The U.S. dollar, though devalued relative to gold, would not be convertible into gold. Following the conference, President Nixon characterized the agreement to the media as "the most significant monetary agreement in the history of the world."

GROUP OF TEN (G10) Belgium, Canada, France, Germany, Italy, Japan, the Netherlands, Sweden, the United Kingdom, and the United States.

Shortly after the Smithsonian Agreement, on March 7, 1972, the six member nations of the European Economic Community (France, West Germany, Italy, Belgium, the Netherlands, and Luxembourg), announced a plan to move toward greater monetary union. The member countries intended to maintain the exchange values of their currencies relative to each other within 2.25 percent. This arrangement became known as the *snake in the tunnel*. Participating nations would maintain exchange values by selling or buying each other's currencies. Collectively, the EEC currencies represented the snake. Whenever the "snake" would move to the allowable edge of the Smithsonian exchange value, the "tunnel,"—the EEC nations—would buy and sell U.S. dollars as needed.

By the middle of 1972, the exchange markets were in turmoil once again. Britain took action first, abandoning the snake in the tunnel in June, only two months after joining. Early in 1973, failure of the Smithsonian Agreement was on the horizon. Despite enormous diplomatic efforts and a 10 percent devaluation of the dollar against gold by the U.S. Treasury, the European nations participating in the snake announced that they would no longer maintain their parity values relative to outside nations, such as the United States. Thus ended the "most significant monetary agreement in the history of the world," just fifteen months after it began.

THE FLEXIBLE EXCHANGE RATE SYSTEM

FLEXIBLE EXCHANGE RATE SYSTEM An exchange rate arrangement whereby a nation allows market forces to determine the international value of its currency.

Although there were attempts to return to some form of an adjustable pegged system, a de facto system of flexible exchange rates emerged. A floating, or **flexible exchange rate system,** as described in Chapter 2, is one in which the forces of supply and demand determine a currency's exchange value in the private market. Leading U.S. economists, such as Milton Friedman, had argued in favor of a flexible exchange rate arrangement since the early 1950s.

The Economic Summits and a New Order

Although the world was operating under a floating rate system, it was not an official system, because the constitution of the IMF forbade floating rates. In 1975, French President Valery Giscard d'Estaing decided to host an informal gathering of the leaders of the major industrialized nations, France, the United States, Germany, Japan, Italy, and the United Kingdom.

Discussions on the exchange rate system continued between the representatives of the United States and France. On the eve of the summit, the two agreed to a system of flexible exchange rates with coordinated interventions in the foreign exchange market whenever they felt such interventions were required to ensure stability of exchange rates. President Giscard announced the breakthrough at the summit and received immediate endorsement for it from the other participating leaders.

JAMAICA ACCORDS A meeting of the member nations of the IMF, occurring in January 1976, amending the constitution of the IMF to allow, among other things, each member nation to determine its own exchange rate arrangement.

With the leaders of the major industrialized countries endorsing the system envisioned in the French–United States negotiations, the members of the IMF rapidly went about completing the details and revising the constitution of the IMF. Member nations completed the negotiations, known as the **Jamaica Accords,** in Jamaica in 1976.

Within six months of the first economic summit, U.S. president Gerald Ford decided to host an economic summit of his own. President Ford, to the disapproval of President Giscard, also invited Canada to participate. With this action, President Ford institutionalized the summits, now held during the summer of each year and known as the Economic Summit. In 1997, summit host U.S. President William Clinton invited Russian President Boris Yeltsin to attend the summit from beginning to end, although he was excused from the economic meetings. At the 1998 Birmingham summit, British Prime Minister Tony Blair invited President Yeltsin to participate in all the summit meetings, formally expanding the participating nations to eight.

ON THE WEB
Learn more about the annual economic summits from the University of Toronto G8 Research Group at:
http://www.g7.utoronto.ca

Performance of the Floating Rate System

The flexibility of the current exchange rate system has allowed the major economies to endure some tumultuous economic conditions. Since 1973, which economists recognize as the beginning of the floating exchange rate period, the major economies have experienced divergent macroeconomic policies, major internal and external economic shocks, and unprecedented fiscal and current account deficits. By allowing its currency's exchange value to be determined by market forces, a floating rate country is able to focus monetary policies on domestic objectives. Most nations, however, have experienced periods of dramatic increases and decreases in the exchange values of their currencies.

Arguably, the greatest challenges to the leading industrialized economies and the exchange rate system occurred between 1973 and 1974 and in 1979. The outbreak of the Middle East War and an oil embargo imposed in October 1973 resulted in a significant appreciation of the dollar relative to many European currencies and the Japanese yen. In 1979, the Organization of Oil and Petroleum Exporting Countries (OPEC) undertook a series of actions that eventually tripled the price of crude oil on the world market. Already struggling with inflation, oil-importing countries were hard hit by the increase in oil prices. At the end of the 1970s and early 1980s, Canada, France, Italy, the United Kingdom, and the United States were experiencing double-digit or near double-digit rates of inflation.

Also in 1979, U.S. President Jimmy Carter appointed Paul Volcker as chair of the Federal Reserve. Paul Volcker made it publicly known that the Federal Reserve would pursue a single objective of reducing inflation. The Fed's policy actions resulted in a U.S. recession in 1981 and 1982. More important to our discussion, they resulted in very high interest rates and put upward pressure on the value of the dollar relative to other major currencies. (Later chapters, particularly Chapters 12 through 15, examine the effect of monetary policy on interest rates, output, and exchanges rates.) As a result, the dollar began an appreciation that continued until early 1985.

Figure 3–4 illustrates the Federal Reserve's nominal effective exchange value of the dollar relative to the currencies of the G10 nations since 1973. The rise of the dollar's value from 1981 through 1985 is one prominent feature of the diagram. The other is the dramatic decline in the dollar's value from 1985 through 1987. We have explained why the dollar appreciated from 1981 through 1985, but why did it peak in 1985 and reverse direction until 1987?

The Plaza Agreement and the Louvre Accord

GROUP OF FIVE (G5) The nations of France, Germany, Japan, the United Kingdom, and the United States.

PLAZA AGREEMENT A meeting of the central bankers and finance ministers of the G5 nations that took place at the Plaza Hotel in New York in September 1985. The participants announced that the exchange value of the dollar was too strong and that the nations would coordinate their intervention actions in order to drive down the value of the dollar.

For some time, the central bankers and finance ministers of a subset of the G10 nations had been meeting to discuss macroeconomic conditions and policies. This subgroup included the United States, the United Kingdom, Germany, Japan, and France, and is known as the **Group of Five,** or **G5.** The content, conclusions, and policy outcomes of these meetings had always been secret. In September 1985, the G5 met at the Plaza Hotel in New York to discuss, primarily, the status of the dollar. In an unprecedented move, the participants issued a statement to the media following the meeting. In what is now known as the **Plaza Agreement,** the G5 announced that it was their belief that the dollar was at a level inconsistent with underlying economic

---

FIGURE 3-4 THE U.S. G10 NOMINAL EFFECTIVE EXCHANGE RATE SINCE 1973

Between 1981 and 1985 the U.S. dollar experienced a considerable appreciation in average value relative to the currencies of ten major nations. Within two years, the appreciation had been reversed.

SOURCE: Data from Federal Reserve Board.

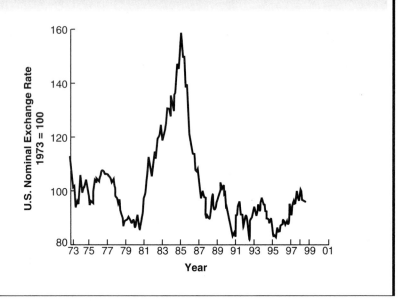

conditions. The G5 said that they would intervene *collectively* to drive down the value of the dollar.

The purpose of the press statement was to convince currency traders that the G5 meant business. The statement and periodic surprise interventions by the G5 appeared to have convinced currency traders. As shown in Figure 3–4, the dollar reversed its prior four-year appreciation within the subsequent two years.

Over the next two years, the G5 increased in ranks to include Italy and Canada (becoming consistent with the membership of the annual economic summits at that time). This expanded group is the **Group of Seven (G7).** In February 1986, the G7 met at the Louvre in France. Once again the dollar was the focus of discussion. Following the meeting, known as the **Louvre Accord,** the finance ministers and central bankers announced that the dollar had reached a level now consistent with underlying economic conditions. The G7, therefore, would only intervene in the foreign exchange market as needed to ensure stability.

This meeting defined the exchange rate management approach of the G7 and G10 economies since 1986. These nations intervene, usually on a collective and unannounced basis, only when a currency or currencies have reached a critical threshold. What is the critical threshold? This is unknown to traders, who are always trying to predict the actions of the finance ministers and central bankers.

Under the Louvre Accord, nations will intervene on behalf of their currencies from time to time. Consequently, the system is not a true flexible

GROUP OF SEVEN (G7) The G5 plus Canada and Italy.

LOUVRE ACCORD A meeting of the central bankers and finance ministers of the G7 nations, less Italy, that took place in February 1987. The participants announced that the exchange value of the dollar had fallen to a level consistent with "economic fundamentals" and that central banks would intervene in the foreign exchange market only to ensure stability of exchange rates.

MANAGED OR DIRTY FLOAT An exchange rate arrangement in which a nation allows the international value of its currency to be primarily determined by market forces, but intervenes from time to time to stabilize its currency.

exchange rate system. This type of exchange rate system is a **managed float (or dirty float),** which is a system of flexible exchange rates but with periodic intervention by official agencies.

FUNDAMENTAL ISSUE #4

What post–Bretton Woods system of "flexible" exchange rates prevails today? Economists typically characterize the post–Bretton Woods exchange rate system as one of floating exchange rates. Individual nations, however, have adopted a wide variety of exchange rate arrangements, ranging from pegged to fully flexible exchange rates. Further, the leading industrialized nations periodically intervene in the foreign exchange markets to stabilize their currencies, making the system a managed float as opposed to a truly flexible exchange rate system.

OTHER FORMS OF EXCHANGE RATE ARRANGEMENTS TODAY

In the previous sections of this chapter, we used an earlier period of the foreign exchange system to illustrate the workings of a gold standard, the Bretton Woods system to illustrate an adjustable-peg dollar standard, and the post–Bretton Woods system to illustrate a floating exchange rate system. Since the break-up of the Bretton Woods system, nations have adopted a wide variety of exchange rate arrangements.

Figure 3–5 illustrates the general types of exchange rate arrangements that IMF member nations have adopted. The figure shows the percent of those nations that peg the exchange value of their currencies to single currencies, currency composites, limited flexibility arrangements, managed float, and floating arrangements. As shown in Figure 3–5, the U.S. dollar and the French franc are the currencies to which other currencies most commonly are pegged. Many nations peg their currencies to a composite, or basket of currencies. (We explain in detail the workings of a basket peg later in this chapter.) Finally, the pie chart shows that a great number of nations have a managed float or an independently floating exchange rate arrangement.

As Figure 3–5 illustrates, nations have adopted a wide variety of exchange rate arrangements. The figure, however, does not provide details on the operation of these arrangements. As the 1997 Southeast Asian currency crises painfully showed, the operation of a nation's currency arrangement is of vital importance. Hence, we shall now consider three specific types of arrangements: a crawling peg, a currency basket peg, and a currency board (or independent currency authority).

FIGURE 3-5 CURRENT FOREIGN EXCHANGE RATE ARRANGEMENTS

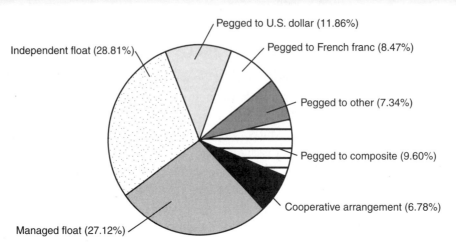

Currently 56 percent of the member nations of the IMF have an independent float or managed float exchange rate arrangement. For those countries that peg their currency, the U.S. dollar is the most common currency for a peg and a composite or basket peg is the second most common arrangement.

SOURCE: Data from International Monetary Fund, *International Financial Statistics.*

Crawling Pegs

Even after the collapse of the Bretton Woods system, some nations have decided to peg their currencies to the currencies of other nations. There are a number of reasons why a nation may choose to do this. The most common argument for pegged exchange rates is that reducing exchange rate volatility and uncertainty may yield gains in economic efficiency. Thus, nations that have a large volume of trade with another nation, but a less stable currency, may choose to peg their currency. Pegging to another nation's currency and reducing exchange rate volatility, therefore, may promote greater trade and capital flows between the two nations.

The macroeconomic conditions of the two nations, however, may be quite different. In later chapters, particularly Chapters 12 through 15, you will see that when the macroeconomic conditions of two nations differ, the paths of their exchange rates will likely differ. This situation would make it difficult, if not impossible, to maintain a pegged exchange rate. In this situation, nations that peg the value of their currencies to the currencies of other nations, may allow the parity value to continuously change. This type of exchange rate arrangement is a **crawling peg.**

CRAWLING PEG An exchange rate arrangement in which a country pegs its currency to the currency of another nation, but allows the parity value to change at regular time intervals.

Mexico's Crawling Peg Arrangement of the Early 1990s The exchange rate arrangement of Mexico during the early 1990s provides a very good example of a crawling peg. Large volumes of Mexico's trade and capital flows are with the United States. To promote exchange rate stability and facilitate these transactions, Mexico pegged the peso to the U.S. dollar. Macroeconomic conditions were quite different between the two economies, however. The difference between the inflation rates of these two nations was most notable; Mexico had a much higher rate of inflation. Because of these differences, officials realized that, according to the theory of relative purchasing power parity presented in Chapter 2, there would be a general tendency for the Mexican peso to depreciate against the U.S. dollar. In light of this recognition, Mexico adopted a crawling peg.

The Parity Band   As in the gold standard and the Bretton Woods system, nations that peg their currencies usually allow the exchange rate to deviate from the parity value by a certain amount, typically expressed as a percentage, on either side of the parity value. The exchange rate, therefore, is not a fixed value, but can fluctuate within a band, known as an **exchange rate band.**

In November 1991, Mexican authorities established a lower and upper limit within which the peso-per-dollar exchange rate could fluctuate. The lower limit, which represents the maximum allowable amount the peso could appreciate against the dollar, was a fixed value of 3.051 pesos per U.S. dollar. The upper limit, which represents the maximum allowable amount the peso could depreciate against the dollar, increased by 0.0002 pesos per U.S. dollar per day. Officials changed the allowable increase to 0.0004 pesos per U.S. dollar per day on October 21, 1992.

Figure 3–6 illustrates the exchange rate band and the actual exchange rate for the Mexican peso between November 1991 and December 1994. Note that a horizontal line represented the lower limit because it was a fixed amount. The upper limit, however, sloped upward, illustrating the crawling peg.

A nation may choose to change its parity value from time to time, either devaluing or revaluing its currency against the currencies to which it pegs. In December 1994, Mexican officials were rapidly depleting Mexico's U.S. dollar reserves trying to maintain the exchange rate arrangement. Officials decided to change the central parity rate, or devalue the peso, for the first time in fifteen years, increasing the parity value by 15 percent. As a result, however, individuals lost confidence in the management of the exchange rate arrangement. Massive outflows of capital led officials to abandon the crawling peg and float the peso two days after the devaluation.

Currency Baskets

The previous section outlined the most common argument for pegging one's currency, that reducing exchange rate volatility and uncertainty may yield gains in economic efficiency. For this same reason, a nation might choose to peg its currency to a weighted average of a number of foreign currencies, known as a **currency basket peg.** The additional motivation for pegging to a currency basket is that the weighted average of a basket of currencies is likely to be less variable than the exchange rate of a single currency.

EXCHANGE RATE BAND A range of exchange values, with an upper and lower limit within which the exchange value of the domestic currency can fluctuate.

ON THE WEB
Obtain more information on the Mexican economy from the Bank of Mexico at:
http://www.banxico.org.mx

CURRENCY BASKET PEG An exchange rate arrangement in which a country pegs its currency to the weighted average value of a basket or selected number of currencies.

FIGURE 3-6 THE MEXICAN PESO EXCHANGE RATE ARRANGEMENT

Mexico's crawling peg exchange rate arrangement had an exchange rate band with a fixed lower exchange value, shown by the horizontal line. The upper limit increased daily by 0.0004 pesos. The actual exchange value of the peso remained within the bands until December 1994.

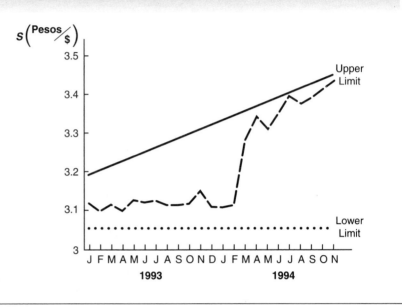

To better understand what a currency basket is, imagine that you have six different coins in your hand, each from a different country. Next imagine that you place all of the coins in a basket. Let's allow the sum of the coins in the basket to equal one unit of your own fictitious currency. The value of the coins in the basket is the value at which you would try to maintain your own currency under a currency basket arrangement.

Selecting a Currency Basket Typically, a nation that adopts a currency basket peg will have a small number of currencies in the basket. The reason for this is that as the number of currencies to which the nation pegs increases, managing the basket peg becomes more difficult. Most nations using a currency basket arrangement peg to six or fewer currencies.

The choice of currencies to be included in the basket is similar to the choice made in constructing an effective exchange rate, as discussed in Chapter 2. A basket typically includes selected currencies most prominent in the nation's international trade, capital flows, or international debt settlement. The basket assigns a weight to each currency, similar to the construction of an effective exchange rate. The weights sum to unity as well. The choice of weights reflects the relative importance of each currency in the nation's international transactions. To better understand the workings of a currency basket peg, let's examine the currency basket of the Czech Republic.

The Currency Basket of the Czech Republic Economic reform and transition to a market-based economy in Czechoslovakia began in 1990. The primary economic goals of the nation were to maintain macroeconomic stability while privatizing many government-controlled industries. One part of the economic measures taken was to peg the domestic currency to a currency basket. In 1993, the Czech Republic and Slovakia separated, though both continued the practice of pegging to a currency basket.

The central bank of the Czech Republic, the Czech National Bank, had the responsibility for pegging the value of the currency, the koruna, or crown, Kc. The currency basket consisted of 0.0125 U.S. dollars and 0.0329 deutsche marks, and was equivalent to one Czech crown. The value of the basket could deviate by 0.5 percent against either one of these two currencies.

For a considerable period, the crown-per-U.S. dollar exchange rate was 28 Kc/$ (which is equivalent to 0.0357 $/Kc). An actual exchange rate between the dollar and the deutsche mark during this period was 1.4176 DM/$ (which is equivalent to 0.7054 $/DM). Using these values, we can calculate the cross rate between the deutsche mark and the crown, which is 0.0506 DM/Kc (0.0357 $/Kc × 1.4176 DM/$ = 0.0506 DM/Kc). Using all of the information available thus far, we can express the currency basket in its currency content and in its exchange rate value.

Determining the Basket Value and Weights The currency content of the basket is simply the sum of the monetary amounts in the basket, set equal to one unit of the domestic currency. In our example, the currency content is

$$\$0.0125 + DM0.0329 = Kc1.$$

The exchange rate value of the basket is the weighted average of the foreign currency per domestic currency exchange rates, which is equal to unity. We will let W represent the weight assigned to a particular currency. In the example, the exchange value of the basket is

$$W_{US}(0.0357 \text{ \$/Kc}) + W_{DM}(0.0506 \text{ DM/Kc}) = 1.$$

Comparing the equation for the currency content against the equation for the exchange rate value, we can determine the weights assigned to each currency. (This can be an important task, because authorities might not publish the weights assigned to currencies.) Suppose we multiply the equation for the exchange value of the basket by Kc. The equation then becomes:

$$W_{US}(\$0.0357) + W_{DM}(DM0.0506) = Kc1.$$

Because this equation and the equation for the currency content of the basket are equal, $W_{US}(\$0.0357)$ must equal $0.0125 and $W_{DM}(DM0.0506)$ must equal DM0.0329. Let's solve for the weights on the dollar, determined by

$$W_{US}(\$0.0357) = \$0.0125.$$

We can divide each side of the equation by \$0.0357, yielding

$$W_{US} = \$0.0125/\$0.0357 = 0.35,$$

or 35 percent. Because the weights must sum to one, W_{DM} equals 0.65, or 65 percent. In words, in the Czech currency basket the dollar receives a weight of 35 percent and the mark receives a weight of 65 percent.

Managing the Currency Basket Under a pegged exchange rate arrangement, the nation's monetary authority maintains the exchange rate between the domestic currency and the currency that the nation is pegging to. A currency basket arrangement introduces an interesting wrinkle. The authority must concentrate on the exchange rate between the domestic currency and the currencies included in the currency basket *and* the cross rates between the currencies in the basket. If these cross rates change, the monetary authority must take action, either depreciating or appreciating the nation's currency so as to maintain the currency basket value. The weights determine the amount of appreciation or depreciation.

FUNDAMENTAL ISSUE #5

What are crawling peg and basket peg exchange rate arrangements? Crawling peg and basket peg exchange rate arrangements are types of pegged exchange rate arrangements. Under a crawling peg, the parity value and the exchange rate bands are allowed to change at regular intervals, providing more flexibility in the arrangement than a true pegged exchange rate arrangement. Under a basket peg arrangement, officials peg the domestic currency to a weighted average value of a small number of currencies. A weighted average value of currencies tends to be less volatile than the exchange value of a single currency.

Independent Currency Authorities

Earlier in this chapter, we explained that a gold standard does not require a central bank. Changes in a nation's official gold reserves govern changes in the nation's money stock. A gold standard only requires an official monetary agency that will increase or decrease the money in circulation as required. Some nations today do not have a central bank. Instead, they have an independent monetary authority or currency board.

A **currency board, or independent monetary authority,** is an independent monetary agency that links the growth of the money stock to the foreign exchange holdings of the currency board. It does this by issuing domestic money in exchange for foreign currency at a fixed exchange rate.

CURRENCY BOARD OR INDEPENDENT CURRENCY AUTHORITY An independent monetary agency that substitutes for a central bank. The currency board pegs the value of the domestic currency, and changes in the foreign reserve holdings of the currency board determine the level of the domestic money stock.

Currency boards were an invention of the British Empire, first established in Mauritius in 1849. The currency board system peaked in the 1940s and virtually disappeared during the 1960s. The currency board was a means of providing a British colony with a stable and convertible currency. The colony issued its monetary instruments—at a fixed rate of exchange—against the pound sterling assets that the currency board held in London. The colony's money, therefore, was convertible at a fixed rate and was as stable as the pound sterling. The colonies saved considerable resources because they did not need to hold and handle sterling coins and notes.

As practiced today, a currency board pegs its nation's currency to the currency of another nation and buys or sells foreign currency reserves as appropriate to maintain the parity value. When the monetary authority buys or sells foreign reserves, it changes the amount of domestic money in circulation. This, and this alone, governs changes in the nation's money stock.

The currency board has very limited responsibilities. The currency board does not hold notes or bills issued by the domestic government, does not set reserves requirements on the nation's banks, and does not serve as a lender of last resort to the nation's banks, as a central bank typically does.

Because of these limited responsibilities, a currency board cannot engage in discretionary monetary policy, and therefore, is shielded from political influence. For this reason, the last few years have seen an increased interest in currency boards. Some economists see currency boards as the best means for some nations to establish a credible approach to price stability.

ON THE WEB

Learn more about the Bank of Lithuania (Lietuvos Bankas) at: **http://www.lbank.lt**

There are a few independent monetary authorities or currency boards today. Some have been established very recently. Estonia, Lithuania, Hong Kong, and Argentina have each established a currency board arrangement. Some currency boards have been successful while others have failed. (See "Management Notebook: Lithuania Abandons its Currency Board.")

FUNDAMENTAL ISSUE #6

What is a currency board or an independent currency authority? A currency board or independent currency authority supplants a central bank. The responsibilities of a currency board, however, are much more limited than those of a typical central bank. A currency board pegs the value of the domestic currency and buys and sells foreign reserves in order to maintain the pegged value. Changes in the stock of foreign reserves solely determine the domestic money stock. Currency boards, therefore, better isolate monetary policy from domestic political pressures.

Lithuania Abandons Its Currency Board

In 1994, Lithuania introduced a currency board system and pegged its currency, the *lit*, to the U.S. dollar at a fixed rate. The rigid discipline of a currency board has had some undesirable effects on the Lithuanian economy. By 1997, a rise in the value of the U.S. dollar caused an appreciation of the lit against the currencies of Lithuania's major trading partners, leading to a trade deficit equivalent to 10 percent of GDP. A banking crisis forced the currency board to ignore the rule that a board is not a lender of last resort to private banks. It has been speculated that the board used a large amount of its reserves to bail out two major banks.

Lithuania recently abandoned the currency board and established a central bank and a pegged exchange rate arrangement. Under the arrangement, U.S. dollar reserves determine only 80 percent of the nation's money stock. This, in turn, gives some flexibility, also known as *discretion*, to the central bank. The main con-

cern over this institutional restructuring was how to do it without scaring off foreign investment.

The official stance of the monetary authorities of Lithuania is that becoming members of the European Union and eventually the European Monetary Union required the switch to a central bank and a pegged exchange rate arrangement. Reinoldijus Sarkinas, chairman of the Bank of Lithuania, claimed that authorities never used board reserves to bail out banks and that the credibility of the new arrangement was sound. He further claimed that the switch from a currency board to a fixed exchange rate arrangement will " . . . pass unnoticed by both currency markets and the public."

FOR CRITICAL ANALYSIS:
What did Lithuania give up by abandoning its currency board arrangement?

FIXED OR FLOATING EXCHANGE RATES?

Now that we have examined a number of exchange rate arrangements, an obvious question is which one is best. Unfortunately, there is no clear-cut answer to this question, and the debate over the benefits of fixed versus flexible exchange rates is one of the oldest in economics. This is precisely the reason why there are so many different types of arrangements in existence today.

On the one hand, fixed exchange rates may promote sound macroeconomic policy, helping to reduce inflation and leading to a stable economic environment. This, in turn, can boost an economy's real economic growth. 98

Under a fixed nominal exchange rate arrangement, however, real exchange rates may appreciate and reduce the competitiveness of the nation's exporters (as was the case with the Czech Republic).

Flexible exchange rates, on the other hand, may help a country overcome external shocks, such as an unusual inflow of capital from abroad or a sudden increase in the price of an imported resource. Flexible exchange rates introduce an additional element of uncertainty and additional volatility, which is the common criticism of flexible rates. In the industrialized nations, however, there is not clear evidence showing that volatility of nominal exchange rates dampens foreign trade or investment.

What is more important than the exchange rate arrangement is that the nation conduct sound macroeconomic policy making. This is perhaps the most overlooked reality in the debate over fixed versus flexible exchange rates. Further, the debate often contrasts the current and imperfect regime with a utopian version of another regime in which governments always conduct policymaking such that it is consistent with the exchange rate regime. As was shown throughout this chapter, that is not always the case. We shall return to these issues in more detail in Chapters 12 through 15.

FUNDAMENTAL ISSUE #7

Which is best, a fixed or flexible exchange rate arrangement?
Whether it is better to peg the value of the domestic currency or allow it to be flexible and market determined is one of the longest-running debates in economics. There is no clear-cut answer, as each arrangement has it own advantages and disadvantages. Sound macroeconomic policymaking is more important in creating a stable economic environment than the choice of an exchange rate arrangement.

CHAPTER SUMMARY

1. **Exchange Rate Arrangements or Exchange Rate Systems:** An exchange rate arrangement or exchange rate system is a nation's set of rules that determine the international exchange value of the domestic currency and links a nation's currency value to the currencies of other nations.

2. **A Gold Standard as an Exchange Rate Arrangement or Exchange Rate System:** A gold standard constitutes an exchange rate arrangement for a nation. With a rule of pegging the value of its currency to gold, a nation establishes the international value of its currency in terms of gold. A gold standard also constitutes an exchange rate system among those nations adopting a gold standard. With the value of each currency established relative to gold, the exchange value among currencies is also established.

3. **The Bretton Woods System of "Pegged" Exchange Rates:** Under the Bretton Woods system, nations pegged the value of their currencies to the U.S. dollar, which was linked to gold. The parity values that nations pegged their currencies at could be changed, and thus the currency devalued or revalued, with the

permission of the IMF. The Bretton Woods system was, therefore, a system of adjustable pegged exchange rates.

4. **The Post–Bretton Woods System of "Flexible" Exchange Rates:** In today's world economy, a number of exchange rate arrangements are in place, ranging from flexible exchange rate arrangements to fixed or pegged exchange rate arrangements. The leading industrialized nations intervene from time to time in the foreign exchange markets. The overall system, therefore, is primarily one of managed floating exchange rates.

5. **Crawling Peg and Basket-Peg Exchange Rate Arrangements:** Some nations desire the stability of a fixed exchange but find it difficult to maintain a rigid parity value. As a result, some nations have adopted either a crawling peg or a basket-peg exchange rate arrangement. Under a crawling peg exchange rate arrangement, a nation pegs the value of its currency, but the parity rate is adjusted at given time intervals. Under a basket-peg exchange rate arrangement, a nation pegs the value of its currency to the value of a basket of selected currencies.

6. **A Currency Board or Independent Currency Authority:** A currency board substitutes for a central bank. The responsibilities of the currency board, however, are much more limited than those of a central bank. Under a currency board system, the value of the nation's currency is pegged to another nation's currency. The currency board is responsible for maintaining the pegged value of the domestic currency by conditioning the nation's outstanding stock of money on the amount of foreign reserves that the currency board has.

7. **Fixed versus Flexible Exchange Rate Arrangements:** There is no clear-cut answer as to whether it is better to peg the value of a nation's currency or to allow the value of the currency to be determined in the market for foreign exchange. Each type of exchange rate arrangement has its benefits and its costs. Sound macroeconomic policymaking is actually more important in creating a sound and stable economic environment than is the choice of exchange rate arrangement.

QUESTIONS AND PROBLEMS

1. List all of the various types of exchange rate arrangements described in this chapter. (*Hint:* There are seven described in this chapter.) Order the list of exchange rate arrangements from fixed to most flexible.

2. Describe two primary functions of the International Monetary Fund.

3. Suppose the value of the U.S. dollar is pegged to gold at a rate of $50 per ounce. Next suppose that the value of the British pound is pegged to the U.S. dollar at a rate of 1.5 dollars per pound, and the value of the Canadian dollar is pegged to the U.S. dollar at a rate of 1.38 Canadian dollars per U.S. dollars. Calculate the value of the Canadian dollar and the British pound relative to gold.

4. Using the information in problem 3, calculate the exchange rate between the Canadian dollar and the British pound.

5. Suppose a new nation decides to peg the value of its currency, the newbill, to a basket consisting of 0.625 U.S. dollars and 0.25 British pounds. Further suppose the exchange rate between the U.S. dollar and the British pound is 1.5 dollars per pound. If the basket constitutes one newbill, what is the appropriate exchange value between the newbill and the dollar, and between the newbill and the pound?

6. Based on the information in problem 5, what is the weight assigned to the U.S. dollar in the currency basket? What is the weight assigned to the British pound in the currency basket?

ON-LINE APPLICATION

Along with the IMF and the World Bank, the Bank for International Settlements (BIS) is an important international financial institution. The BIS, however, is perhaps the least known and understood of the three institutions.

Internet URL: http://www.bis.org

Title: The Bank for International Settlements

Navigation: Begin at the home page for the BIS located at the internet URL provided. Click on *About the BIS*. Next click on *Profile of the BIS* in the general information window.

Application: After reading the document titled Profile of the BIS, answer the following questions.

1. When was the BIS founded, and what nations were involved in its foundation?

2. What are the four principal functions of the BIS?

REFERENCES AND RECOMMENDED READINGS

Grabbe, Orlin J. *International Financial Markets, Second Edition.* New York: Elsevier, 1991, Chapter 1.

Humpage, Owen F., and Jean M. McIntire. "An Introduction to Currency Boards." *Economic Review.* Federal Reserve Bank of Cleveland (Second Quarter, 1995): 1–11.

Kenen, Peter B. "Ways to Reform Exchange Rate Arrangements." *Reprints in International Finance,* no. 28 (November 1994).

Logue, Dennis E. *The WG&L Handbook of International Finance.* Cincinnati, Ohio: South-Western Publishing, 1995, Chapter 1.

Solomon, Robert. *The International Monetary System, 1945–1976: An Insider's View.* New York: Harper and Row Publishers, 1977.

Williamson, John. *What Role for Currency Boards?* Washington, D.C.: Institute for International Economics, September 1995.

International Financial Instruments, Markets, and Institutions

THE FORWARD CURRENCY MARKET AND INTERNATIONAL FINANCIAL ARBITRAGE

FUNDAMENTAL ISSUES

1. What is foreign exchange risk?

2. What is the forward currency market, and how are forward exchange rates determined?

3. What is covered interest parity?

4. What is uncovered interest parity?

5. What is the Eurocurrency market, and how is it related to the forward currency market?

International investors once considered the bond issues of Italy and Spain as comparable to those of emerging economies. Because of high budget deficits, political instability, and exchange rate volatility, these countries had to offer high interest rates in order to attract foreign funds.

The past two years have seen considerable changes in the political and economic environments of these two nations. Each will be among the first-round entrants to the planned European Monetary Union with its single currency. As a result, each has reduced its inflation rate and budget deficit and has linked its currency more closely to the relatively stable German deutsche mark.

These changes have attracted foreign investment and led to lower interest rates. In 1995, issuers of Italian and Spanish bonds had to offer in excess of 11 percent in order to attract foreign funds. By 1998, the rates had declined to a little more than 5 percent. The decline in interest rates has stimulated the economies of these two nations and brought considerable capital gains to their bondholders.

What is the relationship between exchange rates and interest rates? How does exchange rate instability result in higher interest rates? How do political and fiscal uncertainty affect interest rates? In this chapter we examine these questions, particularly the relationship between interest and exchange rates.

FOREIGN EXCHANGE RISK

In Chapter 2 we examined the role of exchange rates in the international marketplace. In Chapter 3 you learned that the exchange values of many currencies float and are determined in the foreign exchange market. Consequently, exchange rates vary over time. These exchange rate changes expose households, firms, and others who engage in international transactions to potential risk.

Let's construct an example to show how an international transaction may involve risk from exchange rate changes. Suppose you work for an international property developer based in the United States, and your firm has an interest in commercial real estate in the United Kingdom. The property agents will consider "substantial offers" on the property for a period of three months, at which time they will arrange sale of the property to the party submitting the highest offer. It will take approximately three more months for your employer to close on the transaction and assume possession of the property.

Based on an estimate of the income potential of the property, your managers instruct you to submit a bid of £9.5 million. Further, suppose that the exchange rate is currently 1.6877 dollars per pound ($/£). From your firm's perspective, the current price of the bid that you are submitting is $16,033,150, which is the dollar price of the offer (£9.5 million × 1.6877 $/£ = $16,033,150). What your managers have communicated to you is that they value the property in the neighborhood of $16,033,150.

If the sellers of the property accept your offer, you will pay the owner of the property £9.5 million upon closing, six months from now. Upon acceptance of the offer, your firm has a foreign-currency-denominated obligation that

FOREIGN EXCHANGE RISK
The risk that the value of a future receipt or obligation will change due to a change in foreign exchange rates.

spans time and, therefore, creates a *foreign exchange risk exposure.* **Foreign exchange risk** is the prospect that the value of a foreign-currency-denominated liability or asset will change because of a change in the exchange rate.

Suppose that over the course of the next six months the dollar were to depreciate against the British pound by 5 percent, to 1.7721 dollars per pound. In our example, the British pound price of the commercial estate would still be £9.5 million. The dollar price, however, would change because of the change in the spot rate. The dollar price of the property would then be $16,834,950 (£9.5 million × 1.7721 $/£ = $16,834,950). Because of the change in the exchange rate, the dollar price of the property would rise 5 percent, or $801,800. By agreeing to the future foreign-currency-denominated transaction, your firm would have incurred an additional 5-percent cost from foreign exchange risk exposure.

Types of Foreign Exchange Risk Exposure

An individual or firm may be exposed to foreign exchange risk in any of three different ways. The first type of foreign exchange exposure, as in our example, is transaction exposure. **Transaction exposure** is the risk that the cost of a transaction, or the proceeds from a transaction, in terms of the domestic currency, may change. A transaction exposure is created when a firm agrees to complete a foreign-currency-denominated transaction some time in the future.

TRANSACTION EXPOSURE
The risk that the cost of a transaction, or the proceeds from a transaction, in terms of the domestic currency, may change due to changes in exchange rates.

The second type of foreign exchange risk is **translation exposure,** which arises when translating the values of foreign-currency-denominated assets and liabilities into a single currency value. It is easier to understand translation exposure by considering the balance sheet of a multinational corporation. The assets and liabilities, say, of a Swiss multinational corporation, may be denominated in many different currencies. At the end of the year, the accountants at the Swiss corporation tabulate the corporation's balance sheet and value all its assets and liabilities in a common currency, the Swiss franc. As the exchange value of the Swiss franc changes, so does the value of assets and liabilities denominated in a foreign currency. The net worth of the company, as reported in the balance sheet, also changes.

TRANSLATION EXPOSURE
Foreign exchange risk that results from the conversion of the value of a firm's foreign-currency-denominated assets and liabilities into a common currency value.

ECONOMIC EXPOSURE The risk that changes in exchange values might alter a firm's present value of future income streams.

The final type of foreign exchange risk is **economic exposure,** which is the effect that exchange rate changes have on a firm's present value of future income streams. Economic exposure affects the ability of a firm to compete in a particular market over an extended period. Some economists believe that at least a portion of foreign direct investment results from firms trying to avoid economic exposure. By owning a plant or office in a foreign location of operation, the firm may avoid some of the foreign exchange risk that it would have incurred if all its plants and offices were in domestic locations only.

Hedging Foreign Exchange Risk

When considering foreign exchange risk, it is important to understand that a change in the exchange rate may be positive or negative from the perspective

HEDGING The act of offsetting or eliminating risk exposure.

COVERED EXPOSURE A foreign exchange risk that has been completely eliminated with a hedging instrument.

of an individual or firm. Nonetheless, the possibility that the exchange rate may change introduces uncertainty that can make successful planning difficult. An individual or firm decreases or mitigates this uncertainty by reducing or eliminating the foreign exchange risk. **Hedging** is the act of offsetting exposure to risk. An exposure is a **covered exposure** if the hedging activity eliminates *all* of the exposure to risk.

A number of financial instruments are available to offset foreign exchange risk. In this chapter we examine both covered and uncovered transactions. Chapter 5 examines a variety of hedging instruments, which may or may not fully cover an exposure to foreign exchange risk. (See an example of the dilemma a firm faces in attempting to hedge foreign exchange risk in the "Management Notebook: Trends and Trade-Offs in Currency Hedging.")

MANAGEMENT NOTEBOOK
Trends and Trade-Offs in Currency Hedging

For nearly a decade, the U.S. dollar's value declined against the Japanese yen. For managers at Nissan, Mitsubishi, Sony, and other big Japanese companies that regarded the United States as their biggest export market, hedging against changes in the dollar–yen spot exchange rate became routine in the early 1990s. During this period, declines in the dollar's value became expected from month to month. For Nissan, which had about $8 billion in annual overseas receivables, each unhedged one-yen decline in the value of the dollar during the dollar's long and steady fall translated into an $80 million drop in yen revenues. Consequently, hedging made a lot of sense. By 1995, some Japanese companies had established automatic hedging systems.

Beginning in the mid-1990s, however, the dollar's fortunes sprang back to life in world currency markets. After reaching a low of 79 yen per dollar (¥/$) in 1995, the exchange rate rose above 100 ¥/$ in early 1996. Indeed, a new upward trend in the dollar's exchange value seemed to be in place.

This left Japanese exporters in a quandary. When the dollar rose from 1995 to 1996, many firms missed out on some big exchange-related profits because they had hedged against the dollar. If they had not hedged, these companies could have traded each dollar in export receivables for 17 percent more yen. In 1996, Honda could not resist the urge to speculate and began delaying its hedges to reap some profits from the dollar's rise. At Hitachi Limited, managers effectively flipped a coin and decided to hedge half their dollar receivables and reap trading profits on the other half. According to one Honda executive, "We tried to hedge using our brains, but it wasn't successful so we gave up."

FOR CRITICAL ANALYSIS:
Was Honda's strategy really "mindless," in light of the trade-off between less risk and lower profitability that firms can face in hedging foreign-exchange risks?

FUNDAMENTAL ISSUE #1

> **What is foreign exchange risk?** Foreign exchange risk is the effect that uncertain future values of the exchange rate may have on the value of a foreign-currency-denominated obligation, receipt, asset, or liability. There are three types of exposure to foreign exchange risk: transaction exposure, translation exposure, and economic exposure. In principle, an individual or firm can offset, or hedge, some or all of the exposure to foreign exchange risk. The individual or firm covers the exposure by completely eliminating the risk.

THE FORWARD EXCHANGE MARKET

FORWARD EXCHANGE MARKET
A market for contracts that ensure the future delivery of a foreign currency at a specified exchange rate.

Chapter 2 examined the spot market for foreign exchange, which is the market for immediate delivery of a foreign currency. Let's assume again that you work for the U.S. property developer with an offer on a U.K. property. It is highly unlikely that your firm would want to purchase the British pound at the time of notification of acceptance of your company's offer. By immediately purchasing the pound, the firm would have more than $16 million of working capital tied up in a foreign currency for six months. Your firm, therefore, would desire the future delivery of the British pound.

The **forward exchange market** is a market for contracts ensuring the future delivery of a currency at a specified exchange rate. Most forward exchange trades are in the amount of $1 million or more and occur between large commercial banks. Table 2–1 of Chapter 2 on page 38, provides forward exchange rates as well as spot exchange rates. The figure shows one-month, three-month, and six-month forward exchange rates for the British pound of 1.6626, 1.6580, and 1.6516 dollars per pound, respectively. One-year forward and longer-term contracts are also available, but are not listed in the *Wall Street Journal*.

Covering a Transaction with a Forward Contract

Because a forward contract guarantees a rate of exchange at a future date, it can eliminate foreign exchange risk, or *cover* an exposure. In our example, following acceptance of your firm's offer on the commercial property, the firm has a *short position* in the pound, which is a future obligation denominated in a foreign currency, the pound. As explained earlier, the firm now has a foreign exchange risk exposure. You could suggest to your superiors that the firm purchase a six-month forward contract on the pound, which would cover the transaction.

Suppose that at the time the property agents accept your firm's offer, the six-month forward rate on the pound is 1.6688 \$/£. A six-month forward contract for £9.5 million guarantees that your firm can purchase the £9.5 million six months from now at an exchange rate of 1.6688 \$/£. The forward contract guarantees that the final price of the commercial property will be \$15,853,600 (£9.5 million × 1.6688 \$/£ = \$15,853,600). There is no uncertainty about the price of the property, so the transaction is covered.

Firms also can experience transaction exposures that result from foreign-currency-denominated payments that they will receive in the future. In these situations, firms have *long positions,* because they will receive amounts denominated in foreign currencies in the future. In this case, the firms could purchase forward contracts enabling them to sell foreign currencies at guaranteed exchange rates. The forward sell contracts would eliminate all of their foreign exchange risks and would thus cover their receipts.

In both of these examples, firms eliminated positions that had foreign exchange risks by purchasing forward contracts with opposite positions. Firms with short positions in foreign currencies can assume long positions in the forward market by purchasing forward contracts guaranteeing payments denominated in foreign currencies. Firms with long positions in foreign currencies can assume short positions in the forward market by selling currencies in the forward exchange market. By assuming equal and offsetting positions in the forward market, firms can eliminate transaction risk and cover their risk positions.

Determination of Forward Exchange Rates

For most currencies in Table 2–1 on page 38, the forward exchange rates differ from the spot rate, and the forward rates for contracts with different maturity periods typically differ. What determines forward exchange rates?

If there are no currency restrictions or government interventions, the market forces of supply and demand determine forward exchange rates. Figure 4–1 illustrates the downward-sloping demand and upward-sloping supply schedules of the forward exchange market for the British pound. Suppose that a large number of firms and individuals increase their demands for British pounds to be delivered six months from now, perhaps because they have short positions in the pound, as in our previous example.

Figure 4–1 shows the effect on the equilibrium forward exchange rate for the pound. The initial equilibrium forward rate, F_1, is 1.6688 \$/£. A rightward shift of the demand curve illustrates an increase in the demand for the pound six months forward. For a given supply of pounds forward, the increase in demand generates a rise in the pound forward exchange rate to F_2. Hence, the increase in the demand for the pound in the forward market causes an appreciation of the pound in the forward market.

FIGURE 4–1   THE FORWARD MARKET FOR THE POUND

Initially the forward market for the pound is in equilibrium at the forward rate of 1.6688 $/£, or F_1. With an increase in the demand for the pound forward, the demand schedule shifts to the right from $D_£$ to $D'_£$. For a given supply, the increase in the demand causes the forward rate to rise to F_2, which is an appreciation of the pound forward.

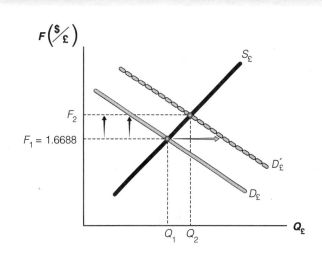

The Forward Exchange Rate as a Predictor of the Future Spot Rate

The forward exchange rate reflects the supply and demand for a currency for future delivery. It is possible, therefore, that the forward rate provides information on the future spot exchange rate.

Suppose again that the six-month forward rate on the British pound is 1.6688 $/£ and that the spot rate is 1.6877 dollars per pound. Because the pound forward exchange rate is less than the pound spot exchange rate, the pound trades at a **forward discount.** If the forward exchange rate of a currency exceeds the spot exchange rate, in contrast, the currency trades at a **forward premium.** Economists usually state the forward premium or discount in a standardized manner by calculating the *standard forward premium* or *discount* as a percentage and expressing it in annual terms. To do this they use the following formula:

FORWARD PREMIUM OR DISCOUNT The difference between the forward exchange rate and the spot exchange rate, expressed as a percentage of the spot exchange rate.

$$\text{Standard forward premium/discount} = (F_N - S)/S \times 12/N \times 100,$$

where F_N is the forward rate, S is the spot rate, and N is the number of months of the forward contract. This formula has three parts. The first part is the forward premium, which is the difference between the forward exchange rate and the spot exchange rate relative to the spot rate, expressed as $(F_N - S)/S$. The second part annualizes the forward premium by dividing by the number of months of the contract, expressing the forward premium on a monthly basis, and then multiplying by 12 to express the forward premium on an annual basis. The last part multiplies the annual forward premium by 100 to express it as a percentage. In our example the standard forward discount is

$$(F_N - S)/S \times 12/N \times 100 = (1.6688 - 1.6877)/1.6877 \times 12/6 \times 100$$
$$= -2.24 \text{ percent.}$$

Now let's suppose that a foreign currency trader believes that the pound will depreciate against the dollar by 1 percent over the next six months. The trader's expectation of future depreciation of the pound is different from the forward discount of the pound. Hence, the trader may attempt to profit through a forward currency transaction.

Suppose the trader exchanges $1 million for pounds in the forward market at a forward exchange rate equal to 1.6688 dollars per pound. Six months from now, the trader will receive £599,232 [$1 million × 1/(1.6688 $/£) = £599,233]. Next let's suppose that the trader's expectations are correct and the pound depreciates by 1 percent, from a rate of 1.6877 dollars per pound to 1.6708 dollars per pound. In the assumed absence of transaction and opportunity costs, the trader then will pay $1 million to buy £599,233 pounds forward. The £599,233 exchange on the spot market at a rate of 1.6708 dollars per pound to obtain $1,001,212.30 (£599,233 × 1.6708 $/£ = $1,001,212.30), netting a profit of $1,212.30.

If other traders share the same expectation, then there is an increase in the total demand for the pound on the forward market. As shown in Figure 4–1, an increase in the demand for the pound on the forward market places upward pressure on the value of pound in the forward market, thereby reducing the amount of the forward discount and eliminating the difference between the forward discount and the expected depreciation. Hence, the following equilibrium condition would hold:

$$(F_N - S)/S = (S_N^e - S)/S,$$

where S_N^e is the spot exchange rate expected to prevail N months from now. In words, this condition states that the forward discount must equal the expected depreciation of the currency, and the forward premium must equal the expected appreciation of the currency.

Based on this equilibrium condition, we might expect a close relationship between the forward exchange rate and the realized future spot exchange rate. This is the reason that we might also expect the forward exchange rate to have some predictive power for movements in the spot rate. Many empirical studies indicate that there is some co-movement between the forward premium or discount and the actual future spot rate. The co-movement is not one-to-one, however. The forward exchange rate sometimes overestimates the future spot exchange rate and sometimes underestimates the future spot exchange rate. We must conclude, therefore, that the forward premium has limited ability in forecasting the future spot exchange rate.

FUNDAMENTAL ISSUE #2

What is the forward currency market? The forward currency market is the market for contracts that oblige the future delivery of a foreign currency at a specified exchange rate. If there are no exchange controls or government intervention, the forces of supply and demand determine the forward exchange rate in the forward currency market. Some consider the forward exchange rate to be a predictor of the expected future spot rate. In practice, however, the forward exchange rate does not predict the future spot exchange rate.

INTERNATIONAL FINANCIAL ARBITRAGE

Chapter 2 presented the theories of absolute and relative purchasing power parity. As was explained, these are theories of international arbitrage in goods and services. Individuals can also seek profits in the financial markets by shifting funds into interest-bearing assets of other nations.

For example, suppose the interest rate on a German financial instrument is 3.25 percent while the interest rate on a British financial instrument with all the same characteristics, such as risk and length to maturity, is 6.25 percent. Would a saver want to move funds from Germany to Britain? The answer depends on whether the actual return *realized* upon maturity is greater for the British financial instrument as compared with the German financial instrument. The realized return, in turn, depends on the net change in the exchange rate of the British pound relative to the deutsche mark over the life of the asset.

The International Flow of Funds and Interest Rate Determination

If the expected exchange-rate-adjusted return on a similar instrument were greater in one nation as compared with another, and if there were no restrictions on capital flows, then we would see savers move funds from one nation to another. This flow of funds could potentially affect interest rates in both nations, as well as the exchange rate between their currencies. In a competitive market, the supply of and demand for funds available for lending, or *loanable funds*, determine interest rates.

Supply   Individuals who save supply loanable funds. There is a positive relationship between the quantity of funds that individuals are willing to save and the rate of return on those funds, or the interest rate. As the interest rate rises, the opportunity cost of accumulating wealth in a non-interest-bearing form increases. This induces individuals to increase their saving by holding more interest-bearing assets.

Various combinations of total saving at different rates of interest compose the market supply schedule for loanable funds. Because there is a positive relationship between the quantity supplied of loanable funds and the rate of interest, the market supply schedule for loanable funds is an upward-sloping curve, as shown in Figure 4–2.

Several factors, including foreign factors, may cause a change in position of the market supply of loanable funds. For instance, if the realized rate of return in another nation rises above that in the domestic nation, households move their savings, or loanable funds, from the domestic country to the foreign country. The market supply of loanable funds in the domestic country would decline, so the supply schedule would shift to the left.

Demand Those who borrow, such as firms that desire to finance investment projects, demand loanable funds. Consistent with the law of demand, as the interest rate on loans increases, the quantity of loanable funds demanded decreases. The market demand schedule for loanable funds is the various combinations of interest rates and quantities of loanable funds demanded.

Because there is a negative relationship between the quantity demanded and the rate of interest, the market demand schedule slopes downward, as illustrated in Figure 4–2. Factors that cause a change in the market demand for loanable funds induce a shift of the demand schedule.

Determination of the Market Interest Rate Point A in Figure 4–2 illustrates a point of market equilibrium, at which the quantity of loanable funds

---

FIGURE 4–2 THE MARKET FOR LOANABLE FUNDS

In a competitive market setting, the supply and demand of loanable funds determine interest rates. The market determined equilibrium interest rate is where the quantity demanded of loanable funds is equal to the quantity supplied, shown by point A, with an interest rate R_1. If the interest rate were equal to R_2, the quantity demanded would exceed the quantity supplied, $Q_2^D > Q_2^S$. The excess quantity demanded would cause the interest rate to rise. At point A and interest rate R_1 there is no longer an excess quantity demanded.

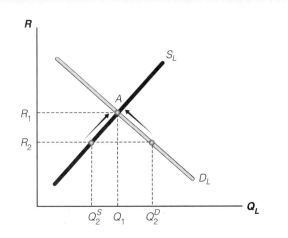

demanded is equal to the quantity of loanable funds supplied. The market interest rate adjusts to satisfy this condition. For example, if in Figure 4–2 the interest rate were equal to R_2, the quantity of loanable funds demanded, Q_2^D, would exceed the quantity of loanable funds supplied, Q_2^S. This excess quantity demanded of loanable funds would put upward pressure on the interest rate, which would rise to R_1 at point A.

Figure 4–3 illustrates how a shift in the market for loanable funds supply schedule affects the market rate of interest. Initially the market for loanable funds is in equilibrium at point A. As in our earlier example, suppose the expected rate of return on foreign instruments became greater than the expected rate of return on similar instruments in the domestic nation. Savers would move funds from the domestic nation to the foreign nation, so the supply of loanable funds in the domestic nation would decline from S_A to S_B. At the interest rate R_A there would now be an excess quantity of loanable funds demanded, which would cause the interest rate to rise to R_B.

Interest Parity

If expected returns on two similar instruments are different, savers would move funds from one instrument to another. In equilibrium, these rates would be equal. That is, we would have *interest parity*, in which interest rate equalization across nations would ensure that no such flow of funds would occur.

To understand interest parity, consider a resident of Germany who is willing to place her deutsche mark savings in either a German treasury bill or a United Kingdom treasury bill. Both instruments have the same risk characteristics. Each is a one-year instrument that is denominated in its home currency.

FIGURE 4–3   A SHIFT IN THE SUPPLY OF LOANABLE FUNDS

Initially the market for loanable funds is in equilibrium at point A with interest rate RA. The shift of the supply schedule from SA to SB illustrates a decrease in the supply of loanable funds. At interest rate RA, the quantity demanded exceeds the quantity supplied. The interest rate will increase until there is no longer an excess demand, which occurs at interest rate RB.

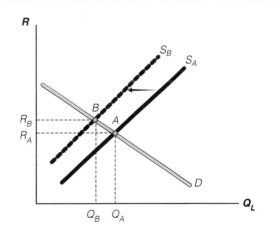

Let's denote the German rate of interest as R, the U.K. rate of interest as R^*, and the spot exchange rate of deutsche marks per U.K. pounds, expressed as DM/£, as S.

First let's consider the outcome if the individual places her deutsche mark savings in the German treasury bill. Following one year, she will have accumulated $1 + R$ deutsche marks for each deutsche mark saved.

Next consider the outcome if the individual places her deutsche mark savings in the U.K. treasury bill. First she must exchange each deutsche mark for British pounds at the spot exchange rate of S marks per pound, to obtain $1/S$ pounds with each deutsche mark. The German resident could then use the $1/S$ British pounds to buy a one-year British treasury bill. After one year, the individual would have accumulated $(1/S)(1 + R^*)$ *British pounds*. As a German resident, the saver will likely wish to convert her pound proceeds into deutsche marks. If S_{+1} is the spot exchange rate at the time of maturity, then the realized return on the U.K. treasury bill will turn out to be $(1/S)(1 + R^*)S_{+1}$ deutsche marks.

At the time the individual is deciding on which instrument to purchase, however, the German saver does not know what the spot rate will be when the instrument matures. The individual must base her decision on their expectation of what the spot rate will be at the time of maturity. If we denote this expectation as S^e_{+1}, then the *expected return* on the U.K. treasury bill is $(1/S)(1 + R^*)S^e_{+1}$ deutsche marks. In other words, the saver anticipates that the accumulated $(1/S)(1 + R^*)$ British pounds will exchange at the expected future spot exchange rate, S^e_{+1}, for an accumulated savings in deutsche marks of $(1/S)(1 + R^*)S^e_{+1}$.

Exchange Uncertainty and Covered Interest Parity

If the German saver in our example were to purchase the U.K. treasury bill, she would have a long position in the pound and would be exposed to foreign exchange risk. She incurs a foreign exchange risk exposure because the actual spot rate that prevails at maturity may turn out to be different from her expectation.

The individual could cover her risk by assuming a short position on the U.K. pound in the forward market, selling the pound forward for the deutsche mark. By purchasing a forward contract, the individual guarantees a rate of exchange at the time of maturity, thereby eliminating all foreign exchange risk.

To cover the foreign exchange risk the individual incurs with the purchase of the British financial instrument, she makes two separate foreign exchange transactions. She buys the pound on the spot market, for the purpose of purchasing the U.K. treasury bill, and sells the pound on the forward market. The amount of savings accumulated with the British treasury bill then depends on the forward exchange rate, as opposed to the future spot exchange rate. If the individual covers her foreign exchange risk, then after one year she would have accumulated $(1/S)(1 + R^*)F$ *deutsche marks*.

The German resident who covers her foreign exchange risk with a forward contract, therefore, will be willing to hold both German and U.K. financial instruments if the return on each deutsche mark held in the German financial instrument is equal to the return on each deutsche mark held on the British financial instrument:

$$1 + R = (F/S)(1 + R^*).$$

Now we can use the fact that

$$F/S = (S/S) + (F - S)/S = 1 + (F - S)/S$$

to rewrite the condition as

$$1 + R = [1 + (F - S)/S](1 + R^*).$$

Now we can cross-multiply the right-hand side to get

$$1 + R = 1 + (F - S)/S + R^* + R^*(F - S)/S.$$

Because R^* and $(F - S)/S$ are both typically small fractions, their product is approximately equal to zero. Making this approximation and subtracting 1 from both sides of the yields

$$R - R^* \cong \frac{F - S}{S}.$$

<table>
<tr><td>Covered Interest Parity
A condition relating interest differentials to the forward premium or discount.</td><td>This equation is called the covered interest parity condition. Covered interest parity is a condition that says that the difference between the interest rate on a domestic financial asset and the interest rate on a foreign financial asset should equal the forward premium or discount.</td></tr>
</table>

Covered Interest Arbitrage If the covered interest parity condition is not satisfied, then a covered interest arbitrage opportunity exists. Let's continue with our example and show how an individual conducts covered interest arbitrage. Suppose the spot rate for the deutsche mark per U.K. pound is 2.9450 DM/£ and the one-year forward rate is 2.8424 DM/£. Because the forward price of the pound is less than the spot price of the pound, the pound trades at a discount against the deutsche mark.

The German saver in our example will incur a loss if she buys the pound on the spot market and sells the pound in the forward market. For each deutsche mark she exchanges at the spot exchange rate of 2.9450 she will receive 0.3396 pounds (1/2.9450 = 0.3396). In six months, the forward exchange contract ensures that the 0.3396 pounds she received in exchange for each deutsche mark will trade for 0.9653 deutsche marks (£0.3396 × 2.8424 DM/£ = DM0.9653). The loss on the spot exchange and forward exchange transactions is 3.47 percent [(0.9653 − 1)/1 × 100 = −3.47 percent].

The return on the pound-denominated instrument is greater than the return on the mark-denominated instrument. Returning to our original question, which instrument should the saver choose? Given that the 6.25 percent return on the pound-denominated instrument exceeds the 3.25 percent return on the deutsche-mark-denominated instrument, she will gain 3 percent on the pound-denominated instrument. She will, however, lose 3.47 percent on the spot exchange and forward exchange transactions required to cover the foreign exchange risk associated with the purchase of the pound-denominated instrument. The loss on the foreign exchange transactions on the pound exceeds the higher rate of return on the pound-denominated asset. Therefore, the German resident should purchase in the German treasury bill.

Covered Interest Parity Grid   A *covered interest parity grid,* which is a figure that illustrates various combinations of interest-rate differentials and forward premiums or discounts, is a convenient way to illustrate the covered interest parity condition.

   Figure 4–4 is a covered interest parity grid, plotting the interest differential on the horizontal axis and the forward premium or discount on the vertical axis. When the covered interest parity condition is satisfied, the interest differential and the forward premium are approximately equal. These combinations of interest-rate differentials and forward premiums or discounts lie on, or very close to, a 45-degree ray through the origin. A narrow band around the

---

FIGURE 4–4   THE COVERED INTEREST PARITY GRID

The covered interest parity grid illustrates all of the interest differentials and forward premium or discount combinations that satisfy the covered interest parity condition. These combinations lie on, or near, the 45-degree ray that intersects the origin.

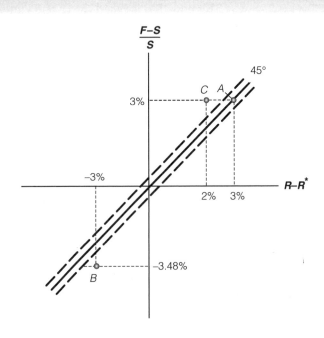

45-degree ray reflects the fact that the covered interest parity condition is an approximation and that brokerage and sales fees on the various financial instruments cause actual returns to be less than the interest rate. As a result, interest-rate differentials and forward premium or discounts need not be exactly equal. Point *A* in Figure 4–4 is an example of a combination that satisfies the covered interest parity condition.

Covered Interest Arbitrage and Savings Flows   If the covered interest parity condition is not satisfied, savers will move funds from one nation to the other as they seek the highest return.

In the previous example, the forward discount on the foreign currency, 3.48 percent, exceeds the negative interest differential, 3 percent. This situation, illustrated by point *B* in Figure 4–4, lies below the 45-degree ray. In this case, and for all situations where the combination of interest differential and forward premium or discount lie below the 45-degree ray, the interest differential between the domestic and foreign financial instruments exceeds the forward premium and individuals should purchase the domestic financial instrument. As a result, savings will flow from abroad into the domestic economy.

Point *C* in Figure 4–4 illustrates a situation where the combination of interest differential, 2 percent, and forward premium or discount, 3 percent, lies above the 45-degree ray. In this case, individuals should purchase the foreign financial instrument, so that savings will flow from the domestic economy into the foreign economy.

Adjustment to an Equilibrium   In our previous example we determined that savings will flow from the United Kingdom to Germany. As a result, there will be pressure on the spot exchange rate, forward exchange rate, and the German and British interest rates to adjust.

To illustrate how the interest rates in the two nations might adjust, we consider the loanable funds markets and the spot and forward markets for foreign exchange. Figure 4–5 displays each of these market frameworks at an initial equilibrium indicated by point *A*. Panel *a* shows the spot market for the British pound, panel *b* displays the forward market for the British pound, panel *c* illustrates the loanable funds market in the United Kingdom, and panel *d* displays the market for loanable funds in Germany.

To move savings into Germany, individuals must exchange the British pound for the deutsche mark, so there is an increase in the demand for the deutsche mark. As explained in Chapter 2, the increased demand for the deutsche mark corresponds to an increase in the supply of the British pound, shown by a shift of the supply curve in panel *a* from $S_\pounds$ to $S_\pounds'$. As shown in panel *a*, the increase in the supply of the British pound in the spot market causes a decline in the spot rate, or a depreciation of the pound relative to the mark, shown by the movement from S_1 to S_2.

British individuals who purchase the German treasury instrument will likely desire to receive their principal and interest in British pounds upon maturity.

FIGURE 4-5 **COVERED INTEREST PARITY EXAMPLE**

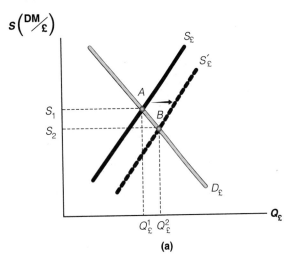

(a)

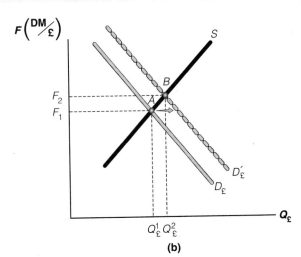

(b)

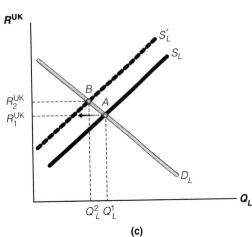

(c)

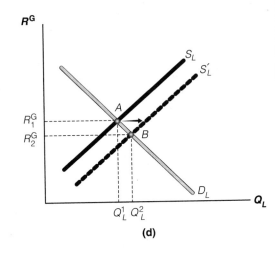

(d)

Panel *a* illustrates the spot market for the British pound. Panel *b* displays the forward market for the British pound. Panel *c* displays the loanable funds market in the United Kingdom. Panel *d* illustrates the loanable funds market in Germany. As individuals move funds from pound-denominated to mark-denominated financial instruments, there is an increase in the demand for the deutsche mark, which is equivalent to an increase in the supply of the pound on the spot market. At the same time, there is an increase in the demand for the pound on the forward market. The flow of funds out of the United Kingdom decreases the supply of loanable funds in the United Kingdom. The flow of funds into Germany increases the supply of loanable funds in that country.

If these individuals cover their exposure to foreign exchange risk, they will purchase the pound forward. This is illustrated by an increase in the demand for the pound in the forward market, shown by a shift from $D_£$ to $D'_£$ in panel *b*. The increase in the demand for the pound on the forward market will cause the pound to appreciate relative to the deutsche mark, as shown by an increase in the forward rate from F_1 to F_2.

The flow of savings out of the United Kingdom causes a decrease in the supply of loanable funds, shown by the shift of the supply curve from S_L to S'_L in panel *c*. A decrease in the supply of loanable funds in the United Kingdom causes an increase in the British interest rate from R_1^{UK} to R_2^{UK}. The flow of savings into Germany causes an increase in the supply of loanable funds from S_L to S'_L in panel *d*, which causes the German interest rate to decline from R_1^G to R_2^G.

FUNDAMENTAL ISSUE #3

What is covered interest parity? Covered interest parity is a condition relating the interest rate differential on similar financial assets in two nations to the spot and forward exchange rates. In equilibrium, the interest differential on the two assets is equal to the forward premium or discount. If covered interest parity does not hold, financial arbitrage is possible, and individuals will move savings from one nation to another.

UNCOVERED INTEREST PARITY

In the previous section, we considered financial arbitrage by an individual who hedged all of the foreign exchange risk by making use of a forward exchange contract. Now we consider a situation in which the individual does not use a forward exchange contract.

There are a number of reasons why someone might choose not to use a forward exchange contract to hedge risk. For example, it might be that the transaction is not large enough to warrant a forward contract, which typically has a denomination of at least $1 million. In this situation, the individual might choose not to hedge the transaction at all, or might decide to use some other hedging instrument. Chapter 5 examines alternative hedging instruments. Here, we consider an uncovered transaction, in which the individual does not hedge the exposure to foreign exchange risk at all.

Uncovered Interest Arbitrage

Earlier, we considered a German saver with a choice between a German treasury instrument and a U.K. treasury instrument. At the time of the investment decision, the anticipated return on the U.K. financial instrument was $(1/S)(1+R^*)S_{+1}^e$, where S_{+1}^e is the individual's expectation of next period's actual spot exchange rate. If the German saver does not purchase a forward exchange contract or hedge the foreign exchange risk in any other manner, then her transaction is uncovered and depends in part upon their expectation of the future spot rate. Following the same basic steps as in our discussion of covered interest parity, we can derive the equilibrium condition representing uncovered interest parity.

UNCOVERED INTEREST PARITY
A condition relating interest differentials to an expected change in the spot exchange rate of the domestic currency.

Uncovered interest parity is a condition relating the interest differential of similar financial instruments of two nations to the expected change in the spot exchange rate between the two nations. The condition representing uncovered interest parity is

$$R - R^* = \frac{(S_{+1}^e - S)}{S}.$$

In words, in equilibrium the interest differential between two similar financial instruments should be approximately equal to the expected depreciation or appreciation of the foreign currency.

Let's use the information from the covered interest arbitrage example, but now suppose the German saver decides not to cover her foreign exchange risk and bases her savings decision on her expectation of the future spot exchange rate. Let's further assume that the German saver expects the future spot exchange rate to be 2.8272 deutsche marks per pound.

As in the covered interest arbitrage example, the interest differential between the German treasury bill and the U.K. treasury bill is −3 percent. If this German saver expects the spot exchange rate to be 2.8272 DM/£ upon maturity of the British treasury bill, then she expects the British pound to depreciate relative to the deutsche mark by 4.0 percent [(2.8272 − 2.9450)/2.9450 × 100 = 4.0 percent]. If the individual had her savings in the U.K. treasury instrument for the year, the number of deutsche marks she would receive in exchange for each British pound would decline by 4.0 percent.

We can state this problem in another manner. The known return on the German financial instrument, paid in deutsche marks, is 3.25 percent. The expected return on the U.K. financial instrument is the difference between the 6.25 percent interest paid on the instrument, in pounds, and the loss of value of the U.K. pound of 4.0 percent, for a total *expected* return on the U.K. treasury bill, in deutsche marks, of 2.25 percent. The individual would take advantage of this financial arbitrage opportunity by purchasing the German treasury bill.

If many people undertook the same transaction, the effect on the spot and loanable funds markets would be the same as in the covered interest parity example. Because the transaction is uncovered, there is no effect on the forward market. The effect on next period's spot exchange rate, however, would be the same as on the forward market in the covered interest parity example.

Risk and Uncovered Interest Parity

Because the purchase of the foreign financial instrument is unhedged in this example, the German saver has a foreign exchange risk exposure. It is very possible that the individual's expectation about the value of the future spot rate may turn out to be incorrect. If this is the case, the realized return on the foreign financial instrument would differ from the expected return.

RISK PREMIUM An increase in the return offered on a higher-risk financial instrument to compensate individuals for the additional risk they undertake.

If a nation's currency value is highly variable, the ability to predict its future value becomes more difficult. If this is the case, individuals will become less confident in their ability to accurately predict the spot rate. This makes the purchase of a foreign financial instrument a much riskier proposition. To induce savers to purchase a risky financial instrument, borrowers may have to offer a higher rate of return on the debt instruments they issue. The inclusion of a risk premium in the uncovered interest parity condition captures this aspect. A **risk premium** is an increase in the return offered on a higher-risk financial instrument to compensate individuals for the additional risk they undertake. The risk premium, ρ, augments the uncovered interest parity condition:

$$R - R^* = \frac{S^e_{+1} - S}{S} + \rho.$$

Hence, if the domestic financial instrument is the higher-risk instrument, then the positive interest differential should equal the expected depreciation of the domestic currency *plus* an additional amount to compensate individuals for the additional risk they assume with the purchase of the domestic financial instrument. (A risk premium associated with a greater exchange rate uncertainty is the topic of the "Policy Notebook: Asian Currency Woes Require Higher Interest Rates.")

Risks Other than Foreign Exchange Risk

The risk premium may reflect risks other than foreign exchange risk. The individual financial instruments may have characteristics that affect their degree of risk. We discuss these instrument-specific risks in Chapter 5.

COUNTRY RISK The possibility of losses on holdings of financial instruments issued in another nation because of political uncertainty within that nation.

In addition to foreign exchange and instrument-specific risks, there may be **country risk,** which is the risk due to the political and fiscal environment of the nation itself. A government with a considerable amount of external debt may eventually default on that debt, so holding its bonds is a risky proposition. Savers would risk losing the return on their funds, and perhaps their principal as well. Changes in government leadership may lead to increased taxes on foreign investment or restricted outflows of foreign funds. Hence, risk premium may reflect both foreign exchange risk and country risk. See the On-Line Application at the end of this chapter for more on country risk.

POLICY NOTEBOOK

Asian Currency Woes Require Higher Interest Rates

The summer of 1997 was tumultuous for many Southeast Asian economies. A currency crisis that spread through the region forced some nations, such as Thailand, the Philippines, Indonesia, and Malaysia, to abandon their currency arrangements and move from pegged to more flexible exchange rates. The currencies of these nations depreciated considerably. The currencies of Thailand, Indonesia, and South Korea depreciated by more than 40 percent against the U.S. dollar.

The depreciation itself was a mixed blessing. Companies dependent upon exports benefited from the depreciation as their products became more price competitive in the international market. Companies dependent on imported inputs, and who had debts to repay in U.S. dollars or other foreign currencies, found their outlays to be much greater with a depreciating currency.

Moving from stable and pegged exchange rates to a more flexible exchange rate arrangement had other consequences. Because of the additional risk and uncertainty inherent in a new and more flexible exchange rate arrangement, lenders demanded higher interest rates to compensate for the additional foreign exchange risk. Within a few months, the prime rate in the Philippines rose 15 percentage points before settling to a net increase around 6 to 7 percent. In Malaysia, the interest rate on short-term loans rose by more than 4 percent, while in Thailand rates on short-term corporate loans rose 15 to 20 percent.

Companies that tried to avoid the cost of higher rates on bank loans issued bonds denominated in foreign currencies. These companies found that their costs of borrowing increased substantially. Many Southeast Asian companies forced to pay higher interest rates due to a risk premium had to postpone capital investment projects that required foreign lending, and some even felt obliged to lay off workers.

FOR CRITICAL ANALYSIS:
In what ways would the currency depreciation affect the business prospects of a Southeast Asian corporation that is heavily indebted in loans denominated in foreign currencies?

ON THE WEB
Learn more about Thailand's economy and its leaders' attempts to stabilize the baht from the Bank of Thailand at:
http://www.bot.or.th

Foreign Exchange Market Efficiency

In this chapter we found that covered interest parity is a condition relating interest differentials to the forward and spot exchange rates. We also learned that uncovered interest parity is a condition relating interest differentials to the spot exchange rate and the expected future spot exchange rate. What is the relationship between these two conditions?

The two conditions are linked through interest rate differentials. Let's suppose that both conditions are satisfied. We can then relate the two conditions through the interest differential as

$$\frac{F-S}{S} = R - R^* = \frac{S^e_{+1} - S}{S},$$

that is, the forward premium is equal to the expected change in the spot rate. We can simplify this relationship by adding S/S to each side, yielding

$$F = S_{+1}^e.$$

In words, the uncovered and covered interest parity conditions imply that the forward exchange rate should equal the spot exchange rate expected to prevail at the time of the settlement of the forward contract.

If the forward rate systematically differs from the spot rate, then, in absence of a risk premium, a profit opportunity exists. An *efficient market* is one in which market prices adjust quickly to new and relevant information. Hence, **foreign exchange market efficiency** means that the spot and forward exchange rates adjust quickly to new information and a systematic profit opportunity does not exist. In other words, if the foreign exchange market is efficient, then, in the absence of any risk premium, the forward exchange rate should, on average, equal the expected future spot exchange rate.

As discussed earlier in this chapter, economists have studied this relationship quite extensively. As stated before, the evidence indicates that there is some co-movement between the forward exchange rate and the actual future spot rate. The forward exchange rate, however, has limited ability in forecasting the future spot exchange rate. Most economists attribute the poor predictive power of the forward rate to the existence of a risk premium.

FOREIGN EXCHANGE MARKET EFFICIENCY When the spot and forward exchange rates reflect, and adjust quickly to, new and relevant information.

FUNDAMENTAL ISSUE #4

What is uncovered interest parity? Uncovered interest parity is a condition relating the nominal interest rate differential on two similar financial instruments to the expected change in the spot exchange rate. If there is a sizable amount of foreign exchange risk or country risk, the interest rate differential may also reflect a risk premium, which compensates individuals for the additional risk they assume.

THE EUROCURRENCY MARKET

As businesses expand their operations to foreign markets, and as individuals and funds managers consider new opportunities in foreign markets, international borrowing and lending activities continue to increase. New markets have developed over time to meet these expanded lending and borrowing preferences. One market in particular, the *Eurocurrency market,* which began in the mid-1950s, has grown considerably to facilitate these activities.

Origins of the Eurocurrency Market

EUROCURRENCY A bank deposit denominated in a currency other than that of the nation in which the bank deposit is located.

EUROCURRENCY MARKET A market for the borrowing and lending of Eurocurrency deposits.

A **Eurocurrency** is a bank deposit denominated in a currency other than that of the nation in which the bank deposit is located. For example, a Eurodollar deposit is a bank deposit denominated in U.S. dollars, but located in a bank outside of the United States. The **Eurocurrency market** is a market for the borrowing and lending of Eurocurrency deposits. There are at least two competing views on how the Eurocurrency market originated.

The first account of how eurocurrencies began gives credit to Soviet financiers. From the end of World War II to the collapse of the Soviet Union, the Soviet Union conducted many of its international transactions using barter, but it conducted monetary transactions in U.S. dollars, because the dollar was the predominant reserve currency. This required the Soviet Union to maintain dollar-denominated deposits in U.S. banks to conduct these transactions.

As tension between the United States and the Soviet Union increased during the Cold War, the Soviet Union became fearful that U.S. officials might freeze these funds. Soviet financial officials sought to move their funds outside of the United States and outside of the U.S. banking system. Soviet financial officials, therefore, moved the funds to banks located in Paris and London. These deposits were Eurodollar deposits, or dollar-denominated deposits, located in Europe.

A second and more likely theory of the origins of the Eurocurrency market begins in the mid-1950s. In 1956 the Egyptian government seized control of the Suez Canal, operated by a firm with French and British ties. Over objections of the United States, the United Kingdom and France retook control of the Suez Canal. In retaliation, the U.S. government soon began selling British pounds in the foreign exchange market.

As an attempt to support the pound by restricting its supply in the foreign exchange market, the British government restricted the foreign lending activities of British banks. These lending activities were a very profitable and sizable portion of the British banks' business. British banks soon began advertising that they would accept dollar-denominated deposits. As an inducement, they offered attractive rates on the deposits. When dollar deposits flowed into the British banks, the banks, in turn, deposited the funds in U.S. banks. This allowed the British banks to resume their international lending activities, which they conducted in U.S. dollars instead of British pounds. The media eventually dubbed the dollar-denominated deposits held in the British banks Eurodollars.

Growth of the Eurocurrency Market

Regardless of the origin of the Eurocurrency market, it has grown considerably since the 1950s. There is no exact number on the size of the Eurocurrency market, but some estimates are available on the currency composition and nationality of banks engaged in this market.

ON THE WEB

Get the most recent statistics on international banking activity from the Bank of International Settlements Annual Report, Statistical Annex, at:
http://www.bis.org

Panel *a* in Figure 4–6 shows that the top five currencies traded in the Eurocurrency markets were the U.S. dollar, the Japanese yen, the deutsche mark, the French franc, and the British pound, making up more than 78 percent of the market. Panel *b* illustrates that the five nations most active in the Eurocurrency markets were Japan, the United States, Germany, France, and the United Kingdom, accounting for approximately 68 percent of the market activity. Borrowing and lending activities among the largest banks in the world dominate the Eurocurrency market with London as the center of the market. Recently, however, traders have arranged smaller-denominated transactions of as little as $50,000. This has attracted a wider variety of participants into the market.

Leading financial papers, such as *The Financial Times,* publish Eurocurrency borrowing and lending rates. Table 4–1 shows recent Eurocurrency interest rates for the fourteen most active currencies and their maturity periods, from overnight to one year. The table presents all of the rates on an annual basis. Each column shows two rates. The first is the rate at which major banks would be willing to lend a Eurocurrency deposit. The second displays the rate they would be willing to pay on a Eurocurrency deposit.

Relationship to the Forward Market

As you can see in Table 4–1, the maturity and composition of Eurocurrency deposits are similar to those of the forward exchange market. The Eurocurrency market and the forward market are highly integrated because they fulfill

---

FIGURE 4–6   THE EUROCURRENCY MARKET

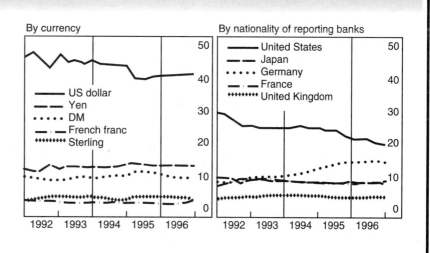

The top five currencies traded in the Eurocurrency markets are the U.S. dollar, the Japanese yen, the deutsche mark, the French franc, and the British pound. The five nations most active in the Eurocurrency markets are Japan, the United States, Germany, France, and the United Kingdom.

SOURCE: From "International Financial Markets" in *Bank for International Settlements–67th Annual Report,* June 9, 1997. Copyright © 1997 Bank for International Settlements. Reprinted by permission.

TABLE 4–1 EUROCURRENCY INTEREST RATES

JUN 30	SHORT TERM	7 DAYS NOTICE	ONE MONTH	THREE MONTHS	SIX MONTHS	ONE YEAR
Belgian Franc	$3\frac{3}{4}-3\frac{1}{4}$	$3\frac{11}{32}-3\frac{5}{16}$	$3\frac{3}{8}-3\frac{1}{4}$	$3\frac{3}{8}-3\frac{1}{4}$	$3\frac{11}{32}-3\frac{5}{16}$	$3\frac{13}{32}-3\frac{3}{8}$
Danish Krone	$3\frac{1}{2}-3\frac{5}{16}$	$3\frac{19}{32}-3\frac{15}{32}$	$3\frac{9}{16}-3\frac{7}{16}$	$3\frac{3}{8}-3\frac{1}{2}$	$3\frac{11}{16}-3\frac{9}{16}$	$3\frac{29}{32}-3\frac{3}{4}$
German Mark	$3\frac{1}{16}-2\frac{15}{16}$	$3\frac{3}{32}-2\frac{31}{32}$	$3\frac{3}{4}-3\frac{1}{4}$	$3\frac{1}{8}-3\frac{1}{32}$	$3\frac{1}{4}-3\frac{5}{32}$	$3\frac{5}{16}-3\frac{3}{16}$
Dutch Guilder	$4-3\frac{3}{4}$	$3\frac{5}{32}-2\frac{15}{16}$	$3\frac{5}{32}-2\frac{29}{32}$	$3\frac{7}{32}-2\frac{31}{32}$	$3\frac{5}{16}-3\frac{1}{16}$	$3\frac{7}{16}-3\frac{3}{16}$
French Franc	$3\frac{9}{32}-3\frac{5}{32}$	$3\frac{5}{16}-3\frac{5}{32}$	$3\frac{11}{32}-3\frac{7}{32}$	$3\frac{13}{32}-3\frac{9}{32}$	$3\frac{7}{16}-3\frac{11}{32}$	$3\frac{17}{32}-3\frac{13}{32}$
Portuguese Esc.	$5\frac{29}{32}-5\frac{27}{32}$	$6-5\frac{15}{16}$	$6\frac{1}{32}-5\frac{15}{16}$	$5\frac{7}{8}-5\frac{13}{16}$	$5\frac{21}{32}-5\frac{9}{16}$	$5\frac{15}{32}-5\frac{3}{8}$
Spanish Peseta	$5\frac{13}{32}-5\frac{1}{4}$	$5\frac{3}{8}-5\frac{9}{32}$	$5\frac{11}{32}-5\frac{1}{4}$	$5\frac{9}{32}-5\frac{3}{16}$	$5\frac{7}{32}-5\frac{1}{8}$	$5\frac{5}{32}-5\frac{1}{16}$
Sterling	$6\frac{9}{16}-6\frac{1}{2}$	$6\frac{17}{32}-6\frac{13}{32}$	$6\frac{21}{32}-6\frac{17}{32}$	$6\frac{7}{8}-6\frac{25}{32}$	$7\frac{1}{16}-6\frac{15}{16}$	$7\frac{5}{16}-7\frac{3}{16}$
Swiss Franc	$1\frac{3}{4}-1\frac{1}{2}$	$1\frac{3}{8}-1\frac{9}{32}$	$1\frac{3}{8}-1\frac{9}{32}$	$1\frac{7}{16}-1\frac{11}{32}$	$1\frac{1}{2}-1\frac{13}{32}$	$1\frac{5}{8}-1\frac{3}{8}$
Canadian Dollar	$3\frac{9}{16}-3\frac{7}{16}$	$3\frac{3}{8}-3\frac{3}{16}$	$3\frac{7}{16}-3\frac{1}{4}$	$3\frac{17}{32}-3\frac{13}{32}$	$3\frac{13}{16}-3\frac{11}{16}$	$4\frac{9}{32}-4\frac{5}{32}$
US Dollar	$6\frac{7}{16}-6\frac{5}{16}$	$5\frac{21}{32}-5\frac{9}{16}$	$5\frac{21}{32}-5\frac{17}{32}$	$5\frac{25}{32}-5\frac{21}{32}$	$5\frac{7}{8}-5\frac{3}{4}$	$6\frac{1}{8}-6$
Italian Lira	$7\frac{21}{32}-6\frac{21}{32}$	$6\frac{7}{8}-6\frac{3}{4}$	$6\frac{27}{32}-6\frac{3}{4}$	$6\frac{25}{32}-6\frac{11}{16}$	$6\frac{11}{16}-6\frac{19}{32}$	$6\frac{7}{16}-6\frac{3}{8}$
Japanese Yen	$\frac{5}{8}-\frac{19}{32}$	$\frac{1}{2}-\frac{3}{8}$	$\frac{9}{16}-\frac{7}{16}$	$\frac{19}{32}-\frac{1}{2}$	$\frac{9}{16}-\frac{15}{32}$	$\frac{15}{16}-\frac{7}{8}$
Asian $Sing	$3\frac{7}{16}-3\frac{5}{16}$	$3\frac{9}{16}-3\frac{7}{16}$	$3\frac{5}{8}-3\frac{1}{2}$	$3\frac{5}{8}-3\frac{1}{2}$	$3\frac{5}{8}-3\frac{1}{2}$	$3\frac{3}{4}-3\frac{5}{8}$

SOURCE: From *Financial Times*, June 30, 1997. Reprinted by permission.

some similar roles. These markets allow a bank, firm, or individual to structure a financial arbitrage denominated in the domestic currency. Because of this, Eurocurrency interest-rate differentials and the forward premium or discount tend to be in equilibrium, meaning that covered interest arbitrage in the Eurocurrency market is typically not profitable.

Using the equations of our previous examples, let's consider using the Eurocurrency market to conduct financial arbitrage. Suppose you decide to borrow U.S. dollars in the Eurocurrency market, which you then plan to convert into Belgian francs (BFr) to lend in the Eurocurrency market.

Using Table 4–1, let's consider borrowing $1 million for three months. Further, on the same day, the spot rate on the Belgian franc is 35.95 BFr/$, and the three-month forward rate is 35.7235 BFr/$. The borrowing rate in Table 4–1 is $5\frac{25}{32}$, or 5.78125. First let's calculate how much we will have to pay back, the principal and interest, on the $1 million. Remember that the interest rate is stated on an annual basis, so we will do a simple conversion to put it on a three-month basis, by dividing the interest rate by twelve and multiplying it by 3 (or simply dividing by 4). The principal and interest due on the three-month $1 million loan is

$$\$1{,}000{,}000 \times [1 + (0.0578125/4)] = \$1{,}014{,}453.$$

Using the $1 million we borrowed, we can exchange it for BFr35.95 million ($1 million × 35.95 BFr/$ = BFr35.95 million). Next we use the BFr35.95 million to purchase a Eurocurrency deposit with a return of 3¼, or 3.25. At the end of three months the principal and interest on the Belgian franc Eurocurrency deposit is

$$\text{BFr35.95 million} \times [1 + (0.0325/4)] = \text{BFr36.2 million.}$$

We will have to repay the Eurodollar loan in dollars in three months, so we will sell the Belgian franc forward at a rate of 35.7235 Belgian francs per dollar. The BFr36.2 million will net $1,014,516 on the forward transaction (BFr36.2 million / 35.7235 BFr/$). After we repay the Eurodollar loan, we have $1,014,516 million – $1,014,453 million = $63. It is most likely that the $63 would not even pay our transaction costs!

FUNDAMENTAL ISSUE #5

What is the Eurocurrency market, and how does it relate to the forward currency market? The Eurocurrency market is a market for the borrowing and lending of Eurocurrency deposits, which are bank deposits denominated in currencies other than those of the nations in which the deposits are located. Eurocurrency transactions typically take place among large banks and in amounts of $1 million or more. The Eurocurrency market and the forward market are highly integrated, fulfilling some of the same roles in financial arbitrage. Therefore, covered interest arbitrage tends to hold in the Eurocurrency market.

CHAPTER SUMMARY

1. **Foreign Exchange Risk:** Foreign exchange risk is the possibility that the value of a foreign receipt or payment to be made in the future may vary due to a change in the exchange rate. There are three types of exposure to foreign exchange risk: transaction risk, translation risk, and economic risk. Some financial instruments can partially or completely offset foreign exchange risks. The exposure is *covered* when it is completely offset. The exposure is *uncovered* if it is not offset at all.

2. **The Forward Currency Market and the Determination of Forward Exchange Rates:** The forward currency market is a standardized market for the future delivery of a currency at a guaranteed exchange rate. When there is no government intervention in the market or exchange rate restrictions, the forces of supply and demand determine forward exchange rates.

3. **Covered Interest Parity:** Covered interest parity is a condition relating interest differentials to the forward premium or discount. In equilibrium, the interest differential is equal to the forward premium or discount. If equilibrium does not hold, the covered interest parity condition postulates that savings will flow from one nation to another in search of higher, exchange-rate-adjusted returns. A parity grid illustrates the covered interest parity condition.

4. **Uncovered Interest Parity:** Uncovered interest parity is a condition relating the nominal interest rate differential on two similar financial instruments to the expected change in the spot exchange rate. Under uncovered interest parity, transactions are not covered and are subject to foreign exchange risk.

5. **The Eurocurrency Market and Its Relationship to the Forward Currency Market:** The Eurocurrency market is the market for the borrowing and lending of Eurocurrency deposits. A Eurocurrency deposit is a deposit denominated in a currency other than that of the nation in which the deposit is located. The Eurocurrency market and the forward currency market are highly integrated. As a result, covered financial arbitrage in the Eurocurrency market is not likely to be profitable.

Questions and Problems

1. Suppose the following information on U.S. dollar and deutsche mark rates prevails in the international money market.

Spot rate	1.740 DM/$
One-month forward rate	1.735 DM/$
Interest rate (DM)	3.0% per year
Interest rate ($)	6.0% per year

   a. Illustrate the covered interest parity grid and plot the above information in the diagram.

   b. Suppose transaction costs are approximately 0.2 percent. Incorporate this information into the parity grid.

   c. Based on the diagram you constructed, would you move funds to the deutsche mark instrument, move them to the U.S. dollar instrument, or maintain your current portfolio?

2. Ignoring transaction costs, use the covered interest parity condition to explain your answer in problem 1.

3. Construct diagrams representing the spot exchange market for the deutsche mark relative to the U.S. dollar, the forward exchange market for the deutsche mark relative to the U.S. dollar, loanable funds market in Germany, and the loanable funds

market in the United States. Based on your answer to problem 1, show the potential effects within each of these markets as individuals reallocate their portfolios.

4. Suppose the following situation prevails in the foreign exchange and Eurocurrency markets for the Dutch guilder (Fl) and the British pound (£).
   One-month Eurocurrency rates:

Dutch guilder	3½ – 3¼
British pound	6¾ – 6½

   Exchange rates:

Spot	3.261 Fl/£
One-month forward	3.252 Fl/£

   Explain how an individual would profit from financial arbitrage in this situation. Calculate the percentage return the individual would earn from undertaking arbitrage activity. Keep all of your calculations to four decimal points for accuracy.

5. Suppose the spot exchange rate between the U.S. dollar and the British pound is 1.664 $/£, the interest rate on a three-month U.S. financial instrument is 5.5 percent, and the interest rate on a similar U.K. financial instrument is 6.5 percent.
   a. Rewrite the uncovered interest parity equation to show how it is a guide for the future spot rate.
   b. Based on the given information, calculate the implied expectation of the spot rate between the U.S. dollar and the British pound.

On-Line Application

This chapter presented the concepts of foreign exchange risk and country risk. Quantifying country risk is an important yet subjective task. A variety of methods exist and a number of investment agencies provide such estimates. Since the World Bank (IBRD) lends to many nations, country risk is an important consideration.

Internet URL: http://www.worldbank.org

Title: The World Bank

Navigation: Begin with the home page of the World Bank. Extend the Internet URL by adding: /html/extdr/faq/97219.htm

Application: Based on the report provided at this site, answer the following questions.

1. Explain how the World Bank evaluates the credit risk of a country, or country risk.

2. In addition to country risk, the World Bank faces "market risk" on its loans. List and describe the types of market risk.

REFERENCES AND RECOMMENDED READINGS

Bakshi, Gurdip S, and Naka, Atsuyuki. "Unbiasedness of the Forward Exchange Rates." *Financial Review,* 32(1) (February 1997): 145–162.

Frachot, Antoine. "A Reexamination of the Uncovered Interest Rate Parity Hypothesis." *Journal of International Money & Finance,* 15(3) (June 1996): 419–437.

Grabbe, J. Orlin. *International Financial Markets, 2d edition,* Chapter 1. New York: Elsevier, 1991.

Hakkio, Craig S., and Sibert, Anne. "The Foreign Exchange Risk Premium: It is Real?" *Journal of Money, Credit & Banking,* 27(2) (May 1995): 301–317.

Hu, Xiaoqiang. "Macroeconomic Uncertainty and the Risk Premium in the Foreign Exchange Market." *Journal of International Money & Finance,* 16(5) (October 1997): 699–718.

Logue, Dennis E. *The WG&L Handbook of International Finance,* Chapter 4. Cincinnati, Ohio: South-Western Publishing Company, 1995.

Madsen, Erik Strojer. "Inefficiency of Foreign Exchange Markets and Expectations." *Applied Economics,* 28(4) (April 1996): 397–403.

INTEREST YIELDS,
INTEREST RATE RISK,
AND DERIVATIVE SECURITIES

FUNDAMENTAL ISSUES

1. How are interest yields, financial instrument prices, and interest rate risk interrelated?

2. Why do market interest yields vary with differences in financial instruments' terms to maturity?

3. How does risk cause market interest yields to differ?

4. What are derivative securities?

5. What are the most commonly traded derivative securities?

Since its founding in 1762, Barings Bank of Britain had been a bank with a significant presence in international markets. For instance, Barings Bank financed the United States' purchase of the Louisiana Territory from France in 1803. During the Napoleonic wars (1803–1815), Barings Bank provided credit to the British government, which gratefully granted lordly titles to the Baring family. The bank's ownership passed to a charitable foundation in 1970, although some members of the original Baring family continued to perform management roles.

In 1995, this esteemed bank collapsed when speculative market positions taken by a 27-year-old manager in Singapore generated billions of dollars worth of losses. The failure of Barings Bank resulted from senior managers' inattention to the risks inherent in the portfolios of financial instruments purchased by a security manager. Included in these portfolios were complex and risky instruments purchased by the Singapore officer of the bank, which ultimately caused the bank's downfall.

In this chapter we shall discuss various types of financial instruments, including those that were involved in the collapse of Barings Bank, which are called *derivative securities,* otherwise known more simply as *derivatives.* As you will learn, if properly managed these securities can reduce an institution's overall risk of loss. If poorly managed, however, derivatives can *add* to overall risk, potentially causing an institution, such as Barings Bank, to fail.

Banks and others use derivatives to manage the risks in their portfolios of foreign currencies, foreign bonds, and other financial instruments. In Chapter 4 you learned about *foreign exchange risk* that arises from holding financial assets denominated in currencies of more than one country. Another important type of risk is *interest rate risk.* Banks and other financial institutions can use derivatives to reduce their exposure to both types of risk. Therefore, before you can try to understand the nature and uses of derivatives, you must first understand the sources of interest rate risk. This requires that you also understand the relationships among interest rates on various financial instruments and how interest rates influence the market prices of financial instruments.

INTEREST RATES

Naturally, anyone who chooses to hold a financial instrument must contend with the risks associated with the instrument. For one thing, there is always the possibility that the issuer of the instrument may default. But even financial instruments with extremely low risk of default, such as bonds issued by governments of the United States, Germany, and the United Kingdom, can pose significant risks of loss owing to the potential for the market values of these instruments to vary as their interest rates change in the marketplace. To understand how individuals and businesses can seek either to minimize risks owing to interest rate variations or to profit from them (at least, in most nations; see the "Policy Notebook: Islamic Banking without Interest"), it is necessary first to understand how to calculate interest yields and prices of financial instruments.

POLICY NOTEBOOK
Islamic Banking without Interest

As interpreted by many adherents of the religion of Islam, the Koran, or holy book of tenets and laws of the faithful, the paying or receiving of interest is forbidden. This has induced Islamic bankers to develop an interest-free banking system that still allows Muslims to borrow, for example, to purchase a house.

To assist banking institutions offering Islamic financial services, the Malaysian central bank recently instituted special check-clearing arrangements. Those banks adhering strictly to the anti-interest interpretation of the Koran operate on the basis of profit-sharing and commissions, or deferred payments. For instance, a "loan" for the purchase of a home has the following structure: The purchaser provides a 20 percent down payment and agrees to participate in a partnership agreement with a bank. Under the terms of this agreement, the bank provides the rest of the funds and leases its prorated portion of the house to the purchaser. The purchaser of the home, therefore, pays the bank rent based on the bank's share in the home, plus a small amount each month to increase equity ownership in the home. If the purchaser defaults on his or her payments, then the bank can sell the house and return the purchaser's accumulated equity share. Essentially, the bank does not really grant a "loan" to the purchaser. Instead, it provides a lease.

Likewise, those individuals who place funds in Islamic savings instruments do not receive interest earnings. Instead, Islamic banks classify them as shareholders who receive dividends when the bank earns a profit.

FOR CRITICAL ANALYSIS:
What additional risks do Islamic banks incur that Western banks do not?

ON THE WEB
Visit Malaysia's home page at:
http://www.jaring.my

PRINCIPAL The amount of credit extended when one makes a loan or purchases a bond.

NOMINAL YIELD The coupon return on a bond divided by the bond's face value.

Interest Yields and Financial Instrument Prices

Holding financial instruments, such as loans or securities, issued by individuals, companies, or governments entails an extension of credit. The amount of credit extended via the purchase of a financial instrument is the **principal** amount of the loan or the security. Payments from the issuers that compensate the purchasers for the use of their funds constitutes *interest*. The amount of interest as a percentage of the principal of a financial instrument is the *interest rate*. For example, the annual interest rate on a simple-interest, one-year loan is equal to the amount of interest divided by the loan principal, expressed as a percentage.

Alternative Measures of Interest Yields   The holder of a financial instrument typically regards interest payments as part of a financial instrument's income yield. Therefore, securities traders commonly wish to determine the overall interest *yield* of a financial instrument. There are different ways to measure interest yields on financial instruments. One of these is the **nominal yield.** For instance, suppose that the Indian government, whose currency is the rupee, issues a bond in an amount of 500,000 rupees (about $12,500). The bond bears 45,000 rupees in interest each year. This fixed amount of interest

COUPON RETURN A fixed interest return that a bond yields each year.

that the bond yields each year is the bond's annual **coupon return,** because many bonds actually have coupons representing legal titles to interest yields. The nominal yield on this bond is equal to

$$R_N = C / F,$$

where R_N is the nominal interest yield, C is the coupon return, and F is the face amount of the bond. Hence, the annual nominal yield for the 500,000-rupee bond with its 45,000-rupee coupon return is equal to 45,000 rupees / 500,000 rupees = 0.09, or 9 percent.

The current market price of a bond typically does not equal the bond's face value. As a result, anyone thinking of purchasing a bond typically considers the bond's *coupon yield.* This is equal to

$$R_C = C / P_B,$$

CURRENT YIELD The coupon return on a bond divided by the bond's market price.

where R_C denotes **current yield,** C is the coupon return, and P_B is the current market price of the bond. For example, if the market price of an Indian government bond with a face value of 500,000 rupees is 450,000 rupees, and if the bond's coupon return is 45,000 rupees per year, then the annual current yield on this bond is equal to 45,000 rupees / 450,000 rupees = 0.10, or 10 percent.

YIELD TO MATURITY The rate of return on a bond if it is held until it matures, which reflects the market price of the bond, the bond's coupon return, and any capital gain from holding the bond to maturity.

A financial instrument's **yield to maturity** is a third way to express the interest yield. This is the rate of return that the owner of the instrument would earn by holding the instrument until maturity, or the stated date at which final principal and interest payments are due. To an individual contemplating whether to hold an instrument until it matures or to sell it at its current market price, the yield to maturity is arguably the most important yield to consider. To calculate the financial instrument's yield to maturity, however, we must first understand how to determine the instrument's price.

Discounted Present Value, the Market Price of a Bond, and Yield to Maturity
The issuer of a bond often sells the bond at a *discount*, meaning that the bond's selling price is less than its face value. Therefore, the holder of the bond automatically earns a **capital gain.** This is an increase in the bond's market value, relative to its market value at the time of purchase, if he or she holds the bond until maturity. Calculating the yield to maturity on any bond takes into account both the capital gain and the coupon returns that a bond yields to its owner. This is why we first determine the price of a bond before computing its yield to maturity.

CAPITAL GAIN A rise in the value of a financial instrument at the time it is sold, as compared with its market value at the time it was purchased.

To illustrate the relationship between coupon returns and capital gains in computing bond yields, consider a specific bond whose maturity is three years. The bond's face value is $10,000. Its annual coupon return is $600. Hence, its nominal yield per year is $600 / $10,000 = 0.06, or 6 percent.

To calculate the yield to maturity on this bond, we must determine its market price. The bond's owner receives three payments: $600 at the end of the first year, $600 at the end of the second year, and $10,600 (the principal plus the third year's interest) at the end of the third year. Consequently, the amount that an individual is willing to pay for this bond must equal the value of these payments from the purchaser's perspective at the time that the purchase occurs.

DISCOUNTED PRESENT VALUE The value today of a payment to be received at a future date.

The value today of payments to be received at future dates is the **discounted present value** of those payments. The discounted present value of any future amount is how much that amount is currently worth to us, *given* current market interest rates. Table 5–1 displays the discounted present value of a dollar received at various future dates. As you can see, the future value of a dollar declines faster at higher interest rates. This implies that the discounted present value of future payments that a holder of a bond receives falls as interest rates increase. As interest rates rise, therefore, the amount that a buyer is willing to pay for the bond declines. Hence, computing bond prices requires an understanding of how to calculate the discounted present value of a future sum.

For our example of a bond with a face value of $10,000 and three annual payments of $600 each, let's suppose that the prevailing market interest rate is $R = 0.07$, or 7 percent. Let's also begin by considering the bond's first year's

TABLE 5–1   PRESENT VALUES OF A FUTURE DOLLAR

This table shows how much a dollar received a given number of years in the future would be worth today at different rates of interest. For instance, at an interest rate of 8 percent, a dollar to be received 25 years from now would have a value of less than 15 cents, and a dollar to be received 50 years from now is worth about 2 cents.

YEAR	COMPOUNDED ANNUAL INTEREST RATE				
	3%	5%	8%	10%	20%
1	.971	.952	.926	.909	.833
2	.943	.907	.857	.826	.694
3	.915	.864	.794	.751	.578
4	.889	.823	.735	.683	.482
5	.863	.784	.681	.620	.402
6	.838	.746	.630	.564	.335
7	.813	.711	.583	.513	.279
8	.789	.677	.540	.466	.233
9	.766	.645	.500	.424	.194
10	.744	.614	.463	.385	.162
15	.642	.481	.315	.239	.0649
20	.554	.377	.215	.148	.0261
25	.478	.295	.146	.0923	.0105
30	.412	.231	.0994	.0573	.00421
40	.307	.142	.0460	.0221	.000680
50	.228	.087	.0213	.00852	.000109

return of $600. Furthermore, let's note that saving $560.75 for one year at an interest rate of 7 percent would yield an amount of $560.75 (the initial amount saved) plus 0.07 times $560.75 (the interest earned). This is equivalent to $560.75 times the factor 1.07, which works out to be equal to $600.

Hence, from today's perspective, a $600 payment to be received one year from now at a market interest rate of 7 percent is worth $560.75. It follows that $560.75 is the *discounted present value* of $600 a year from now at the interest rate of 7 percent. This amount is equal to the future payment of $600 divided by 1 + 0.07, or $600 / (1.07) = $560.75. We can conclude that the formula for calculating the discounted present value of a payment to be received a year from now is

$$\text{Discounted present value} = \frac{\text{Payment one year from now}}{1+R}.$$

The three-year bond in our example also pays $600 two years following the date of issue. Note that at a market rate of interest of 7 percent, holding $524.06 for two years would yield $600. This is so because if you were to save $524.06 for one year at this interest rate, the accumulated saving after the year would be equal to $524.06 times 1.07, or $560.75. Then if you were to save $560.75 for another year, you would end up with $560.75 times 1.07, or $600 at the end of the second year. This leads us to the conclusion that the discounted present value of $600 to be received two years from now is equal to $600 / [(1.07)(1.07)] = $600 / (1.07)^2 = $524.06.

Based on the logic of this calculation, we can determine that a general formula for computing the discounted present value of a payment to be received n years in the future is

$$\text{Discounted present value} = \frac{\text{Payment } n \text{ years from now}}{(1+R)^n}.$$

In our two-year example, $n = 2$, $R = 0.07$, and the payment two years from now is $600.

At the conclusion of the third year, the holder of the three-year bond stands to receive the principal amount of $10,000 and a concluding $600 interest payment. We can calculate the discounted present value of this amount using the earlier formula:

$$\text{Discounted present value of \$10,600 three years hence} = \frac{\$10,600}{(1.07)^3} = \$8,652.76.$$

Thus, today's value of the $10,600 that the bondholder will receive at the time when the three-year bond matures is $8,652.76.

In the absence of transactions costs and risks, the *price* of this three-year bond should be the amount that a buyer perceives the bond to be worth at the purchase date, given a market interest rate of 7 percent. This is the sum of the discounted present values of the payments received in each of the three years. From our previous computations, this sum is

$$\begin{array}{l} \text{Price of} \\ \text{3-year} \\ \text{bond} \end{array} = \frac{\$600}{(1.07)} + \frac{\$600}{(1.07)^2} + \frac{\$10{,}600}{(1.07)^3}$$

$$= \$560.75 + \$524.06 + \$8{,}652.76$$

$$= \$9{,}737.57.$$

Thus, \$9,737.57 is the market value of the three-year bond with a face value of \$10,000 and coupon return of \$600 when the market interest rate is 7 percent.

What is the yield to maturity on this bond? To answer this question, let's write our formula in a different way:

$$\$9{,}737.57 = \frac{\$600}{(1+R_m)} + \frac{\$600}{(1+R_m)^2} + \frac{\$10{,}600}{(1+R_m)^3},$$

where R_m denotes the bond's yield to maturity. By construction of our example, we know that the value for R_m that satisfies this expression is 0.07. Hence, the yield to maturity for this bond is 7 percent (the market interest rate).

We can see that 7 percent is the yield to maturity for the bond because we constructed the example. If the market price on the left-hand side of the equation were to rise from \$9,737.57 to some larger number, however, then the value for R_m would have to decline somewhat. Computing the new value for R_m would then require us to solve a cubic equation. Bond traders commonly use programmed calculators or bond yield tables to evaluate yields to maturity on long-term bonds, which require solving equations of even higher power!

Perpetuities and the Relationship between Interest Yields and Bond Prices

There are many types of bonds. One particularly useful bond to think about, however, is a **perpetuity,** or a bond that never matures. For instance, the British government has issued perpetuities called *British consols.* The British Parliament called these perpetuities *2.5% Consolidated Stock of 1921,* because they first were introduced in that year and at that nominal interest rate. British consols have no fixed maturity date, although Parliament could redeem these bonds at their par values and in any amounts that it may choose.

Perpetuities such as consols pay a fixed coupon return forever. Let's again denote this annual coupon return as an amount C. If the nominal interest rate is R, then anyone contemplating buying a perpetuity must determine how much to pay for this infinite-life bond. If an individual purchases a perpetuity, then she earns C dollars next year, the year after that, and every year following. This implies that the discounted present value of the perpetuity is the sum of the discounted present values of C dollars every year into the future. This is an *infinite sum* equal to

$$C / (1+R) + C / (1+R)^2 + C / (1+R)^3 + C / (1+R)^4 + \ldots$$

ON THE WEB
Track U.S. Interest Rates via the Federal Reserve Bank of New York at:
http://www.ny.frb.org/ pihome/mktrates/dlyrates/

PERPETUITY A bond with an infinite term to maturity.

If we assume that this individual does not have to worry about risks or transactions costs, then this is the amount that she is willing to pay for this bond. This is so because this amount is today's value of the coupon returns the bond will yield. If everyone else uses the same reasoning, then the actual market price of the perpetual bond, P_B, will equal this sum of discounted present values of coupon returns:

$$P_B = C / (1+R) + C / (1+R)^2 + C / (1+R)^3 + C / (1+R)^4 + \ldots$$

Although this is an infinite sum, it results in a simple expression for the price of the perpetuity. To see this, notice that if we multiply both sides of the above equation by $(1 + R)$, we obtain:

$$(1+R) \times P_B = C + C / (1+R) + C / (1+R)^2 + C / (1+R)^3 + C / (1+R)^4 + \ldots$$

Recall that we can always subtract one equation from another equation. So let's subtract the first equation from the second:

$$[(1+R) \times P_B] - P_B = [C + C / (1+R) + C / (1+R)^2 \\ + C / (1+R)^3 + C / (1+R)^4 + \ldots] \\ - [C / (1+R) + C / (1+R)^2 + C / (1+R)^3 + C / (1+R)^4 + \ldots]$$

We can simplify the left-hand side of the equation by performing the multiplication and reducing:

$$[P_B + (R \times P_B)] - P_B = P_B - P_B + (R \times P_B) = R \times P_B.$$

In addition, all the terms on the right-hand side of the last equation cancel out, except for C. Therefore, this complicated equation involving differences between infinite sums reduces to something quite simple:

$$R \times P_B = C.$$

If we now divide both sides of this much simpler equation by R, we get a final expression for the price of a perpetuity, which is

$$P_B = C / R.$$

This expression tells us that the price of a perpetual, nonmaturing bond is its annual coupon payment divided by the market interest rate. This tells us that if the perpetuity pays $C = \$100$ per year forever, and if the market interest rate is 8 percent, then the price of the bond is equal to

$$P_B = C / R = \$100 / (0.08) = \$1,250.00.$$

Suppose that the market interest rate R increases 9 percent. Then the ratio C / R falls, and the price of the bond declines. In our earlier numerical example, if the market interest rate increases to 9 percent, then the price of the perpetuity with a $100 annual coupon return declines to

$$P_B = C / R = \$100 / (0.09) = \$1,111.11.$$

We can reach the following important conclusion from this pricing formula for a perpetuity:

> **Holding the coupon payment and all other factors unchanged, the price of an existing bond varies inversely with the nominal interest rate.**

This means that if the market nominal interest rate falls, then bond prices rise, and those who hold bonds earn a nominal capital gain. In contrast, if the market nominal interest rate rises, then bond prices decline, and people who hold bonds incur a nominal capital loss.

This inverse relationship between the market interest rate and the market price holds for all types of bonds. For instance, if you take a look back at the market price calculation in our earlier example of a three-year bond on page 137, you will note that if the interest rate had been higher, we would have computed a lower market price for the three-year bond. As you can see, the formula for the price of a perpetuity clearly illustrates this inverse relationship that exists for all financial instruments.

Term to Maturity and Interest Rate Risk   Perpetuities are useful bonds to study because the formula for their market price is so simple. Most bonds, however, have a fixed *term to maturity,* or a finite period between the initial purchase of the instrument and the eventual receipt of principal and promised interest payments. It turns out that the term to maturity is a key factor influencing the degree of **interest rate risk** associated with a financial instrument. This is the risk of variations in the market value of the financial instrument due to interest rate variations. Interest rate risk may arise from length of maturity and frequency of payments.

To see why time to maturity plays a key role in determining a financial instrument's interest rate risk, consider an example of two simple instruments. One is a British bond that pays 10,000 pounds sterling after a single year, while the other is a bond that pays 10,000 pounds after the two years have passed. Bonds that pay lump-sum amounts when they mature are called **zero coupon bonds.**

In Table 5–2 we calculate the prices of these two bonds for market interest rates of 6 percent and 7 percent. As the table indicates, an interest rate increase from 6 percent to 7 percent induces a fall in the price of each bond. As a result, those holding the bonds would incur **capital losses,** meaning that the market values of the bonds as components of their financial wealth would fall.

The calculations in Table 5–2 indicate that the percentage capital loss on the two-year bond is 1.9 percent, which is more than double the 0.9 percent capital loss on the one-year bond. This is so because the increase in the market interest rate from 6 percent to 7 percent would be applied to both years during which the two-year bond matures. By way of contrast, the

INTEREST RATE RISK The possibility that the market value of a financial instrument will change as interest rates vary.

ZERO COUPON BONDS Bonds that pay lump-sum amounts at maturity.

CAPITAL LOSS A decline in the market value of a financial instrument at the time it is sold, as compared with its market value at the time it was purchased.

TABLE 5–2 **CAPITAL LOSSES ON BONDS WITH DIFFERING MATURITIES**

This example illustrates that the prices of bonds with longer maturities fall in greater proportion following an expected rise in the market interest rate. Consequently, bonds with longer lifetimes have greater exposure to interest rate risk.

	ONE-YEAR 10,000-POUND ZERO-COUPON BOND	**TWO-YEAR 10,000-POUND ZERO-COUPON BOND**
Bond Price at 7% Rate	10,000 pounds / (1.07) = 9,345.79 pounds	10,000 pounds / $(1.07)^2$ = 8,734.39 pounds
Bond Price at 6% Rate	10,000 pounds / (1.06) = 9,433.96 pounds	10,000 / $(1.06)^2$ = 8,899.96 pounds
Pound Price Change	– 88.17 pounds	– 165.57 pounds
Percentage Price Change	$(-88.17 / 9,433.96) \times (100)$ = –0.9%	$(-165.57 / 8,899.96) \times (100)$ = –1.9%

---

same interest rate increase influences the price of the one-year bond only during the one-year lifetime of the bond.

This illustrates that financial instruments' terms to maturity are key determinants of the proportionate capital losses that their owners experience if market interest rates increase. Instruments with longer terms to maturity expose their owners to greater risk of capital loss. Consequently, holding bonds with longer maturities increases one's exposure to interest-rate risk.

Frequency of Coupon Returns and Interest Rate Risk   An additional factor influencing interest rate risk is the frequency of a bond's coupon returns. For instance, consider a zero-coupon bond that pays 10,000 pounds sterling to the bearer after two years, as compared with a bond that pays 10,000 pounds in a stream of quarterly payments over two years. The bearer of the latter bond receives returns on the bond at a faster rate. Thus, if market interest rates were to increase, the effective capital loss on the bond that pays out quarterly coupon returns would be lower, even though both bonds have the same two-year maturity.

We can conclude that *two* factors influence interest rate risk. One is a bond's term to maturity, or its lifespan. The other factor is the frequency at which the holder of the bond earns returns. To evaluate the interest rate risks that they bear, bond traders must measure these factors simultaneously. They accomplish this by using a concept known as **duration,** which is a measure of the average time necessary to receive all payments of principal and interest. Bond traders use computer spreadsheet programs or financial calculators to compute duration as a weighted average of the present values of payments during the full maturity of a financial instrument. Then they compare computed duration measures for various bonds to determine how to allocate bond holdings so as to reduce overall exposure to interest rate risk in their complete bond portfolios.

DURATION A measure of the average time during which all payments of principal and interest on a financial instrument are made.

FUNDAMENTAL ISSUE #1 ———————————

How are interest yields, financial instrument prices, and interest rate risk interrelated? Interest yields are rates of return derived from holding financial instruments, which traders can compute based on the face value, price, or term to maturity of a financial instrument. The current price of any financial instrument should reflect traders' assessments of the value of the instruments from today's perspective. It follows that a financial instrument's price should depend directly on the discounted present value of current and future returns, which, in turn, depends negatively on the interest rate. Hence, upward movements in interest rates can cause capital losses by unexpectedly depressing market prices, thereby exposing the holder to interest rate risk.

The Term Structure of Interest Rates

What factors determine the actual values of market interest rates? As we shall discuss in Chapters 11–15, the overall level of interest rates depends upon a number of economic factors. Once the general level of interest rates is determined, the interrelationships among interest rates on various financial instruments depend largely on two key factors. One of these is the instruments' terms to maturity. The other is the underlying risks associated with the financial instruments.

TERM STRUCTURE OF INTEREST RATES The relationship among yields on financial instruments with identical risk, liquidity, and tax characteristics but differing terms to maturity.

YIELD CURVE A chart giving the relationship among yields on bonds that differ only in their terms to maturity.

The relationship among interest yields on financial instruments that possess the *same risk, liquidity (ease of convertibility into cash), and tax characteristics* but differing terms to maturity is called the **term structure of interest rates.** Bond yields normally differ even if bonds with different maturities are identical in every other respect.

Yield Curves We can plot the differences among interest yields for various terms to maturity on a **yield curve,** or a chart showing yields on similar bonds with different terms to maturity. Figure 5–1 displays yield curves for selected nations.

As you can see, the yield curves in Figure 5–1 slope upward. Most of the time, this is the typical shape of a yield curve, indicating that interest yields normally rise with an increase in the term to maturity of a financial instrument. Nevertheless, at various times nations can experience downward-sloping yield curves. If this circumstance arises, then a country's yield curve is said to be an *inverted* yield curve, because interest yields fall as the term to maturity increases.

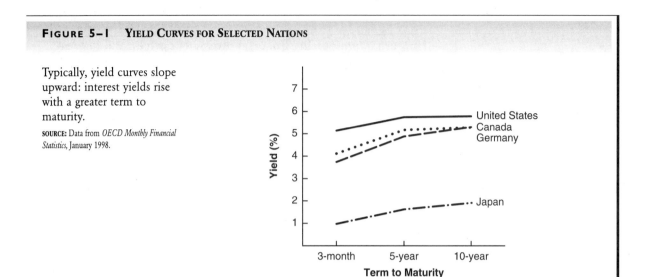

FIGURE 5–1   YIELD CURVES FOR SELECTED NATIONS

Typically, yield curves slope upward: interest yields rise with a greater term to maturity.

SOURCE: Data from *OECD Monthly Financial Statistics,* January 1998.

SEGMENTED MARKETS
THEORY A theory of the term structure of interest rates that views bonds with differing maturities as nonsubstitutable, so that their yields differ because they are determined in separate markets.

Why is it that yield curves typically slope upward? Economists have advanced three fundamental explanations in an effort to answer this question. These are known as the segmented markets theory, the expectations theory, and the preferred habitat theory.

Segmented Markets Theory   The key idea behind the **segmented markets theory** of the term structure of interest rates is that financial instruments with differing terms to maturity are not perfect substitutes. Consequently, they essentially are traded in separate financial markets, even though they may be nearly identical instruments in all respects other than their terms to maturity. Then the interactions between supply and demand conditions within each individual market determine each instrument's yield.

For example, banks around the world issue deposit liabilities with maturities of six months to three years. To match the maturities of these liabilities with assets of corresponding maturities, these institutions often hold government bonds that have maturities of six months to three years. By way of contrast, life insurance companies often issue policy liabilities with intermediate to long-term maturities of five to thirty years. Therefore, they typically desire to "match" these liabilities by holding government notes and bonds with five- to thirty-year maturities.

The basic point of the segmented markets theory is that interest yields of financial assets with differing terms to maturity should reflect these natural differences in desired holdings of financial assets based on their terms to maturity. For example, imagine a situation in which the interest yields on French government bonds with differing maturities were the same. If French banks were to increase their desired holdings of French government bonds with six-month to three-year maturities, however, there would be a rise in the demand for such shorter-term bonds and a resulting increase in their prices. Consequently, the market yields on these shorter-term French government bonds would decline, assuming all other factors were unchanged. As a result, yields on short-term French government bonds would be lower than yields on longer-term bonds, and the French yield curve would slope upward.

Although the segmented markets theory explains why yields may differ across various terms to maturity, it suffers from two problems. One is that the theory assumes that financial instruments with different maturities are not perfect substitutes, even though there is considerable evidence that the interest yields on bonds with similar characteristics move together over time. Hence, bonds that differ only on the basis of terms to maturity must be somewhat substitutable. The second difficulty with the segmented markets theory is that it fails to explain why an upward-sloping yield curve should be a "normal" outcome, as it so typically is.

The Expectations Theory A theory that can shed light on both of these issues is called the **expectations theory** of the term structure of interest rates. We can illustrate the basic features of the expectations theory by examining a setting in which an individual plans to save funds over a two-year period. The individual confronts two possibilities. One option is to hold a two-year bond for the two years to maturity. We suppose that this bond has an annual interest yield denoted I. The individual's other option is hold one-year bonds each year over the two-year interval. If the individual makes this choice, he would place his funds in a one-year bond for the first year at an interest rate of R_1. At the end of the first year, he would place the principal plus the interest accumulated during the first year in holdings of an additional one-year bond that would mature at the conclusion of the second year. We assume that at the beginning of the two-period planning horizon when the individual must make his choice about which savings strategy to pursue, he anticipates that the one-year bond's interest yield during the second year will be R_2^e.

Naturally, the individual would be willing to hold *either* one-year or two-year bonds only if he expects that his return over the two years would be the same under either option. This would be the case if

$$I = (R_1 + R_2^e) / 2.$$

Hence, the individual would be indifferent between the alternative savings strategies if the annual interest rate on the two-year bond, I, were equal to the expected *average* annual interest rate from holding one-year bonds, $(R_1 + R_2^e)/2$. If the two-year bond rate were to rise above this expected average of one-year rates, then the individual would hold only two-year bonds. If the two-year bond rate were to fall below this expected average of one-year rates, however, then the individual would hold only one-year bonds each year. As this individual and others participating in financial markets seek to arbitrage between these two choices, the two sides of the equation would, in fact, be driven to an equality in the marketplace.

EXPECTATIONS THEORY
A theory of the term structure of interest rates that views bonds with differing maturities as perfect substitutes, causing their yields to differ solely because traders anticipated that short-term interest rates will rise or fall.

To see the implications of the expectations theory for the yield curve, suppose that the one-year bond were to pay $R_1 = 0.07$ during the first year and that people expect the one-year bond yield for the next year to be $R_2^e = 0.09$. In equilibrium, therefore, the two-year bond rate I should, under the expectations theory, turn out to be equal to the average of 0.07 and 0.09, which is $(0.07 + 0.09) / 2 = 0.08$. In this situation, the current one-year bond rate would be 7 percent, while the rate on a two-year bond would be 8 percent. Hence, the yield curve for bonds of one- and two-year maturities would slope upward.

Now consider what would happen if people were to expect a sharp decline in the future one-year bond rate, to $R_2^e = 0.05$. As a result, the two-year bond rate would have to decline to

$$I = (R_1 + R_2^e) / 2 = (0.07 + 0.05) / 2 = 0.06.$$

Thus, the two-year bond now would yield 6 percent per year. Because the one-year bond yield would be higher, at 7 percent, the yield curve now would be downward-sloping, or inverted.

As you can see, unlike the segmented markets theory, the expectations theory of the term structure offers an explanation for why yield curves may slope upward or downward: An upward-sloping yield curve indicates a general expectation that short-term interest rates will rise, while a downward-sloping yield curve indicates a general expectation that short-term interest rates will fall. A glaring problem with this conclusion is that yield curves normally slope upward. If interest yields are as likely over long intervals to fall as they are to rise, then the expectations theory cannot provide an explanation for why yield curves generally slope upward.

The Preferred Habitat Theory   To resolve this problem with the expectations theory, the **preferred habitat theory** of the term structure of interest rates puts together key features of the segmented markets theory and the expectations theory. According to the preferred habitat theory, financial instruments are *imperfectly substitutable* if they have differing maturities but are identical in other respects. The preferred habitat theory proposes that the expectations theory otherwise constitutes an acceptable theory of the term structure.

The key assumption of the preferred habitat theory is that, holding all other factors constant, people usually prefer to hold financial instruments with shorter maturities. The reason is that short-maturity instruments typically are more liquid instruments, making them somewhat more desirable to hold as compared with longer-term instruments. Thus, people have a natural "preference for the habitat" of trading in shorter-term instruments, and so a **term premium** on longer-term bonds is necessary to induce them to hold these instruments alongside short-term instruments, if all other factors were the same.

In relating the interest yields on short- and long-term bonds, the preferred habitat theory modifies the expectations theory by adding a term premium. In

PREFERRED HABITAT THEORY A theory of the term structure of interest rates that views bonds as imperfectly substitutable, so that yields on longer-term bonds must be greater than those on shorter-term bonds even if short-term interest rates are not expected to rise or fall.

TERM PREMIUM An amount by which the yield on a long-term bond must exceed the yield on a short-term bond to make individuals willing to hold either bond if they expect short-term bond yields to remain unchanged.

the case of one- and two-year bonds, for instance, the interest yield on the two-year bond thereby would equal

$$I = TP + [(R_1 + R_2^e) / 2],$$

where *TP* is the term premium for the two-year bond. Suppose that $R_1 = R_2^e = 0.07$, so that people expect that the one-year bond rate will remain at 7 percent for both years. In addition, suppose also that people have a decided preference to hold one-year bonds. This leads to a sizable term premium of $TP = 0.01$, or 1 percent, to induce holdings of two-year bonds alongside one-year bonds. As a result, the two-year bond rate is equal to

$$I = TP + [(R_1 + R_2^e) / 2]$$
$$= 0.01 + [(0.07 + 0.07) / 2]$$
$$= 0.01 + 0.07 = 0.08.$$

Hence, the two-year bond rate would equal 8 percent even though people anticipate that the one-year bond rate will stay unchanged at 7 percent. The resulting yield curve relating the yields on one- and two-year bonds slopes upward. This implies that over a long period in which interest rates are equally likely to rise or fall, the yield curve normally would have a positive slope. The preferred habitat theory appears to fit the facts: It indicates that yield curves typically should slope upward. It further predicts that yield curves should steepen if people generally expect short-term interest rates to rise and that they should flatten out, or in extreme cases even become inverted, if people expect sharp declines in short-term interest rates.

FUNDAMENTAL ISSUE #2

Why do market interest yields vary with differences in financial instruments' terms to maturity? Yields on financial instruments with differing maturities will not be equal for two reasons. One is that differences in short-term and long-term rates may arise from differing expectations about whether future short-term interest rates are likely to rise or fall relative to current interest rates on longer-term instruments. Another is that short-term financial instruments generally are more liquid and less risky than longer-term instruments, so that a term premium is needed to induce individuals to be indifferent between holding either long-term or short-term instruments.

The Risk Structure of Interest Rates

RISK STRUCTURE OF INTEREST RATES The relationship among yields on financial instruments that have the same maturity but differ because of variations in default risk, liquidity, and tax rates.

DEFAULT RISK The possibility that an individual or business that issues a financial instrument may be unable to meet its obligations to repay the principal or to make interest payments.

RISK PREMIUM The amount by which one instrument's yield exceeds another because it is riskier and less liquid.

Differences in terms to maturity provide one reason that interest rates differ across financial instruments. The **risk structure of interest rates** constitutes the other key reason. This refers to the relationship among yields on financial instruments that have the *same maturity* but differ as a result of default risk, liquidity, and tax considerations.

Default Risk A fundamental reason that financial instruments offer different yields is that savers must take into account **default risk.** This is the possibility that the issuer of a financial instrument may be unable to honor obligations to pay off the principal or interest. The bonds issued by many national governments, and particularly those of the United States and other developed countries, have relatively low default risk. The reason is that, as long as governments can enforce their power to tax and to create new money, they can raise taxes to make interest and principal payments on bonds that they issue.

In contrast, financial market traders typically regard bonds issued by governments of a number of less-developed nations as much riskier. The reason is that political instability in these nations makes traders wary of holding these bonds. For instance, a twenty-year bond issued by a nation that has had fifteen changes of government during the past seven years, including perhaps a military coup that led to a renunciation of some past government debt obligations, possesses considerable default risk. Thus, even if the government bond issued by the developing country were to have the same term to maturity, traders would require a higher exchange-rate-adjusted yield to induce them to hold both bonds in their portfolios.

The amount by which this developing country's government bond rate exceeds the Treasury bond rate because of greater risk of debt default risk is the **risk premium.** In this situation, in which the main source of risk stems from political uncertainty, the risk premium arises from perceived *country risk* differences. As we discussed in Chapter 4, country risk can account for risk premiums on bonds issued by various nations for reasons other than political uncertainty. For example, if reports were to emerge that the oil reserves of an otherwise politically stable, oil-producing nation were being depleted, then traders likely would consider bonds issued by that nation as possessing greater country risk as well. We shall discuss issues involving country risk in greater detail in Chapter 6.

Private risks also can account for interest rate risk premiums. For example, consider a twenty-year Italian corporate bond. Even if the Italian company issuing the bond were to have a very good current credit rating, the possibility nonetheless exists that its profitability could decline at any future date within the next twenty years. In contrast to the Italian government, this company could not assess taxes or print money to pay its debt obligations if its fortunes turned sour during that span. Thus, the perceived default risk for the Italian corporate bond would be greater than for a twenty-year Italian government bond. The interest rate on the Italian corporate bond typically would equal the rate on the government bond plus a risk premium.

Liquidity An additional rationale for why bonds of most developing nations typically have yields exceeding exchange-rate-adjusted yields on developed-country bonds with the same terms to maturity is that bonds of developing nations most often are less-liquid financial instruments. This is true because financial markets of a number of developing nations have low trading volumes. Thus, the holder of bonds issued by, say, the British, German, or Japanese government knows that these bonds will be easier to sell in a time of a need for cash, as compared with bonds issued by the governments of Rwanda, Bangladesh, or Vietnam.

Likewise, within many countries markets for private bonds are not as active as markets for government bonds. On the one hand, someone who wishes to convert a bond issued by a private Russian company into cash may enter the St. Petersburg markets and discover that few traders stand ready to buy such a bond. On the other hand, the market for bonds issued by the Russian government typically experiences a larger number of buy and sell orders each day. Consequently, a private bond is less liquid than a government bond in Russia. The same point usually holds true in most other nations. As a result, bondholders generally require a higher yield on private bonds, as compared with government bonds with the same term to maturity. The higher private bond yield makes up for the possibility that bondholders may experience greater difficulties selling the private bonds at a future date.

We may conclude that default risk is not the only factor that can cause differences between yields on bonds with the same terms to maturity. Another portion of the difference between yields on bonds with the same maturity is *liquidity premium*. Nevertheless, it is very difficult for economists to distinguish between risk and liquidity premiums. For instance, bonds issued by the Russian government are less liquid than U.S. Treasury bonds of the same maturity. A key reason for this liquidity difference is that fewer traders are willing to take on the additional country risk associated with holding Russian bonds.

For this reason, economists apply the term "risk premium" to refer to interest rate differences resulting both from diverging degrees of default risk *and* from distinctive levels of liquidity. When traders or the financial media refer to a risk premium on one bond relative to another, they generally have in mind a yield difference arising because a bond has greater default risk *and* lower liquidity.

Figure 5–2 gives plots of monthly observations of the average annual yields of long-term U.S. Treasury bonds, the highest-rated long-term investment grade securities (Moody's Aaa), and medium-rated investment grade securities (Moody's Baa). As you can see, the yields on both classes of corporate bonds are always higher than the yield on Treasury bonds, because Treasury bonds have lower default risk and greater liquidity. Likewise, medium-rated corporate bonds have higher yields than highly-rated corporate bonds for the same reasons.

FIGURE 5–2   **U.S. LONG-TERM BOND YIELDS**

U.S. corporate bonds have lower liquidity and higher default risk, as compared with Treasury bonds, so they consistently have higher yields. In addition, the lowest-rated corporate bonds (Moody's Baa) have higher default risk, as compared with the highest-rated corporate bonds (Moody's Aaa), so the lowest-rated corporate bonds also have higher yields.

SOURCE: Data from *Federal Reserve Bulletin* (various issues).

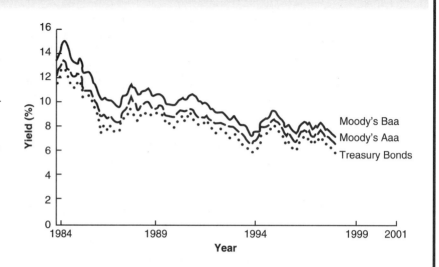

Tax Differences   One more reason that bonds with identical maturities may have different interest yields is that nations' tax laws sometimes treat some bonds differently from others. For example, in the United States bondholders generally have not been required to pay either federal or state taxes on their interest earnings from holdings of municipal bonds, which are bonds issued by state and local governments. Hence, the pretax and aftertax yields on U.S. municipal bonds are the same, but aftertax yields on U.S. Treasury bonds are lower than their pretax yields.

As a result, higher pretax interest rates are necessary to induce traders to hold both U.S. Treasury bonds and U.S. municipal bonds simultaneously. This can be seen in Figure 5–3, which plots pretax (market) U.S. Treasury bond yields and market yields on municipal bonds. The latter bonds have lower yields.

FUNDAMENTAL ISSUE #3

How does risk cause market interest yields to differ?   Differences in degrees of default risk and liquidity cause risk premiums to be imbedded in the yields on financial instruments. Because risk premiums differ across instruments, their market yields typically differ even if they have the same terms to maturity. National and state governments also tax some instruments at different rates, which causes their market rates to diverge.

FIGURE 5–3   U.S. MUNICIPAL AND TREASURY BOND YIELDS

Interest earnings from U.S. municipal bonds are exempt from federal taxation, but interest earnings on U.S. Treasury bonds are subject to federal taxation.

Consequently, Treasury bond yields exceed the yields on municipal bonds.

SOURCE: Data from *Federal Reserve Bulletin* (various issues).

HEDGING, SPECULATION, AND DERIVATIVE SECURITIES

As we discussed in Chapter 4, exchange rate movements cause those who trade in international financial markets to face risks arising from variations in asset returns. They also experience interest rate risks that arise from interest rate volatility. Let's consider how traders confront this additional source of risk.

Possible Responses to Interest Rate Risk

Interest rate risk poses both rewards and challenges to an individual or firm. The rewards arise if an individual or a company finds ways to profit from increases in financial instruments' market values following reductions in market interest rates. The challenges, on the other hand, entail balancing the potential for such capital gains against the possibility of capital losses, or losses incurred if market interest rates decline, thereby reducing the market values of financial instruments.

Some Strategies for Limiting Interest Rate Risk   There are various ways that one might seek to limit exposure to interest rate risks. One approach might be to hold bonds with shorter durations, to avoid zero-coupon bonds, and to strive to make certain that all bond holdings yield frequent coupon returns. Another strategy might be to hold mostly short-term financial instruments. Financial instruments with short-term maturities, as we noted earlier, have lower risk of capital losses when interest rates rise as compared with instruments of longer maturity.

There are three problems with this second strategy, however. One is that if the yield curve slopes upward, it is more likely that long-duration instruments will provide greater returns. This is so because if all other factors are unchanged, duration increases with the term to maturity. The higher is the term to maturity, the higher is the interest yield when the yield curve exhibits its normal shape. Consequently, holding only short-duration instruments constitutes a low-return strategy.

REINVESTMENT RISK The possibility that available yields on short-term financial instruments may decline, so that holdings of longer-term instruments might be preferable.

Second, continually selling and repurchasing—"rolling over"—short-term instruments can be costly. There are opportunity costs of time that must be devoted to this activity, and traders also incur direct costs in the form of expended effort. Furthermore, rolling over instruments with short terms to maturity entails potentially significant exposure to **reinvestment risk.** This is the possibility that market yields decline by the time the short-term instrument matures, so that a trader could have earned a higher net yield by holding longer-term instruments instead.

PORTFOLIO DIVERSIFICATION Holding financial instruments with different characteristics so as to spread risks across the entire set of instruments.

Furthermore, holding only short-maturity instruments sacrifices potential benefits that financial market traders could gain from **portfolio diversification,** or spreading risks across holdings of financial instruments with different characteristics. For instance, short-term yields may fall at the same time that long-term yields are rising. Thus, placing funds in a portfolio consisting only of short-term instruments could lead to a lower return than one could otherwise earn by holding a broader mix of instruments. If traders allocate their funds to a portfolio including longer-term instruments, then the rise in yields on these instruments helps offset the effect on the total portfolio return from declines in short-term yields.

Hedging   Allocating most funds to holdings of short-term instruments is a potentially costly strategy for addressing interest rate risk. An alternative strategy is to **hedge** interest rate risk using other financial instruments in ways that reduce portfolio risks. A *perfect hedge* constitutes a strategy that fully eliminates such risks.

HEDGE A financial strategy that reduces the risk of capital losses arising from interest rate risks or currency risks.

Market interest and exchange rate conditions can vary from one hour to the next. Consequently, holders of financial instruments must meet two key requirements to hedge against portfolio risks, including interest rate risks and foreign exchange risks. One is sufficient *flexibility* to adapt to various situations. Another is the capability to conduct necessary transactions *rapidly*. The desire to find hedging strategies that combine both flexibility and speed has led to the development of sophisticated financial instruments called *derivative securities,* or *derivatives.*

Derivative Securities

A *forward contract,* such as forward currency contract that calls for delivery of a financial instrument at a predetermined price on a specific date, represents one type of **derivative security.** In general, a derivative security is any financial instrument with a return that is linked to, or derived from, the returns of other financial instruments. Forward currency contracts fit this definition, because their payoffs to traders depend on spot exchange rates.

Hedging with Forward Contracts   As you learned in Chapter 4, foreign exchange market participants use forward currency contracts to protect themselves from foreign exchange risks, or the potential for losses owing to unanticipated variations in spot exchange rates. In a like manner, financial market traders hedge against variability in interest rates by using **interest-rate forward contracts,** which are contracts guaranteeing the future sale of a financial instrument at a specified interest rate as of a specific date.

To see how an interest-rate forward contract can be a *perfect* hedge for two parties to such a contract, consider an example. Suppose that a London bank feels certain that next year it will receive 10 million pounds sterling in future interest and principal payments from creditworthy customers who have borrowed from the bank. As part of a new management strategy, the bank's managers have decided to reduce the bank's lending next year and to place half of that amount, or 5 million pounds, in default-risk-free five-year notes issued by the British government. The bank's managers wish to guarantee that at the same time the following year, the bank will still find itself earning the current market interest yield on the British government notes, which we shall suppose is equal to 7 percent. At the same time, a German bank's securities portfolio contains several million pounds worth of five-year British government notes that will mature in three years. The German bank's managers think that market interest rates may rise above 7 percent during the next three years, which would imply a fall in the prices of the notes, causing the bank to incur a capital loss on its British note holdings.

To try to hedge against the risks that they face, the London and German banks negotiate an interest-rate forward contract. The London bank agrees to purchase five-year British notes valued at 5 million pounds *one year from now* at a price that would yield the 7 percent interest yield currently in effect for those notes. The London bank thereby guarantees that it will earn today's 7 percent market rate a year from now. The German bank also relieves itself of the risk of capital loss within the next year on a significant portion of its portfolio of five-year British notes. This is because the contract guarantees the German bank that the price of the notes will be consistent with a 7 percent yield in the following year.

DERIVATIVE SECURITY
A financial instrument in which the return depends on the returns of other financial instruments.

INTEREST-RATE FORWARD CONTRACT Contracts committing the issuer to sell a financial instrument at a given interest rate as of a specific date.

Speculation with Derivatives   As this example and those in Chapter 4 concerning forward currency contracts indicate, traders use derivative securities as hedging instruments for the purpose of protecting a portfolio from risks of loss. This does not mean, however, that traders do not use derivative securities for purposes of risky speculation in the pursuit of profits.

To understand how derivatives transactions may *increase* overall risk, let's slightly change the conditions of the previous example involving the London and German banks. Suppose now that the London bank's managers currently think that the interest cost of their bank's funds, which now averages 6 percent, is likely to be lower by this time next year. Their belief, however, is not consistent with the widespread views of other financial market participants, who generally expect a significant increase in average funding costs that London banks will face during the next year. Nevertheless, the London bank managers are so sure that their expectation will turn out to be correct that they are willing to enter into the interest-rate forward contract with the German bank that we already discussed.

Recall that this contract commits the London bank to buy the British government notes at a price consistent with the *current* market yield of 7 percent. This means that if the widespread expectation that banks' average interest funding costs will rise significantly by the following year are correct, then the net interest profit that the London bank would earn on the British government notes would be much lower next year than the London bank's managers currently *speculate* that it will be. For example, if banks' average funding costs were to rise to as high as 7 percent or more, then the London bank would earn a net profit on its British notes of zero or less. Thus, to the extent that the consensus forecast of higher bank funding costs indicates a strong likelihood that this actually will occur, the London bank would have negotiated a speculative contract and added to its overall risk.

This example indicates that while financial market participants can use derivative securities to hedge against risks, they also can use them to engage in speculative activities. Worldwide derivatives trading has increased dramatically since the early 1980s as financial managers found ways to use derivative securities in hedging strategies. At the same time, however, many traders determined that they could earn significant short-run profits by speculating with derivative securities.

Some traders learned that such derivatives speculations can turn out to be wrong. The results were sizable speculative losses, the most notable of which we tabulate in Table 5–3. Particularly dramatic among these were the 1994 loss of more than $1.5 billion by Orange County, California and the 1995 loss of about $1.4 billion by Britain's Barings Bank. The broader consequences of these losses were layoffs for Orange County employees and the collapse of Barings Bank.

Where did all the "lost" funds tabulated in Table 5–3 end up? The answer is that the funds did not evaporate. Instead, they fell into the possession of

---

TABLE 5–3   MAJOR DERIVATIVES LOSSES IN THE 1990s

Many companies and municipalities experienced multimillion-dollar losses from derivatives in the 1990s.

ESTIMATE OF LOSS	COMPANY/MUNICIPALITY	PRIMARY DERIVATIVES
$50 million	First Boston	Options
$260 million	Volkswagen	Currency futures
$100 million	Cargill Fund	Mortgage derivatives
$157 million	Procter & Gamble	Currency futures
$100 million	Florida State Treasury	Mortgage derivatives
$20 million	Gibson Greeting Cards	Swaps
$35 million	Dell Computer	Swaps and options
$20 million	Paramount Communications	Swaps
$150 million	Glaxo, Inc.	Mortgage derivatives
$1,500 million	Orange County, California	Mortgage derivatives
$50 million	Capital Corp. Credit Union	Mortgage derivatives
$195 million	Wisconsin Investment Funds	Swaps
$25 million	Escambia County, Florida	Mortgage derivatives
$1,400 million	Barings Bank, UK	Stock index futures
$65 million	PacifiCorp	Currency options

individuals, businesses, financial institutions, and government agencies that made the right choices in their own speculative strategies. For instance, in our example involving the London and German banks, if the London bank's managers turn out to be incorrect in their anticipation of a fall in average bank funding costs, then the London bank experiences losses from the interest-rate forward contract. The "lost" funds flow to the German bank, which is able to remove the British notes from its portfolio at a 7 percent yield, and hence at an above-market price, in the following year.

This leads us to the following conclusion about losses in derivatives transactions:

> **For each "loser" in derivatives speculation, there also must be a "winner" on the other side of the transaction.**

From society's perspective, gains and losses from derivatives speculation must, in a purely accounting sense, "cancel out." As we shall discuss, however, this does not mean that governments have not become concerned about the potential for broader fallout from large derivatives losses.

FUNDAMENTAL ISSUE #4

What are derivative securities? Derivative securities are financial instruments that have returns based on the returns of other financial instruments. Traders may use derivative securities to hedge against interest rate and foreign exchange risks. They also may use derivatives to try to earn profits based on speculations about future movements in interest rates and exchange rates.

COMMON DERIVATIVE SECURITIES AND THEIR RISKS

There are several categories of derivative securities. The characteristic that they all share is that their returns stem from returns on other financial instruments. In addition, traders may use them as hedging instruments. Traders also may use these instruments in speculative strategies.

Forward Contracts

LONG POSITION An obligation to purchase a financial instrument at a given price and at a specific time.

SHORT POSITION An obligation to sell a financial instrument at a given price and at a specific time.

In the example of an interest-rate forward contract between London and German banks, the London bank agreed to purchase British government notes in the following year at a price consistent with the current market yield. In the terminology of forward contracts, the London bank took a **long position,** meaning that the London bank is obliged to *purchase* the British governments notes next year at a fixed yield. By way of contrast, the German bank selling the notes took a **short position,** meaning that the German bank must *sell* the British government notes the following year at the contracted price. By entering into the forward contract, however, the German bank's managers were able to remove the British government notes from their portfolios more quickly, thus avoiding the possibility of incurring a capital loss if market yields were to rise.

Two factors that may limit the market for forward contracts are setting terms of the contract and default risk. Participants in forward contracts must agree to specific contract terms. Sometimes it is difficult for two parties to reach agreement. In our example, we simply assumed that the London and German banks could reach mutually satisfying terms. In reality, reaching an agreement on the terms of forward contracts can be a complex undertaking.

Default risk also somewhat deters the use of forward contracts. In our banking example, the London bank might be better off defaulting on the contract if its funding costs were to rise sharply within a year's time. This could make the German bank less likely to agree to the terms of the contract. Such potential incentives for default make interest-rate forward contracts more risky and less liquid, thereby restraining trading volumes somewhat.

Futures

FUTURES CONTRACT
An agreement to deliver to another a given amount of a standardized commodity or financial instrument at a designated future date.

A **futures contract** is an agreement by one party to deliver to another a quantity of a commodity or financial instrument at a specific future date. In contrast to forward contracts, futures contracts specify *standardized* quantities and terms of exchange. Futures contracts specify in advance the amounts to be traded and the guidelines for transactions. Because futures contracts are standardized, parties do not have to spend time working out contract terms.

Holders of futures experience profits or losses on the contracts at any time before the contract expires. This is because futures contracts require daily cashflow settlements. By way of contract, profits or losses occur only at the expiration date of a forward contract, which requires settlements only at maturity.

The futures exchange is an organized market that simplifies the task of selling of a futures contract to another party. This makes futures contracts highly liquid. Consequently, futures trading has grown much more rapidly than transactions in forward contracts. This does not mean that derivatives trading outside public futures exchanges is "small potatoes"; the estimated value of worldwide forward contracts and other derivatives transactions amounts to over $40 trillion, or nearly six times the amount of *annual* U.S. nominal national income.

INTEREST RATE FUTURES Contracts to buy or sell a standardized denomination of a specific financial instrument at a given price at a certain date in the future.

Interest Rate Futures   Contracts requiring delivery of standard quantities of a financial instrument at a specified price and rate of return and on a certain date are **interest rate futures.** Traders undertake transactions in these contracts at the Chicago Board of Trade (CBOT) futures exchange and other exchanges around the world. Each exchange establishes requirements that parties to such a transaction must meet. The financial instruments of futures contracts usually are U.S. Treasury bonds and other government bonds. For example, a trader may enter into a five-year U.S. Treasury note futures contract, which constitutes an agreement to purchase or sell U.S. Treasury notes in standard denominations of $100,000.

STOCK INDEX FUTURE Promises of future delivery of a portfolio of stocks represented by a stock price index.

Stock Index Futures   Standardized agreements to deliver, on a specified date, a portfolio of stocks represented by a stock price index are **stock index futures.** For example, in the case of Standard & Poor's (S&P) 500 futures traded at the Chicago Mercantile Exchange, the stock portfolio is representative of market value of the 500 companies listed in the S&P index. Likewise, Nikkei-225 Stock Average futures are based on a portfolio of 225 stocks traded in the Tokyo Stock Exchange. It was a series of bad bets about Nikkei-225 futures traded in the Singapore International Monetary Exchange (Simex) that led to the downfall of Barings Bank in 1995.

To see how to calculate the value of a futures contract, let's consider an example involving an S&P 500 index futures contract. Computing the dollar value of such a contract requires multiplying the current market price of the futures contract times $500. For instance, if the S&P 500 futures price is 400, then the value of the contract is equal to $200,000. If an individual were to take a *short position* with an S&P 500 futures contract, then she would agree to deliver a cash amount of $500 times whatever the futures price turns out to be at the date in the contract. A party on the other end of the transactions, in contrast, would take a *long position* and agree to pay 400 times $500 for this contract today. Thus, if the market price of the futures contract when the date arrives were to equal to 500, then the contract would have a dollar value of $250,000. The individual in the short position would lose $50,000. The buyer in the long position, in turn, would gain $50,000. The buyer in the long position would have paid $200,000 for the $250,000 cash payment that the seller in the short position is obligated to make.

Currency Futures   Futures contracts entailing the future delivery of national currencies are **currency futures.** The world's largest currency futures market is the International Monetary Market of the Chicago Mercantile Exchange, in which traders conduct futures transactions in the currencies of Australia, Canada, Germany, Japan, Mexico, Switzerland, and the United Kingdom.

Currency futures contracts, like other futures, entail daily cash flow settlements, whereas currency forward contracts entail a single settlement only at the date of maturity. As a result, the market prices of forward and futures contracts usually differ. In addition, futures contracts typically involve smaller currency denominations, as compared with forward contracts. Large banking institutions and corporations that transmit large volumes of foreign currencies in their normal business operations are the primary users of forward contracts. Individuals and smaller firms that wish to undertake hedging or speculative strategies typically trade currency futures instead. Figure 5–4 explains how to read currency futures quotes published in the *Wall Street Journal*.

Hedging with Currency Futures   How might one act on a current currency futures quote? Suppose that a British firm has a franchise operation in the United States. The firm's managers anticipate that the current year's profits from this operation will be $3 million, which they plan to convert to British pounds. If the dollar were to depreciate relative to the pound during the year, then the pound-denominated value of the $3 million would be lower at the end of the year. That is, the British firm's exposure to translation risk would cause it to lose a portion of its dollar-denominated profits from its U.S. operation. To hedge against this risk, the firm's managers could take a long position via a pound future that expires in December. As the dollar-denominated profit earnings of the firm decline in value relative to the British pound, the pound-denominated value of the firm's December future will rise, thereby offsetting, at least partially, the effect of the dollar's depreciation against the pound.

Reducing translation risk requires the firm to establish a *margin account* with a futures broker. The firm posts an *initial margin* (sometimes called the *bond performance requirement*) in this account by paying a small portion of the total value of futures that the broker will purchase on the firm's behalf. Typically the initial margin is less than 2 percent of the total value of futures purchased. During the year, the firm must maintain a *maintenance margin* (sometimes

CURRENCY FUTURE An agreement to deliver to another a standardized quantity of a specific nation's currency at a designated future date.

ON THE WEB
Learn about the Chicago Mercantile Exchange at:
http://www.cme.com

FIGURE 5–4   READING QUOTES ON FOREIGN CURRENCY FUTURES

Each day the *Wall Street Journal* reports Chicago
Mercantile Exchange futures prices using the format
shown above. To understand how to read published
currency futures quotes, consider the information for
each column in the March 5, 1998 quote for the German
deutsche mark:

First column:	Maturing month; contract matures on the second business day preceding the third Wednesday of the month.
Open:	Price of futures contract at the opening of business. On this day, a contract for 125,000 deutsche marks for June 1998 began trading at $0.5555 per deutsche mark.
High:	Highest price of the futures contract reached during the day; $0.5559 per deutsche mark on this day.
Low:	Lowest price of the futures contract reached during the day; $0.5470 per deutsche mark on this day.
Settle:	Price of the futures contract settled upon by the close of business on this day; $0.5474 per deutsche mark.
Change:	Change in price during the day; a decrease of $.0058 per deutsche mark.
Lifetime high:	Highest price at which this futures contract has ever traded, or $0.5995 per deutsche mark.
Lifetime low:	Lowest price at which this futures contract has ever traded, or $0.5470 per deutsche mark.
Open interest:	Number of contracts outstanding on the previous trading day.

SOURCE: Reprinted by permission of *Wall Street Journal,* © 1998 Dow Jones & Company, Inc. All Rights Reserved Worldwide.

CURRENCY

	Open	High	Low	Settle	Change	Lifetime High	Lifetime Low	Open Interest
JAPAN YEN (CME)-12.5 million yen; $ per yen (.00)							
Mar	.7905	.7919	.7825	.7826	– .0075	.9375	.7512	90,500
June	.8005	.8015	.7924	.7925	– .0077	.9090	.7637	7,202
Sept	.8035	.8035	.80357	.8025	– .0079	.8695	.7735	566
Est vol 36,325; vol Wd 21,825; open int 98,308, +1,140.							
DEUTSCHEMARK (CME)-125,000 marks; $ per mark							
Mar	.5502	.5530	.5440	.5445	– .0058	.6160	.5383	66,352
June	.5555	.5559	.5470	.5474	– .0058	.5995	.5470	15,734
Sept	.5526	.5580	.5498	.5502	– .0058	.5944	.5498	1,570
Est vol 45,284; vol Wd 33,888; open int 83,667, 1,168.							
CANADIAN DOLLAR (CME)-100,000 dlrs.; $ per Can $							
Mar	.7034	.7057	.7008	.7034	+ .0003	.7670	.6807	49,288
June	.7044	.7072	.7020	.7046	+ .0003	.7470	.6825	14,187
Sept	.7047	.7075	.7030	.7058	+ .0003	.7463	.6845	2,377
Dec	.7075	.7080	.7074	.7069	+ .0003	.7400	.6860	1,133
Mr99	....	....	....	.7080	+ .0003	.7247	.6875	....
Est vol 17,895; vol Wd 6,901; open int 67,387, –1,078.							
BRITISH POUND (CME)-62,500 pds.; $ per pound							
Mar	1.6468	1.6506	1.6270	1.6300	– .0174	1.7020	1.5680	29,692
June	1.6344	1.6418	1.6190	1.6228	– .0170	1.6940	1.5610	3,959
Sep	1.6260	1.6260	1.6260	1.6156	– .0168	1.6870	1.5690	568
Est vol 16,729; vol Wd 6,800; open int 34,222, +525.							
SWISS FRANC (CME)-125,000 francs; $ per franc							
Mar	.6767	.6818	.6692	.6699	– .0068	.7450	.6687	45,121
June	.6843	.6893	.6768	.6775	– .0068	.7304	.6750	12,139
Sept	....	....	....	.6849	– .0068	.7310	.6840	1,193
Est vol 31,072; vol Wd 33,810; open int 58,465, +11,427.							
AUSTRALIAN DOLLAR (CME)-100,000 dlrs.; $ per A.$							
Mar	.6752	.6752	.6665	.6679	– .0067	.7590	.6328	17,051
June	.6740	.6740	.6675	.6691	– .0067	.7050	.6343	4,495
Est vol 2,121; vol Wd 1,521; open int 21,554, +371.							
MEXICAN PESO (CME)-500,000 new Mex. peso, $ per MP							
Mar	.11520	.11620	.11495	.11545	– 0032	.12340	.09700	20,359
June	.11120	.11190	.11085	.11142	– 00032	.11985	09200	7,402
Sept	.10730	.10790	.10725	.10755	– 00035	.11680	.08000	4,019
Dec	.10402	.10440	.10360	.10400	– 00035	.11440	.08000	7,836
Est vol 8,249; vol Wd 7,452; open int 39,616, +227.							

called the *minimum bond performance requirement*), which is a minimum balance
that must remain in its account with the futures broker. The broker and firm
also establish a *marked-to-market* procedure for applying the future contract
gains and losses to the firm's account at the close of each trading day.

Suppose that the agreed price for a March pound future is 1.630 per pound,
as shown in Figure 5–4. In the figure, we see that the standard size of a pound
future is 62,500 pounds. Also suppose that the initial margin is $2,000 per

contract and that the maintenance margin is $1,500. If the current spot exchange rate is 1.726 per pound, then the firm purchases an amount of pound futures equal to

$$\frac{(\$3 \text{ million}/\$1.726 \text{ per pound})}{62,500 \text{ pounds}}$$

which is approximately equal to 28. Therefore, purchasing 28 standard pound futures contracts provides the best possible futures hedge for the British firm. Note that the firm's initial margin is $28 \times \$2,000 = \$56,000$. Thus, for a $3 million futures account with its broker, the firm must post only $56,000 in its margin account with its broker.

Daily Futures Settlement To illustrate the daily settlement process of a typical futures contract, let's extend our example by supposing that on the first trading day the market closes at a futures price of $1.632 per pound, so that the firm's twenty-eight pound futures appreciate. To keep things simple, let's also assume that the firm pays no brokerage fees. On the first day, the firm earns a dollar profit equal to ($1.632 per pound − $1.630 per pound) × 62,500 pounds × 28 = $3,500. The firm's margin account thereby rises from $56,000 (the initial margin) to $56,000 + $3,500 = $59,500.

If the closing futures price on the second trading day drops to $1.629 per pound, then the firm experiences a dollar loss on the pound futures equal to

($1.629 per pound − $1.632 per pound) × 62,500 pounds × 28 = $5,250.

The firm's margin account thereby falls from $59,500 to $59,500 − $5,250 = $54,250.

Now suppose that the futures price rises to $1.633 per pound on the third trading day. Then the firm earns a dollar profit equal to

($1.633 per pound − $1.629 per pound) × 62,500 pounds × 28 = $7,000

and the firm's margin account thereby rises from $54,250 to $54,250 + $7,000 = $61,250.

Note how the set of twenty-eight futures contracts serves as a hedging instrument for the British firm. If during the course of the year the pound appreciates against the dollar, then the firm's realized pound-denominated value of profits from its U.S. franchise operation decline, so that each dollar of profits from those operations has a smaller pound-equivalent value at the end of the year. As the pound appreciates against the dollar, however, the British company's futures margin position improves, thereby offsetting some or all of the firm's translation risk exposure.

Options

OPTION A financial contract giving the owner the right to buy or sell an underlying financial instrument at a certain price within a specific period of time.

Another type of derivative instrument is an **option,** which is a financial contract providing the holder the right to purchase or sell an underlying financial instrument at a given price. This right does not require the holder to buy or sell. It gives the buyer the *option* to do so. The given price at which the holder

EXERCISE PRICE The price at which the holder of an option has the right to buy or sell a financial instrument; also known as the strike price.

CALL OPTION An option contract giving the owner the right to purchase a financial instrument at a specific price.

PUT OPTION An option contract giving the owner the right to sell a financial instrument at a specific price.

AMERICAN OPTION An option in which the holder may buy or sell a security any time before or including the date at which the contract expires.

EUROPEAN OPTION An option in which the holder may buy or sell a financial instrument only on the day that the contract expires.

FUTURES OPTIONS Options to buy or sell futures contracts.

STOCK OPTIONS Options to buy or sell firm equity shares.

CURRENCY OPTION A contract granting the right to buy or sell a given amount of a nation's currency at a certain price within a specific period of time.

of an option can exercise the right to purchase or sell a financial instrument is the option's **exercise price,** which traders also call the *strike price.*

Call options are options that allow the holder to *purchase* a financial instrument at the exercise price. **Put options** are options that allow the buyer to *sell* a financial instrument at the exercise price. Traders call an option granting the holder the right to exercise the right of purchase or sale at any time before or including the date at which the contract expires an **American option.** They call an option that allows the holder to exercise the right of purchase or sale *only* on the date that the contract expires a **European option.**

Stock Options and Futures Options Many individuals and firms use options to hedge against risks owing to variations in interest rates or stock prices. To do this, they trade **futures options,** which are options to buy or sell stock index futures or interest rate futures, and **stock options,** which are options to buy or sell shares in corporations.

Trading volumes in the stock index futures market have risen considerably since the 1980s. Paralleling this growth has been broadened trading in the futures options market. In fact, today more options on stock index futures—essentially derivatives of derivatives—are traded than options based on actual stocks.

Currency Options Contracts that give the owner the right to buy or sell a fixed amount of a given currency at a specified exchange rate at a certain time are **currency options.** Currency *put* options grant the holder the right to sell an amount of currency, while currency *call* options grant the holder the right to purchase an amount of the currency. Multinational corporations can purchase currency options directly from banks via *over-the-counter* contracts, but they can also purchase them in organized exchanges. Figure 5–5 explains how to read currency option quotes published in the *Wall Street Journal.*

Limited Losses and Potential Profits from Using Currency Call Options Let's consider how a U.S. importer buying 2 million deutsche marks of finished goods for an April payment might hedge against foreign exchange risk using a currency call option. If the current spot rate is $0.51 per deutsche mark, then the 2 million deutsche marks are equal to $1,020,000. To hedge against an unanticipated change in the exchange rate between now and April, the importer purchases April deutsche mark call options. At an exercise price of $0.55 in Figure 5–6, the upper limit on the dollar cost of the imported goods is $1,100,000. In Figure 5–6, an April option with this exercise price has a *premium* of $0.0083 per deutsche mark, which is the effective cost of purchasing the contract. Consequently, one contract for the standard amount of 62,500 deutsche marks requires an expenditure of $518.75. Covering the 2 million deutsche marks in standard allotments of 62,500 deutsche marks requires exactly thirty-two contracts, for a total expenditure, or *total premium,* of 32 × $518.75 = $16,600.

Once the importer purchases the thirty-two option contracts for $16,600, if the dollar depreciates above $0.55 per deutsche mark, and if we ignore exercise fees that the contract might specify, then the importer would choose to

FIGURE 5–5 READING QUOTES ON FOREIGN CURRENCY OPTIONS

OPTIONS
PHILADELPHIA EXCHANGE

	Calls Vol.	Last	Puts Vol.	Last
CDollr		70.43		
50,000 Canadian Dollars-cents per unit.				
72 Mar	...	...	68	1.56
Australian Dollar		67.90		
50,000 Australian Dollars-European Style.				
66 Apr	...	...	50	0.29
66 Jun	...	...	20	0.62
50,000 Australian Dollars-cents per unit.				
66 Jun	4	2.72	...	...
67 Mar	5	1.15	...	...
69 Apr	60	0.54	...	...
British Pound		165.29		
31,250 Brit. Pounds-cents per unit.				
165 Apr	10	1.62	...	...
31,500 Brit. Pounds-European Style.				
176 Jun	64	0.25	...	...
British Pound-GMark		299.08		

	Calls Vol.	Last	Puts Vol.	Last
31,250 British Pound-German Mark cross.				
302 Apr	10	1.36	...	...
French Franc		164.82		
250,000 French Francs-10ths of a cent per				
16¾ Mar	2	0.22	...	...
250,000 French Francs-European Style				
17½ Mar	...	...	2	10.66
German Mark		55.27		
62,500 German Marks-cents per unit.				
54½ Mar	...	...	100	0.16
55 Mar	...	...	10	0.25
55 Apr	600	0.83	600	0.54
57½ Apr	100	0.10	...	...
Japanese Yen		79.27		

	Calls Vol.	Last	Puts Vol.	Last
6,250,000 J.Yen-EuropeanStyle.				
80 Jun	4	2.32	...	...
Swiss Franc		68.07		
62,500 Swiss Francs-European Style.				
62 Mar	24	6.20	...	...
66 Apr	20	2.60	...	...
67 Mar	35	1.30	...	...
68 Mar	35	0.52	10	0.34
68 Jun	2	2.07	...	...
69 Mar	...	...	10	0.95
69 Apr	...	...	20	1.16
70 Apr	16	0.35	...	...
62,500 Swiss Francs-cents per unit.				
69 Mar	200	0.20	...	...
69½ Apr	15	0.46	...	...
Call Vol 3,480		Open Int ... 103,214		
Put Vol 1,929		Open Int ... 123,387		

Each day the *Wall Street Journal* reports Philadelphia Exchange currency options prices using the format shown above. To understand how to read published currency options quotes, consider the information for each column in the quote for the German deutsche mark:

First column: Exercise or strike price of an option contract on 62,500 deustche marks; $0.55 per deustche mark for American options maturing in April.

Second column: Month of option's maturity (option matures on the Friday before the third Wednesday of the month).

Calls/Vol.: Number of call options traded; 600 for call options with an April maturity.

Calls/Last: Price of the last call option settled upon by the close of business on this day; $0.083 per deutsche mark for an April contract.

Puts/Vol: Number of put options traded; 600 for put options with an April maturity.

Puts/Last: Price of the last put option settled upon by the close of business on this day; $0.054 per deutsche mark for an April contract.

Call Vol/Open Int: Total volume of call options traded during day (3,480) and total amount of call options outstanding at the beginning of the day's trading (103,214).

Put Vol/Open Int: Total volume of put options traded during day (1,929) and total amount of put options outstanding at the beginning of the day's trading (123,387).

exercise the option. For example, if the dollar depreciates to an exchange rate of $0.60 per deutsche mark, then it costs the importer $1,200,000 to obtain 2 million deutsche marks in the spot market. The exchange-rate change increases the importer's costs by $1,200,000 – $1,020,000 = $180,000. Exercising the option and obtaining the 2 million deutsche marks at the exercise price of $0.55 per deutsche mark, or at a total dollar expenditure of $1,100,000, thereby saves $100,000. Considering the premium that the importer paid for the options, the importer comes out ahead by an amount equal to $100,000 – $16,600 = $83,400.

Note that the firm did not completely hedge against losses if the spot exchange rate turns out to be $0.60 per deutsche mark, because the firm pays

FIGURE 5–6   POTENTIAL PROFIT AND LIMITED LOSS OF A CALL OPTION

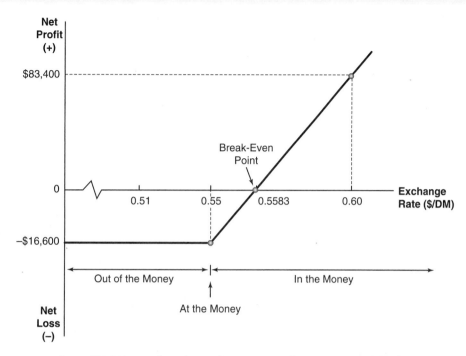

At a per-contract premium of $0.0083 per deutsche mark, each 62,500-deutsche mark contract entails a premium expenditure of $518.75, so that the total premiums that the holder of the options pays would be 32 × $518.75 = $16,600. The maximum loss that the holder can incur on the option is limited to this amount. At or above the exercise exchange rate of $0.55 per deutsche mark, the holder of the options can exercise the options and recoup at least a portion of the premiums paid for the options. At the spot exchange rate of $0.5583 per deutsche mark, the holder's earnings from exercising the options just cover the total premiums paid for the options. At a higher spot exchange rate, the holder of the options earns a net profit. For example, at the spot exchange rate of $0.60 per deutsche mark, the holder earns a net profit of $83,400.

a total of $1,100,000 + $16,600 = $1,116,600 using its option contracts. This is $96,600 more than the $1,020,000 that the firm would have to pay if the exchange rate had remained at its initial value of $0.51 per deutsche mark. Hence, the firm still incurs a net loss of $13,200 as a result of a rise in the exchange rate from $0.51 per deutsche mark to $0.60 per deutsche mark. This is much better than the $180,000 loss it otherwise would have incurred without the currency options.

A spot exchange rate of $0.60 per deutsche mark is just one possible outcome, however. Figure 5–6 illustrates the limited loss and potential profit resulting from the importer's call options for a range of possible values of the spot exchange rate. The maximum loss that the importer can experience is the total premium of $16,000 for the thirty-two option contracts. Below the strike exchange rate of $0.55 per deutsche mark, the importer is "out of the money," meaning that the firm cannot exercise the options. If the spot exchange rate rises to $0.55 per deutsche mark, however, then the importer has the option to exercise the options. At this strike exchange rate, the importer is "at the money." Above the strike exchange rate, the firm is "in the money," meaning that it earns gross receipts that begin to offset the total premium it pays for its options.

If the spot exchange rate rises to $0.5583 per deutsche mark, then the gross earnings from exercising the option increases to $16,600, which exactly recoups the total premium of $16,600. Hence, the spot exchange rate of $0.5583 per deutsche mark is the *break-even point* for the importer's option contracts. If the spot exchange rate rises above $0.5583 per deutsche mark, then the importer earns net profits from its options; that is, its gross earnings exceed the total premium paid for the option contracts. Note that if the spot exchange rate turns out to be $0.60 per deutsche mark in Figure 5–6, then the importer's net gain from the option contracts is equal to

$$(\$0.60 \text{ per deutsche mark} - \$0.5583 \text{ per deutsche mark})$$
$$\times 2,000,000 \text{ deutsche marks} = \$83,400,$$

which is the amount we calculated previously.

Limited Losses and Potential Profits from Using Currency Put Options Suppose that the U.S. firm previously discussed also sells export goods through its German distributor and that its receipt for an April shipment will amount to 1,250,000 deutsche marks. If the current spot exchange rate is $0.58 per deutsche mark, then the 1,250,000 deutsche marks are equivalent to $725,000. To hedge against the possible loss of dollar receipts from this sale of goods, the firm purchases twenty deutsche mark put options.

If the deutsche mark declines in value against the dollar, say to $0.53 per deutsche mark, then the 1,250,000 deutsche marks would yield only $662,500 in December. The firm would lose $62,500 in dollar-denominated receipts that month. Using put options would allow the firm to sell the deutsche marks it received from this transaction at a guaranteed price if the deutsche mark were to depreciate to, or below, the strike exchange rate for the put options. An April put option for the deutsche mark has a strike exchange rate of $0.55 per deutsche mark and a premium of $0.0054 per deutsche mark. One option for 62,500 deutsche marks would thereby entail a dollar premium of $337.50, so twenty deutsche mark put options would entail a total premium expenditure of 20 × $337.50, or $6,750.

Figure 5–7 illustrates the limited loss and potential profit associated with the importer's put options. In the case of put options the option is "out of the money" if the spot exchange rate is *above* the strike exchange rate of $0.55 per deutsche mark. If the spot exchange rate happens to be equal to the strike

FIGURE 5–7   POTENTIAL PROFIT AND LIMITED LOSS OF A PUT OPTION

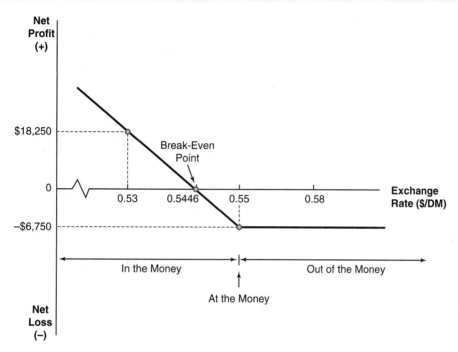

Given a premium payment of $337.50 for each 62,500-deutsche mark contract, the total premiums that the holder of 20 put option contracts pays would be 20 × $337.50 = $6,750, and the holder's maximum loss is limited to this amount. At or below the strike exchange rate of $0.55 per deutsche mark, the holder of the options can exercise the options and recover at least part of the premiums paid for the options. At the spot exchange rate of $0.5446 per deutsche mark, the earnings that the holder receives just cover the total premium payment. At a lower spot exchange rate, the holder earns a net profit. For instance, at the spot exchange rate of $0.53 per deutsche mark, the holder earns a net profit equal to $18,250.

exchange rate, then the option is "at the money." If the spot exchange rate falls *below* the strike exchange rate, then the option is "in the money." This means that as the spot exchange rate declines further below the strike exchange rate, the firm gains progressively higher gross earnings from the option contracts. At the spot exchange rate of $0.5446 per deutsche mark, the firm's gross earnings equal

$$(\$0.55 \text{ per deutsche mark} - \$0.5446 \text{ per deutsche mark})$$
$$\times 1{,}250{,}000 \text{ deutsche marks} = \$6{,}750,$$

which exactly offsets the $6,750 total premium for the option contracts. The spot exchange rate of $0.5446 per deutsche mark is the break-even exchange rate for the put options.

Suppose that the deutsche mark settles at a dollar value of $0.53 in the foreign exchange market. The U.S. firm will lose $62,500 in receipts from the deutsche mark payment. In this instance, the firm can profit from the option contracts by exercising its options and selling deutsche marks at the strike exchange rate of $0.55 per deutsche mark. If the firm purchases 1,250,000 deutsche marks at the prevailing spot exchange rate of $0.53 per deutsche mark, then its payment for the deutsche marks in the spot market is $662,500. Then it can sell the 1,250,000 deutsche marks to the issuer of the option contracts at an exchange rate of $0.55 per deutsche mark. The firm's gross option profit thereby is equal to

$$(\$0.55 \text{ per deutsche mark} - \$0.53 \text{ per deutsche mark})$$
$$\times 1,250,000 \text{ deutsche marks} = \$25,000.$$

Again, the firm will not be perfectly hedged if the spot exchange rate turns out to fall from its initial value of $0.58 per deutsche mark to a level of $0.53 per deutsche mark. But the net option profit of $18,250 (the gross option profit of $25,000 less the $6,750 premium) reduces the $62,500 loss to a net amount of $44,250.

Netting Many multinational firms have both expenditures and receipts that are denominated in foreign currencies, much like the importer in our call option and put option examples earlier. The foreign currency expenditures and receipts may cancel out, on net, much of the risk exposure to exchange rate variations. To see how this works, let's combine the two examples.

If the deutsche mark appreciates from, say, $0.58 per deutsche mark to $0.60 per deutsche mark, then the importer's 2,000,000 deutsche mark expenditure rises by

$$(\$0.60 \text{ per deutsche mark} - \$0.58 \text{ per deutsche mark})$$
$$\times 2,000,000 \text{ deutsche marks} = \$40,000.$$

Simultaneously, the firm's deutsche mark receipts rise by

$$(\$0.60 \text{ per deutsche mark} - \$0.58 \text{ per deutsche mark})$$
$$\times 1,250,000 \text{ deutsche marks} = \$25,000.$$

Hence, the firm's *net* loss due to the change in the spot exchange rate is $15,000.

Because the firm's two translation-risk exposures tend to offset each other in this way, the firm may choose to *consolidate* these exposures into a single *net* risk exposure. The process of combining currency risk exposures of payments and receipts into a net risk exposure is called **netting.** For the firm in our example, consolidating its payments and receipts yields a net exposure of 2,000,000 deutsche marks in expenditures minus 1,250,000 deutsche marks in receipts, or 750,000 deutsche marks in net expenditures. Hence, the firm could try to hedge against this *net* risk exposure to a deutsche mark appreciation solely

NETTING The process of combining separate risk exposures that a firm faces in its foreign-currency-denominated payments and receipts into a single net risk exposure.

through call options. The firm uses call options because the 750,000-deutsche mark net risk exposure requires the *delivery* of the currency in the future. Specifically, the firm hedges the net risk by purchasing twelve deutsche mark call options contracts at a total premium of

($0.0083 per deutsche mark) × (12 × 62,500 deutsche marks) = $6,225.

Netting saves the firm from having to use both call and put options to hedge against exposures relating to both expenditures and receipts. If the firm had not used a netting arrangement, then using both thirty-two call options and twenty put options (as in the separate call and put option examples), the total premiums the firm would have had to pay would have been $16,600 + $6,750 = $22,750. Netting reduces the firm's total premium to $6,225 and thereby reduces its premium expense by $16,525.

Swaps

SWAP A contract entailing an exchange of payment flows between two parties.

INTEREST-RATE SWAP A contractual exchange of one set of interest payments for another.

CURRENCY SWAP An exchange of payment flows denominated in different currencies.

Swaps are financial contracts in which parties to the transactions exchange flows of payments. An **interest-rate swap** is one important type of swap on international financial markets. This is a contract under which one party commits itself to exchange a set of interest payments that it is scheduled to receive for a different set of interest payments owed to another party.

Another key swap contract is a **currency swap,** which is an exchange of payment flows denominated in different currencies. Figure 5–8 illustrates a sample currency swap, in which we suppose that International Business Machines (IBM) Corporation earns a flow of yen-denominated revenues from computer sales in Japan, while Toshiba Corporation earns dollar revenues from selling computers in the United States. IBM pays dollar dividends and interest to its owners and bondholders, and Toshiba pays yen-denominated dividends and interest to its owners and bondholders. Therefore, IBM and Toshiba could, in principle, use a currency swap as a mechanism for trading their yen and dollar earnings for the purpose of paying income streams to their stockholders and bondholders.

There are various types of interest-rate and currency swaps. The most common swap is the *plain vanilla swap* (sometimes called a *bullet swap*), in which two parties to the swap arrangement agree simply to trade streams of payments to which each is entitled. There are other, more sophisticated swap contracts, however. For instance, a *forward swap* delays the actual swap transaction for a period ranging from a few days to a few years. A *swap option* (sometimes called a *swaption*) grants the owner the right to enter into a swap when the swap's market price reaches an exercise or strike price. Determining the effective returns on these and other derivatives of swaps can be fairly complicated. This has led to the development of a group of financial economists who call themselves *financial engineers* and who seek to develop methods for computing the appropriate market prices of these derivative securities.

Figure 5–8   A Sample Currency Swap

IBM receives yen earnings from selling computers in Japan, and Toshiba receives dollar earnings from selling computers in the United States. The two companies could use a currency swap contract to trade their yen and dollar earnings to make payments to holders of their stocks and bonds.

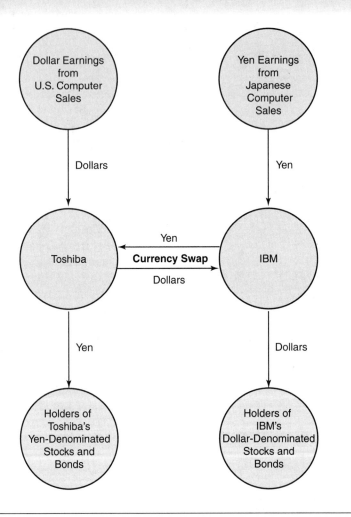

Derivatives Risks and Regulation

Financial engineers also seek to determine the risks that traders incur by speculating via derivative securities. This is a conceptually challenging task, partly because simply determining the dollar amounts of derivatives trading can be difficult.

Measuring Derivatives Risks   A widely used measure of aggregate derivatives volume, which some use as a rough measure of exposure to derivatives risk, is the *notional value* of derivatives, or the amount of principal that serves

MANAGEMENT NOTEBOOK

Are Credit Derivatives the New Wave of the Future?

Credit derivatives constitute a variety of financial instruments intended to separate out and transfer underlying credit risks of bonds and loans. Although hardly any of these instruments existed as recently as 1993, today more than $40 billion in credit derivative transactions occur each year. Half of these transactions involve credit risks relating to the debts of developing nations.

The mechanics of a credit derivative transaction can be complex, but the basic idea is relatively simple. If a bank thinks that it has taken on too much risk of default in a big loan to a single client, then the bank could use a credit swap in an effort to reduce its risk exposure. The counterparty in the transaction would take on this risk in exchange for payment of a regular fee from the bank. In the event of a default, the counterparty to the swap would reimburse the bank for its losses. Such an arrangement would not hurt the bank's standing with their clients, because borrowers are not even informed of the existence of most credit derivative contracts.

Why would a counterparty be willing to take on the default risk associated with a loan? In the case of debt issued by developing nations, some other bank might wish to diversify its own portfolio. By agreeing to take on part of the risks of loans to such nations that have been originated by other banks, this institution thereby diversifies its portfolio without actually going to the trouble to initiate or provide loans to such nations.

Out of trillions of dollars of worldwide derivatives transactions, $40 billion in credit derivatives is currently a drop in the bucket. Nevertheless, the prospects for growth in this area of derivatives trading are considerable. So are the implications for standard credit risk measurement and loan pricing.

FOR CRITICAL ANALYSIS:

As discussed below, regulators often worry about risks associated with derivatives contracts. Are there any potential risk-reduction features associated with credit derivatives?

---

as a basis for computing streams of payments. The notional value of U.S. bank derivatives holdings grew from $1.4 trillion in 1986 to more than $2 trillion in 1997. The estimated notional value of derivative contracts worldwide in 1997 was $55 trillion, up from just over $43.2 trillion in 1996.

Replacement-cost credit exposure is another popular measure of derivatives-related risk. This is the cost that a party to a derivatives contract faces at current market prices if the other party in the derivative contract defaults before contract settlement. Between 1992 and 1994, the total derivatives replacement-cost credit exposure of U.S. commercial banks amounted to about 5 percent of their assets, By 1997 this figure had risen to 8 percent.

DERIVATIVE CREDIT RISKS Risks stemming from the potential default by a party in a derivative contract or from unexpected changes in credit exposure because of changes in the market yields of instruments on which derivative yields depend.

Types of Derivatives Risks   By holding derivatives, firms expose themselves to three basic types of risk. One type is **derivative credit risk.** This is the risk associated with potential default by a contract party or of an unexpected change in credit exposure resulting from changes in market prices of underlying instruments on which derivative yields depend. The replacement-cost-credit-exposure measure focuses on this form of derivatives risk.

DERIVATIVE MARKET RISKS Risks arising from unanticipated changes in derivatives market liquidity or payments-system failures.

Another type of risk is **derivative market risk,** which is the risk of potential losses stemming from unexpected payments-system glitches or unusual price changes at the time of settlement. Such events can cause derivative traders' liquidity levels to drop and can slow their normal efforts to adjust their derivatives holdings, thereby exposing them to risks of loss. For instance, if a multinational firm decides to execute a currency option before an anticipated unfavorable price movement, it may try to do so but find that a critical computer link temporarily is "down," thereby causing it to experience a loss when the price changes. In like manner, the price of an underlying asset in a derivatives transaction might fluctuate unexpectedly at the last moment before settlement, also causing the holder to incur a loss.

DERIVATIVE OPERATING RISKS Risks owing to a lack of adequate management controls or from managerial inexperience with derivative securities.

Finally, derivatives traders must confront **derivative operating risks,** which are risks of loss due to unwise management. Many of the notable derivatives losses summarized in Table 5–3 on page 153 resulted from situations in which firm managers incorrectly valued derivatives and discovered their errors only at settlement. Institutions such as Bankers Trust, which settled several large lawsuits concerning derivatives trading that it performed on behalf of client firms, experienced problems due to inadequate internal controls that resulted in poorly supervised trading by mid-level managers.

As individuals, banks, and companies have become more adept at sorting out the ways in which they can use various derivatives for both hedging and speculation, the markets for these instruments have continued to grow around the world. These markets also have, like those for other financial instruments, become increasingly interconnected. We turn our attention to this development in the next chapter.

FUNDAMENTAL ISSUE #5

What are the most commonly traded derivative securities?
The most commonly held and traded derivatives are forward contracts, futures, options, and swaps. Forward contracts include interest-rate forward contracts as well as forward currency contracts. Interest rate futures, stock index futures, and currency futures are the most common types of futures contracts, which differ from forward contracts because traders exchange them in standardized quantities in organized markets in which flows of profits or losses take place daily, rather than only at maturity. The most common options, which are contracts giving the holder the right to buy or sell a financial instrument, are stock options, futures options, and currency options. Interest rate and currency swaps are contracts committing parties to exchanging flows of interest income or payments denominated in different currencies.

CHAPTER SUMMARY

1. **Interest Yields, Financial Instrument Prices, and Interest Rate Risk:** Interest yields are rates of return derived on financial instruments based on their face values, prices, or terms to maturity of a financial instrument. The prices of financial instruments should incorporate traders' assessments of the current perceived values of such instruments. Thus, any financial instrument's price should depend directly on the discounted present value of current and future returns that it yields, which is inversely related to the interest rate. Unanticipated increases in market interest rates can thereby cause capital losses by reducing market prices, exposing the holder of financial instruments to interest rate risk.

2. **Why Market Interest Yields Vary with Differences in Financial Instruments' Terms to Maturity:** One factor accounting for differences between short-term and long-term interest yields is expectations about whether future short-term interest rates are likely to rise or fall relative to current longer-term interest rates. Another factor is the generally greater liquidity and lower perceived risk of short-term instruments as compared with longer-term instruments, which leads traders to require a term premium to make them indifferent between holding either long-term or short-term instruments.

3. **Effect of Risk on Market Interest Yields:** Because the extent of default risk and liquidity varies across financial instruments, risk premiums also differ across instruments. Traders require market yields to reflect risk premiums, so financial instruments normally differ even if the instruments have the same terms to maturity. In addition, governments often tax some instruments, which ultimately causes their market yields to diverge.

4. **Derivative Securities:** These are financial instruments whose returns depend on the returns of other financial instruments. As a result, traders can use these securities to hedge against or speculate on interest rate risks or foreign exchange risks.

5. **The Most Commonly Traded Derivative Securities:** The derivative securities that are most widely held and traded include forward contracts, futures, options, and swaps. Traders commonly use both interest-rate forward contracts and forward currency contracts. The most widely traded futures contracts include interest rate futures, stock index futures, and currency futures. In contrast to forward contracts, futures contracts call for exchange of a standardized amount of financial instruments in highly organized markets, and flows of profits or losses stemming from futures contracts occur daily. The most commonly traded options, or contracts giving the holder the right to buy or sell a financial instrument, are stock options, futures options, and currency options. Swaps are agreements to exchange flows of payments, so interest-rate swaps entail exchanges of flows of interest payments, while currency swaps are exchanges of payments denominated in different currencies.

QUESTIONS AND PROBLEMS

1. Suppose that a Japanese bond has a face value of 10,000 yen, a coupon return of 600 yen, and a market price of 9,000 yen. What is its coupon yield? What is its nominal yield? Show your work.

2. A British consol has a market price of 10,000 pounds sterling. Its annual coupon return is 800 pounds. What is the current market interest yield on this bond?

3. Consider the following data on three Russian bonds, denoted as bond *A*, bond *B*, and bond *C*:

Bond	Term of Maturity	Current Annual Yield
A	5 years	20 percent
B	10 years	17 percent
C	20 years	15 percent

   If these bonds are equally risky, then what factor might most likely explain the pattern of yields exhibited by these bonds?

4. Explain, in your own words, why a financial instrument's duration influences the degree of interest rate risk incurred by holding the instrument.

5. In what ways does a currency futures contract differ from a forward currency contract?

6. Why is a currency futures option a "derivative of a derivative"? Explain briefly.

ON-LINE APPLICATION

Internet URL: http://www.cme.com

Title: The Chicago Mercantile Exchange (CME)

Navigation: Begin with the CME home page (**http://www.cme.com**). Click on *About the Exchange,* and then click on *Background about the Merc, its membership, and its products.*

Application: Read the discussion, and then answer the following questions:

1. How many total memberships are available in the CME? How many memberships permit the owner to execute trades on any CME contract?

2. Back up to the home page, and then click on *Current Membership Prices.* What was the last price at which a full CME membership traded? Why would someone be willing to pay that much to have the right to execute a trade on the CME?

3. Based on what you learned about bond prices in this chapter, what factors do you think might determine the price of a CME membership? [*Hint:* Imagine holding this membership for a number of years and earning an annual return each year, and then think about how to price the anticipated stream of returns from a CME membership.]

REFERENCES AND RECOMMENDED READINGS

Abken, Peter A. "Beyond Plain Vanilla: A Taxonomy of Swaps." Federal Reserve Bank of Atlanta, *Financial Derivatives: New Instruments and Their Uses* (December 1993): 51–69.

Abken, Peter A. "Globalization of Stock, Futures, and Options Markets." Federal Reserve Bank of Atlanta, *Financial Derivatives: New Instruments and Their Uses* (December 1993): 3–24.

Cohen, Hugh. "Beyond Duration: Measuring Interest Rate Exposure." Federal Reserve Bank of Atlanta, *Financial Derivatives: New Instruments and Their Uses* (December 1993): 130–138.

Federal Reserve Bank of Chicago. *Derivatives and Public Policy*, 1996.

Fieleke, Norman. "The Rise of the Foreign Currency Futures Market," *New England Economic Review* (March/April 1985): 38–47.

Gilbert, R. Alton. "Implications of Netting Arrangements for Bank Risk in Foreign Exchange Transactions." Federal Reserve Bank of St. Louis, *Review* (January/February 1992): 3–16.

Kawaller, Ira G., Paul D. Koch, and Timothy W. Koch. "The Relationship between the S&P 500 Index and S&P 500 Index Futures Prices." Federal Reserve Bank of Atlanta, *Financial Derivatives: New Instruments and Their Uses* (December 1993): 40–48.

Kuprianov, Anatoli. "Derivatives Debacles: Case Studies of Large Losses in Derivatives Markets." Federal Reserve Bank of Richmond, *Economic Quarterly* (Fall 1995): 1–40.

Wall, Larry D., and John J. Pringle. "Interest Rate Swaps: A Review of the Issues," Federal Reserve Bank of Atlanta, *Financial Derivatives: New Instruments and Their Uses* (December 1993): 70–85.

6

A Single World Marketplace— International Financial Market Integration

FUNDAMENTAL ISSUES

1. What are international capital markets?

2. What are international money markets?

3. What are the Eurobond, Euronote, and Eurocommercial paper markets?

4. What are vehicle currencies?

5. What is capital market integration?

Plagued by recent currency problems, the stock exchanges of Southeast Asia took a dramatic plunge in late October 1997, as nervous traders launched a frenzied sell-off. In Southeast Asia, the sell-off started Monday, October 20, when Hong Kong's Hang Seng Index began a four-day decline of more than 23 percent. By Thursday, the declines spread to markets in China, Japan, Europe, and the United States.

On Monday, October 27, there was a dramatic decline in all stock markets, which market participants dubbed "Bloody Monday." The Hang Seng index fell 13.7 percent, leading declines in other Asian markets, Europe, and the United States. By the time the New York markets closed, Wall Street's Dow Jones index declined by 7.2 percent. The following day, however, the Dow Jones index enjoyed a 4.7 percent gain. Optimism returned in Hong Kong, where the stock market experienced an 18.8 percent gain. The markets reversed direction on the following Wednesday and flipped again on Thursday.

Coincidentally, only six days before the market turbulence began, the financial world's most closely listened-to individual, Alan Greenspan, Chair of the U.S. Federal Reserve, delivered a speech on the globalization of finance at an annual monetary conference in Washington, D.C. In a prophetic statement, Mr. Greenspan said, "Some argue that market dynamics have been altered in ways that increase the likelihood of significant market disruptions. Whatever the merits of this argument, there is a clear sense that the new technologies, and the financial instruments and techniques they have made possible, have strengthened interdependencies between markets and market participants, both within and across national boundaries. As a result, a disturbance in one market segment or one country is likely to be transmitted far more rapidly throughout the world economy than was evident in previous eras."

What changes led to a greater linkage of the world's financial markets? To what degree are financial markets now integrated? What are some of the key international financial instruments? To answer these important questions, we begin by examining recent developments in the international capital markets and the international money markets.

INTERNATIONAL CAPITAL MARKETS

Following the end of World War II, the industrialized nations pursued a goal of greater trade liberalization. To improve the prospects for achieving this objective, they established the General Agreement on Tariffs and Trade

(GATT), which became the World Trade Organization (WTO). Over time, trade barriers and transportation costs declined, which led to greater flows of goods and services between most of the world's nations. Not until the 1970s, however, did most industrialized nations begin to liberalize financial markets.

Changes in communications technology, combined with the introduction of innovative new financial instruments, has moved even reluctant nations to liberalize and deregulate their financial markets. Instant and low-cost communications and information innovations allow a wider range of firms and individuals to participate in international financial markets and to manage their risk exposure more effectively. As a result, since the 1970s the growth of international financial markets has far outpaced the growth of international trade in goods and services. Between 1973 and 1998, for example, daily foreign exchange turnover increased from $15 billion to $1.4 trillion, and U.S. cross-border transactions of bonds and equities increased from 9 percent of GDP in 1980 to 164 percent in 1995.

To examine the effect of these developments on the international financial markets, we shall make a general distinction between *capital markets* and *money markets*. **International capital markets** are the markets for cross-border exchange of financial instruments that have a maturity of a year or more. International capital market traders also exchange instruments with no distinct maturity, such as perpetuities (described in Chapter 5). In contrast, **international money markets** are the markets for cross-border exchange of financial instruments with maturities of less than one year. Hence, traders exchange short-term financial instruments, such as Eurocurrencies, in the international money markets.

INTERNATIONAL CAPITAL MARKETS Markets for cross-border exchange of financial instruments that have maturities of one year or more.

INTERNATIONAL MONEY MARKETS Markets for cross-border exchange of financial instruments with maturities of less than one year.

The Size and Growth of the International Capital Market

Table 6–1 presents evidence on the dramatic growth of financing in the international capital markets. Between 1986 and 1998 total financing activity on the international capital markets increased by $1,379.8 billion, an increase of 354.2 percent.

In Table 6–1, the securities category includes two very important components: *international bonds* and *international equities*. A third component of the international capital markets is foreign direct investment. Chapter 5 discussed

TABLE 6–1   GROWTH OF THE INTERNATIONAL CAPITAL MARKET–1986 TO 1997

$ BILLION	1986	1997	CHANGE	PERCENTAGE CHANGE
Total	389.5	1,769.3	1,379.8	354.2
Securities	195.5	916.7	721.2	368.9
Loans	88.5	390.4	301.9	341.1

SOURCE: Data from OECD Financial Market Trends.

EQUITIES Ownership shares that might or might not pay the holder a dividend, whose values rise and fall with savers' perceived value of the issuing enterprise.

bonds in detail. **Equities,** like bonds, are financing instruments. Equities, however, are ownership shares that might or might not pay the holder a dividend. Equity values rise and fall with savers' perceptions of the value of an enterprise.

As Table 6–1 shows, the international securities market, which represents 52 percent of the international capital markets, experienced the greatest absolute growth, with an increase of $721.2 billion. The international loans market also experienced a rapid rate of growth, with nearly a fivefold increase over the period.

Institutional Investors

INSTITUTIONAL INVESTORS Institutions, such as insurance companies, investment companies, and pension funds, that manage funds on the behalf of designated groups of individuals.

A great deal of attention has been given of late to the increased participation of *institutional investors.* Deregulation, liberalization, and the technological advances described at the beginning of the chapter created a wider range of savings opportunities for individuals through institutional investors. **Institutional investors** are institutions—such as insurance companies, investment companies, and pension funds—that manage funds on the behalf of designated

POLICY NOTEBOOK

Is Capital Market Liberalization the Right Policy?

For some developing nations, capital market liberalization can be a mixed blessing. In 1997 alone, more than $225 billion of foreign capital flowed into developing economies. Representing less than 1 percent of world GDP and approximately 3 percent of developing nations' GDP, these funds allow developing countries to finance trade and investment opportunities that otherwise would be impossible. A portion of these funds, however, can flow out of a nation just as quickly as they flow in, putting severe strains on a nation's financial system and affecting the exchange value of the nation's currency.

As a result, some nations continue to have capital restrictions in order to prevent "hot" capital flows. During the early 1990s, Chile, for example, placed a number of constraints on foreign capital flows that included restrictions on borrowing from abroad. Some economists think these capital controls contributed to Chile's solid macroeconomic and exchange value performance.

Others, though, see the capital controls as a hindrance to optimal capital allocation and credit Chile's economic performance to appropriate macroeconomic policymaking.

In 1997 and 1998, the International Monetary Fund began discussions on amending its articles of agreement and extending its jurisdiction to capital flows. This action would allow the IMF to pursue its stated goal of promoting free capital flows. Under the proposal, however, nations with capital market barriers could remove restrictions gradually in order to achieve an 'orderly' liberalization.

FOR CRITICAL ANALYSIS:
As a policymaker in a developing or emerging economy, what types of capital flows would you encourage? What policy actions would you take to encourage the desired capital flows?

TABLE 6–2 **FINANCIAL ASSETS OF INSTITUTIONAL INVESTORS**
(**CALCULATED AS PERCENT OF GDP**)

	1995	PERCENT CHANGE: 1990–1995
Canada	87.9	50.0
Luxembourg	2,132.8	*
Netherlands	158.4	18.7
Sweden	114.8	34.4
United Kingdom	162.3	41.7
United States	170.8	34.1

---

*1990 data incomplete, so no growth rate is calculated.
SOURCE: Data from OECD Financial Market Trends.

groups of individuals. For example, the pension funds of the employees of most U.S. universities, colleges, and other educational institutions are managed by TIAA/CREF, one of the world's largest institutional investors.

A special study by the Organization for Economic Cooperation and Development (OECD) details the size and growth of the financial instruments managed by institutional investors. Table 6–2 presents the OECD's data for the six nations with the largest institutional investor activity. As Table 6–2 shows, the United States and the United Kingdom are two of the nations with the greatest relative amounts of institutional investor activity. Table 6–2 also shows that during the 1990s the financial assets of institutional investors increased by one-third to one-half for the United States, the United Kingdom, and Canada.

ON THE WEB
To learn more about the history and functions of the OECD, visit their web page at: **http://www.oecd.org**

Portfolio Diversification

The development and growth of the international capital market allows individuals and businesses greater opportunities to manage risk and increase potential returns. Nonetheless, savers do not utilize the international capital market to the extent we might expect. Economists Kenneth French of the University of Chicago and James Poterba of Massachusetts Institute of Technology find that savers demonstrate a low level of *international diversification* in their portfolios and that most corporate equity is held by domestic residents.

Table 6–3 provides estimates of equity portfolio weights for U.S., Japanese, and U.K. savers. French and Poterba also estimate the additional return that savers must expect in order to justify the low level of international diversifi-

TABLE 6–3   EQUITY PORTFOLIO DIVERSIFICATION

	PORTFOLIO SHARES (IN PERCENTAGE TERMS)		
	UNITED STATES	**JAPAN**	**UNITED KINGDOM**
United States	93.8	1.3	5.9
Japan	3.1	98.1	4.8
United Kingdom	1.1	0.2	82.0
France	0.5	0.1	3.2
Germany	0.5	0.1	3.5
Canada	1.0	0.1	0.6
	EXCESS RETURN REQUIRED TO JUSTIFY DOMESTIC SHARE OF EQUITY PORTFOLIO (AS PERCENT)		
	0.9	2.5	4.4

SOURCE: Data from French, Kenneth, and James Poterba, "Investor Diversification and International Equity Markets," in *American Economic Review Papers and Proceedings,* Vol. 81 #2, May 1991, pp. 222-226.

cation. As the table shows, U.S. savers hold almost 94 percent of their portfolios in domestic equities.

The estimates of the return on an internationally diversified portfolio are compared with estimated returns on portfolios with distributions comparable to British, Japanese, and U.S. investors. To justify the low level of international diversification, U.S. savers must anticipate a return on their domestic equity holdings that exceeds the actual return by almost 1 percent. U.K. savers, due to a smaller overall equity market, have the most internationally diversified portfolios of the three nations. To justify 82 percent of their portfolio in U.K. equities, however, U.K. savers must anticipate a return on their domestic holdings that exceeds the actual return by more than 4 percent.

French and Poterba conclude that these low levels of international diversification are not due to any national or institutional constraints. The three countries in their study have few, if any, capital controls in place today, and tax differences and transaction costs are also very small for these nations. The authors conclude, therefore, that the low levels of diversification are due to savers' tastes. They speculate that savers perceive a greater degree of risk in foreign equity markets because they are less familiar with those markets than they are with domestic equity markets.

Because of deregulation, liberalization, and technological innovation, international capital markets have undergone considerable growth since the early 1970s. Savers, however, have yet to take full advantage of these new opportunities. How integrated are capital markets? This is a question we address later in the chapter.

FUNDAMENTAL ISSUE #1

What are international capital markets? International capital markets are markets for cross-border exchange of financial instruments that have a maturity of a year or more. Because of deregulation, liberalization, and technological innovation that has taken place since the early 1970s, international capital markets have undergone considerable growth. Since the early 1970s, financing activity in international capital markets has grown by an impressive amount. Though these markets have experienced remarkable growth, savers still have very low levels of international portfolio diversification.

INTERNATIONAL MONEY MARKETS

International money markets are markets for cross-border exchange of financial instruments with maturities of less than one year. Although traders exchange a number of different types of instruments in international money markets, foreign exchange instruments are most actively traded. Recall from Chapter 2 that the foreign exchange market consists of spot and forward exchanges of foreign currencies and that the majority of the foreign exchange market is the trading of foreign-currency-denominated deposits among major banks in amounts of $1 million or more.

As noted earlier, the international capital markets have experienced considerable growth since the early 1970s. The international money markets, however, have experienced *astounding* growth. Economists periodically estimate the volume of transactions in the foreign exchange markets based on surveys of the largest banks and foreign exchange trading firms. Current estimates of the daily activity on the foreign exchange markets indicate that the daily turnover is approximately $1.4 billion. On average, the daily volume of the foreign exchange market approximates two months of activity in the New York Stock Exchange.

The international money markets are comprised of a number of financial instruments other than spot and forward exchange contracts. These instruments include short-term international bank, government, and corporate notes, and international commercial paper.

Because transactions among large banks constitute the bulk of international money markets exchanges, we can use reports of these banks' cross-border asset and liability positions to estimate the size of the market. Table 6–4 provides data on the cross-border positions for December 1997 and the change in cross-border positions for the year 1997. As shown in Table 6–4, reporting

---

TABLE 6–4   REPORTING BANKS' CROSS-BORDER POSITIONS

$ BILLIONS	ASSETS DECEMBER 1997	ASSETS ESTIMATED CHANGE YEAR 1997*
INDUSTRIAL COUNTRIES	7123.6	1019.4
U.S. Dollar	3178.1	461.3
Other Currencies	3945.5	558.1
ALL OTHER COUNTRIES	1914.7	137.3
Total	9038.3	1156.7
	LIABILITIES	
INDUSTRIAL COUNTRIES	6948.7	963.6
U.S. Dollar	3215.7	419.3
Other Currencies	3733.0	544.3
ALL OTHER COUNTRIES	1892.2	183.2
Total	8840.9	1146.9

*Exchange Rate Adjusted Change
SOURCE: Data from Bank for International Settlements, *Annual Report,* 1998.

ON THE WEB

For the most recent data on the cross-border positions of banks and aspects of the international money and capital markets, obtain the Annual Report of the Bank for International Settlements at: **http://www.bis.org**

banks had more than $8 trillion in both outstanding assets and liabilities. The change in these positions for the year 1997 was approximately $1 trillion.

Table 6–4 also shows the dominance of the industrialized countries' banks in international money markets. Cross-border positions of the industrialized countries represents more than 78 percent of the total. The dominance of the U.S. dollar is also apparent, with the dollar denominating more than one-third of outstanding positions.

FUNDAMENTAL ISSUE #2

What are international money markets? International money markets are markets for cross-border exchange of financial instruments with maturities of less than one year. Traders exchange a number of different types of instruments that include foreign exchange spot and forward contracts in international money markets. Foreign exchange transactions dominate the international money market. Current estimates indicate that turnover in the foreign exchange market is approaching $1.5 billion daily.

EUROCURRENCIES, EURONOTES, EUROBONDS, AND EUROCOMMERCIAL PAPER

Eurocurrencies, Euronotes, and *Eurocommercial paper* are financial instruments traded in the international capital and international money markets. The Euro markets, however, are *nontraditional* markets, because traditional financing activity takes place within the domestic economy and is denominated in the domestic currency. Recall from Chapter 4 that Eurocurrencies are bank deposits and loans denominated in a currency other than that of the nation in which the bank is located, and that the Eurocurrency market is a market for the borrowing and lending of Eurocurrencies.

The Euromarkets allow a corporation to raise funds in other nations or to denominate debt in another currency. For example, a U.K. firm may issue a

MANAGEMENT NOTEBOOK

Foreign-Currency-Denominated Debt Threatens to Bring Down Southeast Asian Economies

Prior to the currency collapse in October 1997, businesses of Southeast Asian nations were the beneficiaries of low-cost foreign financing. When the currency crisis occurred, the foreign-denominated debt became an enormous burden to many of these same businesses.

This situation became particularly bleak for Indonesia. From July though October 1997, the rupiah declined by 40 percent against the U.S. dollar. Indonesian companies reportedly amassed more than $56 billion in foreign-currency-denominated debt, most denominated in the U.S. dollar. The problem was that most of this debt was not hedged, leaving the companies exposed to foreign exchange risk. When the exchange value of the rupiah declined against the U.S. dollar, the rupiah value of the outstanding debt rose, raising the risk of companies going bankrupt and defaulting on the debt.

One Indonesian company in particular, Indofood, admitted to having most of its $900 million foreign-currency-denominated debt unhedged. A Philippines-based manufacturer of coffee makers and fans, Nikon, also borrowed heavily in the international markets. When filing for bankruptcy, Nikon stated that "at the time (they borrowed) there was no cause for alarm because the market situation was very bright and very promising."

Foreign capital proved to be very important for the expansion of the Southeast Asian economies. However, foreign-currency-denominated debt exposed many Southeast Asian firms to foreign exchange risk in the late 1990s.

FOR CRITICAL ANALYSIS:

As a corporate manager, what types of internal controls would you recommend for your company when borrowing from abroad?

EUROBONDS Long-term debt
instruments denominated in a
currency other than that of the
country in which the
instrument is issued.

**EUROCOMMERCIAL
PAPER** Unsecured short-term
debt instrument issued in a
currency other than that of the
country in which the
instrument is issued.

EURONOTES Short- and
medium-term debt instruments
issued in a currency other than
that of the country in which the
instrument is issued.

ON THE WEB
*For recent information on
international investment
issues, visit the publication*
Euromoney *at:*
http://www.euromoney.com

debt instrument denominated in deutsche marks in the United States. Note
that this instrument is a *Euro-instrument,* being a financial instrument
denominated in a currency other than that of the country in which the
instrument is issued. Hence, these nontraditional markets give businesses
the opportunity to borrow from individuals or firms that were previously
inaccessible.

Eurobonds are long-term debt instruments issued in a currency other than
that of the country in which the instrument is issued. For example, a Canadian business may issue Canadian-dollar-denominated ten-year debt instruments in London. This is a Eurobond, because it is denominated in a currency, the Canadian dollar, other than that of the country in which it is issued,
the United Kingdom. In 1996, $590 billion in Eurobonds were offered in the
international capital market. This amount represents a 59 percent increase
from 1995. Of this amount, the U.S. dollar denominated 46 percent of the
value of market issues.

Eurocommercial paper is an unsecured short-term debt instrument issued
in a currency other than that of the country in which the instrument is issued.
Euronotes are short- to medium-term debt instruments issued in a currency
other than that of the country in which the instrument is issued. These instruments, with typical maturities of a few months to one year, have a longer term
than Eurocurrencies and a shorter term than Eurobonds. In 1996, $81.3 bil-
lion in Eurocommercial paper was issued and $374.1 billion of Euronotes was
issued. The U.S. dollar denominated 63 percent of the Eurocommercial paper
market and 48 percent of the Euronote market.

FUNDAMENTAL ISSUE #3

**What are the Eurobond, Euronote, and Eurocommercial paper
markets?** Eurobonds, Euronotes, and Eurocommercial paper are
nontraditional financial instruments denominated in a currency
other than that of the nation in which the instrument is issued.
These nontraditional markets have experienced remarkable
growth. In 1996 alone, there were more than $1 trillion of
Eurobond, Euronote, and Eurocommercial paper issues. The
largest of these three markets, the Eurobond market, experienced
nearly a 60 percent growth rate from 1995 through 1996. Most
national governments now borrow in these nontraditional
markets, giving them access to lower-cost financing than they
would have in domestic markets alone.

VEHICLE CURRENCIES

VEHICLE CURRENCY A currency that individuals and businesses most often use to conduct international transactions.

As shown in the previous sections, issues of securities and money market instruments can be denominated in any number of currencies. *Vehicle currencies* are used worldwide to denominate international transactions and international financial instruments. Specifically, a **vehicle currency** is a currency that individuals and businesses most often use to conduct international transactions. For example, Japan may issue a bond denominated in U.S. dollars that is purchased by a European household. In this situation, the U.S. dollar serves as a vehicle currency. The transaction is denominated in the U.S. dollar, but a U.S. household is not party to the transaction at all.

Since the end of World War II, the U.S. dollar has been the dominant vehicle currency. Since the early 1980s, however, there has been a gradual shift toward the use of multiple currencies in international transactions. As a result, there have been periods when it appeared that the dollar might lose its dominant position. For example, during the 1960s' dollar crises that preceded the break-up of the Bretton Woods system and the dollar depreciation of the early 1990s, there was speculation as to whether the dollar would remain the leading vehicle currency. Even today, with the single currency of Europe, the *euro,* being introduced, individuals question whether the U.S. dollar can retain its position as the world's leading currency.

Table 6–5 presents evidence on the use of the three leading vehicle currencies, the U.S. dollar, the deutsche mark, and the Japanese yen. As shown by the data, the U.S. dollar remains the dominant vehicle currency, used to denominate nearly 50 percent of banks' cross-border positions and more than one-third of international bond and Euronote issues.

Will the euro replace the dollar as the primary vehicle currency? To try to answer this question, consider the total of all financial instruments in the three categories shown in Table 6–4 denominated in European currencies and the ECU. These currencies represent slightly more than 35 percent of banks' cross-border positions, 27 percent of the Euronote issues, and 35 percent of interna-

TABLE 6–5	**LEADING VEHICLE CURRENCIES**			
SHARE OF MARKET%	**BANKS' CROSS-BORDER POSITIONS IN FOREIGN CURRENCIES (ASSETS)**	**BANKS' CROSS-BORDER POSITIONS IN FOREIGN CURRENCIES (LIABILITIES)**	**EURONOTES**	**INTERNATIONAL BONDS**
U.S. Dollar	51.8	48.9	57.3	43.6
Deutsche Mark	13.3	12.9	6.6	9.9
Japanese Yen	6.9	6.6	3.6	13.6
All Other	28.0	31.6	32.5	32.9

SOURCE: Data from Bank for International Settlements, *Annual Report,* 1998.

tional bond issues. These numbers indicate that the euro may indeed rival the status of the dollar. This conclusion is supported by research conducted by Federal Reserve economist Michael Leahy, who examined the effect of European unification on the dollar holdings of European nations. Leahy finds that these dollar holdings may decline as much as 35 percent with unification. Hence, the euro may indeed rival the U.S. dollar's vehicle currency status.

FUNDAMENTAL ISSUE #4

What are vehicle currencies? Vehicle currencies are currencies that individuals and businesses most often use to conduct international transactions. Since the end of Word War II, the U.S. dollar has been the world's primary vehicle currency. The German deutsche mark and the Japanese yen are the next two predominant vehicle currencies. Collectively, the currencies of the European Union (EU) nations rival the vehicle currency status of the U.S. dollar. The euro, the single currency of the EU, may eventually compete with the dollar's vehicle currency position.

CAPITAL MARKET INTEGRATION—TESTS AND EVIDENCE

As explained earlier in this chapter, capital market liberalization, deregulation, and technological innovation spurred the dramatic growth of the international capital markets. Nonetheless, savers continue to have low levels of international portfolio diversification. How integrated are international capital markets? Economists typically use four definitions of capital market integration to frame their empirical studies; covered interest parity, uncovered interest parity, real interest parity, and the Feldstein–Horioka saving–investment definition. We shall consider each of these definitions in turn.

Covered Interest Parity

Chapter 4 presented covered interest parity. This condition indicates that the difference between the interest rate on a domestic financial instrument and the interest rate on a foreign financial instrument that are similar in all characteristics, such as time to maturity, should equal the forward premium. Covered interest parity pertains to individuals who hold short-term instruments and wish to avoid exchange rate risk. As explained in Chapter 4, these individuals may engage in forward contracts to completely eliminate, or cover, the foreign exchange exposure. Hence, covered interest parity can be used to test the integration of short-term capital or money markets.

As also explained in Chapter 4, an individual with a short-term foreign exchange risk exposure may cover this exposure using Eurocurrency instruments instead of forward and spot exchange contracts. Hence, we should expect the forward and spot exchange markets and the Eurocurrency markets to be highly integrated. Economists test the integration of these markets using the covered interest parity condition. This condition is:

$$R - R^* = (F-S)/S,$$

where R is the domestic interest rate, R^* is the foreign interest rate, F is the forward exchange, and S is the spot exchange rate, defined as the number of domestic currency units required to purchase one foreign currency unit. Recall that the right-hand side of this equation is the forward premium on foreign exchange.

To use this condition as a test of the degree of integration, economists typically take the average of the offer and ask rates in the Eurocurrency markets. The relationship between the domestic and foreign Eurocurrency rate differential and the forward premium is then examined. If these two markets are highly integrated, then there should not be any persistent difference between the interest differentials and the forward premium. Thus, as explained in Chapter 4, for covered interest parity to hold, there must not be any country risk.

Economists Jeffrey Frankel and Alan MacArthur provide evidence on covered interest parity among twenty-four industrialized nations. Their results indicate that differences between Eurocurrency interest differentials and the forward premium are quite small. Hence, the Eurocurrency markets and the foreign exchange markets have become more integrated. Frankel and MacArthur conclude that country risk has been effectively eliminated among the leading industrialized nations, yet currency risk still remains.

In general, these results do not hold for all types of short-term instruments. Economists Jacob Frenkel and Richard Levich investigated the covered interest parity condition for Euro deposit rates and Treasury bill discount rates. Frenkel and Levich show that there are few deviations from covered interest parity when Euro deposit rates are used. Treasury bill returns, however, display substantial deviations from covered interest parity. Recent studies also show that returns on financial instruments of many less-developed nations still exhibit large deviations from covered interest parity, indicating that their short-term capital markets are still relatively closed.

Uncovered Interest Parity

Uncovered interest parity, our second measure of capital market integration, is a broader definition than covered interest parity. Uncovered interest parity states that the interest differential for financial instruments of two nations, which are similar in all characteristics such as risk and time to maturity, should be equal to the expected change in the spot exchange rate between the two nations currencies. Hence, uncovered interest parity is expressed as:

$$R - R^* = (S_{+1}^e - S)/S,$$

where S_{+1}^e is the spot exchange rate expected to prevail in the next period.

According to the uncovered interest parity condition, if capital markets are integrated, the interest differential of financial instruments of two nations that are similar in all characteristics equals the expected change in the spot exchange rate. For uncovered interest parity to hold, there cannot be a country risk premium or an exchange risk premium. Because uncovered interest parity requires that there be no country risk premium, it requires covered interest parity to hold as well.

One problem with testing uncovered interest parity is determining how to measure individuals' expectations of the future spot exchange rate. Economists typically use either survey data on currency traders' expectations or the actual spot exchange rate that prevails at the time the financial instruments mature. Using either measure, the evidence does not indicate that uncovered interest parity holds to the extent that covered interest parity does.

Figure 6–1 plots the difference between interest differentials on three-month treasury bills and the actual change in the spot rate over the maturity period of the financial instruments for Germany and the United Kingdom relative to the United States. As the figure shows, deviations from uncovered interest parity exist even among the most liberalized developed nations and can persist for extended periods. The average of the deviations shown in Figure 6–1 are 2.7 percent for Germany and 2.8 percent for the United Kingdom. The average of the absolute values of the deviations, however, are 5.3 percent for Germany and 5.1 percent for the United Kingdom.

Chapter 4 explained that if both covered and uncovered interest parity hold, then the forward exchange rate equals the expected future spot exchange rate. This condition is known as *foreign exchange market efficiency*. Although the evidence indicates that there is some co-movement between the forward exchange rate and the actual future spot rate, the forward exchange rate has limited ability in forecasting the future spot exchange rate. Many economists attribute the poor predictive power of the forward rate to the existence of an exchange risk premium.

Figure 6–2 plots the percentage difference between the U.S. dollar forward rate and the actual prevailing U.S. dollar spot rate for Germany and Japan. As the figure shows, the forward rate often overestimates or underestimates the realized spot rate. The averages of the deviations shown in Figure 6–2 are 0.4 percent for Germany and 0.6 percent for Japan. The averages of the absolute values of the deviations, however, are 4.8 percent for Germany and 5.2 percent for Japan.

At this point, we can conclude that although there is sufficient capital market integration to eliminate the country risk among the leading industrialized nations, some exchange risk probably remains.

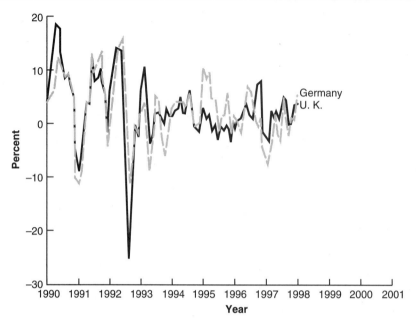

FIGURE 6–1 UNCOVERED INTEREST PARITY DEVIATIONS

Deviations from uncovered interest parity for U.S. and German three-month treasury bills, and U.S. and U.K. three-month treasury bills are plotted by subtracting the three-month change in the spot rate from the interest differential. For national financial instruments such as treasury bills, deviations from uncovered interest parity can persist for extended time periods.

SOURCE: Data from *International Financial Statistics,* International Monetary Fund.

Economists Kenneth Froot and Jeffrey Frankel employed survey data of exchange market traders in a novel test of uncovered interest parity. This survey data is important because it allows economists to separate the errors of traders' forecasts of exchange rate movements from risk premia. Froot and Frankel found very strong evidence that foreign exchange traders had systematic forecast errors. Richard Marston expanded on their work and concluded that deviations from uncovered interest parity are due to currency traders' chronic forecast errors and a risk premium.

Real Interest Parity

Covered and uncovered interest parity conditions relate *nominal* interest rate differentials to spot and forward exchange rates and expected spot exchange rates. These conditions are appropriate definitions for capital market integration if we consider only short- or medium-term financial instruments. Over longer time horizons, however, changes in price levels may affect saving decisions.

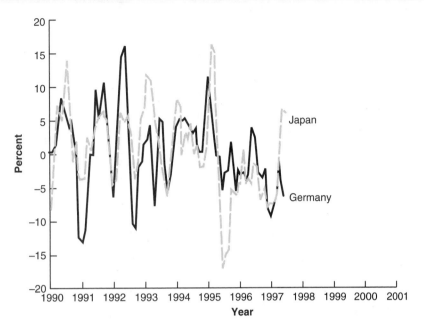

FIGURE 6-2   FORWARD AND SPOT EXCHANGE RATE DIFFERENTIALS

We can plot the difference between the U.S. dollar three-month forward exchange rate and the actual U.S. dollar spot rate that prevailed three months later for Germany and Japan. The forward exchange rate often overestimates the actual spot exchange rate and often underestimates the actual spot exchange rate. Though there is a high degree of co-movement between the two, the forward rate remains a poor predictor of the future spot rate.

SOURCE: Data from *International Financial Statistics,* International Monetary Fund.

For example, if the rate of inflation is fairly low, the purchasing power of one dollar of principal changes very little over a three-month time horizon. In the same inflation environment, however, the purchasing power of one dollar of principal can change significantly over a ten-year time horizon. Hence, holders of long-term financial instruments are likely to be motivated by *real* yields as opposed to *nominal* yields.

REAL INTEREST RATE The nominal interest rate less the rate of price inflation expected to prevail over the maturity period of the financial instrument.

FISHER EQUATION A condition that defines the real interest rate as the nominal interest rate less the expected rate of inflation.

Real Interest Rates: The Fisher Equation   Economist Irving Fisher defined a financial instrument's **real interest rate** as the nominal interest rate less the rate of price inflation expected to prevail during the life of the financial instrument. In what is now known as the *Fisher equation,* Fisher expressed this definition of the real interest rate as:

$$r \equiv R - \pi^{e}$$

where r denotes the real interest rate, R denotes the nominal interest rate, and π^{e} denotes the expected rate of inflation. In words, the **Fisher equation** is a condition that defines the real interest rate as the nominal interest rate less the expected rate of inflation.

Typically the Fisher equation is rewritten as

$$R = r + \pi^e.$$

That is, the nominal interest rate is equal to the sum of the real interest rate and the expected rate of inflation. For example, suppose that the nominal rate of interest on a newly issued one-year note is 5 percent. In addition, suppose you expect the rate of inflation to be 3 percent over the next year. Then, according to the Fisher equation, the real interest rate is 2 percent (5 percent minus 3 percent).

Combining Relative Purchasing Power Parity and Uncovered Interest Parity
The Fisher equation provides an approximation of the real interest rate. By combining uncovered interest parity and relative purchasing power parity, we can use the Fisher equation to establish a condition relating the real rate of interest on financial instruments of two nations that share all of the same characteristics, such as time to maturity and risk.

Chapter 2 examined relative purchasing power parity, which is a theory relating changes in the price levels of two nations to changes in the spot exchange rate. For expected price changes, we can express (*ex ante*) purchasing power parity as:

$$\pi^e - \pi^{*e} = (S_{+1}^e - S)/S,$$

where π^e denotes the expected rate of inflation in the domestic nation, π^{*e} denotes the expected rate of inflation in the foreign nation, S_{+1}^e denotes the spot exchange rate that is expected to prevail over the time period considered, and S is the current spot exchange rate. (Recall that in this equation, the spot exchange rate, S, is defined as the number of domestic currency units required to purchase one foreign currency unit.) In words, the difference in expected rates of inflation is equal to the expected rate of depreciation or appreciation of the domestic currency relative to the foreign currency.

Note that the same term, $(S_{+1}^e - S)/S$, appears on the right-hand side of the equations representing relative purchasing power parity and uncovered interest parity. Hence, we can set these two conditions equal to each other:

$$\pi^e - \pi^{*e} = (S_{+1}^e - S)/S = R - R^*,$$

or

$$\pi^e - \pi^{*e} = R - R^*.$$

We can rearrange this expression to obtain:

$$R - \pi^e = R^* - \pi^{*e}.$$

Note that, according to the Fisher equation, the left-hand side of the equation is equivalent to the domestic real interest rate, r, and the right-hand side of the equation is equivalent to the foreign real interest rate, r^*. Hence, we can also express the equation as:

$$r = r^*.$$

REAL INTEREST PARITY A condition that postulates that in equilibrium the real rate of interest on similar financial instruments of two nations is equal.

This final equation is the **real interest parity** condition. It indicates that in equilibrium the real interest rates of financial instruments of two nations that share all of the same characteristics, such as time to maturity and risk, are equal. In addition to defining the real rate of interest, Irving Fisher also postulated that the real rate of interest is stable in the long run. Hence, real interest parity is implied by relative purchasing power parity and uncovered interest parity.

Real Interest Parity as a Definition of Financial Market Integration   Real interest parity holds if international capital market integration permits differences in real interest rates to be arbitraged away. Hence, if international capital markets are integrated, real interest rate differentials should not persist over extended time periods. Thus, the existence of persistent real interest differentials would cast doubt on the assumption that international capital markets are fully integrated. In general, the evidence on real interest parity indicates that sizable real interest differentials still exist.

Figure 6–3 displays the real interest differentials of national treasury bills for selected industrialized nations. The real interest rates are based on the actual rate of inflation that prevailed over the life of the financial instrument. We then subtract foreign real interest rates from the U.S. real interest rate to yield the differentials plotted in the diagram. As shown in Figure 6–3, negative differences persisted for the first half of the 1990s, while positive differentials persisted over the latter part of the decade. The average of the deviations shown in Figure 6–3 are –1.3 percent for Germany and –2.5 percent for the United Kingdom. The average of the absolute values of the deviations, however, are 2.5 percent for Germany and 3.8 percent for the United Kingdom.

Economist Richard Marston of the University of Pennsylvania shows that real interest rate differentials among the industrialized nations are, on average, small. Marston explains that deviations from real interest parity can be decomposed into deviations from relative purchasing power parity and uncovered interest parity. Because deviations from relative purchasing power parity and uncovered interest parity are small, on average, it is no surprise that deviations from real interest parity are small. Nonetheless, these deviations may still lead one to conclude that real interest parity does not hold.

Saving and Investment

In 1980, Economists Martin Feldstein and Charles Horioka of Harvard University offered an additional definition of the degree of capital market integration. Feldstein and Horioka argued that in a world of full capital market integration, there should be little long-term correlation between a nation's saving rate and investment rate. In an environment of no capital mobility, a nation's saving rate should be related to its investment rate.

FIGURE 6–3   REAL INTEREST RATE DIFFERENTIALS

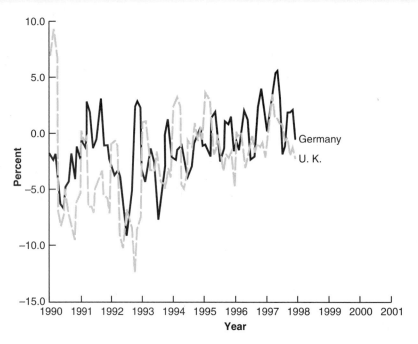

Real interest rate differentials can be persistent, indicating that real interest parity does not hold. The real interest rate differentials in this diagram are for U.S. and German three-month treasury bills and U.S. and U.K. three-month treasury bills. The real interest rates are based on actual rates of inflation.

SOURCE: Data from *International Financial Statistics,* International Monetary Fund.

In a no-capital-mobility setting, a nation's investment possibilities are limited by its available pool of domestic savings. In a fully integrated capital market environment, however, investment opportunities are not limited by the domestic saving pool. In this setting, individuals and firms can fund investment opportunities with either domestic or foreign savings, so that only the global pool of savings limits investment. The correlation of the domestic saving rate and the domestic investment rate in this setting should be near or equal to zero.

The authors calculated the correlation between the ratio of gross domestic investment to GDP and gross domestic saving to GDP for twenty-one OECD member nations. They found that for the period 1960 through 1974, the correlation of saving and investment was nearly 90 percent. This study sparked a great deal of research using this indicator of international capital market integration. Although many refinements have been made, there still appears to be a high correlation among nations' saving rates and investment rates during the period that Feldstein and Horioka examined.

Feldstein and Horioka's test of capital market integration is a long-run test that rests on a number of implicit assumptions. Most important is the assumption that saving and investment decisions are based on anticipated real interest rates. Hence, this test of international capital market integration requires that real interest parity hold in the long run. As we discussed earlier, this is not necessarily the case. Hence, some economists reject the high correlation of national saving and investment as evidence that capital markets are not integrated.

Eventually, as described in Chapter 1, when the United States began borrowing heavily in the international markets in the latter half of the 1980s, the saving and investment relationship for the United States disappeared. Many take this as evidence that considerable capital market liberalization and integration has occurred since the period of Feldstein and Horioka's study.

FUNDAMENTAL ISSUE #5

What is capital market integration? There are four definitions that economists use as a framework for testing the degree of international capital market integration; covered interest parity, uncovered interest parity, real interest parity, and the Feldstein–Horioka saving–investment definition. Evidence using the covered interest parity definition indicates that the Eurocurrency markets are well integrated. The evidence on the remaining definitions indicates that capital markets have become *more integrated* but may not be *fully integrated* after all. Individuals appear to prefer holding their savings in domestic markets, even though greater gains may be had by diversifying internationally. There is also evidence that currency risk and, for the developing nations, country risk may persist as well.

CHAPTER SUMMARY

1. **International Capital Markets:** These are the markets for cross-border exchange of financial instruments that have maturities of a year or more. Deregulation, liberalization, and technological innovation have led to considerable growth in international capital markets. Over the period of 1986 through 1998, financing activity in the international capital market grew considerably. Savers, however, still maintain very low levels of international diversification.

2. **International Money Markets:** These are markets for cross-border exchange of financial instruments with maturities of less than one year. These markets consist of exchanges of a number of different types of instruments, including foreign exchange and international notes and commercial paper. Nonetheless, foreign exchange transactions dominate the international money market. Current estimates indicate that turnover in the foreign exchange market exceeds $1.4 billion daily.

3. **The Eurobond, Euronote, and Eurocommercial Paper Markets:** Eurobonds, Euronotes, and Eurocommercial paper are nontraditional financial instruments denominated in a currency other than that of the nations in which the instruments are issued. Currently, there are more than $1 trillion of Eurobond, Euronote, and Eurocommercial paper issues. The largest of these three markets, the Eurobond market, experienced a 60 percent growth rate since 1995. Most national governments now borrow in these nontraditional markets, giving them access to cheaper financing than they would have in domestic markets alone.

4. **Vehicle Currencies:** Vehicle currencies are currencies that individuals and businesses most often use to conduct international transactions. The U.S. dollar is the world's primary vehicle currency. The deutsche mark and the Japanese yen are the next two predominant vehicle currencies. Collectively, the currencies of the European Union nations are comparable to the vehicle currency status of the U.S. dollar. Hence, the euro, the proposed single currency of the EU, may eventually compete with the dollar's vehicle currency position.

5. **Evidence of Capital Market Integration:** Economists have evaluated evidence for or against international capital market integration in four ways: covered interest parity, uncovered interest parity, real interest parity, and the Feldstein–Horioka saving–investment measure. Evidence indicates that Eurocurrency markets are well integrated but other international capital markets may not be fully integrated. Individuals appear to prefer holding their savings in domestic markets, even though diversifying internationally may yield additional returns. There is also evidence that currency risk and country risk may be prevalent.

QUESTIONS AND PROBLEMS

1. Characterize each of the following financial instruments as either a global equity, global bond, Eurocurrency, Euronote, Eurobond, or Eurocommercial paper.
   a. A Brazilian firm offers a ten-year debt instrument for sale to international savers.
   b. The government of Mexico offers a three-year debt instrument, denominated in the U.S. dollar, for sale on the London market.

    c. Citibank of New York borrows a pound-denominated deposit from Royal Bank of Canada.

    d. A Brazilian firm offers shares of its stock for sale to international savers.

2. Suppose that the interest rate on a domestic debt instrument is 5 percent and that the expected rate of inflation is 2 percent. Further suppose that the foreign nominal interest rate on a similar instrument is 6 percent while the expected rate of inflation is 4 percent.

    a. Based on the nominal interest rates, what would you expect to happen to the exchange value of the domestic currency over the life of the instrument?

    b. Based on the inflation rates, what would you expect to happen to the exchange value of the domestic currency over the life of the instrument?

3. Based on the information in problem 2, what are the domestic and foreign real interest rates?

4. Based on the information in problem 2, does real interest parity hold? Why or why not? What type of adjustment might take place between the two economies?

5. Draw a diagram depicting demand and supply schedules for the spot exchange market of a small developing nation.

    a. Using this diagram, explain how capital inflows might affect the exchange value of the domestic currency.

    b. Explain how capital outflows might affect the exchange value of the domestic currency.

    c. Based on a and b, can you conclude whether capital restrictions would or would not be desirable?

ON-LINE APPLICATION

This chapter described the increasing importance of international financial markets. The volume of international financial transactions has increased enormously over the last ten years.

Internet URL: http://www.oecd.org/publications/figures/

Title: The Organization for Economic Cooperation and Development

Navigation: Begin with the Internet URL provided above. Scroll down the index to *Capital* and click on the *Capital* link. Scroll down to the table titled *Capital II.*

Application: Solve for answers to the following questions.

1. Find the amount of Eurobonds and foreign loans for the United States, the European Union, and the entire OECD group of nations.

2. Calculate the rate of increase in the volume of transactions in these two types of financial assets for the United States, the European Union, and the entire OECD group of nations.

References and Recommended Readings

Bank for International Settlements. *Annual Report.*

Feldstein, Martin, and Charles Horioka. "Domestic Saving and International Capital Flows." *The Economic Journal,* 90 (June 1980): 314–329.

Fisher, Stanley. "Capital Account Liberalization and the Role of the IMF." *International Monetary Fund* (September 1997).

Frankel, Jeffrey. "Quantifying International Capital Mobility in the 1980's." In Dilip Das, ed., *International Finance: Contemporary Issues.* New York: Routledge (1993): 27–53.

Frankel, J., and A. MacArthur. "Political versus Currency Premia in International Real Interest Rate Differentials: A Study of Forward Rates for 24 Countries." *European Economic Review,* 32 (June 1988): 1083–1114.

French, Kenneth, and James Poterba. "Investor Diversification and International Equity Markets." *American Economic Review Papers and Proceedings,* 81, no.2 (May 1991): 222–226.

Frenkel, Jacob, and Richard Levich. "Transaction Costs and Interest Arbitrage: Tranquil versus Turbulent Periods." *Journal of Political Economy,* 85, no.6 (December 1977): 1209–1226.

Froot, Kenneth, and Jeffrey Frankel. "Forward Discount Bias: Is It an Exchange Risk Premium?" *Quarterly Journal of Economics,* 104 (February 1989): 139–161.

Leahy, Michael. "The Dollar as an Official Reserve Currency Under EMU." *Open Economies Review,* 7(4) (1996): 371–390.

Marston, Richard, C. *International Financial Integration: A Study of Interest Differentials Between the Major Industrialized Countries.* New York: Cambridge University Press (1997).

Organization for Economic Cooperation and Development, *International Financial Trends.*

Taylor, Mark. "The Economics of Exchange Rates," *Journal of Economic Literature,* 33 (March 1995): 13–47.

INTERNATIONAL BANKING AND PAYMENT SYSTEMS

It is June 30, 1934, and John Dillinger is the U.S. Federal Bureau of Investigation's (FBI's) "public enemy number one." Dillinger and his gang hold up Merchants National Bank in South Bend, Indiana, thinking that the local post office has just deposited more than $100,000 (about $1.25 million in today's dollars). The robbery does not go according to plan. Following a gun battle in which Baby Face Nelson lets loose bursts of machine-gun bullets at police officers on a street crowded with innocent citizens, the five gangsters drive off with three hostages in a bullet-riddled getaway car in the direction of the Indiana–Illinois border. After releasing their hostages, the gangsters seek medical attention for one of their number who has been mortally wounded by a police bullet. Later, Baby Face Nelson divides the money into neat piles. Dillinger's face falls when he sees his share of the loot: $4,800 (about $60,000 in today's dollars), or less than 25 percent of what he had anticipated. Dillinger has to postpone his plans to flee to Mexico. Three weeks later, he is gunned down by FBI agents outside a Chicago theater.

Now fast forward sixty-one years, to July 20, 1995. Citibank sets up a "war room" in Manhattan to monitor its global funds transfer system and to provide its customers with early warnings of unauthorized funds transfers that its computer security force recently has begun to detect. So far, all the bank knows is that a computer hacker has accessed secret codes and procedures that have permitted the transfer of funds between Citibank computers in Buenos Aires and New York. Then word spreads in the "war room" that security officials have detected a $400,000 withdrawal from the system via transfers to a BankAmerica account in San Francisco. This withdrawal turns out to be the break that the FBI investigators need to crack the case. Ultimately, law enforcement officials arrest Russian gang members not only in New York and San Francisco, but also in Britain, Israel, and the Netherlands. The orchestrator of the computer theft turns out to be a biochemistry graduate in St. Petersburg, Russia. He and his globally distributed gang did not brandish weapons, take hostages, or use getaway cars. Nevertheless, Citibank eventually discovers that during the weeks prior to his arrest, the Russian computer gangster managed to transfer about $12 million out of Citibank customer accounts. Henceforth, bankers realize, the modus operandi for bank robberies will never be the same.

ON THE WEB
*Visit the Financial Crimes
Network Site at:*
**http://www.ustreas.gov/
treasury/bureaus/fincen/**

These contrasting crime stories illuminate the dramatic changes that took place in the banking industry during the latter part of the twentieth century. Banks no longer are isolated storehouses for cash and checks. Today, banks in the smallest communities have access to computer and communications systems that permit them to electronically transfer funds to nearly any other financial institution on the planet. In this chapter we shall discuss the international banking and payment system that modern-day bank robbers seek to pilfer in front of computer consoles in quiet, air-conditioned rooms, rather than behind the nose of a pointed gun on a crowded street.

INTERNATIONAL DIMENSIONS OF FINANCIAL INTERMEDIATION

What accounts for the existence of the banks that latter-day and modern-day gangsters have sought to rob? To answer this question, let's think about the role that such institutions perform in channeling saving to investment projects.

When savers allocate some of their wealth to the purchase of a bond issued by a company, they effectively make a direct loan to that business. In this way, they assist in the *direct finance* of domestic capital investment projects that the company chooses to undertake.

The financing of capital investment projects is not always so direct. It is also possible that a saver may obtain a long-term time deposit at a banking firm chartered by its nation's government. This bank allocates these funds, together with those of other deposit holders, to holdings of bonds issued by the same company as before. In this instance, the saver *indirectly finances* domestic capital investment. The bank, in turn, *intermediates* the financing of the domestic investment.

Financial Intermediation

Figure 7–1 illustrates the distinction between direct and indirect finance. With direct finance, a financial intermediary such as a bank is not involved. A saver lends directly to individuals or firms who undertake capital investment. With indirect finance, however, another institution channels the funds of savers to those parties who desire to undertake capital investments.

FINANCIAL INTERMEDIATION
Indirect finance through the services of financial institutions that channel funds from savers to those who ultimately make capital investments.

The process of indirect finance, or **financial intermediation,** is the most common way in which funds are channeled from saving to investment. *Financial intermediaries* are the institutions that serve as the "go-betweens" in this process. These intermediaries exist solely to take the funds of savers and allocate those funds to ultimate borrowers. Commercial banks that issue deposits and allocate funds to issuing loans or to holding other types of financial instruments are an example of a financial intermediary.

ASYMMETRIC INFORMATION
Possession of information by one party in a financial transaction that is not available to the other party.

Asymmetric Information   Why would any savers desire to direct their funds through some other institution instead of lending them directly to another party? One important reason is **asymmetric information,** or the fact that one

---

FIGURE 7–1 **INDIRECT FINANCE THROUGH FINANCIAL INTERMEDIARIES**

Those savers who exchange funds for the financial instruments of companies in financial markets undertake direct finance of the capital investments of those companies. Financial intermediaries make indirect finance possible by issuing their own financial instruments and using the funds that they obtain from savers to finance capital investments of businesses.

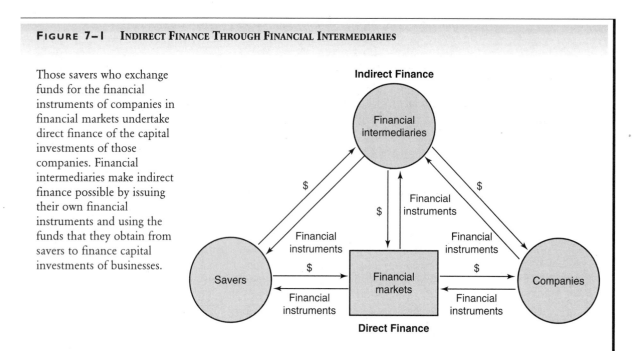

---

party in a financial transaction, such as a borrower, often possesses information not available to another party, such as a lender.

Suppose, for instance, that a Mexican citizen has the opportunity to buy a high-yield bond issued by a public utility located 600 miles from where he resides. The firm plans to use the funds to build an experimental power plant designed to increase electrical-generation efficiency while significantly reducing atmospheric pollution. Unless this Mexican saver happens to be well versed on electrical power generation, it is very difficult for him to assess the true riskiness of this bond. This makes it difficult for him to compare the yield on this bond with yields on alternative financial instruments.

By way of contrast, the public utility that issues the bond surely has much more information about the prospects for its proposed power plant. It may be that the chances of success in both improved fuel efficiency and better low-pollution performance are very good. Or it could be that the public utility's managers propose the project because of political pressures to increase expenditures in the locale in which the proposed plant would be built, in an effort to increase employment in a high-vote region. In either case, the public utility that issues the bond has information about its riskiness that the saver does not possess.

Suppose that, in fact, the public utility's managers know at the outset that the long-term prospects for financial success are poor, yet they have chosen to invest in the construction of the power plant in hopes of future support from

ADVERSE SELECTION The potential for those who issue financial instruments to intend to use borrowed funds to undertake unworthy, high-risk investment projects.

the Mexican government. In this instance, the public utility's managers know that their bond may have *adverse,* or "bad," consequences for those who buy the public utility's bonds. This is an example of an asymmetric-information situation known as **adverse selection.** This is the potential for those who desire funds for unworthy projects to be among the most likely to want to borrow or to issue debt instruments. A consequence of adverse selection is that savers are less willing to lend to those seeking to finance high-quality projects: the presence of poor-quality debt instruments (such as the bonds in our public utility example) makes lenders skeptical.

In contrast, suppose that the managers of the public utility issuing the bond have an honest intention to achieve the specified goals for the power plant and to earn the highest return possible from operating the plant. Nonetheless, after the public utility sells bonds to finance the project, a management change occurs. The new managers, in an effort to cut costs, use inferior materials and techniques in constructing the plant, which ultimately are both inefficient and unprofitable. The result is an increased probability that savers will fail to receive promised interest yields on the public utility's bonds. Such a possibility that a borrower might engage in behavior that increases risk after financial instrument has been purchased is **moral hazard.** This term refers to the potential "immoral" behavior, from the lender's perspective, that the borrower would have exhibited.

MORAL HAZARD The possibility that a borrower might engage in more risky behavior after receiving the funds from a lender.

Certainly, one way that the Mexican saver might deal with either problem posed by asymmetric information is to make a number of 600-mile trips to initially evaluate and then continue to monitor the public utility's progress on its capital investment project. By acquiring as much direct information as possible, the saver reduces the asymmetry of information about the bond's risks. Doing this, however, may be very costly to the saver, who incurs direct costs to make the trips, as well as the opportunity costs of lost time.

One reason that financial intermediaries exist is to save potential holders of financial instruments from incurring such costs. Although these institutions cannot eliminate adverse selection and moral hazard problems, they collect information about the underlying riskiness of financial instruments and monitor the continuing performance of those who issue such instruments. For example, intermediaries may specialize in assessing the prospects of bonds that public utilities issue to finance major capital investments, thereby reducing the extent of potential adverse selection problems in the market for these bonds. These intermediaries also keep track of the performances of public utilities in implementing their investments. Public utilities that fail to do a good job of managing their investment projects might have a harder task issuing new bonds in the future, which reduces the potential for moral hazard problems.

ECONOMIES OF SCALE Cost savings from pooling funds for centralized management.

Economies of Scale Another important reason that financial intermediaries exist is **economies of scale.** Some financial intermediaries make it possible for many people to pool their funds together, thereby increasing the size, or *scale,* of the total amount of savings managed by a central authority. This centralization of management reduces the average fund management costs below the levels savers would incur if they all were to manage their savings alone.

If financial intermediaries manage funds for many people at an average cost that is lower than the cost each faces individually, then financial economies of scale exist. *Pension fund companies,* which are institutions that specialize in managing individuals' retirement funds, largely owe their existence to their abilities to provide such cost savings to individual savers. Likewise, *investment companies–* institutions that manage portfolios of financial instruments called *mutual funds* on behalf of shareholders–also exist largely because of economies of scale.

ON THE WEB
Check the latest international equity quotes at:
http://www.fid-inv.com/

INTERNATIONAL FINANCIAL DIVERSIFICATION Holding financial instruments issued in various countries to spread portfolio risks.

WORLD INDEX FUND A portfolio of globally issued financial instruments with yields that historically have moved in offsetting directions.

Financial Intermediation across National Boundaries

In our example, the Mexican saver contemplates purchasing a bond issued by a Mexican public utility. Another possibility is for the Mexican resident to purchase a bond issued by a public utility located across the border in the United States. There are a number of reasons that the Mexican saver might wish to hold bonds issued by a U.S. company. One reason might be to earn an anticipated higher return. Another reason might be to avoid country risk specific to Mexico by placing at least a portion of his savings in U.S. public utility bonds. More broadly, the saver's goal might be to achieve overall risk reductions via **international financial diversification,** or holding bonds issued in various nations and thereby spreading portfolio risks across both Mexican-issued *and* foreign-issued financial instruments.

A really sophisticated Mexican saver does not just hold financial instruments issued in Mexico and the United States. The saver would place a portion of the wealth with an investment company that offers a **world index fund,** which is a carefully designed grouping of globally issued financial instruments that yield returns that historically tend to move in offsetting directions. By holding a world index fund, the saver consequently earns the average yield on securities of a number of nations while keeping overall risk to a minimum.

International Financial Intermediation Holding shares in a world index fund makes the Mexican saver a part of the process of *international financial intermediation.* This refers to the indirect finance of capital investment across national borders by financial intermediaries such as banks, pension fund companies, or investment companies.

The rationales for international financial intermediation are the same as the justifications for the existence of domestic intermediation. For the Mexican saver, for instance, asymmetric-information problems are likely to be at least as severe, as compared with evaluating the riskiness of Mexican bonds, when attempting to assess the risk characteristics of U.S. bonds. By placing some wealth in a world index fund managed by an investment company, the saver transfers the task of evaluating and monitoring the prospects and performances of bond issuers across the globe. In exchange for this service, the saver pays the investment company management fees.

Banks located in various countries take part in the process of international financial intermediation by using some of the funds of domestic deposit holders to finance loans to individuals and companies based in other nations. As discussed in Chapter 6, a large portion of such lending takes place in the Eurocurrency markets. These markets constitute a key channel through which the process of international financial intermediation takes place.

Economies of Scale and Global Banking   The Eurocurrency markets are at the center of international banking activities. Today, very few nations' capital investment projects are purely domestically financed. Even bank-financed investment in the United States increasingly stems from loans by non-U.S. banks. The largest U.S. corporations on average use the services of more foreign banks than domestic institutions.

As you saw in Chapter 6, the dollar remains the world's primary vehicle currency. Nevertheless, as Table 7–1 indicates, the world's largest banks are not based in the United States. Today most of the largest banking institutions, sometimes called *megabanks,* are located in Europe and Japan. These megabanks typically take in deposits and lend throughout the world. Although they report their profits and pay taxes in their home nations, these megabanks are otherwise fully international banking institutions.

What accounts for the existence of megabanks whose operations span the globe? One possible answer is economies of scale. By increasing their asset portfolios through regional or worldwide expansion, megabanks may be able to reduce average operating costs, thereby gaining efficiency. A recent study by Yener Altunbas and Philip Moyneux of the University College of North Wales in the United Kingdom found that French, German, and Spanish banks stand to experience considerable cost reductions as European banking extends

TABLE 7–1   THE WORLD'S LARGEST BANKS

BANK	COUNTRY	ASSETS ($ BILLIONS)
Tokyo Mitsubishi Bank	Japan	752
United Bank of Switzerland	Switzerland	590
Deutsche Bank AG	Germany	575
Sumitomo Bank	Japan	513
Dai-Ichi Kangyo Bank	Japan	476
Fuji Bank	Japan	474
Sanwa Bank	Japan	470
ABN Amro Holdings	The Netherlands	444
Industrial Bank of Japan	Japan	436
HSBC Holdings	United Kingdom	405

SOURCE: Data from *Wall Street Journal,* December 8, 1997.

more broadly across national borders. The evidence for economies of scale in banking is more mixed for U.S. banks, although U.S. bank managers themselves commonly offer economies of scale as a key rationale for large-scale mergers in the United States.

Some economists believe that a particular form of economies of scale may explain the existence of megabanks: *economies of scale in information processing.* According to this view, the expanding size of these banks reflects the fact that many businesses now have operations that stretch across and among the world's continents. To be able to evaluate and monitor the creditworthiness of these multinational enterprises, banks must also have offices around the globe. This, goes the argument, allows banks to overcome asymmetric-information problems more efficiently than they could if they were purely domestic intermediaries. Hence, a key explanation for megabanks hinges on the existence of *both* asymmetric information *and* economies of scale in international banking operations.

FUNDAMENTAL ISSUE #1

Why do financial intermediaries exist, and what accounts for international financial intermediation? A key reason that financial intermediaries exist is to address problems arising from asymmetric information. One such problem is adverse selection, or the potential for the least creditworthy borrowers to be the most likely to seek to issue financial instruments. Another is moral hazard, or the possibility that an initially creditworthy borrower may undertake actions that reduce its creditworthiness after receiving funds from a lender. Another reason for the existence of financial intermediaries is the existence of economies of scale, or the ability to spread costs of managing funds across large numbers of savers. A potential justification for international financial intermediation by global banking enterprises is that they may experience economies of scale in information processing by spreading their credit evaluation and monitoring operations around the world.

BANKING AROUND THE GLOBE

Multinational businesses have relationships with megabanks based in many nations. Indeed, by the 1990s a typical multinational U.S. firm had accounts with at least as many banks abroad as it maintained with U.S.-based banking institutions. Likewise, individuals and firms residing in other countries increasingly retain the services of banks based elsewhere, including large U.S. banks with overseas offices.

The business of banking, however, varies from nation to nation. Each country has its own unique banking history, and this fact alone accounts for distinctive features of national banking systems.

There are several ways in which countries' banking systems differ. In some countries, banks are the key vehicle for financial intermediation, whereas in others, banking is only one component of a highly diversified financial system. Furthermore, the structure of banking markets differs from country to country. Some nations have only a few large banks, while others, such as the United States, have relatively large numbers of banks of various sizes. The legal environments governing bank dealings with individual and business customers also differ across countries, as does governments' treatment of bank accounts for tax purposes.

Bank versus Market Finance

One key dimension along which national banking systems differ concerns the extent to which banks are the predominant means by which firms finance their working capital needs. For instance, British, German, and Japanese businesses use bank loans to finance significantly larger shares of their investment as compared with businesses located in the United States. In the United Kingdom, nearly 70 percent of funds raised by businesses typically stem from bank borrowings. The proportions for Germany and Japan are the order of 50 percent and 65 percent, respectively. In contrast, U.S. businesses normally raise fewer than 30 percent of their funds through bank loans.

This difference helps to account for why German and Japanese banks more than doubled their sizes between the 1970s and the 1990s. Though British banks grew by less in relative terms, their importance in British business finance permitted them to grow faster than U.S. banks, whose overall size, adjusted for inflation, failed to change significantly in the two decades following the 1970s.

Differences in Bank Market Structure

MARKET STRUCTURES The organization of the loan and deposit markets in which bank rivals compete.

There also are differences in **market structures**—the organization of the loan and deposit markets in which banking institutions interact—across nations' banking systems. In particular, the extent of potential rivalry, often measured by the portion of total deposits concentrated among a nation's largest banks, vary considerably. The top five banks in Belgium, Denmark, France, Italy, Luxembourg, Portugal, Spain, and the United Kingdom have more than 30 percent of the deposits of their nations' residents. In Greece and the Netherlands, this figure is more than 80 percent. In contrast, the top five U.S. banks account for fewer than 15 percent of the deposit holdings of U.S. residents. On the asset side of banks' balance sheets, the U.S. banking system appears to exhibit more potential for rivalry among its banks, as fewer than a third of total bank assets are concentrated among the top ten U.S. banks. In Germany, Japan, and the United Kingdom, this figure is about two-thirds.

The degree of banking competition within a nation also depends on how open the nation's borders are to rivalry from foreign-based banking operations. By the 1990s, foreign banks made many loans to U.S. individuals and firms, but foreign banks had barely penetrated the German and Japanese loan markets. This undoubtedly has played a role in producing the high levels of bank asset concentration in Germany and Japan.

Universal versus Restricted Banking

UNIVERSAL BANKING Banking environment under which depository institutions face few if any restrictions on their authority to offer full ranges of financial services and to own equity shares in corporations.

Another feature that distinguishes national banking systems is the extent to which they permit **universal banking,** under which there are few if any limits on the ability of banks to offer full ranges of financial services and to own equity shares in corporations. In Germany and the United Kingdom, as well as in several other European nations, banks face few such restrictions. European banks may issue insurance, but U.S. banks confront strict limits on their ability to offer insurance policies to their customers. As compared with European banks, Japanese banks face greater restrictions on their activities, but in contrast to U.S. banks, many Japanese banks have unrestricted authority to underwrite stocks and bonds.

Arguments against Universal Banking   In the United States universal banking has been prohibited since 1933, when the U.S. Congress passed the Glass–Steagall Act. A key rationale for this U.S. prohibition barring universal banking is that equity shares tend to be riskier than government securities and municipal bonds. Since 1933, the U.S. Congress has stood by an assessment that taking on greater risk would increase the likelihood of bank failure.

Another concern has been that universal banking might engender conflicts of interest. For instance, if a bank were to buy a significant equity stake in a new Internet firm, then it would be in the bank's interest for that company's share price to remain high. The bank might try to induce its other customers to purchase the company's shares, or it might buy shares in the company for inclusion in portfolios that it manages on behalf of clients, even if these actions were not in its customers' best interests. The bank might even cut back on its lending to a rival Internet company.

Finally, there is also a long U.S. tradition of concern, dating back to Thomas Jefferson's famous remark that "banking establishments are more dangerous than standing armies," about the centralization of financial resources. Those opposed to universal banking worry about the potential for a few large banks to own large portions of common stock in U.S. corporations, which would give the owners of those banks considerable power to shape the U.S. corporate landscape.

Justifications for Universal Banking   Those who favor universal banking point out that there are potentially significant advantages of universal banking.

One of these, they contend, is that it is possible that bank holdings of individually risky equity shares may *reduce* overall bank risk. This may occur, universal-banking proponents argue, if some equity returns were to rise during periods in which many bond yields or returns on loans were declining. Holding equity shares would reduce the riskiness of a bank's full asset portfolio.

INSIDER INFORMATION
Information that is available to inside directors and officers of a corporation but that generally is unavailable to the general public or to depository institutions that lend to the corporation.

Another justification for universal banking is that holding ownership shares in companies gives banks **insider information,** or knowledge about the internal affairs of firms available to inside directors and officers of the firms but not generally available to the general public. Obtaining such information would make evaluating and monitoring these businesses' creditworthiness an easier task for banks, thereby reducing the banks' operating costs. In addition, banks might be less likely to force firms into bankruptcy when the companies experience problems that banks' inside information indicates are simply short-term liquidity difficulties rather than long-term solvency problems. Indeed, those favoring universal banking argue that universal banking could reduce market expectations of bankruptcies, so that firms end up paying lower risk premiums on their borrowings. One case that casts some doubt on this claim is the experience of the U.S. subsidiary of the German company Metallgesellschaft AG, which in late 1993 and early 1994 experienced derivatives losses that initially were not revealed to bank owners by its supervisory board. In the end, the losses reached 3.4 billion deutsche marks before German banks with shares in the firm recapitalized the company at significant cost.

Finally, those favoring universal banking point to the European experience as a possible model for the United States. Although Europeans sometimes raise concerns about the potential for conflicts of interest, many indicate that they feel that they gain from the ability to engage in "one-stop shopping," conducting all their financial dealings at a single banking institution. So far, there has been little evidence that banks in nations with universal banking are significantly more risky than U.S. counterparts. In fact, one complaint heard from customers of European universal banks is that the banks may be overly stodgy and conservative in their portfolio management strategies.

The U.S. appears on the verge of adopting the European universal-banking model. In 1987, J. P. Morgan Bank found and exploited a loophole in a portion of the Glass–Steagall Act known as "Section 20," which says that a bank may not be affiliated with any firm "engaged principally" in underwriting and dealing in firm securities. J. P. Morgan and two other big banks, Bankers Trust and Citicorp, promptly established "Section-20 affiliates" to engage in the equities business in a limited fashion. The Federal Reserve sanctioned these subsidiaries on condition that they earned no more than 5 percent of their revenues from securities, and more than 20 U.S. banks then established Section-20 affiliates. In 1989 the Federal Reserve raised the limit to 10 percent. By 1996, several U.S. banks were bumping up against that limit, and the Federal Reserve responded by proposing an increase to 25 percent. In 1998, the U.S. Congress responded by passing legislation to repeal several elements of the Glass–Steagall Act.

ON THE WEB
See Federal Reserve Regulations at:
http://www.ny.frb.org/ bankinfo/legal

Secrecy and Taxation

The South American nation of Uruguay has experienced greater per-capita income growth over the past fifteen years than every Latin American country except for Chile. A key to its success has been its provision of services, which account for more than 60 percent of Uruguayan GDP. Banking accounts for a significant portion of Uruguay's service industries. Under Uruguayan law, information about ownership of bank deposits cannot be revealed, and funds held in Uruguayan banks cannot be taxed. This has induced many residents of Argentina, Brazil, Chile, and Paraguay to hold deposits in Uruguayan banks. All told, foreign-owned deposits account for more than one-third of the funds held in banks based in Uruguay.

In achieving its banking successes, Uruguay has stolen a page out of Switzerland's book. Under Swiss law, a banker who betrays a depositor's secret risks six months in jail and fines of as much as 50,000 Swiss francs (about $34,000). In 1993, the Swiss government reacted to a growing international concern about money-laundering in drug trading by waiving the secrecy provisions for certain criminal proceedings. Nevertheless, Swiss banks can still refuse to provide information on depositors to tax authorities, and so Swiss bank accounts remain a haven from taxes. This has helped to make Switzerland a European–and, indeed, a world–banking center.

In many other nations, holders of bank accounts can expose themselves to considerable public scrutiny. In the United States, for instance, banks must report the interest earnings of their depositors, upon which depositors must pay income taxes. Banks also must provide special reports to the federal government if they make particularly large dollar transfers on behalf of their customers. To avoid taxes or make payments without public knowledge, U.S. citizens must resort to cash holdings and cash-based transactions–or they must obtain bank accounts in locales such as Uruguay and Switzerland.

ON THE WEB

Get answers to your questions about Swiss banks at:

http://www.swconsult.ch/ chbanks/index.html

FUNDAMENTAL ISSUE #2

How do national banking systems differ? One key factor that distinguishes national banking systems is the extent to which companies finance their operations via bank loans versus direct placement of debt instruments in financial markets. A second factor is the differences in bank market structures. In some nations, a few relatively large banks dominate national loan and deposit markets, whereas in others many banks compete. Another important difference among national banking systems is the extent to which universal banking takes place. Universal banking is widespread in Europe, but in the United States and other nations banking activities typically are more restricted. Finally, nations have different laws regarding secrecy and tax treatment of bank accounts.

BANK REGULATION AND CAPITAL REQUIREMENTS

Clearly, different legal and tax treatments of bank accounts can influence the structure of national banking systems. Indeed, general regulatory frameworks established by national authorities play a considerable part in explaining differences among banking systems around the globe. Before we discuss some of the key aspects of international banking regulation, let's first address why national governments regulate banks in the first place.

The Goals of Bank Regulation

The common rationale for governmental supervision and regulating of banking institutions is that leaving these institutions to their own devices might result in socially undesirable outcomes, such as banking panics, losses of people's savings, and business collapses. Actual national experiences with such events have led to today's broad systems of national banking regulations.

INSOLVENCY A situation in which the value of a bank's assets falls below the value of its liabilities.

Limiting the Scope for Bank Insolvencies and Failures   A key objective of bank regulation, therefore, is to reduce the potential for widespread failures of banking institutions. A bank reaches a point of **insolvency** if the value of its assets falls below the value of its liabilities, so that its equity, or net worth, is negative. In the absence of governmental action to keep an insolvent bank operating, the bank must declare bankruptcy and halt its operations.

A common feature of bank regulation worldwide is the periodic *examination* of banks' accounting records to verify that the institutions are solvent. Another typical feature of bank regulation is the *supervision* of these institutions via the establishment and enforcement of rules and standards that banks must follow and meet.

Maintaining Bank Liquidity   In most countries, banks issue liabilities, such as checking and savings accounts, that function as means of payment or from which customers can withdraw funds on very short notice. An individual bank that has insufficient funds available to meet the cash requirements of its depositors is *illiquid*. If a significant portion of a nation's banking system were illiquid, then there could be adverse effects on the country's flow of payments for goods and services. In the short term, this could depress the nation's gross domestic product.

Consequently, a further objective of bank regulation is to reduce the potential for episodes of widespread bank illiquidity. Governmental regulators thereby conduct bank examination and supervision with this additional goal in mind. Distinguishing illiquidity and insolvency is not always an easy task, however. A bank can experience short-term liquidity problems while remaining solvent, just as someone as wealthy as Donald Trump might lack sufficient ready cash to pull off a big business deal without the aid of other investors. Nevertheless, a bank on the verge of insolvency typically experiences illiquidity. Thus, efforts by government regulators to keep banks liquid sometimes end up perpetuating the lives of insolvent banks that actually should close (see the "Policy Notebook: Bank Bailouts Worldwide"). This is a key rationale that national regulators often give for conducting periodic examination of banks' accounting ledgers.

Promoting an Efficient Banking System   The final goal of bank regulation is to promote low-cost provision of banking services and the banks' attainment of **normal profits.** These are levels of profit just sufficient to compensate bank owners for holding equity shares of banks instead of other businesses.

A basic problem that national bank regulators must confront is the potential for their three regulatory objectives to conflict. On the one hand, one way to improve the likelihood of high bank liquidity and solvency is through a regulatory system that protects existing banks from additional rivalry for customers, thereby allowing banks to earn above-normal profits. On the other hand, a regulatory environment that promotes considerable competition would give banks an incentive to operate efficiently, yet their profit margins might be so low that unexpected declines in economic activity could bring about bouts of bank illiquidity or insolvency. Hence, a nagging issue for any country's banking regulators is deciding to what extent one objective may need to be sacrificed if another is to be attained.

NORMAL PROFIT A profit level just sufficient to compensate bank owners for holding equity shares in banks rather than other enterprises.

ON THE WEB
See the Bank of England's objectives of supervision at:
http://www.bankofengland.co.uk/

FUNDAMENTAL ISSUE #3

What objectives do national banking regulators seek to achieve?
One typical goal of bank regulation is to prevent banks from becoming insolvent, or from having negative net worth. Another regulatory goal is to keep banks from becoming illiquid, or lacking sufficient cash assets to meet the needs of their depositors. A third regulatory goal is for banks to operate at low cost and at normal levels of profit.

Bank Capital Requirements

Since the late 1980s, a major focus of bank regulation has been on bank capital positions, or the extent to which the financial stakes of bank shareholders provide a cushion against losses. In 1989 the regulators of banks in most advanced-market-based economies gathered at the Bank for International Settlements in Basel, Switzerland, to announce a system of **risk-based capital requirements.** As its name indicates, this international program for bank capital standards intends to account for varying asset risk characteristics into the calculation of required bank capital. Under the Basel capital standards, currently followed by thirty-five nations, banks must compute ratios of capital in relation to their **risk-adjusted assets.** This is a weighted average of all the bank's assets, in which the weights reflect regulators' perception of distinctive asset risks.

RISK-BASED CAPITAL REQUIREMENTS Regulatory capital standards that account for different risk factors that distinguish banks' assets.

RISK-ADJUSTED ASSETS A weighted average of bank assets that regulators compute to account for risk differences across assets.

Bank Bailouts Worldwide

Countries do not always share the same cultures, languages, or political systems. One thing, however, that countries all over the world do have in common is their recent propensity to experience major banking catastrophes. The Argentinian government's efforts to recover from a banking crisis in the early 1980s probably cost more than half of that country's GDP. In the United States, the final bill for the government-arranged bailout of the nation's savings and loan industry during the early 1990s totaled at least $200 billion. Between 1992 and 1993, Norway's government effectively purchased more than half of its nation's banking system to keep it financially afloat, and in 1992 the government of Sweden took control of two of the country's four largest banking institutions.

Since 1994, Venezuela has spent more than 20 percent of its nation's annual output repairing its banking system, and the cost of Mexico's 1995 banking collapse has been estimated at nearly 15 percent of that country's output. In Japan, more than $250 billion in bank loans soured in 1995 when home-mortgage companies known as *jusen* went bankrupt following a collapse in Japanese real-estate prices. In 1996, Bulgaria's banking system imploded and had to be rescued by the country's government. In 1998, South Korea's banking system also teetered on bankruptcy, as more than 10 percent of all loans by that country's banks—nearly $25 billion, or the combined market value of all South Korean banks—were "nonperforming," meaning that the banks will be lucky to recover significant portions of the principal amounts of the loans. In India, nearly a fifth of the loans extended by 27 government-owned banks are nonperforming loans, and the Bank of China estimates that about the same portion of Chinese bank loans also are nonperforming.

The International Monetary Fund estimates that since 1980, 133 of 181 IMF member nations have suffered banking problems that it judges to be "significant." Moody's Investors Service, which rates the riskiness of banks in 61 nations on a scale ranging from A (best risk) to E (worst risk), has determined that 31 countries have "average banks" that rate D or E.

Why have so many countries' banking systems faltered in recent decades? There are two basic viewpoints on this issue. One is that banking is an inherently unstable business whose fortunes ebb and flow with the performances of national economies. From this perspective, government regulation and "safety nets," such as deposit insurance or "last-resort" governmental lending agencies, must be put in place to prevent periodic banking collapses from taking place.

Another argument, however, is that governmental safety nets themselves may be responsible for recent banking crises. According to this view, if bankers know that governments stand ready to bail them out if their "bets" should turn sour, then they have every incentive to make highly profitable loans whose yields include hefty risk premiums. Thus, goes this argument, banking safety nets create moral hazard problems for taxpayers, who ultimately must back up governmental guarantees.

FOR CRITICAL ANALYSIS:
Even critics of governmental deposit insurance programs tend to agree that if such insurance systems are established, all banks should be required to participate and pay required insurance premiums. Can you think of a justification for this argument? [Hint: Think about the adverse selection problem that might exist if banks had the option of paying to participate in a deposit insurance program or of not participating at all.]

ON THE WEB
Learn more about the South Korean economy at:
http://www.ait.ac.th/Asia/infokr.html

OFF-BALANCE-SHEET BANKING Bank activities that earn income without expanding the assets and liabilities that they report on their balance sheets.

CORE CAPITAL Defined by the Basel capital standards as shareholders' equity plus retained earnings.

TOTAL CAPITAL Under the Basel bank capital standards, this is the sum of core capital and supplementary capital.

SUPPLEMENTARY CAPITAL A measure that many national banking regulators use to calculate required capital, which includes certain preferred stock and most subordinated debt.

CAPITAL REQUIREMENTS Minimum equity capital standards that national regulatory agencies impose on banks.

Computing Required Capital In the computation of risk-adjusted assets, cash assets and most government securities receive zero weight and hence, do not count, because regulators view these as relatively risk-free assets. Assets that regulators view as having a slight possibility of default, such as interbank deposits, bonds issued by cities, states, or regions, and partially government-guaranteed securities, receive a weight of 20 percent. Somewhat more risky but highly collateralized assets, such as the bulk of private mortgage loans, receive a weight of 50 percent. All other loans and securities receive a 100 percent weight. Additionally, national banking regulators calculate "credit exposure dollar equivalents" for **off-balance-sheet banking.** These are banking activities, such as derivatives trading, that do not affect the reported assets and liabilities of banks but that expose banks to risk of loss. Regulators assign a risk weight of 10 percent to most off-balance-sheet activities. After computing these various weighted figures, regulators sum them together to obtain an individual bank's total risk-adjusted assets. This weighted sum constitutes the denominator of capital ratios that banks must satisfy.

Under the Basel capital standards, banks must compute two ratios of capital relative to risk-adjusted assets. The ratios are based on two separate capital *tiers*. The first, "Tier 1 capital," or **core capital,** is equal to the sum of common shareholders' equity (shares of stock held by voting stockholders) and retained earnings (income not paid out to shareholders). A bank's **total capital** is equal to core capital plus "Tier 2 capital," or **supplementary capital.** This latter measure includes some types of preferred stock (stock shares held by nonvoting stockholders) and most types of subordinated debt.

The Basel **capital requirements** apply to both banks and their parent companies. Banks must satisfy two specific minimum capital ratio requirements: (1) the ratio of core capital to risk-adjusted assets must exceed 4 percent, and (2) the ratio of total capital to risk-adjusted assets must be greater than 8 percent. In addition, banks' parent companies must meet a simple ratio standard in which the ratio of total capital to *total, risk-unadjusted assets* must exceed 4 percent.

To understand the effect of adjusting assets for risk when applying capital requirements, think about a situation in which two U.S. banks each have $15 million in assets. One bank has $1 million in cash, $2 million in government securities, and $12 million in loans to businesses. The bank has $0.5 million in common stockholders' equity and retained earnings and $1 million in subordinated debt. Hence, its core capital is $0.5 million, and its total capital is $1.5 million. The $3 million in cash and Treasury securities do not count toward its risk-adjusted assets. Its $12 million in commercial loans count 100 percent, and so its total risk-adjusted assets equal $12 million. Consequently, its ratio of core capital to risk-adjusted assets is equal to $0.5 million / $12 million, or about 4.2 percent. Its ratio of total capital to risk-adjusted assets is equal to $1.5 million/$12 million, or about 8.3 percent. Its unadjusted capital ratio is $1.5 million/$15 million, or about 10.0 percent. This bank meets the required capital standards.

Now consider a second bank that also has $15 million in assets. This bank, however, has $0.5 million in cash, $0.5 million in securities, and $14 million in commercial loans. Furthermore, the second bank engages in enough off-balance-sheet activities to merit a "credit exposure dollar equivalent" rating of $6 million. The second bank, like the first, has $0.5 million in core capital and $1.5 million in total capital. Therefore, the second bank's unadjusted capital ratio is, like that of the first bank, equal to 10.0 percent. Nonetheless, the second bank clearly is in a riskier position, because it has extended more loans and engaged in off-balance-sheet activities. The current risk-based capital standards take this into account. For the second bank, its $1 million in cash and securities do not count toward its risk-adjusted assets, but its $14 million in commercial loans and $6 million in "credit exposure dollar equivalents" from its off-balance-sheet activities count fully, giving it a risk-adjusted asset total of $20 million. This bank's ratio of core capital to risk-adjusted assets is equal to $0.5 million/$20 million, or 2.5 percent. Its ratio of total capital to risk-adjusted assets is $1.5 million/$20 million, or 7.5 percent. Even though the second bank has the same dollar amounts of assets and capital as the first bank, the second bank fails both the 4 percent and 8 percent standards for core capital and total capital, respectively.

Effects of Capital Requirements   Figure 7–2 shows how the adoption of the risk-based capital standards induced changes in the core capital ratios of U.S. banks. As the figure indicates, the new standards reversed a long trend toward lower capital ratios.

The Basel standards had a significant effect on international banking competition in the late 1990s. During the 1980s, Japanese banks had emerged as global powerhouses, establishing major presences as lenders in Africa, Asia, Europe, the Middle East, South America, Mexico, and even the United States. By 1998, however, Japanese banks were shutting down offices all around the globe. Key reasons for this worldwide cutback, which reinforced one another, were the declining value of the yen in late 1996 and 1997, the simultaneous decline in Japanese stock market prices, and the Basel capital standards. Because the dollar has remained the world's dominant currency, most international customers of Japanese banks prefer to obtain their loans in dollars. Indeed, more than one-fifth of all loans by Japan-based banks were dollar-denominated. The 1997 surge in the dollar's value swelled the *yen*-denominated values of these dollar loans, thereby increasing the value of their loans for purposes of computing their capital requirements. By February 1997, a number of large Japanese banks barely held sufficient capital to meet the risk-adjusted capital ratio requirement of 8 percent. Because their share values also were declining in the Japanese stock market, Japanese banks found their capital ratios squeezed from both directions: rising values of yen assets and declining values of yen-denominated capital measures. They had no choice but to reduce their presence in global lending markets. Indeed, a few large banks had to sell some of their loans, in what some analysts called a great "fire sale." (See "Management Notebook: The Japan Premium.")

FIGURE 7–2 EQUITY AS A PERCENTAGE OF BANK ASSETS IN THE UNITED STATES, 1840–1998

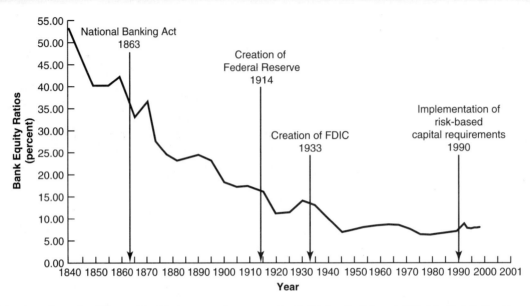

US. bank equity ratios fell considerably between the mid-nineteenth and mid-twentieth centuries. Recently they have risen slightly.

SOURCES: Data from Allen N. Berger, et al. "The Role of Capital in Financial Institutions," in *Journal of Banking and Finance*, 1995; and Federal Deposit Insurance Corporation.

REGULATORY ARBITRAGE
The act of attempting to avoid banking regulations established within one's home country by moving banking offices and funds to nations with less stringent regulations.

Regulatory Arbitrage Why have so many nations joined forces in adopting and enforcing common bank capital standards? One key rationale for this development has been the potential for banks to engage in **regulatory arbitrage.** This is the process by which banks try to escape the effects of regulations imposed by authorities in their home nations by shifting operations and funds to offices in locales where regulatory constraints are less substantial. Because all banks in such nations as Germany, Japan, the United Kingdom, the United States, and more than thirty other countries now must meet the same basic capital requirements, the scope for world regulatory arbitrage has declined significantly. In addition, the coordination of bank capital standards helped to ensure that major banks would not face competitive advantages or disadvantages in international competition for loans and deposits.

Despite international regulation, there are still structural differences across national banking systems and regulations. As discussed earlier, considerable numbers of idiosyncrasies remain in place in various nations. Nevertheless, banking functions, structures, and regulations around the world are becoming more, rather than less, similar with each passing year.

MANAGEMENT NOTEBOOK

The "Japan Premium"

Even though Table 7–1 shows that Japanese banks dominate the listing of the world's largest banks, the end of the twentieth century was not a good time for them. As noted, in the latter 1990s many Japanese banks had to shrink their lending to meet regulatory capital requirements. Others got into trouble as declines in real estate values accompanied the fall in Japanese stock prices, thereby increasing the banks' losses on real estate loans.

One bit of market "fallout" from these problems was the *Japan premium*. During 1997 and 1998, Japanese banks had to pay 0.20 to 0.25 percentage points more for interbank loans, as compared with U.S., British, German, and other Western banks. Two-tenths of a percentage point might not seem like much until one takes into account the hundreds of billions of dollars of worldwide money-market funds that Japanese banks must raise to make loans. For each billion-dollar increment of fund-raising in global money markets, a 0.20 percent "Japan premium" translated into an additional $2 million that Japanese banks had to pay for funds. This extra funding cost, of course, placed Japanese banks at a considerable competitive disadvantage in international lending markets.

FOR CRITICAL ANALYSIS:

If Japanese banks, in the face of the "Japan premium," chose to lend at the same rates as other banks around the world, what was the effect on their profitability?

FUNDAMENTAL ISSUE #4

What are bank capital requirements, and how have national banking regulators implemented these requirements in recent years? Bank capital requirements are minimum permitted standards for shareholder ownership stakes relative to measures of bank assets. Since 1989, bank regulators in thirty-five countries have imposed risk-based capital requirements in which banks must maintain minimal allowable ratios of capital relative to total assets and to risk-adjusted assets.

GLOBAL TRADING AND PAYMENT SYSTEMS

International financial trading and interbank payments increasingly take place electronically. In the United States, although nonelectronic payments media such as cash and checks account for 98 percent of all payments, these media account for less than 15 percent of the *dollar value* of these transactions. This implies that the bulk of large-dollar payments, such as interbank payments, are accomplished via electronic transactions.

This revolution in trading and payments technology has reshaped the technical landscape of international finance. The word *bank* derives from the Italian merchant's bench, or *banco,* across which money changed hands in medieval Europe. In the electronic trading environment of today and the near future, however, this word is becoming a relic of bygone days.

International Financial Trading Systems

FINANCIAL TRADING SYSTEMS Institutional mechanisms linking traders of financial instruments.

What do CORES, MATIF, and CATS all have in common? They are fully automated **financial trading systems,** or institutional structures that link buyers and sellers of financial instruments such as government securities and corporate bonds and stocks, thereby permitting them to initiate exchanges of these instruments. CORES, or the Computer-Assisted Order Routing and Execution System, is a trading system based in Tokyo. MATIF, or the Marché à Terme International de France, is located in Paris; and CATS is the Toronto-based Computer-Assisted Trading System. Most other developed nations have similar systems. The Chicago Mercantile Exchange (CME) in the United States operates a system known as "Globex," and a similar system called "Soffex" operates in Switzerland. All these trading systems—plus others in such locales as Denmark, Singapore, Sweden, and the United Kingdom—share the common feature that they permit traders in financial markets to place orders for purchases and sales of securities via computers.

ON THE WEB
Visit MATIF at:
http://www.matif.fr

Mechanics of Automated Financial Trading   Most nations' automated trading systems have their own special features, but the basic features are similar to those used by the U.S.-based Globex system. Individuals conduct trades on Globex via computer terminals using Globex software programs to call up information on current market terms for many financial instruments, such as futures contracts. The system displays on the trader's computer screen the best bid and offer with the amounts involved, the most recent sale price and quantity traded, and related spot market prices for reference. A trader may then use the computer's keyboard to interact with the system to attempt to make trades via appropriate commands.

For example, if the trader wants to accept a bid for a futures contract, then the trader places a sell order into the system. The system automatically checks to see that this sell order is at a price equal to or less than the buy order and that it is for the same contract for which the earlier bid was made. If these conditions are met, then the system automatically checks to be certain that the quantities of the bid and offer to sell are compatible and that earlier offers to sell have not been received by the system. If so, the system automatically places orders "in line" according to the time the system received them. Finally, the system transmits information on the trade it arranges to the clearing houses of individual exchanges (in the case of a futures contract, the CME) to be executed. Then, the trade is executed.

This is not to say that automatic systems have completely revolutionized futures trading. The CME, the French MATIF, and the Chicago Board of Trade (CBOT) plan to cooperate in developing automatic clearing networks for use during regular trading hours by the beginning of the twenty-first century. One proposed innovation, which has not yet been adopted, would permit traders to use hand-held computers to communicate with the system from trading floors. Currently, floor clerks in exchanges continue to use hand signals to waiting traders or ask another clerk to rush to the trading floor with paper buy or sell orders. Fewer than 10 percent of the CME's and CBOT's regular trading orders reach the trading floor via computer. The CME, MATIF, and CBOT also have proposed further modernization of, or perhaps even a replacement of, the Globex after-hours trading system within the next few years.

Policy Implications of Automated Financial Trading   One clear implication of automated trading is that it allows traders to buy or sell financial instruments at any time of the day—or night. For example, a trader who logs onto the Globex system at 9 P.M. central time, when the CME is closed, may see an acceptable bid price and initiate a transaction on the system. If the trader can transact business at 9 P.M., however, there is no reason that he should confine himself to trading in the Chicago Mercantile Exchange. After all, it is also possible to trade at an exchange in Tokyo, where 9 P.M. in the midsection of the United States is mid-morning in Australia, Hong Kong, Japan, and Singapore.

The globalization of financial markets brought about by automated trading has raised two thorny issues for policy makers. One concerns rules for securities trading on various national trading systems, which typically are similar but not identical. Nations with more demanding requirements for trading in their securities exchanges may incur fewer risks to their systems as globalization of trading continues to take place. At the same time, however, they also may see their exchanges lose business to nations with less stringent rules.

For example, Taiwan has one of the world's busiest and, recently, most volatile stock markets, losing nearly 30 percent of its value in 1995, only to gain much of it back in 1996. Confronted with such volatility, Taiwanese market traders lobbied hard for the development of markets in Taiwanese stock futures and stock options to ease their ability to hedge trading risks without needing to buy or sell individual stocks. In 1997, the Singapore International Monetary Exchange (SIMEX) and the CME began trading futures and options based on Taiwanese stock indices in the face of strong opposition from Taiwan's financial regulators. Although one basis for the opposition might have been the regulators' desire to protect the Taiwan Stock Exchange from competition from SIMEX and the CME, another regulatory complaint was the SIMEX and the CME had looser trading rules than those used in Taiwan. Initially, Taiwan's authorities threatened to stop supplying Taiwanese stock price data to Dow Jones and Morgan Stanley, the companies that compute stock index data for the SIMEX and the CME. Ultimately, however, Taiwanese regulators relaxed their standards so that the Taiwanese Stock Exchange could compete with the other trading systems.

Second, even in areas in which national regulators have agreed about the proper supervisory rules for trading systems, automated trading raises some thorny issues. For example, national authorities almost uniformly express the common view that individual and institutional traders should have equal access to trading systems. Nevertheless, it is infeasible for an individual to stay awake twenty-four hours a day, glued to a computer screen. For large institutions, however, it is simply a matter of employing people in daytime, evening, and night shifts. Consequently, automated trading has the potential to give institutional traders some advantages over individual traders. This has, for example, been a continuing issue for the New York Stock Exchange since it implemented after-hours electronic trading in 1991. Some have argued that this has led to a "two-tiered" stock market in which large traders can gain at the expense of individual traders.

Global Payment Systems

PAYMENT SYSTEM A term that broadly refers to the set of mechanisms by which consumers, businesses, governments, and financial institutions make payments.

Financial trading systems permit traders to execute exchanges of financial instruments. Actual payments of funds, however, take place on **payment systems,** which are institutional structures through which individuals, businesses, governments, and financial institutions process payments of funds for goods, services, or financial assets. Table 7–2 lists the world's largest payment systems and gives data on transactions and flows of funds on these systems. There are several types of payment systems, falling into two broad categories: nonelectronic and electronic.

Nonelectronic Payment Systems   Since the dawning of human society, people have used physical means of payment to accomplish exchanges. The earliest form of exchange was *barter,* or the direct exchange of one good or service for another. Ultimately, this gave way to *monetary exchange,* or the use of a medium of exchange such as standardized units of gold or silver, gold or silver coins, or bank- or government-issued paper currency. In most nations, people continue to use coins and currency for the bulk of exchanges. For instance, U.S. residents use coin and currency for more than three-fourths of the total *number* of exchange *transactions* they make.

When an individual makes a purchase using coins and currency, the transaction is final at the moment that the exchange occurs. In contrast, check transactions are final only after banks transfer funds from the account of the purchaser to the seller. Using checks, therefore, requires parties to a transaction to rely upon banks as *payment intermediaries,* or go-betweens in clearing payments that arise from exchanges of goods, services, or financial assets.

In many nations, checks are the other main noncash form of nonelectronic payment. Other forms of noncash nonelectronic payments include credit card, money order, and paper-based *giro* transactions. Like check-based systems, giro systems, which entail transfer of payment orders between banks and other financial institutions, involve payment intermediaries. Giro systems are

| TABLE 7–2 | TRANSACTIONS AND PAYMENT FLOWS IN MAJOR NATIONAL PAYMENT SYSTEMS | |

COUNTRY/PAYMENT SYSTEM	TRANSACTIONS (THOUSANDS)	VALUE ($ BILLIONS)
France		
SAGITTAIRE	4,500	27,532
Germany		
EIL-ZV	5,500	18,840
EAF	17,800	103,514
Italy		
ME	1,800	11,300
SIPS	4,462	16,807
Japan		
FEYCS	8,839	81,624
BOJ-NET	3,849	434,677
Switzerland		
SIC	95,990	27,235
United Kingdom		
CHAPS	12,596	42,171
United States		
Fedwire	75,900	222,954
CHIPS	51,000	310,021

SOURCE: Data from Bank for International Settlements, *Annual Report*, 1997.

common in both Europe and Asia and link a number of payment intermediaries besides banks, such as post offices.

As Table 7–3 indicates, U.S. residents use paper-based, nonelectronic—mainly check–transactions much more than people in most other nations. An average U.S. resident made 234 such transactions each year in the mid-1990s, which amounted to between about 3 and 100 times more than average residents of other nations.

Electronic Payment Systems   Table 7–3 shows that most non-U.S. residents, except for those in Italy, use electronic means of payment much more regularly, as compared with residents of the United States. There are a number of electronic payment systems. One that has grown considerably in many European nations is *electronic giro* systems, in which banks, post offices, and other payment intermediaries transfer funds by telephone lines or via other forms of electronic communication.

The closest U.S. counterpart to the giro system is the **automated clearing house (ACH),** which is a computer-based clearing and settlement facility for the interchange of credits and debits via electronic messages instead of checks. Typically, U.S. automated clearing houses process payments within one or two days after the request for a funds transfer. Typical forms of ACH transfers are

AUTOMATED CLEARING HOUSE (ACH) A computer-based payments facility that interchanges credits and debits electronically.

**TABLE 7–3   ANNUAL NONCASH TRANSACTIONS PER PERSON
IN SELECTED COUNTRIES**

	NUMBER OF TRANSACTIONS PER PERSON		
COUNTRY	PAPER-BASED	ELECTRONIC	ELECTRONIC PAYMENTS AS PERCENT OF NONCASH TRANSACTIONS
Italy	23	6	20%
Japan	9	31	78
Switzerland	2	65	97
Sweden	24	68	74
Norway	58	40	41
Belgium	16	85	84
United Kingdom	57	58	50
Finland	40	81	67
Denmark	24	100	81
Canada	76	53	41
Germany	36	103	74
Netherlands	19	128	87
France	86	71	45
United States	234	59	20

SOURCE: Data from David Humphrey, et al., "Cash, Paper, and Electronic Payments: A Cross-Country Analysis," in *Journal of Money, Credit, and Banking,* 28, November 1996, Part 2, pp. 914–939.

automatic payroll deposits, in which businesses make wage and salary payments directly into employees' deposit accounts. The U.S. government distributes Social Security benefits via ACH direct-deposit mechanisms and disperses an increasing percentage of welfare and food stamp payments using an *electronic benefits transfer (EBT) system.* The U.S. government's EBT system functions much like an ACH, but to a welfare and food stamp recipient it works much like an ATM, because EBT machines disperse welfare funds or food stamps just as an ATM machine disperses cash.

AUTOMATED TELLER MACHINE (ATM) NETWORKS Bank-operated computer terminals that individuals can use to perform operations such as cash withdrawals.

In the United States, people commonly use **automated teller machine (ATM) networks,** which are depository-institution computer terminals activated by magnetically encoded bank cards. There are more than 90,000 automated teller machines in the United States, and on average consumers undertake roughly 100,000 transactions each year at a typical ATM machine, yielding an annual total of nearly 9 billion total ATM transactions. This makes cash more readily available to U.S. consumers, thereby actually reducing the extent to which they might use alternative media, such as European-type electronic giro systems, to make smaller payments.

POINT-OF-SALE (POS) NETWORKS Systems in which people make payments for retail purchases via direct deductions from their deposit accounts at banks.

Technology has existed since the 1970s for **point-of-sale (POS) networks,** which are systems allowing consumers to make immediate payments via direct deductions from their deposit accounts at depository institutions. POS networks have developed in only a few nations, such as Norway, most likely because of the significant start-up costs of such systems that banks, businesses, and individuals have shied away from incurring. Nevertheless, current trends in the direction of increased consumer use of on-line banking via the Internet could spur greater worldwide interest in POS networks in the future. Although a growing number of U.S. grocery-store chains are making POS systems available to customers, consumer-oriented electronic payments systems process a negligible percentage of the value of U.S. electronic payments.

LARGE-VALUE WIRE TRANSFER SYSTEMS Payments systems such as Fedwire and CHIPS that permit the electronic transmission of large volumes of funds.

Nevertheless, about 85 percent of the *dollar value* of U.S. electronic payments take place via **large-value wire transfer systems.** These U.S. wire transfer systems handle fewer than 1 percent of the total *number* of payment transactions. Thus, they clearly specialize in transferring large sums. Such large-value wire transfer systems also are commonplace in other developed nations and handle the bulk of the values of electronic payment transfers. Among these are the Paris Clearing House, the Bank of Japan-NET system, and the British CHAPS system (see Table 7–2 on page 217).

FEDWIRE A large-value wire transfer system operated by the Federal Reserve that is open to all banking institutions that legally must maintain required cash reserves with the Fed.

In the United States, there are two key large-value wire transfer systems. One is **Fedwire,** which is owned and operated by the Federal Reserve System on behalf of all financial institutions that must hold reserves at Federal Reserve banks. These institutions pay fees to use Fedwire in transferring funds for two key types of transactions. One is *book-entry security transactions,* which are electronic payments for U.S. Treasury securities. The other main type of Fedwire transaction is interbank payments among bank deposit accounts at Federal Reserve banks that involve credit extensions among banks in an interbank market called the *federal funds market.* The average Fedwire payment is just about $4 million. The average daily payment volume on the Fedwire system now is well over $1 trillion ($1,000,000,000,000).

CLEARING HOUSE INTERBANK PAYMENTS SYSTEM (CHIPS) A privately owned and operated large-value wire transfer system linking about 120 U.S. banks, which allows them to transmit large payments relating primarily to foreign exchange and Eurocurrency transactions.

The other major US. large-value wire transfer system is the **Clearing House Interbank Payments System (CHIPS).** This is a privately owned system managed by the New York Clearing House Association, which has nearly a hundred member banks. These banks primarily use CHIPS to transfer funds for foreign exchange and Eurocurrency transactions. The average value of a CHIPS transaction is about $7 million, and the average daily payment flow on the CHIPS system now exceeds $1.5 trillion.

The Bank of Japan's large-value wire transfer system is about the same size as Fedwire and CHIPS and performs similar functions. The same is true of the British CHAPS system, the Paris Clearing House, and other wire transfer systems around the world.

ON THE WEB
Visit CHIPS at:
http://www.chips.org

Efficiency of U.S. Payment System   If you take another look at Table 7–3, you will note that the United States joins Italy in "last place" on the list, in terms of the portion of noncash payments made electronically by the average resident. Economists estimate that the per-unit cost of an electronic payment is between one-third and one-half the cost of a check payment. Consequently, many observers have argued that the widespread use of checks for small and medium-valued U.S. payment transactions implies that the United States is much less efficient in its payments technology, as compared with other developed nations. Estimates are that the total cost of operating a typical country's overall system of payments constitutes about 2 to 3 percent of its gross domestic product, which implies that U.S. residents could incur a sizable social cost if its paper-based check system truly is inefficient.

One main area of recent criticism of the U.S. check system is the heavy involvement of the Federal Reserve System. Most of the Federal Reserve's annual $2 billion budget, 25,000 employees (only about 1,600 of which have job functions related to monetary policy), and small air force of 47 Learjets and cargo planes are devoted to check-clearing services conducted by clearing houses that are owned and operated by the twelve Federal Reserve banks and their twenty-five branches. Even though these Federal Reserve banks earn gross revenues of more than $800 million per year from check-clearing and related services that they perform for private banking institutions, in recent years the Federal Reserve has had trouble covering the costs of providing such services. In some years, the Federal Reserve actually had a net loss on its check-clearing operations.

Some critics have compared the Federal Reserve with the U.S. Postal Service, with Federal Reserve banks increasingly handling $1 to $5 consumer rebate checks and clearing checks for small, rural banks, much as U.S. Post Offices handle large volumes of mail at taxpayer-subsidized rates. According to the critics, the Federal Reserve also has kept the vast U.S. check-based system operating by subsidizing check-clearing operations and inhibiting competition for more efficient, electronic-based systems for small payments, such as European-style giro systems.

Defenders of the Federal Reserve and of the U.S. check system point out that the key economic issue is really social welfare rather than social cost. As a standard of comparison, they point to health expenditures by the United States and other nations. Critics of the volumes of such expenditures complain about their growing shares of nations' levels gross domestic product, without taking into account the potential willingness of people to incur such expenses because they highly value the improved health that such expenses now make possible. Likewise, defenders of the U.S. check system argue, it may be that U.S. residents derive considerable satisfaction from being able to use a payment system that gives them a paper record of every transaction at a per-check cost that is now dramatically lower than in years past. The use of magnetic ink encryption that enables machines to read and sort checks for computer crediting and debiting of accounts, they argue, actually combines elements of both nonelectronic and electronic payment technologies, perhaps capturing the best elements of both. These features of the U.S. check system, they argue, could make it more efficient than the electronic giro systems so widely used in Europe, where many residents otherwise must depend even more fully upon cash for relatively small transactions.

FUNDAMENTAL ISSUE #5 ————

What are the most commonly used financial trading and payment systems? Today people initiate a significant portion of financial transactions on automated trading systems such as Globex. Although people still widely use currency and coins as a means of payment for small transactions, the bulk of the aggregate value of payments take place via payment intermediaries such as banks. Nonelectronic payment systems requiring the use of such intermediaries are paper-based giro and check systems. Electronic payment systems in which payment intermediaries are active participants are electronic giro systems, automated teller machine networks, automated clearing houses, point-of-sale systems, and large-value wire transfer systems.

PAYMENT SYSTEM RISKS AND POLICIES

Central banks are heavily involved in payment systems. As already noted, one reason is that central banks themselves own and manage such systems. In addition, central banks often establish minimum standards for private payment systems. To understand why central banks feel justified in engaging in such supervisory activities, let's begin by discussing the ways in which payment systems produce both private and public risks.

Risk in Payment Systems

There is some element of risk inherent in any financial transaction. For instance, when any retail outlet accepts currency or coins from a customer, there is a remote possibility that the customer's payment might be counterfeit. Nonetheless, a retailer typically accepts currency and coin payments, because the risk of loss is limited to each individual customer and normally involves a relatively small payment value. By way of contrast, the risks incurred in multimillion-dollar transactions on large-value wire transfer systems generally are much greater. For this reason, as we discuss in more detail shortly, central banks have become heavily involved in monitoring and supervising the functioning of large-value payment systems.

Three types of risk naturally arise in any payments system: *liquidity risk, credit risk,* and *systemic risk.* Payment intermediaries such as banks take on such risks on behalf of their fee-paying customers. Central banks commonly regard some of these risks as "special" social risks that require a role for regulation. In the realm of international payments, central banks also are concerned about a particular form of payment system risk known as *Herstatt risk.* Before outlining why central banks might desire to enact policies intended to reduce payment system risks, let's consider each type of risk separately.

Liquidity Risk   You may have noticed that many people are not always punctual in keeping scheduled appointments. Some almost seem to plan on being late to meetings and other engagements. Likewise, many individuals do not always make payments at times that they had promised. This behavior means that those who are to receive promised payments face a risk of loss, perhaps in the form of an opportunity cost, given that late funds could be used for other purposes. In addition, explicit costs could arise from late receipt of a payment. For example, failure to receive a payment at a time it was due could complicate the payment recipient's ability to honor another financial commitment made under the assumption that the payment would arrive on time.

Liquidity risk is the risk that such losses may arise from late receipt of payments. The development of large-value wire transfer systems and other forms of electronic payment systems largely stems from a desire by banks and other payment intermediaries to reduce the amount of liquidity risk by speeding up payment processing. Prior to the advent of modern computer technology that made electronic mechanisms possible, payment intermediaries had to depend on courier or postal services to hand-deliver paper orders for payment. Unanticipated delays in these services exposed payment intermediaries to significant implicit or explicit costs. In contrast, payment intermediaries can initiate wire transfers within minutes, and the actual transfers take place nearly instantaneously.

Credit Risk   A common occurrence in an exchange is for one party to transfer funds before the other party reciprocates with transfer of a good, service, or financial asset. As a result, the party who transfers the funds essentially extends credit to the other party in the transaction, thereby taking on **credit risk.** This is the possibility that the other party in the exchange ultimately might not honor the complete terms of the exchange.

Payment intermediaries that participate in large-value wire transfer systems have developed intricate systems of rules intended to reduce the exposures to credit risks. These rules detail the responsibilities of both parties to a wire transfer, and they clearly spell out the role of the systems' administrators in mediating disagreements that may arise if parties fail to settle transactions on a timely basis.

In an international context, problems may arise because of different rules and legalities that apply to payments that span national payment systems. For instance, a U.S. payment intermediary may use the CHIPS system to transmit a payment to a Japanese bank that is part of the British CHAPS system. These two large-value wire transfer systems may have slightly different rules about settling payments. Furthermore, the U.S. and British legal systems also may

LIQUIDITY RISK The risk of loss that may occur if a payment is not received when due.

CREDIT RISK The risk of loss that could take place if one party to an exchange were to fail to abide by terms under which both parties originally had agreed to make the exchange.

ON THE WEB
*For more about the
Lamfalussy standards, see:*
**http://www.chips.org/
lamfal.html**

have different interpretations of the duties and responsibilities of parties to an exchange. To deal with the potential for such problems in international transactions, central banks of the Group of Ten (G10) nations have developed a common set of rules called *Lamfalussy standards.* These clarify the basic legal payment responsibilities of any payment intermediary that participates in a large-value wire transfer system operated within a G10 nation.

Systemic Risk   Liquidity and credit risks are payment system risks that payment intermediaries assume on an individual basis. Because the payment intermediaries that participate in large-value wire transfer systems are all interconnected, however, the payment intermediaries share some payment system risks. As a result, payment flows among these intermediaries are interdependent. Consider, for instance, a Los Angeles-based bank expecting a wire transfer from a Philadelphia bank at 1:30 P.M. eastern standard time (EST). Based on this anticipation, the Los Angeles bank commits to wire funds to a bank in St. Louis at 1:45 EST. The St. Louis bank, in turn, agrees to wire funds to a Seattle bank at 2:00 EST, using the funds that it anticipates receiving from the Los Angeles bank. Consequently, if the Philadelphia bank fails to deliver the funds promised at 1:30 EST to the Los Angeles bank, the Los Angeles bank might wire legal title to funds to the St. Louis bank at 1:45 EST that are not really in its possession. In addition, if the Philadelphia bank discovers that some event has occurred that will keep it from sending the funds at all that afternoon, then a full chain of payments may take place, even though there are insufficient funds to cover the payments.

In this example, the risk of an inability by the Philadelphia bank to settle its transaction with the Los Angeles bank is a liquidity or credit risk for the latter bank. For the St. Louis and Seattle banks, however, this situation constitutes **systemic risk.** This is a risk that some payment intermediaries, such as the St. Louis and Seattle banks in our example, may not be able to honor financial commitments because of payment settlement breakdowns in otherwise unrelated transactions.

For these payment intermediaries, systemic risk is a negative **externality,** or an adverse spillover effect stemming from transactions in which they were not participants. Another example of a negative externality is air pollution, which can cause those who do not consume the products of manufacturers who pollute the air to incur costs of the polluters actions, nonetheless. Governments often point to the existence of negative externalities as air pollution as a justification for government regulation of the activities of polluters. In like manner, central banks typically cite systemic risk arising from the interdependence of payment intermediaries on large-value wire transfer systems as a justification for their supervision and regulation of these systems.

SYSTEMIC RISK The risk that some payment intermediaries may not be able to meet the terms of payment agreements because of failures by other institutions to settle transactions that otherwise are not related.

EXTERNALITY A spillover from the actions of one set of individuals to others who otherwise are not involved in the transactions among that group.

Herstatt Risk   Systemic risk spans national borders. On June 26, 1974, a German bank called Bankhaus I.D. Herstatt collapsed. When Herstatt failed, German regulators closed the bank at 3:30 P.M. Frankfurt time. That was after the bank had received foreign currency payments from banks based elsewhere in Europe but before the bank had made dollar payments that it owed to banks in the United States. After all the accounting had been unraveled following Herstatt's collapse, U.S. banks determined that they had lost as much as $200 million. The Herstatt episode unsettled U.S. financial markets and payment systems, and several other payment systems in other countries temporarily shut down.

Since this event, bankers have broadly referred to international payment system risks as **Herstatt risk.** This form of risk actually encompasses two types of risk that arise primarily from payments processing relating to foreign-currency transactions between payment intermediaries based in different countries. First, Herstatt risk refers in part to the direct liquidity and credit risks that payment intermediaries face if they enter into agreements to receive payments from institutions based in other nations in different time zones. For the U.S. banks that had to wait for millions of dollars of payments or that lost $200 million outright when Herstatt collapsed in 1974, these direct risks turned out to be significant.

Second, and more broadly, however, Herstatt risk also refers to the systemic risks owing to global linkages among national payment systems. Because of time differences separating large payment intermediaries around the globe, these intermediaries face the potential for events that occur in one time zone, such as the German Herstatt failure, to have broader effects on the functioning of payment systems in another time zone. In this sense, Herstatt risk constitutes an *international externality* that arguably requires the cooperative supervisory and regulatory efforts of many central banks.

HERSTATT RISK Liquidity, credit, and systemic risks across international borders.

Central Banks and Payment Systems

The Herstatt failure was the most dramatic example, to date, of the potential for breakdowns and resulting losses to take place in large-value wire transfer systems. This event led many central banks to begin to reexamine their payment system policies. As we shall discuss, central banks in various parts of the world have reached differing conclusions about the types of policies that are most appropriate for addressing payment system risks.

The U.S. Daylight Overdraft Problem In the United States, a potential source of systemic risk has been the existence of **daylight overdrafts.** These are bank overdrawals of their reserve deposit accounts at Federal Reserve banks that occur when they transmit funds by wire, via Fedwire or CHIPS, that they actually do not yet have in those accounts. As long as the banks can settle their accounts by the end of a given day, they can send such payments even if they do not have funds to honor the payments at the time of transmission.

DAYLIGHT OVERDRAFTS Bank overdrawals of reserve deposit accounts at Federal Reserve banks, which take place when they wire funds in excess of their balances in those accounts.

Figure 7–3 shows the typical pattern of daylight overdrafts by major U.S. banks that engage in this practice. The banks tend to initiate overdrafts beginning at around 10:00 A.M. when significant payment activity first begins. As a result, their reserve account balances at Federal Reserve banks often drop below zero shortly after this time. Around mid-afternoon, total

FIGURE 7-3   DAYLIGHT OVERDRAFTS AT A U.S. BANK

This figure shows the typical pattern of daylight overdrafts for a large U.S. bank. The bank overdraws its reserve account shortly after the regular business day begins. Its overdrafts peak early in the afternoon, and during the remainder of the day the bank begins to receive funds from other sources. By the end of the day, its reserve balance again is positive.

SOURCE: Data from Board of Governors of the Federal Reserve System.

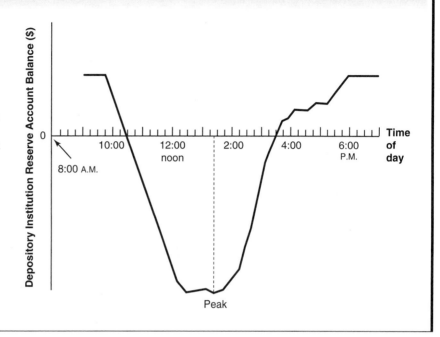

daylight overdrafts reach their "peak," so that the reserve balances of over-drawing banks reach their most negative positions for the day. Then, after overdrawing banks receive transfers of funds from other payment interme-diaries, their reserve account balance at Federal Reserve banks eventually return to positive levels before the day ends.

The aggregate volumes of U.S. daylight overdrafts have been significant sums. Between 1985 and 1990, the average daily peak for daylight overdrafts on both Fedwire and CHIPS combined rose from about $125 billion to over $200 billion, which represented an amount that was nearly three times the size of the total reserves of all U.S. banks. By the early 1990s, it was commonplace for as many as a thousand US. banks to overdraw their Federal Reserve accounts every day.

From the Federal Reserve's perspective, there are two potential problems with daylight overdrafts by U.S. banks. One is the possibility that a U.S. bank might fail to settle on a series of multibillion-dollar overdrafts some day, result-ing in failure to settle by other U.S. banks and a complete payment system breakdown. Hence, the Federal Reserve regards daylight overdrafts as a key source of systemic risk in the United States' large-value wire transfer systems. Another reason that daylight overdrafts concern the Federal Reserve is that overdrafts of reserve accounts essentially amount to loans from Federal Reserve banks to the overdrawing banks. As the owner and operator of Fedwire, the Federal Reserve is the legally responsible party if major settlement failures occur on that payment system. Thus, daylight overdrafts constitute a significant source of credit risk to the Federal Reserve System.

Despite Federal Reserve efforts to hinder daylight overdrafts during the 1980s via various sorts of limitations on permitted volumes of overdrawals, aggregate Fedwire and CHIPS overdrafts continued to grow. For this reason, in April 1994 the Federal Reserve began charging a fee on the amount by which a bank's average per-minute daylight overdraft exceeds a deductible amount equal to 10 percent of the institution's risk-based capital. This deductible recognizes that some daylight overdrafts may be unintentional. From April 1994 until April 1995, this fee on an eighteen-hour basis was equal to eighteen **basis points,** where one basis point equals 0.01 percent. Thus, the initial fee amounted to an interest charge of one-tenth of one percent (0.10 percent).

BASIS POINT One hundredth of one percent.

Figure 7–4 shows that this policy induced U.S. banks to reduce their average and peak overdrafts substantially. Even though one-tenth of one percent does not sound like a sizable fee, this interest charge applies to a single day. Over the course of a year, this fee amounts to an interest charge close to 30 percent that applies if a bank persistently overdraws its account at a Federal Reserve bank. This gave banks clear incentives to reduce their Fedwire and CHIPS overdrafts. To try to cut aggregate daylight overdrafts even further, in April 1995 the Fed increased the fee to twenty-seven basis points. It remains at this level.

FIGURE 7–4   AVERAGE AND PEAK DAYLIGHT OVERDRAFTS AT FEDERAL RESERVE BANKS

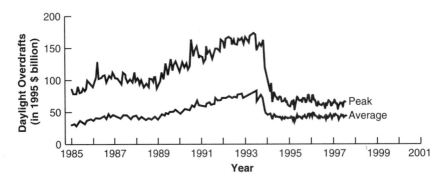

This figure shows the average and peak amounts of reserve account overdrafts by depository institutions at all twelve Federal Reserve banks. The Federal Reserve's imposition of a fee on such overdrafts in April 1994 induced a sharp reduction in total overdrafts. Nevertheless, depository institutions continue to overdraw their accounts by tens of billions of dollars each day.

SOURCES: Data from Board of Governors of the Federal Reserve System; and Diana Hancock and James Wilcox, "Intraday Bank Reserve Management: The Effects of Caps and Fees on Daylight Overdrafts," in *Journal of Money, Credit, and Banking*, 28, November 1996, Part 2, pp. 870–908.

An Intraday Funds Market? When the Federal Reserve implemented its interest charge on daylight overdrafts, some economists speculated that the policy might spur the development of an *intraday funds market,* in which banks would lend sums to each other for periods spanning a few hours within a day. This does not appear to have occurred, however, which Federal Reserve critics see as an indication that the Federal Reserve's current interest charge on daylight overdrafts is below the interest rate that an unhindered private market would yield.

The main experience with intraday lending has been in Japan, where daylight overdrafts also have occurred. Before market interest rates in that country fell to very low levels in the mid-1990s, Japanese banks often negotiated interest surcharges on overnight loans that were not repaid at the time that they were due the next day. For example, failure to repay an overnight loan due at 10 A.M. the following day would subject the borrower to additional interest payments applying to periods beyond that hour. This surcharge effectively amounted to an intraday interest charge.

Net Payment Settlement versus Real-Time Gross Settlement The European approach to payment system policymaking has been much different than in the United States and Japan. The large-value wire transfer systems in these latter two countries have generally used *net payment settlement,* in which banks send payments to each other at various times during the day but settle their accounts vis-à-vis one another only at the end of the day. The failure of payment transmissions to match up with receipts thereby leads to daylight overdrafts.

In Europe, by way of contrast, most large-value wire transfer systems aim to achieve *real-time gross settlement,* in which a payment directly alters a bank's reserve account at the moment the system transmits the payment. In a real-time gross settlement system, therefore, a daylight overdraft cannot occur. If a bank incurred a daylight overdraft, then it would officially exhaust its reserve balances, requiring the bank to convert other assets into cash to make good on the payment it had made. The Swiss SIC system has been at the forefront of efforts to achieve real-time gross settlement. Other European nations, such as the United Kingdom, Italy, and Germany, have begun to institute computer technology to make second-by-second monitoring of payments and bank reserve balances possible (see "Policy Notebook: Are European Payment-System Policies on 'TARGET'?").

Although real-time gross settlement systems eliminate daylight overdrafts, they accomplish this at the cost of reduced liquidity. The ability to make daylight overdrafts permits U.S. and Japanese banks to make the speediest possible transmission of payments. In a real-time gross settlement system, however, a bank is not able to send a payment until it is certain that it has the funds on hand. This may require the bank to wait for additional minutes or hours to receive payments due from others in the payment system before it transmits its own payment messages. Thus, real-time gross settlement can slow the processing of payments. This tends to undercut a key advantage of electronic payment systems, which has been their great speed and liquidity.

POLICY NOTEBOOK

Are European Payment-System Policies on "TARGET"?

The key to the European Union's plans to institute real-time gross payment settlement is the Trans-European Automated Real-time Gross-settlement Express Transfer (TARGET) system. The TARGET system, which has a target completion date of 1999, will handle large-value payments among current European central banks and the planned European Central Bank. This system will permit these institutions to transmit funds exchanges nearly instantaneously, thereby allowing real-time gross settlement.

It remains to be seen whether the central banks of Europe can agree either about the primary purpose of TARGET or even about what central banks will have access to the system. Officials of the German Bundesbank, the Bank of France, and the Bank of England have been embroiled in a dispute over these issues that has spilled over into public view. German and French central banking officials contend that TARGET should play a key role in the conduct of European-wide monetary policy once European nations adopt a single currency. The reason, they argue, is that intraday credit provided to banks via TARGET could influence the aggregate European money stock. Thus, the Germans and French argue, only the central banks of those nations opting to join the proposed European Monetary Union should have access to the system.

British officials, in contrast, argue that TARGET's main function should be efficient payment processing. Monetary policymaking, they contend, is independent from European payment-system issues. As a result, TARGET should, from the British point of view, be open to all nations in the European Union.

The disagreement about TARGET has major implications for the functioning of the payment systems of Europe. In addition, however, it does not bode well for future European efforts to coordinate other technical banking operations, such as settlements of foreign exchange and securities transactions.

FOR CRITICAL ANALYSIS:

What would be the main advantage, from the perspective of overall systemic risk in Europe, of a full-scale adoption of the TARGET system for the entire European Union?

Essentially, the operation and regulation of large-value wire transfer systems entails choosing a point along a trade-off between systemic risk and payment system liquidity. The most liquid payment systems are net settlement systems that permit banks to send funds as quickly as possible, but these systems permit daylight overdrafts that magnify systemic risks. The least risky payment systems, from a systemic perspective, are real-time settlement systems that constrain banks to match receipts and payments of funds, thereby reducing overall payment system liquidity.

FUNDAMENTAL ISSUE #6

What are payment system risks, and how have central banks sought to contain these risks? Payment system risks that payment intermediaries face on an individual basis include liquidity risk, or the possibility of incurring losses as a result of delayed receipt of payments, and credit risk, or the possibility that another party may fail to honor fully the terms of a transaction. Systemic risk is the possibility that payment settlement failures among some payment intermediaries may cause further failures in payment settlement among others, potentially resulting in the breakdown of the payment system as a whole. Herstatt risk refers broadly to liquidity, credit, and systemic risks that arise specifically from the international transmission of payments. To help contain liquidity and credit risks, central banks of the most developed nations have agreed on relatively uniform standards of conduct for payment system participants. In the United States, the Federal Reserve has sought to contain systemic risk by limiting daylight overdrafts on the Fedwire and CHIPS systems. European central banks have further limited systemic risk by inducing the adoption of real-time gross settlement of payments.

CHAPTER SUMMARY

1. **The Existence of Financial Intermediaries and the Process of International Financial Intermediation:** A key reason that financial intermediaries exist is to address problems arising from asymmetric information. One such problem is adverse selection, or the potential for the least creditworthy borrowers to be the most likely to seek to issue financial instruments. Another is moral hazard, or the possibility that an initially creditworthy borrower may undertake actions that reduce its creditworthiness after receiving funds from a lender. Another reason for the existence of financial intermediaries is the existence of economies of scale, or the ability to spread costs of managing funds across large numbers of savers. A potential justification for international financial intermediation by global banking enterprises is that they may experience economies of scale in information processing by spreading their credit evaluation and monitoring operations across the world.

2. **How National Banking Systems Differ:** An important feature that induces differences among national banking systems is the degree to which firms fund their operations through borrowings from banks, as compared with directly issuing debt instruments in financial markets. Another key factor is that a small number of relatively large banks dominate national loan and deposit markets in some countries, whereas in other nations bank market structures display greater rivalry among larger numbers of banking institutions. In addition, universal banking is more common in some regions of the world than it is in others, in which the scope of permissible banking activities often is more restricted. Finally, different laws concerning secrecy and tax treatment of banking accounts can lead to differences in the functioning of national banking systems.

3. **The Objectives that National Banking Regulators Seek to Achieve:** A key regulatory goal is the prevention of bank insolvency, or negative net worth. An additional objective is the prevention of widespread bank illiquidity, or general inability of banks to meet the cash requirements of their depositors. A third regulatory goal is to induce banks to operate at low cost and at normal profit levels.

4. **Bank Capital Requirements and Their Implementation in Recent Years:** Bank capital requirements are minimum standards that national bank regulators impose for shareholder ownership shares in relation to bank asset measures. Currently, bank regulators in thirty-five nations require banks based in their countries to meet risk-based capital standards. Under these requirements, banks must maintain minimal allowable ratios of capital relative to total assets and to risk-adjusted assets.

5. **The Most Commonly Used Financial Trading and Payment Systems:** Currently, traders initiate and undertake many financial exchanges using automated trading systems. Currency and coins continue to predominate as a means of payment in small-value trades for goods, services, and financial assets. Nevertheless, most of the total value of payments are intermediated by institutions such as banks. Non-electronic payments transmitted via payment intermediaries are paper-based giro transfers and check transactions. Today payment intermediaries increasingly participate in electronic payment systems, such as electronic giro systems, automated clearing houses, automated teller machine networks, point-of-sale systems, and large-value wire transfer systems.

6. **Payment System Risks and Central Bank Approaches to Containing These Risks:** An individual payment system participant faces liquidity risk, which is the potential for losses to arise from delayed payment receipts, and credit risk, which is the potential for another party in a payment transaction to live up to the terms of the exchange. Systemic risk is the potential for the failure of some payment intermediaries to settle their transactions to result in further payment settlement failures. Herstatt risk is a general term for liquidity, credit, and systemic risks that payment intermediaries face when they transmit payments across national borders. To limit the extent of liquidity and credit risks, many central banks have agreed to institute somewhat uniform responsibilities for payment system participants. The Federal Reserve has tried to restrain systemic risk on the Fedwire and CHIPS systems by limiting daylight overdrafts on these systems. European central banks have reduced systemic risk further by promoting real-time gross payment settlement.

QUESTIONS AND PROBLEMS

1. Why might a U.S. resident choose to hold a deposit in a U.S. bank that allocates a significant portion of its assets to international loans and securities, instead of making such loans or purchasing such securities personally?

2. In your view, what does a Dutch resident gain, relative to a U.S. resident, from the fact that there are only a few banking institutions offering deposit accounts in the Netherlands? What does a Dutch resident potentially lose? Explain your reasoning.

3. In your view, what does a German resident potentially gain, relative to a U.S. resident, from the fact that universal banking is permitted in Germany but currently is sharply restricted in the United States? What does a German resident potentially lose? Explain your reasoning.

4. Do you view high levels of bank secrecy in Uruguay and Switzerland as socially desirable? Why or why not?

5. In your own words, explain why U.S. banking regulations may have helped to produce the current environment in which there are more than 9,000 banks in the United States.

6. Suppose that a Japanese bank has total assets of 1,000 million yen. Of these assets, 80 percent are loans to businesses, and the remainder are holdings of cash assets and government securities. The bank engages in derivatives trading that Japanese regulators assign a credit equivalence exposure value of 400 million yen. The bank's equity capital amounts to 100 million yen, and the bank has no subordinated debt. Does this bank meet current capital requirements?

7. In your own words, define a negative externality. Explain how such externalities can arise in a nation's payment system.

8. How do daylight overdrafts cause both credit and systemic risks of concern to a central bank? In light of the Federal Reserve's concerns about this issue, can you rationalize why the Federal Reserve does not simply *ban* such overdrafts? Do you think that the Federal Reserve could enforce such a policy? Explain.

ON-LINE APPLICATION

Internet URL: http://www.bis.org

Title: Statistics on Payment Systems in the Group of Ten Countries

Navigation: Begin with (**http://www.bis.org**). In the left margin, click on *Publications* and then click on *Committee on Payment and Settlement Systems*. Scan down the publications list and click on *Statistics on Payment Systems in the Group of Ten Countries*. Download the entire PDF file, which contains tables payment-system data for G10 countries listed in alphabetical order, and answer the following questions.

Application: You can use the data in this report to make a number of cross-country comparisons. Here, let's focus on comparing the relative use of checks and automated teller machines (ATMs) in Belgium and the United States.

1. Look at Table 1 ("Basic statistical data") for Belgium (the first country in the report) and the United States (the last country in the report). On a separate sheet of paper, write down each nation's population in the latest available year, and write down the average exchange rate for the Belgian franc, or "BEF," (given in francs per dollar) for that year. Next, scroll to Table 13 ("Indicators of use of various cashless payment instruments: value of transactions") for each country. What was the *dollar value* of total checks (spelled "cheques" in the tables) issued in each nation during this year (use the average BEF exchange rate for the year to convert the Belgian value of checks issued into dollars)? What was the average *per-capita dollar value* of checks issued in each nation (divide each nation's dollar value of checks issued by its population)? Based on your per-capita figures, in which of the two nations are checks a relatively more important means of payment for the average resident?

2. Now consider Table 6 ("Cash dispensers, ATMs, and EFTPOS terminals") for each nation. For the most recent year, what was the total *dollar value* of all transactions on ATMs in each country? What was the average *per-capita dollar value* of ATM transactions in each nation? Based on your per-capita figures, in which of the two nations are ATM transactions a more common means of transferring funds?

REFERENCES AND RECOMMENDED READINGS

Altunbas, Yener, and Philip Molyneux. "Cost Economies in EU Banking Systems." *Journal of Economics and Business,* 48 (August 1996): 217–230.

Fokerts-Landau, David, Peter Garber, and Dirk Schoenmaker. "The Reform of Wholesale Payment Systems and Its Impact on Financial Markets." *International Monetary Fund Working Paper.* WP/96/37, April 1996.

Frankel, Allen, and David Palmer. "The Management of Financial Risks at German Nonfinancial Firms: The Case of Metallgesellschaft." Paper Presented at the Federal Reserve Bank of Chicago Conference on Bank Structure and Competition, May 1997.

Frieden, Jeffrey. *Banking on the World.* Blackwell: Oxford, 1989.

Giddy, Ian, Anthony Saunders, and Ingo Walter. "Alternative Models for Clearance and Settlement: The Case of the Single European Market." *Journal of Money, Credit, and Banking,* 28 (November 1996, Part 2): 986–1001.

Hall, Brian, and David Weinstein. "Bank versus market Based Financial Systems: Evidence from Financial Distress in Japan and the United States." Paper Presented at the Federal Reserve Bank of Chicago Conference on Bank Structure and Competition, May 1997.

Hancock, Diana, and James A. Wilcox. "Intraday Management of Bank Reserves: The Effects of Caps and Fees on Daylight Overdrafts." *Journal of Money, Credit, and Banking,* 28 (November 1996, Part 2): 870–909.

Humphrey, David B., Lawrence B. Pulley, and Jukka M. Vesala. "Cash, Paper, and Electronic Payments: A Cross-Country Analysis." *Journal of Money, Credit, and Banking,* 28 (November 1996, Part 2): 914–939.

Lindgren, Carl-Johan, Gillian Garcia, and Matthew I. Saal. *Bank Soundness and Macroeconomic Policy.* Washington, D.C.: International Monetary Fund, 1996.

The Economist. "Survey: Financial Centers," (May 9, 1998).

Unit Three

CENTRAL BANKS, EXCHANGE RATES, AND BALANCE-OF-PAYMENTS DETERMINATION

THE ROLE OF CENTRAL BANKS

FUNDAMENTAL ISSUES

1. What are the main assets and liabilities of central banks?

2. Who owns and manages central banks?

3. What are the primary functions of central banks?

4. What are key perspectives about the appropriate duties of central banks?

5. How do central banks intervene in foreign exchange markets?

6. How effective are foreign exchange interventions?

It is a wintry Philadelphia evening in late 1790. Thirty-five-year-old Alexander Hamilton, former aide-de-camp of George Washington, co-author of The Federalist Papers, *and now the first U.S. Treasury secretary, is engaged in a desperate battle with Secretary of State Thomas Jefferson and U.S. Representative James Madison (another co-author of* The Federalist Papers) *for Washington's mind. Hamilton seeks the establishment of the Bank of the United States, a national bank that he has modeled after the Bank of England. He has crafted his proposal after years of intellectual study of how a central bank may be able influence the general levels of money and credit in an economy.*

Hamilton is drafting reports to the U.S. House of Representatives. He furiously searches for the right words to convince skeptical members of the fledgling republic's Congress that the U.S. economy will benefit from the establishment of a banking system with a "national" bank at its center. Finally, he dips his pen into a bottle of ink and writes that the Bank of the United States could, through proper use of its proposed powers, help an otherwise "dead stock" of funds to "acquire life, or in other words, an active and productive quality." Hamilton concludes that, "by contributing to enlarge the mass of industrious and commercial enterprise," his proposed bank and other private banks in the new republic would "become nurseries of national wealth."

Weeks later, Hamilton's reports convince Congress to enact a law establishing the bank. Shortly thereafter, Hamilton defeats Jefferson and Madison in another "war of the pen" and convinces Washington not to veto the law. The American republic's first experiment with a "national" bank begins.

In 1790, Hamilton's ideas about central banking represented a minority view, and he realized this. After all, England and Sweden were the only nations in the world with central banks. Consequently, Hamilton was careful to appeal to the interests of farmers, shopkeepers, and working people who had only recently concluded a long and bloody conflict to achieve independence from a nation with a strong central government. Toward this end, Hamilton sacrificed the idea of the establishing a true central bank in favor of a semi-public banking institution with sharply constrained authority. The best he could hope for was that the Bank of the United States might eventually evolve into a central bank with a level of prestige rivaling that of the Bank of England. Hamilton probably could never have guessed that two centuries hence there would be 170 central banks around the world. Nor is it likely that he could have foreseen that each of these institutions would possess broader powers than he would have dared to propose for the Bank of the United States.

CENTRAL BANK BALANCE SHEETS AND INSTITUTIONAL STRUCTURES

The first central bank was the Swedish Sveriges Riksbank (called the Risens Standers Bank until 1867), which began operations as a state-owned institution in 1668. A charge from the Riksdag, the parliament of Sweden, placed day-to-day management of the Riksbank under control of a commission. Initially, the Riksbank did not issue money, but by 1701 the Riksbank had authority to issue "transfer notes" that basically functioned as a form of currency. In 1789, the Riskdag established a National Debt Office that formally

ON THE WEB
Visit the Swedish Riksbank
at: **http://www.riksbank.se**

issued Swedish government currency, but the Riksbank Act of 1897 made the Riksbank the only legal issuer of currency in Sweden.

In 1694, the British parliament established the Bank of England. It authorized the Bank of England to issue currency notes redeemable in silver. The Bank of England's notes circulated along with other forms of money used at the time, which included notes issued by the government and private finance companies. Until 1800, the Riksbank and Bank of England were the only central banks. The total number of central banks worldwide remained a single digit as late as 1873.

As Figure 8–1 indicates, considerable expansion in the number of central banks occurred beginning in the latter part of the nineteenth century and particularly during the latter part of the twentieth century. Part of this growth stemmed from the establishment of central banks by former colonial states that achieved independence. Although, as we discussed in Chapter 3, some countries have established currency boards, several nations that previously had conducted their monetary and financial dealings without central banks have decided that it is in their best interests to establish these institutions.

FIGURE 8–1   THE NUMBER OF CENTRAL BANKING INSTITUTIONS, 1670–1998

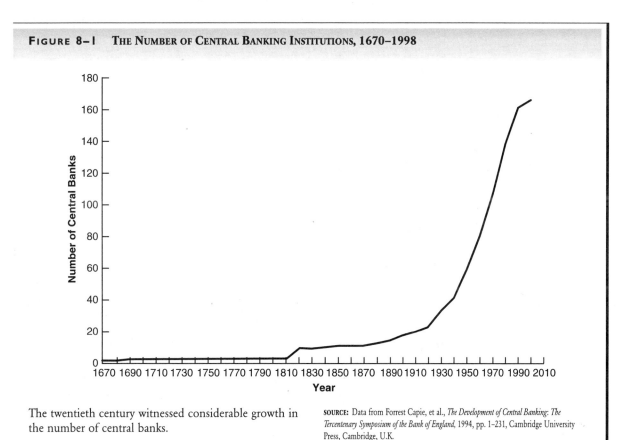

The twentieth century witnessed considerable growth in the number of central banks.

SOURCE: Data from Forrest Capie, et al., *The Development of Central Banking: The Tercentenary Symposium of the Bank of England*, 1994, pp. 1–231, Cambridge University Press, Cambridge, U.K.

Why has nearly every independent nation established its own central bank? Before addressing this question, we first discuss the typical functions of central banks. This will help us to identify the reasons that central banks have become so prevalent.

Central Bank Assets, Liabilities, and Net Worth

The best place to begin any examination of the functions of a central bank is its balance sheet, which is a tabulation of the central bank's assets, liabilities, and net worth. Table 8–1 displays consolidated balance sheets of the three major central banks of the world—the U.S. Federal Reserve, the Bank of Japan, and the German Bundesbank—as of 1998. The table displays dollar, yen, and deutsche mark amounts and percentages relative to total assets and to total liabilities and net worth. Because nominal values of central bank assets, liabilities, and net worth change considerably over time while proportionate allocations tend to remain stable, you should concentrate most attention on the percentages in Table 8–1.

Central Bank Assets Examination of Table 8–1 shows that the balance sheets of the Federal Reserve, the Bundesbank, and the Bank of Japan share some common features. They hold some analogous assets; among these are securities issued by their nations' governments, which account for at least three-fourths of the assets of the Federal Reserve and the Bank of Japan. German government securities account for a smaller proportion of assets at the Bundesbank because of institutional features that we shall discuss later in this chapter.

The remaining assets of the central banks include various types of securities, loans, and certificates of ownership. The Federal Reserve, for instance, lends to private banks via the *discount-window* facilities of the Federal Reserve banks. Banks, in turn, must pay an interest charge, called the **discount rate,** to obtain loans from the Federal Reserve. Panel (*a*) of Table 8–1 indicates that the dollar amount of discount-window lending and proportionate Federal Reserve asset allocation to such lending is very small in comparison with the Bank of Japan and the Bundesbank. Nevertheless, Federal Reserve discount-window lending can be an important aspect of U.S. monetary policy, as we shall discuss later in this chapter. Panels (*b*) and (*c*) show that purchases and sales of private securities such as commercial paper and central bank lending to banks and other financial institutions are much more conspicuous central banking functions in Japan and Germany. As you will learn shortly, this reflects differences in the implementation of monetary policy by the Bank of Japan and the Bundesbank as compared with procedures used by the Federal Reserve.

All three central banks maintain holdings of assets denominated in the currencies of other nations. These are foreign-currency-denominated securities and deposits. As we have noted in earlier chapters, a key reason that central banks hold such securities and deposits is so that they can trade the assets when they wish to try to change the values of their nations' currencies in foreign exchange markets. This will be discussed in greater detail in this chapter.

DISCOUNT RATE The interest rate that the Federal Reserve charges on discount window loans that it extends to depository institutions.

TABLE 8–1 THE CONSOLIDATED BALANCE SHEETS OF THE FEDERAL RESERVE SYSTEM, THE BUNDESBANK, AND THE BANK OF JAPAN

(A) THE FEDERAL RESERVE SYSTEM
($ BILLIONS, AS OF FEBRUARY 28, 1998)

ASSETS			LIABILITIES AND CAPITAL		
ASSET	DOLLAR AMOUNT	PERCENT OF TOTAL ASSETS	LIABILITY	DOLLAR AMOUNT	PERCENT OF TOTAL LIABILITIES AND EQUITY
U.S. Treasury Securities	$ 429.5	87.4%	Federal Reserve Notes	$ 447.1	91.0%
Federal Agency Securities	2.8	0.6%	Bank Reserve Deposits	17.5	3.6%
Loans to Depository Institutions	–	–	U.S. Treasury Deposits	5.0	1.0%
Gold & SDR Certificates	20.3	4.1%	Deferred Credit Items	4.7	1.0%
Foreign Currency Assets	17.2	3.5%	Other Liabilities	5.3	1.0%
Cash Items in Process of Collection	4.5	0.9%	Total Liabilities	479.6	97.6%
Other Assets	16.9	3.5%	Equity Capital	11.6	2.4%
Total Assets	$ 491.2	100.0%	Total Liabilities & Capital	$ 491.2	100.0%

SOURCE: Data from *Federal Reserve Bulletin*, May, 1998, Board of Governors of the Federal Reserve System.

(B) THE BUNDESBANK
(BILLIONS OF DEUTSCHE MARKS, AS OF FEBRUARY 28, 1998)

ASSETS			LIABILITIES AND CAPITAL		
ASSET	DEUTSCHE MARK AMOUNT	PERCENT OF TOTAL ASSETS	LIABILITY	DEUTSCHE MARK AMOUNT	PERCENT OF TOTAL LIABILITIES AND CAPITAL
Domestic Securities and Bills	DM 228.3	62.6%	Currency Notes	DM 252.2	69.2%
Direct Loans to Private Banks	2.6	0.7%	Bank Reserve Deposits	49.3	13.5%
Other Loans	9.4	2.6%	Government Deposits	0.1	–
Gold and SDR Certificates	17.0	4.7%	Other Liabilities	49.3	13.5%
Foreign Currencies and Claims on European Monetary Institute	88.5	24.3%	Total Liabilities	350.9	96.3%
Other Assets	18.7	5.1%	Equity Capital	13.6	3.7%
Total Assets	DM 364.5	100.0%	Total Liabilities & Capital	DM 364.5	100.0%

SOURCE: Data from Deutsche Bundesbank, *Monthly Report*, April 1998.

(C) THE BANK OF JAPAN
(BILLIONS OF YEN, AS OF APRIL 30, 1998)

ASSETS			LIABILITIES AND CAPITAL		
ASSET	YEN AMOUNT	PERCENT OF TOTAL ASSETS	LIABILITY	YEN AMOUNT	PERCENT OF TOTAL LIABILITIES AND CAPITAL
Japanese Government Securities	¥ 58,862	73.5%	Currency Notes	¥ 49,659	62.0%
Loans to Deposit Insurance Corp.	1,851	2.3%	Bank Reserve Deposits	3,961	4.9%
Other Loans	4,150	5.2%	Government Deposits	1,305	1.6%
Bills Purchased and Discounted	4,650	5.8%	Other Liabilities	23,008	28.7%
Foreign Currency Assets	3,137	3.9%	Total Liabilities	77,933	97.2%
Other Assets	7,415	9.3%	Equity Capital	2,132	2.8%
Total Assets	¥ 80,065	100.0%	Total Liabilities & Capital	¥ 80,065	100.0%

SOURCE: Data from Bank of Japan, April 1998.

The *gold certificates* on the Federal Reserve's balance sheet remain from the days when the gold standard was in force (see Chapter 3). During that period, the U.S. Treasury Department sold gold to the Federal Reserve in exchange for money. The U.S. Treasury issued gold certificates to the Federal Reserve to indicate the Federal Reserve's ownership of the gold that the Treasury continued to hold (and still does hold) in reserve. As we discussed in Chapter 3, *Special Drawing Rights (SDR) certificates* are assets issued by the International Monetary Fund (IMF) as a type of international currency intended to compensate for the declining role of gold as a basis for the world's currency system. The U.S. Treasury financed U.S. SDR shares with the IMF by issuing a fixed-dollar amount of SDR certificates to the Federal Reserve. The Bank of Japan and Bundesbank also hold gold and SDR certificates, though in smaller absolute quantities. The amounts of these holdings for the Bank of Japan and Bundesbank are subsumed in the "other assets" categories of panels (*b*) and (*c*).

All central banks receive payments from other parties that they credit to their accounts but that have not yet "cleared" the payments system. Panel (*a*) of Table 8–1 shows these as *cash items in the process of collection,* a term that the Federal Reserve applies because such payments may be subject to cancellation at the time of collection. The amounts of these items for the Bank of Japan and Bundesbank also are subsumed in the "other assets" categories of panels (*b*) and (*c*).

Central Bank Liabilities   At least three-fourths of each central bank's total liabilities and equity capital is composed of *currency notes* (known as "Federal Reserve notes" in the United States). Accountants designate currency notes as liabilities to indicate that the central banks "owe" holders of the notes something in exchange. For instance, if you had sought to redeem a $1 Federal Reserve note at a Federal Reserve bank before the early 1930s, you could have received gold in exchange. Now, however, you would receive a new $1 Federal Reserve note. Likewise, if you turned in yen- or DM-denominated notes to the Bank of Japan or Bundesbank, you also would receive new yen notes or DM notes in exchange. So in what sense are these notes really liabilities? The answer is that if the United States, Japanese, or German governments were to close down their central banks, they would be liable to holders of their notes for the dollar, yen, or deutsche mark value of goods and services at the time of the closures.

Another important liability of the three central banks is bank reserve deposits. Private banks may hold some of these deposits to meet legal requirements established by the central banks. In addition, however, they also hold a portion of these deposits as *excess* reserves to help facilitate check clearing and transactions with the central bank and other private banks, including transfers of funds that they may lend to one another in their nations' **interbank funds markets.** These are markets for very short-term loans among banks. These loans have large denominations and typically have maturities between one day and one week. As we will discuss, the market interest rates on these loans perform important roles in U.S., Japanese, and German monetary policymaking.

INTERBANK FUNDS MARKETS
Markets for large-denomination interbank loans and one-day to one-week maturities.

Table 8–1 also indicates that a common type of deposit liability at all three central banks is government deposits. The U.S. Treasury, Japanese Ministry of Finance, and German Ministry of Finance draw on these deposit funds to make payments such as purchases of goods and services or tax refunds.

The *deferred availability cash items* in panel (*a*) are payments that the Federal Reserve has promised to another party or payments it has made but that have yet to "clear." The Bank of Japan and Bundesbank have analogous liabilities that are subsumed in the "other liabilities" category of panels (*b*) and (*c*).

Like private companies, central banks issue ownership shares. Table 8–1 shows that the Federal Reserve's equity capital is comparatively low in relation to its assets. Another difference not revealed by the numbers in the table is that Federal Reserve equity shares are privately owned, while Bank of Japan and Bundesbank shares are not. Let's turn to this issue next.

FUNDAMENTAL ISSUE #1

What are the main assets and liabilities of central banks? The primary assets of central banks are government securities, loans to private banking institutions, and foreign-currency-denominated securities and deposits. Key central bank liabilities are currency notes and reserve deposits of private banking institutions.

Central Bank Ownership and Organizational Structures

Even though central bank balance sheets are similar, each central banking institution has its own organizational structure. Some governments formally own their central banks, but others do not. In some nations, central banks are a part of the government, but in others central banks have considerable independence from government.

Central Bank Ownership   Central banks may be owned by their nations' governments, they may be privately owned, or they may be owned by both their government and by private individuals, banks, or businesses. As shown in Table 8–2, the German Bundesbank is owned solely by the German government, while private banks that are members of the U.S. Federal Reserve System own all Federal Reserve equity shares. The Japanese government owns 55 percent of the shares issued by the Bank of Japan, and private citizens own the remainder of its equity shares.

Table 8–2 indicates, however, that most governments have at least partial ownership of their nations' central banking institutions. Furthermore, all governments receive at least a portion of the profits generated by central banks. Even though central banks in South Africa and the United States are privately owned, the governments of these nations are entitled to nearly all central bank

---

TABLE 8–2 **THE OWNERSHIP OF CENTRAL BANKS IN SELECTED NATIONS**

STATE OWNERSHIP	PRIVATE OWNERSHIP	MIXED OWNERSHIP*
Argentina	South Africa	Austria (50%)
Australia	Switzerland	Belgium (50%)
Canada	United States	Chile (50%)
Denmark		Greece (10%)
France		Japan (55%)
Finland		Mexico (51%)
Germany		Turkey (25%)
Ireland		Italy**
India		
The Netherlands		
New Zealand		
Norway		
Spain		
Sweden		
United Kingdom		

*Percentages are government ownership shares.
**The Banca d'Italia is publicly incorporated and can only be owned by other public companies.
SOURCE: Data from Forrest Capie, et al., *The Development of Central Banking: The Tercentenary Symposium of the Bank of England,* 1994, pp. 1-231, Cambridge University Press, Cambridge, U.K.

SEIGNIORAGE Central bank profits resulting from the value of a flow increase in a country's money stock over and above the cost of money production.

profit flows. A large part of these profits is **seigniorage,** which is the value of a flow increase in a nation's money stock in excess of the cost of producing the new money. Central banks earn considerable seigniorage, and governments regard seigniorage as a supplement to explicit taxes for funding public expenditures (see "Policy Notebook: Central Bank Profit Sharing–An Impediment to European Monetary Union?"). As noted in Chapter 7, central banks can also earn profits from other central banking operations besides money creation, such as profits from check clearing and other payment-system-related services that they provide to private banks.

Central Bank Organization and Management Table 8–3 provides information about the governing boards that are responsible for managing the affairs of central banks in selected nations. Central banks typically have a chief executive officer. The chief's title–which might be "president," "governor," or "board chairperson"–varies from country to country, as does the individual's term in office. This is also true of other directors who serve on central bank governing boards. As Table 8–3 indicates, qualifying credentials for directors vary among nations.

In most countries, laws enacted by parliaments or congresses specify the structures of central bank governing boards and the selection procedures for

TABLE 8–3 TERMS OF OFFICE AND REQUIREMENTS FOR CENTRAL BANK BOARDS IN SELECTED NATIONS

COUNTRY	CHIEF	DIRECTORS	REQUIREMENTS OF BOARD OF DIRECTORS
Australia	7	5	Academic, agricultural, or business backgrounds
Austria	5	5	At least one representative each from among banking, industry, trade and small business, salaried employees, and labor
Canada	7	3	Selected from "diversified occupations"
Chile	5	10	Three general representatives; one representative of republic president
Denmark	Unlimited	5	Eight directors with seats in Parliament; one economist; one lawyer
Greece	4	8	At least five representatives of industry, commerce, and agriculture
Ireland	7	4	Two representatives of banking and one or two civil servants
Italy	Unlimited	5	Minimal regional representation
Japan	5	4	Two nonvoting government representatives and four representatives from city banks, regional banks, commerce and industry, and agriculture
Norway	Unlimited	5	Determined by political balance in Parliament
Sweden	Unlimited	3	Determined by political balance in Parliament
Switzerland	6	3	Minimal representation from regions and economic sectors
United States	4	14	No more than one director from any Federal Reserve District

SOURCE: Data from Forrest Capie, et al., *The Development of Central Banking: The Tercentenary Symposium of the Bank of England,* 1994, pp. 1–231, Cambridge University Press, Cambridge, U.K.

chief executive officers and boards of directors. Selection processes vary widely. In some countries, such as the United Kingdom, the prime minister or president of the nation appoints members of the central bank governing board. In others, such as Norway, the Parliament or Congress elects chief executive officers and directors. Some nations use procedures in which both the country's president and its Parliament or Congress have a role. For instance, in the United States the president nominates potential new members of the Federal Reserve's Board of Governors, but the Senate votes on whether to confirm the president's selection.

In a number of countries, central bank boards must include representatives of government. The Australian government's treasury secretary, for example, is automatically a voting member of the board of the Bank of Australia, and government ministers or representatives are granted "advisory roles" at the Banques de France, the Bank of Denmark, and the Bank of Canada. In Italy,

POLICY NOTEBOOK

Central Bank Profit Sharing—An Impediment to European Monetary Union?

As noted earlier in this chapter, most of the profits of central banks stem from seigniorage earnings, or profits earned on assets held against the currencies that they issue. These assets include domestic and foreign bonds that bear interest and gold reserves that central banks lend in world commodity markets. Earnings from such activities can be significant. For instance, in a typical year the German Bundesbank earns more than $8 billion. Like other central banks in Europe, the Bundesbank transfers the bulk of its earnings to its nation's government as a supplement to the government's tax revenues.

Under the Maastricht Treaty's blueprint for European Monetary Union, however, the Bundesbank and the other central banks of Europe are to become part of a "European System of Central Banks" modeled after the U.S. Federal Reserve System. This central banking system would continue to earn seigniorage, but the seigniorage is to be distributed to nations according to each country's percentage share of GDP and its percentage share of the monetary union's total population. As a result, European Monetary Union is to result in a redistribution of European seigniorage earnings. Estimates of the effects of this redistribution are displayed in Figure 8–2. Panel (*a*) shows the current distribution of

seigniorage among the fifteen central banks of the European Union. Note that at present Germany earns almost one-third of all seigniorage in the EU, while Sweden and Spain together earn just over one-fourth of the total.

Panel (*b*) of Figure 8–2 shows the estimated seigniorage shares if all fifteen nations were to join the proposed European Monetary Union. As you can see, Germany's share would decline to less than one-fourth, and Sweden's and Spain's shares would decline by even greater amounts. Thus, these nations would have to find new revenue sources, following the loss of central bank seigniorage earnings, if they wished to maintain their current levels of government expenditures. Clear beneficiaries of joining the monetary union would be France and Italy and—ironically, given its ambivalence about joining the proposed monetary union—the United Kingdom.

FOR CRITICAL ANALYSIS:
France and Italy have been key proponents of European Monetary Union, and leaders of those two nations sometimes complain that Germany's government dragged its heels in the movement toward EMU. Could the panels in Figure 8–1 provide one possible rationale for the behavior of these nations' governments?

---

by way of contrast, Banca d'Italia shareholders appoint the central bank's board of directors at regional meetings, and the government has no direct role in the process.

As with private companies, the boards of directors choose officers to manage central banking operations. The amount of discretion that central bank chiefs, boards of directors, and officers have in managing the affairs of their institutions differs considerably from country to country. As discussed earlier in this chapter, some central bank boards can operate relatively independently from their nation's governments, while others cannot.

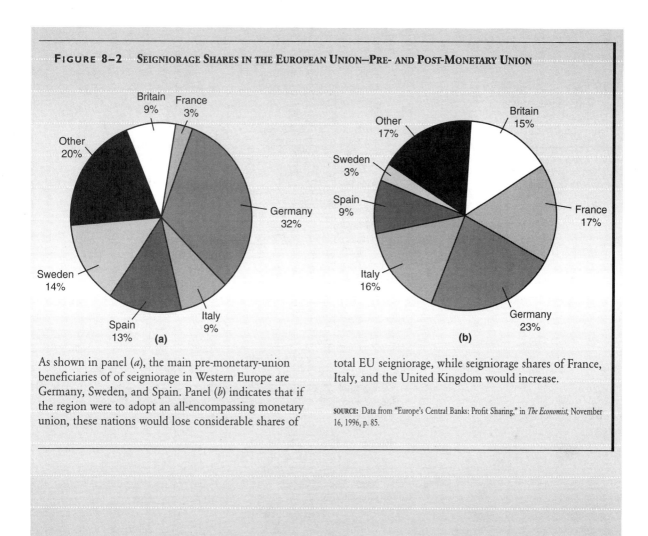

FIGURE 8–2   SEIGNIORAGE SHARES IN THE EUROPEAN UNION—PRE- AND POST-MONETARY UNION

As shown in panel (*a*), the main pre-monetary-union beneficiaries of of seigniorage in Western Europe are Germany, Sweden, and Spain. Panel (*b*) indicates that if the region were to adopt an all-encompassing monetary union, these nations would lose considerable shares of total EU seigniorage, while seigniorage shares of France, Italy, and the United Kingdom would increase.

SOURCE: Data from "Europe's Central Banks: Profit Sharing," in *The Economist*, November 16, 1996, p. 85.

Typically, central banks are large institutions with hundreds or thousands of employees. Figure 8–3 displays the approximate number of central bank employees per 10,000 residents for selected nations. Note that central banks in some countries (e.g., Costa Rica, the Dominican Republic, France, and Greece) have very large staffs relative to their nations' populations. Central banks in other countries (e.g., Ethiopia, Brazil, India, and Mexico) have many fewer employees relative to their total populations. Roland Vaubel of the University of Mannheim, Germany, found that central banks' revenues, the per capita income of the nations in which they are based, and the extent of the

Figure 8–3 **Central Bank Employees Per 10,000 Residents for Selected Nations**

The number of central bank employees per 10,000 residents varies considerably from country to country.

sources: Data from World Bank, *1997 World Development Indicators;* and Roland Vaubel, "The Bureaucratic and Partisan Behavior of Independent Central Banks: German and International Evidence," in *European Journal of Political Economy,* 13, May 1997, pp. 201–224.

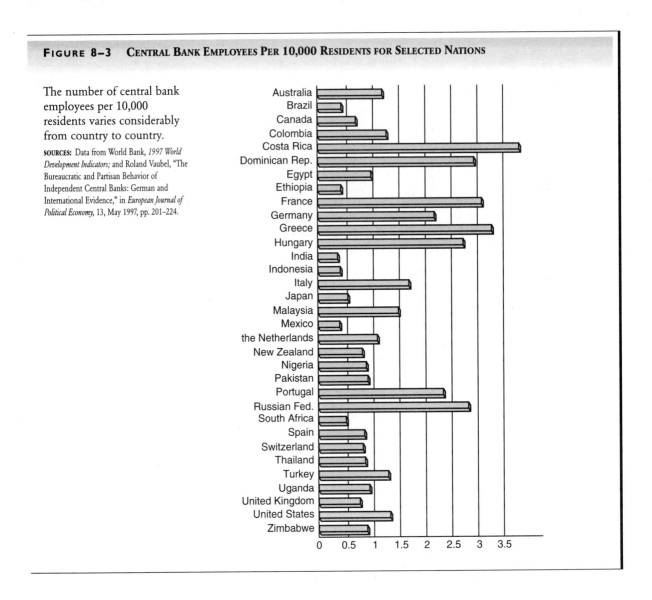

banks' budgetary independence are key determinants of the number of employees at central banks.

Presumably another key determinant of the staff sizes of central banks should be the kinds of functions that central banks perform. Some central banks' duties are limited to conducting monetary policy actions. Other central banks have many regulatory responsibilities and may, as discussed in Chapter 7, provide significant payment system services. Consequently, central banks would likely have varying levels of employment, even after taking into account differences in national populations and per capita incomes and differing levels of central bank earnings and degrees of independence.

FUNDAMENTAL ISSUE #2

Who owns and manages central banks? In many countries, governments are the owners of central banking institutions. In others, however, central banks are both publicly and privately owned. In a few countries, central bank ownership is completely private. Nevertheless, governments typically determine the structure of their nations' central banks, and in many nations governments influence how central banks are managed.

WHAT DO CENTRAL BANKS DO?

Today's central banks put their employees to work on a large number of tasks. These tasks fall into three broad categories, however. First, central banks perform banking functions for their nations' governments. Second, central banks provide financial services for private banks. Third, central banks conduct their nations' monetary policies. Let's consider each of these categories in turn.

Central Banks as Government Banks

Governments often argue that they "need" central banks. For instance, a primary motivation for the founding of the Bank of England in 1694 was the desire for the Bank to raise government funds to finance one of Britain's wars with France. In like manner, a justification that the French government gave for establishing the Banques de France in 1800 was to better manage the nation's public debt that had ballooned as France and Britain continued their military buildups.

Even in countries where providing financial services to governments has not been the key justification for a central bank, central banks typically have become the main governmental banking institution. For example, in the United States, in which there had been long-standing opposition to central banks before the founding of the Federal Reserve System in 1913, the U.S. Treasury quickly began to rely on Federal Reserve banks as providers of depository services.

Central Banks as Government Depositories As we noted earlier, a significant liability of central banks is government deposits. National governments may hold these deposits at a single central bank office or in various regional branch offices of central banks.

For instance, the U.S. Treasury holds deposits at each of the twelve Federal Reserve banks. These regional banks clear checks drawn on those accounts. They also accept deposits of fees and taxes paid by U.S. residents and firms. Furthermore, they make payments at the direction of the U.S. Treasury, just as a private bank makes payments on behalf of a private customer.

FISCAL AGENT A term describing a central bank's role as an agent of its government's finance ministry or treasury department, in which the central bank issues, services, and redeems debts on the government's behalf.

Central Banks as Fiscal Agents Central banks typically operate as **fiscal agents** for national governments, meaning that they issue, service, and redeem government debts. Treasury departments or finance ministries issue securities such as bills, notes, and bonds to cover shortfalls between tax receipts and expenditures on goods and services. In nations with highly developed financial markets, treasury departments of finance ministries issue these securities at auctions.

In their role as fiscal agents, central banks often review, tabulate, and summarize bids to purchase the securities, issue securities to successful bidders, and process the purchasers' payments to the government. For example, in the United States the Federal Reserve banks operate **book-entry security systems,** which are systems of computerized accounts of U.S. Treasury sales of bills, notes, and bonds and of interest and principal payments on these instruments. When an institution with a book-entry security account desires to sell U.S. Treasury securities, it instructs the Federal Reserve bank that maintains its book-entry security account to transfer the title of ownership from its account to the book-entry security account of the institution that has agreed to purchase the security. The Federal Reserve bank then makes the transfer electronically.

BOOK-ENTRY SECURITY SYSTEMS Computer systems that the Federal Reserve uses to maintain records of sales of treasury securities and interest and principal payments.

In emerging nations with less developed financial markets, central banks may play more direct roles. They may effectively act as investment banks for their governments by lining up private individuals or firms willing to purchase new government security issues. In nations with particularly thin secondary securities markets, central banks even purchase the securities directly from government treasury departments or finance ministries. To help broaden the markets for government securities, central banks in some countries, such as South Korea, have even imposed regulations requiring private banks to purchase government bills, notes, and bonds. Economists say that such rules make private banks *captive buyers* of government debt.

Central Banks as Bankers' Banks

Although the immediate rationale for the 1694 founding of the Bank of England was to improve government's ability to finance wartime expenditures, the British Parliament also justified creating the Bank of England to stabilize London financial markets and limit periodic fluctuations in the availability of currency and credit throughout England.

Do Banks "Need" a Central Bank? In later years, governments of other nations offered similar rationales for the establishment of central banks. Many proponents of these institutions, in fact, have contended that private banks *need* a central bank. As we discussed in Chapter 7, the key rationale for such a "need" is the idea that financial markets are subject to *externalities,* or situations in which transactions among individuals or firms can spill over to affect others.

According to this view, central banking institutions perform socially useful roles in supervising and regulating the processes and systems through which individuals, firms, and banks exchange payments. Hence, private banks "need" a central bank to keep payment systems operating smoothly on a day-to-day basis and to repair any breakdowns in these systems.

Lenders of Last Resort   We noted in Chapter 7 that the most dramatic sort of financial breakdown is a *systemic* failure, in which large numbers of banking institutions fail. The classic example of this type of systemic failure is a *bank run,* in which large numbers of bank customers lose confidence in the ability of banks to maintain their asset values and, hence, anticipate depletion of the banks' net worth. As a result, customers seek to liquidate their deposits, which actually does push large numbers of banks into insolvency.

In principle, a central bank can keep bank runs from occurring by serving as the financial system's **lender of last resort** that stands ready to lend to any temporarily illiquid but otherwise solvent bank. By lending funds when necessary, the central bank might prevent such illiquidity from leading to a general loss of confidence that can lead to a system-wide "run on the bank." In the years following its establishment, the Bank of England also came to function as a lender of last resort for banks suffering temporary liquidity problems that posed short-term threats to their individual solvency and to the broader stability of the British financial system. In response to critics' attacks on the Bank of England's policies, supporters of the Bank offered this as another justification for the Bank's existence.

Central Banks as Monetary Policymakers

Even though most central banks devote the bulk of their resources, including the time and effort of their employees, to the tasks of providing services to their nations' governments and banking institutions, most media attention on central bankers focuses on their monetary policymaking function. As you will learn in Chapters 11 through 15, there is a good reason for this: In a number of economic settings, central banks can considerably affect the price level and, potentially, real economic activity.

Instruments of Monetary Policy   Central banks, of course, do not set a nation's price level. Nor do they add much to a nation's real output, aside from the services that they provide to governments and private banks. Nevertheless, they have access to a number of **policy instruments,** which for central banks are financial variables that they can control, either directly or indirectly. By altering these policy instruments, a central bank can bring about variations in market interest rates, thereby changing the volumes of money and credit in its nation's economy and generating changes in the value of its nation's currency. Such financial-market effects can, in turn, induce changes in the level of a country's economic activity.

1. Interest Rates on Central Bank Advances   Traditionally, a key central bank policy instrument has been the interest rate charged on *advances,* or loans, to private banks.

LENDER OF LAST RESORT A central banking function in which the central bank stands willing to lend to any temporarily illiquid but otherwise solvent banking institution to prevent its illiquid position from leading to a general loss of confidence in that institution.

POLICY INSTRUMENTS A financial variable that central banks can control in an effort to attain its policy objectives.

Subsidy versus penalty rates As we noted earlier, in the United States the Federal Reserve's discount rate is the interest rate on U.S. central bank advances. In contrast to some other central banks, the discount rate is the *only* rate on advances that the Federal Reserve sets. Generally, the Federal Reserve sets the discount rate slightly below other market interest rates, such as the *federal funds rate*, which is the market interest rate in the U.S. interbank funds market known as the *federal funds market.* Because the Federal Reserve's discount rate is lower than the rate at which banks can borrow from one another in the federal funds market, it is a **subsidy rate,** meaning that access to advances from the Federal Reserve effectively amounts to central-bank-subsidized credit. To keep banks from borrowing unlimited amounts at its subsidy rate, Federal Reserve banks ration credit to private banks. The Federal Reserve banks do this through administrative guidelines that banks must satisfy to be eligible for Federal Reserve advances.

In Germany and Switzerland, the Bundesbank and the Swiss National Bank (the Swiss central bank) establish *two* interest rates on central bank advances. One of these rates is, like the Federal Reserve's discount rate, a rate below prevailing interbank funds rates. The Bundesbank and Swiss National bank establish credit quotas for all private banks in Germany and Switzerland, and these banks often borrow up to these limits. Consequently, the volume of loans that these central banks make to private banks is relatively larger than in the United States, though it is smaller than the typical volume in Japan (see below).

The other interest rate on central bank advances in Germany and Switzerland is the **Lombard rate,** which is an interest rate that these nations' central banks set *above* current market interest rates. Hence, the Lombard rate is a **penalty rate,** meaning that private banks can get Lombard credit from the Bundesbank and Swiss National Bank only by incurring an above-market penalty. Banks can borrow at this penalty rate whenever they unexpectedly find themselves illiquid. Because German and Swiss banks can finance a known amount of daily funds borrowings at the below-market discount rate and cover unanticipated credit requirements at the above-market Lombard rate, the market interest rate in German and Swiss interbank funds markets tends to vary between these two central bank rates. Consequently, when they establish values for the discount and Lombard rates, the Bundesbank and Swiss National Bank place lower and upper limits on daily interest-rate variations.

The Bank of Japan also advances credit to private banks. Like the Federal Reserve, Bundesbank, and Swiss National Bank, the Bank of Japan sets its discount rate below the current interbank funds rate. It does not restrict access to credit at this rate with the same zeal as the Federal Reserve, so the loans it extends to private banks account for a larger portion of its assets (about 6 percent, as shown in Table 8–1 on page 239). In contrast to the Bundesbank and Swiss National Bank, however, the Bank of Japan does not establish fixed credit quotas for banks. Instead, it engages in discretionary rationing of discount-window credit on a daily basis. The effective value of the Bank of

SUBSIDY RATE An interest rate on central bank advances that is set below other market interest rates.

LOMBARD RATE The specific name given to the interest rate on central bank advances that German and Swiss central banks set above current market interest rates.

PENALTY RATE The general term for any interest rate on central bank advances that is set above prevailing market interest rates.

Japan's discount rate also varies with the term of its discount-window loans. To accomplish this, the Bank of Japan calculates the total interest charge on advances to private banks based on the period of the loan *plus* one additional day. As a result, if the Bank of Japan were to restrict advances to a bank to one-day maturities on a Tuesday, whereas on the previous Monday it had permitted two-day advances, its action on Tuesday effectively would raise the interest charge on advances to that bank. Thus, Japanese banks can face several different discount-rate charges by the Bank of Japan from day to day.

The Bank of England and the Bank of Canada each set a single discount rate, but they choose to use their discount rates solely as penalty rates. Hence, these central banks typically establish discount rates slightly above prevailing market interest rates. Private banks then borrow at these rates only when they have little other recourse.

Central bank interest rates and other market interest rates   Even though every central bank has its own policy regarding the interest rate (or rates) it establishes for advances of credit to private banks, in principle each central bank can influence other short-term interest rates by varying the rate (or rates) that it charges. In Germany, for instance, the Bundesbank can induce a rise in the average interbank funds rate by pushing up both the discount rate and the Lombard rate, thereby raising both the lower and upper limits for movements in the interbank rate. Alternatively, it can induce less "dramatic" changes in the level of the interbank funds rate by raising just one of its interest rates, and this is a more common manner in which the Bundesbank tries to bring about gradual interest-rate adjustments in Germany.

The adjustments in other market interest rates occur as a result of the term structure of interest rates, which we discussed in Chapter 5. For instance, a rise in the one-day interbank funds rate induced by an increase in the Bundesbank's rates on advances will cause bond traders, provided that they do not regard the policy action as transitory, to expect higher one-day rates in the future. Because other market rates are averages of one-day funds rates, they will increase following a long-lived rise in the one-day interbank funds rate.

In Japan, the Bank of Japan can try to generate an increase in the interbank funds rate, either by raising its quoted discount rate or by shortening the maturity of its advances, thereby raising the effective discount rate. Either action tends to raise the effective cost to Japanese banks of raising funds through central bank advances, which induces them to offer higher rates to borrow privately in the interbank market. The result is a rise in the average Japanese interbank funds rate and, via the term structure of interest rates, an increase in the general level of interest rates on other Japanese financial instruments.

Finally, in nations with a single subsidy rate and administered rationing of central bank advances, such as the United States, or with a single penalty rate that automatically rations advances, such as Canada and the United Kingdom, an increase in the discount rate often induces increases in other interest rates via an **announcement effect.** In connection with rates on central bank

ON THE WEB
Visit the Bundesbank at:
http://www.bundesbank.de/

ANNOUNCEMENT EFFECT
A change in private market interest rates or exchange rates that results from an anticipation of near-term changes in market conditions signaled by a central bank policy action.

advances, this is a change in private market interest rates that results from an *anticipation* of near-term changes in interest rates. A rise in the discount rate *signals* to private banks that an increase in other rates is likely. Central banks already strenuously ration advances in these countries, so a discount-rate increase does not necessarily induce further declines in private-bank borrowing from these central banks. Nevertheless, because of the announcement effect, private banks will respond by increasing their current borrowing in the interbank market today, before the interbank funds rate rises. The result is a self-fulfilling prophesy. As private banks raise their demand for loans from other banks, they bid up the general level of the interbank funds rate.

OPEN-MARKET OPERATIONS
Central bank purchases or sales of government or private securities.

2. Open-Market Operations A second fundamental type of monetary policy instrument available to many central banks is **open-market operations.** This term refers to central bank purchases or sales of government or private securities. Most central banking institutions that engage in open-market operations—such as the U.S. Federal Reserve—buy or sell only government securities. Some, such as the Federal Reserve, buy securities in secondary markets, rather than purchasing them directly from the government. At the Federal Reserve, voting members of the *Federal Open Market Committee (FOMC)*—the seven Federal Reserve Board governors and five Federal Reserve bank presidents—set the overall strategy of open-market operations at meetings that take place every six to eight weeks. They explain this strategy in the *FOMC Directive,* which outlines the FOMC's policy objectives, establishes short-term federal funds rate goals, and lays out specific target ranges for monetary aggregates. The Federal Reserve Bank of New York's *Trading Desk* then implements the *Directive* from day to day during the weeks between FOMC meetings.

Outright transactions versus repurchase agreements The Trading Desk's open-market operations typically occur within a one-hour interval each business morning. The Trading Desk conducts two types of open-market operations. One is called an *outright transaction.* This is an open-market purchase or sale in which the Trading Desk is not obliged to resell or repurchase securities at a later date. The other kind of operation is a *repurchase agreement transaction,* which commits the seller of a security to repurchase the security at a later date. The Trading Desk often buys securities from dealers under agreements for the dealers to repurchase them at a later date. The Trading Desk also commonly uses *reverse repurchase agreements* when conducting open-market sales, which are agreements for the Trading Desk to repurchase the securities from dealers at a later time.

When a central bank purchases a security, it typically makes payment to the prior owner by crediting the owner's deposit account at a banking institution. When the bank receives the funds, its reserves increase. The Trading Desk often uses outright purchases or sales when it wishes to permanently change the aggregate level of bank reserves. In contrast, it typically uses repurchase agreements when its main goal is to keep the current level of reserves from changing for some external reason. Nevertheless, the Trading Desk can substitute repurchase agreement transactions for outright purchases or sales to change the overall reserve level by continuously mismatching repurchase-agreement transactions as needed.

Alternative procedures for open-market operations   Because Germany's Bundesbank is able to use its discount rate–Lombard rate system for advances to constrain market interest rates from day to day, it does not conduct open-market operations each day. Instead, it offers a set of repurchase agreements at a regular weekly auction. This enables the Bundesbank to maintain a desired level of bank reserves from week to week.

The Bank of Canada also conducts open-market operations once per week. However, it usually participates directly in the Canadian Treasury's weekly auction of government bills of indebtedness. Thus, many of the Bank of Canada's open-market operations are outright transactions, with some purchases made directly from the government.

At the Bank of Japan, most open-market operations involve the purchase or sale of *privately issued* financial instruments, including commercial bills and paper and bank certificates of deposit. In the past, this has allowed the Bank of Japan to try to directly influence a variety of market interest rates. Since the late 1980s, however, the Bank of Japan has aimed its open-market operations primarily at influencing the Japanese interbank funds rate. As we shall discuss shortly, this procedure parallels the approach adopted by most central banks in industrialized countries.

Open-market operations are much less common in less developed and emerging economies. The reason for this is simple: These nations do not have well-developed markets for government securities and other short-term instruments. This makes it difficult for central banks in these countries to find a critical mass of banks and other institutions that regularly trade securities on a daily or weekly basis.

3. Reserve Requirements   As we will discuss in greater detail, a key objective of a central bank's policies typically is to influence the aggregate reserves in its banking system. In years past, therefore, an important instrument of monetary policy has been **reserve requirements.** These are rules specifying portions of transactions (checking) and term (time and savings) deposits that private banks must hold either as vault cash or as funds on deposit at the central bank.

Today, however, reserve requirements are less important instruments of monetary policy (see "Policy Notebook: Bank Reserve Requirements—On the Way Out, or In?"). Certainly, central banks rarely change reserve requirements in an effort to exert direct effects on the quantities of money and credit or on the levels of market interest rates. Central banks offer reserve requirements mainly to ensure that private banks are sufficiently liquid to be able to make rapid day-to-day reserve adjustments in response to unexpected events. To assist banks in this endeavor, most central banks assess reserve requirements on an average basis: Banks must meet their reserve requirements, but they need do so only on average over a period of one or two weeks.

RESERVE REQUIREMENTS
Central bank regulations requiring private banks to hold specified fractions of transactions and term deposits either as vault cash or as funds on deposit at the central bank.

POLICY NOTEBOOK

Bank Reserve Requirements—On the Way Out, or In?

To many economists, reserve requirements constitute an anachronism. These economists argue that reserve requirements might prove useful as a stabilizing tool if central banks really desire to achieve targets for monetary aggregates, but they note that most central banks today pay little attention to variations in money growth. Hence, they contend, reserve requirements around the world should be sharply reduced, if not eliminated.

Table 8–4 shows that, as compared with a decade ago, banks in many industrialized countries face lower required reserve ratios. Relative to the required reserve ratios of other nations in the table, the official 10 percent

ratio for transactions deposits in the United States stands out. The *effective* U.S. required reserve ratio is much lower, however, because most large U.S. banks evade the bulk of reserve requirements that they would otherwise face via *sweep accounts*. These accounts, which appeared in the United States beginning in early 1993, shift funds from transactions deposits that are subject to reserve requirements to interest- or noninterest-bearing savings deposits that are exempt from reserve requirements. As panel (*a*) of Figure 8–4 shows, total funds in U.S. sweep accounts (and, thus, total funds exempt from the 10 percent required reserve ratio) increased dramatically after

TABLE 8–4   REQUIRED RESERVE RATIOS IN SELECTED INDUSTRIALIZED NATIONS

REQUIRED RESERVE RATIO FOR TRANSACTIONS DEPOSITS (IN PERCENTAGE POINTS)	1989	1998
Canada	10.0	0.0
France	5.5	1.0
Germany	12.1	2.0
Japan	1.75	1.2
New Zealand	0.0	0.0
United Kingdom	0.45	0.35
United States	12.0	10.0
REQUIRED RESERVE RATIO FOR NONTRANSACTIONS DEPOSITS (IN PERCENTAGE POINTS)	**1989**	**1998**
Canada	3.0	0.0
France	3.0	0.0
Germany	4.95	2.0
Japan	2.5	1.3
New Zealand	0.0	0.0
United Kingdom	0.45	0.35
United States	3.0	0.0

SOURCE: Data from Gordon Sellon, Jr. and Stuart Weiner, "Monetary Policy without Reserve Requirements: Analytical Issues," in Federal Reserve Bank of Kansas City *Economic Review*, 81, Fourth Quarter 1996, pp. 5–24.

June 1995. Panel (*b*) indicates that the result was a significant decline in the actual reserves that U.S. banks held at Federal Reserve banks.

Even as the United States has joined the movement toward significant reductions in effective reserve requirements, however, some European central bank officials—notably officials of Germany's Bundesbank and the Bank for International Settlements—have proposed *higher* reserve requirements for banks in European Union countries. Their rationale for this proposal is simple: If European banks have to hold more reserves with European central banks or with a future European Central Bank, then these central banks would be able to earn interest on the funds, which would give central banks a steady source of income to fund their operations. This justification for higher reserve requirements relies on their usefulness as a tax on banks and their customers. It has nothing to do with issues of monetary, financial, or economic stability.

FOR CRITICAL ANALYSIS:
Why do bank customers as well as banks incur a tax from the imposition of reserve requirements?

FIGURE 8–4   SWEEP ACCOUNTS AND U.S. BANK RESERVES AT FEDERAL RESERVE BANKS

(a)

(b)

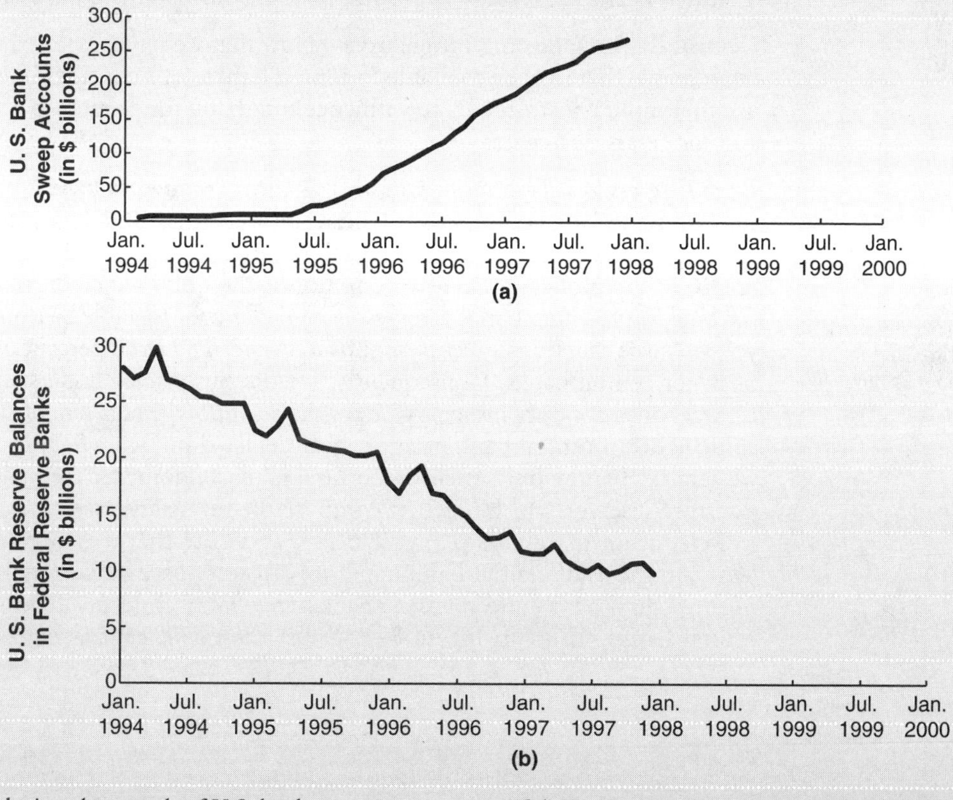

Panel (*a*) depicts the growth of U.S. bank sweeps accounts, or shifts of funds from transactions deposits subject to reserve requirements to nontransactions deposits with no legal required reserve ratios. The effect of these sweeps is shown in panel (*b*): Reserve balances that U.S. banks hold with Federal Reserve banks have declined at a fairly steady pace.

4. Interest Rate Regulations and Direct Credit Controls In a number of nations, and especially in those with less-developed financial markets, central banks traditionally have used more blunt means of influencing the quantities of money and credit. In East Asia, for instance, central banks commonly place restrictions on interest rates that private banks may pay their depositors. They sometimes use these limits as monetary policy instruments. For example, raising the allowable interest rate that banks may pay on deposits potentially can induce individuals and firms to hold more deposits, thereby increasing the amount of deposits, including those that circulate as money.

In nations such as China and Russia, central banks also use *direct credit controls,* which are explicit quantity constraints on how much credit banks and other financial institutions may extend to individuals and firms. If central banks in these nations wish to contract the growth of money and credit, perhaps in an effort to contain inflation, then they tighten credit constraints. If the central banks wish to induce higher growth in money and credit, perhaps to encourage increased near-term economic growth, then they loosen the controls somewhat.

Central Bank Operating Procedures Now that we have reviewed the policy instruments that may be available to central banks, let's consider how they can use their policy instruments to influence interbank funds rates, bank reserves, and monetary aggregates.

MONETARY BASE Central bank holdings of domestic securities and loans plus foreign exchange reserves, or the sum of currency and bank reserves.

DOMESTIC CREDIT Total domestic securities and loans held as assets by a central bank.

Bank Reserves and the Monetary Base A nation's **monetary base** is equal to the sum of central bank holdings of domestic securities and loans and foreign exchange reserves. Economists call total domestic securities and loans **domestic credit,** so the monetary base by definition is the domestic credit plus the central bank's foreign exchange reserves. If you refer back to Table 8–1 on page 239, you will note that this sum corresponds to between 80 to 90 percent of the assets of major central banks. Consequently, for the purpose of understanding how central banks conduct monetary policy, let's simplify things by considering the stripped-down central bank balance sheet depicted in Figure 8–5. In the figure, we assume that the only assets of a central bank are domestic credit and foreign exchange reserves, which together compose the monetary base.

Refer again to Table 8–1 on page 239, and note that it is also true that at least two-thirds of central bank liabilities are composed of currency issued by major central banks and reserves that private banks hold on deposit with the central banks. Thus, in Figure 8–5 we list these two central bank liabilities.

FIGURE 8–5 A SIMPLIFIED CENTRAL BANK BALANCE SHEET

ASSETS	LIABILITIES
Domestic Credit	Currency
Foreign Exchange Reserves	Bank Reserves
Monetary Base	Monetary Base

Because assets must equal liabilities in this simplified balance sheet, we reach an important conclusion:

> **The monetary base constitutes the bulk of central bank assets and liabilities. Viewed from the asset side of a central bank's balance sheet, the monetary base is equal to domestic credit plus foreign exchange reserves. Viewed from the liability side of the central bank's balance sheet, the monetary base is equal to currency plus bank reserves.**

It follows that a central bank can expand the monetary base by increasing its liabilities and bringing about a corresponding rise in its assets. One way to do this would be for the central bank to produce and distribute additional currency, and in bygone years that was the primary means by which emperors and empresses, kings and queens, and parliaments increased a nation's monetary base. Today, however, central banks usually bring about changes in the monetary base by inducing changes in bank reserve balances. They use their available policy instruments to achieve objectives for the level of reserves and, consequently, for the size of the monetary base. Central banks in industrialized nations accomplish this by undertaking policy actions that influence the equilibrium interbank funds rate and the quantities of reserves demanded by banks. Therefore, to understand how central bank policies ultimately affect interest rates, reserves, and the monetary base, you must understand the factors that determine the amount of reserves that banks wish to hold.

The Demand for Bank Reserves From the day-to-day perspective of a country's private banking institutions, the most important interest rates are the interbank funds rate and the interest rate(s) that the nation's central bank established. The reason is that these are the rates of interest at which these institutions can lend or borrow reserves from day to day to fund their extensions of credit to households and firms.

EXCESS RESERVES Cash assets that banks hold as a contingency against a need for liquidity.

Excess reserves are the reserves that banks hold in excess of central bank reserve requirements. Banks normally hold excess reserves as a contingency against a need for cash. Such a need could arise because of unanticipated deposit withdrawals or because of unexpected opportunities for profitable loans or security purchases. In most countries, holding reserves as vault cash or as reserve deposits with central banks yields no interest return to banks. (A few central banks, such as the Banca d'Italia, pay interest on required reserves, though at rates below market rates, and the Federal Reserve pays a market interest rate on special reserve-clearing accounts held by private banks.) Thus, banks could lend excess reserves to other private banks in their nation's interbank funds market.

This means that the interbank funds rate is the best measure of the opportunity cost of holding excess reserves. If the interbank funds rate is relatively low, then the opportunity cost that banks incur by holding excess reserves is relatively small, and they will be more likely to hold larger amounts of excess reserves. If the interbank funds rate rises significantly, however, then this increases the opportunity cost of holding excess reserves. Under this circumstance, banks are more likely to lend these reserves to other banking institutions in the interbank funds market. This reasoning indicates that the demand for excess reserves by banks should be *inversely related* to the interbank funds rate. If the interbank funds rate rises, then the desired amount of excess reserve holdings at banks will decline. In contrast, if the interbank funds rate falls, then depository institutions will be more willing to maintain larger balances of excess reserves.

Consequently, Figure 8–6 shows a downward-sloping demand schedule for total bank reserves, which is equal to the sum of required reserves (denoted RR) that banks must hold irrespective of the interbank funds rate and excess reserves (denoted ER). The figure denotes the interbank funds rate as R_I. Note that above some sufficiently high interbank funds rate, such as R_I^2, banks choose not to hold any excess reserves, and the total reserve holdings of banks

FIGURE 8–6 **THE DEMAND FOR AND SUPPLY OF BANK RESERVES**

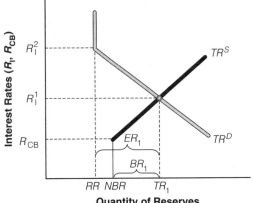

The minimal amount of reserves that private banking institutions demand is the amount of required reserves, RR. Banks desire to hold excess reserves only as the federal funds rate falls below the interbank funds rate R_I^2, so the total reserve demand schedule for depository institutions (TR^D) slopes downward below this rate. If the central bank supplies an amount of nonborrowed reserves equal to NBR and sets its interest rate on advances equal to R_{CB}, then banks desire to borrow additional reserves from the central bank whenever the interbank funds rate exceeds the interest rate on advances. Hence, the total reserve supply schedule (TR^S) slopes upward above R_{CB}. The equilibrium interbank funds rate is R_I^1, at which the total quantity of reserves demanded by private banks is equal to the total amount of reserves supplied by the central bank. The amount of excess reserves demanded by banks at this rate is equal to the distance ER_1, the amount of borrowed reserves supplied via central bank advances is equal to the distance BR_1, and the equilibrium reserve level in the nation's banking system is TR_1.

are equal to the constant amount of required reserves. As the interbank rate drops below this level, however, banks are increasingly willing to hold excess reserves, which accounts for the downward slope of the reserve demand schedule, denoted TR^D.

The Supply of Bank Reserves and the Equilibrium Interbank Funds Rate and Reserve Level Figure 8–6 also depicts a reserve supply schedule, which slopes upward over much of its range. The quantity NBR is the amount of **nonborrowed reserves,** which are reserves that the central bank supplies to the banking system through means other than direct advances of credit, such as open-market operations. This quantity does not vary with the interbank funds rate. Hence, if nonborrowed reserves were the only means by which a central bank were to supply reserves to the banking system, the reserve supply schedule would be vertical.

Because central banks in most nations extend advances at subsidy rates, however, the reserve supply schedule slopes upward. In Figure 8–6, R_{CB} denotes a central bank's subsidy discount rate. If the interbank funds rate is below the discount rate, then private banks generally borrow funds from other banks rather than borrowing reserves directly from the central bank. If the interbank funds rate is above the discount rate, however, then private banks have an incentive to increase their borrowings from the central bank. Thus, the amount of **borrowed reserves,** or the amount of reserves supplied through central bank advances, increases as the interbank funds rate rises, so that the total reserve supply schedule, denoted TR^S, slopes upward along the range above the discount rate. The elasticity of the supply schedule would depend on the extent to which the central bank rations advances. If the central bank is relatively more willing to grant advances, then the reserve supply schedule would be relatively more elastic, but if the central bank is relatively more restrictive in its willingness to extend loans to banks, then the schedule would be relatively less elastic.

In Figure 8–6, R_1^1 is the equilibrium interbank funds rate, or the interbank funds rate at which the total quantity of reserves that banks demand from the central bank is just equal to the total quantity of reserves that the central bank supplies through open-market operations and advances. The amount of excess reserves demanded by banks at that rate is equal to the distance ER_1, and the sum of RR and ER_1 is equal to TR_1, which denotes the total quantity of reserves demanded by banks. The amount of borrowed reserves supplied via central bank advances equal to the distance BR_1, and the sum of NBR and BR_1 also equals TR_1. Thus, we can say

$$TR_1 = RR + ER_1 = NBR + BR_1.$$

Consequently, TR_1 is the equilibrium reserve level in the nation's banking system. This reserve level is the amount of reserves that would appear on the central bank's balance sheet in Figure 8–5. Together with the quantity of currency in circulation, it determines the size of the monetary base. It follows that a central bank can influence the size of the monetary base through policy

NONBORROWED RESERVES Reserves that central banks supply to private banks through open-market operations rather than via advances.

BORROWED RESERVES Reserves that central banks supply directly to private banks in the form of advances.

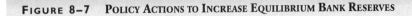

FIGURE 8–7   POLICY ACTIONS TO INCREASE EQUILIBRIUM BANK RESERVES

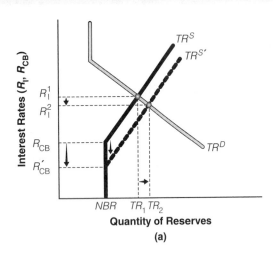

(a)

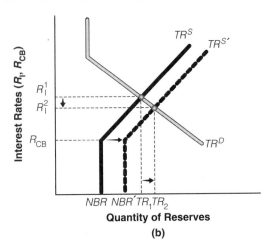

(b)

There are two ways that the central bank can raise the supply of reserves to increase equilibrium bank reserves. One approach, displayed in panel (*a*), is to reduce the interest rate on central bank advances, from R_{CB} to R'_{CB}, thereby pushing down the point of the kink in the reserve supply schedule. This action effectively shifts the reserve supply schedule to the right, inducing a downward movement in the equilibrium interbank funds rate, from R_I^1 to R_I^2 and an increase in the

equilibrium amount of total reserves in the banking system from TR_1 to TR_2. The other approach, shown in panel (*b*), is to conduct an open-market purchase. This increases the amount of nonborrowed reserves in the banking system, from NBR to NBR' and thereby also shifts the reserve supply schedule rightward. Hence, this policy action also pushes down the equilibrium interbank funds rate and raises the equilibrium amount of total reserves in the banking system.

actions that alter the equilibrium interbank funds rate and the equilibrium level of bank reserves.

Figure 8–7 shows two ways that a central bank can induce an increase in bank reserves and, consequently, in the monetary base. One method, shown in panel (*a*), is to reduce the interest rate on advances. A reduction in this rate, to R'_{CB}, pushes down the point of the "kink" in the reserve supply schedule, effectively shifting the schedule to the right over most of its range, from TR^S to $TR^{S'}$. Following this shift, there is an excess quantity of reserves supplied by the central bank at the initial interbank funds rate, R_I^1. In the interbank funds market, banks reduce their demand for loans from other institutions, and so the interbank funds rate is bid downward, to R_I^2. As the interbank funds rate declines, banks increase their excess reserve holdings, causing a rightward movement down along the reserve demand schedule, and reduce their borrowings from the central bank, causing a leftward movement down along the new reserve supply schedule. At the new equilibrium interbank funds rate, the equilibrium total quantity of reserves demanded is equal to TR_2. Hence, a reduction in the central bank interest rate on advances expands bank reserves, thereby generating a rise in the monetary base.

Panel (*b*) of Figure 8–7 depicts the effect of an open-market purchase of securities. This injects additional nonborrowed reserves directly into the financial system, so nonborrowed reserves rise to NBR', causing the reserve supply schedule to shift rightward to $TR^{S'}$. Again, the result is a decline in the equilibrium interbank funds rate, an increase in the equilibrium level of total bank reserves, and a rise in the monetary base.

Alternative Central Bank Operating Procedures   We can use the reserve demand and supply diagrams developed in Figure 8–6 to examine basic approaches that central banks have adopted in pursuing their monetary policy objectives. Central banks typically implement monetary policy by following an established **operating procedure,** which is a self-imposed guideline for conducting monetary policy over a period of several weeks or months.

OPERATING PROCEDURE
A central bank guideline for conducting monetary policy over an interval spanning several weeks or months.

Central bank operating procedures fall into two broad categories. One category includes *reserve-oriented operating procedures,* under which central banks seek to attain targets for bank reserve aggregates. In practice, this might entail targeting borrowed reserves, nonborrowed reserves, or total reserves. Panel (*a*) of Figure 8–8 illustrates how a central bank can target total reserves. To do so, the central bank first has to determine the likely position of total reserve demand. If the central bank forecasts that total reserve demand will be TR_1^D, then to achieve a target level of total reserves denoted TR^*, the central bank must adjust the interest rate on advances and the amount of nonborrowed reserves to levels that place the total reserve supply schedule at the location given by TR_1^D. These levels are given by R_{CB}^1 and NBR_1, respectively. If banks increase their demand for excess reserves, causing the total reserve demand schedule to shift to the right, to TR_2^D, then to maintain its total reserve target the central bank must reduce the supply of reserves, causing the total reserve supply schedule to shift leftward to TR_2^S. It can do this either by increasing the interest rate on advances, as illustrated by the increase to R_{CB}^2 in panel (*a*), or by conducting open-market sales that would reduce nonborrowed reserves. Consequently, this reserve-oriented operating procedure often trades off reduced stability of interest rates for increased stability of bank reserves.

Panel (*b*) of Figure 8–8 depicts an *interest-rate-oriented operating procedure.* Here, a central bank establishes a target for the interbank funds rate, denoted R_1^*. If the central bank anticipates that the total reserve demand schedule will be at the position given by TR_1^D, then achieving this target for the interbank funds rate requires setting the interest rate on advances at R_{CB}^1 and the level of nonborrowed reserves at NBR_1. Under this operating procedure, if a rise banks' demand for excess reserves causes total reserve demand to shift rightward to TR_2^D, then the central bank must *increase* the supply of reserves. It can do so either by reducing the interest rate on advances, as illustrated in panel (*b*) by

FIGURE 8–8 **RESERVE- VERSUS INTEREST-RATE-ORIENTED OPERATING PROCEDURES**

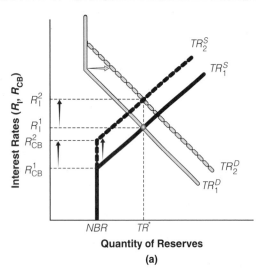

(a)

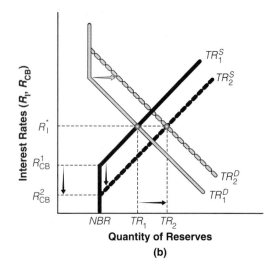

(b)

If a central bank targets bank reserves, then, as shown in panel (*a*), an increase in total reserve demand resulting from a rise in desired excess reserve holdings by banks requires a leftward shift in the reserve supply schedule to maintain the target reserve level, denoted TR^*. The central bank induces this shift by increasing the interest rate on central bank advances, from R_{CB}^1 to R_{CB}^2. Hence, with a reserve-oriented operating procedure, stabilizing the level of bank reserves often entails greater variability in interest rates. Panel (*b*)

illustrates an interest-rate-oriented operating procedure, in which the central bank sets an interbank funds rate target of R_I^*. In the face of an increase in reserve demand, keeping the interbank funds rate at this target level would require an increase in the supply of reserves, which the central bank could bring about by reducing the interest rate on central bank advances, from R_{CB}^1 to R_{CB}^2, and allowing the equilibrium level of bank reserves to rise from TR_1 to TR_2.

the reduction from R_{CB}^1 to R_{CB}^2, or by engaging in open-market purchases that would increase nonborrowed reserves. Hence, this interest-rate-oriented operating procedure can achieve greater stability of interest rates but can produce larger variations in bank reserves.

Central banks around the world have experimented with many varieties of reserve- and interest-rate-oriented operating procedures. In the United States, for instance, the Federal Reserve targeted nonborrowed reserves from 1979 to 1982, borrowed reserves from 1982 to 1987, and the federal funds rate from 1987 to the present. The Federal Reserve's current targeting of the interbank funds rate corresponds to the approach followed by most central banks today, which by and large have adopted interest-rate-oriented operating procedures for monetary policy.

FUNDAMENTAL ISSUE #3

> **What are the primary functions of central banks?** Central banks are the main depository institutions for national governments, and they serve as fiscal agents operating the systems through which governments issue debt instruments and make interest and principal payments, and by promoting broader markets for government debt instruments. Central banks also provide banking services for private banking institutions and function as lenders of last resort, providing liquidity in the event of systemic failures such as bank runs. Finally, central banks conduct monetary policy by determining values for their policy instruments, which may include interest rates on central bank advances, open-market operations, reserve requirements, and interest-rate and credit restrictions. They vary these policy instruments to influence total bank reserve levels and interbank funds rates.

WHAT SHOULD CENTRAL BANKS DO?

As already discussed, central banks in most countries perform three broad functions: government depository and fiscal agent; banking regulator, lender of last resort, and payment-system supervisor; and monetary policymaker. This does not, however, mean that economists agree that central banks necessarily should be involved in all three spheres of influence within the economy. Furthermore, even when economists generally concur that a central bank should have a broad role within a general area of responsibility, they may not agree with the specific *assignment* of a particular role for the central bank.

Alternative Perspectives on Central Banking

Since the advent of central banking, economists have grappled with the problem of what central banks *ought* to do. Although nearly every observer has her or his own notion of the specific tasks that central banks should attempt to perform, economists have developed three broad perspectives about alternative central banking arrangements that might be best for society as a whole.

1. Multifunction Central Banks   Today, when most people think about central banks, they envision a multifunction central bank that performs all the various roles that we have discussed. This includes consulting closely with and providing services to government officials and agencies, supervising and regulating private banking institutions and payment systems, and influencing overall economic performance through their abilities to affect interest rates and levels of bank reserves.

This is a natural image of central banking, because it corresponds closely to the reality of modern central banking in major nations. The Federal Reserve, the Bundesbank, and the Bank of Japan, which are the key central banks today, are good examples of multifunction central banks. These institutions take on all possible central banking tasks within their nations' economies. Their leaders, therefore, are powerful individuals.

2. Compartmentalized Central Banks A number of economists question whether giving a few individuals such sweeping responsibilities is really in the best interests of the world's nations. Their concerns do not necessarily stem from worries about centralization of power with a few central bankers. Instead, they arise from a belief that multipurpose central banks may find themselves pursuing conflicting objectives and, as a result, may not always act in society's broad interest.

Suppose, for example, that a nation has experienced accelerating inflation in recent years. You will learn in Chapter 14 that appropriate monetary policy actions to reduce the inflation rate typically entail higher interest rates. From the perspective of a nation's government, however, higher interest rates push up the cost of issuing new government debt. At the same time, higher interest rates also may lead to reductions in borrowing by households and firms, thereby forcing private banks to halt or even contract profitable credit extensions. In its other roles as government fiscal agent and banker's bank, therefore, a multipurpose central bank may resist pushing up interest rates as much as may be necessary to attain its purely monetary policy goal of halting inflationary pressures within the economy.

Thus, many economists argue that central banks ought to be *compartmentalized* institutions, in which separate "departments" pursue specific central banking objectives. Under most proposals for compartmentalized central banks, one central banking department would be preeminent and proactive, and other departments would be subsidiary units of the central bank that would react to the actions of the preeminent department. For example, a central bank might have a monetary policy department, a fiscal department, and a banking department. In such a compartmentalized central banking institution, the monetary policy department might be the preeminent unit of the central bank that focuses on attaining the central bank's overarching goal, which might be achieving low or even zero inflation. If interest rate increases were necessary to attain this overarching central bank objective, the monetary policy department would act accordingly. Then the fiscal and banking departments of the central bank would react to contain the fiscal and banking complications that might arise from the *proactive* anti-inflationary policies of the monetary policy department.

3. Streamlined Central Banks Some who promote compartmentalizing central banking functions go a step further and argue that central banks would be better off as *streamlined* institutions that pursue one specific goal. For instance, many proponents of streamlining central banks contend that central banks should be monetary-policy-oriented institutions that aim for specific economic objectives, such price stability. Bank regulation, they argue, should be entrusted to another institution, such as a government banking agency. Likewise, other institutions, such as private banks, could act as government depositories and serve as the government's fiscal agents. This, proponents argue, would keep the streamlined central bank from losing sight of its key monetary policy objectives.

ON THE WEB
Visit the Bank of England at:
**http://www.bankofengland.
co.uk/**

In 1997, the United Kingdom opted for a somewhat less extreme form of central bank streamlining by assigning the regulation and supervision of private banks, which previously had been a key duty of the Bank of England, to a separate agency of the British government. The Bank of England retained its fiscal agent function, however. In the United States, Congress recently has considered bills proposing a similar separation of powers, in which a single federal regulator would supervise U.S. banks, leaving the Federal Reserve with only the duties of pursuing monetary policy objectives and serving as fiscal agent for the U.S. Treasury.

4. Private Central Banks Some economists argue that society would be better served if private market forces determined the appropriate scope of at least some central banking functions. They point to historical episodes in which private banks developed their own regulatory institutions and payment-system supervisors to limit the scope for systemic failures. They also cite past examples in which governments used private banks as depositories for their funds without the need for a central bank to fulfill this and other fiscal functions. Hence, a number of economists contend that central banks really ought to concern themselves primarily with conducting monetary policy, leaving their other functions to the marketplace.

Indeed, at least a few economists go even further by arguing that even monetary arrangements should be left to private markets to sort out. Many proponents of *free banking,* or banking and monetary structures determined by private market forces rather than by governmental policies, promote the end of a active monetary management by national central banks. For example, George Selgin of the University of Georgia has argued that once society has established a fiat money (see Chapter 3), unregulated private banks would foster greater economic stability as compared with a system overseen by a proactive central bank.

The Assignment Problem

As discussed earlier in this chapter, nearly all nations have chosen government ownership or management of their central banks. Thus, government-appointed individuals or boards establish central bank monetary policies,

ASSIGNMENT PROBLEM
The problem of determining
whether the central bank or the
finance ministry should assume
responsibility for achieving
a nation's domestic or
international policy objectives.

supervise and regulate private banks, and manage the provision of financial services to the government. At the same time, however, elected or appointed officials of the government finance ministries or treasury departments implement policies regarding public expenditures and taxation. In the realm of monetary policy, this situation gives rise to the policy **assignment problem,** or the task of determining the appropriate policy objectives for the central bank and the finance ministry (or treasury) to pursue. A nation's central bank can vary the monetary base and thereby influence the total quantity of money in circulation, while the nation's finance ministries can alter the composition of its budget. In principle, each authority can conduct policies aimed to achieve a specific objective.

Suppose, for instance, that both the central bank and the finance ministry agree that the nation has two key economic goals for the current year. One is to achieve a desired level of real GDP. Another is to maintain balanced trade with the nation's key trading partners. Hence, for the current year the nation in this example has a domestic objective (the desired GDP level) and an international objective (balanced trade). Its central bank could seek to conduct monetary policy with an intent to achieve the domestic GDP objective or the trade objective. At the same time, the finance ministry could vary its spending and taxation policies in an effort to attain one objective or the other. It would be redundant for both authorities to aim at the same objective, so it makes sense for one authority to seek to achieve the domestic objective of a desired real GDP level while the other authority aims to achieve the international objective of a balanced trade account.

Would it be in the nation's best interest for the central bank to vary the monetary base in an effort to achieve the desired real GDP level while the finance ministry varies the composition of its budget as necessary to promote attainment of balanced trade? Or should the central bank seek to attain an exchange rate consistent with trade balance, leaving the finance ministry with the responsibility for altering real GDP through its budgetary policies? This example illustrates the fundamental nature of the assignment problem.

There is a problem in determining the appropriate assignment of policy objectives only in situations in which a central bank's monetary policies could be aimed more efficiently at one objective, while a finance ministry's budgetary policies could more efficiently be directed toward achievement of the other objective. As it turns out, it can be true in certain situations that a nation's central bank can better attain domestic goals, while a finance ministry can do a more creditable job of achieving international objectives. In some cases, however, it could be better for the central bank to work toward attaining international objectives while the finance ministry focuses on purely domestic goals. You will learn in Chapters 12 and 13 that the effects of central bank monetary policies and finance ministry budgetary policies on a nation's domestic performance and its balance of payments depend on whether the exchange rate floats or is fixed and on the extent to which financial resources can flow across national borders. Consequently, these two factors are crucial to determining the appropriate assignment of objectives.

Hence, the appropriate assignment of policy objectives varies from nation to nation, depending on the various circumstances that they face. As a result, the assignment problem can become a contentious central banking issue. A nation's central bank officials may be confident that it would be more efficient for the finance ministry to restrict its policy interests to domestic issues, leaving the international sphere to the central bank. Finance ministry officials, however, may be reluctant to accept this assignment. It is not unusual, therefore, for central banks and finance ministries to squabble about these issues. Sometimes disagreements about the appropriate solution to a nation's policy assignment problem can become public spats and escalate into serious political disputes. Whether a nation's central bank or its finance ministry ultimately emerges victorious depends in large part on the degree of independence possessed by its central bank. As we shall discuss in Chapter 14, in recent years this has led economists to devote considerable attention to the issue of how much political and economic independence governments should grant to central bank officials.

FUNDAMENTAL ISSUE #4

What are key perspectives about the appropriate duties of central banks? Most of the world's central banks are multifunction institutions that undertake the full range of central banking tasks. Some economists think that it might be better for society if central banks were compartmentalized institutions composed of separate departments with specific, prioritized duties. Others argue that central banks should be streamlined institutions that pursue a single, narrowly defined goal. Still others contend that societal interests would be better served if central banks were private institutions that arose from the interplay of market forces. In today's world of government-influenced central banks, however, central banks and government finance ministries face an assignment problem, which is the issue of determining which type of policy authority should pursue domestic versus international objectives.

MANAGED EXCHANGE RATES: FOREIGN EXCHANGE INTERVENTIONS

If central banks seek to attain international objectives, then they typically do so in part through foreign exchange interventions, buying or selling financial assets denominated in foreign currencies in an effort to influence exchange rates. Nevertheless, even if central banks focus on domestic policy objectives, leaving finance ministries the task of pursuing international goals, they often still find themselves intimately involved in the mechanics of foreign exchange interventions. The reason is that in their role as government depositories and fiscal agents, they usually conduct foreign exchange interventions on behalf of their governments. Under these circumstances, as we shall discuss, central banks may wish to undertake actions to prevent the interventions from complicating their strategies for attaining their domestic objectives.

Mechanics of Foreign Exchange Interventions

To attain international goals, central banks often attempt to alter the values of their nations' currencies in the foreign exchange markets via interventions. Now that you have learned about the balance-sheet compositions, structures, and functions of central banks, we can consider how they conduct foreign exchange market interventions in an effort to influence exchange rates.

Intervention Transactions   Central banks normally conduct foreign exchange interventions via *spot market* transactions. A key reason is that central banks often wish for their interventions to convey clear signals of their policy intentions to foreign exchange market traders. Sizable spot transactions are readily detectable by traders, thereby improving the likelihood that traders will observe central bank interventions and be able to infer the objectives of the central banks.

Most central banks do not use forward market transactions in their interventions. Central banks commonly use swap transactions, however, to adjust the composition of their portfolios of foreign exchange reserves. In this respect, swaps, which we discussed in Chapter 5, are a useful means of adding to a central bank's holdings of a particular currency shortly before a period of spot market intervention with one of those currencies. As we noted in Chapter 6, the U.S. dollar, the Japanese yen, and the German deutsche mark are the key vehicle currencies of the world, so these are the currencies that central banks commonly stockpile using swap transactions in advance of interventions.

Leaning with or against the Wind   A central bank intervenes either on its own account or on behalf of its national government in an effort to influence the value of its nation's currency in the foreign exchange market. If a central bank intervenes to support or speed along the current trend in the value of its nation's currency in the foreign exchange market, then economists say that its interventions are **leaning with the wind.**

LEANING WITH THE WIND Central bank interventions to support or speed along the current trend in the market exchange value of its nation's currency.

LEANING AGAINST THE WIND Central bank interventions to halt or reverse the current trend in the market exchange value of its nation's currency.

In contrast, economists say that a central bank's interventions intended to halt or reverse a recent trend in the value of its nation's currency are **leaning against the wind.** Most often central banks lean against the wind solely to halt, at least temporarily, sharp swings in market exchange rates. Consequently, a key rationale for many instances of leaning against the wind is simply to reduce volatility in exchange rates. A central bank does not necessarily lean against the wind with an aim to bring about long-term reversals in the trend value of their currencies, although in some instances this might be an ultimate goal of a central bank or finance ministry upon whose behalf the central bank conducts a policy of leaning against the wind.

Financing Interventions   If central banks intervene in foreign exchange markets on their own behalf, then they do so using their own reserves of assets denominated in foreign currencies. Many central banks have "war chests" of foreign currency reserves in the event that they should desire to conduct interventions on their own account. In like manner, governments often maintain reserves of foreign-currency-denominated assets.

To better understand how central banks and finance ministries fund their interventions, it is helpful to review the mechanics of foreign exchange market interventions in the United States, Germany, and Japan. In the United States, the U.S. Treasury has primary responsibility for undertaking foreign exchange interventions. Consequently, the Treasury usually determines the timing and extent of U.S. interventions, even though the Federal Reserve conducts these interventions on the Treasury's behalf. The U.S. Treasury's position is that it has the legal authority to order the Federal Reserve to use its own foreign exchange reserves as well as those of the Treasury, and in the past the Federal Reserve has conducted Treasury interventions using its own reserves as well as those of the Treasury. Recently, this has become a source of tension within the Federal Reserve System, as some Federal Reserve officials have openly questioned this "subservience" of the Federal Reserve to the Treasury.

Nonetheless, the U.S. government maintains a separate *Exchange Stabilization Fund (ESF)* that it can use to finance its interventions when Federal Reserve foreign exchange reserves are not involved. If ESF officials intervene in support of the dollar's value by selling assets denominated in foreign currencies, they initially deposit the dollars obtained in the transaction in a Treasury deposit at the Federal Reserve. The Treasury Department then issues a nonmarketable security to the ESF, which purchases the Treasury security from its account with the Federal Reserve, which credits the Treasury's deposit account. To ensure that this sequence of transactions has no ultimate effect on the Federal Reserve's balance sheet, and hence on the monetary base, the Treasury then withdraws these funds from its deposit account at the Federal Reserve and redeposits them at private banks.

The Japanese mechanism for official interventions is much like that of the United States. The national budget of Japan includes the Foreign Exchange Fund Special Account, through which the Ministry of Finance can fund

ON THE WEB

Visit the Bank of Japan at:
**http://www.boj.or.jp/en/
index.htm**

interventions, using the Bank of Japan as its agent for actually conducting transactions in foreign exchange markets. The Ministry of Finance uses this account much like the U.S. Treasury uses the Exchange Stabilization Fund, although it does not take any steps to automatically shield the Japanese money stock from the effects of its actions.

In Germany, the government's Ministry of Finance has formal responsibility for determining Germany's exchange rate arrangement. Thus, the German finance ministry can decide to commit Germany to a fixed exchange rate or to a pure float. In contrast to the U.S. and Japanese institutional frameworks, however, the Ministry of Finance itself does not conduct foreign exchange interventions. Once the Ministry of Finance establishes the arrangement for the determination of the deutsche mark's value, it is up to the Bundesbank alone to conduct interventions that it views to be necessary to support that arrangement.

The Bundesbank, therefore, initiates and implements all German foreign exchange interventions. It does so either using its own foreign currency reserves or by drawing on reserves supplied by the *European Monetary Cooperation Fund (EMCF)*. The EMCF was established as a source of funds to finance interventions by central banks of nations who participate in the European Monetary System (EMS). Hence, the Bundesbank draws upon EMCF reserves whenever it wishes to conduct interventions designed to maintain the deutsche mark's value vis-à-vis currencies of other EMS nations. The Bundesbank uses its own reserves if its interventions are unrelated to its obligations to other EMS countries.

Sterilization of Interventions

STERILIZATION A central bank policy of altering domestic credit in an equal and opposite direction relative to any variation in foreign exchange reserves so as to prevent the monetary base from changing.

A central bank **sterilizes** foreign exchange interventions when it buys or sells domestic assets in sufficient quantities to prevent the interventions from influencing the domestic money stock. As we noted earlier in this chapter, a key money measure is the *monetary base*, which we can view as either the sum of domestic credit plus foreign exchange reserves or as the sum of domestic currency and bank reserves. Thus, sterilization of the sale of foreign exchange reserves requires an equal-sized expansion of domestic credit, perhaps via a central bank open-market purchase, that would maintain an unchanged monetary base.

The mechanics of U.S. foreign exchange interventions entail accounting entries that lead to nearly immediate and complete sterilization. Germany and Japan also follow policies intended to assure at least long-term sterilization of interventions.

Many other countries officially espouse a policy of sterilizing foreign exchange interventions, but in practice some find it difficult to fully offset the effects of the resulting changes in net foreign assets. Thus, many interventions by central banks around the world are at least partly nonsterilized, so that interventions cause changes in relative quantities of national moneys in circulation. It is through this channel, as we shall discuss in more detail in the following chapters, that many economists think that interventions actually may influence market exchange rates. As you will learn in the following chapters, nonsterilized interventions can, at least in principle, lead to a number of adjustments in national economies.

Indeed, a number of economists believe that *only* nonsterilized interventions can affect exchange rates. If central banks are able to sterilize interventions, they argue, then interventions really just amount to changes in the currency compositions of domestic and foreign assets that individuals and firms around the world regard as essentially perfect substitutes. Hence, changes in the relative supplies of these assets can have no effects on foreign exchange market equilibrium.

FUNDAMENTAL ISSUE #5

How do central banks intervene in foreign exchange markets?
Central banks typically intervene in the spot market for foreign exchange, using swap transactions primarily to adjust the currency compositions of their portfolios of foreign exchange reserves. If a central bank intervenes to support the current trend in the value of its currency, then it leans with the wind. If it intervenes in an effort to halt or reverse the current trend in the value of its currency, then it leans against the wind. Both central banks and government finance ministries can intervene in foreign exchange markets. Although some nations seek to ensure that their interventions are sterilized, many others fail to sterilize interventions fully.

DO INTERVENTIONS ACCOMPLISH ANYTHING?

If sterilized interventions have no effects, then the implication would be that interventions would be redundant policies. After all, any central bank can vary the amount of money it places in circulation relative to other world currencies through purely domestic policy actions, such as varying interest rates on advances or engaging in open-market operations, that alter the monetary base. Consequently, an important issue for international monetary economists is whether foreign exchange interventions can and do have independent short- and long-term effects on market exchange rates.

Gauging the Short-Term Effects of Interventions

PORTFOLIO BALANCE EFFECT
An exchange rate adjustment resulting from changes in government or central bank holdings of foreign-currency-denominated financial instruments that influences the equilibrium prices of the instruments.

Most economists believe that sterilized foreign exchange interventions can, at least in theory, have at most two types of immediate effects on exchange rates. They call one of these the **portfolio balance effect:** If the exchange rate is viewed as the relative price of imperfectly substitutable assets such as bonds, then changes in government or central bank holdings of bonds and other assets denominated in various currencies can influence exchange rates by affecting the equilibrium prices at which traders are willing to hold these assets. For example, if an intervention reduces the supply of domestic assets relative to foreign assets held by individuals and firms, then the expected return on domestic assets must fall to induce individuals and firms to readjust their portfolios. A reduction in the anticipated rate of return on domestic assets, in turn, requires an appreciation of the domestic currency. Hence, a finance ministry or central bank purchase of domestic currency can, through the portfolio balance effect, cause the value of the domestic currency to rise.

The other possible effect is an intervention *announcement effect,* in which foreign exchange interventions may provide traders with previously unknown information that alters their willingness to demand or supply currencies in the foreign exchange markets. The announcement effect can exist, therefore, only if a government or central bank intervention clearly reveals some kind of "inside information" that traders did not have prior to the intervention. For instance, a central bank that plans to conduct a future anti-inflation policy by contracting its money stock may reveal this intention by leaning against the wind in the face of a recent downward trend in the value of its nation's currency. If currency traders believe this message provided by the central bank's intervention, then they will expect a future appreciation and will increase their holdings of the currency. This concerted action by currency traders then causes an actual currency appreciation. Thus, the announcement effect of the intervention, like the portfolio balance effect, induces a rise in the value of the domestic currency.

A major study of foreign exchange market interventions during the 1980s and early 1990s by Kathryn Dominguez of Harvard University and Jeffrey Frankel of the University of California at Berkeley found evidence that both effects were at work during that period, especially in the latter part of the 1980s when many of the world's governments conducted sizable interventions. Dominguez and Frankel found that during this interval, in which central banks coordinated several interventions, the *announcements* of the interventions actually had larger effects on exchange rates than the actual magnitudes of the interventions themselves. This, in their view, provides strong evidence of announcement effects in interventions. Particularly in the case of coordinated interventions during the late 1980s, traders seem to have viewed interventions as signals of government and central bank commitments to future policy changes and reacted by altering their desired holdings of domestic and foreign assets. The result was changes in market exchange rates, at least in the short run.

Can Even Coordinated Interventions Work in the Long Run?

As we discussed in Chapter 3, one of the most significant episodes of coordinated currency interventions took place beginning in 1985. In September of that year, at the Plaza Hotel in New York, the finance ministers and central banks of G5 nations made an announcement that "in view of the present and prospective change in fundamentals, some orderly appreciation of the main non-dollar currencies against the dollar is desirable. We stand ready to cooperate more closely to encourage this when to do so would be helpful." The Plaza Agreement was followed in 1987 by a reaffirmation of the Plaza principles at the Louvre Palace in Paris, called the Louvre Accord. Much official rhetoric since these policy agreements has indicated that the G5 nations believed they largely accomplished their objective of stabilizing exchange rates at "desired" levels.

Some economists, however, believe this is an overstatement. Among these doubters are Michael Bordo of Rutgers University and Anna Schwartz of the National Bureau of Economic Research. In their view, central bank interventions really did not accomplish much except to distort exchange markets and to subject central banks to excessive risks of loss.

The Extent of Foreign Exchange Interventions in the Late 1980s   In support of this argument, Bordo and Schwartz conducted a study in which they tabulated data on the foreign exchange interventions coordinated by the United States, Germany, and Japan between early 1985 and late 1989. Figure 8–9 displays their estimates of the combined dollar amounts of interventions by central banks and finance ministries during that period.

Bordo and Schwartz reach two conclusions from their analysis of these interventions. First, the interventions were sporadic and highly variable, which potentially may have *added to,* instead of reducing, foreign exchange market volatility and uncertainty. These variable—and therefore often unexpected—central bank exchange market interventions likely caused individuals and firms to experience unintended wealth transfers. In addition, the increased risk of such transfers probably induced many traders to undertake more efforts to hedge against the risks of unexpected central bank interventions. This, as we discussed in Chapter 5, can be an effective, yet costly, activity.

Second, interventions during the late 1980s were very small in size relative to total trading in foreign exchange markets. Bordo and Schwartz note, for instance, that in April 1989 total foreign exchange trading amounted to $129 billion per day, yet the Fed purchased only $100 million in marks and yen in that entire month, on a single day. In fact, Fed purchases of marks and yen for all of 1989 amounted to about $17.7 billion, or the equivalent of less than 14 percent of the amount of an average day's trading in April of that year. Given the meager relative size of foreign exchange trading by even a coalition of the world's largest central banks during the 1985–1989 period, Bordo and Schwartz question the likelihood that central bank exchange market interventions can really have long-lasting effects on exchange rates.

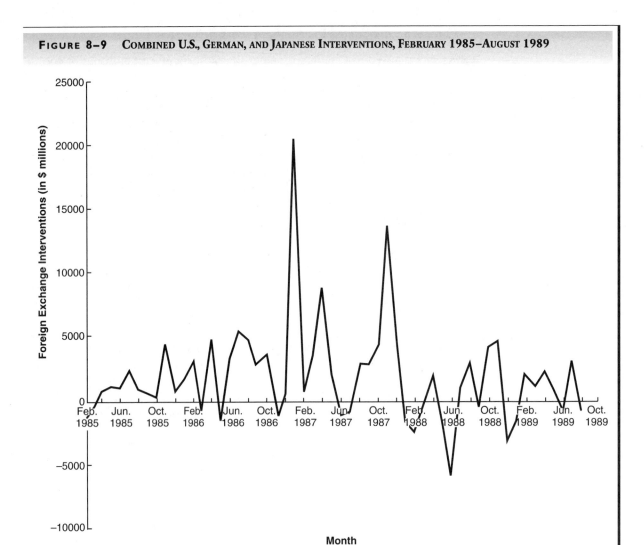

FIGURE 8-9 COMBINED U.S., GERMAN, AND JAPANESE INTERVENTIONS, FEBRUARY 1985–AUGUST 1989

The total dollar amount of the foreign exchange interventions by these nations during the late 1980s varied considerably from month to month.

SOURCE: Data from Michael Bordo and Anna Schwartz, "What Has Foreign Exchange Market Intervention Since the Plaza Agreement Accomplished?" in *Open Economies Review*, 2:1, 1991, pp. 39–64.

Are the Direct Costs of Foreign Exchange Interventions Worth the Benefits?
Bordo and Schwartz argue that efforts by central banks to manipulate
exchange rates have significant direct costs. Financing interventions require
expenditures of foreign exchange reserves, which either directly or indirectly
(via ownership shares in central banks) are assets of national governments.
During the late 1980s, Bordo and Schwartz argue, governments that participated in the coordinated effort to reduce the dollar's value exposed their governments, and hence their taxpaying citizens, to risks of sizable foreign
exchange losses.

For instance, they point out that while the Federal Reserve and Treasury combined for more than $1 billion in realized gains from foreign exchange transac-
tions in 1985 through 1989, the Netherlands lost 600 million Dutch guilders on
dollar interventions in 1986 and 1987, and Germany reportedly lost 9 billion
deutsche marks in the fourth quarter of 1987 alone. Bordo and Schwartz question the wisdom of central bank and finance ministry gambles with such large
stakes, given their limited abilities to achieve exchange rate goals.

Although Bordo and Schwartz make a strong case that the experience of the
late 1980s indicates that central banks cannot manipulate exchange rates over
long time horizons, many economists join Dominguez and Frankel in arguing
that foreign exchange interventions can and do influence exchange rates from
time to time. They contend that looking at the gains and losses from foreign
exchange interventions by any single nation is misleading, because coordinated actions by several central banks are likely to have the most pronounced
effects on exchange rates. They also argue that the announced willingness of
central banks to influence exchange rates commonly can cause self-fulfilling
prophecies: If traders believe that central banks can influence exchange rates
and expect them to do so, then the traders themselves will act on their expectations in ways that push exchange rates in the directions central bankers
desire. The coordinated interventions of the late 1980s, they point out, were
unambiguously associated with an interval in which the value of the dollar
declined. This decline, they note, continued even beyond the active period of
interventions, potentially implying longer-term effects.

Efforts to manipulate exchange rates through foreign exchange interventions have been more muted in the 1990s. This may be because nations have
less desire to influence exchange rates or because they have been unable to
reach agreement on how to do so. Or it may be, as we shall discuss in Chapter 15, that modern central bankers and finance ministers have recognized the
limits on their abilities to lean against the wind in today's foreign exchange
markets. Before we reach that point, however, in the following chapters you
will need to learn much more about how policy actions of government
finance ministries and central banks influence economic activity.

FUNDAMENTAL ISSUE #6

How effective are foreign exchange interventions? Economists are divided about the answer to this question, depending in part on whether one has in mind short-run or long-run effects on interventions. Most economists believe that nonsterilized interventions can have direct, short-run effects on exchange rates by changing relative quantities of currencies in circulation. Some economists also contend that sterilized interventions can alter exchange rates through portfolio balance effects or announcement effects. There is evidence that these latter effects mattered, at least in the short run, during the period of widespread foreign exchange interventions in the 1980s. There also is evidence, however, that even coordinated interventions had relatively small effects, may have added to exchange rate volatility, or may have caused taxpayer losses owing to greater currency risks incurred by governments and central banks.

CHAPTER SUMMARY

1. **The Main Assets and Liabilities of Central Banks:** Key central bank assets are government securities, loans to private banks, and foreign-currency-denominated securities and deposits. The primary liabilities of central banks are currency notes and reserve deposits of private banks.

2. **The Ownership and Management of Central Banks:** Central bank ownership may be entirely public, entirely private, or mixed public and private. Nonetheless, national governments determine the organizational structure of central banks, and many governments try to play a hands-on role in managing central bank operations.

3. **The Primary Functions of Central Banks:** Central banks are depositories for funds held by national governments and act as fiscal agents by operating the systems through which governments issue debt instruments, making interest and principal payments to those who hold government debt, and developing markets for government debt instruments. Central banks perform financial services for private banks and operate as lenders of last resort by providing liquidity to stem bank runs or other systemic banking problems. Furthermore, central banks vary policy instruments, such as interest rates on central bank advances, open-market operations, reserve requirements, and interest-rate and credit restrictions, in an effort to affect interbank funds rates and total bank reserves.

4. **Key Perspectives about the Appropriate Duties of Central Banks:** Today's central banks are multifunction institutions that perform the complete spectrum of central banking tasks. Nevertheless, some economists have proposed making central banks compartmentalized institutions composed of separate departments with narrowly focused and prioritized duties, streamlined institutions that seek to achieve one specific objective, or private institutions whose structures reflect market forces. Because governments influence central banks in today's world, however, central banks and government finance ministries must deal with the policy assignment problem, meaning that they must determine which authority should pursue domestic objectives and which authority should seek to achieve international goals.

5. **How Central Banks Intervene in Foreign Exchange Markets:** Most central banks focus their interventions within the spot foreign exchange market. Although many central banks use swap transactions to change the compositions of their foreign exchange reserves, they normally do not engage in many forward exchange market transactions. Leaning with the wind refers to central bank interventions to support the current trend in the value of its currency, while leaning against the wind refers to interventions intended to halt or reverse the current trend in the value of its currency. Central banks and finance ministries both intervene in foreign exchange markets, though institutional frameworks governing the mechanisms for interventions and the extent to which they are sterilized vary from nation to nation.

6. **The Effectiveness of Foreign Exchange Interventions:** Many economists have concluded that nonsterilized interventions can influence market exchange rates by changing relative quantities of money supplied. Some also argue that sterilized interventions can alter exchange rates via portfolio balance effects or announcement effects. Evidence from the experience with interventions in the 1980s indicates that these latter effects were present, but there is also evidence from these episodes that even coordinated interventions may have had limited exchange-rate effects or could have contributed to greater exchange rate variability and taxpayer losses in some nations.

QUESTIONS AND PROBLEMS

1. What are the key assets and liabilities of central banks?

2. In your view, what is the single most important role of a central bank? Could a central bank perform this role without performing its other roles? Explain your reasoning.

3. In 1997, it came to public light that the Bank of Italy (the central bank of Italy) owned shares in a few (but not all) private banks that it regulated. Many observers regarded this as inappropriate. Do you agree? Why or why not?

4. Could a central bank conduct monetary policy solely by varying its interest rate on advances? Explain your reasoning.

5. Total reserves are equal to the sum of required reserves and excess reserves. But total reserves also are equal to the sum of borrowed reserves and nonborrowed reserves. Explain how these two ways of splitting up total reserves make sense from the differing perspectives of a central bank and private banks.

6. Explain, in your own words, how a multifunction central bank could find itself in a quandary in trying to satisfy more than one policy objective at the same time. Do you think that this is a good argument for either a compartmentalized or streamlined central bank?

7. Suppose that a nation's central bank does not use open-market operations to conduct monetary policy. How could the central bank vary the interest rate(s) that it charges on its advances to try to sterilize a foreign exchange intervention intended to raise the value of its nation's currency? Explain.

8. Why might it make a difference whether or not foreign exchange interventions are sterilized? Explain.

9. True or false? Even though most central banks conduct foreign exchange interventions in the spot market, there is no reason that forward market interventions would not be equally effective. Take a stand, and support your answer.

ON-LINE APPLICATION

Internet URL: http://www.frbsf.org/system/econinfo/inbrief/guides.html

Title: How the Federal Reserve Conducts U.S. Monetary Policy

Navigation: Begin at the home page of the Federal Reserve Bank of San Francisco (**http://www.frbsf.org**). If this does directly route you to the FedWest GateWay page, click on that link. Next, click on *Central Banking,* followed by *The Federal Reserve System.* Finally, click on *How the Fed Guides Monetary Policy.*

Application: Read the article, and answer the following questions:

1. According to the article, for which monetary policy instruments does the Federal Open Market Committee (FOMC) establish guidelines? What group of individuals within the Federal Reserve System follows FOMC guidelines in conducting day-to-day U.S. monetary policy operations?

2. Based on the article, what Federal Reserve policymakers determine the remaining instruments of monetary policy? Do these policymakers have any say in FOMC deliberations as well?

REFERENCES AND RECOMMENDED READINGS

Batten, Dallas, Michael Blackwell, In-Su Kim, Simon Nocera, and Yuzuru Ozeki. "The Conduct of Monetary Policy in the Major Industrial Countries: Instruments and Operating Procedures." International Monetary Fund Occasional Paper No. 70, July 1990.

Bordo, Michael, and Anna Schwartz. "What Has Foreign Exchange Market Intervention Since the Plaza Agreement Accomplished?" *Open Economies Review,* 2 (1) (1991): 39–64.

Borio, Claudio. "The Implementation of Monetary Policy in Industrial Countries: A Survey." BIS Economic Papers, No. 47, July 1997.

Broaddus, J. Alfred, and Marvin Goodfriend. "Foreign Exchange Operations and the Federal Reserve." Federal Reserve Bank of Richmond *Economic Review,* 82 (Winter 1996): 1–19.

Capie, Forrest, Charles Goodhart, Stanley Fischer, and Norbert Schnadt. *The Future of Central Banking: The Tercentenary Symposium of the Bank of England.* Cambridge, U.K.: Cambridge University Press, 1994.

Daniels, Joseph, and David VanHoose. "Reserve Requirements, Currency Substitution, Seigniorage, and the Transition to European Monetary Union." *Open Economies Review,* 5 (1996): 257–273.

Dominguez, Kathryn, and Jeffrey Frankel. *Does Foreign Exchange Intervention Work?* Washington, D.C.: Institute for International Economics, 1993.

Giuseppi, John. *The Bank of England: A History from Its Foundation in 1694.* London: Evans Brothers Ltd., 1966.

Goodhart, Charles. *The Evolution of Central Banks,* Cambridge, Mass.: MIT Press, 1988.

Kasman, Bruce. "A Comparison of Monetary Policy Operating Procedures in Six Industrial Countries." *Federal Reserve Bank of New York Quarterly Review,* 17 (Summer 1992): 5–24.

Lewis, Karen. "Are Foreign Exchange Intervention and Monetary Policy Related, and Does It Matter?" *Journal of Business,* 68 (1995): 185–214.

Schwartz, Anna. "From Obscurity to Notoriety: A Biography of the Exchange Stabilization Fund." *Journal of Money, Credit, and Banking,* 29 (May 1997): 135–153.

Selgin, George. "Free Banking and Monetary Control." *Economic Journal,* 104 (November 1994): 1449–1459.

Smith, Vera. *The Rationale of Central Banking and the Free Banking Alternative.* 1936; Reprint, Indianapolis: Liberty Press, 1990.

Vaubel, Roland. "The Bureaucratic and Partisan Behavior of Independent Central Banks: German and International Evidence." *European Journal of Political Economy,* 13 (May 1997): 201–224.

TRADITIONAL APPROACHES TO EXCHANGE-RATE AND BALANCE-OF-PAYMENTS DETERMINATION

9

FUNDAMENTAL ISSUES

1. How does the supply of exports and demand for imports determine the supply of and demand for foreign exchange?

2. What is the elasticity approach to balance-of-payments and exchange-rate determination?

3. What is the J-curve effect?

4. What are pass-through effects?

5. What is the absorption approach to balance-of-payments and exchange-rate determination?

6. How do changes in real income and absorption affect a nation's current account balance and the foreign exchange value of its currency?

In the mid-1990s, the United Kingdom began a strong economic expansion. In addition, between August 1996 and August 1997 the British pound appreciated by 20 percent against a trade-weighted basket of currencies. Because an appreciation of the pound would likely make British exports relatively more expensive on the international market and make British import goods relatively cheaper, many observers anticipated that exports would fall and imports would rise, so that the United Kingdom would experience a sizable current account deficit.

Yet by September 1997, the U.K. current account deficit was a mere 1 percent of GDP. The small deficit mainly resulted from continued strength in U.K. exports. This outcome puzzled many economists and policymakers. Economists with the British government determined there were two possible explanations for the U.K. current account performance. First, there may have been a considerable delay before the pound appreciation exerted its full effect on import and export performance, because many orders for British exports may have been placed before the pound appreciated. As evidence of this, the British Treasury gave the example of a £400 million order for oil exploration equipment placed a year prior to the appreciation. Second, British exporters apparently were willing to reduce their prices to offset the effect of the appreciation and maintain market share. Evidence does show that the price of British exports declined while the pound appreciated.

When, and by how much, does a rise or fall in the exchange value of a nation's currency affect its balance of payments? How does economic growth or an economic contraction affect a nation's balance of payments and the exchange value of its currency? Over the course of time, economists have developed approaches to balance-of-payments and exchange-rate determination in an effort to answer these questions. This chapter considers two traditional approaches to balance-of-payments and exchange-rate determination, while Chapter 10 describes two more modern approaches.

COMMON CHARACTERISTICS OF THE TRADITIONAL APPROACHES

Economists developed the two traditional approaches between the early 1920s through the 1960s, when the world economy was quite different from that of today. These models, therefore, share some common characteristics. Because the major economies had adjustable-peg exchange rate arrangements under both the gold standard and the Bretton Woods system, economists focused their efforts on understanding the effect of a devaluation on a nation's balance of payments. We can, however, use these approaches to examine the effects of a currency depreciation as well, as you will learn in this chapter.

When these approaches were developed, capital flows did not dominate the foreign exchange market as they do today. As a result, both approaches assume that capital flows exist solely to finance international transactions of goods and services. Hence, capital flows are not explicitly considered in the models, which focus only on a nation's trade in goods and services. As explained in Chapter 6, trade flows certainly are important, but are dwarfed by the volume of capital flows. By distinguishing the effects of trade flows from the effects of capital flows, however, these approaches contribute to our understanding of exchange-rate and balance-of-payments determination.

The two traditional approaches differ in their emphasis on the economic variables that influence a nation's balance of payments and the exchange value of its currency. The first approach, the *elasticities approach*, emphasizes price effects, while the second, the *absorption approach*, emphasizes income effects. We begin with the elasticities approach, which emphasizes the relationship between a nation's imports and exports and the supply of and demand for foreign exchange.

EXPORTS, IMPORTS, AND THE DEMAND
FOR AND SUPPLY OF FOREIGN EXCHANGE

As explained earlier, the traditional approaches assume that capital flows occur only as a means of financing current account transactions. Hence, the quantity demanded and the quantity supplied of foreign exchange depend only on international transactions of goods and services.

Derivation of the Demand for Foreign Exchange

We explained in Chapter 2 that when a nation's residents export goods and services, they require foreign exchange as payment for these exports. Thus, the quantity of a currency demanded in the foreign exchange market, or the demand for foreign exchange, is derived from the nation's supply of exports. In this chapter we provide a more complete derivation of the demand for foreign exchange. We shall use a Canadian example to illustrate the derivation of the demand for foreign exchange. In this setting where capital flows are ignored, the quantity of foreign exchange demanded by Canada is equal to the value of Canada's supply of exports.

Suppose that Canada exports wheat and imports hockey pucks. Further suppose that Canada's shares of the world market for these two goods are so small

FIGURE 9–1 **CANADA'S EXPORT SUPPLY CURVE AND THE DEMAND FOR FOREIGN EXCHANGE**

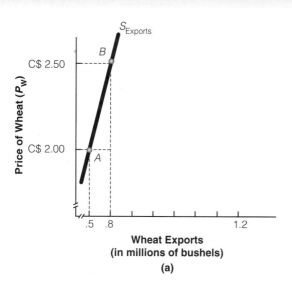

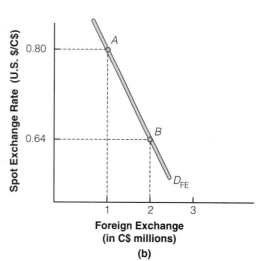

Panel (*a*) illustrates a hypothetical export supply curve for Canada as combinations of the quantity supplied of wheat at various prices, such as those denoted by points *A* and *B*. The value of Canada's exports determines the quantity demanded of the Canadian dollar. For example, at a spot exchange rate of 0.80 U.S.$/C$, the world price of wheat is C$2.00, at which Canada

exports C$1 million of wheat. Point *A*, in panel (*b*) shows the combination of $C1 million of foreign exchange demanded at the spot exchange rate 0.80 U.S.$/C$. Panel (*b*) illustrates the demand for foreign exchange as combinations of the quantity of foreign exchange demanded at various exchange rates, such as those denoted by points *A* and *B*.

that they do not influence the world prices of the goods. Panel (*a*) of Figure 9–1 illustrates a hypothetical export supply curve for Canada. Point *A* shows that at a price of C$2.00 per bushel the quantity of wheat supplied is 0.5 million bushels, while point *B* shows that at a price of C$2.50 per bushel, the quantity of wheat supplied is 0.8 million bushels. We shall further suppose that the world price of wheat, in terms of the U.S. dollar, is U.S.$1.60 per bushel.

At an exchange rate of 0.80 U.S. dollars per Canadian dollar (U.S.$/C$), the world price of wheat, in terms of the Canadian dollar, is C$2.00 per bushel [$1.60/(0.80 U.S.$/C$) = C$2.00], at which Canada exports 0.5 million bushels of wheat. The value of Canada's exports at this exchange rate is C$1 million (C$2.00 × 0.5 million = C$1 million). Thus, at an exchange rate of 0.80 U.S.$/C$, the quantity of foreign exchange demanded is C$1 million. Point *A* in Figure 9–1*b*, illustrates this combination of the quantity of foreign exchange demanded and the spot exchange rate.

If the Canadian dollar depreciates relative to the U.S. dollar from 0.80 U.S.$/C$ to 0.64 U.S.$/C$, the world price of wheat, in terms of the Canadian dollar, rises to C$2.50 per bushel [U.S.$1.60/(0.64 U.S.$/C$) = C$2.50]. As illustrated in Figure 9–1a, at this price Canada exports 0.8 million bushels of wheat. The value of Canada's exports at this new exchange rate, therefore, is C$2 million (C$2.50 × 0.8 million = C$2 million). Thus, at this exchange rate the quantity of foreign exchange demanded is C$2 million. Point *B* in Figure 9–1b shows this combination of the quantity of foreign exchange demanded and the spot exchange rate. Figure 9–1b illustrates the demand curve for the Canadian dollar formed by connecting points *A* and *B*.

Elasticity and the Demand for Foreign Exchange

PRICE ELASTICITY OF SUPPLY
A measure of the proportional change of the quantity supplied of a good, service, or financial instrument to a proportional change in its price.

PRICE ELASTICITY OF DEMAND
A measure of the proportional change of the quantity demanded to a proportional change in price.

Price elasticity of supply is a measure of the responsiveness of the quantity supplied to a change in price. Likewise, **price elasticity of demand** is a measure of the responsiveness of the quantity demanded to a change in price. Elasticity is an important measure, as it tells us the proportional change in quantity demanded or supplied in response to a given proportional change in price.

In Figure 9–1a, the quantity of wheat supplied rose from 0.5 million bushels to 0.8 million bushels when the price of wheat rose from C$2.00 per bushel to C$2.50 per bushel. Suppose that, for the same price change, the quantity of wheat supplied rose to 1.2 million bushels, as denoted by point *B'* in Figure 9–2a. We would say that, in this second case, the quantity of wheat supplied was more responsive to the price increase–it was *more elastic*. Figure 9–2a illustrates the initial export supply curve *S*, and the export supply curve formed by points *A* and *B'* and denoted *S'*. In panel (*a*), the proportional change in quantity supplied in response to the same proportional change in price is greater for the supply curve *S'*. Hence, over the indicated price range, the supply curve *S'* is more elastic than the supply curve *S*.

Because the export supply curve determines the foreign exchange demand curve, the elasticity of export supply determines the elasticity of demand for foreign exchange. As in the previous example, at an exchange rate of 0.64 U.S.$/C$ and a world price for wheat of U.S.$1.60, the world price of wheat in terms of the Canadian dollar is C$2.50. If Canada's exports of wheat are 1.2 million bushels at this exchange rate, then the value of Canada's exports, say to the United States, and thus the quantity of foreign exchange demanded by U.S. residents, is C$3 million (C$2.50 × 1.2 million = C$3 million).

Point *B'* in Figure 9–2b shows this new combination of the spot exchange rate and the quantity of foreign exchange demanded. As the figure shows, the foreign exchange demand curve formed by connecting points *A* and *B'*, denoted *D'*, is more elastic over this range of exchange rates than the original demand curve *D*. It is in this manner that the elasticity of the export supply curve determines the elasticity of the foreign exchange demand curve. The more elastic is the export supply curve, the more elastic is the demand for foreign exchange. Likewise, the less elastic is the export supply curve, the less elastic is the demand for foreign exchange.

FIGURE 9–2   ELASTICITY OF EXPORT SUPPLY AND THE ELASTICITY OF FOREIGN EXCHANGE DEMAND

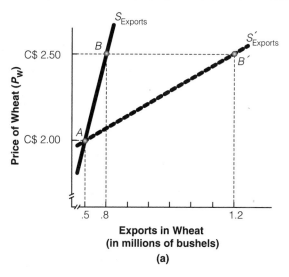

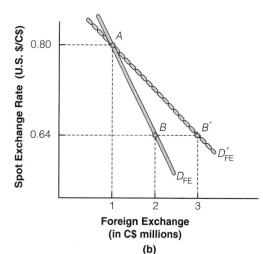

The elasticity of export supply determines the elasticity of demand for foreign exchange. In panel (*b*), *D* denotes the demand curve for foreign exchange derived from the export supply curve *S*, while *D′* denotes the demand curve for foreign exchange derived from the export supply curve *S′*. In panel (*a*), the export supply curve denoted *S′* is more elastic than the supply curve denoted *S*. As a result, the demand curve for foreign exchange denoted *D′* is more elastic than the demand curve for foreign exchange denoted *D*.

Derivation of the Supply of Foreign Exchange

In the traditional, trade-based theory of exchange-rate determination, a nation's supply of foreign exchange results from its imports of goods and services. As a nation purchases foreign goods and services, it pays for these purchases with foreign exchange. Hence, it supplies foreign exchange when it imports foreign goods and services.

Consider Canada's imports of hockey pucks. Figure 9–3*a* illustrates a hypothetical import demand curve for hockey pucks in Canada. Point *A* of panel (*a*) indicates that at a price of C$5.00 per puck, the quantity of hockey pucks demanded is 600,000, while point *B* indicates that at a price of C$6.25 the quantity of hockey pucks demanded is 320,000. The hypothetical import demand curve formed by connecting points *A* and *B* and denoted *D* illustrates all of the various combinations of quantity demanded and price.

The import demand curve described in Figure 9–3*a* determines Canada's supply of foreign exchange in the same way that the export supply curve determined the demand for foreign exchange in our previous example. Suppose the world price of a hockey puck is U.S.$4.00. At a spot exchange rate

FIGURE 9-3 **CANADA'S IMPORT DEMAND CURVE AND THE SUPPLY OF FOREIGN EXCHANGE**

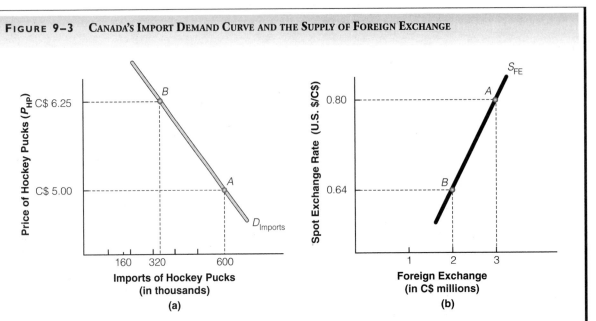

Panel (*a*) illustrates a hypothetical import demand curve for Canada as combinations of the quantity of hockey pucks demanded at various prices, such as those denoted by points *A* and *B*. The value of Canada's imports determines the quantity of foreign exchange supplied. For example, at a spot exchange rate of 0.80 U.S.$/C$, the world price of hockey pucks is C$5.00, at which

Canada imports C$5 million of hockey pucks. Point *A*, in panel (*b*) shows the combination of $C5 million of foreign exchange supplied and the spot exchange rate 0.80 U.S.$/C$. Panel (*b*) illustrates the supply of foreign exchange as combinations of the quantity of foreign exchange supplied at various exchange rates, such as those denoted by points *A* and *B*.

of 0.80 U.S.$/C$, the world price of hockey pucks in Canadian dollars is C$5.00 [U.S.$4/(0.80 U.S.$/C$) = C$5.00]. Hence, at a spot exchange rate of 0.80 U.S.$/C$, Canada imports 600,000 hockey pucks. The value of Canada's imports at this spot exchange rate and, therefore, the supply of foreign exchange is C$3 million (C$5.00 × 600,000 = C$3 million). Point *A* of panel (*b*) shows this combination of the spot exchange rate and the quantity of foreign exchange supplied.

At a spot exchange rate of 0.64 U.S.$/C$, the world price of hockey pucks in Canadian dollars is C$6.25 [U.S.$4.00/(0.64 U.S.$/C$) = C$6.25]. Point *B* of panel (*a*) indicates that at this price, Canada imports 320,000 hockey pucks. The value of Canada's imports at this spot exchange rate and, therefore, the supply of foreign exchange is C$2 million (C$6.25 × 320,000 = C$2 million). Point *B* of panel (*b*) shows this combination of the spot exchange rate and the quantity of foreign exchange supplied. The foreign exchange supply curve formed by connecting points *A* and *B* and denoted S_{FE} in panel (*b*) illustrates

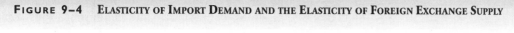

FIGURE 9–4 ELASTICITY OF IMPORT DEMAND AND THE ELASTICITY OF FOREIGN EXCHANGE SUPPLY

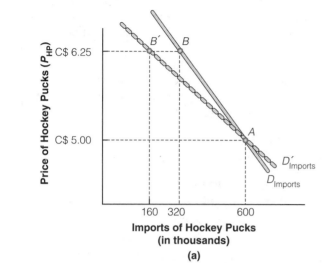

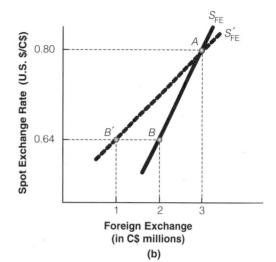

The elasticity of import demand determines the elasticity of foreign exchange supply. In panel (*b*), *S* denotes the foreign exchange supply curve derived from the import demand curve *D,* while *S'* denotes the foreign exchange supply curve derived from the import demand curve *D'*. In panel (a), the import demand curve denoted *D'* is more elastic than the demand curve denoted *D*. As a result, the foreign exchange supply curve denoted *S'* is more elastic than the foreign exchange supply curve denoted *S*.

all of the various combinations of the spot exchange rate and the quantity of foreign exchange supplied.

Elasticity and the Supply of Foreign Exchange

Just as the elasticity of export supply determines the elasticity of foreign exchange demand, so does the elasticity of import demand determine the elasticity of foreign exchange supply. Figure 9–3 shows that as the price of hockey pucks rises from C$5.00 to C$6.25, the quantity of hockey pucks demanded falls from 600,000 to 320,000. Suppose that for the same increase in price, the quantity of hockey pucks demanded falls to 160,000. Point *B'* in panel (*a*) of Figure 9–4 shows this combination of price and quantity demanded. The new demand curve formed by points *A* and *B'* and denoted *D'* is more elastic over the same price range as compared with the previous demand curve *D*.

As explained earlier, at a spot exchange rate of 0.64 U.S.$/C$ the world price of hockey pucks is C$6.25. Using the import demand curve *D'*, at a world price of C$6.25 Canada imports 160,000 hockey pucks. The value of Canada's imports at this spot exchange rate and along the demand curve *D'* and, therefore, the quantity of foreign exchange supplied–is C$1 million (C$6.25 × 160,000 = C$1 million). Point B' of panel (b) illustrates this combination of the spot exchange rate and the quantity of foreign exchange supplied. The new foreign exchange supply curve formed by points A and B' and denoted S' is more elastic over the same range of exchange rates than the previous supply curve S.

Thus, the elasticity of import demand determines the elasticity of foreign exchange supply. The more elastic is the import demand curve, the more elastic is the foreign exchange supply curve. The less elastic is the import demand curve, the less elastic is the foreign exchange supply curve.

FUNDAMENTAL ISSUE #1

How does the supply of exports and demand for imports determine the supply of and demand for foreign exchange? In an environment where capital flows occur only to finance current account transactions, the supply and demand for foreign exchange is determined by a nation's imports and exports of goods and services. When a nation's residents import goods and services, they must pay for these imports with foreign exchange. Thus, the demand for imports generates a supply of foreign exchange. Likewise, when a nation's residents export goods and services, they require foreign exchange as payment for these exports. Thus, the supply of exports generates a demand for foreign exchange.

THE ELASTICITIES APPROACH

ELASTICITIES APPROACH
An approach that emphasizes changes in the prices of goods and services as the main determinant of a nation's balance of payments and the exchange value of its currency.

The **elasticities approach** centers on changes in the prices of goods and services as the determinant of a nation's balance of payments and the exchange value of its currency. As already explained, elasticity is a measure of the responsiveness of quantity to a change in price.

The previous section also showed that a change in the exchange rate affects the domestic currency price of goods and services. As an example, the Canadian dollar price of imported hockey pucks rises when the Canadian dollar depreciates against the U.S. dollar. As a result, Canada imports fewer hockey pucks. Hence, a change in the exchange rate affects the domestic prices of imported and exported goods and services. In turn, the quantity of imports demanded and the quantity of exports supplied changes as the domestic price changes. Elasticity measures thereby help us to determine how much the quantity of imports demanded and the quantity of exports supplied will change in response to a change in the exchange rate. In principle, this can be a useful tool when considering how to correct a balance of payments deficit.

The Exchange Rate and the Balance of Payments

To understand the effects of a currency devaluation or depreciation and the role of elasticity, we begin with a country that currently experiences a current account deficit. Figure 9–5 illustrates the two foreign exchange demand curves, D and D', from Figure 9–2 and the two foreign exchange supply curves, S and S', from Figure 9–4. Suppose that the spot exchange rate between the Canadian dollar and the U.S. dollar is 0.80 U.S.$/C$. As Figure 9–5 shows, at this spot exchange rate, Canada's quantity of foreign exchange supplied exceeds the quantity of foreign exchange demanded by C$2 million.

Recall that Canada's supply of foreign exchange results from the import of goods and services, while the demand for foreign exchange results from foreign purchases of Canada's exports. Hence, when Canada's quantity of foreign exchange supplied exceeds the quantity of foreign exchange demanded, Canada runs a current account deficit. The difference, C$2 million in this example, is the amount of the current account deficit.

Let's suppose the Canadian government wishes to eliminate the current account deficit by permitting the value of the Canadian dollar to depreciate relative to the U.S. dollar. As Figure 9–5 illustrates, when the number of U.S.

FIGURE 9–5 THE CURRENT ACCOUNT DEFICIT

The current account deficit is equivalent to the difference between the quantity of foreign exchange supplied and the quantity of foreign exchange demanded. At a spot exchange rate of 0.80 U.S.$/C$, Canada supplies C$3 million in foreign exchange and demands C$1 million in foreign exchange. Thus, at an exchange rate of 0.80 U.S.$/C$, the current account deficit is C$2 million. The extent to which a currency depreciation will improve the current account deficit depends on the elasticity of foreign exchange demand and supply. When demand and supply are relatively more elastic, less of a depreciation is required to eliminate the current account deficit.

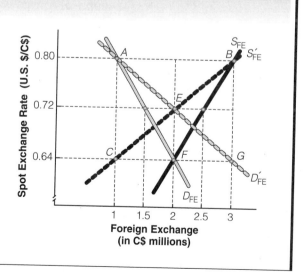

dollars required to purchase each Canadian dollar decreases, the quantity of foreign exchange demanded increases and the quantity of foreign exchange supplied decreases. In other words, Canada's exports of goods and services rise and Canada's imports of goods and services fall.

The Role of Elasticity How much of a depreciation of the Canadian dollar is required to completely eliminate the current account deficit? As Figure 9–5 also illustrates, the answer to this question depends of which set of supply and demand curves we consider. Consider the foreign exchange demand curve denoted D' and the foreign exchange supply curve denoted S'. The difference between the quantity of foreign exchange demanded and the quantity supplied and, therefore, the current account deficit, is eliminated at an exchange rate of 0.72 U.S.\$/C\$. In other words, a 10 percent depreciation of the Canadian dollar relative to the U.S. dollar eliminates the current account deficit:

$$(0.80 - 0.72)/0.80 \times 100 = 10\%.$$

If, on the other hand, we consider the foreign exchange supply and demand curves D and S in Figure 9–5, a 10 percent depreciation of the Canadian dollar relative to the U.S. dollar does not completely eliminate the current account deficit. A deficit of C\$1 million remains. The spot exchange rate would need to decline to 0.64 U.S.\$/C\$ in order to completely eliminate the deficit. Hence, according to the figure, a 20 percent depreciation is required:

$$(0.80 - 0.64)/0.80 \times 100 = 20\%.$$

What these two contrasting examples show is that the elasticities of the supply and demand curves are important when considering the correction of a balance-of-payments deficit. As explained in the previous section of this chapter, elasticity is a measure of the price responsiveness of the demand for and the supply of foreign exchange. Because the demand curve D' is more elastic relative to demand curve D, a 10 percent depreciation generates a larger change in the quantity of foreign exchange demanded along curve D' than it does along the less elastic demand curve D. Likewise, a 10 percent depreciation generates a larger change in the quantity of foreign exchange supplied along the relatively more elastic supply curve S' than it does along the supply curve S.

We must also keep in mind that, though we speak of the elasticities of the demand and supply curves for foreign exchange, the elasticity measures of these two curves merely reflect the elasticities of the export supply and import demand curves. The elasticities of export supply and import demand depend on many factors. These measures also vary across countries. Table 9–1 provides import price elasticity measures for Canada, Germany, Japan, the United Kingdom, and the United States. This table shows how price elasticity measures vary across countries. For example, Canada's and Germany's import

TABLE 9–1   MEASURES OF THE PRICE ELASTICITY OF IMPORT DEMAND

IMPORTING COUNTRY	SOURCE COUNTRY				
	CANADA	GERMANY	JAPAN	U.K.	U.S.
Canada	–	–0.84	–1.28	–0.46	–0.99
Germany	–0.67	–	–1.51	–0.11	–0.89
Japan	–0.36	–1.31	–	–0.74	–0.72
U.K.	–1.62	–0.49	–0.29	–	–0.88
U.S.	–0.80	–1.70	–1.13	–0.34	–

SOURCE: Data from Marquez, Jaime, "Bilateral Trade Elasticities" in *Review of Economics and Statistics*, VLXXII (1), February, 1990, pp. 70–77.

ON THE WEB

Learn more about the Canadian economy at:
http://www.statcan.ca/ english/Pgdb/economy.htm

EXCHANGE RATE INSTABILITY
A situation in which a currency depreciation increases the difference between the quantity of foreign exchange supplied and the quantity of foreign exchange demanded instead of reducing the difference.

MARSHALL–LERNER CONDITION A necessary condition for exchange rate stability, in which the sum of the elasticity of import demand and the elasticity of export supply must exceed unity.

demands are most sensitive to changes in the prices of Japanese goods and services, while U.K. import demand is least sensitive to changes in Japanese goods and services and most sensitive to changes in the prices of Canadian goods and services. To understand the implications of the elasticity measures in Table 9–1, consider Canada's elasticity of imports demanded from Japan. The table shows a price elasticity measure of –1.28. This measure indicates that when the prices of Japanese goods and services rise by 1 percent, Canada's demand for imported Japanese goods and services falls by 1.28 percent.

The Marshall–Lerner Condition   Based on the previous example, it appears that a depreciation will always improve a balance of payments deficit to some extent if not in full. This is not necessarily the case. It is theoretically possible that a depreciation can *increase* the difference between the quantity of foreign exchange supplied and the quantity of foreign exchange demanded. Likewise, an appreciation may *increase* the difference between the quantity of foreign exchange demanded and the quantity of foreign exchange supplied. **Exchange rate instability** is this type of situation where a depreciation causes an excess quantity of foreign exchange supplied to increase, and a currency appreciation causes an excess quantity of foreign exchange demanded to increase.

The **Marshall–Lerner condition** specifies the necessary condition for exchange rate stability. The condition and its derivation are quite complex and are beyond the scope of our discussion here. However, we can state the condition as it applies to the single-country example we have considered to this point. According to the Marshall–Lerner condition, exchange rate stability results when the sum of the absolute values of the elasticity of import demand and the elasticity of export supply exceed unity. The Marshall–Lerner condition is met in most situations. It is possible, however, that if we consider a very short time horizon, the Marshall–Lerner condition may not be met.

FUNDAMENTAL ISSUE #2

What is the elasticity approach to balance-of-payments and exchange-rate determination? The elasticity approach is a theory of balance-of-payments and exchange-rate determination that emphasizes the effect of prices changes. A currency depreciation or appreciation may change the domestic currency price paid for imports and the price received for exports, thus leading to changes in the quantity of imports demanded and the quantity of exports supplied. The amounts by which the quantity of imports demanded and the quantity of exports supplied (and, therefore, the balance of payments) change is determined by the elasticity of export supply and the elasticity of import demand.

Short- and Long-Run Elasticity Measures and the J-Curve

Many factors determine the elasticity of export supply and import demand. The time horizon considered is particularly important, however, when considering the correction of a current account deficit.

Short-Run versus Long-Run Time Horizons The Marshall–Lerner condition implies that the elasticities of export supply and import demand must be sufficiently elastic for a depreciation to reduce the nation's balance of payments deficit. Elasticity measures generally differ over the time horizon that is considered. Because a longer time interval provides households and businesses the time needed to adjust to price changes, supply and demand tend to be relatively more price elastic over longer time periods and relatively less elastic over shorter time periods. For example, in the short run, households and businesses may be obligated by contract to complete a purchase of an imported good. Further, households and businesses might not have the opportunity to find domestic suppliers of imported goods and services, and thus might alter their planned expenditures on imports.

Over longer time horizons, however, if the prices of imported goods and services rise, households and business can adjust their planned expenditures. They can seek out alternatives to imported goods and services and reduce their reliance on imports. Hence, over longer time intervals, households and businesses are more responsive to price changes, and over shorter time intervals they are less responsive to price changes. We can conclude, therefore, that import demand and export supply tend to be relatively more elastic over long time intervals and relatively less elastic over short time intervals.

J-CURVE EFFECT
A phenomenon in which a depreciation of the domestic currency causes a nation's balance of payments to worsen before it improves.

The J-Curve Effect Because import demand and export supply tend to be less elastic in the short run, a depreciation of the domestic currency is unlikely to immediately improve a nation's balance-of-payments deficit. It is even possible that a depreciation could cause a nation's balance of payments to worsen before it improves, a phenomenon known as the **J-curve effect.** (See "Policy Notebook: The United States and Canada–J-Curves or S-Curves?").

To understand how the J-curve effect might arise, consider an extreme example where, in the short term, Canada's quantity of imports demanded and quantity of exports supplied are completely unresponsive to price changes–they are completely *inelastic.* Using the original import demand curve *D* and export supply curve *S*, at an exchange rate of 0.80 U.S.$/C$, the value of Canada's imports is C$3 million (C$5.00 × 600,000 = C$3 million) and the value of Canada's exports is C$1 million (C$2.00 × 500,000 = C$1 million). Hence, Canada has a current account deficit of C$2 million.

Next consider how a depreciation of the Canadian dollar to a spot exchange rate of 0.64 U.S.$/C$ affects the current account deficit in this situation. Because the quantity of exports supplied and the quantity of imports demanded are unresponsive to price changes, these quantities do not vary with a change in the spot exchange rate. As explained earlier, when the spot exchange rate falls to 0.64 U.S.$/C$, the world price of wheat, as expressed in Canadian dollars, is C$2.50, and the world price of hockey pucks is $6.25. Thus, the value of Canada's exports rises to C$1.25 million (C$2.50 × 500,000 = C$1.25 million), while the value of Canada's imports rises to C$3.75 million (C$6.25 × 600,000 = C$3.75 million). Canada's current account deficit actually widens to C$2.5 million, for an increase of C$500,000.

As the time period considered lengthens, Canadian households and businesses are able to find alternatives to the relatively more expensive imported goods and services. Thus, the quantity of imported goods and services begins to decline, as indicated by the import demand curve *D* in Figure 9–3*a.* Likewise, foreign households and businesses are able to shift their expenditures to the relatively cheaper Canadian exports. Consequently, the quantity of Canadian goods and services exported begins to rise, as indicated by the supply curve *S* in Figure 9–1*a.* Eventually, as shown in Figure 9–5, the current account deficit is eliminated.

Figure 9–6 illustrates the hypothetical J-curve that results for this example. Initially, in time period t_1, Canada has a current account deficit of C$2 million. With a depreciation of the Canadian dollar to a spot exchange rate of 0.64 U.S.$/C$, the deficit widens to C$2.5 million in time period t_2. As time continues, the deficit narrows, until it is eventually eliminated in time period t_3. The graph shows the initially worsening of the trade deficit before it improves, forming a J-shaped curve.

FIGURE 9–6 THE "J-CURVE"

Initially Canada has a current account deficit of C$2 million. At time period t_1 the currency depreciates. In the short run, import demand and export supply may be relatively inelastic. In this situation, the current account actually widens to C$2.5 million at time period t_2. Eventually, as business and households have time to adjust their planned expenditures on imports and exports, the deficit narrows.

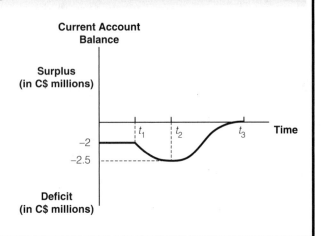

FUNDAMENTAL ISSUE #3

What is the J-curve effect? The J-curve effect is a phenomenon where, following a depreciation of the domestic currency, a nation's balance-of-payments deficit may actually worsen before it improves, forming a J-shaped curve. The J-curve effect results from the demand for imports and supply of exports being inelastic in the short-run. Hence, following a depreciation of the domestic currency, the quantity of imports demanded and the quantity of exports supplied do not change much. As a result, the balance-of-payments deficit, as valued in the domestic currency, widens. The J-curve effect is sometimes, but not always, observed following a domestic currency depreciation or devaluation.

Pass-Through Effects

In our example, a depreciation of the Canadian dollar improved Canada's current account deficit. Part of the improvement was brought about by a decrease in the quantity of imports demanded. This reduction in the quantity of imports demanded resulted from an increase in the Canadian dollar price of imported goods caused by the currency depreciation. Economists refer to this effect, in which a currency depreciation results in higher domestic prices of

POLICY NOTEBOOK

The United States and Canada—"J-Curves" or "S-Curves?"

Do the trade accounts of the United States and Canada display a "J-curve" effect following a depreciation of their respective currencies? This is the question examined by economists Kanta Marwah of Carleton University in Canada, and Lawrence Klein of the University of Pennsylvania in the United States.

Marwah and Klein investigate the behavior of the trade accounts of these two countries between 1975 and 1994. Using trade data and spot exchange rates between the United States, Canada, the United Kingdom, France, Germany, and Japan, the authors are able to detect a long- and short-run relationship between exchange rate changes and the trade balance. They find that, in general, following a currency depreciation there is a "distinct tendency" for trade balances to worsen before they improve. In the case of Canada, the trade balance worsens in the first quarter following a depreciation before it begins to improve in the second quarter. They find that the U.S. trade balance worsens in the first and second quarters following a depreciation before it begins to improve in the

third quarter, so that the J-curve effect appears to last slightly longer in the United States.

Consequently, Marwah and Klein find that although the U.S. and Canadian patterns of adjustment are similar, the "J-curve" effect is less regular for Canada than it is for the United States. In addition, they conclude that the adjustment pattern for Canada is also much quicker than that of the United States. They also find that trade balances worsen and then improve again later in the adjustment process. This observation, referred to as an "S-curve," has been made by other economists as well. Nonetheless, Marwah and Klein's main conclusion is that the trade balances of the United States and Canada do worsen following a depreciation, before they improve.

FOR CRITICAL ANALYSIS:

Why might the trade balance of a nation such as Canada adjust more quickly in response to exchange-rate changes as compared with the trade balance of the United States?

PASS-THROUGH EFFECT
The effect of a currency depreciation that results in higher domestic prices of imported goods and services.

imported goods and services, as the **pass-through effect.** In other words, the currency depreciation is *passed through* to domestic prices.

If, for some reason, the currency depreciation is not passed through to domestic prices of imported goods and services, the currency depreciation may not improve the current account deficit. Similarly, if a currency appreciation does not reduce the price of imported goods and services, the appreciation may not reduce a current account surplus. Hence, it is important to understand how much of a change in the exchange value of the domestic currency is passed through to domestic prices because of the implications for a nation's balance of payments.

There have been a number of studies conducted on pass-through effects. Economists have found that the degree of pass-through varies across nations, across time, and across industries within nations. Some industries, such as

Changes in the Value of the U.S. Dollar and the Price of Luxury German Autos

During the early 1980s, the U.S. dollar appreciated considerably against most other major currencies. A dollar appreciation should result in lower prices of imported goods and services relative to the prices of these goods and services abroad as the appreciation is passed-through to U.S. prices. For example, when the U.S. dollar appreciates, the U.S. price of an imported German luxury automobile should be less than the U.S. dollar price of the same auto in Europe, after subtracting for transportation costs.

Following the appreciation of the U.S. dollar in the early 1980s, however, luxury German automobiles became more expensive in the United States than in most European nations: German auto exporters had increased the prices of luxury automobiles to more than offset the appreciation of the dollar. In contrast, when the dollar reversed course and depreciated in the latter half of the 1980s, U.S. dollar prices of imported luxury German automobiles dropped back toward European prices. Hence, German exporters allowed the depreciation of the U.S. dollar to pass through to U.S. imported luxury automobile prices.

There are a number of reasons why exchange rate changes may not be passed through to domestic prices of imported goods and services. Some production costs, such as advertising, may be conducted in the domestic nation. These costs rise when the domestic currency appreciates. In addition, it may be that foreign exporters cannot easily expand their sales abroad when the domestic currency appreciates. Hence, domestic prices of imported goods and services may not fall. Further, it may be that foreign firms wish to maintain their market share and are willing to alter the prices of their exports to the domestic nation to offset the effects of a currency depreciation.

Economists Kenneth Froot and Paul Klemperer provide evidence in support of an additional hypothesis. Their hypothesis is that foreign firms react differently to changes in the exchange value of the domestic currency. If a change in the exchange value of the domestic currency is viewed as being temporary, foreign firms alter their prices and do not allow a full pass-through to domestic prices. If the change in the exchange value of the domestic currency is viewed as permanent, foreign firms allow pass-through effects to domestic prices. This is a potential explanation of why the degree of pass-through varies across time.

FOR CRITICAL ANALYSIS:

How might the degree of exchange rate pass-through differ during a period of global expansion as compared with a period of global economic contraction?

luxury automobiles, have a very low degree of pass through. (See the "Management Notebook: Changes in the Value of the U.S. Dollar and the Price of Luxury German Autos.") One reason that exchange value changes might not be passed through to domestic prices is that foreign producers may choose to alter the prices of their products to offset the change in a currency's exchange value and thereby maintain their market share in the domestic nation.

THE ABSORPTION APPROACH

The two traditional balance-of-payments and exchange-rate approaches emphasize different variables. The elasticities approach emphasizes prices as a determinant of the balance of payments and exchange rate. The absorption approach, however, assumes that prices remain constant and emphasizes changes in real domestic income. Hence, the **absorption approach** is a real-income theory of balance-of-payments and exchange-rate determination. Because of the assumption of constant prices, economists view the absorption approach as a short-run approach to balance-of-payments and exchange-rate determination.

ABSORPTION APPROACH
A theory of balance-of-payments and exchange-rate determination that emphasizes the role of a nation's expenditures, or absorption, and income. According to the absorption approach, if a nation's real income exceeds the amount of goods and services that it absorbs, then the nation will run a current account surplus. If a nation's real income is less than the amount of goods and services it absorbs, then the nation will run a current account deficit.

Modeling the Absorption Approach

The absorption approach separates the market values of a nation's expenditures on final goods and services into four basic categories. These categories are consumption expenditures, investment expenditures, government expenditures, and expenditures on imports. Exports are not included, because they represent another nation's expenditures on domestic final goods and services. Because prices are assumed to be constant, the values in each category are *real* measures.

Absorption Economists refer to the total of these four categories of expenditures as *domestic absorption*. That is, a nation absorbs goods and services for

ABSORPTION A nation's total expenditures on final goods and services net of exports.

consumption, investment, and public sector purposes, as well as imports from abroad. Hence, **absorption** is a nation's total expenditures on final goods and services. We shall express the identity representing a nation's absorption as:

$$a \equiv c + i + g + im,$$

where a denotes absorption, c denotes real consumption expenditures, i denotes real investment expenditures, g denotes real government expenditures, and im denotes the nation's real expenditures on imported goods and services.

Real Income   A nation's real income, on the other hand, is equivalent to the real expenditures on its output of final goods and services. Hence, real income is equal to real consumption expenditures, real investment expenditures, real government expenditures, and other nations' real expenditures on its output, or its real exports. We shall represent a nation's real income as:

$$y \equiv c + i + g + x,$$

where y denotes real income and x denotes real exports.

The Current Account   As explained earlier in this chapter, capital flows were not very important at the time the elasticities and absorption approaches were developed. Hence, the current account was the focus of economists' attention. In the absorption approach, the current account balance, ignoring any unilateral transfers, is represented by the difference between foreign real expenditures on exports and domestic real expenditures on imports. This is represented as:

$$ca = x - im,$$

where ca denotes the real current account balance. If real exports exceed real imports, the nation is running a current account surplus. If real exports are equal to real imports, the nation's current account is balanced. If real exports are less than real imports, the nation is running a current account deficit.

Determination of the Current Account Balance

According to the absorption approach, a nation's current account balance is determined by the difference between its income and absorption. This can be seen by subtracting the equation representing absorption from the equation for the nation's real income:

$$y - a = (c + i + g + x) - (c + i + g + im).$$

Combining terms on the right-hand side, we obtain:

$$y - a = x - im.$$

Finally, we can substitute ca for the value $x - im$, as the difference between the two is the current account balance. Doing so, we obtain the standard equation representing the absorption approach:

$$y - a = ca.$$

Hence, a nation's current account balance is determined by the difference between its real income and its absorption.

For example, suppose the nation's income exceeds its absorption, $y > a$; that is to say, it is producing more output than it absorbs. In this situation, the right-hand side of the equation is positive, which implies that the nation is running a current account surplus ($y > a$: current account surplus). Likewise, when a nation's incomes is less than its absorption, it runs a current account deficit ($y < a$: current account deficit). Finally, when a nation's income is equal to its absorption, its current account is balanced.

Economic Expansion and Contraction

Though it is a simple theory, the absorption approach is useful in understanding the performance of a nation's current account balance and the exchange value of its currency during periods of economic expansion and during periods of economic contraction, or recessions. It is often presupposed, particularly in popular media reports, that a nation experiencing an economic contraction will spend less on imported goods and services, so that its current account balance will improve and its currency will appreciate. Likewise, observers typically argue, a country undergoing an economic expansion will spend more on imported goods and services so that its current account balance will deteriorate and its currency will depreciate. In the real world things do not always turn out this way. The absorption approach helps explain why this is so.

Consider a nation whose current account initially is balanced. Suppose that this nation experiences an economic expansion. As real income rises, so, typically, do real expenditures, or absorption. Returning to the equation for the absorption approach:

$$y - a = ca,$$

when real income, y rises and absorption, a, rises, it is unclear whether the nation will have a current account deficit or surplus. This depends on which element, real income or absorption, rises *faster*. If real income rises faster than absorption—that is, if domestic output rises faster than domestic expenditures—the nation will experience a current account surplus. If absorption rises faster than real income, the nation will experience a current account deficit. If real income and absorption rise at the same rate, the current account will remain in balance.

We can examine the impact on the exchange value of the domestic currency in a similar manner. We return to our previous equation that appeared in our derivation of the absorption approach:

$$y - a = x - im.$$

If, during the course of an economic expansion, real income rises faster than absorption, then the nation's exports must rise relative to its imports. As a result, the domestic currency appreciates. If absorption rises faster than real income, the nation's imports must rise relative to its exports. As a result, the domestic currency depreciates.

Likewise, during the course of an economic downturn, if real income falls faster than absorption, then exports decline relative to imports, and the domestic currency depreciates. If absorption declines faster than real income, then the nation's exports rise relative to its imports, and the domestic currency appreciates.

In conclusion, the absorption approach shows us why a nation enjoying an economic expansion often experiences a currency appreciation, while a nation in a recession often experiences a currency depreciation. What is important is the *relative* change in real income and absorption. The absorption approach, as we shall discuss next, also illustrates the limited effectiveness of policy actions designed to reduce a current account deficit.

FUNDAMENTAL ISSUE #5

What is the absorption approach to balance-of-payments and exchange-rate determination? The absorption approach emphasizes a nation's real income and expenditures as determinants of its balance of payments and the exchange value of its currency. According to the absorption approach, if a nation's real income exceeds the amount of goods and services that it absorbs, then the nation will run a current account surplus. If a nation's real income is less than the amount of goods and services it absorbs, then the nation will run a current account deficit. If real income and absorption are equal, the nation's current account will be balanced.

Policy Instruments

We must recall the economic environment during which the absorption model was developed to fully appreciate its policy implications. The absorption approach was developed in the 1950s, with credit typically given to Sidney Alexander, an economist at the International Monetary Fund. As explained in Chapter 3, during this period most nations participated in the Bretton Woods system of adjustable-peg-exchange-rate arrangements.

As we noted in Chapter 8 and will be discussing in much greater detail in Chapter 12, policymakers have access to a number of *policy instruments*, which are variables that they can determine, either directly or indirectly. In the

ABSORPTION INSTRUMENT
A government's ability to increase or decrease a nation's absorption by changing its own purchases of domestic output or by influencing consumption and investment expenditures.

absorption approach, and under adjustable-pegged exchange rates, policymakers have two instruments, an *absorption instrument* and an *expenditure-switching instrument*. The **absorption instrument** refers to a government's ability to raise or reduce a nation's absorption by changing its own purchases of domestic output (g), or by influencing consumption and investment expenditures through changes in taxes. A change in government spending results in a change in g, whereas a change in taxes affect households' planned consumption expenditures and businesses investment expenditures, resulting in a change in c and i. It is unclear, however, how a decrease in expenditures might affect real income in the context of the absorption model. Thus, it is also unclear as to whether the use of an absorption instrument will be effective in reducing a current account deficit.

Nevertheless, the absorption approach also shows the potential consequences of attempting to stimulate the domestic economy through increased government expenditures. Suppose that policymakers in an economy experiencing a recession increase government spending, g, in an attempt to stimulate output. If the increase in government expenditures causes absorption to rise faster than output, then the nation's current account balance will worsen.

EXPENDITURE-SWITCHING INSTRUMENT   A government's ability to alter, or switch, expenditures among imports and exports by enacting policies that change their relative prices.

The **expenditure-switching instrument** is the ability of the government to alter, or "switch," private expenditures among imports and exports by adopting policies that change their relative costs. This can be accomplished in two ways. First, the government can impose trade restrictions. These commercial policies would raise the price of imported goods and services, leading consumers and business to purchase fewer imports and more goods and services produced domestically. Domestic income rises as the domestic production of the imported goods and services rises, while the absorption of imported goods and services declines and the absorption of domestic goods and services rises. These types of policies, however, often lead to retaliation from the nation's trading partners.

Another way to induce expenditure switching is by changing the exchange value of the domestic currency. A devaluation of the domestic currency causes foreign goods and services to become relatively more expensive. Consequently, domestic consumers and businesses may switch from imported to domestically produced goods and services. A revaluation of the domestic currency would have the opposite effect.

Expenditure switching, according to the absorption approach, does not necessarily improve the current account balance. If households and businesses switch directly between imported goods and services and domestically produced goods and services, leaving overall absorption the same, and if the level of real income remains the same, then there is no change in the current account balance. As demonstrated earlier, the current account balance changes only if there is an increase in real income relative to absorption. This is accomplished only if a policy action stimulates greater output of exports relative to expenditures on imports. Hence, a devaluation alone may have limited usefulness in correcting a current account deficit.

FUNDAMENTAL ISSUE #6

How do changes in real income and absorption affect a nation's current account balance and the exchange value of its currency? According to the absorption approach, if real income rises faster than absorption, then exports rise relative to imports, the nation's balance of payments improves, and the domestic currency appreciates. If absorption rises faster than real income, then imports rise relative to exports, the nation's balance of payments deteriorates, and the domestic currency depreciates. The two types of policy instruments in the absorption model, the absorption instrument and the expenditure-switching instrument, may have negligible effects on a nation's current account imbalance. Hence, it is unclear if these instruments will increase real income relative to absorption.

CHAPTER SUMMARY

1. **A Nation's Supply of Exports and Demand for Imports Determine its Demand for and Supply of Foreign Exchange:** If capital flows occur only to finance current account transactions, then the supply and demand for foreign exchange is determined by a nation's imports and exports of goods and services. When a nation's residents import goods and services, they must pay for these imports with foreign exchange. Hence, the nation's residents supply foreign exchange. Likewise, when a nation's residents export goods and services, they require foreign exchange as payment for these exports, which yields their demand for foreign exchange.

2. **The Elasticity Approach to Balance-of-Payments and Exchange-Rate Determination:** The elasticity approach is a theory of balance-of-payments and exchange-rate determination that focuses on the effects of price changes. A currency depreciation or appreciation may change the domestic currency price paid for imports and the price received for exports, thus leading to changes in the quantity of imports demanded and the quantity of exports supplied.

3. **The J-Curve Effect:** The J-curve effect is a phenomenon in which a nation's balance of payments deficit may actually worsen before it improves following a currency depreciation or devaluation. What results is a "J-shaped" curve as the balance of payments adjusts over time. The J-curve effect results from low short-run price elasticities of demand for imports and supply of exports. In the long run, however, these elasticities are larger because consumers and businesses have more time to adjust to the price changes. Hence, in the long run, the balance of payments is likely to improve following a depreciation of the domestic currency.

4. **Pass-Through Effects:** A pass-through effect arises when a change in the exchange value of the domestic currency results in a change in the domestic prices of imported goods and services. Hence, when the exchange value of the domestic currency changes, it may or may not be passed through and result in a change in the domestic prices of imported goods and services. The degree of pass-through varies across nation, across time, and across industries. The degree of pass-through is very important because it influences the response of a nation's balance of payments to a change in value of the domestic currency.

5. **The Absorption Approach to Balance-of-Payments and Exchange-Rate Determination:** The absorption approach to balance-of-payments and exchange-rate determination emphasizes a nation's real income and expenditures. According to the absorption approach, if a nation's real income exceeds the amount of goods and services that is absorbs, then the nation will run a current account surplus. If a nation's real income is less than the amount of goods and services it absorbs, then the nation will run a current account deficit. If real income and absorption are equal, the nation's current account will be balanced.

6. **Changes in Real Income and Absorption and a Nation's Current Account Balance and the Exchange Value of Its Currency:** The absorption approach illustrates that if real income rises faster than absorption, then exports rise relative to imports, the nation's balance of payments improves, and the domestic currency appreciates. If absorption rises faster than real income, then imports rise relative to exports, the nation's balance of payments deteriorate, and the domestic currency depreciates. A similar argument holds when real income and absorption decline.

QUESTIONS AND PROBLEMS

1. Price elasticity is calculated as the percentage change in quantity divided by the percentage change in price. If we let a subscript A denote the old value and a subscript B denote the new value, price elasticity is calculated as:

$$\frac{\left[\dfrac{Q_B - Q_A}{1/2(Q_A + Q_B)}\right]}{\left[\dfrac{P_B - P_A}{1/2(P_A + P_B)}\right]}$$

If the absolute value of the price elasticity measure is greater than unity, we say it is elastic. If it is less than unity, we say it is inelastic. If it is equal to unity, we say it is unit elastic. Using this formula, calculate the elasticity of foreign exchange demand in Figure 9–1b and the elasticity of foreign exchange supply in Figure 9–3b.

2. Based on the elasticity calculations in problem 1, what is the change in the quantity of imports demanded and the quantity of exports supplied when the Canadian dollar depreciates relative to the U.S. dollar by 1 percent? Answer this question both in absolute terms and in percentage change.

3. Slovakia is an international supplier of hockey pucks. Suppose that Slovakia prices and sells its hockey pucks on the international market in the U.S. dollar. What happens to Slovakia's exports when the currency of a major consumer of hockey pucks, Canada, depreciates against the U.S. dollar? Suppose Slovakia hockey puck producers desire to maintain the market share they have in Canada. Thus, they are willing to adjust their price for hockey pucks so that the quantity of hockey pucks demanded remains constant. Based on the depreciation illustrated in Figure 9–3, how much would Slovakia have to reduce the price of hockey pucks to maintain its current level of exports to Canada?

4. Suppose that real consumption expenditures in a nation are $10,000, real investment expenditures are $8,000, real government expenditures are $5,000, real expenditures on imports are $1,000, and real exports are $500. What is the nation's levels of real income and absorption? What is its trade balance?

5. Suppose that the government of the nation described in question 4 devalues the domestic currency and, as a result, imports fall by $50, exports rise by $50, and real consumption expenditures rise by $25. What is the trade balance now? Did the devaluation improve the balance of payments?

6. Explain how a "Buy American" advertising campaign is similar to an expenditure switching policy. What is the potential impact the campaign might have on the balance of payments in the context of the absorption approach?

ON-LINE APPLICATION

This chapter presented the elasticities approach to balance-of-payments and exchange-rate determination and the J-curve effect. A J-curve effect is sometimes observed for a nation's external balance following a devaluation or depreciation. The size and length of time of the effect is determined by elasticity of demand for exports and imports.

Internet URL: http://www.banxico.org.mx

Title: The Bank of Mexico

Navigation: Begin with **(http://www.banxico.org.mx)**. Click on *English* if an English version is desired. Next click on *Economic Information*. From the list of options, select *External data, time series*. Click on *Trade Balance*. From the bottom of the first list of options, click on *Trade Balance*.

Application: View the list of data, examining the period from January 1994 through 1995, and answer the following questions.

1. Prior to the depreciation of the Mexican peso in December 1994, was Mexico experiencing a trade surplus or deficit?

2. How long of a period was required before the balance changed signs?

3. Can you give any reasons why the balance changed so quickly? (It might be helpful to find out by how much the peso depreciated. This information is available at this web site.)

4. Examining the data from 1994 to the present, can you find any evidence of an S-curve effect?

REFERENCES AND RECOMMENDED READINGS

Alexander, S. S. "Devaluation versus Import Restriction as an Instrument for Improving the Foreign Trade Balance." *International Monetary Fund Staff Papers*, I (1951): 379–392.

Alexander, S. S. "Effects of a Devaluation on a Trade Balance." *International Monetary Fund Staff Papers*, II (1952): 263–278.

Corden, W. M. *Inflation, Exchange Rates, and the World Economy: Lectures on International Monetary Economics*, Chapter I: A Model of Balance of Payments Policy. Chicago: The University of Chicago Press, 1977.

Froot, Kenneth, and Paul Klemperer. "Exchange Rate Pass-Through When Market Share Matters." *American Economic Review*, 79 (September 1989): 637–654.

Gagon, Joseph E., and Michael Knetter. "Markup Adjustment and Exchange Rate Fluctuations: Evidence from Panel Data on Automobile Exports." *Journal of International Money and Finance*, 14(2) (April 1995): 289–310.

Jones, R. W., and W. M. Corden. "Devaluation, Non-Flexible Prices, and the Trade Balance for a Small Country." *Canadian Journal of Economics*, 9 (February 1976): 275–297.

Marquez, James. "Bilateral Trade Elasticities." *Review of Economics and Statistics*, 73 (February 1990): 70–77.

Marwah, Kanta, and Lawrence Klein. "Estimation of J-curves: United States and Canada." *Canadian Journal of Economics*, 29(3) (August 1996): 523–539.

Tsiang, S. C. "The Role of Money in Trade-Balance Stability: Synthesis of the Elasticity and Absorption Approaches." *American Economic Review*, 51 (1961): 912–936.

10

MONETARY AND PORTFOLIO APPROACHES TO EXCHANGE-RATE AND BALANCE-OF-PAYMENTS DETERMINATION

FUNDAMENTAL ISSUES

1. How do a central bank's foreign exchange market interventions alter the monetary base and the money stock?

2. What is the monetary approach to balance-of-payments and exchange-rate determination?

3. How is the monetary approach a theory of exchange-rate determination in a two-country setting?

4. What is the portfolio approach to exchange-rate determination?

5. Should central banks sterilize foreign exchange interventions?

In July 1997, Mr. George Soros, manager of one of the largest international investment funds, announced that he had completed a $980 million investment in Svyazinvest, a Russian telecommunications firm. This transaction was the largest single portfolio investment in Russia at the time. Mr. Soros added that he thought Russia had become "the most interesting emerging market in the world."

This event happened to coincide with a barrage of criticism against Mr. Soros from Southeast Asian politicians. Malaysian Prime Minister Mahathir Mohamad accused "a certain powerful American financier," namely Mr. Soros, for attacking Southeast Asian currencies, causing declines in their values in foreign exchange markets.

Only a few years earlier, the economies of Southeast Asia were the recipients of major portfolio investments from funds managers like Mr. Soros. This inflow of funds caused Asian currency values to rise and lending activity to expand. When international funds managers began directing funds elsewhere, most of the currencies of Southeast Asia tumbled. Mr. Soros claimed that sales of Malaysian ringgit and Thai baht-denominated-assets were made solely on an evaluation of return and risk.

How can a change in the demand for foreign-currency-denominated assets affect the exchange value of a nation's currency? This is an important question, particularly for emerging and transitional economies experiencing sizable inflows of foreign funds. Economists have developed financial-markets-oriented approaches to balance-of-payments and exchange-rate determination that help us understand this issue.

INTERVENTION, STERILIZATION, AND THE MONEY SUPPLY

Chapter 8 detailed the various objectives and functions of a central bank. In that chapter you learned that in many countries the central bank acts as the government's agent, conducting transactions in the foreign exchange markets at the government's request. We now consider how foreign exchange market interventions alter the nation's *monetary base* and its *money stock*.

A Nation's Monetary Base

Figure 8–5 on page 256 illustrates a simplified balance sheet of the central bank. In the figure, domestic credit (*DC*), which is the central bank's holdings of securities and loans, and foreign exchange reserves (*FER*), valued in terms of the domestic currency, constitute the central bank's assets. Currency outstanding (*C*) and the total reserves of banks (*TR*) constitute the central bank's liabilities. Because the assets of the central bank equal its liabilities, we can express the nation's monetary base as either the sum of domestic credit and foreign exchange reserves or the sum of currency outstanding and the total reserves of banks:

$$MB = DC + FER, \text{ or } MB = C + TR.$$

For our discussion in this chapter, it will be convenient to focus on the asset side of the central bank's balance sheet and express the nation's monetary base (*MB*) as the sum of domestic credit and foreign exchange reserves. Hence, allowing Δ to denote the change in a variable, we can express the change in a nation's monetary base as:

$$\Delta MB = \Delta DC + \Delta FER.$$

This expression tells us that a nation's monetary base will change because of a change in domestic credit or in foreign exchange reserves, or in both.

A Nation's Money Stock

There are a variety of measures of a nation's money stock, which we shall denote *M*. The simplest measure, and the one we shall use, is the sum of the amount of currency in circulation and the amount of transactions deposits in the banking system. As explained in Chapter 8, most nations have a fractional-reserve banking system. Central banks typically require that private banks maintain a fraction of their customers' transactions deposits as reserves. This fraction determines the maximum increase in the money stock that a change in the total reserves of the banking system can create.

An Open-Market Transaction　To see why this is so, consider an example. Suppose the reserve requirement is 10 percent. Next consider an open-market operation, as described in Chapter 8, in which the U.S. Federal Reserve System (the "Fed") purchases $1 million of securities from a securities dealer. When the Fed purchases the $1 million in securities, the domestic credit component of the Fed's balance sheet rises by $1 million, so the monetary base rises by $1 million. The securities dealer may have the Fed wire the payment to the dealer's account, say at a bank in Chicago. The Fed completes the transaction by applying a $1 million credit to the Chicago bank's reserve account at the Federal Reserve Bank of Chicago, and the amount of total reserves of the private bank increases by $1 million. The private bank then earmarks these funds for the dealer's transactions deposit account with the bank. The Fed has, therefore, created an additional $1 million in total reserves, and the nation's money stock immediately rises by $1 million.

The effect of the Fed's action does not end here, however. Of the $1 million in total reserves, 10 percent, or $100,000 are required reserves and

$900,000 are excess reserves. The bank in Chicago is free to lend out the $900,000 in excess reserves. If the individuals who receive the $900,000 in loans spend these funds, then the recipients of these funds ultimately may redeposit them at other banks, thereby creating $900,000 in new transactions deposits. Because of this lending activity, the amount of domestic credit, and thus the money stock, can rise by an additional $900,000, for a total increase of $1 million + $900,000 = $1.9 million.

Once again the story does not necessarily end here. Of the $900,000 in new transactions deposits, 10 percent, or $90,000 are required reserves and $810,000 are excess reserves. Banks with the new $810,000 in excess reserves are free to lend the excess reserves, which will be spent and again may create new deposits at other banks.

This process continues, with excess reserves being 10 percent smaller at each step and thus the amount of new transactions deposits created being 10 percent larger at each step. Consequently, we can conclude that the $1 million open-market purchase by the Fed leads to an increase in the money stock that is a multiple of the $1 million purchase. The Fed's security purchase, therefore, has a multiplier effect on the total quantity of transactions deposits included in the nation's money stock.

The Money Multiplier To determine the magnitude of the multiplier effect in this example, let's denote the amount of transactions deposits of private banks as TD and the amount of total cash reserves of these banks as TR. Finally we denote the reserve requirement as rr. If banks were to hold only the amount of reserves required by the Fed, then total reserves in the banking system would be $TR = (rr \times TD)$. Any change in total reserves due to changes in transactions deposits at banks would be

$$\Delta TR = rr \times \Delta TD.$$

Solving this equation for ΔTD by dividing each side of the equation by rr yields

$$\Delta TD = (1/rr) \times \Delta TR.$$

Thus, the *maximum* amount by which transactions deposits may rise is equal to the change in total reserves times a *multiplier* equal to $1/rr$.

In our example, the Fed's security purchase causes an initial increase of $1 million in the private bank's reserves, so ΔTR equals $1 million. Further, the reserve requirement is 10 percent, so rr equals 0.10 and $1/rr$ equals 10. As a result, the maximum possible change in total transactions deposits in the banking system, ΔTD, equals 10 times $1 million, or $10 million. Therefore, in our example, the Fed's $1 million securities purchase ultimately can increase the amount of transactions deposits, and thus the money stock, by $10 million. The ratio $1/rr$ is the transactions deposit multiplier. Under an assumption that the monetary base is comprised solely of transactions deposits, the transactions deposit multiplier is also the **money multiplier** (m),

MONEY MULTIPLIER
The number by which a reserve measure is multiplied to obtain the total money stock of an economy.

which is the number by which a reserve measure is multiplied to obtain the amount of the money stock of an economy.

Realistically, the final multiplier effect of an open-market transaction is less than the amount given by the money multiplier as derived here. One reason is that most people hold some money in the form of currency and do not deposit all of their funds in transactions deposits accounts. Hence, at each step in the process banks have fewer funds to lend than that given in the example. Another reason that the multiplier typically is smaller than the ratio $1/rr$ is that many banks hold some excess reserves—or, in other words, they do not lend out all excess reserves at each step of the multiplier process.

The Relationship between the Monetary Base and the Money Stock

This example, in which we assume that the monetary base consists solely of transactions deposits, describes a relationship between the monetary base and the money stock. That is, the money stock is equal to the monetary base times the money multiplier. As we include the amount of currency in circulation as a component of the monetary base, the money multiplier becomes more complex and is no longer equal to the ratio $1/rr$. (The derivation of the money multiplier in a situation where the monetary base includes currency in circulation is left as a problem at the end of this chapter.) Regardless of the complexity of the money multiplier, we can express the relationship between the money stock and the monetary base as:

$$M = m \times MB = m(C + TR) = m(DC + FER).$$

Further, we can express a change in the nation's money stock as the value of the money multiplier times the change in the nation's monetary base:

$$\Delta M = m \times \Delta MB = m(\Delta C + \Delta TR) = m(\Delta DC + \Delta FER).$$

Using this equation, we can examine the effect of an open-market operation, as depicted in our previous example, on the nation's money stock. First we must recognize that the change in total reserves of the banking system—the initial $1 million increase in the private bank's reserve account at the Chicago Fed—is equivalent to a $1 million change in domestic credit, because the Fed purchased $1 million in securities. The change in cash outstanding and foreign exchange reserves, however, is zero. Assuming that the money multiplier is 10, substituting these values into the previous equation yields

$$\Delta M = 10 \times \$1 \text{ million} = \$10 \text{ million}.$$

Thus, $10 million is the maximum possible change in the nation's money stock.

Foreign Exchange Interventions and the Money Stock

Chapter 8 explained that foreign exchange interventions are purchases or sales of foreign-currency-denominated assets. To show how central banks conduct

---

The simplified balance sheets of the Federal Reserve and the Bank of England express the monetary base as the sum of the central bank's assets, domestic credit and foreign exchange reserves, and as the sum of its liabilities, currency, and bank reserves.

Simplified Balance Sheet of the Federal Reserve

Assets	Liabilities
Domestic credit	Currency
Foreign exchange reserves	Bank reserves
Monetary base	Monetary base

Simplified Balance Sheet of the Bank of England

Assets	Liabilities
Domestic credit	Currency
Foreign exchange reserves	Bank reserves
Monetary base	Monetary base

their interventions through the private banking system, changing the monetary base and thereby altering the money stock, we consider only the purchase or sale of foreign-currency-denominated bank deposits. These deposits are assets of domestic individuals, firms, brokers, and banks, which they hold on deposit at foreign banks. Hence, foreign exchange transactions of the central bank affect the balance sheets of domestic private banks *and* the balance sheets of foreign private banks. Indirectly, therefore, foreign exchange interventions influence the domestic money stock *and* potentially the foreign nation's money stock.

An Example of a U.S. Foreign Exchange Transaction   To illustrate the consequences of a central bank's foreign exchange interventions, we shall focus on a two-country example using the simplified central bank balance sheet presented in Chapter 8. For purposes of illustration, let's suppose that the two countries are the United States and the United Kingdom. Figure 10–1 presents the simplified balance sheets of the Federal Reserve and the Bank of England. As our example unfolds, we use these balance sheets to show the change in the components of the monetary base of each nation.

Let's suppose that the money multiplier of the United States is 2.6 while the money multiplier of the United Kingdom is 2.1. Also, let's suppose that the Federal Reserve purchases a £1 million bank deposit from a New York foreign exchange dealer at a spot rate of 1.6 U.S. dollars per pound ($/£).

FIGURE 10–2 **THE EFFECT OF A FOREIGN EXCHANGE PURCHASE ON THE FED'S BALANCE SHEET**

When the Federal Reserve purchases $1.6 million of foreign reserves, the foreign exchange reserves component of the monetary base rises. The Federal Reserve pays the foreign exchange dealer by applying a $1.6 million credit to the reserves of the dealer's bank.

Simplified Balance Sheet of the Federal Reserve

Assets	Liabilities
Domestic credit	Currency
Foreign exchange reserves +$1,600,000	Bank reserves +$1,600,000
Monetary base +$1,600,000	Monetary base +$1,600,000

If the dealer instructs the Fed to wire the payment to his account at a New York bank, the Fed applies a $1.6 million (£1 million × 1.6 $/£) credit to that bank's reserve account at the Federal Reserve Bank of New York. The private bank then earmarks those funds for the transactions deposit account at the dealer's bank. As a result, the transactions deposits of the U.S. banking system rise by $1.6 million and the foreign exchange reserves of the Fed rise by £1 million (or, if valued in dollar terms, by $1.6 million). Figure 10–2 shows the effect of the foreign exchange purchase on the Fed's balance sheet as an increase in the foreign exchange reserves component of $1.6 million, with a resulting increase in the U.S. monetary base of $1.6 million.

As discussed earlier, the initial increase in transactions deposits leads to a multiple increase in the U.S. money stock. The increase in the U.S. money stock is equal to the U.S. money multiplier times the $1.6 million increase in the monetary base. Using the same equations as in our open-market-operation example, we can express the impact on the U.S. money stock as

$$\Delta M_{US} = m_{US} \times \Delta MB = m_{US} \times (\Delta DC + \Delta FER).$$

In this instance, the change in domestic credit is zero, the change in foreign exchange reserves is $1.6 million, and the U.S. money multiplier is 2.6. Substituting these values into the last equation, the change in the U.S. money stock is

$$\Delta M_{US} = 2.6 \times (\$0 + \$1.6 \text{ million})$$
$$= 2.6 \times \$1.6 \text{ million} = \$4.16 \text{ million}.$$

Hence, the foreign exchange transaction of the Fed increases the U.S. money stock by $4.16 million.

The Effect on the U.K. Money Stock Following a purchase of the pound-denominated deposit, the Fed has a £1 million claim on a U.K. bank. The Fed presents this claim to the Bank of England. The Bank of England "clears" the

---

FIGURE 10–3   THE EFFECT OF FOREIGN EXCHANGE PURCHASE BY THE FED ON THE BANK OF ENGLAND'S BALANCE SHEET

When the Federal Reserve purchases £1 million of British-pound-denominated bank deposits, it then presents the deposits to the Bank of England. The Bank of England assumes the liability and reduces the British bank's reserve account by £1 million. This, in turn, reduces domestic credit and the monetary base by £1 million.

Simplified Balance Sheet of the Bank of England

Assets	Liabilities
Domestic credit	Currency
Foreign exchange reserves −£1,000,000	Bank reserves −£1,000,000
Monetary base −£1,000,000	Monetary base −£1,000,000

Federal Reserve's claim on the U.K. bank by assuming the liability itself. This action reduces the reserves of the U.K. bank by £1 million. As shown in Figure 10–3, the domestic credit component of the U.K. monetary base decreases by £1 million. The U.K. money stock declines by a multiple of the change in the monetary base. Using the previous equations, the change in the U.K. money stock is

$$\Delta M_{UK} = m_{UK} \times \Delta MB_{UK} = m_{UK} \times (\Delta DC + \Delta FER).$$

In the example here, the U.K. money multiplier is 2.1, the change in domestic credit is a negative £1 million, and the change in foreign reserves is zero. The change in the U.K. money stock, therefore, is:

$$\Delta M_{UK} = 2.1 \times (-\text{£1 million} + \text{£0})$$
$$= 2.1 \times (-\text{£1 million}) = -\text{£2.1 million}.$$

The foreign exchange market transaction of the Fed that results in a $4.16 million increase in the U.S. money stock also results in a £2.1 million decrease in the U.K. money stock.

Sterilization

In Chapter 8 we noted that central banks may have internal economic goals, such as price stability and full employment, and external economic objectives, such as exchange rate stability and balanced trade. In the example just given, the Fed may have intervened in the foreign exchange market in pursuit of an external objective. The consequence is a change in the domestic money stock. Suppose, however, that the change in the U.S. money stock conflicts with the internal objectives of the Fed. In this case, the Fed desires to offset, or *sterilize*, the effect of the foreign exchange intervention on the U.S. money stock. As explained in Chapter 8, the Fed can sterilize the foreign exchange transaction through an offsetting U.S. open-market transaction.

FIGURE 10–4 **THE COMBINED EFFECTS OF A FOREIGN EXCHANGE TRANSACTION AND STERILIZATION**

When the Federal Reserve purchases $1.6 million of foreign exchange reserves, the foreign exchange reserves component of the monetary base rises. The Federal Reserve pays the foreign exchange dealer by applying a $1.6 million credit to the bank reserves of the dealer's bank. The Fed sterilizes the foreign exchange transaction through an open-market sale of securities. This reduces the domestic credit component of the monetary base. To complete the open-market transaction the Fed reduces bank reserves. Thus, the monetary base is unchanged.

Simplified Balance Sheet of the Federal Reserve

Assets	Liabilities
Domestic credit −$1,600,000	Currency −$1,600,000
Foreign exchange reserves $1,600,000	Bank reserves $1,600,000
Monetary base	Monetary base

To sterilize the effect of the foreign exchange transaction, the Fed must offset the increase in foreign exchange reserves with an equivalent decrease in domestic credit. To do this, the Fed must engage in an open-market sale of securities. When the Fed sells $1.6 million of U.S. Treasury securities to a domestic dealer, domestic credit falls by $1.6 million. The dealer pays for the securities by wiring funds from a transactions deposit account to the Fed. The Fed clears the transaction deposit by reducing the total reserves of the dealer's bank. Thus, transactions deposits fall by $1.6 million.

Figure 10–4 illustrates the combined effect of the foreign exchange transaction and the open-market transaction on the Fed's balance sheet. When both transactions are conducted simultaneously, domestic credit falls by $1.6 million, and foreign exchange reserves rise by $1.6 million. The foreign exchange transaction results in a $1.6 million increase in private bank reserves while the open-market transaction results in a $1.6 million decrease in private bank reserves. The net effect on private bank reserves is zero. Furthermore, Figure 10–4 illustrates that the net effect on the U.S. monetary base is zero.

The sterilized foreign exchange transaction leaves the U.S. monetary base, and, therefore, the U.S. money stock unchanged. Combining the foreign exchange transaction and the open-market transaction in the equations representing the relationship between the money stock and the monetary base, we can express the effect on the money stock as:

$$\Delta M_{US} = m_{US} \times (\Delta DC + \Delta FER)$$
$$= 2.6 \times (-\$1,600,000 + \$1,600,000) = 0.$$

Hence, a fully sterilized foreign exchange intervention has no effect on the U.S. money stock.

The Bank of England may also desire to sterilize the effect of the U.S. foreign exchange transaction on the U.K. money stock. If so, the Bank of England can also undertake an offsetting open-market transaction.

FUNDAMENTAL ISSUE #1

How do a central bank's foreign exchange market interventions alter the monetary base and the money stock? Central bank foreign exchange market interventions increase or reduce the foreign exchange reserves component of the monetary base. Thus, purchases (sales) of foreign assets increase (reduce) the monetary base. A nation's money stock is a multiple of the monetary base. Hence, foreign exchange transactions change the nation's money stock by a multiple of the change in the monetary base. Sterilization changes the domestic credit component of the monetary base in an opposite direction, thereby eliminating the effect of the foreign exchange transaction on the monetary base and the money stock.

THE MONETARY APPROACH TO BALANCE-OF-PAYMENTS AND EXCHANGE-RATE DETERMINATION

Chapter 9 presented the two traditional approaches to balance-of-payments and exchange-rate determination, the elasticities and absorption approaches. As explained earlier, these approaches focused on transactions in goods and services and ignored financial markets. After the collapse of the Bretton Woods system, economists sought to develop approaches to understanding balance-of-payments and exchange-rate determination that allowed for floating exchange rates and greater integration of goods and financial markets across economies. Their efforts yielded the *monetary approach,* which quickly became popular among many economists. As you will now learn, the preceding material laid all the groundwork for understanding the role of money in determining a nation's balance of payments and the exchange value of its currency.

MONETARY APPROACH Relates changes in a nation's balance of payments and the exchange value of its currency to differences between the quantity of money demanded and the quantity of money supplied.

The **monetary approach** to balance-of-payments and exchange-rate determination postulates that changes in a nation's balance of payments and the exchange value of its currency are a monetary phenomenon. That is, balance of payments deficits or surpluses or exchange rate variations result from differences between the quantity of money supplied and the quantity of money demanded.

Although the monetary approach is a recent development relative to the theories presented in Chapter 9, its roots can be traced back to the philosopher David Hume and his price-specie flow model (see the "Policy Notebook: David Hume's Price-Specie Flow Model"). This approach begins with a formal model of the demand for, and supply of, money balances.

POLICY NOTEBOOK
David Hume's Price-Specie Flow Model

David Hume was a noted philosopher and historian who also made significant contributions to the classical school of economic thought. Hume, who was born in 1711, entered the University of Edinburgh at the age of twelve. At the age of twenty-three, Hume left England to further his studies in France, where he wrote *A Treatise of Human Nature.* Although Hume's writings on religion were controversial and prevented him from gaining a professorship at Edinburgh, he eventually became a librarian there.

Hume's writings continue to influence scholarship in religion, philosophy, and economics. One of Hume's contributions to economics was the price-specie flow model. Hume argued that if a trade imbalance existed between two nations, over time an automatic adjustment would occur, eliminating the imbalance. This theory, known as the *price-specie flow model,* challenged the predominate view of the period that a nation could sustain a trade surplus indefinitely, with no effect on the domestic economy.

To understand the automatic adjustment process, consider a nation experiencing a trade surplus. Because goods, on net, flow out of the nation, *specie* (or coined money) flows into the domestic economy from abroad. The inflow of specie causes an increase in the domestic

money stock and, in turn, causes wages and prices to rise. The increase in prices, all other things constant, makes domestic goods and services more expensive internationally and, therefore, causes imports to rise and exports to fall. This adjustment process eventually eliminates the trade surplus.

Likewise, a nation with a trade deficit would experience an outflow of specie, and the resulting decline in the nation's money stock reduces wages and prices. The change in prices, all other things constant, makes domestic goods and services less expensive internationally. Thus, exports rise and imports fall, eventually eliminating the trade deficit.

This example illustrates how the price-specie model emphasizes the role of the nation's money stock in the adjustment process. The focus on the money stock is also the central feature of the monetary approach to balance-of-payments and exchange-rate determination developed by economists since the early 1970s, demonstrating the importance of Hume's work.

FOR CRITICAL ANALYSIS:
Would Hume's price-specific flow model function in a setting in which people use flat money instead of coined money? How would the model work in a world of electronic money?

The Cambridge Approach to Money Demand

The monetary approach begins with the **Cambridge equation,** which is a theory of the demand for money developed in the late nineteenth century by economists at Cambridge University. The Cambridge equation is

$$M^d = kPy,$$

where M^d denotes the total quantity of nominal money balances that all households desire to hold, k is a fraction between zero and one, P is the aggregate price level in the economy, and y is total real income. Because P is the

ON THE WEB
Learn more about David Hume and his influential work from the Hume Archives at:
http://www.utm.edu/research/hume/

aggregate price level and *y* is real income, multiplying the two together yields nominal income. Hence, the Cambridge equation constitutes a hypothesis that people hold a fraction of their nominal incomes as money.

Money, the Balance of Payments, and the Exchange Rate

As discussed earlier, a nation's quantity of money is equal to a money multiplier times the monetary base:

$$M = m(DC + FER).$$

As before, we have expressed the monetary base as the sum of domestic credit and foreign exchange reserves.

The Relationship between the Money Stock and the Balance of Payments

Chapter 1 examined the identities that make up a nation's balance of payments system. Recall that the current account balance plus the capital account balance is equal to the official settlements balance. The official settlements balance consists mainly of changes in the central bank's foreign exchange reserves. However, we shall assume the nation's foreign exchange reserves are equivalent to its official settlements balance.

Using this accounting identity, we can relate a nation's money stock to its balance of payments. Remember also from Chapter 1 that an increase in the official settlements balance (or in this case, the foreign exchange reserves component of the monetary base) is equivalent to a balance-of-payments surplus. Likewise, a decrease in foreign exchange reserves is equivalent to a balance-of-payments deficit. If foreign exchange reserves are unchanged, then the nation's overall balance of payments continues to be zero. Hence, we can relate changes in the nation's money stock to changes in its balance of payments.

The Relationship between Domestic Prices, Foreign Prices, and the Spot Exchange Rate

Economists who use the monetary approach assume that purchasing power parity holds in the long run. As explained in Chapter 2, absolute purchasing power parity postulates that the equilibrium domestic price level of traded goods and services is equal to the foreign price level of traded goods and services times the spot exchange rate between the two nations' currencies. Hence, absolute purchasing power parity is expressed as

$$P = SP^*,$$

where *P* is the domestic price level, *S* is the spot exchange rate (expressed in domestic currency units per foreign currency unit), and *P** is the foreign price level.

The Monetary Equilibrium Condition

The relationship among the Cambridge equation of money demand, the money stock (and, therefore, the balance of payments), the foreign price level, and the spot exchange rate can be determined through an equilibrium condition in which the quantity of money demanded equals the money stock:

$$M^d = M.$$

First we substitute the equation for the quantity of money and the Cambridge equation into the equilibrium condition $M^d = M$ to yield:

$$kPy = m(DC + FER).$$

Next we use the expression for absolute purchasing power parity to substitute in for the domestic price level to obtain

$$m(DC + FER) = kSP^*y.$$

In words, in equilibrium the actual money stock equals the quantity of money demanded. Proponents of the monetary approach, however, use this relationship to explain how key variables affect the nation's balance of payments and the exchange value of its currency.

The Monetary Approach and a Fixed Exchange Rate Arrangement

According to the monetary approach, an event that causes a difference between the quantity of money demanded and the quantity of money supplied generates a change in the nation's balance of payments or in the spot exchange value of its currency. In addition, the monetary approach postulates that the event triggers an automatic adjustment process that eventually brings the economy back to an equilibrium at which the quantity of money demanded equals the quantity of money supplied.

To understand the automatic adjustment process of the monetary approach, we must take into account the type of exchange rate arrangement the nation has adopted. Hence, we must examine the monetary approach under both fixed and flexible exchange rate arrangements.

A Change in Domestic Credit Consider a nation that is small, so that its economy has no effects on the price levels of foreign nations. In addition, suppose that its central bank pegs the exchange value of its currency. If the nation's central bank increases domestic credit through an open-market purchase of securities, then the open-market purchase causes the nation's money stock to rise through the multiplier process. All other things constant, the open-market operation thereby causes the actual money stock to exceed the quantity of money demanded.

In this situation, households find that the quantity of money that they hold exceeds the quantity they desire to hold. Households reduce their money holdings by increasing their purchases of goods and services. Some of these additional purchases are purchases of foreign goods and services. Depending on the type of exchange rate arrangement, the increase in the demand for foreign goods and services will have one of two effects. Under a fixed exchange rate arrangement, the additional purchases of foreign goods and services will generate a balance-of-payments deficit, with no change in the exchange value of the domestic currency. Under a flexible exchange rate arrangement, the additional purchases of foreign goods and services will cause the domestic currency to depreciate, with no change in the balance of payments.

We shall consider in detail a fixed exchange rate arrangement. Under a fixed exchange rate arrangement the nation's monetary authorities must intervene via a sale of foreign exchange reserves in order to maintain the pegged exchange value of its currency through a sale of foreign exchange reserves. As a result, foreign exchange reserves decline, while the spot exchange rate remains constant.

Let's consider the size of the foreign exchange intervention that the monetary authorities must undertake to maintain the pegged exchange value of the domestic currency. We shall denote the pegged exchange value of the domestic currency as $\bar{S}$ and the new level of domestic credit as DC'. At this new level of domestic credit, the money stock exceeds the quantity of money demanded, expressed as

$$m(DC' + FER) > k\bar{S}P^*y.$$

To prevent the domestic currency from depreciating, the domestic central bank must reduce the quantity of money supplied so that it equals the quantity of money demanded. To do so, the central bank must sell sufficient foreign reserves to exactly offset the increase in domestic credit, returning the money stock to its original level. At this level, households' desired quantity of money again equals the quantity of money supplied.

As discussed earlier, a decline in foreign exchange reserves is equivalent to a balance of payments deficit. The amount of the balance of payments deficit, therefore, is equal to the change in the foreign exchange reserves component of the monetary base, which is equal to the change in domestic credit brought about by the central bank's open-market transaction. We can conclude that, under a fixed exchange rate arrangement, the monetary approach indicates that an increase in domestic credit generates a balance-of-payments deficit, while a decrease in domestic credit results in a balance-of-payments surplus.

A Change in the Quantity of Money Demanded   Let's continue our example of a small nation that pegs the exchange value of its currency. Suppose that instead of a change in domestic credit there is an increase in either the foreign price level or real income. According to the Cambridge equation that we modified by including absolute purchasing power parity, an increase in either of these two variables causes an increase in the quantity of money demanded.

In this situation, households find that their desired quantity of money falls short of their current money holdings. Households will increase their money holdings by reducing their expenditures on goods and services. As a result, households' demands for domestic *and* foreign goods and services decline. The decline in demand for foreign goods and services results in either a balance-of-payments surplus or an appreciation of the domestic currency. To maintain the pegged exchange value of the domestic currency, the central bank must buy foreign reserves.

Let's consider the size of foreign exchange intervention the central bank must undertake to maintain the pegged exchange value of the domestic currency. Let's also continue to denote the pegged exchange value of the domestic currency as $\overline{S}$, and let's denote the higher foreign price level or higher level of real income as $(P^*y)'$. The higher foreign price level or higher level of real income causes the quantity of money demanded to exceed the quantity of money supplied, expressed as

$$m(DC + FER) < k\overline{S}(P^*y)'.$$

To prevent the domestic currency from appreciating, the domestic monetary authorities must increase the quantity of money supplied so that it equals the quantity of money demanded. To accomplish this, the central bank buys foreign exchange reserves. The increase in foreign exchange reserves is equivalent to a balance-of-payments surplus, with the size of the surplus equal to the change in foreign exchange reserves. We can conclude that a rise in either the foreign price level or domestic real income results in a balance-of-payments surplus. Likewise, a decline in either the foreign price level or domestic real income results in a balance-of-payments deficit.

The Monetary Approach and a Flexible Exchange Rate Arrangement

Suppose now that our small nation that we have been considering no longer pegs the exchange value of the domestic currency. Initially, its central bank allows the spot exchange rate to be freely determined in the foreign exchange market. Under a flexible exchange rate arrangement such as this, the domestic central bank does not intervene in the foreign exchange market. The foreign exchange reserves component of the monetary base, therefore, remains unchanged, and the nation has neither a balance-of-payments surplus, nor a balance-of-payments deficit. The spot exchange rate, as we have seen, is determined by the quantity of money supplied and the quantity of money demanded.

A Change in Domestic Credit Suppose that, as in the earlier example, the domestic central bank increases domestic credit through a purchase of securities. Domestic credit and the domestic money stock rise, and the money stock exceeds the quantity of money demanded.

In this situation, households find that their money holdings exceed the quantity of money they desire. Households reduce their money holdings by increasing their expenditures on goods and services, with some of these expenditures on foreign goods and services. As households increase their expenditures on foreign goods and services, the domestic currency depreciates.

The domestic currency will continue to depreciate until the quantity of money supplied equals the quantity of money demanded. It is in this regard that the spot exchange rate is determined by the quantity of money supplied and the quantity of money demanded. We can conclude, therefore, that under a flexible exchange rate arrangement, the monetary approach indicates that an increase in domestic credit results in a depreciation of the domestic currency, while a decline in domestic credit results in an appreciation of the domestic currency.

A Change in the Quantity of Money Demanded   If the foreign price level or domestic real income increases, then according to the Cambridge equation, the quantity of money demanded increases. As a result, the quantity of money demanded exceeds the quantity of money supplied.

In this situation, households find that their current money holdings fall short of the quantity desired. Households increase their money holdings by reducing their expenditures on domestic and foreign goods and services. The decrease in demand for foreign goods and services causes the domestic currency to appreciate. This appreciation continues until the quantity of money supplied once again equals the quantity of money demanded, so that households find that their actual money holdings match their desired money holdings.

We can conclude, therefore, that under a flexible exchange rate arrangement, the monetary approach theorizes that an increase in the foreign price level or domestic real income results in an appreciation of the domestic currency. By way of contrast, a decline in the foreign price level or domestic real income results in a depreciation of the domestic currency.

FUNDAMENTAL ISSUE #2

What is the monetary approach to balance-of-payments and exchange-rate determination? The monetary approach postulates that changes in the balance of payments or exchange rate result from differences between the quantity of money supplied and the quantity of money demanded. Additionally, the monetary approach assumes that when an event causes a difference between the quantity of money supplied and the quantity of money demanded, it triggers an automatic adjustment that eventually eliminates the difference. Under a fixed exchange rate arrangement, a difference between the quantity of money supplied and the quantity of money demanded causes a change in the nation's balance of payments. Under a flexible exchange rate arrangement, the exchange value of the domestic currency changes.

APPLYING THE MONETARY APPROACH: A TWO-COUNTRY SETTING

We have not yet considered how changes in the quantity of money supplied and demanded *in another nation* might affect the spot exchange rate. Economists have, however, found the monetary approach very illuminating in examining how the balance-of-payments accounts and currency values of *two nations* interact.

A Two-Country Monetary Model

To extend the monetary approach in a two-country setting, we must specify a Cambridge equation of money demand for each nation. We shall denote the individual nations with subscripts A and B. The Cambridge equations, equilibrium conditions, and absolute purchasing power parity condition for the two nations are

$$M_A^d = k_A P_A y_A, \qquad\qquad M_B^d = k_B P_B y_B,$$
$$M_A = M_A^d, \qquad\qquad M_B = M_B^d,$$
$$P_A = SP_B,$$

where the spot exchange rate S is expressed as the number of units of Country A's currency per unit of Country B's currency.

To derive a single expression for the spot rate, we first substitute the Cambridge equation for each nation into the equilibrium conditions to yield

$$M_A = k_A P_A y_A, \qquad\qquad M_B = k_B P_B y_B.$$

Next we substitute the absolute purchasing power parity condition into the equilibrium condition for Country A, which yields

$$M_A = k_A SP_B y_A, \qquad\qquad M_B = k_B P_B y_B.$$

Now we divide Country A's equilibrium condition by Country B's equilibrium condition:

$$\frac{M_A}{M_B} = \frac{k_A SP_B y_A}{k_B P_B y_B},$$

or, more simply:

$$\frac{M_A}{M_B} = S \times \frac{k_A y_A}{k_B y_B}.$$

Finally, we rearrange the expression by dividing each side of the equation by the ratio of each nations' quantity of money demanded, to obtain:

$$S = \frac{M_A}{M_B} \times \frac{k_B y_B}{k_A y_A}.$$

This expression illustrates the monetary approach to exchange-rate determination in a two-country setting. That is, the spot exchange rate is determined by the *relative quantities of money supplied* and the *relative quantities of money demanded.*

With this specification we can see how a change in the relative money stocks or in the relative quantities of money demanded brings about a change in the spot exchange rate. For example, if there is an increase in the money stock of Country A, all other things unchanged, then the spot exchange rate rises. That is, Nation A's currency depreciates relative to Nation B's currency. If there is an increase in the real income of Country A, then the relative quantity of money demanded declines and the spot exchange rate falls, or Nation A's currency appreciates relative to Nation B's currency.

An Example of Exchange-Rate Determination for Two Nations

Suppose that the monetary base in Australia is 37,780 million Australian dollars, (A\$37,780 million) and that the Australian money multiplier is approximately 2.22. Also, suppose that the monetary base in New Zealand is 10,091 million New Zealand dollars (NZ\$10,091 million) and that the New Zealand money multiplier is approximately 3.37. In addition, suppose that Australian nominal GDP is A\$473,390 million and that Australian real GDP is A\$432,960, while New Zealand's nominal GDP is NZ\$91,045 million and that New Zealand's real GDP is NZ\$79,269.

Using this information, the money stock in Australia, which is determined by multiplying the monetary base by the multiplier, is equal to A\$83,847. Likewise, the money stock in New Zealand is NZ\$34,050. Now we can calculate the fraction of nominal income held as money, k, for each nation by dividing the money stock by nominal GDP. These calculations show that the fraction of nominal income held as money balances in Australia is 0.177 and that the fraction of nominal income held as money balances in New Zealand is 0.374.

Using this information, we can employ the two-country monetary approach to calculate the equilibrium spot exchange rate between the Australian dollar and the New Zealand dollar. Using a subscript A to denote Australia and a subscript NZ to denote New Zealand, we can express the two-country monetary approach for this example as:

$$S = \frac{M_A}{M_{NZ}} \times \frac{k_{NZ}\, y_{NZ}}{k_A\, y_A}.$$

Substituting the values of the money stock and real GDP for each nation into this equation yields

$$S = \frac{A\$83,847}{NZ\$34,050} \times \frac{0.374(NZ\$79,269)}{0.177(A\$432,960)},$$

or

$$S = 0.9526.$$

Thus, the equilibrium spot exchange rate between the Australian dollar and the New Zealand dollar is 0.9526 Australian dollars per New Zealand dollar.

Now let's consider the effect of an increase in the Australian monetary stock. Suppose the Australian money stock rises by 5 percent to A\$88,039, while the New Zealand money stock remains the same. Substituting this new value for the Australian money stock in the previous equation yields a new value for the spot exchange rate of

$$S = \frac{A\$88,039}{NZ\$34,050} \times \frac{0.374(NZ\$79,269)}{0.177(A\$432,960)},$$

or

$$S = 1.00.$$

Hence, the increase in the Australian money stock causes the equilibrium spot exchange rate to increase from 0.9526 A\$/NZ\$ to 1.00 A\$/NZ\$. The resulting depreciation of the Australian dollar relative to the New Zealand dollar is 5 percent $[(1.00 - 0.9526)/0.9526 \cong 0.05]$.

Thus, the two-country monetary approach indicates that the spot exchange rate is determined by the relative quantity of money demanded and the relative quantity of money supplied. A nation that increases its money stock causes its currency to depreciate. Similarly, a nation that experiences an increase in the quantity of money demanded, all other things constant, experiences an appreciation of its currency.

ON THE WEB

To learn more about the New Zealand economy, visit the Internet site of the Reserve Bank of New Zealand at:
http://www.rbnz.govt.nz/10-years.htm

FUNDAMENTAL ISSUE #3

How is the monetary approach a theory of exchange-rate determination in a two-country setting? According to the monetary approach in a two-country setting, the spot exchange rate is determined by the relative quantity of money supplied and the relative quantity of money demanded. In general, if all other things are the same, a nation that increases its money stock causes it currency to depreciate. In contrast, a nation whose households demand a larger quantity of money experiences an appreciation of its currency.

THE PORTFOLIO APPROACH TO EXCHANGE-RATE DETERMINATION

The monetary approach to balance-of-payments and exchange-rate determination focuses on the quantity of money demanded and the quantity of money supplied. The portfolio approach expands the monetary approach by

PORTFOLIO APPROACH Relates changes in a nation's balance of payments and the exchange value of its currency to the quantities demanded and supplied of domestic money, domestic securities, and foreign securities.

recognizing that households may desire to hold other financial instruments, such as domestic and foreign securities. Hence, the **portfolio approach** postulates that the exchange value of a nation's currency is determined by the quantities of domestic money and domestic and foreign securities demanded and the quantities of various financial instruments supplied in the markets for these instruments.

Households' Allocation of Wealth

To make our exposition of the portfolio approach simple, we focus on only three types of financial instruments: domestic money, domestic bonds, and foreign bonds. The portfolio approach assumes that individuals earn interest for holding bonds but receive no interest for holding money. It follows that households have no incentive to hold the foreign currency, which they can obtain in the spot exchange market if they wish to conduct a foreign transaction.

As discussed in Chapters 4 and 5, however, the domestic and foreign bonds have elements of risk that money does not. To balance the risk and returns on these instruments, households desire to distribute their wealth over all three types of instruments. A **wealth identity** expresses this notion as

WEALTH IDENTITY Shows the types of assets that constitute the household's total stock of wealth.

$$W \equiv M + B + SB^*,$$

where W denotes household wealth, M denotes the wealth that households desire to hold as money, B denotes the wealth that households desire to hold as domestic bonds, S denotes the spot exchange value of the domestic currency defined as domestic currency units per foreign currency units, and B^* denotes the wealth that households desire to hold as foreign bonds. A wealth identity shows the types of assets that constitute the household's total stock of wealth.

The portfolio approach, therefore, assumes that the exchange value of a nation's currency is determined by the quantities of each of these financial instruments supplied and the quantities demanded. Hence, in contrast to the monetary approach, differences between the quantities of domestic and foreign bonds demanded and supplied are as important as the differences in the quantities of domestic money demanded and supplied.

A Change in the Domestic Money Stock Let's consider, within the context of the portfolio model, the effect of an open-market operation on the exchange value of the domestic currency. Suppose the central bank wishes to increase the domestic money stock and undertakes an open-market purchase of domestic bonds. As explained in Chapter 8, the open-market purchase causes the domestic money supply to rise and the domestic interest rate to decline.

As the domestic interest rate declines, households find they are no longer satisfied with their current allocation of wealth. The decline in the domestic interest rate causes a decline in the quantity of domestic bonds demanded by households. Households have the same stock of wealth to allocate over all three instruments, however. Hence, as the quantity of domestic bonds demanded falls, the quantity of domestic money and foreign bonds demanded increases.

FIGURE 10–5 A DECREASE IN THE DOMESTIC INTEREST RATE

FIGURE 10–5 A DECREASE IN THE DOMESTIC INTEREST RATE

Initially the spot exchange market is in equilibrium at point A with the initial domestic interest rate denoted R_1. When the domestic interest rate declines, households buy more foreign bonds. As a result, their demand for the foreign currency rises, shown by the rightward shift of the demand curve from $D_{FC}(R_1)$ to $D_{FC}(R_2)$. The increase in the quantity demanded of the foreign currency causes the domestic currency to depreciate from S_1 to S_2.

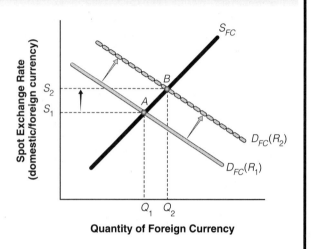

Figure 10–5 illustrates the effect on the spot exchange rate of the change in households' quantity demanded of all three instruments. Initially, the spot exchange market is in equilibrium at point A, at which the domestic interest rate is equal to R_1. As households buy more foreign bonds, the demand for the foreign currency rises, shown by the rightward shift of the demand curve from $D_{FC}(R_1)$ to $D_{FC}(R_2)$. As a result of the increase in demand for the foreign currency, the spot exchange rate rises from S_1 to S_2. Thus, the domestic currency depreciates. We can conclude, therefore, that the portfolio approach postulates that a decline in the domestic interest rate results in a depreciation of the domestic currency, and a rise in the domestic interest rate results in an appreciation of the domestic currency.

Consistent with the monetary approach to exchange rate determination, the portfolio approach predicts that an open-market purchase of securities leads to a domestic currency depreciation. There is a striking difference between the two approaches, however. The monetary approach attributes a currency depreciation to changes in the quantity of *money* demanded and supplied. The portfolio approach attributes a currency depreciation to changes in the quantities demanded and supplied of *all the instruments* that constitute households' stock of wealth.

A Change in the Foreign Interest Rate Consider the effect of a rise in the foreign interest rate on the spot exchange rate. Because of the change in the foreign interest rate, households desire to hold larger quantities of foreign bonds and smaller quantities of domestic money and domestic bonds.

FIGURE 10–6 AN INCREASE IN THE FOREIGN INTEREST RATE

Initially the spot exchange market is in equilibrium at point A with the initial foreign interest rate denoted R_1^*. When the foreign interest rate rises to R_2^*, households buy more foreign bonds. Households' demand for the foreign currency rises, shown by the rightward shift of the demand curve from $D_{FC}(R_1^*)$ to $D_{FC}(R_2^*)$. As a result, the domestic currency depreciates from S_1 to S_2.

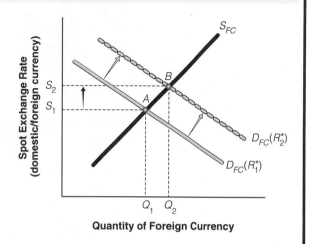

Figure 10–6 shows the effect of a change in the foreign interest rate on the spot exchange rate. Initially, the spot exchange market is in equilibrium at a spot exchange rate denoted S_1 at which the foreign interest rate is equal to R_1^*. As households liquidate some of their holdings of domestic money and domestic bonds and begin buying foreign bonds, the demand for the foreign currency rises, shown by the rightward shift of the demand curve from $D_{FC}(R_1^*)$ to $D_{FC}(R_2^*)$. The increase in demand for the foreign currency causes the spot exchange rate to rise from S_1 to S_2. Thus, the domestic currency depreciates. We can conclude that the portfolio approach indicates that an increase in the foreign interest rate causes a depreciation of the domestic currency, and that a decline in the foreign interest rate causes an appreciation of the domestic currency.

FUNDAMENTAL ISSUE #4

What is the portfolio approach to exchange-rate determination?
The portfolio approach assumes that households desire to hold domestic and foreign securities along with their holding of money. Hence, the portfolio approach postulates that the value of a nation's currency is determined by the quantity of money and securities demanded and the quantity supplied. An increase in the domestic interest rate causes the domestic currency to appreciate, while an increase in the foreign interest rate causes the domestic currency to depreciate.

To Sterilize or Not to Sterilize?

Chapter 8 explained that many nations, such as the United States, fully sterilize their foreign exchange market interventions as a matter of routine. Should nations routinely sterilize their interventions? The answer to this question depends on whether sterilized foreign exchange interventions affect the exchange value of the domestic currency. The monetary and portfolio approaches to exchange-rate determination offer conflicting answers to this question.

Sterilized Foreign Exchange Interventions and the Monetary Approach
According to the monetary approach to exchange-rate determination, differences between the nominal quantity of money supplied and the nominal quantity of money demanded determine the spot exchange rate. Recall the expression for the money stock:

$$M = m(DC + FER),$$

where DC denotes domestic credit, FER denotes foreign exchange reserves, and m is the money multiplier. In the monetary approach, foreign exchange interventions affect the spot exchange value of the domestic currency by increasing or decreasing the domestic monetary base, thereby increasing or decreasing the domestic money stock.

For example, a foreign exchange market intervention that increases foreign exchange reserves leads to a multiple increase in the money stock. Complete sterilization of this intervention entails an open-market sale of securities that reduces domestic credit by an amount equivalent to the increase in foreign exchange reserves. As a result of the open-market transaction, the domestic monetary base remains unchanged, and so does the domestic money stock.

Because sterilized intervention leaves the domestic money stock unchanged, there is no difference between the quantity of money supplied and the quantity of money demanded. Therefore, there is no effect on the exchange value of the domestic currency. Thus, according to the monetary approach, fully sterilized foreign intervention is *ineffective*, because it leaves the exchange value of the domestic currency unchanged.

Sterilized Foreign Exchange Interventions and the Portfolio Approach
According to the portfolio approach, changes in the exchange value of the domestic currency result from differences between the quantities of money and bonds supplied and the quantities demanded. The simple portfolio model assumes that households allocate their wealth across three types of financial instruments—domestic money, domestic bonds, and foreign bonds. Now let's consider the effect of a fully sterilized foreign exchange intervention in this portfolio model.

As explained in Chapter 8, foreign exchange reserves typically are foreign-currency-denominated financial instruments, such as treasury bills and bonds.

When domestic monetary authorities purchase foreign exchange reserves, the quantity of foreign bonds demanded increases. The increase in the quantity of foreign bonds demanded causes the domestic currency to depreciate.

The purchase of foreign exchange reserves results in an increase in the domestic monetary base and an increase in the domestic money stock. The central bank sterilizes the intervention through an open-market sale of domestic bonds, reducing domestic credit, and leaving the domestic monetary base and money stock unchanged. The open-market transaction, however, increases the quantity of domestic bonds available. Hence, sterilized foreign exchange intervention is, in effect, an exchange of domestic bonds for foreign bonds. According to the portfolio approach, the exchange of domestic for foreign bonds results in a depreciation of the domestic currency. Thus, sterilized intervention can be effective. As noted in Chapter 8, a recent study by Kathryn Dominguez and Jeffrey Frankel provides evidence that sterilized interventions do affect exchange rates. Further, their work indicates that both a portfolio effect and a news effect was present during coordinated interventions of the 1980s.

FUNDAMENTAL ISSUE #5

Should central banks sterilize foreign exchange interventions? According to the monetary approach to exchange-rate determination, sterilized foreign exchange interventions are not effective, meaning that these interventions leave the domestic money supply unchanged. According to the portfolio approach, sterilized interventions can be effective, as they alter households' holdings of domestic and foreign bonds. The empirical evidence indicates that sterilized interventions may have some effect on the spot exchange value of a currency through both a news effect and a portfolio effect.

CHAPTER SUMMARY

1. **Central Bank Foreign Exchange Market Interventions, the Monetary Base, the Money Stock, and Sterilization:** Central bank foreign exchange interventions alter the nation's monetary base by changing foreign exchange reserves. The change in the monetary base eventually leads to a change in the money stock that is a multiple of the change in the monetary base. Sterilization of a foreign exchange intervention by an open-market transaction can partially or fully offset the effect of the foreign exchange intervention on the monetary base and, therefore, the money stock.

2. **The Monetary Approach to Balance-of-Payments and Exchange-Rate Determination:** The monetary approach to balance-of-payments and exchange-rate determination postulates that changes in a nation's balance of payments or the exchange value of its currency are a monetary phenomenon. That is, these changes are due to a difference between the quantity of money supplied and the quantity of money demanded. In a fixed-exchange-rate arrangement, differences between the quantity of money supplied and the quantity of money demanded determine a nation's balance of payments, while in a flexible exchange rate arrangement differences between the quantity of money supplied and the quantity of money demanded determine the spot exchange value of the nation's currency.

3. **The Two-Country Monetary Approach to Exchange-Rate Determination:** Economists often use a two-country monetary approach to exchange rate determination. According to the two-country monetary approach, the spot exchange rate is determined by the relative quantities of money supplied and the relative quantities of money demanded. A rise in the money stock of one nation causes that nation's currency to depreciate, while a rise in one nation's quantity of money demanded causes that nation's currency to appreciate.

4. **The Portfolio Approach to Exchange-Rate Determination:** The portfolio approach assumes that households desire to hold both domestic money and domestic and foreign bonds. Households allocate their wealth across these instruments in order to balance risk and return. As a result, the exchange value of a nation's currency is determined by the quantities of money and domestic and foreign bond demanded and supplied. According to the portfolio approach, an increase in the domestic interest rate results in an appreciation of the domestic currency, while an increase in the foreign interest rate results in a depreciation of the domestic currency.

5. **Sterilized versus Nonsterilized Foreign Exchange Interventions:** According to the monetary approach to exchange-rate determination, sterilized foreign exchange interventions are not effective, meaning that they leave the domestic money supply unchanged. According to the portfolio approach, however, sterilized interventions can be effective, because they alter households' holdings of domestic and foreign bonds and, therefore, their relative demands for the foreign currency. Empirical evidence indicates that sterilized interventions may have some effect on the spot exchange value, indicating the possibility of a portfolio effect.

QUESTIONS AND PROBLEMS

1. Illustrate a simple balance sheet of the central banks of Japan and Australia. Show in your diagram the effect on the components of the monetary base of each nation of the Bank of Japan selling A$1 million bank deposits. Assume that the spot exchange rate is 87.5 yen-per-Australian dollar (¥/A$).

2. This chapter presented a simple example of a money multiplier where it was assumed that as the money stock expands, households wish to hold all of their money balances as transactions deposits. Suppose that households wish to hold some fraction of their money balances as currency. Let b denote households' ratio of currency balances to transactions deposits (C/TD). Finally, assume the reserve requirement is 10 percent.
   a. What is the value of the money multiplier if b is zero? (*Hint:* This is the same as the example presented earlier in the text.)
   b. What is the value of the money multiplier if b is 25 percent? (*Hint: b* enters the money multiplier formula in the same way that the reserve requirement does.)

3. Suppose the reserve requirement in Australia is 20 percent and the reserve requirement in Japan is 8 percent and that the monetary base consists only of transactions deposits. Using the information in question 1, what is the maximum possible change in the money stocks of each nation?

4. Suppose Japan partially sterilizes the foreign exchange transaction in question 1 by buying ¥47.5 million of securities. What is the total change in the Japanese money stock that results from both the foreign exchange transaction and the open-market transaction?

5. Write out an equation representing the monetary approach to balance-of-payments and exchange-rate determination. Suppose that domestic credit equals $1000, foreign exchange reserves equal $80, the money multiplier is 2, the fraction of nominal income that individuals desire to hold in money balances is 20 percent, the foreign price level is 1.2, and the spot exchange value of the domestic currency is 2. Using this information, what is:
   a. the money stock in the domestic economy?
   b. the level of real income of the domestic economy?

6. Using the information in question 5, suppose the domestic monetary authorities increase domestic credit by $135 through an open-market purchase of securities.
   a. Under a fixed exchange rate regime, what in the effect of this open-market transaction on the nation's balance of payments?
   b. Under flexible exchange rates, all other things constant, what is the new exchange value of the dollar? Is this an appreciation or depreciation?

7. Using the information on the Australian and New Zealand economies on page 323 of this chapter, calculate the effect of a 3 percent increase of New Zealand's domestic credit on:
   a. the New Zealand money stock.
   b. the equilibrium spot rate.
   c. New Zealand's balance of payments.

8. Illustrate the spot exchange market for the domestic currency using the supply and demand framework. Explain and illustrate the effect of a central bank open-market sale of bonds on the exchange value of the domestic currency.

ON-LINE APPLICATION

Chapter 3 explained the operation of a currency board. This chapter explained the monetary model of exchange-rate determination. This application combines them by considering Estonia, which operates under a currency board arrangement. Under the currency board arrangement the currency is pegged and is maintained through the accumulation or depletion of foreign reserves. The monetary base adjusts with the change in reserves.

Internet URL: http://www.ee/epbe/

Title: The Bank of Estonia

Navigation: Click on *statistical datasheets*. Next click on *Table 2, foreign exchange reserves backing the kroon*. Record the net amount of foreign reserves found on line X. Click back to the index for the statistical data sheet. Click on *Table 6*, find the line titled *MONEY*, and record the amount for the same period as the reserve data. (*Note:* this item is recorded in millions.)

Application: Based on the data you collected, answer the following questions.

1. Under a currency board the monetary base (MONEY) is a multiple of the volume of foreign exchange reserves. What is that multiple (multiplier) for Estonia?

2. Using the data you collected, your answer to application question 1, and the monetary equation for a fixed exchange rate arrangement provided in this chapter, what must happen to the foreign reserves of Estonia if real income rises by 5 percent?

REFERENCES AND RECOMMENDED READINGS

Batten, Dallas, S., and Mack Ott. "What Can Central Banks Do About the Value of the Dollar?" *Federal Reserve Bank of St. Louis Review* (May 1984): 16–26.

Bordo, Michael, and Anna Schwartz. "What Has Foreign Exchange Market Intervention Since the Plaza Agreement Accomplished?" *Open Economies Review*, 2 (1991): 39–64.

Daniels, Joseph. "Optimal Sterilization Policies in Interdependent Economies." *Journal of Economics and Business*, 48 (1) (January 1997): 43–60.

De Grauwe, Paul, Hans DeWachter, and Mark Embrechts. *Exchange Rate Theory and Chaotic Models of Foreign Exchange Markets.* Oxford: Blackwell Press, 1993.

Dominguez, Kathryn, and Jeffrey Frankel. "Does Foreign Exchange Intervention Matter?" *American Economic Review*, 83 (4) (1993): 1356–1369.

Dornbusch, Rudiger. "Monetary Policy Under Exchange-Rate Flexibility." In *Managed Exchange Rate Flexibility: The Recent Experience.* Federal Reserve Bank of Boston, (1979): 90–122.

Humpage, Owen F. "Institutional Aspects of U.S. Intervention." *Federal Reserve Bank of Cleveland Economic Review*, 30 (Quarter 1, 1994): 2–19.

Taylor, Mark P. "The Economics of Exchange Rates." *Journal of Economic Literature*, 33 (March 1995): 13–47.

OPEN ECONOMY MACROECONOMICS AND POLICY ANALYSIS

11

AN OPEN ECONOMY FRAMEWORK

FUNDAMENTAL ISSUES

1. What are the key relationships implied by a nation's circular flow of income and expenditures?

2. How is equilibrium real income determined in an open economy?

3. What is the *IS* schedule, and what factors determine its position?

4. What is the *LM* schedule, and what factors determine its position?

5. What is an *IS–LM* equilibrium?

6. What is the *BP* schedule, and how can we use the *IS–LM–BP* model to determine a nation's balance-of-payments status?

About thirty years ago, the United States taxpayers provided more than $100 billion in today's dollars to fund efforts to land astronauts on the moon. At one point, expenditures on Project Apollo, which ultimately succeeded in this *endeavor, required about 1 cent of every dollar of U.S. GDP, and space-related research composed more than 20 percent of all private and government research expenditures.*

Proponents of manned space exploration offered three rationales for manned moon shots. One, of course, related to intangible benefits from expanded knowledge of the moon and the solar system. Another was the invention and innovation spillovers to the private economy that could result. A third rationale was that space-related spending would have positive effects on the U.S. economy. Government reports in the 1960s projected sizable "multiplier effects" as the Apollo space program government expenditures poured into the economy. In 1971, the Midwest Research Institute concluded that space-related research and development spending would result in a $7 increase in GDP for every dollar spent. Chase Econometric Associates, Inc. predicted an eventual economic return of $14 for every dollar spent.

What might account for such potential "multiple effects" on aggregate economic activity of government spending on space exploration and other programs? This is one important topic that we shall address in this chapter. In addition, we shall discuss the relationship between money, interest rates, and economic activity and the interaction between domestic economic variables and international factors.

NATIONAL INCOME AND EXPENDITURES: THE *IS* SCHEDULE

To understand the factors that influence a nation's overall economic performance, we must consider the determination of its equilibrium level of real income.

The Circular Flow of Income and Expenditures

Figure 11–1 depicts the flows of income and expenditures in a typical economy. By examining these flows, we can deduce some fundamental relationships that must exist among various components of income and expenditures.

Income Equals Product The first of these relationships concerns the real value of household income, y, and the real value of firms' output. As you can see in Figure 11–1, once households receive income payments, they can allocate them to several uses. Nevertheless, ultimately all real household income flows back to firms. Consequently, the total real value of firms' output also must equal y:

FIGURE 11-1   THE CIRCULAR FLOW OF INCOME AND EXPENDITURES

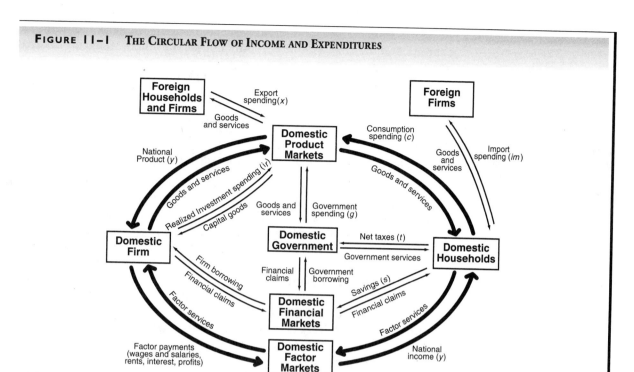

The earnings that firms derive from producing goods and services and supplying them in product markets ultimately flow to households, which own the firms and the factors of production. Households consume domestic goods and services, import foreign goods and services, save, and pay net taxes. Households, firms, the government, and foreign residents purchase the goods and services that firms produce.

REAL CONSUMPTION The real amount of spending by households on domestically produced goods and services.

REAL HOUSEHOLD SAVING The amount of income that households save through financial markets.

REAL NET TAXES The amount of real taxes paid to the government by households, net of transfer payments.

TRANSFER PAYMENTS Governmentally managed income redistributions.

The real value of household income is equal to the real value of the output produced by firms.

By definition, therefore, real income and real output are equivalent.

The Income Identity   The circular-flow diagram in Figure 11–1 indicates that a nation's households can allocate their real income in four ways. One income allocation is to **real consumption,** *c,* which is the real value of household expenditures on domestically produced goods and services. Additionally, households can allocate part of their real income to **real saving,** *s.* Households save by purchasing financial claims issued in financial markets. **Real net taxes,** *t,* are total tax payments net of **transfer payments,** which are governmentally mandated redistributions of income among various households. A final possible household income allocation is to real expenditures

REAL IMPORTS The real flow of spending by households for the purchase of goods and services from firms in other countries.

on *foreign-produced goods* and services, which economists call **real imports,** *im*. (Throughout, we shall assume that only households import foreign-produced goods and services.)

It follows that real income must equal the sum of real consumption, real saving, real net taxes, and real imports:

$$y \equiv c + s + t + im.$$

INCOME IDENTITY A truism that states that real income is allocated among real household consumption, real household saving, real net taxes, and real imports.

This is called the **income identity.** The three-bar equality symbol means that the income identity is a definitional relationship that must always hold true.

The Product Identity   Figure 11–1 shows that a nation's firms borrow part of real household saving and, in exchange, provide financial claims, such as stocks and bonds. Firms issue these claims in financial markets, and they use the funds that they attract from households to purchase services and goods—such as capital goods, from other firms—and to finance inventories of unsold goods. Together, these real expenditures of firms on goods and services constitute **real realized investment spending,** denoted i_r.

REAL REALIZED INVESTMENT SPENDING Actual real firm expenditures in the product markets.

Part of household saving may also be channeled to the nation's government. The government then uses these funds to cover any budget deficit, or the difference between real government spending, *g*, and real net taxes, *t*. Like firms, the government borrows by issuing bonds and other financial claims to savers in financial markets.

As Figure 11–1 indicates, household consumption, firm realized investment, and government spending are the three *domestic* components of total spending on domestically produced output. The final component of spending on domestically produced goods and services is spending by foreign residents on the output that domestic firms export abroad, or the nation's **real exports,** denoted *x*.

REAL EXPORTS Real value of goods and services produced by domestic firms and exported to other countries.

Summing all four spending components yields the **product identity** for a nation's economy:

$$y \equiv c + i_r + g + x.$$

PRODUCT IDENTITY A truism that states that real national product is the sum of real household consumption, real realized investment, real government spending, and real export spending.

This is a definitional relationship that must always hold true, in the absence of measurement errors, so we again use the three-bar equality symbol (see the "Policy Notebook: How Reliable Are Initial GDP Estimates?").

ON THE WEB
Get the most recent firm figures on U.S. GDP and its components from the Federal Reserve Bank of St. Louis at:
http://www.stls.frb.org/fred

FUNDAMENTAL ISSUE #1

What are the key relationships implied by a nation's circular flow of income and expenditures? An examination of a nation's circular flow of income and expenditures reveals three fundamental relationships. One is that the real value of income must equal the real value of output. A second is the income identity, which says that all real income must be split among real

How Reliable Are Initial GDP Estimates?

About fifty days after the conclusion of each quarter, the U.S. government releases estimates of annualized GDP growth for the prior quarter. If, for example, the government determines that real GDP probably grew by 1 percent during the prior quarter, it announces an annualized growth rate of 4 percent for that quarter. In the normal course of events, journalists then run stories trumpeting the high rate of growth of the U.S. economy, and analysts explain why the economy may be on the verge of overheating, slowing down, growing too fast, or growing below its true potential, and so on. Furthermore, journalists, economists, and officials in other nations will often make predictions about the implications for their own countries' economic prospects based on these annualized quarterly U.S. statistics.

There is an important difficulty with these quarterly statistics, however. They commonly are incorrect. In the past, annualized quarterly GDP growth estimates have been off by as much as 75 percent. These errors typically are revealed the next quarter. Then, of course, journalists, economic analysts, and government officials have already turned their attention to the next quarterly statistics—which may be off the mark as well.

FOR CRITICAL ANALYSIS:
In light of the errors in quarterly estimates, some observers argue that it would be better for everyone to wait a few months and pay attention only to revised statistics. Does it make sense for an individual, businessperson, or government official to pay attention to potentially incorrect statistics, if everyone else seems to be doing so?

---

consumption, real saving, real net taxes, and real imports. The third is the product identity, which states that the real value of total output of goods and services must equal the sum of real consumption, real realized investment, real government spending, and real exports.

Private and Public Expenditures

The circular flow diagram in Figure 11–1 shows how a nation's flows of income and expenditures are related, but it does not tell us the *magnitudes* of those flows. The various identities that these flows must satisfy must hold for a nation experiencing a significant expansion of real output and very low labor unemployment, as well as for a nation in the depths of a recession with record unemployment rates.

To understand how the *equilibrium* levels of a nation's real income and expenditures are determined, we must develop more concrete hypotheses about the factors that influence total expenditures on domestically produced goods and services. We shall then be able to combine these hypotheses to develop a complete theory of real income determination in an open economy.

Saving, Import Spending, and Domestic Consumption Spending A key factor influencing household saving and expenditures on domestic- and foreign-manufactured goods and services is **real disposable income,** which is real income net of tax payments, or $y_d \equiv y - t$. Because the income identity states that $y \equiv c + s + t + im$, we can subtract real net taxes t from both sides of the identity to write disposable income as

$$y_d \equiv y - t \equiv c + s + im.$$

Thus, households can use their after-tax income to buy domestically produced goods and services, to save, or to purchase foreign-produced goods and services. If we use the symbol Δ to refer to a change in a variable, then it follows that a change in disposable income can be written as

$$\Delta y_d \equiv \Delta c + \Delta s + \Delta im.$$

In words, households may allocate any additional disposable income to additional domestic consumption, additional saving, and additional import expenditures. Dividing both sides of this identity by Δy_d yields the following expression:

$$\frac{\Delta y_d}{\Delta y_d} = 1 \equiv \frac{\Delta c}{\Delta y_d} + \frac{\Delta s}{\Delta y_d} + \frac{\Delta im}{\Delta y_d}.$$

Thus, the sum of a change in consumption stemming from a change in disposable income $(\Delta c/\Delta y_d)$, a change in saving resulting from a change in disposable income $(\Delta s/\Delta y_d)$, and a change in real imports stemming from a change in disposable income $(\Delta im/\Delta y_d)$ must be equal to 1.

The first ratio on the right-hand side of this identity, $\Delta c/\Delta y_d$, is the **marginal propensity to consume (MPC).** The *MPC* is the change in real consumption induced by a change in real disposable income. If $\Delta c/\Delta y_d$ is equal to a value of 0.75, for example, then this numerical value indicates that a one-unit rise in real disposable income induces households to increase their expenditures of domestically produced goods and services by 0.75 units. In the United States, for instance, each one-dollar rise in after-tax income thereby induces a 75-cent increase in consumption of U.S.-produced output.

The second ratio, $\Delta s/\Delta y_d$, is the **marginal propensity to save (MPS).** The *MPS* is a change in real saving resulting from a change in real disposable income. If $\Delta s/\Delta y_d$ is equal to 0.15, then a one-unit rise in real disposable income spurs households to raise their real saving by 0.15 units. An *MPS* value of 0.15 for the United States, therefore, implies that each one-dollar increase in disposable income leads to a 15-cent rise in saving by U.S. households.

The third ratio, $\Delta im/\Delta y_d$, is the **marginal propensity to import (MPIM).** The *MPIM* is additional real import expenditures stemming from additional income earnings. If $\Delta im/\Delta y_d$ is equal to 0.10, then each additional unit of real

REAL DISPOSABLE INCOME
A household's real after-tax income.

MARGINAL PROPENSITY TO CONSUME (*MPC*)
The additional consumption resulting from an increase in disposable income; a change in consumption spending divided by a corresponding change in disposable income; the slope of the consumption function.

MARGINAL PROPENSITY TO SAVE (*MPS*) The additional saving caused by an increase in disposable income; a change in saving divided by a corresponding change in disposable income; the slope of the saving function.

MARGINAL PROPENSITY TO IMPORT (*MPIM*)
The additional import expenditures stemming from an increase in disposable income; a change in import spending divided by a corresponding change in disposable income; the slope of the import function.

after-tax household income results in a 0.10 unit rise in real import spending. A value of *MPIM* equal to 0.10 for the United States indicates that each one-dollar rise in real after-tax household income causes U.S. households to increase real expenditures on imported goods and services by 10 cents.

Because $MPC \equiv \Delta c/\Delta y_d$, $MPS \equiv \Delta s/\Delta y_d$, and $MPIM \equiv \Delta im/\Delta y_d$, we can rewrite the previous identity as

$$MPC + MPS + MPIM \equiv 1.$$

Using the hypothetical numerical values discussed earlier for the United States, the 75 cents of each new dollar of U.S. real after-tax income used for consumption of U.S. goods and services, the 15 cents of additional disposable real income allocated to saving, and the 10 cents of disposable real income spent on imported goods and services must sum to each 1 dollar of additional disposable real income.

The Saving Function A key determinant of household saving is disposable income. Let's consider a functional relationship, called the *saving function*, that captures this idea:

$$s = -s_0 + (b \times y_d).$$

According to this relationship, total household saving is equal to a constant amount, $-s_0$, plus an amount that depends on disposable income, $b \times y_d$. A graph of the saving function is shown in panel (*a*) of Figure 11–2. The function's intercept is s_0, and its slope is equal to b. This slope is a fraction that indicates the portion of additional real disposable income, y_d, that households allocate to saving. The quantity $b \times y_d$ is *induced saving*, or is the amount of saving spurred by after-tax income earnings.

We assume that the intercept of the saving function, $-s_0$, is a negative number. This is because if disposable income is equal to zero, then households must reduce their existing wealth to buy goods and services. The quantity $-s_0$ is *autonomous dissaving*, which is the amount by which households draw upon their current wealth to purchase domestically produced goods and services and foreign imports, irrespective of their after-tax income earnings.

Note that we assume that s_0 is constant. Consequently, a change in s_0, denoted Δs_0, is equal to zero. From the saving function, it follows that $\Delta s = \Delta s_0 + b \Delta y_d = b \Delta y_d$. If we divide both sides of this equality by Δy_d, we then find that $b = \Delta s/\Delta y_d \equiv MPS$. Thus, the slope of the saving function, b, is equal to the marginal propensity to save (*MPS*).

The Import Function The amount of spending on imported goods and services also varies with the amount of real income. Consider the following *import function*:

$$im = im_0 + (d \times y_d).$$

The intercept of this function, which appears in panel (*b*) of Figure 11–2, is im_0. This is *autonomous import spending*, or household import expenditures that take place irrespective of the amount of total after-tax household income.

FIGURE 11–2 **THE SAVING, IMPORT, AND CONSUMPTION FUNCTIONS**

Panel (*a*) shows the saving function, in which the intercept $-s_0$ represents autonomous dissaving. The marginal propensity to save, $b = \Delta s/\Delta y_d$, is the slope of the saving function. Panel (*b*) displays the import function. This function's intercept, im_0, is the level of autonomous imports, and marginal propensity to import, $d = \Delta im/\Delta y_d$, is the function's slope. Finally, panel (*c*) shows the consumption function. Real consumption of domestic goods and services, *c*, is equal to disposable income less saving and import expenditures, so the intercept of the consumption function is $s_0 - im_0$, which is autonomous consumption. The consumption function's slope is equal to $1 - b - d$, or one minus the marginal propensity to save and the marginal propensity to import.

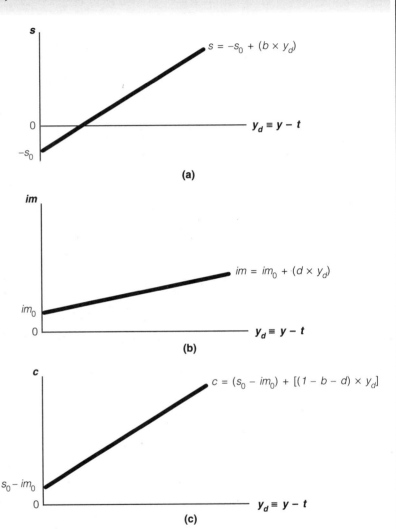

(a)

(b)

(c)

As we discussed in Chapter 9, a currency depreciation or devaluation may induce an increase in a nation's imports, and so we might expect that the magnitude of autonomous import spending depends on the exchange rate. As a simplification, however, we shall assume that this is not the case. As you will see, we shall be able to capture the essential features of the effects of a depreciation or devaluation on total national expenditures and income by assuming that exchange-rate changes influence export spending.

The quantity $d \times y_d$ is *induced import spending,* or the amount of import expenditures that stems directly from the receipt of disposable income. The fraction. d is the slope of the import function, which is equal to $\Delta im/\Delta y_d$ or the marginal propensity to import. Hence, the slope of the import function is the marginal propensity to import (*MPIM*).

The Consumption Function From the disposable income identity, $y_d \equiv c + s + im$, we know that households allocate their disposable income earnings to domestic consumption, saving, and import expenditures. Consequently, a domestic consumption function follows from our hypotheses about the forms of the saving and import functions. If we substitute the saving function, $s = s_0 + (b \times y_d)$, and the import function, $im = im_0 + (d \times y_d)$, into the disposable income identity, the result is:

$$y_d = c + s + im,$$

or

$$y_d = c - s_0 + (b \times y_d) + im_0 + (d \times y_d).$$

We can rearrange the last equation by solving for c. The result is the consumption function:

$$c = (s_0 - im_0) + [(1 - b - d) \times y_d].$$

AUTONOMOUS CONSUMPTION
The amount of household consumption spending on domestically produced goods and services that is independent of the level of real income.

This straight-line function appears in panel (c) of Figure 11–2. The consumption function's intercept is equal to $s_0 - im_0$. This is **autonomous consumption,** or the amount of real expenditures on domestically produced goods and services that would occur regardless of the magnitude of real disposable income. As long as the majority of total disposable income stays within the nation's borders, its autonomous consumption is a positive number. Thus, the intercept $s_0 - im_0$ is greater than zero, as shown in panel (c) of Figure 11–2.

The slope of the consumption function is equal to $1 - b - d = \Delta c/\Delta y_d \equiv$ *MPC*. Thus, the slope of the consumption function is the marginal propensity to consume (*MPC*). It follows that if we sum together the *MPC*, the *MPS*, and the *MPIM*, we can make substitutions to obtain

$$MPC + MPS + MPIM = (1 - b - d) + b + d = 1.$$

And so, as we noted earlier, the three marginal propensities add up to a value of 1.

Desired Investment Spending Expenditures on capital goods comprise the bulk of firm investment spending. In principle, domestic firms could import capital goods from other nations. To keep things simple, however, we shall assume that firms' investment spending is on domestic goods only.

Although variations in real income can potentially influence real investment, a key factor determining the amount of investment expenditures is the rate of interest. The interest rate that matters for investment is the *real interest rate,* denoted r. As in Chapter 4, we denote the nominal interest rate as R. We denote expected inflation rate as π^e, where we use the Greek letter pi to denote the inflation rate and the e superscript to denote the expected inflation rate. Then we can express the real interest rate as

$$r = R - \pi^e.$$

The real interest rate is equal to the nominal interest rate minus the expected inflation rate.

To produce goods and services, firms typically purchase or install capital goods, such as office buildings, computer equipment, factories, and the like. When evaluating the long-term profitability of such investment expenditures, firm owners compare the real return on investment–the real value of the annual flow of production that new capital goods makes possible–with the opportunity cost of incurring the investment expenditure. This opportunity cost is the real rate of interest that firm owners could earn if they were to save the funds instead. Consequently, if the real interest rate, r, increases, then desired real investment, i, declines. This inverse relationship between desired investment spending and the interest rate is shown as the *investment schedule,* labeled i in panels (*a*), (*b*), and (*c*) of Figure 11–3.

As shown in panel (*a*) of Figure 11–3, a decrease in the real interest rate from r_0 to r_1 causes desired real investment spending to rise from i_0 to i_1. Such a fall in the real interest rate could take place because of an decrease in the nominal interest rate or an increase in the expected inflation rate.

Panel (*b*) of Figure 11–3, however, displays another way in which desired investment may rise from i_0 to i_1. The desired investment schedule itself may shift to the right, meaning that an increase in desired investment could take place without a change in the real interest rate. Such a shift in the investment schedule may result from an increase in the anticipated real return on investment projects.

Panel (*c*) of Figure 11–3 shows that, whether induced by a fall in the real interest rate or expectations of higher real returns on investment, an increase in desired investment causes investment to rise at any given level of aggregate income, y. Thus, even though some amount of investment may be income-induced in the real world, to keep things as simple as possible we shall assume that investment is *autonomous,* or unrelated to income. And so, if we measure investment along the vertical axis, as in panel (*c*), and measure real income along the horizontal axis, an increase in desired investment results in an upward shift in a horizontal desired investment schedule, from $i = i_0$ to $i = i_1$.

Government Spending and Net Taxes The levels of public expenditures and net taxes chosen by a nation's government typically depend on a variety of factors, including the political structure that defines the government's role in the economy. These factors lie outside the scope of this text, as our objective is to understand how a government's spending and taxation decisions affect the economy once they have been adopted.

Government Expenditures We shall assume that political and other factors that lead a government to choose any particular level of public expenditures

---

FIGURE 11–3   FACTORS CAUSING CHANGES IN DESIRED INVESTMENT

Panels (*a*) and (*b*) show two key factors that can induce an increase in desired real investment expenditures. One, which panel (*a*) depicts, is a decline in the real interest rate resulting from a fall in the nominal interest rate or a rise in anticipated inflation. This causes a movement along the investment schedule. The other, shown in panel (*b*), follows from a shift in the investment schedule itself, so that a rise in desired investment takes place at any given real interest rate, which could arise from an increase in firms' expectations of future profitability from new investment. As panel (*c*) indicates, either cause of an increase in desired investment spending generates an upward shift in the investment curve graphed against real income.

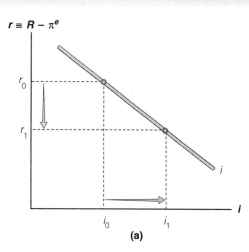

(a)

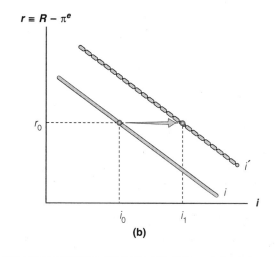

(b)

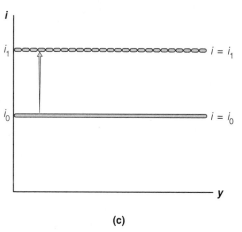

(c)

---

are determined outside our model. Thus, we shall assume that real government spending is equal to an autonomous amount, $g = g_0$. Panel (*a*) of Figure 11–4 shows that this implies that the *government spending schedule* is horizontal. If the government raises its spending from $g = g_0$ to $g = g_1$, then the government spending schedule shifts upward by the increase in spending.

Net Taxes   The governments of countries around the world assess a wide variety of taxes, including income taxes, value-added taxes, sales taxes, excise taxes, property taxes, and the like. The dependence of many governments' tax revenues on the levels of consumption expenditures and incomes indicates that, realistically, net taxes depend on their nations' real income levels. Nonetheless, we again shall simplify by assuming that net taxes are

FIGURE 11–4 THE GOVERNMENT SPENDING AND NET TAX SCHEDULES

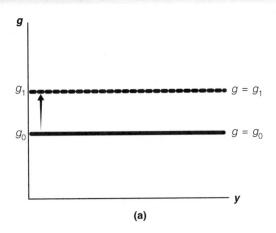

(a)

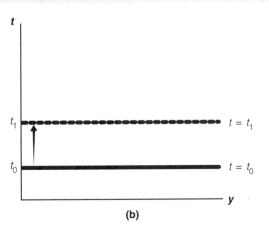

(b)

A key assumption of the basic open-economy framework is that government spending is autonomous, so that the government spending schedule is horizontal, as shown in panel (*a*). An increase in government spending thereby causes an upward shift in this schedule. Another assumption is that net taxes are autonomous, so that the net tax schedule in panel (*b*) also is horizontal. An increase in net taxes results in an upward shift in this schedule.

autonomous and equal to a lump-sum quantity. Panel (*b*) of Figure 11–4 shows that with this simplification, the *net tax schedule* is, like the government spending schedule, horizontal. Consequently, an increase in net taxes from an amount $t = t_0$ to a larger amount $t = t_1$ shifts the net tax schedule upward by the amount of the tax hike, as depicted in panel (*b*).

Export Spending There are two key factors that determine foreign expenditures on a nation's exports. One is the real incomes of foreign residents who buy domestically produced goods. If real income levels rise in other countries, export spending on a nation's domestic output would tend to increase.

As discussed in Chapter 9, the other key factor affecting the volume of spending on a nation's exports is the exchange rate. For instance, if the domestic currency *appreciates,* so that obtaining a unit of domestic currency requires additional units of foreign currency, then domestic exports become more expensive to foreign residents, and they will reduce their spending on domestic exports.

The domestic level of real income, y, has no effect on real exports, however. This implies that foreign expenditures on domestic exports are strictly autonomous with respect to *domestic* income. As a result, the *export schedule* is horizontal, as depicted in Figure 11–5. An increase in foreign real income levels

FIGURE 11-5 THE EXPORT SCHEDULE

FIGURE 11-5 THE EXPORT SCHEDULE

Changes in domestic income have no direct effect on export expenditures. Thus, the export schedule is horizontal. If foreign incomes rise or the domestic currency's value depreciates, however, export spending rises, causing an upward shift in the export schedule.

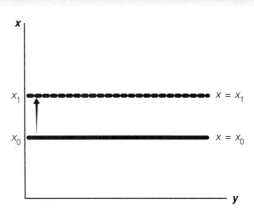

or a depreciation of the domestic currency causes exports to increase from an amount x_0 to a larger amount x_1. Thus, either occurrence results in an upward shift in the export schedule, as shown in the Figure 11-5.

Equilibrium Income and Expenditures

We shall define the equilibrium flow of total expenditures and real income as follows:

In equilibrium, the aggregate desired expenditures on domestically produced goods and services by households, firms, the government, and foreign residents are equal to total real income.

Because real income and the real value of domestically produced goods and services are equivalent, the equilibrium flow of real income is that level of all domestically produced and sold output that households, firms, the government, and foreign residents desire to purchase. If any real income remains unspent, then this indicates that firms produced "too much" output, giving them an incentive to cut back on sales and causing real income to change. In equilibrium, however, there is no tendency for the flow of real income and expenditures to change, so the equilibrium level of real income and expenditures must satisfy the condition that all income ultimately is spent.

Aggregate Desired Expenditures The aggregate amount of spending on domestically produced goods and services is the total of household consumption expenditures, desired investment spending, government expenditures, and spending on exports of domestic output by residents of other nations.

FIGURE 11–6   DERIVING THE AGGREGATE EXPENDITURES SCHEDULE

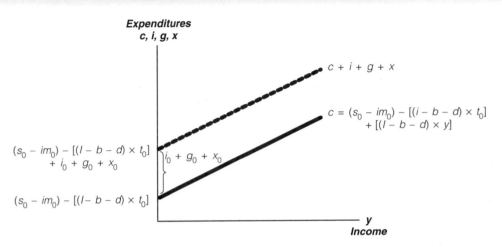

Summing the combined amount of desired investment spending, government spending, and export expenditures with the level of consumption at each

point along the consumption function yields the aggregate expenditures schedule, $c + i + g + x$.

Hence, aggregate desired expenditures on domestic goods and services are equal to $c + i + g + x$.

Figure 11–6 shows how to sum these components of aggregate desired expenditures. We begin by graphing the upward-sloping household consumption function, $c = (s_0 - im_0) + [(1 - b - d) \times y_d]$. We now take into account, however, that disposable income, y_d, by definition is equal to total real income, y, minus the current lump-sum amount of real net taxes, $t = t_0$. Substituting $y - t_0$ for y_d allows to rewrite the consumption function as

$$c = (s_0 - im_0) + [(1 - b - d) \times (y - t_0)],$$

or

$$c = (s_0 - im_0) - [(1 - b - d) \times t_0] + [(1 - b - d) \times y].$$

This means that if we measure real income along the horizontal axis, the intercept of the consumption function, $(s_0 - im_0) - [(1 - b - d) \times t_0]$, accounts for the consumption-reducing effect of taxes. The slope of the consumption function is still equal to the marginal propensity to consume, $MPC = 1 - b - d$.

By adding the vertical distance $i_0 + g_0 + x_0$ to the amount of consumption at each possible real income level, we obtain the **aggregate expenditures schedule,** $c + i + g + x$. The aggregate expenditures schedule displays the total amount of spending on domestically produced goods and services by house-

AGGREGATE EXPENDITURES SCHEDULE A schedule depicting total desired expenditures by households, firms, and the government at each and every level of real national income.

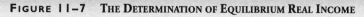

FIGURE 11–7 THE DETERMINATION OF EQUILIBRIUM REAL INCOME

Equilibrium real income arises at the point at which aggregate desired real expenditures, $c + i + g + x$, equal aggregate real income. This is true at the single real income level, y_e, at which the aggregate expenditures schedule crosses the 45-degree.

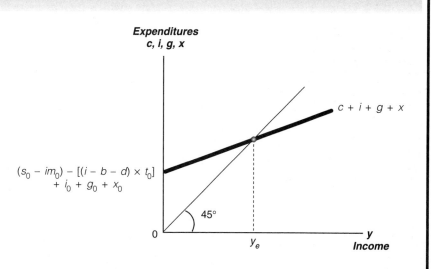

AGGREGATE NET AUTONOMOUS EXPENDITURES The total amount of autonomous consumption, autonomous investment, autonomous government spending, and autonomous export spending, which are assumed to be independent of the level of national income.

holds, firms, the government, and foreign residents at any given level of domestic real income. The vertical intercept of this schedule is **aggregate net autonomous expenditures,** or $(s_0 - im_0) - [(1 - b - d) \times t_0] + i_0 + g_0 + x_0$. This quantity is the net level of spending that is determined independently from the current real income level. The slope of the schedule is the same as the slope of the consumption function, $1 - b - d$.

Equilibrium National Income As noted earlier, the equilibrium flow of real income is that level at which households, firms, the government, and foreign residents desire to purchase all domestically produced goods and services. Hence, a nation's *equilibrium real income* is the real income level at which aggregate desired expenditures are equal to the real value of domestically produced output. From the circular flow diagram in Figure 11–1, we know that the real value of output is equal to real income. Thus, in equilibrium real income is equal to aggregate desired expenditures on domestic goods and services, or $y = c + i + g + x$.

45-DEGREE LINE A line that cuts in half the 90-degree angle of the coordinate axes on a diagram relating real income to aggregate desired expenditures and that provides a potential set of equilibrium points at which real income equals aggregate desired expenditures.

The Income–Expenditure Equilibrium Figure 11–7 shows the determination of a single income–expenditure equilibrium. The aggregate expenditure curve is taken from Figure 11–7; it displays all combinations of real income and desired expenditures by households, firms, the government, and foreign residents. A **45-degree line** cuts in half the 90-degree angle of the coordinate axes on the diagram. At any point along this 45-degree line, the level of real income is equal to the level of aggregate desired expenditures, so each point on the 45-degree line potentially can satisfy our definition of equilibrium. Hence, the *single point* at which the two schedules intersect is the single point that satisfies the equilibrium condition $y = c + i + g + x$. The equilibrium level of real income at this point is denoted y_e.

FUNDAMENTAL ISSUE #2

How is equilibrium real income determined in an open economy? In equilibrium, aggregate desired expenditures equal real income. In an open economy, household consumption of domestically produced goods and services, firm-desired investment spending, government spending, and export spending by foreigners make up aggregate desired expenditures. Desired investment, government spending and net taxes, and export spending are autonomous, while consumption spending is positively related to disposable income, and so the aggregate expenditures schedule has the same slope as the consumption function. Equilibrium real income is determined by the intersection of this schedule and the 45-degree line.

The *IS* Schedule

Figure 11–7 makes clear that the equilibrium level of real income depends on the position of the aggregate expenditures schedule. This schedule's position, in turn, depends on the amount of net autonomous expenditures, including **autonomous investment** spending. Because autonomous investment spending is negatively related to the real interest rate, however, changes in the real interest rate alter autonomous investment spending, total net autonomous expenditures, and the position of the aggregate expenditures schedule. Thus, interest rate variations induce variations in equilibrium real income.

The Derivation of the *IS* Schedule   Figure 11–8 shows how a rise in the nominal interest rate can affect equilibrium real income. Panel (*a*) displays the desired investment schedule as graphed, with the *nominal* interest rate measured along the vertical axis. This schedule slopes downward because of the negative relationship between real investment spending and the real interest rate. A rise in the nominal interest rate, from R_1 to R_2, given the expected inflation rate, π^e, causes desired real investment spending to decline from i_1 at point A to i_2 at point B.

Such a decline in desired investment, as shown in panel (*b*), results in a fall in net autonomous expenditures. Consequently, a rise in the nominal interest rate causes the aggregate desired expenditures schedule to shift downward,

AUTONOMOUS INVESTMENT
Desired investment that is independent of the level of real income.

FIGURE 11-8   THE DERIVATION OF THE *IS* SCHEDULE

A rise in the nominal interest rate, given the expected inflation rate, raises the real interest rate and induce a reduction in investment spending. Therefore, as indicated in panel (*a*), an increase in the nominal interest rate induces a movement from point *A* to point *B* along the investment schedule and causes a decline in desired investment spending. This, as panel (*b*) shows, reduces aggregate desired expenditures, resulting in a reduction in equilibrium real income, from y_1 at point *A* to y_2 at point *B*. Consequently, the new combination of real income and the nominal interest rate consistent with equilibrium real income and expenditures, which is y_2 and R_2 at point *B* in panel (*c*), lies above and to the left of the original combination y_1 and R_1 at point *A*. It follows that the *IS* schedule, which shows all combinations of real income and the nominal interest rate consistent with equilibrium real income and expenditures, slopes downward.

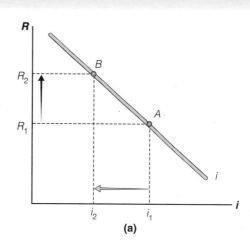

(a)

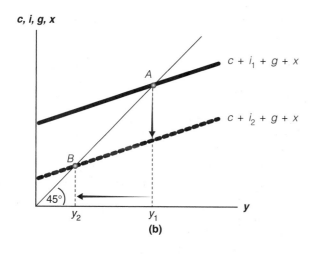

(b)

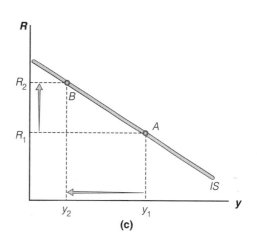

(c)

***IS* SCHEDULE** A set of possible combinations of real income and the nominal interest rate that are necessary to maintain the income–expenditure equilibrium, $y = c + i + g + x$ for a given level of aggregate net autonomous expenditures.

resulting in a decline in equilibrium real income, from y_1 to y_2. As a result, as displayed in panel (*c*), there is a movement from the initial real income–nominal interest rate combination, y_1 and R_1 at point *A* consistent with equilibrium real income, to a new combination, y_2 and R_2 at point *B*.

Point *A* and point *B* represent real income–nominal interest rate combinations that lie on an ***IS* schedule,** which is a set of combinations of real income levels and nominal interest rates that maintain equilibrium real income. The *IS* schedule was first developed in 1937 by Sir John Hicks of Oxford University. Hicks derived the schedule by assuming a simple economy with no government sector or international trade, so that aggregate desired expenditures were equal to $c + i$. From the income identity, with no taxes and no imports, real income therefore would, by definition, equal $y \equiv c + s$. Thus, when Hicks imposed the equilibrium condition $y = c + i$, he could write it as $c + i = c + s$. After subtracting c from both sides, this yielded $i = s$, or investment equals saving, hence the term "*IS*" as a label for the resulting relationship that we have derived more generally in Figure 11–8.

Determining the Position of the *IS* Schedule   To derive the *IS* schedule in Figure 11–8, , we consider only the effects of a rise in the nominal interest rate on desired investment spending. We assume that all other factors affecting autonomous desired expenditures are unchanged. These factors include autonomous consumption saving, government expenditures, autonomous net taxes, autonomous imports, and autonomous export spending. Increases in government expenditures or autonomous export spending, for example, cause a rise in aggregate desired expenditures, as shown in panel (*b*) of Figure 11–9. Likewise, reductions in autonomous saving, imports, or net taxes also generate such an upward shift in the aggregated desired expenditures schedule by inducing a rise in consumption spending at any given interest rate.

As panel (*c*) of Figure 11–9 indicates, the result of any one of these possible sources of an increase in autonomous expenditures is a new real income–nominal interest rate combination, y_2 and R_1 at point *B*, that lies to the right of the original combination, y_1 and R_1 at point *A*. Therefore, any of the factors just listed that cause an increase in aggregate desired expenditures generate a *rightward shift* in the *IS* schedule, such as the shift depicted in panel (*c*).

By way of contrast, any factor that causes a *reduction* in aggregate desired expenditures shifts the *IS* schedule *leftward*. Such factors include reductions in government spending or autonomous export expenditures or increases in autonomous saving, net taxes, or autonomous import expenditures.

The Multiplier Effect   The amount by which the *IS* schedule shifts in response to a change in net autonomous expenditures depends on the size of the **multiplier effect.** This term refers to the fact that a given one-unit change in aggregate net autonomous expenditures causes a greater-than-one-unit change in equilibrium real income in the same direction. In panel (*b*) of Figure 11–9, a one-unit movement in the intercept of the aggregate desired expenditures schedule $c + i + g + x$ induces an increase in equilibrium real income that exceeds one unit.

Some algebra helps to illustrate how to determine the size of the multiplier effect. The income–expenditure equilibrium condition is $y = c + i + g + x$. Let's substitute from our consumption function, $c = (s_0 - im_0) - [(1 - b - d) \times t_0] + [(1 - b - d) \times y]$, and, for purposes of illustrating the multiplier effect, assume that net taxes and desired investment, government spending, and export spend-

FIGURE 11-9   A CHANGE IN AUTONOMOUS EXPENDITURES AND THE POSITION OF THE *IS* SCHEDULE

An increase in aggregate desired expenditures, which might result from a reduction in autonomous saving, autonomous import expenditures, or net taxes or from an increase in autonomous government spending or autonomous export expenditures, causes the aggregate expenditures schedule to shift upward, as shown in panel (*b*). Hence, at a given interest rate and level of investment expenditures, displayed in panel (*a*), equilibrium real income increases following the movement from point *A* to point *B* in panel (*b*). This implies that a new real income–interest rate combination maintaining equilibrium real income and expenditures, y_2 and R_1 at point *B* in panel (*c*), lies on a new *IS* schedule to the right of the original combination y_1 and R_1 at point *A* on the initial *IS* schedule. Thus, a rise in autonomous expenditures shifts the *IS* schedule to the right.

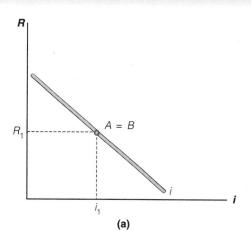

(a)

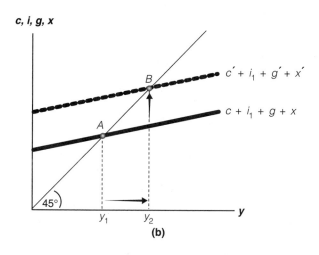

(b)

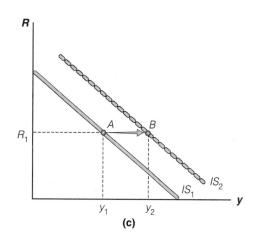

(c)

ing are all autonomous. This permits us to rewrite the income–expenditure equilibrium condition as:

$$y = (s_0 - im_0) - [(1 - b - d) \times t_0] + [(1 - b - d) \times y] + i_0 + g_0 + x_0.$$

Subtracting $(1 - b - d) \times y$ from both sides of this equation, we obtain:

$$y - [(1 - b - d) \times y] = (s_0 - im_0) - [(1 - b - d) \times t_0] + i_0 + g_0 + x_0.$$

Because the left-hand side is equal to $[1 - (1 - b - d)] \times y$, which reduces to $(b + d) \times y$, we can write this equation as:

$$(b + d) \times y = (s_0 - im_0) - [(1 - b - d) \times t_0] + i_0 + g_0 + x_0.$$

Finally, let's divide both sides of the equation by $(b + d)$ to obtain a final expression for equilibrium real income:

$$y = \frac{1}{b+d}\{(s_0 - im_0) - [(1 - b - d) \times t_0] + i_0 + g_0 + x_0\}.$$

The expression tells us that equilibrium real income is equal to the ratio $1/(b + d)$ times aggregate net autonomous expenditures, $(s_0 - im_0) - [(1 - b - d) \times t_0] + i_0 + g_0 + x_0$. The ratio $1/(b + d)$ is the **autonomous expenditures multiplier,** which determines the size of the multiplier effect on equilibrium real income resulting from a variation in net autonomous expenditures. We know that b is the marginal propensity to save (MPS) and that d is the marginal propensity to import ($MPIM$). Hence, we can rewrite the multiplier as $1/(MPS + MPIM)$. Earlier we noted that the marginal propensities to consume, save, and import must sum to 1, or that $MPC + MPS + MPIM = 1$. It follows that $MPS + MPIM$ is equal to $1 - MPC$. Thus, another way to write the multiplier is $1/(1 - MPC)$. The MPC is a fraction, so the multiplier is greater than 1. For example, if the marginal propensity to save is equal to 0.10 and the marginal propensity to import is equal to 0.15, then the marginal propensity to consume is equal to $MPC = 0.75$. Then the multiplier is equal to $1/(1 - MPC) = 1/(1 - 0.75) = 1/0.25 = 4$. A \$1 billion increase in aggregate net autonomous expenditures in Figure 11–9 causes a \$4 billion rise in equilibrium real income.

Why is there a multiplier effect? To answer this question, let's again suppose that $MPC = 0.75$ and that the nation we are considering is the United States. Then each one-dollar rise in disposable income raises consumption spending by 75 cents. If autonomous export expenditures, for example, rise by an amount equal to \$1 billion, then such a spending increase immediately raises U.S. real income by \$1 billion. Because we have assumed that taxes are a lump sum, real disposable income rises by \$1 billion, spurring household consumption spending to increase by 75 percent of \$1 billion, or \$750,000. This raises the disposable income of all firms from whom the government or foreign residents purchases domestically produced goods and services by \$750,000. At this point, therefore, the \$1 billion increase in autonomous export spending increases total real income by \$1.75 billion.

The total process of spending increases is not yet finished, however. Owners and employees at exporting domestic firms that have gained \$750,000 in new sales and income earnings are now able to raise their consumption spending by 75 percent of this amount, or by $0.75 \times \$750,000 = \$562,500$. Furthermore, this spending increase causes a rise in disposable income of \$562,500 for other domestic firm owners and workers, who then raise their consumption spending by $0.75 \times \$562,500 = \$421,875$.

In the end, the total rise in real income caused by the initial $1 billion increase in autonomous export expenditures is equal to the sum of all these increases ($1 billion + $750,000 + $562,500 + $421,875 + ...) in spending. As we determined earlier, if the *MPC* is equal to 0.75, then the total rise in real income caused by a $1 billion increase in autonomous exports is equal to $1 billion × 1/(1 − 0.75) = $1 billion × 4 = $4 billion. This, then, is the amount that the *IS* schedule shifts to the right in panel (*c*) of Figure 11–9 following an upward shift of the aggregate expenditures schedule equal to $1 billion in additional autonomous export spending in panel (*b*).

FUNDAMENTAL ISSUE #3

What is the *IS* schedule, and what factors determine its position? The *IS* schedule is a downward-sloping set of all combinations of real income and the nominal interest rate for which aggregate desired expenditures equal real income. The *IS* schedule shifts rightward if there is an increase in autonomous desired expenditures arising from a fall in autonomous saving, import spending, or taxes, or from a rise in autonomous government spending, investment, or export spending. In contrast, a rise in autonomous saving, import spending, or taxes or a fall in autonomous government spending, investment, or export spending would shift the *IS* schedule to the left.

THE MARKET FOR REAL MONEY BALANCES: THE *LM* SCHEDULE

In Chapters 8 and 10, you learned that the two key liabilities of central banks—reserves held by private financial institutions and currency held by the non-bank public—together comprise the monetary base. In addition, you learned that there are two important central bank assets corresponding to these liabilities. These are domestic credit and foreign exchange reserves. Consequently, we can consider the quantity of money issued by a central bank from the perspective of either the asset or liability side of the central bank's balance sheet.

How much of the money that a central bank issues do people really want to hold? A friend might mention that a common acquaintance "has lots of money," and the friend might enviously state that one of her goals in life is to "make just as much money." It might seem apparent that we all would like to have as much money as possible. Yet central banks typically must *require* financial institutions to hold minimal amounts of reserves by imposing legal reserve requirements. If they did not do this, many financial institutions would hold nearly zero reserve balances. Inducing the nonbank public to hold the money that central banks issue sometimes can be an even more difficult proposition. For instance, in Russia during the middle and late 1990s, many people preferred to use U.S. dollars, rather than the ruble, for transactions.

We may conclude that people around the world do not necessarily really "want more money" than they already possess. What they really want is more *wealth*. Although money is a way to hold part of one's wealth, in many circumstances holding money balances issued by a central bank is not in one's best interest. How much of an individual's wealth that a person desires to hold as money balances is the individual's *demand for money*.

The Demand for Money

To see why holding as much money as possible might not be a good idea, think for a moment about how much interest you earn on the central-bank-issued currency you have on hand at the moment. The amount of interest that you earn on such currency holdings is zero. In contrast, if you had sufficient currency to place in a bank deposit or to buy a government bond, then you could convert that currency into an interest-bearing asset that would yield you a return greater than zero.

The Transactions and Precautionary Motives for Holding Money   Viewed from this perspective, why would anyone hold non-interest-bearing forms of money? The answer, of course, is the reason that you probably have some currency on hand yourself at this moment: You desire to hold money to buy things, because money is a widely accepted medium of exchange.

TRANSACTIONS MOTIVE
The motive to hold money for use in planned exchanges.

The early twentieth-century British economist John Maynard Keynes referred to this basic motive for holding money as the **transactions motive.** This is the incentive to hold non-interest-bearing money for use as a medium of exchange in planned transactions. For example, it is handy to have some cash or coins on hand to use in payment for a snack and soft drink or juice after each round of afternoon classes. Money also can be very useful for purchasing groceries from week to week and for making rent and utility payments from month to month.

PRECAUTIONARY MOTIVE
The motive to hold money for use in unplanned exchanges.

Keynes coined the term **precautionary motive** to describe a related reason to hold money. This is the desire to hold money in case a need arises to make previously unplanned transactions. For instance, there is always a chance that the hard disk in your personal computer will malfunction and need repair, or that you might be in a clothing retailer and discover a sale on jeans that you "need" but nonetheless did not previously plan to purchase. Most people try to keep additional cash on hand to cover such contingencies.

A key determinant of how much money any of us chooses to hold to satisfy our own transactions and precautionary motives depends largely on our relative incomes. If you happen to be a student whose income is relatively low, so that you spend the bulk of your income on tuition, rental payments, and the like, then you may have to limit the number of times that you purchase a soft drink each week. You also may be more less likely to buy an article of clothing that happens to be on sale, because your budget for such contingencies may be limited. By way of contrast, a wealthier student who receives a large monthly allowance may purchase afternoon snacks along with soft drinks, and that student may keep significant sums of cash on hand to purchase sale merchandise on shopping trips.

These commonsensical considerations led Keynes, as well as many of his predecessors, to argue that one key determinant of desired money holdings is one's income. A rise in income leads, via the transactions and precautionary motives for holding money, to an increase in the demand for money balances.

The Portfolio Motive for Holding Money   In addition to the transactions and precautionary motives for holding money, Keynes also proposed the existence of a *speculative motive.* This incentive to hold non-interest-bearing cash, he reasoned, stems from the interaction between changes in the nominal interest rate and the price of an interest-bearing financial asset such as a bond. The modern term for this incentive to hold money is the **portfolio motive,** which refers to the motive for people to adjust their desired mix of money and bond holdings based on their speculations about interest-rate movements and anticipated changes in bond prices. To the extent that this motive influences desired money holdings, changes in the nominal interest rate can thereby affect the quantity of money demanded.

Bonds, Money, and Financial Wealth   To understand the essential elements of the reasoning behind the portfolio motive, let's suppose a person allocates her financial wealth only between money holdings, M, and holdings of another financial asset that we shall call a "bond," B. The distinguishing characteristic of money is that the nominal price of money is always equal to 1 unit of money (for instance, $1, 1 franc, 1 yen, etc.), whereas the nominal price of a bond can fluctuate. Thus, as discussed in Chapter 5, a person who holds a bond earns a *capital loss* if the nominal price of the bond declines over a given period or a *capital gain* if the nominal price of the bond rises during another interval. A one-dollar bill issued by the Federal Reserve System, a one-deutsche mark note issued by the German Bundesbank, and a one-yen note issued by the Bank of Japan have the same *nominal* values of $1, 1 DM, or 1 yen, respectively, across time. Therefore, an individual cannot incur a nominal capital loss or earn a nominal capital gain if he holds all his financial wealth in the form of currency notes issued by these or other central banks.

To contemplate how an individual chooses shares of her financial wealth to split between money and bonds, let's suppose that at a given time her nominal financial wealth is equal to some amount W. The individual allocates this amount of wealth between holdings of non-interest-bearing holdings of money, M, and holdings of interest-bearing bonds, B. As before, we shall denote the nominal interest return on bonds as R. Hence, at this given point

PORTFOLIO MOTIVE Modern term for Keynes's essential argument for a speculative motive for holding money, in which people hold both money and bonds and adjust their holdings of both components of financial wealth based on their anticipations concerning interest rate movements.

in time, the individual's financial wealth must equal to her money holdings plus her bond holdings:

$$W \equiv M + B.$$

If wealth is fixed at a point in time, then it must be true that the sum of changes in money and bond holdings must equal zero, or $\Delta M + \Delta B \equiv 0$. In other words, a change in the individual's bond holdings, ΔB, must be countered by an offsetting change in money holdings in the opposite direction, $-\Delta M$. For instance, if this individual had \$12,000 in financial wealth, of which she holds \$6,000 as money and \$6,000 as bonds, then if she wishes to reduce her bond holdings by \$3,000, she must increase her money holdings by \$3,000, leaving \$9,000 in cash and \$3,000 in bonds.

The *wealth constraint* that the individual faces provides the basis for an interaction between interest-rate changes and the individual's demand for money. As we discussed in Chapter 5, the fact that bonds earn a nominal interest return means that variations in the nominal interest rate alter the market prices of bonds and, consequently, the individual's desired bond holdings. Altering her bond holdings, however, requires the individual to vary her money holdings. Thus, interest rate changes will induce her to alter her desired money holdings.

The Portfolio Motive How might an individual alter her money and bond holdings as part of a speculative strategy concerning expected changes in interest rates? The individual will recognize that future capital gains or losses from bond holdings depend directly on whether interest rates rise or fall in the future. Given her *anticipation* of future interest-rate movements, she realizes that as interest rates change, she should change her mix of money and bonds (see "Management Notebook: Are Interest Rates Predictable?").

Suppose that the current market interest rate rises to a level that a given individual believes is rather high. As you learned in Chapter 5, interest yields and bond prices are inversely related. As a result, this individual's anticipation is that if the current interest rate is "high," then the interest rate likely will decline in the future, implying that bond prices likely will rise. This means that she anticipates a future capital gain on bonds that she holds as part of her financial wealth. To further increase her anticipated capital gains from bond holdings, this individual decides allocate more of her financial wealth to bonds in the present. But her financial wealth is fixed now, so this requires her to reduce her holdings of money. Consequently, for this individual a current rise in the market interest rate causes a current reduction in her desired money holdings. *Her demand for money depends negatively on the market interest rate.*

The Demand for Real Money Balances Before we think about combining the transactions, precautionary, and speculative motives to consider the total demand for money, we need to consider the appropriate measure of money holdings.

MANAGEMENT NOTEBOOK

Are Interest Rates Predictable?

Interest rates do more than equilibrate the market for real money balances. Changes in interest rates influence profitability of banks and other financial institutions and determine whether a business investment was a smart decision or a foolish mistake. In addition, many aspects of the formulation of government policies are based on predicted movements in "the" interest rate. For example, central banks must base their decisions about money growth rates on projections of future interest rates that will influence the public's desired holdings of real money balances. In addition, governmental budgetary authorities must try to forecast interest rates to make estimates of interest payments that they will have to make to holders of government bonds.

Most interest-rate predictions turn out to be incorrect. One analyst has said that "predicting interest rates is like shooting a gun out the window of your house and hoping that a game bird will fly by." Studies of interest-rate forecasts in the 1990s concluded that all points at which key interest-rate moves occurred were

missed by forecasters. Furthermore, studies examining long series of interest-rate data and forecasts consistently find that forecasters typically could have done as well by flipping a coin.

The values of real and financial assets are linked to interest rates, so any individual who might be able to predict a change in interest rates thereby could predict changes in many asset prices. Thus, any forecaster who could predict interest-rate variations with certainty potentially could make hundreds of millions of dollars in a very short time period. Such a person would have every incentive to trade financial assets based on her or his forecasts, rather than share those with central banks or government budgetary authorities.

FOR CRITICAL ANALYSIS:
How are interest rates and financial asset prices related? How could a good forecaster of interest-rate variations earn sizable profits if others in the economy were inferior forecasters?

When asked how much cash you have on hand, you might take a look and reply, "Oh, about $25." This would be the nominal, face value of the currency and coins in your possession. But if you think about it for a moment, you will realize that what really matters to you is the purchasing power of the money that you hold.

Real Money Balances   Suppose, for instance, that you decide to carry $25 in cash to cover a day's purchases. You might plan to spend $15 to purchase lunch and $5 to purchase an afternoon snack between classes, which would leave you with $5 in precautionary balances for that day. Now suppose that the price level doubles shortly after you leave for campus. This doubles the price of the lunch you had planned to buy, to $30. In addition, the price of the intended afternoon snack rises to $10. Now the $25 that you had carried from home does not even cover all the lunch items that you had planned to purchase. Furthermore, you have to give up your afternoon snack. Effectively, the purchasing power of the $25 in cash drops to half its previous value. Purchasing the same lunch and snack during the coming day requires twice as much money, or $50. Thus, doubling of prices requires a doubling of your nominal money balances if you wish to maintain the purchasing power necessary to cover the day's expenses.

This example indicates that the real purchasing power of a person's nominal cash balances is the price-adjusted value of one's nominal money holdings, or **real money balances,** denoted by $m \equiv M/P$. Thus, by definition real money balances are equal to nominal money holdings, M, divided by the GDP price deflator, P.

REAL MONEY BALANCES The price-level-adjusted value of the nominal quantity of money, defined as the nominal money stock divided by the price level.

The Demand Schedule for Real Money Balances What matters for determining the transactions and precautionary demands for real money balances is a person's *real* income. Consequently, a rise in aggregate real income raises the total demand for money across all individuals. A decline in aggregate real income, in contrast, reduces the demand for real money balances. The logic of the portfolio motive for holding money continues to apply to the *nominal* interest rate, however, because real financial wealth still must be split between real holdings of money and bonds. Changes in the nominal interest rate thereby induce changes in the split of real wealth between real money balances and real bond holdings that are equivalent to alterations in the split between nominal holdings of money and bonds.

To take into account these determinants of the demand for real money balances, we can draw a *money demand schedule,* or a graphical depiction of the relationship between the quantity of money demanded and the nominal interest rate. Panel (*a*) of Figure 11–10 depicts a sample money demand schedule. The negative slope of the money demand schedule reflects the inverse relationship between the quantity of real money balances demanded and the nominal interest rate implied by the portfolio motive for holding money. In addition, we label the schedule $m^d(y_1)$ to indicate that the *position* of the money demand schedule depends on the current level of real income, such as a real income level y_1.

Panel (*b*) of Figure 11–10 illustrates the effect of an increase in real income, from y_1 to a larger amount y_2. Higher real income increases the volume of planned transactions by all individuals in the economy, thereby increasing their holdings of real money balances for transactions purposes. In addition, the rise in real income raises total precautionary money holdings. Therefore, at any given nominal interest rate, people desire to hold more real money balances, so the money demand schedule shifts rightward, as shown in panel (*b*) by the shift from $m^d(y_1)$ to $m^d(y_2)$.

The *LM* Schedule

As we noted earlier, a central bank cannot force people to hold the nominal stock of money that it issues. People must be willing to hold it. The price level and the nominal interest rate are the factors that influence people's willingness

FIGURE 11–10 THE MONEY DEMAND SCHEDULE

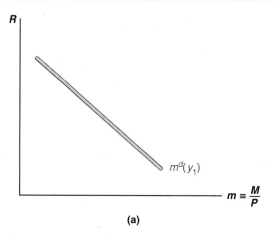

(a)

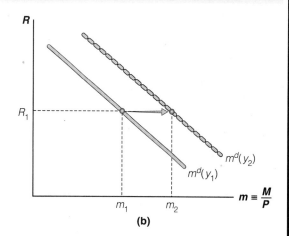

(b)

The demand for real money balances, $m \equiv M/P$, is the total demand for real purchasing power. As shown in panel (*a*), the demand for real money balances slopes downward as a result of the portfolio motive for holding real money balances. The demand for real

money balances shifts rightward when real income rises, as displayed in panel (*b*), because of the transactions and precautionary motives for holding real money balances.

to hold money balances. In Chapter 14 we shall consider how the price level is determined. For now we shall concentrate on how the nominal interest rate adjusts to make people satisfied withholding the quantity of money, *given* a particular price level.

Money Market Equilibrium and the LM Schedule   We shall assume that the central bank sets a given nominal quantity of money supplied, M_1^s, by determining the quantity of domestic credit and foreign exchange reserves. The supply of real money balances then is equal to M_1^s/P_1, where P_1 is the current price level. Figure 11–11 depicts the supply of real money balances, together with the money demand schedule from Figure 11–10. Given the quantity of money supplied $M_1^s = M_1$, the *equilibrium* nominal interest rate is equal to R_1. At this interest rate, people are willing to hold the nominal quantity of money, M_1, issued by the central bank, *given* the current level of prices, P_1. Hence, the market for real money balances is in equilibrium.

Figure 11–12 illustrates the effect of a rise in real income on the equilibrium nominal interest rate. A rise in real income, from y_1 to a higher level y_2, increases the demand for real money balances. As a result, as shown in panel (*a*) of Figure 11–12, the money demand schedule shifts to the right, from $m^d(y_1)$ to $m^d(y_2)$. At the initial equilibrium interest rate R_1 at point A, there is

FIGURE 11–11 **MONEY MARKET EQUILIBRIUM**

The equilibrium nominal interest rate is the interest rate at which the quantity of real money balances demanded equals the quantity of real money balances supplied by the central bank. This occurs at the point where the demand schedule for real money balances crosses the real money supply schedule.

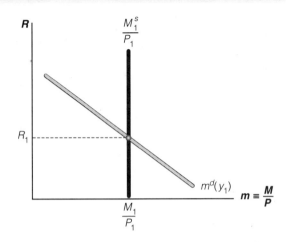

FIGURE 11–12 **THE DERIVATION OF THE *LM* SCHEDULE**

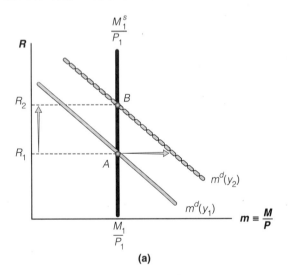

(a)

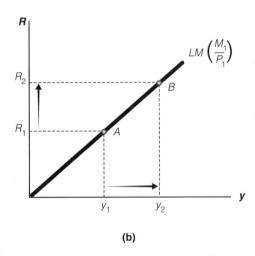

(b)

If real income rises from an initial amount y_1 to a higher level y_2, then the demand for real money balances increases, causing the equilibrium nominal interest rate to rise from R_1 at point A in panel (a) to R_2 at point B. Consequently, as shown in panel (b), the

real income–interest rate combinations y_1 and R_1 at point A and y_2 and R_2 at point B maintain equilibrium in the market for real money balances, given the current supply of real money balances. Both of these points lie on an *LM* schedule.

an excess quantity of real money balances demanded. This implies an excess quantity of bonds supplied, because people desire to hold fewer bonds as they seek to increase their real money balances. As a result, bond prices decline, so the equilibrium nominal interest rate rises, to R_2 at point B. Thus, in panel (b), there is a movement from an initial real income–nominal interest rate combination, y_1 and R_1 at point A, to a new combination, y_2 and R_2 at point B. Both real income–nominal interest rate combinations are representative points of money market equilibrium along the schedule displayed in panel (b), which is labeled *LM*.

LM **SCHEDULE** A set of combinations of real income and the nominal interest rate that maintains money market equilibrium.

An *LM* **schedule** is a set of all combinations of real income levels and nominal interest rates that maintain equilibrium in the money market. John Hicks also gave the *LM* schedule its name in 1937, when he referred to the demand for money as desired liquidity, *L*. Because money market equilibrium required equality between desired liquidity and the quantity of money balances supplied by a central bank, *M*, Hicks noted that $L = M$ must always hold along the schedule for money market equilibrium, hence the term *LM*.

Determining the Position of the *LM* Schedule   It is crucial to recognize that our derivation of the *LM* schedule in Figure 11–12 depended on an unchanging supply of real money balances equal to M_1/P_1. For this reason, we have labeled the *LM* schedule as $LM(M_1/P_1)$ in panel (b) of the figure, to indicate that we have derived this set of real income–nominal interest rate combinations *given* the nominal money stock M_1 and the price level P_1. If there had been a different position for the real money supply schedule, then we would have developed a different set of combinations of real income and the nominal interest rate consistent with money market equilibrium. That is, we would have derived a different *LM* schedule.

To see this, suppose that the central bank increases the nominal money stock while real income and the price level remained unchanged. As shown in panel (a) of Figure 11–13, this causes a rise in the real money stock, from M_1/P_1 to M_2/P_1. Real income remains unchanged at y_1, but the equilibrium nominal interest rate declines, from R_1 at point A to R_2 at point B.

After the increase in the nominal money stock, a new real income–interest rate combination, y_1 and R_2 at point B in panel (b) of Figure 11–13, maintains equilibrium in the market for real money balances. This combination is on a new *LM* schedule, $LM(M_2/P_1)$, that lies below and to the right of the initial *LM* schedule, $LM(M_1/P_1)$. Holding the price level fixed, therefore, a rise in the nominal money stock raises the supply of real money balances and shifts the *LM* schedule downward and to the right. In contrast, a decline in the money stock with an unvarying price level shifts the *LM* schedule upward and to the left.

A change in the price level also alters the amount of real money balances, causing the *LM* schedule to shift. For the time being, however, and in Chapters 12 and 13 that follow, we shall assume that the price level is fixed. We shall explore the ramifications of changes in the price level in Chapter 14.

FIGURE 11–13 **CHANGES IN THE REAL MONEY SUPPLY AND IN THE POSITION OF THE *LM* SCHEDULE**

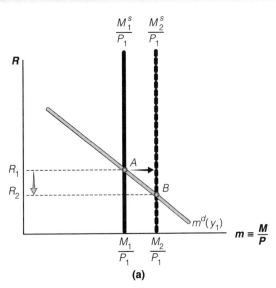

(a)

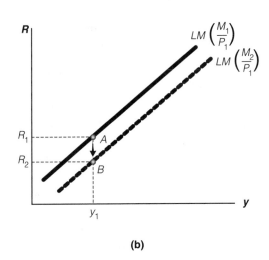

(b)

Panels (*a*) and (*b*) show the effects of a rise in the real money supply owing to an increase in the nominal quantity in circulation by a nation's central bank with an unchanged price level. The result in the market for real money balances, as shown in panel (*a*), is a rise in the supply of real money balances and a resulting movement from equilibrium point *A* to equilibrium

point *B*. Because real income does not change following the decline in the equilibrium interest rate, the new real income–interest rate combination y_1 and R_2 at point *B* in panel (*b*) lies directly below the original combination y_1 and R_1 at point *A*. Consequently, the *LM* schedule shifts downward and to the right.

FUNDAMENTAL ISSUE #4

What is the *LM* schedule, and what factors determine its position? The *LM* schedule is an upward-sloping set of all combinations of real income and the nominal interest rate that maintain equilibrium in the market for real money balances. The *LM* schedule shifts downward and to the right if there is an increase in the nominal money stock or a fall in the price level. A decrease in the money stock or a rise in the price level causes the *LM* schedule to shift upward and to the left.

THE BALANCE OF PAYMENTS: THE *BP* SCHEDULE
AND THE *IS–LM–BP* MODEL

You have seen so far in this chapter that the *IS* schedule is a downward-sloping set of real income–nominal interest rate combinations that yield equilibrium real income. You also have learned that the *LM* schedule is an upward-sloping set of real income–nominal interest rate combinations that maintain money market equilibrium.

In addition, you have learned that the level of real income also affects a nation's import expenditures. This means that the level of real income must influence a country's trade balance and, consequently, its current account balance. Furthermore, you have seen that the nominal interest rate influences bond holdings within a nation, which implies that the nominal interest rate must affect a country's capital account balance. This reasoning indicates that real income and the nominal interest rate together must determine a nation's balance of payments.

Maintaining a Balance-of-Payments Equilibrium: The *BP* Schedule

Recall from Chapter 1 that the *overall* balance of payments is the sum of the current account balance, the private capital account balance, and the official settlements balance. A *balance-of-payments equilibrium,* however, is defined as a situation in which the current account balance and capital account balance sum to zero, so that the official settlements balance also equals zero.

Real Income and the Balance of Payments   What real income levels and nominal interest rates would a nation require to maintain a balance of payments equilibrium?

To consider this question, take a look at Figure 11–14. Suppose that the current account and capital account sum to zero at point *A,* at a nominal interest rate equal to R_1 and a real income level equal to y_1. Thus, at point *A* there is a balance of payments equilibrium. Now suppose that real income rises, to the level y_2 at point *C.* At this point, higher real income stimulates a rise in import spending. This reduces the trade balance and depresses the current account balance. Consequently, under our assumption that a balance of payments equilibrium exists at point *A,* it follows that at point *C* there is a *balance of payments deficit.*

The Nominal Interest Rate and the Balance of Payments   If real income remains at y_2 in Figure 11–14, then what changes are necessary to reattain a balance of payments equilibrium? The answer is that the nominal interest rate must rise by an amount sufficient to make domestic financial assets, such as domestic bonds, more attractive to residents of other nations. Because they could earn higher returns on domestic bonds than they could prior to the rise

---

FIGURE 11-14   THE *BP* SCHEDULE

If real income rises from y_1 at point A, at which the balance of payments balance is equal to zero, to y_2 at point C, then a nation's import expenditures increase, and its trade balance declines. The result is a balance of payments deficit at point C. Reattaining a balance of payments equilibrium requires an increase in the nominal interest rate, which induces foreign residents to hold more of the nation's financial assets, thereby improving its capital account balance. Hence, a point such as point B, which is above and to the right of point A, represents another real income–interest rate combination consistent with a balance of payments equilibrium. The set of all such combinations is the *BP* schedule.

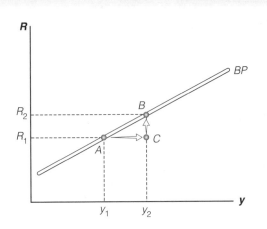

---

in the domestic interest rate, foreign residents would increase their holdings of domestic financial assets.

Thus, if real income remains equal to y_2 but the nominal interest rate rises, then the result is a real income–nominal interest rate combination such as point B in Figure 11–14. If the interest-rate increase from R_1 to R_2 is sufficient to reattain a balance-of-payments equilibrium, then point B, like point A, represents a balance-of-payments equilibrium. In fact, points A and B lie on a set of real income–nominal interest rate combinations that would maintain a balance of payments equilibrium. This set of combinations slopes upward. At higher real income levels, the resulting increases in imports reduce the current account balance, thereby requiring higher nominal interest rates to spur purchases of domestic assets sufficient to raise the capital account balance and reattain balance-of-payments equilibrium.

***BP* SCHEDULE** A set of real income–nominal interest rate combinations that are consistent with a balance-of-payments equilibrium in which the current account balance and capital account balance sum to zero.

The set of real income–nominal interest rate combinations that maintains a balance-of-payments equilibrium, so that along the ***BP* schedule** the sum of the current account and capital account is equal to zero. The implication of the *BP* schedule is that at any given time there is a single set of combinations of real income and the nominal interest rate along which a nation can achieve a balance of payments equilibrium.

Note that our derivation of the *BP* schedule has hinges on an implicit, yet important, assumption–the exchange rate remains unchanged. An important implication is that variations in the exchange rate can alter the position of the *BP* schedule. We shall discuss this point in greater detail in Chapter 13.

FIGURE 11-15 *IS–LM* EQUILIBRIUM

At point *E*, where the *IS* and *LM* schedules cross, the market for real money balances is in equilibrium at the same time that real income equals aggregate desired expenditures.

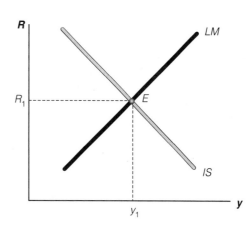

The *IS–LM–BP* Model

We now have three schedules with which to work. The *IS* schedule is a set of real income–nominal interest rate combinations that maintain equilibrium real income; the *LM* schedule consists of real income–nominal interest rate combinations that maintain equilibrium in the market for real money balances; and the *BP* schedule is the set of real income–nominal interest rate combinations for which the current account and the capital account sum to zero at the current exchange rate. Now let's put the schedules together to consider how equilibrium real income, the equilibrium nominal interest rate, and a nation's balance of payments status are jointly determined.

IS–LM **Equilibrium**   Let's begin by considering the simultaneous determination of the equilibrium real income level and the equilibrium nominal interest rate via the *IS* and *LM* schedules alone. Figure 11-15 shows how to combine these two schedules. At point *E*, the two schedules cross. Real income is equal to aggregate desired expenditures at the real income level y_1, because point *E* is on the *IS* schedule. Point *E* also is on the *LM* schedule, and so the money market is in equilibrium at the nominal interest rate R_1.

Point *E* is a point of *IS–LM* **equilibrium.** It is a point that is shared by both the *IS* schedule and the *LM* schedule. At this point, equilibrium real income is attained simultaneously with the nominal interest rate that maintains equilibrium in the money market.

IS–LM EQUILIBRIUM
A single point shared in common by the *IS* and *LM* schedules, at which the economy simultaneously attains both an income–expenditure equilibrium and equilibrium in the money market.

FUNDAMENTAL ISSUE #5

What is an *IS–LM* equilibrium? An *IS–LM* equilibrium is a single point that the *IS* and *LM* schedules share in common. At this point, both real income and the nominal interest rate are consistent with an equilibrium flow of real income and equilibrium in the market for real money balances.

Determining a Nation's Balance-of-Payments Position Panel (*a*) of Figure 11–16 shows a situation in which a nation's current account and capital account sum to zero at the current *IS–LM* equilibrium. Because an *IS–LM* equilibrium occurs at point *E* on the *BP* schedule, both the equilibrium nominal interest rate and the equilibrium real income level are consistent with a balance of payments equilibrium.

In panel (*b*), the *IS–LM* equilibrium point *E* lies below and to the right of the *BP* schedule. Consequently, the current equilibrium real income level, y_1, induces import expenditures that are too high, at the current equilibrium interest rate, R_1, to maintain a balance of payments equilibrium. At this interest rate, real income would have to fall to y_2 at point *A* to reduce import spending and, thus, raise the current account balance. Alternatively, the nominal interest rate would have to rise to R_2 to induce sufficient capital inflows at point *B*. From either perspective, it is clear that point *E* in panel (*b*) is an *IS–LM* equilibrium point at which, given the current exchange rate, there is a *balance-of-payments deficit*, meaning that the sum of the current account balance and the capital account balance is less than zero.

Finally, panel (*c*) in Figure 11–16 displays a situation in which the *IS–LM* equilibrium point *E* lies above and to the left of the *BP* schedule. In this situation, the current equilibrium real income level, y_1, yields import spending that is too low, at the current equilibrium interest rate, R_1, to produce a balance-of-payments equilibrium. At the interest rate R_1, real income would have to rise to y_2 at point *A* to spur import expenditures and reduce the current account balance. Alternatively, the nominal interest rate would have to decline to R_2 to induce offsetting capital outflows at point *B*. We may conclude that point *E* in panel (*c*) is an *IS–LM* equilibrium point at which, given the current exchange rate, there is a *balance-of-payments surplus*, so that the sum of the current account balance and the capital account balance exceeds zero.

As you can see, the *IS–LM–BP* model is a useful tool for examining the determination of the equilibrium nominal interest rate, equilibrium real income, and the state of the balance of payments. In the following two chapters, we shall use this open-economy framework to help understand how monetary and fiscal policy actions influence these variables in alternative exchange-rate settings.

FIGURE 11–16   *IS–LM* EQUILIBRIUM AND THE *BP* SCHEDULE

At an *IS–LM* equilibrium point *E* that lies along the *BP* schedule in panel (*a*), the equilibrium nominal interest rate and equilibrium real income level yield import expenditures and capital flows consistent with a balance of payments equilibrium. An *IS–LM* equilibrium point *E* that lies to the right of the *BP* schedule, as in panel (*b*), however, corresponds to a real income–nominal interest rate combination that yields import expenditures and capital outflows sufficiently high to produce a balance-of-payments deficit. Panel (*c*) shows the final possibility, which is an *IS–LM* equilibrium point *E* that lies to the left of the *BP* schedule. This point corresponds to a real income–nominal interest rate combination that yields import expenditures and capital outflows sufficiently low to yield a balance of payments surplus.

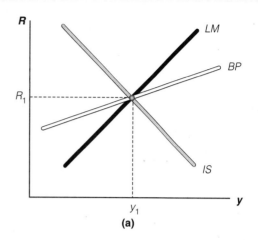

(a)

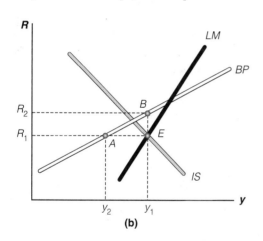

(b)

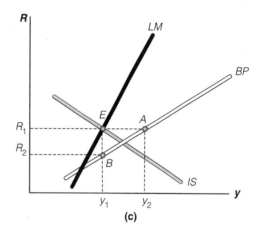

(c)

FUNDAMENTAL ISSUE #6

> **What is the *BP* schedule, and how can we use the *IS–LM–BP* model to determine a nation's balance of payments status?**
> The *BP* schedule is a set of real income–nominal interest rate combinations for which the sum of the current account balance and the capital account balance is equal to zero. Hence, if an *IS–LM* equilibrium occurs at a point on the *BP* schedule, then a balance of payments equilibrium results. An *IS–LM* equilibrium above or below the *BP* schedule, however, results in a balance of payments surplus or deficit, respectively.

CHAPTER SUMMARY

1. **The Key Relationships Implied by a Nation's Circular Flow of Income and Expenditures:** The circular flow of income and expenditures implies three fundamental relationships. One is that the real value of income must equal the real value of output. Another is the income identity, which states that all real income must be allocated to real consumption, real saving, real net taxes, and real imports. The third relationship is the product identity, which states that the real value of total output of goods and services must equal the sum of real consumption, real realized investment, real government spending, and real exports.

2. **The Determination of Equilibrium Real Income in an Open Economy:** The equilibrium level of real income is equal to aggregate desired expenditures at that income level. The components of aggregate desired expenditures in an open economy are household consumption spending on domestically produced goods and services, firm desired investment expenditures, government spending, and export expenditures by residents of other nations. If desired investment, government spending and net taxes, and export spending are autonomous, while consumption spending is positively related to disposable income, then the aggregate expenditures schedule has the same upward slope as the consumption function, and equilibrium real income is determined by the intersection of this schedule and the 45-degree line.

3. **The *IS* schedule and the Factors that Determine Its Position:** The *IS* schedule is a downward-sloping set of all combinations of real income and the nominal interest rate for which aggregate desired expenditures equal real income. An increase in autonomous desired expenditures arising from a fall in autonomous saving, import spending, or taxes or from a rise in autonomous government spending, investment, or export spending shifts the *IS* schedule rightward. A rise in autonomous saving, import spending, or taxes or a fall in autonomous government spending, investment, or export spending would, in contrast, shift the *IS* schedule leftward.

4. **The *LM* Schedule and the Factors that Determine Its Position:** The *LM* schedule is an upward-sloping set of all combinations of real income and the nominal interest rate that maintain equilibrium in the money market. An increase in the nominal quantity of money or a reduction in the price level shifts the *LM* schedule downward and to the right. In contrast, a decrease in the money stock or a rise in the price level causes the *LM* schedule to shift upward and to the left.

5. ***IS–LM* Equilibrium:** An *IS–LM* equilibrium is the point at which the *IS* and *LM* schedules cross. At such an equilibrium point, real income and the nominal interest rate simultaneously achieve an equilibrium flow of real income and equilibrium in the market for real money balances.

6. **The *BP* Schedule and How We Can Use the *IS–LM–BP* Model to Determine a Nation's Balance of Payments Status:** The *BP* schedule is a set of real income–nominal interest rate combinations for which the sum of the current account balance and the capital account balance is equal to zero. Therefore, attainment of an *IS–LM* equilibrium along the *BP* schedule results in a balance-

of-payments equilibrium. An *IS–LM* equilibrium above or below the *BP* schedule, however, implies a balance-of-payments surplus or deficit, respectively.

QUESTIONS AND PROBLEMS

1. Suppose that in Germany, the value of the *MPS* is 0.20 and the value of the *MPC* is 0.45. What is the marginal propensity to import (*MPIM*)? If disposable income in Germany were to rise from DM90 billion to DM100 billion, by how much would Germany's consumption rise? By how much would its saving rise? By how much would its imports rise? Is the sum of your answers equal to the change in income?

2. Suppose that the value of a nation's autonomous spending multiplier is equal to 4. The marginal propensity to save is equal to 0.15, and the economy is open to international trade. What is the value of the marginal propensity to import? Show your work.

3. Suppose that the U.S. GDP deflator is equal to one and that the U.S. nominal money stock is equal to $1.8 trillion. If the demand schedule for real money balances is given by the straight-line function (measured in trillions of dollars), $m^d = (0.9 \times y) - (100 \times R)$, then what is the equation for the economy's *LM* schedule? Show your work, and solve for R on the left-hand side of the equation that you derive. Finally, if y is equal to $8 trillion, then what is the equilibrium nominal interest rate?

4. Suppose that desired investment spending is determined by the equation (measured in trillions of dollars), $i = 7.4 - (100 \times R)$. If government spending is equal to $2 trillion, real consumption spending is equal to a *fixed* value of $3 trillion, and export spending is equal to $1 trillion, then what is the straight-line equation for the *IS* schedule? (Hint, set y equal to $c + i + g + x$ and solve the resulting expression with R on the left-hand side of your solution.) Finally, if the nominal interest rate is 5.4 percent (that is, 0.054), what is the equilibrium level of real income?

5. Use your answers to questions 3 and 4 to calculate the single real income–nominal interest rate combination for an *IS–LM* equilibrium.

6. Suppose that the current account and capital account sum to a number less than zero at the equilibrium real income–nominal interest combination that you calculated in question 5. Would the *IS–LM* equilibrium point lie above or below the *BP* schedule? Explain your reasoning.

ON-LINE APPLICATION

In the early part of this chapter, we discussed how real income must equal *aggregate* desired expenditures on domestically produced goods and services at the equilibrium *aggregate* real income level. Large nations, such as the United States, can experience considerable differences in *regional* economic activity, however. A good resource for information about the economic performance of different regions of the United States is the Federal Reserve's *Beige Book.* This publication is compiled by the Federal Reserve's Board of Governors in Washington, D.C., but it receives considerable input from staff economists at the twelve Federal Reserve banks.

Internet URL: http://www.bog.frb.fed.us/fomc/Beigebook/

Title: The Beige Book

Navigation: Begin with the Federal Reserve Board's address above. Under Federal Open Market Committee, click on *Beige Book.* Click on *Report* for the most recent date, and read the summary.

Application: Read the Beige Book Summary and answer the following questions:

1. What measures of overall business activity does the *Beige Book's* analysis consider? According to these measures, are there regional variations in business activity at present? What is the outlook for overall U.S. business activity?

2. Have recent variations in exchange rates or in trade with other nations affected the U.S. economy? Have these variations have differential effects across geographical regions of the United States?

REFERENCES AND RECOMMENDED READINGS

Branson, William. *Macroeconomic Theory and Policy.* New York: Macmillan, 1978.

Hansen, Alvin. *A Guide to Keynes.* New York: Macmillan, 1953.

Harris, Laurence. *Monetary Theory.* New York: McGraw-Hill, 1981.

Hicks, John. "Mr. Keynes and the Classics: A Suggested Interpretation." *Econometrica,* 5 (2, April 1937): 147–159.

Keynes, John Maynard. *The General Theory of Employment, Interest, and Money.* New York: Harcourt Brace Jovanovich, 1964.

ECONOMIC POLICY WITH FIXED EXCHANGE RATES

As one of the original founding members of the European Monetary System (EMS) and its "exchange-rate mechanism" linking the currency values of several countries within the European Union, Italy had pulled out all stops to keep in step with Germany, France, and other EMS nations. Although various factors had induced Italy to remove its currency, the lira, from the exchange-rate mechanism in 1992, by 1995 the nation's government and the Bank of Italy had effectively tied the lira's value back to that of the deutsche mark, the franc, and the other major currencies of Europe. The nation appeared to be on track in pursuing its goal of irrevocably fixing the exchange value of the lira in anticipation of the adoption of a single European currency in 1999.

Under another set of criteria required to achieve that goal, however, Italy needed to reduce its government deficit. This required reductions in government expenditures and increases in tax receipts. In a country in which the government's share of GDP traditionally has been large even by European standards, this was a tall order. In addition, even relatively small fiscal policy cutbacks seemed to bring about wrenching economic adjustments, particularly after the lira's value had been stabilized. By the end of 1997, Italy's economic recovery from the recession of the early 1990s had dwindled. Some observers began to wonder if Italy might be better off if it were to lengthen the period of deficit reduction and postpone fixing the lira's value. Italian leaders scoffed at such suggestions, pointing out that adopting them would require postponing Italy's plans to join the countries using a single currency. Nevertheless, many rank-and-file Italian citizens began to openly question whether being part of the proposed currency union would be worth the economic price required by the fiscal adjustments. Some even openly questioned whether deficit reduction with a fixed exchange value for the lira might cripple an already weak economy.

Do fiscal policy adjustments really have stronger effects on economic activity with a fixed exchange rate? If so, could monetary policy actions potentially offset these effects? These are the kinds of questions that have arisen as several European nations have sought to maintain a system of fixed exchange rates with their immediate neighbors.

THE OBJECTIVES OF POLICY

The relative effectiveness of monetary and fiscal policies in a system of fixed exchange rates has not just been an issue faced by countries in Europe. Until the early 1970s, much of the world participated in various types of fixed-exchange-rate systems. Consequently, the appropriate management of monetary and fiscal policies under fixed exchange rates has been an important issue. To contemplate how effective policies conducted by national governments and central banks may be, however, we first need to think about what goals they may desire to pursue.

Internal Balance Objectives

In Chapter 11, we introduced the *IS–LM–BP* framework. We use this framework to examine the factors that determine a nation's equilibrium nominal interest rate, its equilibrium real income, and its balance-of-payments position. Changes in the nominal money stock can influence the position of the *LM* schedule, and variations in government spending and taxation policies can affect the position of the *IS* schedule. Consequently, such policy actions could affect a nation's economic performance, and so central banks and governments might contemplate adopting policy strategies with an explicit intention to achieve specific national economic goals.

As we noted in Chapter 11, one aim of central banks and governments could be to achieve *internal balance,* which refers to the attainment of purely domestic policy objectives. Although national policymakers might seek to achieve a number of internal balance objectives, three objectives typically top any policymaker's list of internal balance goals.

Real Income Goals   One internal balance objective of policymakers might be to achieve the highest possible growth in its citizens' livings standards. Measuring how much a country is growing in terms of annual increases in real national income requires adjusting for population growth. Hence, most economists agree that the best available measure of the growth in overall living standards within any nation is the growth rate of **per-capita gross domestic product,** or per-capita GDP. This is the total value of final goods and services produced within a nation during a given year divided by the number of the nation's residents. Per-capita GDP, therefore, is a measure of material well-being for the average resident of a country, and the growth rate of per-capita GDP is a measure of the improvement of an average resident's living standards over time. As Table 12–1 indicates, average annual growth rates of per-capita real GDP vary considerably across nations.

Is Per-Capita GDP Growth an Appropriate Policy Objective?   Some economists question whether central banks and/or governments should try to fine-tune their nations' real growth. One reason is that there are significant problems in

PER-CAPITA GROSS DOMESTIC PRODUCT The total value of final goods and services produced within a country during a given year divided by the number of people residing in the country.

TABLE 12–1	RATES OF GROWTH IN PER-CAPITA REAL GDP FOR SELECTED NATIONS (%)		
	1970–1979	**1979–1988**	**1989–1998**
Canada	3.4	2.1	0.6
France	3.4	1.7	1.5
Germany	2.9	1.8	2.0
Italy	2.7	2.6	1.5
Japan	4.0	3.2	2.1
United Kingdom	2.2	2.3	1.4
United States	2.1	1.7	1.3

SOURCE: Data from Organization for Economic Cooperation and Development.

measuring and interpreting per-capita GDP data. Although per-capita income growth may be calculated easily if dependable data are available, the governments of many developing nations do not have the resources to collect accurate real income data, and many do not carefully tabulate their nation's populations.

There also are some conceptual problems stemming from using the rise in per-capita GDP as a measure of economic growth. One is that this measure fails to indicate how a nation's income is *distributed* among the residents of a nation. A country's per-capita GDP might grow very rapidly during years in which the incomes of its poorest residents decline even further. In addition, the rate of increase in per-capita real GDP is at best an *indicator* of improvements in the average well being of a nation's residents. This is so because real living standards can improve without per-capita income growth, if people, on average, enjoy more leisure time while producing as much as they did before. Furthermore, measured per-capita GDP growth does not fully account for *quality* changes that take place over time. Improvements in goods and services that residents of a nation produce and consume are not taken into account in the compilation of GDP statistics. Finally, the well being of a country's citizens likely depends on more than just the value of the nation's output of goods and services. For instance, if the act of producing those goods and services significantly damages the environment, then overall living standards could decline, on net, even if the country's citizens have higher real incomes and more goods and services available for consumption.

ON THE WEB

Learn about cross-country per-capita income growth and inequality from the World Bank at:

http://www.worldbank.org

Can National Policymakers Influence Real Living Standards? Despite these problems, economists generally regard growth in per-capita GDP as the best available overall measure of a nation's economic growth. For this reason, policymakers might wish to conduct policies intended to maintain high and stable rates of growth in per-capita GDP.

This does not necessarily mean, however, that such policies of central banks and governments *can* influence nations' economic growth rates. As we shall discuss in greater detail in Chapter 14, many economists believe that over intervals longer than several years, the monetary policies of central banks have meager effects on real output growth. Furthermore, a number of economists have concluded that over periods spanning decades, the ability of nations' governments to spur economic growth via their spending and taxation policies is secondary in comparison with broader factors, such as the tastes, preferences, education, and other attributes of those nations' residents.

Nevertheless, it might be possible that trying to attain high and stable per-capita GDP growth could help limit fluctuations in aggregate real income relative to **natural GDP,** or the level of real GDP along the long-run growth path that the economy otherwise would tend to follow in the absence of cyclical fluctuations. Intervals in which such fluctuations take place are known as **business cycles.** Even if policymakers were to agree that they might not have much influence on a nation's natural GDP, they still might feel obligated to try to conduct policies that might reduce the frequency and extent of business-cycle fluctuations.

Employment Goals   Labor is a key factor of production, and in most democratic countries workers account for the bulk of the electorate. Even leaders of nondemocratic societies are likely to feel obliged to pay attention to the interests of workers. Thus, governments and central banks usually feel pressure to follow policies intended to reduce the size and volatility of worker unemployment rates.

To track the extent of aggregate unemployment within their nations, governments tabulate **unemployment rates.** A nation's unemployment rate is the percentage of its labor force that is unemployed. Governments define the term *labor force* in various ways, so national unemployment rates are not always strictly comparable across countries. Nevertheless, Table 12–2 shows recent average unemployment rates for several nations. As you can see, there has been considerable variation in unemployment rates. Many nations have experienced double-digit unemployment rates, while in other countries average unemployment rates have been much lower.

There are three components of the unemployed portion of a nation's labor force. One is **frictional unemployment.** This is the portion of the labor force made up of people who are out of work temporarily, perhaps because they recently left one job and will not begin another for a few weeks. Another is **structural unemployment,** or the portion of the labor force composed of people who would like to have jobs but who do not possess skills and other attributes necessary to obtain gainful employment. The sum of the ratios of those who are frictionally and structurally unemployed as a ratio of the labor force is the **natural rate of unemployment,** or the unemployment rate that would arise if the economy could stay on its long-run growth path. At any point along this path, there would naturally be

NATURAL GROSS DOMESTIC PRODUCT A level of real GDP that lies on a nation's long-run growth path.

BUSINESS CYCLES Periods of fluctuation in real GDP around its natural level.

UNEMPLOYMENT RATE The percentage of a nation's labor force that is unemployed.

FRICTIONAL UNEMPLOYMENT The fraction of a nation's labor force composed of people who are temporarily out of work.

STRUCTURAL UNEMPLOYMENT The fraction of a nation's labor force composed of people who would like to be employed but who do not possess skills and other characteristics required to obtain jobs.

NATURAL RATE OF UNEMPLOYMENT The sum of the rates of frictional and structural unemployment, or the unemployment rate that would arise if a nation's economy were always on its long-run growth path.

TABLE 12-2   UNEMPLOYMENT RATES IN SELECTED NATIONS (%)

	1994	1995	1996	1997	1998*	1999*
Australia	9.7	8.5	8.6	8.6	8.1	7.5
Canada	10.4	9.5	9.7	9.2	8.5	8.2
France	12.3	11.6	12.4	12.5	11.9	11.3
Germany	9.6	9.4	10.3	11.5	11.4	11.2
Hong Kong	1.9	3.2	2.8	2.2	2.5	2.4
Italy	11.3	12.0	12.1	12.3	12.0	11.6
Japan	2.9	3.1	3.3	3.4	3.6	3.6
South Korea	2.4	2.0	2.0	2.7	6.3	3.4
Spain	24.2	22.9	22.2	20.8	19.7	18.5
Sweden	8.0	7.7	8.0	8.1	7.0	6.5
Taiwan	1.5	1.8	2.6	2.7	2.6	2.4
United Kingdom	9.3	8.2	7.5	5.6	4.9	4.8
United States	6.1	5.6	5.4	4.9	5.0	5.0

*IMF estimates.
SOURCE: International Monetary Fund, *World Economic Outlook,* various issues.

CYCLICAL UNEMPLOYMENT
The fraction of a nation's labor force composed of individuals who have lost employment owing to business-cycle fluctuations.

people between jobs or people lacking characteristics necessary to obtain employment. Remaining variations in the overall unemployment rate along an economy's growth path would arise from changes in the third category of unemployment. This is **cyclical unemployment,** or the portion of the labor force composed of individuals who have lost their jobs as a result of business-cycle fluctuations. One possible internal balance objective of national governments is to minimize cyclical unemployment.

Inflation Goals   To some extent all members of society bear inflation costs. Nonetheless, some bear the brunt of these costs to a greater degree than others. Those who are particularly harmed by inflation are business owners who experience forgone profit opportunities and who must incur costs of changing prices, savers, and financial institutions who are creditors, and people who pay the largest portion of taxes. Table 12–3 summarizes these costs.

The inflation costs summarized in Table 12–3 provide a strong rationale for policymakers to try to maintain low inflation and to limit inflation volatility. Most policymakers, therefore, include maintaining low and stable inflation, in addition to attaining high growth in per-capita real income and minimizing cyclical unemployment rates, as a part of their definition of internal balance.

External Balance Objectives

In addition to purely domestic, internal balance objectives, a nation's government and central bank may also be concerned about international payment

---

TABLE 12–3   THE COSTS OF INFLATION AND INFLATION VARIABILITY

TYPE OF COST	CAUSE
Resources expended to economize on money holdings (more trips to banks, etc.)	Rising prices associated with inflation
Costs of changing price lists and printing menus and catalogs	Individual product/service price increases associated with inflation
Redistribution of real incomes from individuals to the government	Inflation that pushes people into higher, nonindexed nominal tax brackets
Reductions in investment, capital accumulation, and economic growth	Inflation variability that complicates business planning
Slowed pace of introduction of new and better products	Volatile price changes that reduce the efficiency of private markets
Redistribution of resources from creditors to debtors	Unexpected inflation that reduces the real values of debts

---

flows. Thus, as discussed in Chapter 11, these policymakers may desire to achieve *external balance,* or the attainment of objectives for international flows of goods, services, income, and assets or for the relative values of their national currencies.

Why would a nation's residents desire for policymakers to pursue external balance objectives? One reason is that international factors help determine domestic outcomes in open economies. If residents of a nation engage in significant volumes of trade with other nations, international considerations may affect a nation's ability to achieve its output, employment, and inflation objectives. Consequently, internal and external balance objectives may go hand in hand. Another reason, however, is that a number of a nation's citizens may have immediate interests in the international sectors of their nation's economies. They may perceive that international variables themselves—such as the nation's merchandise trade balance or its current account balance—should be ultimate policy goals.

International Objectives and Domestic Goals   As we discussed in Chapter 11, two factors that play a role in determining a country's aggregate desired expenditures are export expenditures on the nation's output of goods and services by residents of other nations and import spending by its own residents on foreign-produced goods and services. An increase in export expenditures increases aggregate desired expenditures, whereas a rise in import spending reduces the fraction of disposable income available for consumption of domestically produced output. Therefore, both of these international factors affect the position of a country's *IS* schedule and thereby influence the equilibrium level of real income.

It follows that a government or central bank must take into consideration the volumes of export and import expenditures when contemplating appropriate policy strategies. At a minimum, a national policymaker must account for the real income effects of trade-related expenditures that are unrelated to purely domestic influences. More broadly, however, a policymaker may reach the conclusion that achieving its internal balance objectives may require careful attention to international factors. For example, a policymaker may seek to achieve balanced merchandise trade as part of a general strategy intended to achieve its domestic output, employment, and inflation objectives.

External Balance for Its Own Sake   Policymakers in most countries, however, typically regard external balance objectives as a set of goals that are separable from its internal balance objectives. Workers and business owners in industries that export large portions of their output often push their governments to enact policies that promote exports. At the same time, workers and business owners in industries that rely on domestic sales of their output may pressure government and central bank officials to pursue policies that restrain imports. Persistent efforts by both of these interest groups could induce a nation's policymakers to seek merchandise trade and balance of payments *surpluses* as external balance objectives.

History is replete with examples of nations that have sought to achieve persistent surpluses in their balance-of-payments accounts. For example, in the seventeenth and eighteenth centuries, successive generations of British citizens advocated a national policy of **mercantilism.** The view of this school of thought is that inflows of payments relating to international commerce and trade are a primary source of a nation's wealth. During this period, therefore, British mercantilists advocated governmental and central bank policy actions designed to promote exports and to hinder imports. A fundamental difficulty with mercantilist thought, of course, is that if all countries simultaneously try to attain trade and payments surpluses through import limitations, international commerce likely would be stymied. Realization of this self-defeating aspect of mercantilism led to its decline in the nineteenth century. Mercantilist thought supports the interests of special interest groups in any open economy, however, so these groups still use mercantilist arguments today in an effort to pressure policymakers to maintain trade and current account balances, if not surpluses.

The interests of exporters and importers also may make exchange-rate objectives part of the mix of external balance goals. If export industries are a predominant political interest group, a country's policymakers also face pressures to reduce the exchange value of its currency. By way of contrast, in a nation in which domestic industries have considerable political clout, policymakers may be lobbied to push up the value of the nation's currency.

MERCANTILISM A view that a primary determinant of a nation's wealth is its inflows of payments resulting from international trade and commerce, so that a nation can gain by enacting policies that spur exports while limiting imports.

FUNDAMENTAL ISSUE #1

What are the economic goals of national policymakers? There are two categories of economic goals that governments and central banks often pursue. One consists of internal balance objectives, which are goals for national real income, employment, and inflation. The other consists of external balance objectives, which are goals for the trade balance and other components of the balance of payments.

THE ROLE OF CAPITAL MOBILITY

CAPITAL MOBILITY The extent to which financial resources can flow across a nation's borders.

The manner in which monetary and fiscal policy actions may influence a nation's economic performance relative to either internal or external balance objectives depends considerably on the extent of **capital mobility.** This term refers to the degree to which funds and financial assets are free to flow across a nation's borders. A nation with *high capital mobility* is one that is open to and experiences considerable cross-border flows of funds and financial assets.

After accounting for differing risks across alternative assets and nations that issue the assets, owners of financial assets around the world seek the highest available returns. Many are willing and able to shift their funds from one nation to another. Typically, therefore, flows of funds across national boundaries are significant if the returns to reallocations are high enough and if barriers to such flows are insignificant. A number of nations, however, have imposed legal impediments, called **capital controls,** that restrict the ability of their residents to hold and exchange assets denominated in the currencies of other nations. Capital controls thereby inhibit flows of funds and assets across the borders of a country and can lead to *low capital mobility* for nations that adopt such controls. Furthermore, many less developed nations do not possess well-developed banking systems or financial markets, which often has kept their capital mobility low.

CAPITAL CONTROLS Legal restrictions on the ability of a nation's residents to hold and exchange assets denominated in foreign currencies.

Capital Mobility and the *BP* Schedule

As you learned in Chapter 11, we can infer whether a nation would experience a balance-of-payments surplus or deficit at a given *IS–LM* equilibrium nominal interest rate–real income combination by referring to the *location* of the *BP* schedule. The extent of capital mobility, it turns out, affects the *slope* of the *BP* schedule. As you will see later in this chapter, the degree of capital mobility and the resulting slope of the *BP* schedule determine how monetary and fiscal policy actions ultimately influence a nation's economic performance.

The Case of Low Capital Mobility   As you learned in Chapter 11, a balance of payment equilibrium, in which the current account balance and capital account balance sum to zero, occurs if an *IS–LM* equilibrium arises at a point along the *BP* schedule. Thus, an *IS–LM* equilibrium point below and to the right of the *BP* schedule implies that a nation is experiencing a balance of payments deficit. Below the *BP* schedule, the nominal interest rate is so low at a given level of real income that either capital flows out of the nation, thereby causing a capital account deficit, or capital inflows are too meager to offset the nation's current account deficit. To the right of the *BP* schedule, real income is so high at a given nominal interest rate that the induced level of import spending results in a current account deficit. Either a capital account deficit or a current account deficit contributes to a balance-of-payments deficit, but which is the *predominant* reason for a balance of payments deficit? The answer depends on the degree of capital mobility and the slope of the *BP* schedule.

Let's begin by thinking about required adjustments of real income and nominal interest rates necessary to maintain balance-of-payments equilibrium when there is low capital mobility. This situation arises because of capital controls or other impediments to flows of funds and assets. When there is low capital mobility, the *BP* schedule is relatively *steep*. To see why this is so, consider panel (*a*) of Figure 12–1. Suppose that the real income–nominal interest rate combination y_1 and R_1 at point *A* is consistent with balance-of-payments equilibrium. If real income rises to y_2, then imports increase, generating a current account deficit at point *C*. Thus, low capital mobility requires a very sizable increase in the nominal interest rate to induce residents of other nations to circumvent capital controls and increase their holdings of domestic financial assets in amounts sufficient to improve the capital account balance to reattain balance-of-payments equilibrium.

It follows that a rise in real income from y_1 to y_2 in panel (*a*) requires a relatively large increase in the nominal interest rate, say to R_2 at point *B*, to ensure that the sum of the current account balance and capital account balance would equal zero. Points *A* and *B* thereby lie on a relatively steep *BP* schedule. Stated differently, a relatively steep *BP* schedule indicates that a nation's degree of capital mobility is relatively low.

The Case of High Capital Mobility   In contrast, if capital mobility is relatively high, then the *BP* schedule is relatively shallow, as shown in panel (*b*) of Figure 12–1. As before, if real income rises from y_1 at point *A*, at which there is balance of payments equilibrium, to y_2 at a point *B*, then the result is an increase in imports. This causes a current account deficit at the point *C*.

If capital mobility is high, then a relatively small rise in the nominal interest rate, perhaps from R_1 to R_2 in panel (*b*), is sufficient to induce other nations' residents to raise their holdings of domestic financial assets in sufficient quantities to improve the capital account balance and reattain balance-

FIGURE 12–1 CAPITAL MOBILITY AND THE SLOPE OF THE *BP* SCHEDULE

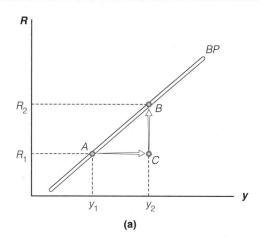

(a)

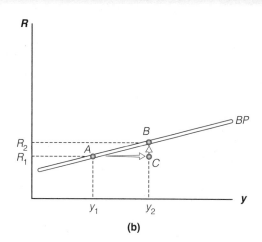

(b)

Panel (*a*) illustrates that the *BP* schedule is relatively steep when there is low capital mobility. If there is a balance-of-payments equilibrium at point *A*, then if real income rises to y_2, imports increase, causing a current account deficit at point *C*. With low capital mobility, a relatively large increase in the nominal interest rate is needed to induce foreign residents to

overcome barriers to capital inflows sufficient to achieve a new balance-of-payments equilibrium at point *B*. In contrast, as shown in panel (*b*), a comparatively smaller increase in the nominal interest rate is required to induce sufficient capital inflows when there are fewer barriers to capital mobility, so that the *BP* schedule is relatively shallow with higher capital mobility.

of-payments equilibrium. Hence, the *BP* schedule containing points *A* and *B* in panel (*b*) has a relatively shallow slope. In other words, a relatively shallow *BP* schedule indicates that the degree of capital mobility is relatively high.

Perfect Capital Mobility

In Chapter 4, you learned about the *uncovered interest parity condition*. This condition states that if bonds denominated in two different currencies otherwise are perfect substitutes, then the difference between the interest rates on the bonds should equal the expected rate of depreciation. You also learned that uncovered interest parity does not always hold, because there may be distinctive risk characteristics of these otherwise similar bonds, thereby requiring the riskier bond to offer a risk premium.

Perfect Capital Mobility and the *BP* Schedule   Another key reason that the uncovered interest parity condition may not hold, however, is that barriers to capital mobility can inhibit substitution between otherwise identical bonds. Imperfect capital mobility, therefore, is a common explanation for the failure of the uncovered interest parity condition to be met in a number of nations.

FIGURE 12–2 **THE *BP* SCHEDULE WITH PERFECT CAPITAL MOBILITY**

We suppose that the bonds issued in foreign nations, which offer the interest return R^*, have the same risks as domestic bonds. In addition, we assume that domestic and foreign residents do not anticipate any depreciation of the domestic currency relative to the currency issued by the central bank of the other nation. With perfect capital mobility, it follows from the uncovered interest parity condition that the domestic interest rate, R, is equal to the foreign interest rate, R^*. This implies that the domestic *BP* schedule is horizontal under perfect capital mobility. Both point A and point B are consistent with balance-of-payments equilibrium, but if the interest rate declines to R' at point C, the domestic interest rate is less than the foreign interest rate, so that capital flows out of the domestic country. There is a domestic balance-of-payments deficit at point C.

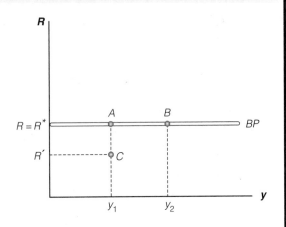

But this means that for a nation with *perfect* capital mobility, we would expect that the uncovered interest parity condition should be satisfied. Let's suppose that a small nation's bonds have the same degree of risk as those issued in a large nation, which offers the interest return R^*. In addition, let's also assume that people do not anticipate any depreciation of the domestic currency relative to the currency issued by the central bank of the other nation. With perfect capital mobility, therefore, the uncovered interest parity condition would imply that the domestic interest rate, R, should be *equal* to the foreign interest rate, R^*. Thus, as shown in Figure 12–2, under these assumptions the domestic interest rate would not vary from the foreign interest rate R^* as domestic real income varies. As a result, the domestic *BP* schedule is *horizontal* under perfect capital mobility.

The Domestic Interest Rate and Balance of Payments with Perfect Capital Mobility Any point along the *BP* schedule in Figure 12–2 is a point at which the current account balance and the capital account balance sum to zero. Thus, the real income–nominal interest rate combination y_1 and R at point A in Figure 12–2 is a point of balance-of-payments equilibrium, because it lies on the *BP* schedule. So is point B. Even though the real income level y_2 is higher at point B, the smallest conceivable rise in the domestic interest rate would be sufficient to generate capital inflows sizable enough to offset the resulting rise in imports. Capital is fully mobile, so the *BP* schedule is horizontal.

It follows that with perfect capital mobility, variations in the nominal interest rate are the only factor that can induce balance-of-payments deficits or surpluses. For instance, at point C directly below point A in Figure 12–2, the lower domestic interest rate R' would induce a significant capital outflow. Savers would reallocate their bond holdings from domestic bonds to equally risky, fully substitutable foreign bonds in pursuits of higher returns available on the foreign bonds.

FUNDAMENTAL ISSUE #2

How does the degree of capital mobility influence the slope of the *BP* schedule? With low capital mobility, a significant rise in a nation's interest rate is required to generate the capital inflows needed to offset the greater imports that result from a rise in the nation's real income level. Because the *BP* schedule is the set of real income–nominal interest rate combinations that maintain balance-of-payments equilibrium, this means that the *BP* schedule is steeply sloped with a low degree of capital mobility. As capital mobility increases, the *BP* schedule becomes more shallow. In the extreme case of perfect capital mobility, the *BP* schedule is horizontal at the level of the foreign interest rate.

FIXED EXCHANGE RATES AND IMPERFECT CAPITAL MOBILITY

As we discussed in Chapter 4, many nations still choose to fix their exchange rates. These nations may consider their residents' costs in hedging against foreign exchange risks to be greater than the benefits of a flexible-exchange-rate system's shock-absorbing features. How does the adoption of a fixed exchange rate influence the transmission of economic policies enacted by governments and central banks?

At this point, we are not in a position to develop complete answers to this question, because the *IS–LM–BP* framework developed in Chapter 11 does not tell us anything about unemployment or inflation. It also is silent concerning the relationship between actual GDP and the natural GDP level. We shall not try to explain how the effects of economic policies relate to these broader internal balance objectives until Chapter 14. Nevertheless, we can still use the *IS–LM–BP* framework to develop some essential answers to this question. To accomplish this, we shall interpret achieving a higher level of real income as a nation's only internal balance objective and maintaining balance-of-payments equilibrium as the overriding external balance objective. Thus, we rule out mercantilist-driven desires for simultaneous current and capital account surpluses. It would be straightforward to account for such goals, but we leave it to you in problem 1 at the end of the chapter. Under this interpretation of the basic *IS–LM–BP* model, we shall demonstrate that our answers depend on the degree of capital mobility.

Monetary Policy under Fixed Exchange Rates and Low Capital Mobility

As we noted in Chapter 8, a key problem of maintaining a fixed exchange rate through foreign-exchange interventions is making a commitment to a particular exchange rate credible. For now, however, let's suppose that a country has established a credible fixed-exchange-rate commitment. We shall revisit the credibility issue in Chapters 14 and 15.

We shall begin by thinking about the effects of monetary policy under fixed exchange rates. First, however, we need to consider how monetary policy actions influence nominal interest rates and real income.

Monetary Policy, the Nominal Interest Rate, and Real Income A country's equilibrium nominal interest rate and the equilibrium level of real income arise in an *IS–LM* equilibrium, such as point *A* in panel (*b*) of Figure 12–3. As shown in panel (*a*), the amount of money demanded at the real income level y_1 crosses the supply of real money balances at the equilibrium nominal interest rate R_1, so that equilibrium is maintained at point *A* in the money market.

Now suppose that the central bank undertakes an expansionary monetary policy by increasing the nominal quantity of money, from M_1 to M_2. At a given price level, P_1, this causes a rise in the supply of real money balances, resulting in a decline in the equilibrium nominal interest rate, to R_3 at point *C* in panel (*a*). This decline in the nominal interest rate at the income level y_1 is the amount by which the *LM* schedule shifts downward in panel (*b*), from point *A* to point *C*. The fall in the nominal interest rate generates a rise in desired real investment spending, which in turn causes equilibrium real income to rise toward y_2 at point *B* in panel (*b*). Thus, there is a movement down along the *IS* schedule from point *A* to point *B*. The result of this increase in real income is an increase in the demand for real money balances in panel (*a*), from $m^d(y_1)$ to $m^d(y_2)$. This causes the equilibrium nominal interest rate to rise back up toward R_2 at point *B* in panel (*a*). In panel (*b*) this can be visualized as movement back up along the *LM* schedule from point *C* to point *B*. Point *B*, therefore, is the final equilibrium point, with a net decline in the equilibrium nominal interest rate, from R_1 to R_2, and an increase in equilibrium real income, from y_1 to y_2.

We may conclude that, provided that the price level is unchanged, an expansionary monetary policy action causes a **liquidity effect**—the term for a fall in the equilibrium nominal interest rate induced by an increase in the nominal money stock—that stimulates desired investment and expands equilibrium real income. Hence, the channel through which monetary policy actions are transmitted to the economy is through a liquidity effect that alters desired investment and thereby changes the real income level.

LIQUIDITY EFFECT A reduction in the equilibrium nominal interest rate stemming from an increase in the nominal quantity of money in circulation.

FIGURE 12–3   THE EFFECTS OF EXPANSIONARY MONETARY POLICY

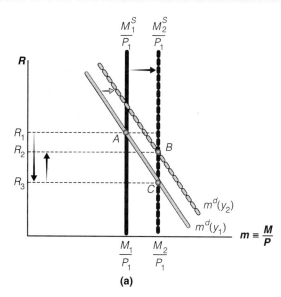

(a)

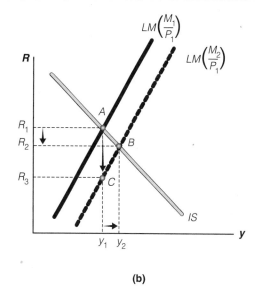

(b)

A central bank policy action that increases the nominal quantity of money in circulation causes, if the price level is unchanged, an increase in the supply of real money balances. This generates a decline in the money-market-equilibrium interest rate from R_1 at point A to R_3 at point C in panel (*a*), which results in a downward shift in the LM schedule by the distance A–C in panel (*b*). The decline in the interest rate, however, induces a rise in desired investment and a consequent movement down along the IS schedule to a new IS–LM

equilibrium point B at the higher real income level y_2. As real income increases, the demand for real money balances rises in panel (*a*), causing the equilibrium interest rate to rise to R_2, which corresponds to an upward movement along the new LM schedule in panel (*b*), from point C to point B. On net, therefore, the rise in the nominal money stock causes a reduction in the equilibrium nominal interest rate and an increase in equilibrium real income.

Monetary Policy and the Balance of Payments with Imperfect Capital Mobility   Now let's contemplate the balance-of-payments implications of an expansionary monetary policy action when a nation has low capital mobility. As shown in panel (*a*) of Figure 12–4, we shall assume that initially the country attains balance-of-payments equilibrium at point A on the relatively steep BP schedule. An increase in the nominal quantity of money, from M_1 to a larger amount M_2, causes the LM schedule to shift downward and to the right, resulting in a new IS–LM equilibrium point below and to the right of the BP schedule. Hence, a monetary expansion generates a balance-of-payments deficit at point B in Figure 12–4.

FIGURE 12–4 **THE INITIAL EFFECTS OF MONETARY POLICY WITH A FIXED EXCHANGE RATE**

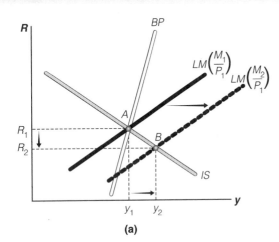

(a)

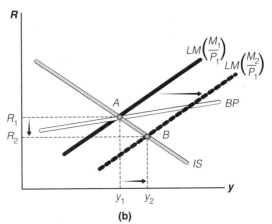

(b)

Both panels show how a monetary expansion initially affects the nominal interest rate and real income under a fixed exchange rate. In panel (*a*) the *BP* schedule is relatively steep, indicating a situation of low capital mobility. The decline in the equilibrium interest rate that occurs following a movement from point *A* to point *B* induces little capital outflow, but the rise in equilibrium real income stimulates greater import

spending. The result is a balance-of-payments deficit at point *B*. In contrast, in panel (*b*) the *BP* schedule is much more shallow, implying a situation of high capital mobility. In this case, the decline in the equilibrium interest rate spurs a significant capital outflow that makes a key contribution to the resulting balance-of-payments deficit at point *B*.

It is important to recognize that because capital mobility is low, the key reason that a balance-of-payments deficit occurs at point *B* is a rise in real income. This rise in real income stimulates an increase in imports and thereby causes a trade deficit to occur. The equilibrium interest rate declines, but because capital mobility is low, relatively little capital flows out of the country. Thus, the primary explanation for the existence of a balance-of-payments deficit at point *B* in panel (*a*) is the trade deficit stemming from increased import expenditures at the higher income level y_2.

Panel (*b*) of Figure 12–4 illustrates a situation in which capital mobility is relatively high, though still imperfect, so that the *BP* schedule is relatively shallow. In contrast to the example in panel (*a*), a decline in the nation's equilibrium interest rate to R_2 causes a significant outflow of capital, so at point *B* the nation experiences a sizable capital account deficit, which is a key contributor to the balance of payments deficit it experiences at this new equilibrium point.

Sterilized versus Nonsterilized Monetary Policies At point *B* in either panel of Figure 12–4, the fact that a nation experiences a balance-of-payments deficit means that there would be market pressures for the nation's exchange rate to change. With low capital mobility, as in panel (*a*), the increase in equilibrium real income at point *B* induces the nation's residents to seek to acquire other nations' currencies so that they may purchase more imports. This raises the demand for foreign exchange and places downward pressure on the nation's currency value. By way of contrast, at point *B* in panel (*b*), in which there is high capital mobility, the fall in the equilibrium interest rate induces residents to acquire more foreign assets. This also entails acquiring greater volumes of foreign currencies, which tends to depress the value of their nation's currency in the foreign exchange markets.

To keep the exchange value of its nation's currency from declining at point *B* in either panel of Figure 12–4, a central bank would have to sell some of its foreign exchange reserves. This would offset the rise in the demand for foreign currencies by its own citizens by raising the supply of foreign currencies in the foreign exchange markets. But if the central bank were to sell some of its foreign currency reserves, its assets would decline. This would require a decline in its liabilities, including some of its money liabilities in circulation. Hence, the domestic money stock would begin to fall. To keep this from happening, the central bank would have to add sufficient *domestic* assets, such as domestic government bonds, to its own portfolio. This action would prevent its total assets from falling. This, as we discussed in Chapters 8 and 10, would be a *sterilized* intervention, because this action would prevent changes in foreign exchange reserves from affecting the nation's money stock.

Both panels of Figure 12–4 illustrate outcomes if a central bank sterilizes its interventions to maintain a fixed exchange rate. But what would happen if the central bank chose not to sterilize, perhaps because its external balance objective is to maintain balance-of-payments equilibrium? Figure 12–5 provides the answer to this question. As in Figure 12–4, panels (*a*) and (*b*) of Figure 12–5 depict the initial effects of a monetary expansion with low capital mobility and high capital mobility, respectively. In each panel, at a new equilibrium point *B* the nation experiences a balance-of-payments deficit. Because this tends to depress the value of the nation's currency in foreign exchange markets, the nation's central bank must sell some of its foreign exchange reserves to keep the exchange rate fixed.

In the absence of sterilization, the central bank's assets would decline, which would require a reduction in the amount of circulating money liabilities that it issues. Consequently, the nation's nominal money stock would begin to decline. As both panels of Figure 12–5 indicate, failure to sterilize ultimately would cause the nation's quantity of money to decline from M_2, the level to which the central bank originally had raised the nation's money stock, back to M_1, the initial quantity of money before the monetary expansion. Thus, the central bank's sales of foreign exchange reserves to maintain a fixed exchange rate eventually cause the *LM* schedule to shift back to its original location, and the initial *IS–LM* equilibrium point *A* ultimately is reattained. A *nonsterilized* monetary expansion with a fixed exchange rate thereby leads to an eventual contraction of the money stock. As long as no

FIGURE 12–5 THE EFFECTS OF A MONETARY POLICY EXPANSION WITH NONSTERILIZED INTERVENTIONS

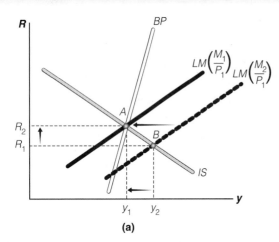

(a)

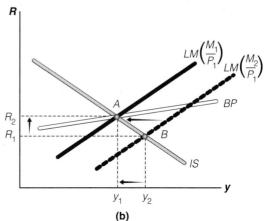

(b)

Panels (*a*) and (*b*) illustrate the final effects of an increase in the nominal quantity of money that, as shown in Figure 12–4, first cause a rightward shift in the *LM* schedule and a movement from point *A* to point *B*. In panel (*a*) there is relatively low capital mobility, so a balance-of-payments deficit stems mainly from higher import expenditures, while in panel (*b*) there is significant capital mobility, so the balance of payments deficit at point *B* results mainly from capital

inflows. In either case, the balance-of-payments deficit implies an increased demand for foreign currencies by the nation's residents, which tends to depress the value of the nation's currency in foreign exchange markets. To keep the exchange rate from changing, the nation's central bank must sell foreign exchange reserves. If the central bank does not sterilize this action, this causes a reduction in the quantity of money in circulation and an ultimate movement back to point *A*.

other factors change, the economy then would reattain its initial equilibrium real income level and interest rate, leading to reattainment of balance of payments equilibrium at point *A*.

Figure 12–5 illustrates the broader implications of the monetary approach to the balance of payments that we outlined in Chapter 10. According to the monetary approach, committing to a fixed exchange rate causes a nation's money stock to vary with changes in foreign exchange reserves that are necessary to keep the exchange rate fixed. If monetary policy actions are nonsterilized, then the result is an automatic adjustment toward balance-of-payments equilibrium and toward the pre-expansion equilibrium real income level and nominal interest rate. Hence, we may conclude that:

> **According to the monetary approach to the balance of payments, efforts to affect real income and the balance of payments via nonsterilized monetary expansions or contractions ultimately are ineffective policy actions if exchange rates are fixed.**

Could sterilization prevent this eventual adjustment to balance-of-payments equilibrium? If a central bank attempts to sterilize indefinitely, so as to maintain real income at y_2 at point B, then a persistent balance-of-payments deficit places continual downward pressures on the value of the nation's currency. No central bank has sufficient foreign exchange reserves to keep the exchange rate fixed and to conduct sterilized monetary expansions for long. Ultimately, nations that try to push up their real income levels by way of monetary expansions either must eventually permit their money stocks to contract or must devalue their currencies.

FUNDAMENTAL ISSUE #3

To what extent can monetary policy actions influence the real income level of a small open economy with imperfect capital mobility and a fixed exchange rate? The initial effects of monetary policy actions with a fixed exchange rate depend considerably on the extent to which the central bank of a small open economy sterilizes by preventing variations in its foreign exchange reserves from affecting the nation's nominal money stock. Under the monetary approach to the balance of payments, the immediate effects of unsterilized monetary policy actions on real income ultimately are reversed by offsetting changes in the quantity of money in circulation.

Fiscal Policy under Fixed Exchange Rates

As with monetary policy, the degree of capital mobility has a major bearing on the real income effects of *fiscal policy actions,* which are variations in the government's spending or taxation policies. In addition, the effects of fiscal policy actions depend in part on whether the central bank sterilizes interventions to maintain a fixed exchange rate. Before we discuss these issues, however, let's determine exactly how fiscal policy actions affect the equilibrium nominal interest rate and the equilibrium level of real income.

Fiscal Policy, the Nominal Interest Rate, and Real Income   Figure 12–6 displays the effects, within the *IS–LM* framework, of a rise in real government spending, from an amount equal to g_1 to a larger amount equal to g_2. As we discussed in Chapter 11, the increase in government spending causes the *IS* schedule to shift to the right by the amount of the rise in spending times the autonomous expenditures multiplier, $1/(1-MPC)$. Hence, at the initial equilibrium interest rate, R_1, real income rises from y_1 to y_3, which is equal to the distance between the initial equilibrium point A and point C. This increase in

FIGURE 12–6   THE EFFECTS OF EXPANSIONARY FISCAL POLICY

An increase in government spending shifts the *IS* schedule rightward by the amount of the rise in spending times the autonomous expenditures multiplier, shown by the movement from point *A* to point *C*. This causes equilibrium real income to rise, thereby inducing an increase in the demand for real money balances. As a result, the equilibrium nominal interest rate rises, as shown by the movement upward along the *LM* schedule from point *A* to point *B*. Holding inflation expectations unchanged, the real interest rate increases, thereby causing a decline in desired investment expenditures and a movement back along the *IS* schedule from point *C* to point *B*. Thus, a rise in government spending crowds out some amount of private investment expenditures. Nevertheless, on net the increase in government spending generates a rise in the equilibrium nominal interest rate and an increase in equilibrium real income.

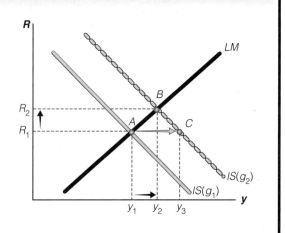

real income, however, raises the demand for real money balances, thereby causing an increase in the equilibrium nominal interest rate, from R_1 to R_2. Thus, there is upward movement along the *LM* schedule from point *A* to point *B*. This increase in the equilibrium nominal interest rate reduces investment expenditures, thereby causing real income to decline somewhat, to y_2, as shown by a movement back along the new *IS* schedule from point *C* to point *B*. The amount of the fall in real income from y_3 back toward y_2 is equal to the decline in investment spending times the autonomous expenditures multiplier, $1/(1-MPC)$.

The *net* effect of the increase in real government expenditures is an increase in the equilibrium real income level. Nevertheless, equilibrium real income no longer rises by the full amount predicted by the basic multiplier analysis discussed in Chapter 11. In fact, a fiscal-policy-induced increase in equilibrium real income typically is smaller, because of the decline in investment stemming from a rise in the interest rate. This fall in investment following a rise in government spending is called the **crowding out effect.** By inducing a rise in the nominal interest rate that reduces private investment expenditures, an increase in government spending "crowds out" some amount of private investment, thereby offsetting to some extent the rise in equilibrium real income that otherwise would occur. Note that a tax reduction has the same sort of crowding out effect.

In contrast, a reduction in government spending or a tax increase, holding other factors constant, generates a decline in the equilibrium interest rate,

CROWDING OUT EFFECT
A decline in real private investment spending induced by a rise in the demand for money and the equilibrium nominal interest rate caused by a rise in equilibrium real income that follows an expansionary fiscal policy action.

POLICY NOTEBOOK
Inducing Russians to Pay Their Taxes

It is said that nothing is certain in life but death and taxes. In Russia in recent years, death has been the only real certainty. Under the yoke of Communist oligarchy before the late 1980s, Russians became adept practitioners of "underground" transactions, so as to avoid governmental entanglements that might otherwise arise. Indeed, since the breakup of the Soviet Union governmental umbrella, the most pressing problem that the Russian government has faced has been just finding the firms and households who ought to be paying taxes. Most Russians have viewed the Russian tax structure, which has specified more than 200 forms of taxation, as a bureaucratic quagmire inherited from the former Communist system. Thus, many Russians simply have not been paying any taxes at all.

This has posed significant problems for the Russian national government. To finance its efforts to modernize its nation's economy, the Russian government has relied upon sizable loans from the International Monetary Fund (IMF). Between 1991 and 1994, however, tax avoidance became so commonplace that the Russian government's tax revenues declined from nearly 40 percent of GDP to closer to 25 percent of GDP. Worried that the Russian government ultimately would fail to raise sufficient future tax revenues to repay its big loans, the IMF handed the government an ultimatum: Either improve and enforce its tax laws or give up its access to IMF credit.

Tax enforcement in Russia can be a risky business. In one year alone, 26 Russian tax collectors were killed and 74 were injured in the course of their work. Six were kidnapped and 41 had their homes burned. In 1997, the Russian president placed a general–who previously had conducted a war against separatists in Chechnya and who commanded the police and 200,000 militia–in charge of a nationwide effort to strike back against tax-dodgers. The general announced that he would "strike economic crime not with an open palm, but with a strong fist."

So far, the Russian government's efforts to enhance its collection of taxes have not paid large dividends in form of higher tax revenues. The inefficiencies that plague the expenditure side of the government's budget–not to mention evidence of widespread corruption and misappropriations of public spending–have not provided the public with much reason to believe the government's promises to reform its tax system. Thus, millions of Russians continue to avoid registering with government tax officials, who, in turn, fail in their duty to track down those who owe taxes to the government.

FOR CRITICAL ANALYSIS:
In your view, which of the following approaches would be most useful in inducing more Russians to pay their taxes: Better enforcement of existing tax laws, or revamped tax laws and greater efficiency in public spending?

ON THE WEB
Learn how to conduct business in Russia at:
http://www.fe.doe.gov/ international/russia.html

thereby stimulating private investment. Of course, national governments may reduce their spending or raise their taxes for reasons other than those associated with their purely macroeconomic effects (see "Policy Notebook: Inducing Russians to Pay Their Taxes"). Nonetheless, the *IS–LM* model indicates that fiscal policy changes may have broad effects on national economic performances, irrespective of governmental objectives in adopting such changes.

FIGURE 12-7 **THE INITIAL EFFECTS OF EXPANSIONARY FISCAL POLICY WITH A FIXED EXCHANGE RATE**

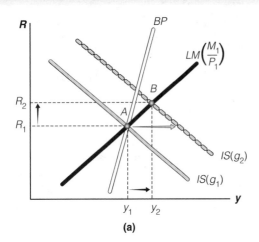

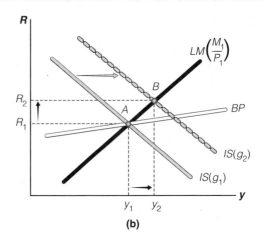

(a) (b)

Both panels show how an increase in real government expenditures initially induces an increase in the equilibrium nominal interest rate and a rise in equilibrium real income. In panel (*a*) the *BP* schedule is relatively steep, which implies a situation of low capital mobility. The increase in the equilibrium interest rate that occurs following a movement from point *A* to point *B* induces little capital inflow, but the rise in equilibrium real income stimulates greater import spending. The net result is a balance of payments deficit at point *B*. In contrast, in panel (*b*) the *BP* schedule is much more shallow, which indicates a situation of high capital mobility. In this case, the rise in the equilibrium interest rate generates a significant capital inflow that more than offsets the higher imports owing to the increase in equilibrium real income. This results in a balance of payments surplus at point *B* in panel (*b*).

Fiscal Policy and the Balance of Payments with Imperfect Capital Mobility

Both panels in Figure 12–7 depict the balance of payments effects stemming from an increase in government spending. In panel (*a*), capital mobility is relatively low, so the *BP* schedule is relatively steep. In contrast, in panel (*b*) there is relatively high capital mobility, and so the *BP* schedule is relatively shallow. The initial equilibrium point in each panel is denoted as point *A,* at which there is an *IS–LM* equilibrium along the *BP* schedule, and so we assume that there is balance-of-payments equilibrium before any fiscal policy action takes place.

In each panel of Figure 12–7, an increase in government spending causes the *IS* schedule to shift to the right, from $IS(g_1)$ to $IS(g_2)$. This yields a new equilibrium point *B* with a higher nominal interest rate R_2 and a higher real income level y_2. In panel (*a*), the rise in equilibrium real income induces a rise in imports that causes the nation to experience a trade deficit. The rise in the equilibrium interest rate generates an inflow of some financial resources from other nations, but with low capital mobility this inflow is not very significant.

Thus, on net there is a balance-of-payments deficit, as point B lies below and to the right of the BP schedule in panel (a).

Panel (b) in Figure 12–7 illustrates a situation in which capital mobility is much greater. In this case, the rise in the equilibrium interest rate owing to the increase in government spending causes a significant inflow of financial resources from abroad. As a result, there is a sizable capital account surplus that more than offsets the trade deficit stemming from the rise in equilibrium income and the consequent increase in imports. Hence, panel (b) shows that with very high capital mobility, an increase in government spending results in a balance-of-payments surplus, with point B above and to the left of the BP schedule.

The Effects of Fiscal Policy Actions with and without Monetary Sterilization

At point B in panel (a) of Figure 12–7, the existence of a balance of payments deficit places downward pressure on the nation's currency value. To keep the exchange rate fixed, the central bank must intervene by selling foreign exchange reserves. If the central bank sterilizes by trading domestic securities to maintain an unchanged quantity of money in circulation, then the nation remains at point B in panel (a) only for as long as the central bank's foreign exchange reserves last. Persistent operations with a balance of payments deficit, however, would likely deplete the central bank's foreign exchange reserves. Eventually the central bank would have to devalue or abandon a fixed exchange rate.

In contrast, in panel (b) of Figure 12–7 there is a balance of payments surplus at point B, so there is *upward* pressure on the nation's currency value in the foreign exchange market. Maintaining a fixed exchange rate thereby requires the central bank to *purchase* additional foreign exchange reserves. To sterilize the effect that an accumulation of more foreign exchange reserves has on the money stock, the central bank has to sell domestic bonds. This allows the economy to remain at point B in panel (b) of Figure 12–7 for as long as the central bank's holdings of domestic bonds remain undepleted.

Figure 12–8 illustrates the outcomes that result if the central bank is unwilling to sterilize in the face of an increase in government spending. Again, both panels of Figure 12–8 display movements from an initial point A with balance-of-payments equilibrium to point B at which there is an international payments imbalance. In the case of low capital mobility depicted in panel (a), nonsterilization results in a decrease in the nation's money stock. This is because the central bank sells foreign exchange reserves to maintain the nation's fixed exchange rate in the face of a balance of payments deficit at point B. The LM schedule shifts upward and to the left as the quantity of money in circulation declined from M_1 to M_2. This ultimately leads to a new IS–LM equilibrium at point C, with a higher equilibrium interest rate R_3 and a somewhat lower equilibrium real income level, y_3. The fall in real income generates a decline in import spending, thereby reducing the trade deficit and yielding balance-of-payments equilibrium at point C. This ends pressure on the central bank to sell foreign exchange reserves to defend the fixed exchange rate.

FIGURE 12-8 **THE FINAL EFFECTS OF AN INCREASE IN GOVERNMENT SPENDING WITHOUT STERILIZATION**

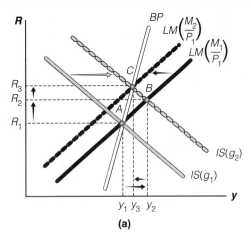

(a)

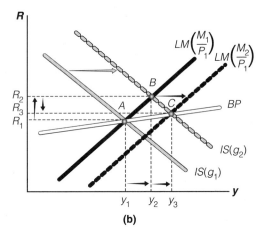

(b)

The panels of this figure illustrate the final effects of an increase in real government expenditures that, as shown in Figure 12–7, first cause a rightward shift in the *IS* schedule and a movement from point *A* to point *B*. In panel (*a*) there is relatively low capital mobility, so a balance of payments deficit results from higher import spending that more than offsets meager capital inflows. Hence, the nation's residents raise their demand for foreign currencies, which reduces the value of the nation's currency. To keep the exchange rate fixed, the nation's central bank sells foreign exchange reserves. Without sterilization, these generate a reduction in the quantity of money in circulation, and a movement to

point *C* tends to offset the effect of the rise in government spending on real income. In contrast, in panel (*b*) there is significant capital mobility. It is so significant that capital outflows more than offset increased imports, resulting in a balance of payments surplus at point *B*. The nation's residents reduce their desired holdings of foreign currencies, which raises the value of the nation's currency in foreign exchange markets. To keep the exchange rate from changing, the nation's central bank purchases foreign exchange reserves. This raises the money stock and induces a movement to point *C* that *reinforces* the real-income effect of the increase in government spending.

In panel (*b*) of Figure 12–8, in which capital mobility is relatively high, there is a balance-of-payments surplus at point *B* following a rise in government spending, because the nation experiences significant capital inflows following the rise in the nominal interest rate from R_1 to R_2. Consequently, the central bank starts to accumulate foreign exchange reserves in its efforts to maintain a fixed exchange rate. If the central bank does not sterilize, then the nation's money stock grows as the central bank's foreign exchange reserves increase, causing the *LM* schedule to shift down and to the right. As a result, the equilibrium interest rate declines to R_3, reducing the capital inflow and eventually yielding balance-of-payments equilibrium at point *C* along the *BP* schedule.

Figures 12–7 and 12–8 illustrate a key implication of the monetary approach to the balance of payments: Under a fixed exchange rate, fiscal policy actions force a central bank to respond to international payments imbalances by reducing or accumulating foreign exchange reserves. As the examples in Figures 12–7 and 12–8 demonstrate, the real income effects of fiscal policy actions hinge on central bank decisions about whether to sterilize and on the degree of capital mobility.

In our examples we have focused on variations in government expenditures, although in most respects the basic analysis also applies to the effects of tax changes. Nevertheless, two factors complicate the ultimate effects that tax variations have on a nation's equilibrium interest rate and real income level. One is the potential for *Ricardian equivalence* to reduce the effect of a tax change on aggregate desired expenditures. Named for David Ricardo, an eighteenth-century British economist, Ricardian equivalence refers to the possibility that a nation's residents may view a tax cut that is deficit-financed tax cut as an indication that a future tax increase will be required to repay government borrowings. This induces them to save the proceeds of the current tax cut to permit such future repayments. To the extent that Ricardian equivalence may hold for a given nation, the economic effects of tax changes are dampened.

The second complication is that governments typically collect the bulk of their revenues via taxation of income. Evaluating the full effects of tax changes requires assessing the interaction among tax-rate changes across ranges of household and firm income levels. Tax changes may also affect household work effort, firm production, and, ultimately, aggregate expenditures (see "Policy Notebook: Tax Assessments Around the Globe").

ON THE WEB
Visit the Hong Kong Monetary Authority at:
http://www.info.gov.hk/ hkma/

FUNDAMENTAL ISSUE #4

To what extent can fiscal policy actions influence the real income level of a small open economy with imperfect capital mobility and a fixed exchange rate? The immediate effect of an expansionary fiscal policy action is an unambiguous rise in the nation's real income level. Ultimately, however, the effects of fiscal policy actions on real income in a small open economy with a fixed exchange rate depend to some extent on a central bank's decision about sterilization. Sterilization can mute this effect somewhat, but nonsterilized interventions in support of a fixed exchange rate reinforce the rise in real income that a fiscal expansion generates.

Tax Assessments Around the Globe

Britain adopted the first income tax in 1799 as a "temporary measure." In the United States, a truly temporary income tax lasted from 1864 to 1872. In 1913 an amendment to the U.S. constitution brought back the income tax, despite the prediction of one lawmaker that ultimately "a hand from Washington will stretch out to every man's house." At that time, the government promised that only those citizens with the highest incomes would owe any taxes. Indeed, in 1913, the U.S. income tax exempted all with annual incomes below $3,000, which at that time meant that 99 percent of U.S. citizens paid no income taxes.

Today residents of most developed nations pay income taxes. These nations typically strive to achieve *progressivity* of their tax structures, meaning that governments seek to assess higher income tax rates on those who earn higher taxable incomes. Panel (*a*) of Figure 12–9 displays estimated *marginal income tax rates*–the additional portion of the next dollar earned that an individual owes in income taxes–for those subject to the highest and lowest tax rates in sixteen nations. Clearly, Japan and several European nations lead the way in the highest marginal tax rates for the highest-income residents, while Singapore and Hong Kong stand out with much lower tax rates for the "rich." These latter two nations also impose lower marginal tax rates on those who have the lowest incomes.

Panel (*b*) of Figure 12–9 shows that some nations are more willing to tax lower-income residents than others.

An individual can earn the equivalent of more than 20,000 U.S. dollars per year before owing any income taxes in Luxembourg, Hong Kong, Sweden, France, Switzerland, and Singapore. In contrast, in the United Kingdom and the Netherlands, a person earning fewer than the equivalent of 10,000 U.S. dollars per year owes taxes.

Of course, some countries' governments rely more than others on the income tax as a key source of tax revenues. For this reason, some international tax analysts like to look at a broader measure of tax assessments. This is the "tax freedom day" for a nation's average resident, or the day each year when sufficient GDP has been earned to meeting the nation's total tax bills, thereby allowing its residents to begin working for themselves. Table 12–4 reports the "tax freedom day" for fourteen nations. Based on this measure of tax assessments, Swedes are the most tax-burdened people among developed nations: An average resident of Sweden begins to earn income on his or her own behalf only after the midpoint of each year!

FOR CRITICAL ANALYSIS:

In recent years, Hong Kong and Singapore have ranked among the fastest-growing nations of the world. Some observers partly attribute their strong employment and GDP performances to the relatively small "tax bites" that they impose on income-earners. Do you see any possible merit to this argument?

FIGURE 12-9 MARGINAL INCOME TAX RATES AND INCOME LEVELS AT WHICH INDIVIDUALS MUST PAY INCOME TAX TAXES IN SELECTED NATIONS

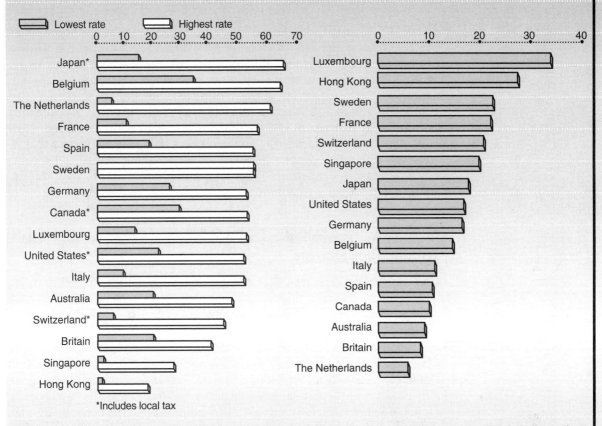

Panel (*a*) displays the highest and lowest percentage marginal income tax rates in sixteen nations. Panel (*b*) shows the income levels, measured in thousands of U.S. dollars, at which an individual must begin to pay income taxes in these nations.

SOURCE: Data from Organization for Economic Cooperation and Development.

TABLE 12-4 "TAX FREEDOM DAY" IN SELECTED NATIONS

Singapore	March 4	**Canada**	May 12
United States	April 11	**Germany**	May 23
Japan	April 12	**Italy**	June 2
Australia	April 25	**France**	June 12
Spain	May 5	**Netherlands**	June 12
Switzerland	May 6	**Belgium**	June 17
Britain	May 9	**Sweden**	July 3

SOURCE: Organization for Economic Cooperation and Development.

FIXED EXCHANGE RATES AND PERFECT CAPITAL MOBILITY

As already discussed, the degree of capital mobility influences the ultimate effects of fiscal policy actions. In Chapter 6 we indicated that there is evidence that capital mobility has increased for many nations of the world, and in particular for countries in North America, Western Europe, and East Asia. If nations were to reach a point at which flows of funds and financial assets were as mobile *across* their borders as *within* their borders, then they would experience *perfect capital mobility,* and the uncovered interest parity condition would hold. Let's begin by considering how economic policies work in a small open economy with perfect capital mobility. Then we shall consider how policy actions that are undertaken in one economy might spill over to affect another nation when capital is fully mobile.

Economic Policies with Perfect Capital Mobility and a Fixed Exchange Rate: The Small Open Economy

If an economy is small relative to the rest of the world, then changes in its real income or its nominal interest rate have negligible repercussions for other nations. Thus, for a small open economy, foreign incomes and interest rates are "given."

Monetary Policy with Perfect Capital Mobility and a Fixed Exchange Rate

Figure 12–10 depicts the effects of a monetary expansion in a small open economy that has perfect capital mobility and a fixed exchange rate. With perfect capital mobility, uncovered interest parity holds, so that the home interest rate is equal to the sum of the foreign interest rate, anticipated home currency depreciation, and a risk premium. If we assume that there is no anticipated depreciation of the domestic currency and no risk premium, then the domestic interest rate must equal the foreign interest rate. Hence, the BP schedule in the figure is *horizontal* at the foreign interest rate, R^*, because with perfect capital mobility even a very small variation in the nation's nominal interest rate induces very large shifts of financial resources across the nation's borders.

An expansionary monetary policy, such as an increase in the money stock from M_1 to M_2, shifts the LM schedule to the right. This results in a movement from an initial $IS–LM$ at point A on the BP schedule to new $IS–LM$ equilibrium at point B below the BP schedule. The equilibrium domestic interest rate declines to R_1, below the foreign interest rate R^*. This induces significant flows of capital out of the small open economy, which results in a balance-of-payments deficit. To prevent a decline in the value of the nation's currency, the central bank sells foreign exchange reserves. If it sterilizes its foreign exchange market interventions, then the central bank can maintains an equilibrium point B for at least some period of time. If the central bank's interventions are not sterilized, however, the

---

FIGURE 12-10   MONETARY POLICY WITH PERFECT CAPITAL MOBILITY AND FIXED EXCHANGE RATES

This figure shows the effects of an unsterilized increase in the quantity of money if there is perfect capital mobility, so that the *BP* schedule is horizontal. The result is a rightward shift of the *LM* schedule along the *IS* schedule, from point *A* to point *B*. The resulting decline in the nominal interest rate induces capital outflows and results in a balance of payments deficit. To keep the nation's currency from depreciating, the central bank sells foreign exchange reserves, which causes the nation's money stock to fall back to its initial value, causing the *LM* schedule to shift back to point *A*. Hence, unsterilized monetary policy actions have no long-lived effects on equilibrium real income.

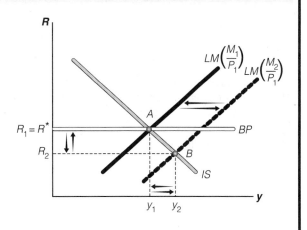

---

resulting decline in foreign exchange reserves ultimately causes the nation's money stock to fall back to its original level.

Once again, we conclude that an expansionary monetary policy action ultimately has no effect on real income when the central bank maintains a fixed exchange rate. Because it must intervene in the foreign exchange market to keep the exchange rate from changing, the central bank effectively must "undo" its own policies.

Fiscal Policy with Perfect Capital Mobility and a Fixed Exchange Rate   In contrast, the extent to which fiscal policy actions can influence real income under a fixed exchange rate are enlarged if capital is completely mobile. To see this, consider Figure 12–11. An increase in government spending from g_1 to g_2 causes the *IS* schedule to shift rightward, resulting in an equilibrium at point *B* above the *BP* schedule. The small open economy's equilibrium nominal interest rate rises above the foreign interest rate, to R_2, so the nation experiences a balance-of-payments surplus as the higher domestic interest rate induces significant inflows of capital from abroad.

At point *B* in Figure 12–11, the central bank begins to accumulate foreign exchange reserves in its efforts to keep the exchange rate from changing. If the central bank sterilizes indefinitely, then the economy remains at point B. In the absence of sterilization, however, the increase in foreign exchange reserves leads to a rise in the quantity of money in circulation, and the *LM* schedule shifts rightward until it again achieves balance of payments equilibrium at a new *IS–LM* equilibrium point *C* on the *BP* schedule. Consequently, fiscal policy has its greatest possible effect on equilibrium real income when capital is perfectly mobile.

FIGURE 12–11   **FISCAL POLICY WITH PERFECT CAPITAL MOBILITY AND FIXED EXCHANGE RATES**

An increase in real government expenditures shifts the *IS* schedule rightward along the *LM* schedule, from point *A* to point *B*. The resulting rise in the nominal interest rate induces capital inflows. This results in a balance-of-payments surplus, which tends to place upward pressure on the value of the nation's currency. To prevent such an appreciation, the central bank must purchase foreign exchange reserves, causing the money stock to increase and shifting the *LM* schedule rightward to a final equilibrium at point *C*.

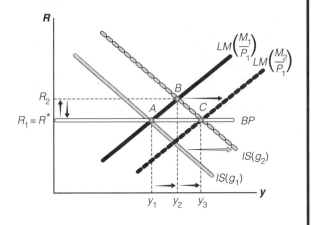

FUNDAMENTAL ISSUE #5

In what ways does perfect capital mobility alter the relative effectiveness of monetary and fiscal policy actions in a small open economy that adopts a fixed exchange rate? With perfect capital mobility and fixed exchange rates, the real income effects of monetary actions are muted. Under a policy of nonsterilized central bank interventions, in fact, monetary policy actions have no effects on a small open economy's real income level. In contrast, fiscal policy actions have their largest possible short-run effects on the nation's level of real income, particularly with nonsterilized central bank interventions.

Economic Policies with Perfect Capital Mobility and a Fixed Exchange Rate: A Two-Country Example

Some nations of the world, such as the United States, Japan, and Germany clearly do not fit the small-open-economy assumption. Variations in the economic performance of such nations can in fact affect economic outcomes in other countries.

A Two-Country Model with Perfect Capital Mobility and a Fixed Exchange Rate   To try to understand how policy actions or other economic developments in one country might have spillover effects on other nations, let's

FIGURE 12–12   A TWO-COUNTRY FRAMEWORK WITH PERFECT CAPITAL MOBILITY AND A FIXED EXCHANGE RATE

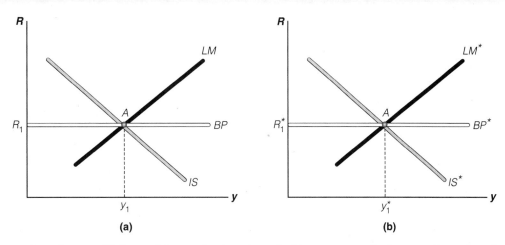

This figure shows how equilibrium real income levels and nominal interest rates arise in two nations whose borders are fully open to flows of financial resources. For the domestic country, an *IS–LM* equilibrium arises at point A in panel (a), at which equilibrium real income is equal to y_1 and the equilibrium nominal interest rate is equal to R_1. In the absence of any domestic currency depreciation, uncovered interest parity implies that the equilibrium domestic interest rate must equal the equilibrium foreign interest rate, R_1^* in panel (b), which is determined by *IS–LM* equilibrium for the foreign nation. This is point A in panel (b), at which the equilibrium level of foreign real income is equal to y_1^*.

imagine a "world" composed of *two* nations that are of roughly equal size and that engage in international trade of goods, services, and financial assets. Clearly, in such a world our small-open-economy assumption is violated, because each nation accounts for about half of the world's output.

Figure 12–12 illustrates the determination of equilibrium real income levels and equilibrium nominal interest rates in the two nations when financial resources flow freely across their borders. In one nation, which we shall call the *domestic economy,* an *IS–LM* equilibrium arises at point A in panel (a), at which equilibrium real income is equal to y_1 and the equilibrium nominal interest rate is equal to R_1. If there is perfect capital mobility, then in the absence of any domestic currency depreciation, the uncovered interest parity condition implies that this equilibrium domestic interest rate must be equal to the equilibrium foreign interest rate, R_1^* in panel (b). This value for the foreign interest rate, in turn, stems from a foreign *IS–LM* equilibrium at point A in panel (b), where the equilibrium level of foreign real income is equal to y_1^*. We continue to assume that prices are unchanged in both the domestic country *and* the foreign country.

An important implication of Figure 12–12 is that perfect capital mobility imposes a constraint on interest rate movements in the domestic and foreign economies. Although the *IS* and *LM* schedules in both nations shift as a result of economic policy actions, their final locations ultimately must be consistent, absent any expected currency depreciation, with equality of the domestic and foreign interest rates. In contrast to the small-open-economy framework we considered earlier, nominal interest rates in both nations may change in response to monetary or fiscal policy actions. Nevertheless, the free movement of financial resources between the two nations ultimately must drive the countries' interest rates to the same value.

The Effects of a Foreign Monetary Expansion   Consider Figure 12–13, which illustrates the effects of an increase in the quantity of money in circulation in the foreign economy. For purposes of illustration, we assume that the domestic nation's central bank wants to keep the value of the domestic currency fixed relative to that of the foreign currency. Consequently, the domestic central bank must intervene as necessary in the foreign exchange market to maintain its nation's goal of a fixed exchange rate. The foreign central bank, in contrast, pursues its own independent monetary policy by increasing the foreign money stock.

FIGURE 12–13   **THE EFFECTS OF A FOREIGN MONETARY EXPANSION IN THE TWO-COUNTRY MODEL WITH A FIXED EXCHANGE RATE**

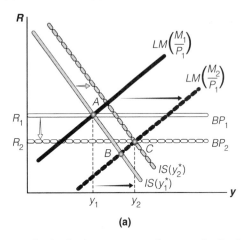
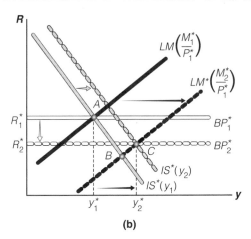

(a)   (b)

An increase in the foreign money stock causes the foreign *LM* schedule to shift rightward in panel (*b*). This causes an initial decline in the equilibrium foreign interest rate, thereby inducing a flow of financial resources from the foreign country to the domestic country. To keep its currency from appreciating relative to the foreign currency, the domestic central bank would have to buy foreign assets, resulting in a rise in the domestic money stock and a rightward shift in the domestic *LM* schedule in panel (*a*). Equilibrium nominal interest rates in both nations fall to the same level, which stems the flow of financial resources from the foreign country to the domestic country, thereby pushing the balance of payments back into equilibrium in each nation. On net, equilibrium real income levels in both nations increase, so there is a locomotive effect associated with a foreign monetary expansion.

Note that an alternative way to examine a system of fixed exchange rates in a two-country framework is to suppose that both countries work together to adjust a "world money stock" as necessary to keep the exchange rate linking their two currencies unchanged. In our two-country example, however, we wish to be more realistic. In real-world fixed-exchange-rate systems, such as the Bretton Woods system of the 1950s and 1960s and the Exchange-Rate Mechanism (ERM) of the European Monetary System (EMS) of the 1980s and 1990s, nations typically fix their exchange rates relative to the currency of a "center country" in the system (the United States in the Bretton Woods system and Germany in the EMS). For instance, you might think of Germany as the "foreign country" that determines its own monetary policy in our two-country framework and of France as the "domestic country" whose central bank seeks to maintain a fixed exchange rate.

A rise in the foreign money stock causes the foreign LM schedule to shift rightward, from $LM^*(M_1^*/P_1^*)$ to $LM^*(M_2^*/P_1^*)$ in panel (b), thereby resulting initially in a decline in the equilibrium foreign interest rate and a rise in equilibrium indicated by a movement from point A to point B. The fall in the foreign interest rate relative to the domestic interest rate induces a flow of financial resources from the foreign country to the domestic country, causing the foreign nation to experience a balance-of-payments deficit and the domestic nation to experience a balance-of-payment surplus. The resulting decline in the demand for foreign currency and rise in the demand for domestic currency in the foreign exchange markets places upward pressure on the value of the domestic currency relative to the foreign currency.

To keep its currency from appreciating relative to the foreign currency, the domestic central bank buys assets denominated in the foreign currency. If the domestic central bank's interventions are nonsterilized, then this action increases the quantity of domestic currency in circulation, thereby increasing the domestic money stock. Thus, in Figure 12–13 the domestic LM schedule shifts to the right, from $LM(M_1/P_1)$ to $LM(M_2/P_1)$ in panel (a), toward the new IS–LM equilibrium point B. At the same time, however, the rise in foreign real income induces an increase in foreign import spending, which corresponds to an increase in domestic exports. Hence, the domestic IS schedule shifts to the right in panel (a), which yields the final equilibrium point C. On net, there is a reduction in the equilibrium domestic interest rate, from R_1 to R_2, and a rise in equilibrium domestic income, from y_1 to y_2 at point B.

Finally, the rise in domestic real income causes the foreign IS schedule to shift to the right, from $IS^*(y_1^*)$ to $IS^*(y_2^*)$, as domestic residents import more foreign goods, which induces an increase in foreign exports. Consequently, the final equilibrium point in panel (b) is point C. Note that in equilibrium, perfect capital mobility requires that the nominal interest rates in both nations fall to the same level. This stems the flow of financial resources from the foreign country to the domestic country, thereby pushing the balance of payments back into equilibrium in each nation.

LOCOMOTIVE EFFECT
A stimulus to real income growth in one nation due to an increase in real income in another country.

We may conclude that a foreign country generates a corresponding domestic monetary expansion, which is required for the domestic central bank to maintain a fixed exchange rate. The outcomes in both nations, under our maintained assumption that the price levels in both countries are unchanged, are interest-rate reductions and rises in income levels. The fact that a rise in foreign income owing to a foreign money expansion theoretically can lead to a rise in *domestic* income is an example of the **locomotive effect.** This is the potential for income growth in one nation to spur income growth in another country. In this case, when the domestic country's central bank fixes the value of its currency relative to the foreign currency, higher foreign income due to a foreign monetary expansion increases domestic income. Thus, if we apply our framework to the Exchange-Rate Mechanism of the EMS, a key implication is that if price levels and other factors are unchanged, we can predict that a German monetary expansion should raise equilibrium income levels both in Germany and in France.

The Effects of a Foreign Fiscal Expansion   In principle, it is also possible for income in one nation to grow *at the expense* of income growth in another nation. To see why this may occur, consider Figure 12–14, which illustrates the effects of a foreign fiscal expansion. As shown in panel (*b*), given the initial level of domestic real income, a rise in foreign government spending, from g_1^* to g_2^*, shifts the foreign IS schedule rightward, from $IS^*(g_1^*, y_1)$ to $IS^*(g_2^*, y_1)$. This causes a movement up along the foreign LM schedule, to point *B*, which generates an initial increase in foreign real income and the foreign interest rate. The resulting differential between the new equilibrium foreign interest and the domestic interest rate induces a flow of financial resources from the domestic country to the foreign country that tends to depress the value of the domestic currency.

To keep the value of its currency fixed relative to the foreign currency, the domestic central bank sells foreign exchange reserves, which depresses the amount of domestic currency in circulation. The resulting decline in the domestic money stock, assuming nonsterilized domestic interventions, causes the domestic LM schedule to shift to the left in panel (*a*), from $LM(M_1/P_1)$ to $LM(M_2/P_1)$, which yields point *B*. At the same time, however, the increase in foreign income stimulates foreign import spending, so domestic exports rise. As a result, the domestic IS schedule shifts rightward, which generates the final equilibrium point *C*. Note that the net effect on equilibrium domestic real income could go either way, but panel (*a*) illustrates a situation in which, on net, equilibrium domestic real income *declines,* from y_1 to y_2, as domestic real investment falls off in response to the higher domestic interest rate by a greater amount than the increase in domestic exports stemming from the rise in foreign real income.

Finally, panel (*b*) shows that the assumed net decline in domestic real income causes the foreign IS schedule to shift back to the left slightly, from $IS^*(g_2^*, y_1)$ to $IS^*(g_2^*, y_2)$. On net, the movement from the initial equilibrium point *A* to the final equilibrium point *C* in panel (*b*) causes foreign real

---

**FIGURE 12–14   THE EFFECTS OF A FOREIGN FISCAL EXPANSION IN THE TWO-COUNTRY MODEL
WITH A FIXED EXCHANGE RATE**

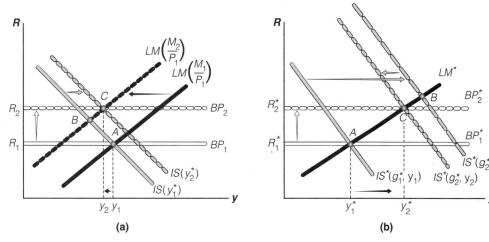

(a)   **(b)**

An increase in foreign government spending shifts the foreign *IS* schedule rightward in panel (*b*), causing a rise in the foreign interest rate that induces a flow of financial resources from the domestic country to the foreign country. To keep the value of its currency fixed relative to the foreign currency, the domestic central bank must sell foreign exchange reserves, causing a decline in the domestic money stock and a leftward shift in the domestic *LM* schedule in panel (*a*). If the rise in domestic exports caused by the rise in foreign real income is insufficient to offset the effect of the decline in domestic investment caused by the rise in the domestic interest rate, then equilibrium domestic real income falls. This is an example of a beggar-thy-neighbor effect.

BEGGAR-THY-NEIGHBOR EFFECT
A policy action in a nation that benefits that nation's economy but that worsens economic performance in another nation.

income to rise from y_1^* to y_2^* and causes the foreign interest rate to rise from R_1^* to R_2^*, which is equal to the domestic interest rate, R_2.

With perfect capital mobility and a domestic policy of maintaining a fixed exchange rate, therefore, a foreign fiscal expansion causes equilibrium foreign income to rise. In principle, however, it can generate a decline in equilibrium domestic income. International economists refer to this type of policy effect as an example of a **beggar-thy-neighbor effect,** in which a policymaker in one nation embarks on a policy action that benefits the policymaker's home economy at the expense of worsened economic performance in another nation. In the example, illustrated in Figure 12–13, the foreign government is able to raise income at home by raising its spending. A possible byproduct of this action is a decline in the income level of the domestic nation, whose central bank maintains a fixed rate of exchange of domestic currency for foreign currency. Many observers argued that such a beggar-thy-neighbor effect took place in Europe in the early 1990s following the significant fiscal expansion during the reunification of Germany. During that period, there was a significant rise in German and French interest rates and a sharp recession in France, as the French central bank maintained its commitment to the ERM.

The Effects of a Domestic Monetary Expansion   If the domestic central bank maintains a fixed exchange rate, then the locomotive or beggar-thy-neighbor effects can only work in one direction, from the foreign economy to the domestic economy. Domestic policy actions cannot influence the foreign economy. Figure 12–15 helps to illustrate this point by examining the effects of a *domestic* monetary expansion, under the assumptions that price levels in both nations are unchanging and that the domestic central bank maintains a fixed rate of exchange between the domestic and foreign currencies.

A rise in the domestic quantity of money causes the domestic *LM* schedule to shift rightward, from $LM(M_1/P_1)$ to $LM(M_2/P_1)$, as shown in panel (*a*) of Figure 12–15. This pushes down the domestic nominal interest rate, from R_1 toward R_2. Consequently, there is a shift of financial resources away from the domestic nation, which begins to experience a capital account deficit and, hence, a balance of payments deficit. The resulting reduction in the demand for domestic currency and rise in the demand for foreign currency places downward pressure on the value of the domestic currency.

To keep the rate of exchange of domestic currency for foreign currency fixed, the domestic central bank sells foreign exchange reserves. As in the

FIGURE 12–15   THE EFFECTS OF A DOMESTIC MONETARY EXPANSION IN THE TWO-COUNTRY MODEL WITH A FIXED EXCHANGE RATE

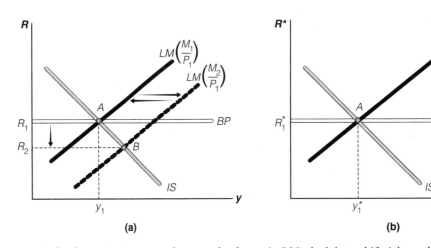

(a)   (b)

An increase in the domestic money stock causes the domestic *LM* schedule to shift rightward in panel (*a*), which pushes down the domestic nominal interest rate and induces a flow of financial resources from the domestic nation to the foreign nation. To keep the exchange rate from changing, the domestic central bank would have to sell foreign exchange reserves. If the domestic central bank's interventions to maintain the fixed exchange rate are nonsterilized, this action would cause the domestic money stock to decline to its initial level. Thus, equilibrium foreign real income is unchanged in panel (*b*), implying that the domestic central bank's policy of a fixed exchange rate insulates the foreign economy from the effects of domestic policy actions.

small-open-economy example that we considered in Figure 12–10 on page 401, if the domestic central bank sterilizes this action by purchasing domestic bonds, then for some time the domestic economy might remain at the equilibrium nominal interest rate R_2 and the corresponding equilibrium real income level y_2. If the domestic central bank's interventions to maintain the fixed exchange rate are nonsterilized, however, then its sales of foreign exchange reserves causes the domestic money stock to decline to its initial level. Ultimately, therefore, the domestic *LM* schedule shifts back to its original position, so that the initial domestic monetary expansion has no long-lived effect on the domestic economy. The domestic policy action also has no effect on the foreign economy. Effectively, the domestic central bank's objective of maintaining a fixed exchange rate *insulates* the foreign economy from the effects of domestic policy actions.

An important implication of this example is that the domestic central bank's commitment to the fixed exchange rate entails a sacrifice of its ability to conduct independent monetary policy actions. A real-world prediction, therefore, is that under the ERM, the Bank of France could not undertake policies to influence French real income.

The Effects of a Domestic Fiscal Expansion   What happens if the domestic country's government seeks to influence domestic real income through fiscal policy actions? Figure 12–16 shows the effects of an expansionary domestic fiscal policy action when the domestic central bank maintains a fixed value of the domestic currency relative to the foreign currency. At the initial level of foreign real income, an increase in government spending from g_1 to g_2 causes the domestic *IS* schedule to shift rightward, from $IS(g_1, y_1^*)$ to $IS(g_2, y_1^*)$ in panel (*a*). This initial movement to point *B* causes domestic real income and the domestic nominal interest rate to rise, and financial resources begin to move from the foreign country to the domestic country. Hence, the domestic nation begins to experience a balance-of-payments surplus.

In panel (*b*), the increase in domestic real income and the resulting rise in domestic import spending generates an increase in foreign exports, so the foreign *IS* schedule shifts to the right. This causes a rise in equilibrium foreign real income that, in turn, stimulates domestic exports and causes the domestic *IS* schedule to shift further to the right in panel (*a*), from $IS(g_2, y_1^*)$ to $IS(g_2, y_2^*)$. At the same time, however, with nonsterilized central bank purchases of foreign exchange reserves to keep the exchange rate unchanged, there is a rise in the domestic money stock. Consequently, the domestic *LM* schedule shifts rightward, causing the domestic nominal interest rate to fall back somewhat at the final domestic equilibrium point *C*, at which balance-of-payments equilibrium is reattained. The expansionary fiscal policy action leads to a rise in domestic real income and also generates a rise in foreign real income. Hence, the domestic fiscal expansion has a locomotive effect in this two-country framework. The implication for the ERM in Europe is that a French fiscal expansion could, given fixed French and German price levels, raise German real income as well as French real income.

FIGURE 12–16 **THE EFFECTS OF A DOMESTIC FISCAL EXPANSION IN THE TWO-COUNTRY MODEL WITH A FIXED EXCHANGE RATE**

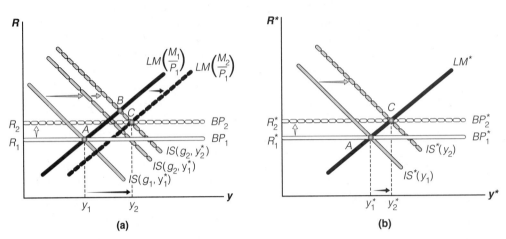

(a)　　　　　　　　　　　　(b)

An increase in domestic government expenditures causes the domestic *IS* schedule to shift rightward in panel (*a*). The initial result is a rise in the domestic nominal interest rate and a flow of financial resources from the foreign country to the domestic country. The increase in foreign exports due to the rise in domestic real income causes the foreign *IS* schedule to shift rightward in panel (*b*). Thus, there is a locomotive effect on foreign real income, which, in turn, causes domestic exports to rise, causing the domestic IS schedule to shift to the right again in panel (*a*). If the domestic central bank conducts nonsterilized purchases of foreign exchange reserves to keep the exchange rate fixed, then the domestic money stock also increases, causing the domestic *LM* schedule to shift rightward and the domestic nominal interest rate to fall back somewhat. At points *C* in both panels, balance-of-payments equilibrium is reattained at higher domestic and foreign interest rates and real income levels.

FUNDAMENTAL ISSUE #6

In a two-country setting in which one nation's central bank fixes the exchange rate, to what extent can policy actions in one nation influence economic activity in the other nation? If there is perfect capital mobility and the domestic nation's central bank fixes the exchange rate, then foreign monetary policy expansions can lead to a rise in real income in both the foreign and domestic countries. In contrast, a foreign fiscal expansion tends to stimulate foreign income while leading to a reduction in domestic income. Domestic monetary policy actions cannot influence foreign real income, because the domestic central bank's efforts to fix the exchange rate insulate the foreign economy from changes in domestic monetary policies.

CHAPTER SUMMARY

1. **The Economic Goals of National Policymakers:** Government fiscal authorities and central banks typically pursue two sets of economic goals. One set is internal balance objectives, which are goals for national real income, employment, and inflation. The other is external balance objectives, which are goals for the trade balance, other components of the balance of payments, and exchange rates.

2. **The Degree of Capital Mobility and the Slope of the *BP* Schedule:** If the degree of capital mobility for a nation is low, then the balance-of-payments deficit stemming from higher imports resulting from a given rise in the nation's real income level could be offset only by capital inflows generated by a sizable increase in the nation's interest rate. The *BP* schedule is the set of real income–nominal interest rate combinations consistent with balance-of-payments equilibrium, and so this reasoning implies that the *BP* schedule is steeply sloped if capital is relatively immobile. A rise in the degree of capital mobility makes the *BP* schedule more shallow. The *BP* schedule is horizontal in the extreme case of perfect capital mobility.

3. **The Influence of Monetary Policy Actions on the Real Income Level of a Small Open Economy with Imperfect Capital Mobility and a Fixed Exchange Rate:** The immediate effects of monetary policy actions with a fixed exchange rate depend considerably on the extent to which the central bank of a small open economy sterilizes the effects of its foreign exchange operations on the nation's nominal money stock. Unsterilized monetary policy actions, which are consistent with an external balance objective of maintaining balance-of-payments equilibrium, require changes in the quantity of money in circulation that ultimately offset initial monetary policy actions undertaken by a central bank.

4. **The Influence of Fiscal Policy Actions on the Real Income Level of a Small Open Economy with Imperfect Capital Mobility and a Fixed Exchange Rate:** Expansionary fiscal policy actions have the direct effect of increasing equilibrium real income in a small open economy with a fixed exchange rate. The size of a given fiscal action's effect on real income depends in part on whether the central bank sterilizes interventions in support of a fixed exchange rate. Nonsterilized interventions that are consistent with an external-balance goal of a balance of payments tend to reinforce a rise in real income from a fiscal expansion.

5. **Perfect Capital Mobility and the Relative Effectiveness of Monetary and Fiscal Policy Actions in a Small Open Economy that Adopts a Fixed Exchange Rate:** With perfect capital mobility and fixed exchange rates, nonsterilized monetary policy actions have no effects on a small open economy's real income level, but fiscal policy actions have their largest possible short-run effects on the nation's level of real income when central bank interventions in support of a fixed exchange rate are nonsterilized.

6. **The Influence of Policy Actions in a Nation on Economic Activity in Another Nation When One Nation's Central Bank Fixes the Exchange Rate:** If there is perfect capital mobility and the domestic nation's central bank fixes the exchange rate, then foreign monetary policy expansions can induce an increase in both nation's real income levels. By way of contrast, a foreign fiscal expansion tends to stimulate foreign income while depressing domestic income.

Because the domestic central bank's efforts to maintain a fixed exchange rate tend to insulate the foreign economy from changes in the domestic interest rate and real income level, domestic monetary policy actions cannot influence foreign real income.

Questions and Problems

1. As noted at the beginning of the chapter, mercantilist interests often press for pursuing a balance-of-payments *surplus* as an external balance objective. Suppose that a nation were to adopt the goal of attaining a *specific* balance-of-payments surplus. How could the *BP* schedule be altered to account for this policy goal? Would the nation's central bank be under more or less pressure to sterilize when confronted with this external balance objective? Explain your reasoning.

2. Suppose that a national government adopts, and is able to enforce, a system of capital controls that permits absolutely no flows of financial resources across its borders. What would be the shape of this nation's *BP* schedule? Explain, in your own words, what effects, if any, that an expansionary fiscal policy action would have on equilibrium real income in such an environment.

3. If the central bank of a small open economy maintains a fixed exchange rate but conducts unsterilized monetary policies, how would a contractionary monetary policy action ultimately affect the nation's balance of payments and its real income level, assuming that the price level is unchanged? Support your answer.

4. If the central bank of a small open economy with very high (though imperfect) capital mobility maintains a fixed exchange rate and conducts unsterilized monetary policies, would a contractionary fiscal policy action induce the nation's money stock to expand or contract as a result? Explain.

5. In our two-country framework with perfect capital mobility, we assumed that the domestic central bank acted alone to maintain a fixed exchange rate. Suppose instead that both the foreign and domestic central banks work together to buy and sell foreign and domestic currencies in sufficient quantities to keep the exchange rate fixed. In such an environment, could a domestic monetary expansion lead to a change in equilibrium real income in the foreign nation? If so, would there be a locomotive effect or a beggar-thy-neighbor effect?

6. Suppose, as in question 5, that both the foreign and domestic central banks work together in the two-country model to keep the exchange rate fixed. In this setting, could a domestic fiscal expansion lead to a change in equilibrium real income in the foreign nation? If so, would there be a locomotive effect or a beggar-thy-neighbor effect?

On-Line Application

Internet URL:
http://www.odci.gov/cia/publication/nsolo/factbook/zi.htm#Economy

Title: The CIA World Factbook–Zimbabwe

Navigation: Start at the home page for the Office of the Director of Central Intelligence **(http://www.odci.gov).** Click on *Central Intelligence Agency,* and if you agree to the listed conditions, click on *Click here to continue.* Then click on *Publications.* Next, click on *1999 World Factbook* (or the Factbook with the latest available date. Click on *countries,* and select *Zimbabwe.*

Application: Scan through the description until you reach the "Economy" discussion. Then answer the following questions:

1. Based on the data provided, what was the government deficit in Zimbabwe for the latest available year?

2. What was per-capita GDP in Zimbabwe for the most recent year for which data are available?

3. Suppose that you are an advisor to the government of Zimbabwe. You are told that the government recently has established a value for a fixed exchange rate, following several years of exchange-rate volatility (see the recent exchange rates listed in the CIA "Economy" description). The country now wishes to eliminate its government deficit within the next year through a combination of spending cuts and tax increases, but it does not desire for its real GDP per capita to decline. Zimbabwe's government has asked you for an assessment of whether the nation can achieve this objective. Assuming that the country's population and price level do not change in the near future, and applying what you have learned in this chapter, provide this assessment.

REFERENCES AND RECOMMENDED READINGS

Argy, Victor. *International Macroeconomics: Theory and Policy.* London: Routledge, 1994.

Bryant, Ralph C. *Money and Monetary Policy in Interdependent Nations.* Washington, D.C.: Brookings Institution, 1980.

Daniels, Joseph, and David VanHoose. "Two-Country Models of Monetary and Fiscal Policy: What Have We Learned? What More Can We Learn?" *Open Economies Review,* 9 (1998): Forthcoming.

Dooley, Michael P. "A Survey of Literature on Controls Over International Transactions." *International Monetary Fund Staff Papers,* 43 (December 1996): 639–687.

Frenkel, Jacob, and Razin, Assaf. "The Mundell–Fleming Model a Quarter Century Later." *International Monetary Fund Staff Papers,* 34 (1987): 567–620.

Heffernan, Shelagh, and Peter Sinclair. *Modern International Economics.* Oxford: Blackwell, 1990.

McCallum, Bennett T. *International Monetary Economics.* Oxford: Oxford University Press, 1996.

Taylor, John B. *Macroeconomic Policy in a World Economy.* New York: W. W. Norton, 1993.

13

Economic Policy with Floating Exchange Rates

FUNDAMENTAL ISSUES

1. How do monetary and fiscal policy actions affect a nation's real income under floating exchange rates?

2. How does perfect capital mobility influence the relative effectiveness of monetary and fiscal policy actions in a small open economy that permits its exchange rates to float?

3. In a two-country setting with a floating exchange rate, to what extent can policy actions in one nation influence economic activity in the other nation?

4. What is the basic economic efficiency trade-off faced in choosing between fixed and floating exchange rates?

5. How does the choice between fixed and floating exchange rates depend in part on its implications for economic stability and monetary policy autonomy?

By most standards, Switzerland is the wealthiest nation in Europe. Until the 1990s, its economy had also been the most stable, with the Swiss unemployment rate rarely rising above 1 percent, even during recessions. After 1990, however, aggregate output stalled, and the nation actually experienced slightly negative overall growth during the 1990s. By 1997, an unheard-of figure of 10 percent of Swiss residents lived below the government's official poverty line. Of those, 40 percent were immigrants from other nations who originally had moved to Switzerland to seek opportunities that its previously booming economy had provided. Fearing social unrest, the Swiss army began to study the experience of U.S. authorities during the Los Angeles riots to increase its preparedness in the event of worker upheavals in Bern or Zurich.

Many Swiss citizens blamed their nation's economic problems on their central bank, the Bank of Switzerland. The central bank, they argued, had permitted the value of the Swiss currency, the franc, to rise in foreign exchange markets and had failed to conduct offsetting monetary policy actions to stabilize the aggregate effects on the nation's economy. What was needed in the face of a floating Swiss franc and a sharp recession, they contended, was greater monetary expansion.

Others contended that the real problem was that the government and central bank had agreed to let the Swiss franc float in the first place. These critics called for efforts to stabilize, and even fix, the franc's value relative to other currencies. Without such a policy change, they argued, the Swiss army's anti-riot preparations might not be in vain.

To what extent might monetary policy help to stabilize a nation's economy under floating exchange rates? Are there conditions under which a nation might be better off fixing its exchange rate rather than letting the value of its currency vary in foreign exchange markets? As the Swiss example illustrates, these are questions of real-world significance. They also are questions that we shall address in this chapter.

FLOATING EXCHANGE RATES AND IMPERFECT CAPITAL MOBILITY

When it chooses to maintain a fixed exchange rate, a nation's central bank shoulders two burdens. First, it must stand ready to intervene in the foreign exchange market by purchasing and selling foreign-currency-denominated assets. Thus, the central bank must be willing to accumulate or expend foreign exchange reserves. Second, it must decide whether or not to sterilize its foreign exchange market interventions. If it fails to sterilize, then the central bank effectively sacrifices control of the quantity of money in circulation.

By permitting the exchange rate to float, a central bank relieves itself from these burdens. You will learn in this chapter that adopting a floating exchange rate also increases the potential for monetary policy actions to exert effects on a nation's economic performance. Fiscal policy, in contrast, may lose at least some of its potency when exchange rates float.

The Effects of Exchange Rate Variations in the *IS–LM–BP* Model

Before we consider how monetary and fiscal policy actions may influence a nation's economic performance under floating exchange rates, we first need to consider how changes in the exchange rate exert effects in the *IS–LM–BP* framework.

Exchange Rate Variations and the *IS* Schedule   Figure 13–1 shows how a depreciation in the value of a nation's currency influences the *IS* schedule. A fall in the value of a nation's currency makes imports more expensive, inducing the nation's residents to reduce their import spending. Simultaneously, the effective prices of the nation's export goods faced by other nations' residents decline. Consequently, expenditures on the nation's exports increase.

Both of these effects generate a rise in the nation's aggregate autonomous expenditures at any given nominal interest rate, such as R_1 in Figure 13–1. As a result, the real income level consistent with an income–expenditure equilibrium increases from y_1 at point *A* to y_2 at point *B*. Hence, the *IS* schedule

---

FIGURE 13–1   THE EFFECTS OF A CURRENCY DEPRECIATION ON THE *IS* SCHEDULE

A decline in the value of a nation's currency corresponding to a rise in the exchange rate from S_1 to S_2 makes imports more expensive for a nation's residents, inducing them to cut back on their import expenditures. At the same time, the nation's export goods become less expensive for foreign residents, so foreign expenditures on the nation's exports rise. Together, these effects cause an increase in the nation's aggregate autonomous expenditures at any given nominal interest rate, such as R_1, so the real income level consistent with an income–expenditure equilibrium increases from y_1 at point *A* to y_2 at point *B*. Consequently, the *IS* schedule shifts rightward.

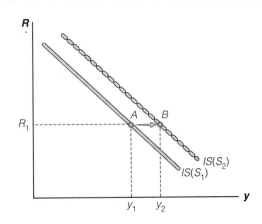

shifts to the right, from $IS(S_1)$ to $IS(S_2)$, following a rise in the exchange rate, from S_1 to S_2, which entails a depreciation of the home currency.

Exchange Rate Variations and the *BP* Schedule The depreciation of a nation's currency also alters the position of the *BP* schedule. Remember that the *BP* schedule consists of all real income–interest rate combinations that maintain balance of payments equilibrium, holding all other factors unchanged. As already discussed, however, a currency depreciation causes a nation's exports to rise and its imports to fall at any given real income level and at any given nominal interest rate. Therefore, as shown in Figure 13–2, at a given real income–nominal interest rate combination, such as y_1 and R_1 at point A on the *BP* schedule labeled $BP(S_1)$, a rise in the exchange rate from S_1 to S_2 generates an improvement in the trade balance that results in a balance-of-payments surplus at point A.

This means that for the balance of payments to return to equilibrium, the nation's real income must increase to a level such as y_2, at which sufficient import spending takes place to return the trade balance to its previous level. As a result, point B lies on a new *BP* schedule, denoted $BP(S_2)$, following the home currency depreciation. We may conclude that a currency depreciation causes the *BP* schedule to shift to the right.

Monetary Policy under Floating Exchange Rates

Panels (*a*) and (*b*) of Figure 13–3 illustrate the effects of an expansionary monetary policy action under floating exchange rates for a small open economy. Each panel assumes that there is an initial *IS–LM* equilibrium at point A on the

---

FIGURE 13–2   THE EFFECTS OF A CURRENCY DEPRECIATION ON THE *BP* SCHEDULE

At a given real income–interest rate combination, such as y_1 and R_1 at point A on the *BP* schedule labeled $BP(S_1)$, an increase in the exchange rate from S_1 to S_2 results in an improvement in the trade balance. Consequently, a balance of payments surplus occurs at point A. Reattainment of balance of payments requires an increase in the nation's real income to a level such as y_2, which generates a sufficient increase in import expenditures to return the trade balance to its previous level. Hence, point B lies on the scheduled denoted $BP(S_2)$ following the home currency depreciation, which implies that a currency depreciation causes the *BP* schedule to shift to the right.

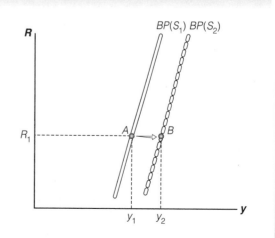

FIGURE 13-3 THE EFFECTS OF AN INCREASE IN THE MONEY STOCK WITH A FLOATING EXCHANGE RATE

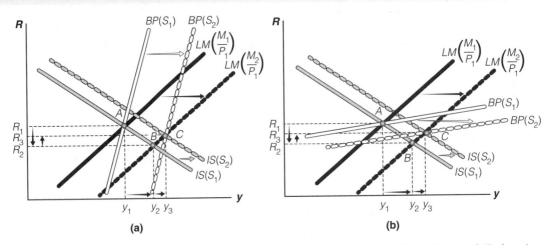

An increase in the money stock causes the LM schedule to shift rightward, so in both panels (*a*) and (*b*) there is an initial movement from point *A* to point *B*. Because point *B* lies below and to the right of the *BP*(S_1) schedule, there is a balance-of-payments deficit at point *B* in both panels. The rise in import spending and acquisition of foreign financial assets by the nation's residents and the reduction in export spending and acquisition of domestic financial assets by foreign citizens causes the home currency to depreciate, so the exchange rate rises from S_1 to S_2. As a result, the *IS* and *BP* schedules shift rightward. At the final equilibrium point *C*, balance of payments equilibrium is reattained in both panels, so that there is no further upward pressure on the exchange rate.

BP schedule labeled *BP*(S_1), so that at the outset there is balance-of-payments equilibrium at the prevailing exchange rate, S_1. The *BP* schedule is very steep in panel (*a*), which indicates low capital mobility. In panel (*b*), the *BP* schedule is much more shallow, implying a much higher degree of capital mobility.

An increase in the money stock from M_1 to M_2 causes the *LM* schedule to shift rightward. Hence, in both panels of Figure 13–3 there is an initial movement from point *A* to point *B*. Because point *B* lies below and to the right of the *BP*(S_1) schedule, there is a balance-of-payments deficit at point *B*. In panel (*a*), in which capital mobility is low, the reason for this balance-of-payments deficit is the rise in import spending owing to an increase in real income from y_1 to y_2. In panel (*b*), in which capital mobility is high, the balance-of-payments deficit results from the outflow of capital spurred by the decline in the interest rate from R_1 to R_2.

The rise in import spending and acquisition of foreign financial assets by the nation's residents and the reduction in export spending and acquisition of domestic financial assets by foreign citizens places downward pressure on the value of the nation's currency. Thus, the domestic currency depreciates; the value of the exchange rate would rise from its initial value S_1 to a higher level, S_2.

The domestic currency depreciation raises the domestic price of foreign goods and reduces the foreign price of domestic goods. Consequently, the rise in the exchange rate from S_1 to S_2 causes export spending to rise and import spending to fall, raising total expenditures on domestic goods. This causes the *IS* schedule to shift to the right, from $IS(S_1)$ to $IS(S_2)$. At the same time, as discussed earlier, the depreciation causes the *BP* schedule to shift to the right, from $BP(S_1)$ to $BP(S_2)$. Following these adjustments in the positions of the *LM*, *IS*, and *BP* schedules, the point *C* represents the new *IS–LM–BP* equilibrium. At this point, balance-of-payments equilibrium occurs on the new *BP* schedule, and so there is additional pressure on the value of the domestic currency.

Figure 13–3 demonstrates that, with either low or high capital mobility, an increase in the money stock tends to induce a rise in equilibrium real income, holding other factors such as the price level unchanged. Under a floating exchange rate, therefore, an increase in the quantity of money unambiguously constitutes an expansionary policy action that induces at least a near-term increase in a nation's real income level.

Fiscal Policy under Floating Exchange Rates

Fiscal policy actions can also alter the value of a small nation's currency if the nation's exchange rate floats. Whether the nation's currency depreciates or appreciates depends on the degree of capital mobility, however.

The Case of Low Capital Mobility   Panel (*a*) of Figure 13–4 depicts the effects of an increase in government spending when the extent of capital mobility is relatively low. With the exchange rate initially unchanged at its initial value of S_1, an increase in government spending causes the *IS* schedule to shift to the right, from $IS_1(g_1, S_1)$ to $IS_1(g_2, S_1)$. This yields a new *IS–LM* equilibrium at point *B*, which lies to the right of the initial *BP* schedule, labeled $BP(S_1)$. Therefore, the immediate effect of the rise in government spending is a balance-of-payments deficit caused by an increase in import spending resulting from a rise in real income from y_1 to y_2.

The nation's currency depreciates in the face of the balance-of-payments deficit. The resulting rise in the exchange rate, from S_1 to a higher level, S_2, induces net export expenditures to increase. This causes the *IS* schedule to shift rightward once more, to $IS_2(g_2, S_2)$. Furthermore, the currency depreciation causes the *BP* schedule to shift to the right, from $BP(S_1)$ to $BP(S_2)$. Following these shifts in the *IS* and *BP* schedules, the new *IS–LM–BP* equilibrium is at point *C*. The exchange rate S_2 constitutes the new equilibrium exchange rate, because there is no tendency for the nation's currency to depreciate further once balance-of-payments equilibrium is reattained at point *C*. The increase in government spending also induces a higher equilibrium real income level, y_3, at this final equilibrium point.

The Case of High Capital Mobility   When capital is very mobile, as in panel (*b*) of Figure 13–4, the ultimate effects of an increase in government spending are different from those shown in panel (*a*). The initial effect of a rise

FIGURE 13–4   THE EFFECTS OF AN INCREASE IN GOVERNMENT SPENDING WITH A FLOATING EXCHANGE RATE

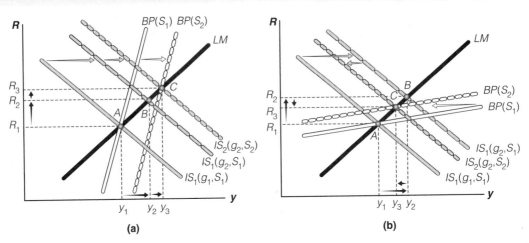

In both panels, an increase in government expenditures causes an initial rightward shift in the *IS* schedule, thereby inducing a movement from point *A* to point *B*, which leads to an increase in the equilibrium nominal interest rate and an increase in equilibrium real income. In panel (*a*), in which the relatively steep slope of the *BP* schedule implies low capital mobility, greater import spending more than offsets a small capital inflow in causing a balance-of-payments deficit to arise at point *B*. This induces a currency depreciation that shifts both the *IS* and *BP* schedules to the right, leading to a final equilibrium with a balance-of-payments equilibrium at point *C*. In panel (*b*), in which the relatively shallow slope of the *BP* schedule implies high capital mobility, significant capital inflows more than offset greater import expenditures in causing a balance of payments surplus to occur at point *B*. This induces a currency appreciation that shifts both the *IS* and *BP* schedules leftward, leading to a final balance of payments equilibrium at point *C*.

in government spending, however, is the same and is shown by the movement from point *A* to point *B* in panel (*b*), as the *IS* schedule shifts rightward, from $IS_1(g_1, S_1)$ to $IS_1(g_2, S_1)$.

Nevertheless, with high capital mobility the resulting rise in the interest rate from R_1 to R_2 causes significant capital inflows into this nation. This induces a balance of payments *surplus* at point *B*, above the initial *BP* schedule, denoted $BP(S_1)$. As foreign residents acquire more of the nation's currency to purchase domestic financial assets, the nation's currency value *appreciates*. The domestic price of foreign goods declines as the foreign price of domestic goods rise, which spurs import expenditures and reduces export spending. Hence, the result of the fall in the exchange rate (which implies a home currency appreciation), from S_1 to S_2, is a decline in total expenditures on the nation's goods, and so the *IS* schedule shifts *leftward*, from $IS(g_2, S_1)$ to $IS(g_2, S_2)$. The currency appreciation also causes the *BP* schedule to shift leftward, from $BP(S_1)$ to $BP(S_2)$.

At the final equilibrium point C in panel (b), equilibrium real income on net is higher than before, at y_3 as compared with the beginning level of y_1. Nonetheless, comparing panel (b) with panel (a) indicates that high capital mobility fundamentally changes the nature of the economy's adjustments following a rise in government spending. The result is a reduction in the extent to which equilibrium real income increases following a given increase in government spending.

FUNDAMENTAL ISSUE #1

How do monetary and fiscal policy actions affect a nation's real income under floating exchange rates? An expansionary monetary policy action results in a balance-of-payments deficit that causes a nation's currency to depreciate, thereby spurring export spending while inhibiting import expenditures. Therefore, expansionary monetary policy actions cause a nation's equilibrium real income to increase in the short run. The effects of fiscal policy actions on a nation's balance of payments and the value of its currency hinge on the degree of capital mobility. Under most circumstances, an expansionary fiscal policy action causes at least a slight short-term increase in a nation's real income level. The extent of the rise in real income declines as the degree of capital mobility rises.

FLOATING EXCHANGE RATES AND PERFECT CAPITAL MOBILITY

How would *perfect* capital mobility affect the transmission of monetary and fiscal policy actions to a nation's balance of payments and real income level under *floating* exchange rates? We consider this question first for the case of a small open economy. Then we contemplate this issue in a two-country framework. As in Chapter 12, we assume throughout that there is no anticipated currency depreciation or appreciation, so that the uncovered interest parity condition implies that the nominal interest rate for the small open economy is equal to the large-country nominal interest rate, R^*.

Economic Policies with Perfect Capital Mobility and a Floating Exchange Rate: The Small Open Economy

Recall that variations in economic activity within a small open economy do not affect the world economy, so variations in its output, interest rate, or price

---

If there is perfect capital mobility under a floating exchange rate, an increase in the amount of money in circulation causes a rightward shift of the *LM* schedule along the *IS* schedule, from point *A* to point *B*, which induces a decline in the nominal interest rate that leads, in turn, to capital outflows. The resulting balance-of-payments deficit causes the nation's currency to depreciate. This results in higher export spending and lower expenditures, so the *IS* schedule shifts rightward to a final equilibrium at point *C*.

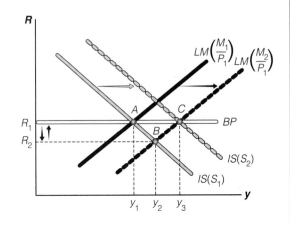

---

level cannot influence corresponding values in the rest of the world. Let's think about how monetary and fiscal policies affect a small open economy's real output and interest rate under the assumption that the price level does not vary.

Monetary Policy with Perfect Capital Mobility and a Floating Exchange Rate
Figure 13–5 depicts the effects of an increase in the money stock in a small open economy with a floating exchange rate and with perfectly mobile capital and, hence, a horizontal *BP* schedule. An increase in the money stock from M_1 to M_2 causes the *LM* schedule to shift rightward, inducing a movement from the initial equilibrium point *A* to a new point of *IS–LM* equilibrium, denoted *B*. At point *B*, the induced decline in the equilibrium interest rate, from R_1 to R_2, generates considerable capital outflows. This causes the country to start to experience a balance-of-payments deficit.

The balance-of-payments deficit, in turn, places downward pressure on the value of the nation's currency, so the exchange rate rises from its initial level, S_1 to a higher value, S_2. Thus, import spending declines, and export spending rises. The resulting increase in net expenditures on the nation's goods causes the *IS* schedule to shift to the right, from $IS(S_1)$ to $IS(S_2)$. At the final equilibrium point *C*, the sum of the nation's current account balance and its capital account balance again is equal to zero, so there is no further pressure on the value of its currency. The exchange rate S_2 is the new equilibrium exchange rate. Finally, real income increases as fully as possible, from y_1 to y_3, or by the amount of the horizontal distance that the *LM* schedule shifts to the right. Monetary policy has the largest possible immediate effect on real income with a floating exchange rate and perfect capital mobility.

FIGURE 13–6 **THE EFFECTS OF AN INCREASE IN GOVERNMENT SPENDING WITH A FLOATING EXCHANGE RATE AND PERFECT CAPITAL MOBILITY**

If there is perfect capital mobility under a floating exchange rate, an increase in government expenditures shifts the *IS* schedule rightward along the *LM* schedule, from point *A* to point *B*. The resulting rise in the nominal interest rate induces capital inflows that lead to a balance-of-payments surplus that causes a currency appreciation. Consequently, export spending declines and export expenditures increase, causing the *IS* schedule to return to its original position at point *A*.

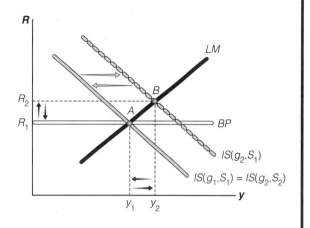

Fiscal Policy with Perfect Capital Mobility and a Floating Exchange Rate

Figure 13–6 illustrates the effects of an increase in government spending, from g_1 to g_2, in a small open economy with a floating exchange rate and perfectly mobile capital. The direct effect of this policy action is a rightward shift in the *IS* schedule at the initial exchange rate, from $IS(g_1, S_1)$ to $IS(g_2, S_1)$, and a movement from point *A* to point *B*. At the new equilibrium point *B*, the initial rise in the interest rate induces significant capital inflows and thereby leads to the onset of a balance-of-payments surplus.

The balance-of-payment surplus at point *B* generates an appreciation of the country's currency, which causes import spending to rise and export expenditures to fall. As a result, total aggregate spending on domestic output declines, and the *IS* schedule shifts leftward, from $IS(g_2, S_1)$ to $IS(g_2, S_2)$, which is the same as the original position of the *IS* schedule. Thus, the final equilibrium is point A once again, and real income is unaffected, on net, by the rise in government spending. We may conclude that with perfect capital mobility, fiscal policy actions have *complete crowding out effects*. Any increase in government spending crowds out an equal amount of net export spending by foreign residents, because of the currency appreciation that the fiscal policy action causes. On net, therefore, equilibrium real income is unaffected by the fiscal policy action.

Perfect Capital Mobility and Fixed versus Floating Exchange Rates Let's compare our conclusions about the effects of monetary and fiscal policies under perfect capital mobility and a *floating* exchange rate with those we reached in Chapter 12 when we considered an environment with perfect capital mobility and a *fixed* exchange rate. Recall from Chapter 12 that nonsterilized central bank interventions to maintain a fixed exchange rate cause a nation's money stock to change in the same direction as resulting movements in its foreign exchange reserves. Thus, an initial effort by a central bank to expand the quantity of money in circulation ultimately is offset fully by a reduction in the quantity of money as the central bank sells foreign exchange reserves to relieve resulting downward pressure on the value of its nation's currency. Nonsterilized monetary policy actions thereby cannot affect equilibrium real income with a fixed exchange rate.

In contrast, an expansionary fiscal policy action, such as an increase in government spending, exerts its largest possible effect on equilibrium real income with fixed exchange rates and perfectly mobile capital. This is true, as you learned in Chapter 12, because maintaining a fixed exchange rate in the face of a rise in government expenditures requires purchases of foreign exchange reserves that, if unsterilized, cause an expansion of the quantity of money in circulation. This equiproportionate rise in the nominal money stock reinforces the expansionary effect that the fiscal policy action has on equilibrium real income.

Under a floating exchange rate, however, there is no automatic adjustment of the quantity of money in response to a fiscal policy action. Instead, as illustrated in Figure 13–6, the *exchange rate* adjusts, which leads to a crowding-out effect on net export spending that fully dampens the effect that an increase in government spending otherwise would have on equilibrium real income.

A monetary policy action, by way of contrast, induces both a direct rise in real income and an exchange-rate adjustment that reinforces this real-income increase, as shown in Figure 13–5. Thus, an expansionary monetary policy action exerts its largest possible effect on the equilibrium level of real income in a small open economy if the exchange rate floats and capital is perfectly mobile.

Table 13–1 summarizes comparisons of the real income effects of economic policy actions with fixed versus floating exchange rates for a small open economy with perfectly mobile capital. This table yields the following important conclusions about the real-income effects of monetary and fiscal policies under perfect capital mobility:

1. **With perfectly mobile capital, monetary policy actions have minimal effects on equilibrium real income in a small open economy if the exchange rate is fixed. Monetary policy actions have their largest possible real-income effects if the exchange rate floats.**
2. **With perfect capital mobility, fiscal policy actions exert their largest feasible effects on equilibrium real income in a small open economy if the exchange is fixed. Fiscal policy actions have minimal real-income effects if the exchange rate floats.**

TABLE 13–1	REAL INCOME EFFECTS OF ECONOMIC POLICIES FOR A SMALL OPEN ECONOMY WITH PERFECT CAPITAL MOBILITY UNDER FIXED VERSUS FLOATING EXCHANGE RATES

EXCHANGE RATE SETTING	MONETARY POLICY EFFECT	FISCAL POLICY EFFECT
Fixed exchange rate	Minimum effect	Maximum effect
Floating exchange rate	Maximum effect	Minimum effect

FUNDAMENTAL ISSUE #2

How does perfect capital mobility influence the relative effectiveness of monetary and fiscal policy actions in a small open economy that permits its exchange rates to float? With perfect capital mobility and floating exchange rates, the monetary policy actions exert their greatest possible effects on equilibrium real income in a small open economy. In contrast, fiscal policy actions have no short-run real income effects under floating exchange rates and perfect capital mobility.

Economic Policies with Perfect Capital Mobility and a Floating Exchange Rate: A Two-Country Example

In Chapter 12, we considered the implications of policy actions for the economic performances of two nations that were completely open to cross-border capital flows, under the assumption that one nation's central bank intervened in the foreign exchange market to keep the rate of exchange for the two nation's currencies fixed. Now let's apply that two-country example to a setting with a floating exchange rate, while maintaining our assumption of no anticipated currency appreciations or depreciations.

The Effects of a Domestic Monetary Expansion First, let's think about the effects of an action by the domestic central bank to increase the amount of domestic money in circulation. As shown in panel (*a*) of Figure 13–7, this shifts the domestic *LM* schedule to the right. As a result, the domestic interest rate falls from its initial equilibrium value of R_1 at point *A* toward a lower value of R' at point *B*, which is below the *BP* schedule, denoted BP_1, that prevails at the initial equilibrium exchange rate. This decline in the domestic interest rate induces a shift in financial resources from the domestic country to the foreign country, thereby raising the domestic demand for foreign currency and reducing the foreign demand for domestic currency. As a result, the

FIGURE 13–7   THE EFFECTS OF A DOMESTIC MONETARY EXPANSION IN THE TWO-COUNTRY MODEL
WITH A FLOATING EXCHANGE RATE

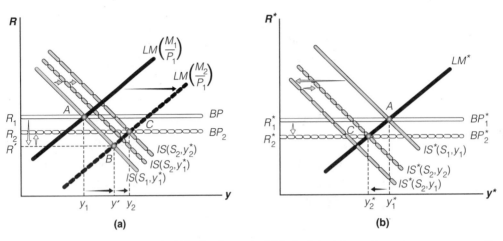

An increase in the domestic money stock shifts the domestic *LM* schedule rightward, causing a movement from point *A* to point *B* in panel (*a*). The resulting decline in the domestic interest rate causes financial resources to flow from the domestic country to the foreign country, thereby causing the domestic currency to depreciate relative to the foreign currency. The rise in the equilibrium exchange rate from S_1 to S_2 induces a rise in net expenditures on domestic output and a decline in net spending on foreign output, so the domestic *IS* schedule shifts rightward in panel (*a*), while the foreign *IS* schedule shifts leftward in panel (*b*). At the final equilibrium points labeled points *C*, domestic real income is higher, and foreign real income is lower. Thus, the domestic monetary expansion has a beggar-thy-neighbor effect on the foreign country.

value of the domestic currency depreciates, and the value of the foreign currency appreciates. Thus, the equilibrium exchange rate rises from its initial value of S_1 to a higher level, S_2.

The domestic currency depreciation induces a rise in net expenditures on domestic output, so at the initial level of foreign real income the domestic *IS* schedule shifts rightward in panel (*a*) of Figure 13–7, from $IS(S_1, y_1^*)$ to $IS(S_2, y_1^*)$. At the same time, the corresponding foreign currency appreciation and induced reduction in net expenditures on foreign output at the initial level of domestic real income causes the foreign *IS* schedule to shift to the left in panel (*b*), from $IS^*(S_1, y_1)$ to $IS^*(S_2, y_1)$. Finally, higher real income levels in both nations induce increased exports, which then shift both nations' *IS* schedules to the right, to $IS(S_2, y_2^*)$ in panel (*a*) and to $IS^*(S_2, y_2)$ in panel (*b*). If domestic imports are highly responsive to a rise in domestic income, then the foreign *IS* schedule could shift farther back toward, or even beyond, point *A*, but panel (*b*) illustrates the more typical case in which foreign real income declines on net.

The equilibrium domestic nominal interest rate converges to an equality with the equilibrium foreign interest rate, with $R_2 = R_2^*$ at points C in both panels, as the BP schedules for both nations shift downward because of the *simultaneous* decline in nominal interest rates in both nations. In contrast to the small-open-economy case considered earlier in this chapter, both nations are sufficiently large that their policymakers can influence the overall world interest rate.

At point C in panel (*a*), the equilibrium level of domestic real income, y_2, exceeds the initial equilibrium value, y_1. At point C in panel (*b*), however, equilibrium foreign real income, y_2^*, lies below its initial level, y_1^*. We may conclude that under a floating exchange rate and perfect capital mobility, a domestic monetary expansion can have a *beggar-thy-neighbor effect* on the foreign country. That is, an increase in the domestic money stock exerts an expansionary effect on the domestic economy but typically tends to depress the equilibrium level of economic activity in the foreign economy.

If you think back to Chapter 12, you will recall that if the domestic monetary authority intervenes in the foreign exchange market to fix the exchange rate, then domestic monetary policy actions have no ultimate effects on either domestic or foreign real income levels or nominal interest rates in a two-country world with perfect capital mobility. Figure 13–7 indicates that if the exchange rate floats, domestic monetary policy can affect levels of real income and interest rates in both nations within the same two-country world. Hence, the foreign economy is no longer insulated from domestic monetary policy actions under a floating exchange rate.

The Effects of a Foreign Monetary Expansion Note that we could have just as easily considered the effect of a foreign monetary expansion in Figure 13–7. Such an example produces a mirror image: A rightward shift of the foreign LM schedule, a rightward shift of the foreign IS schedule as the foreign currency's value depreciates, and a leftward shift of the domestic IS schedule as the domestic currency's value appreciated. Thus, an increase in the foreign money stock generates—with a floating exchange rate and perfect capital mobility—a decline in equilibrium nominal interest rates in both nations, a rise in equilibrium foreign real income, and a decline in equilibrium domestic real income.

You saw in Chapter 12 that if the domestic central bank maintains a fixed exchange rate, then a foreign monetary expansion induces the domestic central bank to increase the domestic money stock, so there is a *locomotive effect* as both nations' real income levels would rise in response. Figure 13–7 shows that the *opposite* result occurs in a two-country world with a floating exchange rate. In such a world, a foreign monetary expansion instead typically generates a *beggar-thy-neighbor effect*.

The Effects of a Domestic Fiscal Expansion In Figure 13–8, we consider the effects of an increase in domestic government spending in the two-country model under a floating exchange rate. The direct effect of a rise in domestic

FIGURE 13-8   THE EFFECTS OF A DOMESTIC FISCAL EXPANSION IN THE TWO-COUNTRY MODEL
WITH A FLOATING EXCHANGE RATE

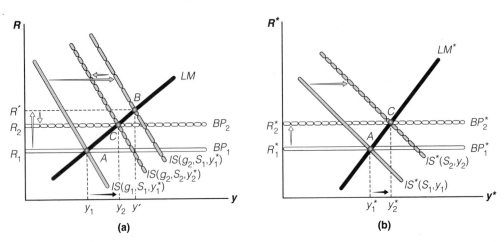

An increase in domestic government expenditures causes the domestic *IS* schedule to shift rightward in panel (*a*), causing a movement from point *A* to point *B*. The resulting decline in the domestic interest rates induces an inflow of financial resources from the foreign country that causes an appreciation of the domestic currency relative to the foreign currency. The fall in the equilibrium exchange rate from S_1 to S_2 induces a reduction in net expenditures on domestic goods and services, which causes the domestic *IS* schedule to shift leftward in panel (*a*), and it causes an increase in net spending on foreign goods and services, which causes the foreign *IS* schedule to shift rightward in panel (*b*). At points *C*, the equilibrium levels of real income in the two nations are higher than their initial values, so the domestic fiscal expansion has a locomotive effect on the foreign country.

government expenditures, at the initial equilibrium exchange rate, S_1, and the initial foreign real income level, y_1^*, is a rightward shift in the domestic *IS* schedule in panel (*a*), from $IS(g_1, S_1, y_1^*)$ to $IS(g_2, S_1, y_1^*)$. As a result, the equilibrium domestic nominal interest rate rises toward R' at point *B* in panel (*a*), which causes an inflow of financial resources from the foreign country. To acquire domestic financial assets, foreign residents would increase their demand for domestic currency. The domestic currency appreciates, and the foreign currency depreciates. Consequently, the equilibrium exchange rate declines from S_1 to a smaller value, S_2.

The domestic currency appreciation generates a reduction in net expenditures on domestic goods and services, causing the domestic *IS* schedule to shift back to the left. At the same time, the foreign currency depreciation leads to an increase in net spending on foreign goods and services, which induces a rightward shift in the foreign *IS* schedule. As equilibrium real income levels in both nations increase, so do exports, which tend to push both nations' *IS* schedules to the right. In panel (*a*), we assume that domestic exports respond more strongly to the domestic currency appreciation than to the rise in foreign real income, so that there is a net leftward shift of the domestic IS schedule, to $IS(g_2, S_2, y_1^*)$, which generates a final equilibrium at point C. In panel (*b*), we show the combined rightward shifts in the foreign IS schedule following the foreign currency depreciation and rise in domestic real income by the movement to $IS^*(S_2, y_2)$ at point C. The equilibrium foreign nominal interest rate rises toward convergence with the equilibrium domestic interest rate, with $R_2 = R_2^*$ at points C in both panels, as the BP schedules for both nations shift upward.

At points C in both panels of Figure 13–8, the equilibrium levels of real income in the two nations exceed their initial values. Thus, under a floating exchange rate and perfect capital mobility, a domestic fiscal expansion has a *locomotive effect* on the foreign country. An increase in domestic government spending results in expansions of real income levels in both nations.

The Effects of a Foreign Fiscal Expansion   The example in Figure 13–8 could have been altered to evaluate the effect of a foreign fiscal expansion. Again, a mirror image of effects takes place: a rightward shift of the domestic IS schedule, a leftward shift of the foreign IS schedule as the foreign currency's value appreciates, and a rightward shift of the domestic IS schedule as the domestic currency's value depreciates. Hence, we may conclude that increase in foreign government spending generates, with a floating exchange rate and perfectly mobile capital, increases in equilibrium nominal interest rates and real income levels in both nations.

In Chapter 12 you learned that if the domestic central bank maintains a fixed exchange rate, then a foreign fiscal expansion induces the domestic central bank to reduce the domestic money stock, which can lead to a *beggar-thy-neighbor effect*. That is, with a fixed exchange rate and perfect capital mobility, an increase in foreign government spending can cause a rise in foreign real income at the expense of a reduction in domestic real income. Figure 13–8 shows that the *opposite* outcome typically occurs in a two-country world with a floating exchange rate, in which a foreign fiscal expansion instead generates a *locomotive effect*. These differences in cross-country policy effects are summarized in Table 13–2.

TABLE 13–2   CROSS-COUNTRY EFFECTS OF ECONOMIC POLICY ACTIONS IN THE TWO-COUNTRY MODEL WITH PERFECT CAPITAL MOBILITY UNDER FIXED VERSUS FLOATING EXCHANGE RATES

EXCHANGE RATE SETTING	MONETARY POLICY EFFECT	FISCAL POLICY EFFECT
Fixed exchange rate	Locomotive effect	Beggar-thy-neighbor effect
Floating exchange rate	Beggar-thy-neighbor effect	Locomotive effect

Fiscal Stimulus by Trading Partners— Good News or Bad News?

It is the spring of 1998. The trade deficits of the United States and several Western European nations are widening. Japan's real GDP growth has slowed significantly. In a March meeting, finance ministers of the G7 nations gather in Washington to discuss appropriate policy steps to try to deal with the situation. Japan finds itself under intense pressure from other member nations to strengthen domestic demand. Both U.S. and European officials complain to the media that Japan has not proposed sufficiently strong "fiscal stimulus," such as tax cuts or increases in government expenditures.

At the same time, European Union leaders have just agreed to stringent restraints on the fiscal policies of nations that wish to become members of the proposed European Monetary Union. The key goal of the restrictions is to *prevent* nations from embarking on undesirably stimulative fiscal policies.

Why would European leaders join U.S. leaders in calling upon Japan to engage in fiscal stimulus in the midst of the recessionary pressures of early 1998 while working toward preventing such stimulus by other European nations? The answer to this question lies in the exchange rate policies pursued by the EU nations at the time. Because most EU nations planned to fix their exchange rates at the beginning of 1999, efforts by specific EU nations to spur real income growth through expansionary fiscal policies would, as discussed in Chapter 12, more than likely have generated beggar-thy-neighbor effects that would have placed downward pressure on equilibrium income levels in other EU nations. At the same time, however, EU nations' currency values *floated* relative to the value of the U.S. dollar and the Japanese yen. This meant that a Japanese fiscal expansion would have been likely to result in a locomotive effect, which would have benefited the EU economies.

Hence, fiscal stimulus by Japan, a trading partner whose exchange rate floated against EU exchange rates, was desirable for the EU. In contrast, fiscal stimulus on the part of other EU nations, trading partners whose currency values were mutually fixed, was not desirable for any nation within the EU. This was why EU nations joined the United States in calling for Japanese fiscal stimulus while agreeing internally to seek to restrain fiscal stimulus. For the EU in 1998, fiscal stimulus by specific trading partners would have been good news, but fiscal stimulus by other trading partners would have been bad news.

FOR CRITICAL ANALYSIS:
What are two key reasons that the United States desired for Japan to engage in fiscal stimulus in 1998?

FUNDAMENTAL ISSUE #3

In a two-country setting with a floating exchange rate, to what extent can policy actions in one nation influence economic activity in the other nation? With a floating exchange rate and interdependent economies, an expansionary monetary policy action expansion in one nation tends to raise equilibrium real income in that nation while reducing equilibrium real income in the other country. In contrast, an expansionary fiscal policy action in one nation tends to stimulate equilibrium real income levels in both countries.

FIXED VERSUS FLOATING EXCHANGE RATES

Which is preferable: a fixed exchange rate, or a floating exchange rate? If this choice were simple, then the wide variety of exchange-rate arrangements that we surveyed in Chapter 3 would not exist. In addition, individual nations would not have fixed their exchange rates during some periods in their history while permitting them to float during other intervals. If it were an easy matter to decide whether to fix exchange rates or to let exchange rates float, all nations would have made the same choice, and they would have maintained the same exchange-rate systems over the years.

This observation indicates that there must be pros and cons associated with these alternative exchange-rate arrangements. That is, nations must confront *economic trade-offs* when choosing between fixed and floating exchange rates. A choice of one type of exchange-rate system or the other must entail balancing the potential gains from that choice with the potential losses.

The fundamental trade-offs between fixed versus floating exchange rates cut across two dimensions: *economic efficiency* and *economic stability.* As you will learn, the most *efficient* exchange rate system may or may not be the one that attains greater stability of an economy's overall real income performance. This is what makes the choice of the "best" exchange-rate system potentially very difficult.

Efficiency Arguments for Fixed versus Floating Exchange Rates

ECONOMIC EFFICIENCY
The allocation of scarce resources at minimum cost.

Economic efficiency is the attainment of the least-cost allocation of scarce resources. Therefore, *the most efficient exchange-rate system is the set of exchange-rate arrangements that permits residents of a nation to direct resources to their alternative uses at minimum cost.* To evaluate whether a fixed exchange rate or a floating exchange rate may better contribute to economic efficiency, we need to contemplate the costs that a nation's residents face under the alternative systems.

Social Costs Stemming from Foreign Exchange Risks In Chapters 4 and 5, you learned about how currency exchanges in the forward exchange market and financial transactions involving various derivative securities may be used to hedge against foreign exchange risks. Such hedging activities entail expenditures of resources. For instance, banks must pay salaries to traders who possess the expertise necessary to plan hedging strategies and to conduct derivatives transactions on their behalf.

In addition, holding and trading derivatives exposes banks and other firms to risks. As we discussed in Chapter 5, these include *credit risks* associated with potential default by a contract counterparty, *market risks* arising from potential liquidity crunches or payment-system failures, and *operating risks* stemming from the potential for poor derivatives management. On the one hand, failure to control these risks can result in sizable losses, as noted in Chapter 5. On the other hand, establishing and maintaining management systems to monitor and contain derivatives risks can entail sizable resource expenses. Losses stemming from derivatives risks and the costs of limiting such losses constitute another set of costs associated with hedging activities.

Furthermore, governmental concerns about the potential for *systemic risks,* such as systemic payment-system risks discussed in Chapter 7, can lead to the establishment of elaborate systems of regulatory oversight of financial institutions. The costs incurred by governments in examining and supervising financial institutions represent further costs that stem from hedging activities in the face of foreign exchange risks..

Efficiency via a Fixed Exchange Rate?   Many observers argue that the efficiency trade-off between fixed and floating exchange rates favors adopting a system of fixed exchange rates. The basis of their argument is simple. If rates of exchange among currencies are fixed, then exchange rate volatility and the related risks by definition should be significantly muted, if not eliminated. As a result, there is little incentive to undertake foreign exchange hedging activities, and so the associated costs are minimized. A system of fixed exchange rates thereby would be most efficient.

Figure 13–9 shows how a trade-weighted index measure of the dollar's value, or effective exchange rate (see Chapter 2), has behaved since the concluding years of the Bretton Woods system of fixed exchange rates. As you can see, the dollar's overall exchange value has varied considerably during the past twenty-five years. Undoubtedly, exchange rate variability under floating exchange rates has spurred increased hedging activities and raised the related costs.

FIGURE 13–9   EXCHANGE RATE VOLATILITY UNDER FLOATING EXCHANGE RATES

Since the last years of the Bretton Woods system of fixed exchange rates, the dollar's value has exhibited several periods of variability. This variability was most pronounced during the 1980s.

SOURCE: Data from *1998 Economic Report of the President, Federal Reserve Bulletin* (various issues).

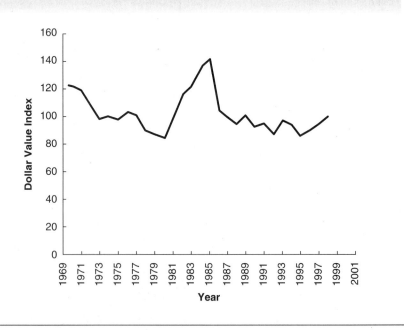

REALIGNMENT A change in an official exchange rate target.

ON THE WEB
Visit the Bank of Mexico at:
**http://www.banxico.org.
mx/html**

Does this mean that social costs resulting from foreign exchange risks are always lower under a system of fixed exchange rates? Not necessarily. "Fixed" exchange rates are never *permanently* fixed. In a system of fixed exchange rates, people face the possibility of exchange rate **realignments,** or changes in official target values for currency values. Consequently, there can be substantial risks arising from political instability or other factors that may influence governmental authorities who determine the "appropriate" exchange rates to fix.

Indeed, foreign holders of Mexican government bonds and firm stocks learned this lesson the hard way in 1994. As we noted in Chapter 3, until December of that year, the Mexican government sought to keep the value of the peso within an official "trading band"—or allowable range of exchange-rate variation—relative to the U.S. dollar. Mexico's objective in pursuing this policy was to keep its inflation rate more in line with U.S. inflation and thereby promote a stable environment for increased trade with the United States, Canada, and other nations. An indication of the apparent success of the Mexican policy was a November 18, 1994, headline in the *Wall Street Journal,* which read, "Mexico Posts Surprisingly Solid Growth, As Turnaround in Economy Advances." A figure accompanying the article, titled "On the Move," showed recent Mexican GDP growth of nearly 5 percent per year.

Nonetheless, between February and December of 1994, the peso's value declined by more than 10 percent relative to the dollar, to the bottom of the Mexican government's trading band. Then, on December 21, the Mexican government unexpectedly devalued the peso. In that single day, the peso's value relative to the dollar shot down by 12.7 percent. During the week following the devaluation, the peso's value fell by a total of more than 35 percent.

For Americans who held peso-denominated financial assets, this meant that within a single week's time they had lost more than *one-third* of the dollar value of their holdings. In early 1995 the Federal Reserve intervened in the dollar-peso exchange market to support the peso's value, and the U.S. Treasury made more than $40 billion loan guarantees to the Mexican government. These actions helped the peso's market value recover considerably. Consequently, for most foreign holders of Mexican bonds and stocks, the devaluation caused short-term "paper losses" that were not actually realized at maturity. Nevertheless, a number of non-Mexican bondholders and stock traders did experience significant losses as a result of the 1994 peso devaluation.

This example shows that a "fixed" exchange rate system is not necessarily risk-free. Indeed, the potential for unhedged losses arguably may be greater under a fixed exchange rate, as compared with a floating exchange rate system. This is because a fixed exchange rate can lull some holders of financial assets into a sense of complacency, leading them to take unhedged trading positions that yield large losses when unexpected devaluations occur.

We may conclude that a system of floating exchange rates increases the potential for day-to-day foreign exchange risks, requiring potentially significant expenditures of resources associated with hedging activities. This is an efficiency-related drawback of permitting the exchange rate to float. Under a system of fixed exchange rates, in contrast, the possibility of unanticipated governmental actions to alter exchange rate targets can pose risks of unhedged foreign exchange losses. Hence, we reach the following conclusion on the efficiency merits of fixed versus floating exchange rates:

> **There is a trade-off between the social costs incurred in hedging against foreign exchange risks in a system of floating exchange rates and the risk of experiencing unhedged losses as a result of unexpected devaluations in a system of fixed exchange rates.**

This means that a key criterion for evaluating the potential efficiency gain that a country might experience by switching from a floating exchange rate to a fixed exchange rate is the risk that the nation's government may face pressures to vary its exchange rate targets. As we shall discuss in Chapter 14, a fundamental implication is that the *credibility* of the government's commitment to a fixed exchange rate is likely to be crucial in determining whether a system of fixed exchange rates is more efficient than a floating exchange rate system.

FUNDAMENTAL ISSUE #4

What is the basic economic efficiency trade-off faced in choosing between fixed and floating exchange rates? On the one hand, members of society must incur large resource costs to hedge against foreign exchange market risks in a system of floating exchange rates. On the other hand, with fixed exchange rates there can be significant risks of unhedged losses stemming from unanticipated currency devaluations. Because these latter risks depend on the behavior of governments, a fixed exchange rate system is not necessarily preferable, on efficiency grounds, to a system of floating exchange rates.

Stability Arguments for Fixed versus Floating Exchange Rates

What should a country do if the fixed and floating exchange rate systems happen to produce the same level of economic efficiency? Can other factors tip the balance in favor of one system? Or, alternatively, if one exchange rate system is more efficient than the other, can other factors induce a nation to adopt the alternative system of exchange rates nonetheless?

One potentially important consideration in choosing between fixed and floating exchange rates is *economic stability*. There are a number of notions of "economic stability," because there are several variables that a nations' citizens may desire for their government to try to stabilize. These include real income, the inflation rate, and the unemployment rate. For now we shall focus on real income stability under fixed versus floating exchange rates. It turns out that the implications for real income stability under the two exchange rate systems are fundamentally the same, even if inflation and unemployment stability also are key policy goals, as we shall explain in Chapter 14. Hence, we can identify the key aspects of the *stability trade-off* entailed in the choice of a fixed or floating exchange rate by concentrating on the single policy goal of stable real income.

Autonomous Expenditure Volatility and Fixed versus Floating Exchange Rates   One possible source of real income instability that any nation faces is variability in aggregate autonomous expenditures. Recall from Chapter 11 that variations in autonomous saving, import spending, investment, government spending, net taxes, or export spending cause changes in the equilibrium real income level, thereby resulting in changes in the position of the *IS* schedule. For example, consider the effect of a significant decline in real income in the rest of the world, denoted by y^* in Figure 13–10, from an initial level of y_1^* to a lower level of y_2^*. With less real income to allocate to purchases of domestic goods, foreign residents reduce their expenditures on domestic exports. This causes aggregate autonomous expenditures on domestic goods and services to decline, so the *IS* schedule shifts leftward, from $IS(y_1^*)$ to $IS(y_2^*)$, causing a movement along the *LM* schedule from point *A* to point *B*. As a result, equilibrium *domestic* real income declines, from y_1 to y_2. Volatility in real income in the rest of the world results in domestic income instability, holding all other factors unchanged.

Does the choice between fixed and floating exchange rates have any bearing on domestic real income stability in the face of a decline in real income

---

FIGURE 13–10   THE EFFECTS OF A DECLINE IN AGGREGATE AUTONOMOUS EXPENDITURES

A decline in real income in the rest of the world, from y_1^* to y_2^*, causes foreign residents to reduce their expenditures on domestic exports, resulting in a fall in domestic aggregate autonomous expenditures and a leftward shift in the *IS* schedule. Consequently, equilibrium domestic real income declines from y_1 at point *A* to y_2 at point *B*, which indicates that volatility in real income in the rest of the world results in domestic real income instability.

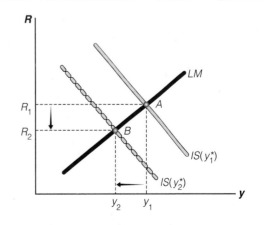

FIGURE 13–11   REAL INCOME STABILITY IN THE FACE OF A DECLINE IN AGGREGATE AUTONOMOUS EXPENDITURES
WITH PERFECT CAPITAL MOBILITY

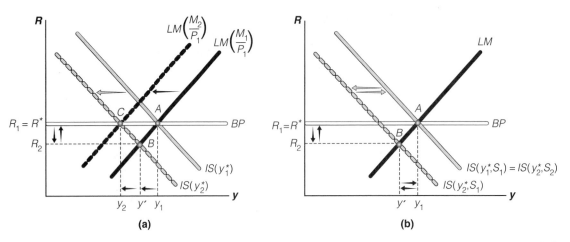

Panel (*a*) shows that a fall in foreign real income with a fixed exchange rate causes the domestic *IS* schedule to shift leftward, inducing a movement from point *A* to point *B*. The resulting domestic balance-of-payments deficit places downward pressure on the value of the nation's currency. To keep the exchange rate fixed, the central bank must reduce the money stock and shift the *LM* schedule leftward. This monetary policy response yields a final equilibrium at point *C* in panel (*a*) and reinforces the real income effect of the fall in foreign real income. Panel (*b*) indicates that under a floating exchange rate, the fall in foreign real income that induces a movement to point *B* causes the equilibrium exchange rate to rise from S_1 to S_2, which induces a rise in net export spending and a rightward shift in the *IS* schedule. Hence, real income is more stable under a floating exchange rate as compared with a fixed exchange rate.

abroad? The answer to this question is yes, as Figure 13–11 illustrates for the case of a small open economy with perfect capital mobility. We draw Figure 13–11 under the assumption that there is no expected exchange rate depreciation, in which case uncovered interest parity yields equality between the domestic nominal interest rate, R_1, and the nominal interest rate in the rest of the world, R^*. Hence, the *BP* schedule is horizontal at this world interest rate.

Panel (*a*) of the figure displays the effect on equilibrium domestic real income of a fall in foreign real income with a fixed exchange rate. As in Figure 13–10, a decline in real income in the rest of the world causes the domestic *IS* schedule to shift leftward, from $IS(y_1^*)$ to $IS(y_2^*)$, along the *LM* schedule, from point *A* to point *B*. At point *B*, however, the equilibrium domestic interest rate, R_2, lies below the world interest rate, R^*. This stimulates capital outflows, thereby resulting in a domestic balance of payments deficit and downward pressure on the value of the nation's currency. As we discussed in Chapter 12, to keep the exchange rate fixed, the central bank must respond by reducing the quantity of money. This causes the *LM* schedule to shift to the left, from $LM(M_1)$ to $LM(M_2)$. The final equilibrium real income level is equal to y_3, at point C in panel (*a*). Under a fixed exchange rate, therefore, a contraction in the money stock required to maintain a fixed exchange rate *reinforces* a decline in domestic real income following a fall in foreign real income.

Panel (*b*) of Figure 13–11 contrasts this result with what happens under a floating exchange rate. As before, a decline in real income in the rest of the world causes the *IS* schedule to shift leftward. This takes place at the *initial equilibrium exchange rate*, denoted S_1, so we label the new *IS* schedule as $IS(y_2^*, S_1)$. At the new *IS–LM* equilibrium point B that results from this shift, there again is a balance-of-payments deficit. This causes the market value of the domestic currency to decline, so the exchange rate rises to a higher value, S_2. The depreciation in the domestic currency spurs net export spending, which causes the *IS* schedule to shift back to its original position, now labeled $IS(y_2^*, S_2)$, at point A. At this point, the nation reattains balance-of-payments equilibrium, and the equilibrium level of domestic real income once again is equal to y_1, its initial value. By permitting the exchange rate to float, a nation's policymakers *automatically* ensure real income stability in the face of a decline in real income in the rest of the world. Real income is more stable, therefore, under a floating exchange rate, as compared with a fixed exchange rate.

Indeed, we would have obtained this same basic conclusion if we had considered *any* factor that causes a decline in aggregate autonomous expenditures and if we had evaluated a situation of imperfect capital mobility. Equilibrium real income is more stable in the face of variations in aggregate autonomous expenditures under a floating exchange rate.

Financial Volatility and Fixed versus Floating Exchange Rates This conclusion does not necessarily mean that a floating exchange rate always promotes real income stability, however. To see why, let's begin by considering another possible source of real income instability, which is volatility in the financial sector of the economy.

For example, suppose that people suddenly lose confidence in long-term prospects in the bond market. This induces them to shift much of their wealth from bonds to holdings of money. Thus, the demand for real money balances increases at any given level of real income. As shown in panel (*a*) of Figure 13–12, at an initial real income level of y_1, this causes a rightward shift in the demand schedule for real money balances, from $m_1^d(y_1)$ to $m_2^d(y_1)$. The result is a rise in the equilibrium interest rate, from R_1 at point A to R' at point B, and, as shown in panel (*b*), an upward shift in the *LM* schedule at the initial income level y_1, from $LM_1(M_1/P_1)$ at point A to $LM_2(M_1/P_1)$ at point B. Thus, the rise in the demand for money causes the *LM* schedule to shift, even though the quantity of real money balances does not change. The rise in the interest rate causes a decline in desired investment, as reflected by an upward movement along the *IS* schedule in panel (*b*), so equilibrium real income declines from y_1 to y_2. At the final *IS–LM* equilibrium point C, therefore, real income is lower than before. The decline in real income causes the demand for real money balances to fall somewhat, so the equilibrium interest rate falls back to R_2 at point C in panel (*a*).

FIGURE 13–12   THE EFFECTS OF A RISE IN THE DEMAND FOR REAL MONEY BALANCES

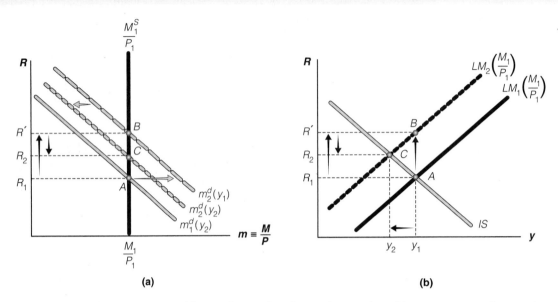

(a)

(b)

A rise in the demand for money caused by any factor other than an increase in real income causes an increase in the equilibrium nominal interest rate, from R_1 at point A in panel (*a*) to R' at point B. At the initial level of real income, new real income–interest rate combination that maintains money-market equilibrium, given by point B in panel (*b*), lies above the initial real income–interest rate combination given by point A. Thus, an increase in the demand for real money balances not stemming from a rise in real income generates an upward and leftward shift in the LM schedule. This causes equilibrium real income to decline to y_2 in panel (*b*), which induces a leftward shift in the money demand schedule in panel (*a*). The net effect is a rise in the equilibrium interest rate and a decline in equilibrium real income.

Figure 13–12 indicates that variations in the demand for real money balances can lead to real income instability. Now let's consider how the extent of such instability can depend on the choice between fixed versus floating exchange rates. Figure 13–13 provides a comparison between the real income effects of money demand variations for the two exchange rate systems, again under the assumption of a small open economy with perfect capital mobility. Panel (a) shows the effect of a rise in the demand for real money balances under a fixed exchange rate. This causes the LM schedule to shift to the left, from $LM_1(M_1/P_1)$ to $LM_2(M_1/P_1)$, which tends to induce a rise in the equilibrium domestic interest rate, from R_1 at point A toward R_2 at point B.

Because R_2 exceeds the world interest rate, R^*, at point B, the domestic economy experiences a capital inflow that contributes to a balance-of-payments surplus. As a result, there is upward pressure on the value of the domestic currency

FIGURE 13–13 **REAL INCOME STABILITY IN THE FACE OF A RISE IN THE DEMAND FOR REAL MONEY BALANCES WITH PERFECT CAPITAL MOBILITY**

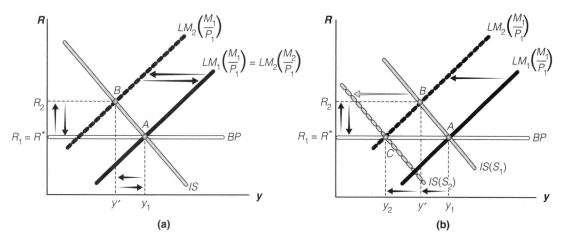

In panel (*a*), a rise in the demand for real money balances under a fixed exchange rate causes the *LM* schedule to shift leftward, inducing a movement from point *A* to point *B*. The resulting rise in the domestic interest rate causes a capital inflow. To keep the exchange rate fixed, the domestic central bank must purchase foreign assets, which leads to a rise in the domestic money stock and causes the *LM* schedule to shift back to the right. In panel (*b*), the movement to point *B* caused by a rise in the demand for real money balances with a floating exchange rate leads to a decline in the equilibrium exchange rate from S_1 to S_2. As a result, there is decline in net export expenditures in the domestic economy that causes the *IS* schedule to shift leftward to the final equilibrium point *C*. At this point, real income is below the initial equilibrium income level, so real income is less stable in the face of money demand variations under a floating exchange rate.

in foreign exchange markets. To keep the exchange rate fixed, the domestic central bank must purchase foreign-currency-denominated assets. If the domestic central bank conducts nonsterilized interventions, this action generates a rise in the domestic money stock, which shifts the *LM* schedule back to the right in panel (*a*), to $LM_2(M_2/P_2)$ at point *A*. By maintaining a fixed exchange rate, therefore, the central bank *automatically* offsets the real income effect of a rise in money demand. Equilibrium real income is more stable in the face of variations in the demand for real money balances under a fixed exchange rate.

Panel (*b*) of Figure 13–13 shows how equilibrium real income responds to a rise in the demand for real money balances in a system of floating exchange rates. The increase in money demand shifts the *LM* schedule leftward, from $LM_1(M_1/P_1)$ to $LM_2(M_1/P_1)$. This places upward pressure on the domestic interest rate, which tends to rise from R_1 at point *A* toward R_2 at point *B*. The result is an inflow of capital and a balance-of-payments surplus. In a floating exchange rate system, this causes the domestic currency to appreciate, so the equilibrium exchange rate declines from an initial value, S_1, to a lower level, S_2.

Consequently, the domestic price of goods imported from abroad falls, and the foreign price of domestic exports rises, thereby inducing a decline in net export expenditures in the domestic economy. This reduces aggregate desired expenditures on domestic goods and services, which causes the *IS* schedule to shift leftward in panel (*b*), from $IS(S_1)$ to $IS(S_2)$. At the final equilibrium point *C*, real income is equal to y_3, which unambiguously is less than the initial equilibrium income level y_1. By adopting a system of floating exchange rates, a nation's policymakers thereby expose real income to *greater* instability as a result of money demand variations.

The Stability Trade-Off These examples illustrate a fundamental *stability trade-off* that nations face when they choose between adopting fixed or floating exchange rates:

1. **Variations in aggregate desired expenditures lead to real income instability under a fixed exchange rate. Permitting the exchange rate to float automatically reduces the real income effects of volatility in desired expenditures.**
2. **Variations in the demand for real money balances contribute to real income instability under a floating exchange rate. Fixing the exchange rate automatically reduces the real income effects of volatility in money demand.**

This stability trade-off indicates that, holding economic efficiency criteria constant, a nation should opt for a fixed exchange rate if the main source of real income instability arises from financial volatility that causes variations in the demand for real money balances. In contrast, in a nation in which there is considerable volatility in desired expenditures, a system of floating exchange rates is preferable.

Clearly, it is possible that a system of floating exchange rates might be preferable on the grounds of stability, yet be less desirable than a system of fixed exchange rates from the perspective of economic efficiency. Alternatively, maintaining a fixed exchange rate could, under some circumstances, be the better policy choice from the standpoint of achieving greater real income stability, but adopting a system of floating exchange rates might lead to a higher level of overall economic efficiency. In either of these situations, a nation would have to make a difficult choice between minimizing real income instability and maximizing economic efficiency.

Monetary Policy Autonomy and Fixed versus Floating Exchange Rates

Our analyses of economic policymaking in Chapter 12 and in this chapter indicate that there is at least one other factor that can influence a nation's choice to fix its exchange rates or to allow them to float in foreign exchange

MONETARY POLICY AUTONOMY
The capability of a central bank to engage in monetary policy actions independent of the actions of other central banks.

ON THE WEB
Visit the Bank of Thailand at:
http://www.bot.or.th/

markets. This is the nation's desire for **monetary policy autonomy,** or the extent to which monetary policies can exert independent effects on overall economic performance.

As you learned in Chapter 12, when nations' economies are interdependent, the choice between a system of fixed or floating exchange rates affects the ability of its central bank to conduct independent policy actions to influence its own nation's economic performance. Under a fixed exchange rate, a central bank's actions to keep the value of its nation's currency unchanged preclude the potential for any efforts to vary the quantity of money for purposes of domestic real income stabilization. In a sense, adopting a fixed exchange rate in a world of interdependent economies makes a nation's monetary policy a "slave" to events in other nations (see "Policy Notebook: Thailand's Penalty for Sticking to Its Guns").

POLICY NOTEBOOK
Thailand's Penalty for Sticking to Its Guns

For years, the Bank of Thailand pegged the value of Thailand's currency, the baht, to a basket of currencies dominated by the U.S. dollar, which observers estimate constitutes about 80 percent of the currency basket. This policy paid big dividends for Thailand in the late 1980s and early 1990s. As the dollar's value declined in foreign exchange markets, the baht's value fell roughly in step. As a result, Thai exports rose dramatically, increasing by more than 20 percent in 1995 alone. As Thailand's export industries boomed, so did its export-driven economy.

In 1996 and 1997, however, the tables turned, as the country began to pay a price for its exchange-rate-pegging policies. The value of the U.S. dollar rose in world markets, and the Bank of Thailand intervened to keep the baht's value unchanged against its dollar-dominated currency basket. On a single day in 1997, the Bank of Thailand spent about $500 million of its dollar reserves buying baht to keep the baht's value from falling below the Bank's target.

Naturally, the baht's value relative to most other world currencies rose along with the dollar's. Shortly afterward, Thai exports declined, and Thailand's annual rate of GDP growth fell from over 8 percent to just over 4 percent. Bangkok stock prices dropped precipitously, and private debt to foreigners soared. By September of 1997, the Bank of Thailand had given up its efforts to peg the value of the baht to the value of the dollar. Ultimately the value of the baht had declined by over 35 percent relative to the dollar. This helped to set off a series of currency declines throughout Southeast Asia in the fall of 1997.

FOR CRITICAL ANALYSIS:
Many Thai residents called on the Bank of Thailand to devalue the baht long before the fall of 1997. Which residents would have stood to gain the most from such a devaluation?

In contrast, earlier in this chapter we noted in our two-economy analysis of a floating exchange rate system that a central bank's policy actions can influence its nation's equilibrium real income level. Hence, adopting a system of floating exchange rates gives a nation's central bank policy autonomy that it does not possess under a system of fixed exchange rates.

As you can see, nations must truly take many considerations into account when they determine the exchange rate policies that are best for their own interests. Economic efficiency trade-offs, economic stability trade-offs, and the issue of monetary policy autonomy all can influence a country's final decision. In the next chapter we will show how one more factor can play a role in affecting this decision. This is the extent to which the price level is flexible. Policymakers must also consider variations in the price level and inflation when they choose the exchange rate systems for their nations.

FUNDAMENTAL ISSUE #5

How does the choice between fixed and floating exchange rates depend in part on its implications for economic stability and monetary policy autonomy? With fixed exchange rates, the effects of variability in aggregate autonomous expenditures on a nation's output of goods and services causes real income instability, whereas flexibility of exchange rates automatically mutes such instability in a system of floating exchange rates. With floating exchange rates, money demand volatility can make a nation's real income level more unstable, whereas maintaining fixed exchange rates automatically offsets the extent to which changes in the demand for real money balances influence equilibrium real income. Hence, a floating exchange rate system is preferable to a system of fixed exchange rates if the variability of aggregate autonomous expenditures is significantly larger than the volatility of money demand. Another consideration favoring a system of floating exchange rates is that central banks can engage in independent policy actions when exchange rates float. Under a system of fixed exchange rates, central banks must sacrifice their policy autonomy.

CHAPTER SUMMARY

1. **How Monetary and Fiscal Policy Actions Affect a Nation's Real Income under Floating Exchange Rates:** An increase in the amount of money in circulation induces a balance of payments deficit. This causes a depreciation of a nation's currency that stimulates net export expenditures and raise equilibrium real income. The effects of fiscal policy actions on a nation's balance of payments and the value of its currency depend on the extent to which a nation's borders are open to flows of financial resources. Under most circumstances, an expansionary fiscal policy action induces a short-run increase in a nation's real income level. The amount of the resulting increase in real income tends to fall as the degree of capital mobility increases.

2. **Perfect Capital Mobility and the Relative Effectiveness of Monetary and Fiscal Policy Actions in a Small Open Economy that Permits its Exchange Rates to Float:** With perfect capital mobility and floating exchange rates, the monetary policy actions exert their greatest possible effects on equilibrium real income in a small open economy. In contrast, fiscal policy actions have no short-run real income effects under floating exchange rates and perfect capital mobility.

3. **The Effects of Policy Actions in One Nation on the Economic Activity in the Other Nation with a Floating Exchange Rate:** With a floating exchange rate and interdependent economies, an expansionary monetary policy expansion in one nation tends to raise equilibrium real income in that nation while reducing equilibrium real income in the other country. In contrast, an expansionary fiscal policy expansion in one nation tends to stimulate equilibrium real income levels in both countries.

4. **The Basic Economic Efficiency Trade-Off Faced in Choosing between Fixed and Floating Exchange Rates:** To shield themselves against risks of loss caused by exchange rate volatility that can arise with floating exchange rates, individuals and businesses must allocate significant resources to hedging activities. By reducing the variability of exchange rates, a system of fixed exchange rates largely eliminates the incentive to engage in such activities, thereby yielding a potential resource saving. Nevertheless, adopting fixed exchange rates exposes individuals and firms to the possibility of incurring sizable unhedged losses as a result of unexpected devaluations.

5. **Economic Stability, Monetary Policy Autonomy, and the Choice between Fixed and Floating Exchange Rates:** Changes in aggregate autonomous expenditures lead to real income instability in a system of fixed exchange rates but do not affect the level of real income under floating exchange rates. Variations in the demand for real money balances cause real income level instability in a system of floating exchange rates but do not affect the level of real income under fixed exchange

rates. Therefore, a system of floating exchange rates promotes greater real income stability if the variability of aggregate autonomous expenditures is sizable relative to the volatility of money demand. A floating exchange rate also allows central banks to conduct independent monetary policies, whereas central banks lose policy autonomy under fixed exchange rates.

QUESTIONS AND PROBLEMS

1. Explain, in your own words, why a currency depreciation shifts the *BP* schedule rightward.

2. Suppose that a national government adopts, and is able to enforce, a system of capital controls that permits absolutely no flows of financial resources across its borders, so that the *BP* schedule is vertical. Explain what effects an expansionary fiscal policy action would have on equilibrium real income in such an environment.

3. In the early 1990s, as the United States struggled to emerge from a short but sharp real income contraction, its government prevailed upon the Japanese government to increase government spending and cut taxes. Assuming that capital mobility between the United States and Japan is nearly perfect and that the dollar-yen exchange rate floats in the foreign exchange market, would this request appear to have been consistent with U.S. interests? Justify your answer.

4. Referring back to the situation described in question 3, what *monetary policy* actions would the U.S. government have preferred the Japanese government to pursue in the early 1990s? Explain your reasoning.

5. Since the late 1950s, most nations of Western Europe have sought to maintain a system of nearly fixed exchange rates, on the grounds that such a system would promote greater efficiency by limiting the need to hedge against foreign exchange risks that would arise under floating exchange rates. Since 1979, Western European nations have realigned their exchange rates well over a dozen times. Does this fact strengthen or weaken the case for fixed exchange rates in Western Europe? Explain.

6. Consider a nation in which the demand for money is relatively stable. Export and import expenditures have fluctuated considerably in recent years, however, and political instability has led to considerable variation in government spending. If the country's primary goal is real income stability, should it adopt a system of fixed or floating exchange rates? Justify your answer.

ON-LINE APPLICATION

Internet URL: http://www.bof.fi

Title: Bank of Finland

Navigation: The above address connects you with the home page for the Bank of Finland. Click on *in English*.

Application: To take a look at Finnish economic data, click on *Statistics,* and answer the following questions:

1. Click on *Monetary Aggregates,* and then click on the box labeled *Money Supply* M_1. Then click on *Time Series.* Use the data for the M_1 measure of the Finnish money stock to calculate rates of money growth in Finland during recent months.

2. Go back to *Statistics,* and click on *Exchange Rates.* Then click on the box labeled *FIM Against USO and DEM, daily.* Use the data for the U.S. dollar exchange rate of the Finnish currency, the *markka,* to calculate rates of Finnish currency depreciation during recent months. Does there appear to be a relationship between the M_1 money growth rate and the rate of depreciation of the *markka?* Does this square with theory?

REFERENCES AND RECOMMENDED READINGS

Argy, Victor. *International Macroeconomics.* London: Routledge, 1994.

Bartolini, Leonardo, and Gordon M. Bodnar. "Are Exchange Rates Excessively Volatile? And What Does 'Excessively Volatile' Mean, Anyway?" *International Monetary Fund Staff Papers,* 43 (March 1996): 72–96.

DeGrauwe, Paul. *International Money,* 2nd Edition. Oxford: Oxford University Press, 1996.

Frenkel, Jacob, and Razin, Assaf. "The Mundell-Fleming Model a Quarter Century Later." *International Monetary Fund Staff Papers,* 34 (1987): 567–620.

Heffernan, Shelagh, and Peter Sinclair. *Modern International Economics.* Oxford: Blackwell, 1990.

McCallum, Bennett T. *International Monetary Economics.* Oxford: Oxford University Press, 1996.

McDermott, C. John, and Robert F. Wescott. "An Empirical Analysis of Fiscal Adjustments." *International Monetary Fund Staff Papers,* 43 (December 1996): 725–753.

14

The Price Level, Real Output, and Economic Policymaking

FUNDAMENTAL ISSUES

1. What is the aggregate demand schedule?

2. What factors determine the extent to which changes in the quantity of money can influence aggregate demand in an open economy?

3. What factors determine the extent to which fiscal policy actions can influence aggregate demand in an open economy?

4. What is the aggregate supply schedule?

5. How are a nation's price level and volume of real output determined, and how might economic policymakers influence inflation and real output?

6. Why does the rational expectations hypothesis indicate that economic policies may have limited real output effects and that the credibility of policymakers is important?

Germany's unemployment rate had just reached its highest level in sixty-four years: 12.2 percent. The value of the German deutsche mark had fallen to a seven-year low against the U.S. dollar, and the German government was facing significant obstacles to its efforts to get its budget under control in anticipation of the proposed 1999 European currency union. In the midst of these economic difficulties, it came time for Germany's constitutionally sanctioned "wage-setting" cartel of major unions and corporations to meet to determine the base wages for a sizable portion of the German labor force. Prior to the cartel's meeting, the German chancellor pleaded with German unions "to go easy for a while, or even forgo a real wage increase."

Nevertheless, the big union–corporation group agreed to maintain high wages. Shortly afterward, one of Germany's largest engineering corporations announced plans to cut employment by 10,000 workers, or over a third of its work force, and a major German electrical company cut 1,200 positions at its medical-technology division. Four other big firms followed suit, slashing their payrolls by a combined 10,000 workers.

Market analysts around the world immediately predicted even higher German unemployment and more pressures on the German central bank, the Deutsche Bundesbank, to keep inflation down in light of the wage increases. In addition, they reduced their already low estimates for the growth of German real GDP, which already had been nearly flat for several years.

Why would an overall German wage increase have such significant adverse effects on unemployment rates, output growth, and inflation? In previous chapters, we have focused on how equilibrium real income and the equilibrium nominal interest rate are determined in open economies. To concentrate on how varying degrees of capital mobility affect the transmission of policy actions, we also have abstracted from the important role that the price level plays in this process. Consequently, at this point we have not developed a complete framework for understanding the factors that affect *real* economic variables, such as aggregate labor employment. Nor have we explored theories of how nominal GDP is split between its price level and real GDP components.

Our objectives in this chapter are to address these issues. To do so, we shall need to explain the determination of the price level in an open economy, how variations in the price level influence the transmission of monetary and fiscal policies, and ways in which the actions of policymakers themselves can affect a nation's price level and its rate of change, the inflation rate. Furthermore, we shall seek to explain the relationships between the price level and real output and between the inflation rate and unemployment rate.

AGGREGATE DEMAND

Any theory of price level determination must begin with a theory of the total demand for all goods and services produced within a nation. Economists refer to this as the *aggregate demand for real output.* As you will now learn, in the preceding three chapters we have laid all the groundwork for understanding the factors that determine aggregate demand.

The Aggregate Demand Schedule

You first learned in Chapter 11 that the point of intersection of the *IS* schedule and the *LM* schedule is a single real income–nominal interest rate combination at which aggregate desired expenditures equal real income *and* at which the market for real money balances is in equilibrium. Subsequently, you learned how variations in aggregate autonomous expenditures can affect the equilibrium real income level and nominal interest rate. In addition, you saw how changes in the nominal money stock and the demand for real money balances can influence these variables.

These factors, it turns out, are also the fundamental determinants of the aggregate demand for a nation's output of goods and services. The reason is that the *IS–LM* framework provides the underpinning for the theory of aggregate demand.

To see why this is so, consider Figure 14–1. Panel (*a*) displays the *IS–LM* diagram. The initial point at which the *IS* and *LM* schedules cross is point *A*. The position of the *LM* schedule, as we discussed in Chapter 11, depends on the quantity of *real money balances.* At point *A*, the nominal money stock is M_1 and the value of the GDP deflator is P_1. Consequently, the quantity of real money balances is equal to M_1/P_1, and the *LM* schedule is $LM(M_1/P_1)$.

Now consider what happens following a rise in the price level from P_1 to a higher level, P_2. This causes real money balances to decline, from M_1/P_1 to M_1/P_2. The effect of such a decline in real money balances on the position of the *LM* schedule is the same as if the nominal money stock had declined with an unchanged price level, which causes the *LM* schedule to shift upward and to the left. Thus, as shown in panel (*a*) of Figure 14–1, a rise in the price level causes a shift in the *LM* schedule $LM(M_1/P_2)$, yielding a new *IS–LM* equilibrium point *B*. The decline in the supply of real money balances resulting from the price level increase causes the equilibrium nominal interest rate to rise. This increase in the interest rate causes desired investment spending to decline. Hence, there is a fall in aggregate desired expenditures, which generates a fall in equilibrium real income. Consequently, at point *B* the equilibrium nominal interest rate is higher, as compared with the initial point *A*, at R_1, and the equilibrium real income level is lower, at y_2.

Panel (*b*) of the figure shows the relationship between equilibrium real income and the price level implied by panel (*a*). Both real income–price level combinations in panel (*a*), y_1 and P_1 at point *A* and y_2 and P_2 at point *B*, are consistent with *IS–LM* equilibrium. Therefore, *both* of these real income–price

FIGURE 14–1   DERIVING THE AGGREGATE DEMAND SCHEDULE

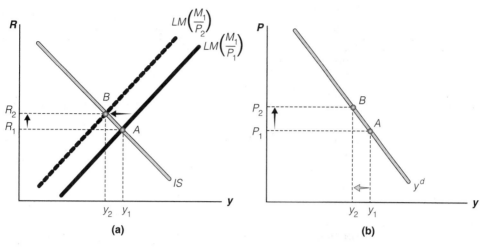

Panel (*a*) shows that a rise in the price level induces an increase in the equilibrium nominal interest rate through the real balance effect, as the *LM* schedule shifts back along the *IS* schedule from point *A* to point *B*. Because equilibrium real income falls as the price level increases, the aggregate demand schedule containing real income–price level combinations *A* and *B* slopes downward in panel (*b*).

AGGREGATE DEMAND SCHEDULE
Combinations of real income
and the price level that
maintain *IS–LM* equilibrium
and thereby ensure that real
income is equal to aggregate
desired expenditures and that
the market for real money
balances is in equilibrium.

level combinations maintain equilibrium real income *and* equilibrium in the market for real money balances. The complete set of real income–price level combinations consistent with *IS–LM* equilibrium, which includes points *A* and *B*, is the **aggregate demand schedule,** denoted y^d. This schedule, by definition, is the set of combinations of real income and the price level that are consistent with *IS–LM* equilibrium, which means that these combinations simultaneously maintain an equality of aggregate desired expenditures and real income *and* money market equilibrium.

FUNDAMENTAL ISSUE #1

What is the aggregate demand schedule? The aggregate demand schedule consists of real income–price level combinations that achieve equality of real income and aggregate desired expenditures while at the same time maintaining equilibrium in the market for real money balances. Consequently, every point along an aggregate demand schedule corresponds to a point of *IS–LM* equilibrium.

Factors that Determine the Position of the Aggregate Demand Schedule in an Open Economy

In Figure 14–1, we derived the aggregate demand schedule by considering the effect on equilibrium real income following an increase in the price level, *holding all other factors unchanged*. This means that variations in other factors that influence the positions of the *IS* or *LM* schedules can alter the position of the aggregate demand schedule. Thus, changes in aggregate autonomous expenditures, which affect the position of the *IS* schedule, and variations in the nominal money stock, which influence the position of the *LM* schedule, can cause the aggregate demand schedule to shift. Via these channels, therefore, fiscal and monetary policy actions can influence the aggregate demand schedule's position.

As you learned in Chapters 12 and 13, however, the degree of capital mobility conditions the extent to which monetary and fiscal policy actions can affect equilibrium real income. In addition, the real income effects of monetary and fiscal policies vary, depending on whether a nation adopts fixed or floating exchange rates. It follows that the extent to which aggregate demand responds to monetary or fiscal policy actions in an open economy depends on the degree of capital mobility and the system of exchange rates that is in place.

Monetary Policy and Aggregate Demand   Before we explore ways in which capital mobility and exchange rate flexibility condition the effects of monetary policy actions on aggregate demand, let's first focus on the basic linkage between changes in the quantity of money and the aggregate demand schedule. To do this, let's initially consider a *closed economy* in which the issues of capital mobility and exchange rate flexibility are irrelevant.

In a closed economy, if a nation's central bank increases the nominal quantity of money supplied from M_1 to a larger amount M_2, then, as shown in panel (*a*) of Figure 14–2, at a given price level such as P_1, the result is a downward and rightward shift in the *LM* schedule from $LM(M_1/P_1)$ to $LM(M_2/P_1)$. Thus, there is a movement from an initial *IS–LM* equilibrium at point *A* to a new equilibrium at point *B*. The increase in the nominal money stock reduces the equilibrium nominal interest rate, from R_1 to R_2, and induces a rise in equilibrium real income, from y_1 to y_2.

As you can see in panel (*b*), the real income–price level combination y_2 and P_2 lies to the right of the original aggregate demand schedule, denoted as $y^d(M_1)$. Nevertheless, this new point *B* in panel (*b*) is consistent with the *IS–LM* equilibrium at point *B* in panel (*a*). By definition, the aggregate demand schedule is a set of real income–price level combinations that maintain *IS–LM* equilibrium, so point *B* in panel (*b*) is on a *new* aggregate demand schedule. Consequently, a rise in the nominal quantity of money shifts the aggregate demand schedule to the right. That is:

FIGURE 14-2   THE EFFECT OF AN INCREASE IN THE MONEY STOCK ON AGGREGATE DEMAND IN A CLOSED ECONOMY

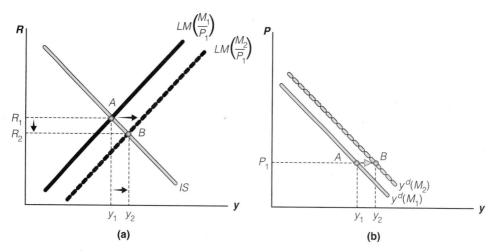

With an unchanged price level, an increase in the nominal quantity of money in circulation causes an increase in the amount of real money balances and shifts the *LM* schedule downward and to the right along the *IS* schedule from point *A* to point *B* in panel (*a*). Because the resulting real income level at point *B* in panel (*b*) corresponds to the same price level, this new equilibrium real income–price level combination lies on a new aggregate demand schedule to the right of the real income–price level combination at point *A* on the original aggregate demand schedule. Thus, an increase in the nominal money stock causes an increase in aggregate demand.

> **In a closed economy, a rise in the nominal money stock always causes an increase in aggregate demand.**

Now that you see how monetary policy actions affect aggregate demand in a closed economy, let's turn our attention to the effects of central bank policies in open economies.

Monetary Policy and Aggregate Demand in an Open Economy with a Fixed Exchange Rate   In Chapters 12 and 13, you learned that the effects of monetary policy actions on equilibrium real income in an open economy depend on whether exchange rates are fixed or flexible and on the degree of capital mobility. Thus, you might expect that the effects of monetary policy actions on aggregate demand should depend on these same factors.

Figure 14–3 illustrates how monetary policy actions might—or might not—affect the position of the aggregate demand schedule in a system of fixed exchange rates. The figure displays three pairs of diagrams in panels (*a*), (*b*),

FIGURE 14–3 **THE EFFECT OF AN INCREASE IN THE MONEY STOCK ON AGGREGATE DEMAND IN AN OPEN ECONOMY WITH A FIXED EXCHANGE RATE**

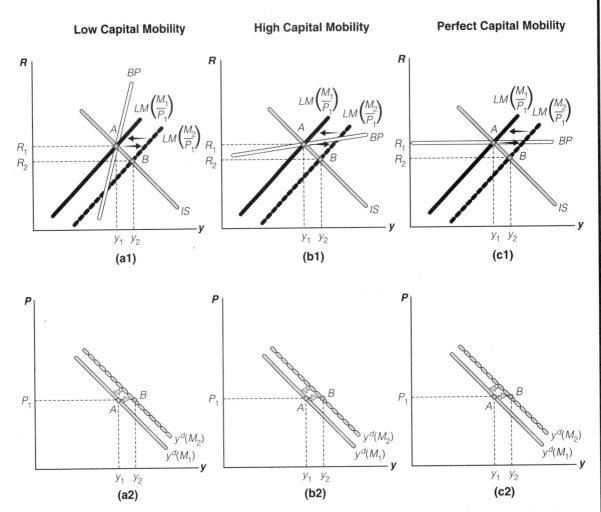

In all three pairs of panels, an increase in the money stock causes the *LM* schedule to shift downward and to the right, resulting in a movement from point *A* to point *B*. The induced increase in real income causes import spending to rise, and the induced decline in the nominal interest rate results in capital outflows, and these effects together lead to a balance-of-payments deficit. If the central bank sterilizes its interventions to maintain a fixed exchange rate, then the money stock remains at its higher level, M_2, and the aggregate demand schedule shifts fully to the position $y^d(M_2)$. With unsterilized interventions, however, the money stock falls back toward its original level of M_1 as the central bank's foreign exchange reserves decline. Consequently, the aggregate demand ultimately returns to its original position, $y^d(M_1)$, in diagram (*a2*), as the *LM* schedule shifts back to its initial position.

and (*c*). Each pair consists of *IS–LM–BP* diagrams above corresponding aggregate demand schedules. Panel (*a*) displays a situation of low capital mobility and a relatively steep *BP* schedule, while panel (*b*) shows a situation of high capital mobility and a more shallow *BP* schedule. Finally, panel (*c*) illustrates an environment in which there is perfect capital mobility, so that the *BP* schedule is horizontal.

In panel (*a*), as in Figure 14–2, an increase in the money stock from M_1 to M_2 causes the *LM* schedule to shift downward and to the right, so there is a movement from point *A* to point *B* in diagram (*a*1). The equilibrium nominal interest rate declines from R_1 toward R_2, and equilibrium real income rises from y_1 toward y_2. Thus, holding other factors constant, at a given price level P_1 there is a rightward shift in the aggregate demand schedule, in diagram (*a*1), from $y^d(M_1)$ toward the dashed schedule denoted $y^d(M_2)$.

The increase in real income spurs import spending, and with low capital mobility the decline in the nominal interest rate induces a meager outflow of capital. Thus, a balance-of-payments deficit arises at point *B*, and there is downward pressure on the value of the nation's currency in foreign exchange markets. If the central bank sterilizes its interventions to maintain a fixed exchange rate, then the money stock remains at its higher level, M_2, and the aggregate demand schedule shifts fully to the position $y^d(M_2)$ in diagram (*a*2). With nonsterilized interventions, however, the money stock falls back toward its original level of M_1 as the central bank's foreign exchange reserves decline. Thus, the aggregate demand ultimately returns to its original position, $y^d(M_1)$, in diagram (*a*2), as the *LM* schedule shifts back to its initial position in diagram (*a*1).

As shown in panels (*b*) and (*c*), these same basic conclusions follow in environments of high and perfect capital mobility. In diagram (*b*1), a balance-of-payments deficit again follows an expansion of the money stock, with more significant capital outflows accounting for much of the deficit. In diagram (*b*2), therefore, aggregate demand again rises only if the central bank were to sterilize its foreign exchange interventions. In diagram (*c*1), the decline in the nominal interest rate generates capital outflows that account fully for the balance-of-payments deficit, and in diagram (*c*2) we again see that the aggregate demand schedule shifts rightward only with sterilized interventions. Otherwise, an increase in the quantity of money in circulation ultimately has no effect on aggregate demand.

Thus, we can reach the following conclusion:

For any degree of capital mobility, in a system of fixed exchange rates the effects on aggregate demand of central bank actions to alter the nominal money stock hinge on the extent to which a nation's central bank sterilizes its foreign exchange market operations. If central bank foreign exchange interventions to maintain fixed exchange rates are unsterilized, then efforts to expand aggregate demand through increases in the money stock ultimately are ineffective.

FIGURE 14–4   THE EFFECT OF AN INCREASE IN THE MONEY STOCK ON AGGREGATE DEMAND IN AN OPEN ECONOMY WITH A FLOATING EXCHANGE RATE

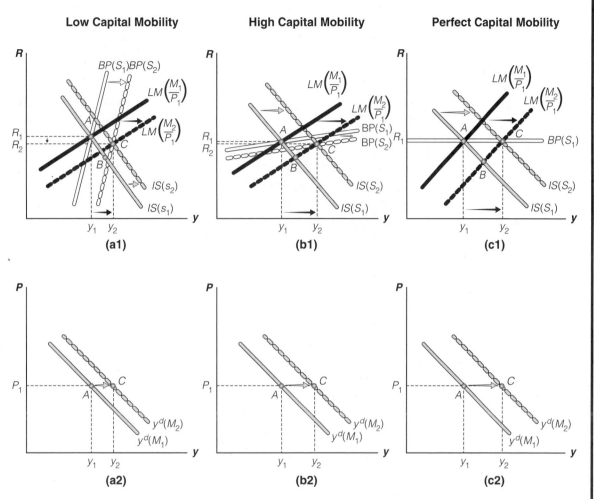

In all three pairs of panels, an increase in the money stock causes the *LM* schedule to shift rightward, resulting in a balance-of-payments deficit, which, in turn, causes a domestic currency depreciation. The rise in the exchange rate stimulates greater net export expenditures and raises equilibrium real income. With higher capital mobility, the extent of capital outflow and, consequently, the size of the resulting depreciation and real income effect, rise. Hence, higher capital mobility enhances the amount of the expansion in aggregate demand induced by a rise in the money stock.

Panels (*b*) and (*c*) of Figure 14–4 illustrate that this same conclusion follows with high and perfect capital mobility. Note in diagram (*b*1), however, that with high capital mobility, a given monetary expansion causes a larger capital outflow and, hence, greater currency depreciation, as compared with the case of low capital mobility in diagram (*a*1). This generates a larger rise in net export spending, and so the *IS* schedule shifts farther to the right. Consequently, equilibrium real income rises by a larger amount under high capital mobility, so that the aggregate demand schedule shifts farther to the right in diagram (*b*2).

In panel (*c*) you can see that the rise in aggregate demand resulting from a monetary expansion is even more pronounced under perfect capital mobility. We may conclude that:

> **In a system of floating exchange rates, an expansionary monetary policy action unambiguously raises aggregate demand. The size of the effect on aggregate demand becomes greater as the degree of capital mobility increases.**

Thus, under floating exchange rates, greater capital mobility enhances the potential strength of monetary policy.

Exchange Rate Policy and Aggregate Demand in an Open Economy   If we interpret the shifts displayed in Figure 14–4 somewhat differently, we can also explain how an exchange-rate devaluation can influence aggregate demand. Suppose that the central bank had held the exchange rate fixed at S_1 but then decided to devalue its nation's currency. This requires an increase in the exchange rate target to a new, higher level, denoted S_2. To bring about this change in the exchange rate, the central bank would need to expand the money stock for a time until the exchange rate settled at the central bank's higher target value. This would shift the *LM* schedule rightward. At the same time, the increase in the exchange rate would cause the *IS* and *BP* schedules to shift to the right.

These effects are the same as those illustrated in panels (*a*), (*b*), and (*c*) of Figure 14–4. Therefore, this figure also illustrates the essential effects of an exchange rate devaluation in a system of fixed exchange rates. Such a devaluation would, as illustrated in Figure 14–4, cause aggregate demand to increase. The amount of the expansion in aggregate demand would be greater with higher degrees of capital mobility.

Fiscal Policy and Aggregate Demand   To understand the basic linkage between fiscal policy actions and the aggregate demand schedule, let's again start by considering the case of a closed economy. Panel (*a*) of Figure 14–5 displays the *IS–LM* effects of a rise in real government expenditures, from g_1 to a higher level g_2, for a given price level, P_1. As discussed in Chapter 13, the direct result is a rightward shift in the *IS* schedule by the amount of the government spending

FIGURE 14–5   **THE EFFECT OF AN INCREASE IN GOVERNMENT SPENDING ON AGGREGATE DEMAND IN A CLOSED ECONOMY**

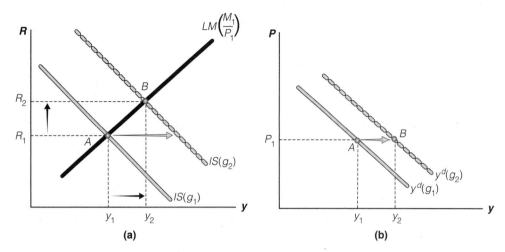

With an unchanged price level, an increase in government spending shifts the *IS* schedule rightward along the *LM* schedule from point *A* to point *B* in panel (*a*). The resulting real income level at point *B* in panel (*b*) corresponds to the same price level, and this new equilibrium real income–price level combination is located on a new aggregate demand schedule to the right of the real income–price level combination at point *A* on the original aggregate demand schedule. Consequently, an increase in government spending causes an increase in aggregate demand.

FUNDAMENTAL ISSUE #2

What factors determine the extent to which changes in the quantity of money can influence aggregate demand in an open economy? The effects of an increase in the money stock on aggregate demand depend on the exchange rate system that is in place and on the degree of capital mobility. Under fixed exchange rates, an unsterilized increase in the quantity of money does not influence aggregate demand. Exchange rate devaluations, in contrast, induce an increase in aggregate demand, and the same effect arises from an increase in the amount of money in circulation under a floating exchange rate. In these latter situations, greater capital mobility enhances the amount of the increase in aggregate demand.

increase times the autonomous spending multiplier, $1/(1 - MPC)$. The rise in real income causes the demand for real money balances to rise, thereby generating an increase in the equilibrium nominal interest rate. As a result, real investment spending declines, but not sufficiently to prevent a net rise in equilibrium real income, from y_1 at point A to y_2 at point B.

Point B in panel (a) is a new IS–LM equilibrium, so the real income–price level combination y_2 and P_1 must lie on a new aggregate demand schedule, $y^d(g_2)$, at point B in panel (b). Thus, in a closed economy the increase in government spending causes an increase in aggregate demand.

Fiscal Policy and Aggregate Demand in an Open Economy with a Fixed Exchange Rate Now consider the implications of an expansionary fiscal policy action in an open economy with a fixed exchange rate. Panels (a), (b), and (c) of Figure 14–6 display the effects of an increase in government spending under low, high, and perfect capital mobility. In the upper diagram in each panel, the rise in government spending causes the IS schedule to shift from $IS(g_1)$ to $IS(g_2)$, generating an initial movement from point A to point B. Thus, the equilibrium nominal interest rate initially rises from R_1 to R', and equilibrium real income increases from y_1 to y'.

As we discussed in Chapter 12, the effects of a fiscal expansion on a nation's balance-of-payments depend on the openness of its borders to flows of financial resources. In the case of low capital mobility, illustrated in diagram (a1), the rise in the equilibrium nominal interest rate resulting from the increase in government expenditures induces a capital inflow that is too small to compensate for an increase in import spending caused by the rise in real income. As a result, there is a balance-of-payments deficit at point B. This places downward pressure on the value of the domestic currency. To keep the exchange rate fixed, the central bank must sell foreign exchange reserves. If the central bank's interventions are unsterilized, this causes a reduction in the nominal money stock, from M_1 to a smaller amount M_2, thereby shifting the LM schedule upward and to the left, from $LM(M_1)$ to $LM(M_2)$. The resulting IS–LM–BP equilibrium is at point C, at which there is still a net rise in the equilibrium interest rate, to R_2, and a net increase in equilibrium real income, to y_2.

Because equilibrium real income rises from its initial level of y_1 to the higher level of y_2 at the current price level, P_1, this new real income–price level combination at point C lies on a new aggregate demand schedule in diagram (a2). Thus, on net the increase in government spending shifts the aggregate demand schedule to the right, from $y^d(g_1, M_2)$ to $y^d(g_2, M_2)$.

Panels (b) and (c) show that aggregate demand also increases following a rise in government spending with high and perfect capital mobility. In each of these cases, however, the initial rise in the equilibrium interest rate generates capital inflows sufficiently large to more than offset higher imports stemming from an increase in real income. Thus, in diagrams (b1) and (c1) in Figure 14–6, there is a balance-of-payments *surplus* at point B. To maintain a fixed exchange rate, therefore, the central bank must add to its foreign exchange reserves. If unsterilized, this action causes the domestic money stock to rise, from an initial value M_1 to a higher level M_2. The LM schedule shifts downward and to

FIGURE 14–6   THE EFFECT OF AN INCREASE IN GOVERNMENT SPENDING ON AGGREGATE DEMAND IN AN OPEN ECONOMY WITH A FIXED EXCHANGE RATE

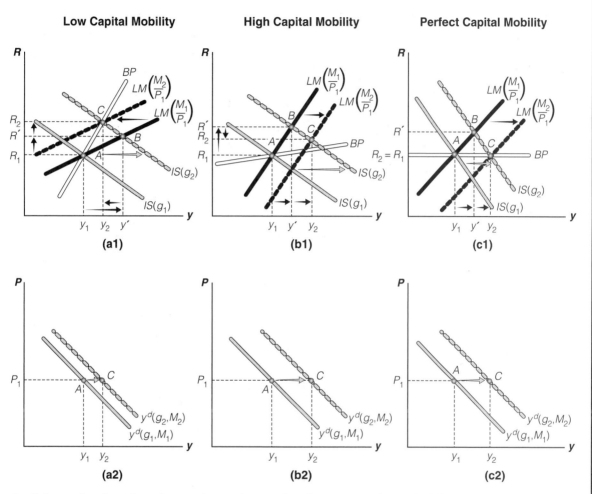

In all three pairs of panels, an increase in government expenditures causes the *IS* schedule to shift rightward, inducing initial increases in the equilibrium nominal interest rate from R_1 to R' and in the level of equilibrium real income from y_1 to y'. Panel (*a*1) shows that with low capital mobility, there is a balance-of-payments deficit at point *B*, which requires the central bank to sell foreign exchange reserves to keep the exchange rate fixed, thereby resulting in a final equilibrium at point *C* and a slight rise in aggregate demand, shown in panel (*a*2). Panels (*b*) and (*c*) show that with higher or perfect capital mobility, a rise in government spending causes a balance-of-payment surplus at point *B*. To keep the exchange rate from declining in both cases, the central bank must purchase foreign exchange reserves, which leads to a final equilibrium at point *C* and larger increases in aggregate demand.

the right, leading to an equilibrium real income–interest rate combination y_2 and R_2 at point C. Consequently, equilibrium real income is greater at the current price level, so the aggregate demand schedule shifts rightward in both diagrams ($b2$) and ($c2$).

Note that panels (a), (b), and (c) indicate that as the degree of capital mobility increases, the extent to which central bank interventions generate money stock changes that reinforce the expansionary effects of fiscal policy actions rises. We may conclude that:

> **In a system of fixed exchange rates, an expansionary fiscal policy action unambiguously raises aggregate demand. The size of the effect on aggregate demand becomes greater as the degree of capital mobility increases.**

Thus, under fixed exchange rates, greater capital mobility enhances the potential strength of fiscal policy.

Fiscal Policy and Aggregate Demand in an Open Economy with a Floating Exchange Rate If a nation's central bank permits exchange rates to float, then fiscal policy actions do not lead to changes in the quantity of money in circulation. Instead, they result in changes in the equilibrium value of the nation's currency.

Panels (a), (b), and (c) of Figure 14–7 show how the relationship between fiscal policy actions and aggregate demand varies with the degree of capital mobility in a system of floating exchange rates. Panel (a) depicts a situation of low capital mobility. At the current market exchange rate S_1, an increase in the amount of government spending, from g_1 to g_2, causes the IS schedule to shift to the right in diagram ($a1$), from $IS(g_1, S_1)$ to $IS(g_2, S_1)$. With low capital mobility, the increase in the equilibrium nominal interest rate stemming from the rise in government spending generates insufficient capital account improvements to counter an increase in import spending caused by the rise in equilibrium real income. Hence, there is a balance-of-payments deficit at point B.

This causes the domestic currency to depreciate, so the equilibrium exchange rate rises to S_2. This depreciation spurs net exports, so the IS schedule shifts farther to the right, to $IS(g_2, S_2)$. In addition, the rise in the exchange rate causes the BP schedule to shift downward and to the right, to $BP(S_2)$. At the final equilibrium point C, there is balance-of-payments equilibrium at the higher exchange rate S_2, the higher nominal interest rate R_2, and the higher real income level y_2. As shown in diagram ($a2$), this produces to a new real income–price level combination, y_2 and P_1, that is consistent with an IS–LM equilibrium. Thus, the rise in government spending causes the aggregate demand schedule to shift rightward, from $y^d(g_1)$ to $y^d(g_2)$.

In a situation in which there is high capital mobility, the effect of a government spending increase on aggregate demand is much more muted, however, as shown in panel (b) of Figure 14–7. In diagram ($b1$), the initial increase in the

**FIGURE 14-7   THE EFFECT OF AN INCREASE IN GOVERNMENT SPENDING ON AGGREGATE DEMAND
IN AN OPEN ECONOMY WITH A FLOATING EXCHANGE RATE**

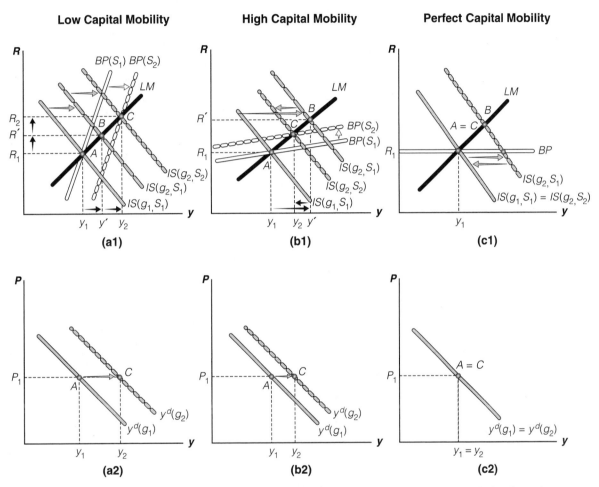

**FIGURE 14-7   THE EFFECT OF AN INCREASE IN GOVERNMENT SPENDING ON AGGREGATE DEMAND
IN AN OPEN ECONOMY WITH A FLOATING EXCHANGE RATE**

In all three pairs of panels, an increase in government expenditures causes the *IS* schedule to shift rightward, inducing initial increases in the equilibrium nominal interest rate from R_1 to R' and in the level of equilibrium real income from y_1 to y' exchange rates. Panel (*a*1) depicts a situation of low capital mobility, which the rise in government spending causes a balance of payments deficit at point *B*, which induces a currency depreciation and an additional rightward shift in the *IS* schedule. At the final equilibrium point *C* there is a potentially sizable expansion in aggregate demand in panel (*a*2). With high or perfect capital mobility, in contrast, an increase in government spending causes a balance of payments surplus, a currency appreciation, and a partially [panel (*b*1)] or fully [panel (*c*1)] offsetting leftward shift in the *IS* schedule. Thus, the aggregate demand effect of a rise in government expenditures is mitigated by higher capital mobility.

equilibrium nominal interest rate, from R_1 at point A to R' at point B, causes a capital account improvement that more than offsets the decline in the current account. Hence, there is a balance-of-payments *surplus* at point B in diagram (*b1*). This causes the exchange rate to *fall* from an initial value S_1 to a *lower* value S_2, which reduces net export spending and causes the *IS* schedule to shift back to the left, to $IS(g_2, S_2)$. Although real income on net is higher, at y_2, at the final equilibrium point C, as compared with the case of low capital mobility in panel (*b*), there is a smaller increase in equilibrium real income following the rise in government spending. The aggregate demand schedule, therefore, shifts by a smaller amount in diagram (*b2*) as compared with diagram (*a2*).

Panel (*c*) depicts a situation of perfect capital mobility. In this case, there is a significant balance-of-payments surplus at point B in diagram (*c1*), as the increase in the nominal interest rate generates sizable capital inflows. As a result, there is a sizable domestic currency appreciation, which ultimately causes the *IS* schedule to shift back to its original position. The final equilibrium point C corresponds to the initial equilibrium point A, and equilibrium real income remains at its initial level, y_1. Thus, there is no movement from point A in diagram (*c2*). Aggregate demand is unaffected by the rise in government expenditures with perfect capital mobility and a floating exchange rate.

This reasoning leads to the following conclusion:

> **Under floating exchange rates, the size of the effect of a given fiscal policy action on aggregate demand declines as the degree of capital mobility increases. Under perfect capital mobility, fiscal policy cannot influence the position of the aggregate demand schedule.**

Consequently, adopting a system of floating exchange rates tends to mute the effects that fiscal policy actions can exert on aggregate demand.

FUNDAMENTAL ISSUE #3

What factors determine the extent to which fiscal policy actions can influence aggregate demand in an open economy? The key factors influencing the aggregate demand effects of fiscal policy actions are capital mobility and the exchange rate system that a government adopts. In a system of fixed exchange rates, an increase in government spending causes aggregate demand to increase, and greater capital mobility enhances this effect. In a system of floating exchange rates, the aggregate demand effects of increased government expenditures are more muted, and they dissipate further as the degree of capital mobility increases.

AGGREGATE SUPPLY

As we shall discuss, the equilibrium price level is the price level at which firms and workers are willing and able to produce the aggregate output of goods and services that is consistent with the aggregate demand for those goods and services. Hence, to contemplate how the price level is determined, we must first consider the behavior of firms and workers.

Output and Employment Determination

Changes in the price of an *individual* good or service typically induce firms to alter the amount of inputs, such as labor, that they use in production and to vary the quantity of the good or service that they produce and offer for sale in the marketplace. A long-standing issue, however, is the extent to which changes in the *overall* price level affect the *aggregate* levels of employment and output. As you will learn, resolving this issue is crucial to determining whether monetary or fiscal policies can influence aggregate employment and output levels in an open economy.

PRODUCTION FUNCTION
The relationship between the quantities of factors of production employed by firms and their output of goods and services using the current technology.

The Production Function   The aggregate **production function** is the relationship between the quantities of production factors–labor, capital, land, and entrepreneurship–employed by all firms in the economy and their total output of goods and services, given the technology currently available. We shall focus on short-run production decisions, which firms must make over a time horizon sufficiently brief that firms cannot adjust fixed factors of production, such as capital, land, and entrepreneurship. Hence, in the short run the factor of production that firms can vary is the quantity of labor that they employ, denoted N.

Economists have three approaches to measuring of the quantity of labor employed by firms. One approach is to measure the number of people employed during a given period. Another approach is to measure the total time worked by all individuals employed by firms, which is just the total hours that workers were employed during a given interval. Finally, economists can combine these approaches by measuring the number of *person-hours*.

Firms use labor in conjunction with other productive factors to produce goods and services. The aggregate production function determines the economy-wide level of real output, y, resulting from firms' employment of the total quantity of labor, N:

$$y = F(N).$$

This equation indicates that the aggregate amount of firms' real output is a *function* of the amount of labor that they employ.

Panel (*a*) of Figure 14–8 displays a diagram of the aggregate production function, $F(N)$. At any point along this function, we can see how much real output firms can produce given a particular level of employment. For example, if firms

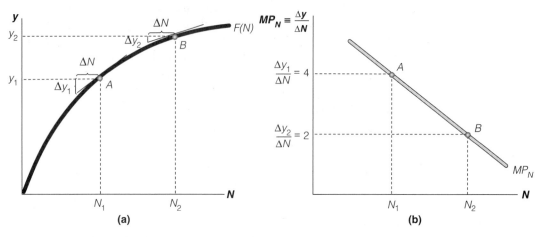

Given a fixed stock of capital and a current state of technology, higher levels of labor employment are necessary to achieve increased production of real output. The bowed, or concave, shape of the production function in panel (*a*) reflects the law of diminishing returns, which states that total output increases at a decreasing rate for each additional one-unit rise in employment of labor. Consequently, as shown in panel (*b*), the marginal product of labor declines as employment rises.

employ N_1 units of labor at point *A*, then aggregate real output would equal y_1. Increasing employment to N_2, at point *B*, leads to production of a higher real output level, y_2.

The Marginal Product of Labor The *slope* of the production function is a change in output resulting from a change in employment, or "rise," divided by a corresponding change in employment, or "run." By definition, the slope of the production function, $\Delta y/\Delta N$, is the additional amount of output that firms can produce by employing an additional unit of labor, which economists call the **marginal product of labor,** or MP_N. That is, $MP_N \equiv \Delta y/\Delta N$, or the slope of the production function at a given quantity of labor.

MARGINAL PRODUCT OF LABOR
The additional quantity of output that firms can produce by employing another unit of labor.

Because the aggregate production function in panel (*a*) of Figure 14–8 is *concave,* or bowed downward, its slope declines as employment increases. For instance, the slope of the function at point *A* is equal to the slope of the line tangent to the function at this point, or $\Delta y_1/\Delta N$, where the symbol Δ denotes a change in a quantity. At the higher employment level N_2 at point *B*, however, an identical change in employment, ΔN, leads to a smaller change in output, Δy_2. As a result, the slope of the production function at point *B*, which is equal to $\Delta y_2/\Delta N$, must be smaller than the slope of the production function at point *A*. Thus, the marginal product of labor declines as labor employment

LAW OF DIMINISHING MARGINAL RETURNS The fact that the additional output produced by an additional unit of labor ultimately falls as firms employ more units of labor.

at firms increases. This is consistent with the **law of diminishing marginal returns,** which states that eventually the additional output produced by an additional unit of labor declines as firms employ more units of labor given at least one fixed input.

Panel (*b*) of Figure 14–8 depicts the marginal-product-of-labor schedule, or MP_N *schedule.* The MP_N schedule shows the marginal product of labor, or slope of the production function, at any given quantity of labor. The schedule's downward slope reflects the law of diminishing marginal returns. At the employment level N_1, the marginal product of labor is equal to $\Delta y_1/\Delta N$, which is the slope of the production function at point *A*, which we assume is equal to a value of four units of output per unit of labor. If total employment were to increase to N_2 at point *B*, then the slope of the production function would fall to $\Delta y_2/\Delta N$, which we assume is equal to two units of output per unit of labor.

The Demand for Labor   To determine how many units of labor to employ, any firm must weigh the revenue gain from the sale of the additional production generated by another unit of labor against the cost of hiring that labor unit. To maximize its profits over a given period, a firm must produce output to the point at which its marginal revenue (*MR*), or additional revenue stemming from production and sale of an additional unit of output, is just equal to its marginal cost (*MC*), or additional production cost that it incurs in this endeavor. On the one hand, if *MR* is greater than *MC* at a given production level, then the firm earns a positive net profit from the last unit of production, which gives the firm an incentive to increase production. On the other hand, if *MC* is greater than *MR*, then the firm's net profit on the last unit produced is negative, which gives the firm an incentive to reduce production. At the output level at which *MR* = *MC*, therefore, the firm earns positive net profits for every unit up to the last unit produced, which thereby maximizes profits on its total output production.

If firms are purely competitive, then no individual firm can influence the market price of a unit of output. Thus, each unit of output yields the same marginal revenue, which is the market price. If follows that purely competitive firms produce output up to the point at which

$$MR \equiv P = MC,$$

which indicates that under pure competition, price equals marginal cost.

A firm's marginal cost of producing output stems from the expense that it incurs by employing labor. This is the *nominal wage,* denoted W and measured in units of domestic currency per labor unit, that it pays for each unit of labor. For example, suppose that the current market wage rate is $W_1 = \$20$ per unit of labor. If, as at point *B* in Figure 14–8, the marginal product of labor at the firm's current output level is $MP_N = \Delta y/\Delta N = 2$ units of output per unit of labor, then we can compute the firm's marginal cost of producing output by dividing W_1 by MP_N. This yields $MC = (\$20$ per unit of labor$)/(2$ units of output per unit of labor) = $10 per unit of output. Hence, marginal cost by definition is equal to W/MP_N.

This implies that we can rewrite a purely competitive firm's profit-maximizing condition, $P = MC$, as

$$P = W/MP_N.$$

Multiplying both sides of this equation by MP_N yields

$$P \times MP_N = (W/MP_N) \times MP_N = W.$$

Therefore, an alternative way to express the firm's profit-maximizing condition is

$$W = P \times MP_N.$$

This equation tells us that a purely competitive, profit-maximizing firm will employ labor to the point at which the money wage that the firm pays each unit of labor is equal to the price it receives for each unit of output that labor produces times the marginal product of labor. Economists call this latter product the **value of the marginal product of labor,** or $VMP_N = P \times MP_N$. For example, if the market price of a firm's output is $5 per unit of output and the marginal product of labor is two units of output per unit of labor, then the value of labor's marginal product is equal to the product of these two figures, or $10 per unit of labor.

Figure 14–9 illustrates the value-of-marginal-product-of-labor schedule, or VMP_N schedule, which we obtain by multiplying the firm's output price, P, times the MP_N schedule in panel (*b*) of Figure 14–8. If the nominal wage that

VALUE OF THE MARGINAL PRODUCT OF LABOR The price of output times the marginal product of labor.

FIGURE 14–9   THE DEMAND FOR LABOR

A profit-maximizing firm employs labor to the point at which the value of labor's marginal product is equal to the nominal wage. Thus, a rise in the nominal wage reduces the quantity of labor demanded by a firm.

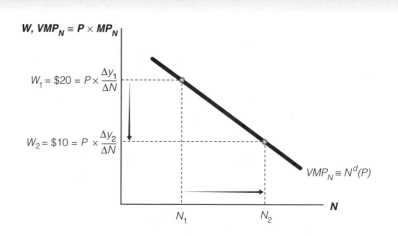

a firm pays each unit of labor is $W_1 = \$20$ per unit of labor, then the firm employs labor to the point at which the value of labor's marginal product is equal to $20 per unit of labor. This, the figure shows, implies employment of an amount of labor N_1. At a lower wage rate of $W_2 = \$10$ per unit of labor, however, the firm requires a smaller value of marginal product to maximize its profit, and so it *increases* the amount of labor it employs, to the quantity of labor N_2. A fall in the market wage rate causes the firm to increase the quantity of labor it demands.

Hence, a firm decides how many units of labor that it desires to employ by moving along its VMP_N schedule. This leads to the following important conclusion:

> The VMP_N schedule for a purely competitive firm is that firm's labor demand schedule showing how many units of labor, N, that the firm demands at any given nominal wage, W.

This means that the quantity of labor actually employed by firms depends on three factors. One is the prices at which firms are able to sell their products. Another is the productivity of labor (see "Policy Notebook: Who Leads the Way in Labor Productivity?"). The third, to which we now turn our attention, is the process by which nominal wages are determined.

Wage Flexibility, Aggregate Supply, and the Price Level

The process by which nominal wages are determined can vary considerably across firms and industries within individual countries. In addition, there is significant variation in the extent to which certain institutional structures for wage determination may predominate. Every nation also has its own laws governing the interactions between firms and workers. As a result, no single theory of wage determination fits every nation. This means that the manner in which total employment and the aggregate output level are determined also differs across countries.

The Determination of Nominal Wages In a number of nations, for example, most workers and firms establish contracts that set the terms, such as wages and benefits, that govern the employment of workers with the firms over a given time period, such as one to three years. In some nations, such as Belgium, Norway, Finland, and Sweden, more than half of all workers are members of unions that negotiate *explicit contracts,* or formal, written agreements between workers and firms. In a few countries, such as Austria and Italy, unions may coordinate wage bargaining, leading to a highly centralized process of determining nominal wages that strengthens the wage-setting powers of unions. In other countries, such as France and Japan, the legal environment extends many aspects of union agreements to nonunionized workers. In

POLICY NOTEBOOK

Who Leads the Way in Labor Productivity?

Table 14–1 displays estimates of index measures of average labor productivity in manufacturing for various nations. The measures are scaled in such a way that U.S. labor productivity is always equal to 100. Consequently, the 1995 figure of 73 for Japan indicates that in 1995 Japan's average labor productivity amounted to 73 percent of average U.S. labor productivity.

The table indicates that between 1960 and 1985, these countries made considerable headway in closing their "productivity gaps" vis-à-vis the United States. Indeed, labor productivity in the Netherlands outstripped U.S. productivity by 1985. During the following decade, however, the U.S. productivity advantage over European nations actually widened somewhat. Canadian average labor productivity also fell off somewhat, relative to productivity in the United States. Because labor productivity is a key determinant of the demand for labor by firms, many economists think that these relative productivity differences help to account for differences in unemployment rates across these countries. Between 1985 and 1995, for instance, German, French, and Dutch unemployment rates increased as labor productivity in those countries declined relative to other nations. At the same time, British unemployment rates declined at the same time that its relative labor productivity increased.

FOR CRITICAL ANALYSIS:
If all international barriers to mobility and other factors of production and to mobility of technological advances were to evaporate, and if nations were to adopt identical industry regulations, what value would you expect the index numbers in Table 14–1 to approach?

TABLE 14–1 **INDEX MEASURES OF AVERAGE LABOR PRODUCTIVITY IN MANUFACTURING FOR SELECTED NATIONS**

	1960	1985	1995
United States	100	100	100
Japan	19	69	73
Germany	56	86	81
France	46	86	85
Britain	45	60	70
Canada	69	84	70
Australia	51	57	52
Netherlands	51	107	97
Sweden	50	87	90

SOURCE: Data from Organization for Economic Cooperation and Development.

Japan, for example, the national government, rather than unions, coordinates the wage-determination process by establishing a synchronized, nationwide schedule for nominal wage adjustments (see "Management Notebook: It's All in a Day's Work–Depending on Where You Live").

In other countries, the process by which workers and firms establish nominal wages is much more decentralized. This is particularly true in countries such as the United Kingdom and the United States, in which the legal setting promotes more individualized labor contracting and the extent of unionization is lower. Of course, wage contracts need not exist only in unionized industries. For instance, most U.S. firms offering employment to new recipients of undergraduate degrees usually extend job offers stating initial salaries and policies on the amount of time that will pass before the next salary review. In addition, *implicit contracts,* or unwritten, tacit agreements, may exist, so even in the absence of explicit wage agreements, workers and firms may follow certain unstated patterns of behavior in establishing standards for wage determination. Nevertheless, most U.S. and British workers and firms establish wage bargains on an individual basis, rather than through a centralized procedure. Indeed, in many industries within these nations, labor markets may function very much like those for goods and services, with the nominal wage adjusting to equilibrate the quantity of labor supplied by workers with the quantity of labor demanded by firms.

Employment and Aggregate Supply with Fixed versus Flexible Nominal Wages   To see why the process of wage determination is so important, consider Figure 14–10 on page 472. In panel (*a*), the overall level of nominal wages is *fixed* at a level W^f. The general level of nominal wages could be inflexible in the short term because of long-term contracts negotiated in concert by national unions or via governmental coordination of a nationwide bargaining process. Another reason for wage stickiness might be minimum wage laws that fix the wages of the lowest-paid workers. Although fewer than 5 percent of workers in the United States, Austria, Belgium, and the Netherlands are covered by minimum wage systems, in France, Greece, and Luxembourg 10 to 20 percent of workers earn a legally mandated minimum wage.

As shown in diagram (*a*1), if wages are inflexible, then the overall level of nominal wages W^f does not vary with a change in the position of the VMP_N schedule resulting from a rise in the price level, from an initial price level P_1 to a higher price level P_2. As a result, employment increases from N_1 at point A to N_2 at point B, as the value of workers' marginal product rises, inducing firms to demand more labor so as to expand their output of goods and services in pursuit of greater profits. In diagram (*a*2), this increase in employment causes a movement from point A to point B along the aggregate production function, so that aggregate real output increases from y_1 to y_2. Therefore, in diagram (*a*3) there is a movement from the initial real output–price level combination y_1 and P_1, at point A, to a new combination y_2 and P_2, at point B. Points A and B in diagram (*a*3) lie along an upward-sloping **aggregate supply schedule,** which shows how real output that all workers and firms in the economy are willing

AGGREGATE SUPPLY SCHEDULE
A schedule depicting volumes of real output produced by all workers and firms at each possible price level.

MANAGEMENT NOTEBOOK

It's All in a Day's Work—Depending on Where You Live

Table 14–2 shows the average wage rate, computed as the U.S. dollar values of nominal hourly wages and benefits, earned by a typical manufacturing worker in 27 nations. Several factors influenced changes in these overall dollar wage rates between 1985 and 1995. One was variations in national labor demand and supply conditions. In Taiwan, for example, labor productivity grew much faster during the 1980s and 1990s as compared with U.S. labor productivity, thereby fueling a rise in the demand for Taiwanese labor. This factor helped lead to a relative increase in Taiwanese manufacturing wages from just over one-tenth of U.S. wages in 1985 to more than one-third of U.S. wages in 1995.

In addition, for nations other than the United States, the changes in the dollar exchange rate accounted for at least part of the change in their dollar-denominated

wage rates over this interval. For example, the sharp rises in German and Japanese wages stemmed largely from the general decline in the dollar's value relative to the deutsche mark and the yen following the mid-1980s. Hence, the dollar's depreciation undoubtedly contributed to the relative improvement in the competitive position of U.S. manufacturing firms into the 1990s.

FOR CRITICAL ANALYSIS:

Between 1985 and late 1994, the dollar value of the Mexican peso was relatively stable. What factors might have accounted for the reduction in Mexican wages relative to U.S. wages—from more than 12 percent ($1.59 in Mexico compared with $13.01 in the United States) to less than 9 percent ($1.51 in Mexico compared with $17.20 in the United States)—during that interval?

ON THE WEB
Visit the Central Bank of China R.O.C. at:
http://www.cbc.gov.tw

and able to produce varies with changes in the price level. The aggregate supply schedule in diagram (a3) includes all real output–price level combinations consistent with the fixed nominal wage W^f in diagram (a1). Hence, if the general level of nominal wages is fixed, a nation's aggregate supply schedule slopes upward: A rise in the price level causes an increase in real output.

In contrast, panel (b) of Figure 14–10 depicts a setting in which nominal wages fully adjust to changes in the price level. In diagram (b1), we assume that W^b is an initial, *base* wage level. At the price level P_1, the value of labor's marginal product is equal to $VMP_N^1 = MP_N \times P_1$, and at the base wage W^b, the quantity of labor demanded by firms is equal to N_1, at point A. In diagram (b2),

TABLE 14-2   HOURLY LABOR COSTS IN MANUFACTURING

	1985	1995
Germany	9.60	31.88
Japan	6.34	23.66
France	7.52	19.34
United States	13.01	17.20
Italy	7.63	16.48
Canada	10.94	16.03
Australia	8.20	14.40
Britain	6.27	13.77
Spain	4.66	12.70
South Korea	1.23	7.40
Singapore	2.47	7.28
Taiwan	1.50	5.82
Hong Kong	1.73	4.82
Brazil	1.30	4.28
Chile	1.87	3.63
Argentina	0.67	1.67
Malaysia	1.08	1.59
Mexico	1.59	1.51
Philippines	0.64	0.71
Thailand	0.49	0.46
Indonesia	0.22	0.30
China	0.19	0.25
India	0.35	0.25

Amounts in U.S. dollars.
SOURCE: Data from Organization for Economic Cooperation and Development.

the real output level produced by this amount of labor is equal to y_1. This yields the real output–price level combination y_1 and P_1 at point A in diagram (b3).

An increase in the price level, to a higher level P_2, again causes a rise in the value of the marginal product of labor in diagram (b1), to $VMP_N^2 = MP_N \times P_2$. Now, however, we suppose that nominal wages flexibly adjusts to this change in the price level to keep the *real* wage unchanged, perhaps because of contractual arrangements that call for such adjustment, from a level W^b to a new level $W^b + \Delta P$, where ΔP denotes a full adjustment to the rise in the price level. At the new equilibrium point B in diagram (b1), the nominal wage thereby rises in proportion to the increase in the price level. As a result, firms demand the same

FIGURE 14–10 **EMPLOYMENT AND OUTPUT DETERMINATION WITH FIXED VERSUS FLEXIBLE NOMINAL WAGES**

Inflexible Wages with Price Level Change

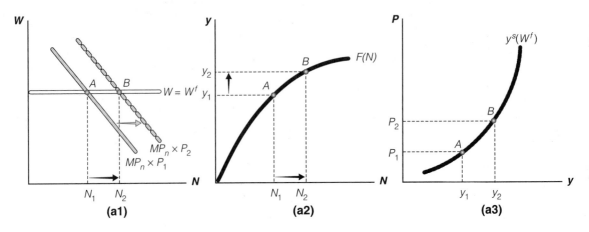

Flexible Wages with Price Level Change

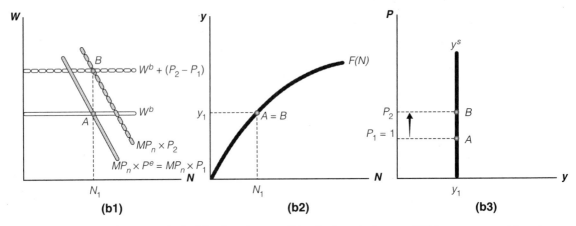

Panels (*a*) show that if wages are inflexible, then the overall level of nominal wages W^f does not vary with a change in the position of the VMP_N schedule resulting from a rise in the price level. Consequently, employment rises from N_1 at point A to N_2 at point B, as the value of workers' marginal product increases, inducing firms to demand more labor. The resulting increase in employment cause a movement from point A to point B along the aggregate production function, so that aggregate real output increases from y_1 to y_2. Hence, the aggregate supply schedule slopes upward with fixed nominal wages. In contrast, panels (*b*) show that if W^b is an initial, base level of wages, then automatic contractual adjustment of wages in response to an increase in the price level, to $W^b + \Delta P$, results in no change in employment or output. Hence, with complete wage adjustment to price changes, the aggregate supply schedule is vertical.

amount of labor as they did before the rise in the price level. Employment remains equal to N_1 at point B in diagram (b1), so the amount of real output produced is equal to y_1 in diagram (b2). As a result, the new real output–price level combination y_1 and P_2 at point B in diagram (b3) lies directly above point A. The *aggregate supply schedule* containing these points is vertical. A rise in the price level does not induce an increase in the nation's real output level.

What types of labor market arrangements can cause nominal wages to adjust equiproportionately to changes in the price level? One possibility is if workers' contracts call for full *indexation* of wages, so that firms automatically ratchet workers' wages upward in response to inflation. Workers' contracts might be indexed directly to price-level variations, or they might be indexed less directly, via arrangements such as profit-sharing contracts (see "Management Notebook: Profit Sharing–Is the Market Working?"). Another possibility would be situations in which markets for labor skills are highly competitive and unregulated, so that they essentially function as *auction markets*, with wages determined via a bidding process. In such markets, firms would bid wages upward in response to increases in the price level, so that nominal wages would vary in direct proportion to prices.

Many economists argue that in the long run, labor markets should function like auction markets. That is, given the passage of a sufficient span of time, labor contracts or other institutional wage arrangements should reflect such factors as the productivity of a nation's workers, the size of its labor force, and general willingness of workers to supply their skills to firms. In a long-run equilibrium, therefore, the nominal wage should adjust equiproportionately to changes in the price level. Thus, the long-run aggregate supply schedule for an economy is vertical, as in Figure 14–10.

The Aggregate Supply Schedule with Partial Wage Adjustment In most nations, the general level of nominal wages is neither completely fixed nor fully flexible in the face of changes in the price level. The overall wage level within a country typically adjusts *partially* to movements in prices, at least over short-run periods.

This means that for most nations, over a short-run interval the aggregate supply schedule, y^s, slopes upward, as shown in Figure 14–12 on page 475. Thus, as compared with the situation that arises if the general level of nominal wages were fixed, as illustrated by the much shallower aggregate supply schedule $y^s(W^f)$, inducing a given rise in real output production may require relatively significant increase in the price level. At the same time, because all wages in a nation generally are not fully indexed to inflation and because institutional arrangements usually prevent labor markets from functioning as auction markets in the short run, the aggregate supply schedule is not vertical. Only in the long run—which is a period sufficiently lengthy that the wage determination process takes into account all the elements influencing worker and firm preferences—does a rise in the price level fail to yield a higher level of real output, as is the case along the vertical schedule denoted y^s_{LR}.

MANAGEMENT NOTEBOOK
Profit Sharing—Is the Market Working?

Many economists have contended that the best wage-setting arrangement entails automatic adjustments of wages to firm profitability. This, they argue, effectively ties workers' rewards to the performance of their companies. As a result, workers may have an incentive to behave more like firm shareholders than purely as employees, thereby raising worker productivity and helping to reduce labor–management strife over wages and benefits. In addition, some economists promote profit sharing as a means of stabilizing employment, because reductions in firm profits would lead to automatic wage reductions, thereby enabling companies to experience lower wage bills without need to lay off workers. Furthermore, some argue that increased profit sharing could actually raise overall employment by effectively reducing the net cost of employing each additional unit of labor.

Figure 14–11 displays estimates of the portions of workers employed under contracts with profit-sharing clauses in the nine countries with the largest shares of workers covered by such contracts. France leads the list, with more than a fourth of its workers covered by profit-sharing schemes, which is well above Japan's 15 percent profit-sharing coverage rate. Somewhat contradictory to proponents' arguments, however, France is infamous for strikes and other manifestations of labor disgruntlement. French labor productivity growth also lags behind many countries, and it suffers from a double-digit unemployment rate.

Nevertheless, there is some evidence that firms with profit-sharing contracts experience higher productivity elsewhere, particularly in the United States. Is France a "special case"? The answer is yes. French laws *require* firms with more than 50 employees to offer government-designed, deferred profit-sharing arrangements to their workers. Hence, government edict rather than market forces determines the structure of the bulk of French profit-sharing plans. This makes it less likely that French workers and firms derive as much benefit from profit sharing.

Nevertheless, the governments of other countries also influence the degree of profit sharing. For example, in the United Kingdom profit-based bonuses are tax-free up to a threshold income level, and in the United States more than 10 percent of workers covered under profit-sharing plans are employed by businesses that receive special tax credits for offering profit-sharing plans. The Japanese government also gives favored tax treatment to certain profit-sharing schemes. Thus, profit sharing currently is not a fully market-determined process. It remains to be seen how widespread profit-sharing arrangements may become in the absence of governmental stimulus.

FOR CRITICAL ANALYSIS:
According to our theory of labor demand discussed earlier, a worker who produces additional output valued at $250 per week will earn a weekly wage of $250. Now suppose that the worker's employer offers to pay $200 per week in wages but a fixed weekly $50 share of profits, so that the worker's wage is unchanged from the worker's perspective. From the employer's perspective, however, what is the additional cost of employing the worker? Could this lead to higher employment at this and other firms?

FIGURE 14–11   PORTIONS OF WORKERS COVERED BY PROFIT-SHARING ARRANGEMENTS

In most nations, fewer than 15 percent of workers have profit-sharing agreements with their employers. In France, more than one-fourth of workers participate in profit-sharing arrangements.

SOURCE: Data from Organization for Economic Cooperation and Development.

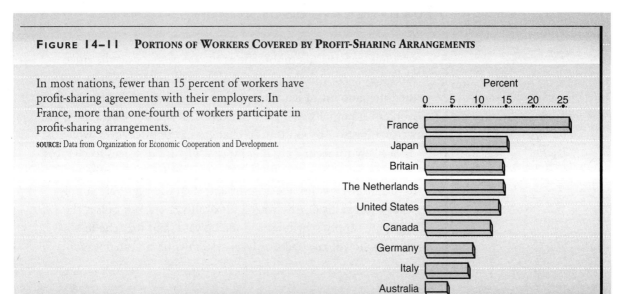

FIGURE 14–12   THE SHORT-RUN AND LONG-RUN AGGREGATE SUPPLY SCHEDULES

Over a short-run period in which nominal wages are fixed and do not adjust to changes in the price level, the aggregate supply schedule, $y^s(W^f)$. In the long run, which is a sufficiently lengthy interval during which the wage determination process can account for an increase in the price level, the aggregate supply schedule is vertical, as illustrated by the schedule denoted y_{LR}^s.

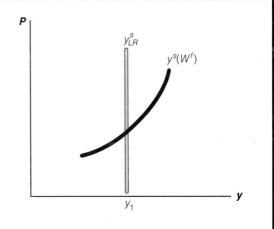

> **FUNDAMENTAL ISSUE #4**
>
> **What is the aggregate supply schedule?** The aggregate supply schedule consists of combinations of real output and the price level that are consistent with firms' production capabilities and the total amount of labor employed, given the process by which workers' nominal wages are determined. If the overall level of wages adjusts in proportion to changes in the price level, which is most likely to occur only if contracts fully index wages to changes in the price level or if sufficient time passes for wages otherwise to make such a complete adjustment, then the aggregate supply schedule is vertical. Any wage inflexibility, however, causes the aggregate supply schedule to slope upward, and the schedule is most shallow if contracts or legal restraints fix nominal wages.

REAL OUTPUT, THE PRICE LEVEL, AND ECONOMIC POLICYMAKING

The aggregate demand and aggregate supply schedules together provide a foundation for understanding the determination of a country's price level and its volume of real output. In addition, as you will learn in this section, they also provide a framework for examining how economic policies may influence a nation's real GDP and inflation rate.

The Equilibrium Price Level and the Equilibrium Real Output Level

The *equilibrium price level* is the price level at which all workers and firms are willing to produce a level of output that maintains both equality of real income and aggregate desired expenditures and money market equilibrium. Thus, at an economy's equilibrium price level, firms are satisfied producing the current output of goods and services at the wages they pay workers, there is no tendency for current real income to change, and the current interest rate is consistent with equilibrium in the market for real money balances.

Figure 14–13 illustrates the determination of the equilibrium price level, P_1, which arises at the single point E where the aggregate demand and aggregate supply schedules cross. At this price level, the equilibrium level of real output, y_1, by definition corresponds to a real income level consistent with an *IS–LM* equilibrium, because point E is on the aggregate demand schedule. Therefore, real income is equal to aggregate desired expenditures, and the market for real money balances is in equilibrium. At the same time, point E is on the aggregate supply schedule, so y_1 also constitutes a level of real output that firms are willing and able to produce, given the current technology available to them

FIGURE 14–13 DETERMINATION OF THE EQUILIBRIUM PRICE LEVEL AND EQUILIBRIUM REAL OUTPUT

The equilibrium price level and the equilibrium level of real output arise at the intersection of the aggregate demand and aggregate supply schedules. This point, denoted E, is on the aggregate demand schedule and corresponds to a point of *IS–LM* equilibrium, so the market for real money balances is in equilibrium and real income is equal to aggregate desired expenditures. At the same time, this point is on the aggregate supply schedule, and so at the price level corresponding to point E, workers and firms are willing and able to produce the equilibrium real output level. If the price level happened to equal P_2, then the level of aggregate desired expenditures is consistent with an output level equal to y_3, but the aggregate output level that firms produce is equal to y_2. Thus, the equilibrium price level must rise to P_1 at point E, which yields the equilibrium output level y_1.

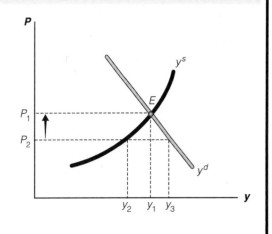

and the nominal wages that they pay workers. It follows that y_1 is the *equilibrium real output level* for the economy.

To see why P_1 and y_1 constitute the equilibrium price level–real output combination, suppose that the actual price level happens to equal P_2. At this price level, the real value of money balances supplied by the central bank is driven upward, thereby pushing down the equilibrium nominal interest rate in the money market. This raises aggregate desired expenditures to an amount consistent with the real income level y_3 in Figure 14–13. At the same time, however, the lower price level P_2 reduces the value of labor's marginal product, inducing firms to demand less labor at any given nominal wage and, therefore, to produce less real output. Thus, the actual level of real output produced is equal to y_2. A rise in the price level thereby must occur to push the value of real money balances downward. This increases the equilibrium interest rate and depresses investment expenditures, thereby reducing aggregate spending and the quantity of real output demanded. In addition, an increase in the price level raises the value of the marginal product of labor, causing firms to increase employment of labor and output production. Hence, there must be upward pressure on the price level if the price level is equal to P_2, and the price level rises toward P_1 to reattain full equilibrium.

The Output and Price Level Effects of Economic Policies with Floating versus Fixed Exchange Rates

Monetary and fiscal policies can affect the position of the aggregate demand schedule. In turn, aggregate demand, together with aggregate supply, determines the equilibrium price level and the equilibrium volume of real output.

It follows that monetary and fiscal policies may play roles in influencing the level of GDP and the inflation rate in an open economy.

Aggregate Demand, Output, and Inflation   To see how monetary or fiscal policy actions might have short-run effects on real output and the price level, consider Figure 14–14. You learned in the opening section of this chapter that monetary and fiscal policies can, under certain circumstances, influence the position of the aggregate demand schedule. Figure 14–14 illustrates a situation in which a policy action induces a rise in aggregate demand, thereby causing the aggregate demand schedule to shift to the right along the short-run aggregate supply schedule.

As a result of the increase in aggregate demand, at the initial equilibrium price level P_1, the desired quantity of real output demanded increases. To induce a rise in the actual amount of production, however, the price level must rise to a new equilibrium level, P_2. This rise in the price level raises the value of the marginal product of labor, thereby inducing firms to employ more workers and produce a larger volume of goods and services. Consequently, the level of real output increases from its initial equilibrium level y_1 to a new, higher level y_2.

Thus, in principle, an expansionary policy action that yields an increase in aggregate demand has the following key effects. First, it produces inflation, because it pushes up the price level. Second, in the short run the rise in the price level generates increased real output. Finally, associated with the rise in real output is an increase in total employment in the economy.

Economic Policies, Output, and Inflation with Floating versus Fixed Exchange Rates   As we discussed earlier, how monetary and fiscal policies influence

---

FIGURE 14–14   THE EFFECTS OF A POLICY-INDUCED INCREASE IN AGGREGATE DEMAND SHORT-RUN AND LONG-RUN AGGREGATE SUPPLY SCHEDULES

An expansionary monetary, exchange rate, or fiscal policy action causes the aggregate demand schedule to shift to the right along the short-run aggregate supply schedule. This results in a rise in the equilibrium price level and an increase in equilibrium real output.

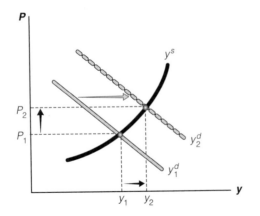

aggregate demand depends both on the degree of capital mobility and whether exchange rates float in the foreign exchange markets or are fixed through central bank interventions. It follows that these same factors condition the potential effects that policy actions may exert on a nation's price level and volume of aggregate real output.

Policy Effects on Real Output and the Price Level under Floating Exchange Rates
In the first part of this chapter, we determined that monetary policy actions always influence aggregate demand in a system of floating exchange rates. In contrast, fiscal policy actions have more limited effects on aggregate demand, and the effects of fiscal policy actions dissipate with increased capital mobility.

For this reason, adopting a system of floating exchange rates enhances the potential for monetary policy actions to have significant short-run effects on real output. Expansions in the money stock also tend to have more inflationary consequences under floating exchange rates, as compared with expansionary fiscal policy actions.

Policy Effects on Real Output and the Price Level under Fixed Exchange Rates
In a system of fixed exchange rates, a nation's central bank must intervene in foreign exchange markets as needed to maintain the value of the nation's currency. Barring sustained sterilization of such interventions, the result is that any efforts to expand aggregate demand via an expansion of the quantity of money in circulation typically place downward pressure on the value of the nation's currency that must be offset by a contraction in the money stock. Therefore, changes in the quantity of money generally have muted effects on aggregate demand and, thus, on real output and the price level, under fixed exchange rates. By way of contrast, maintaining fixed exchange rates enhances the potential influence of fiscal policy actions on aggregate demand and, consequently, on equilibrium real output and prices.

Another manner in which policymakers might bring about an expansion in aggregate demand, a short-run rise in equilibrium real output, and an associated increase in the price level would be through a currency *devaluation*. A devaluation induces a rise in net export spending and, thus, causes an increase in aggregate demand.

FUNDAMENTAL ISSUE #5

How are a nation's price level and volume of real output determined, and how might economic policymakers influence inflation and real output? The intersection of the aggregate demand and aggregate supply schedules determines the equilibrium level of real output and the equilibrium price level. At equilibrium, all workers and firms are willing and able to produce the amount of real output that yields a real income level equal to aggregate desired expenditures and money market equilibrium at the current price level. Under floating exchange rates, changes in the money stock are the key means by which economic policymaking might influence aggregate demand, the price level, and real output. Under fixed exchange rates, fiscal policy actions and devaluations are economic policy actions that are most likely to affect aggregate demand, the price level, and real output.

RULES VERSUS DISCRETION IN ECONOMIC POLICYMAKING

The preceding analysis indicates that there are a number of circumstances under which it appears that monetary, fiscal, and exchange rate policies *potentially* can influence the economy's volume of real output and, by implication, employment level. An important issue, however, is whether such policies *actually* can play a role in affecting a nation's real economic performance.

Expectations and the Flexibility of Nominal Wages

Many economists are skeptical about the likelihood that most monetary, fiscal, or exchange rate policy actions can have significant, long-lived effects on a nation's real output and employment levels. The basis for their skepticism is their doubts that economic policymakers can initiate policy actions without altering the behavior of private individuals and businesses. If workers and firms can *anticipate* the effects of particular policy actions, these economists argue, then it is less likely that such actions can influence real output and employment.

The Rational Expectations Hypothesis The linchpin of this view is called the **rational expectations hypothesis.** According to this hypothesis, a person attempts to make the best possible forecast of an economic variable using all available past *and current* information *and* drawing on an understanding of what factors affect the determination of the economic variable.

For instance, as workers bargain with firms over their nominal wages, they must try to forecast the level of prices so that they can try to maintain a desired purchasing power of their wages. If workers' expectations are *rational*, then they will use all information available to them at the time they negotiate their wages. In addition, they will take into account all the factors that play a role in determining the price level during the period that their wage bargain will be in force.

RATIONAL EXPECTATIONS HYPOTHESIS The hypothesis that people form expectations using all available past and current information, plus their understanding of how the economy operates.

Wages, Employment, and Output When Policy Actions Are Anticipated Figure 14–15 depicts the implication that the rational expectations hypothesis

FIGURE 14–15   NOMINAL WAGES AND EMPLOYMENT UNDER RATIONAL EXPECTATIONS

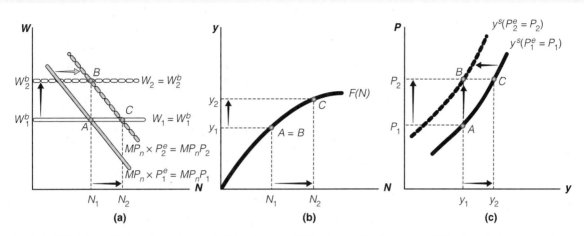

At the initial points labeled A, workers and firms have established an initial base wage, W_1^b, given their expectation of the price level, $P_1^e = P_1$, and their anticipation of the value of the marginal product of labor, $VMP_N^1 = MP_N \times P_1^e = MP_N \times P_1$ in panel (a). If workers and firms form expectations rationally and recognize that a policy action is likely to raise the price level, then they will raise their price expectation to $P_2^e = P_2$ and negotiate a higher base nominal wage W_2^b. As a result, equilibrium real output will remain unchanged in panel (b), so that the aggregate supply schedule will shift upward by the amount of the anticipated increase in the price level, from point A to point B in panel (c). Only if workers and firms fail to anticipate policy actions that cause rise in the price level would movements from point A to point C, and corresponding short-run increases in employment and output, take place.

has for wage and employment determination. At the initial points labeled A in the figure, we assume that workers and firms have established an initial base wage, denoted W_1^b. We assume in panel (a) that they have set this base wage in light of their *expectation* of the price level, $P_1^e = P_1$ (where the superscript e denotes an expectation) and, consequently, their *anticipation* of the value of the marginal product of labor, $VMP_N^1 = MP_N \times P_1^e = MP_N \times P_1$, during the period in which firms pay workers the base wage W_1^b. If the actual price level in fact turns out to equal P_1, then the employment level equals N_1 at point A. As a result, in panel (b) the level of real output is equal to y_1. Hence, in panel (c) the resulting real output–price level combination y_1 and P_1 is at point A on the aggregate supply schedule $y^s(W_1^b)$.

Suppose, however, that just before workers agree to the base wage W_1^b, they learn that an economic policymaker intends to embark on a new policy strategy that is likely to increase the price level. Such a price increase would erode the purchasing power of their wages. Thus, as shown in panel (a), workers have an incentive to renegotiate a higher base wage, W_2^b, in light of their forecast of the higher price level that they would expect to arise following the policy action, denoted $P_2^e = P_2$. To keep the purchasing power of their wages the same, workers thereby insist on an increase in the base wage in proportion to the expected rise in the price level. For instance, if P_2^e were 5 percent higher than P_1^e, workers negotiate a base nominal wage W_2^b that would be 5 percent above W_1^b.

As you can see in panel (*b*), if the actual price level rises to P_2–by the amount workers anticipate when they renegotiate their wages–the result is no change in employment at point *B*. Thus, in panel (*b*), we can see that real output remains unchanged following the correctly anticipated rise in the price level from P_1 to P_2. As shown in panel (*c*), this means that the aggregate supply schedule shifts *upward* by the amount of the anticipated increase in the price level, to $y^s(W_1^b)$. We may conclude that if workers are able to correctly anticipate an increase in the price level resulting from an economic policy action, the result would be no change in real output. Thus, the policy action also would not affect employment.

Wages, Employment, and Output When Policy Actions Are Unanticipated
This is not to say that economic policies could never affect output and employment. For example, consider the points labeled *C* in Figure 14–15. These points denote the outcomes of an *unanticipated* rise in the price level from P_1 to P_2. In this situation workers expected the price level to equal P_1 when they negotiated their contract, but it actually turns out to be equal to P_2. Unless contracts indexed wages fully to such a price increase, the result in panel (*a*) would be an increase in employment at the base wage W_1^b, from N_1 to N_2 at point *C*.

The increase in employment of labor causes real output to rise from y_1 to y_2 at point *C* in panel (*b*), which implies a movement from point *A* to point *C* in panel (*c*). Thus, under the rational expectations hypothesis, an *unexpected* rise in the price level induced by an expansion in aggregate demand can induce an increase in equilibrium real output.

Our reasoning on the effects of anticipated versus unanticipated policies leads to the following conclusion:

> **If workers form price-level expectations rationally and can adjust their wage bargains with their employers in light of those expectations, then correctly anticipated policy actions have no effect on real output and employment. Only unanticipated policy changes can influence the levels of output and employment.**

This conclusion has important policy implications. One is that even if monetary, fiscal, or exchange rate policies affect aggregate demand, from a theoretical standpoint they will not necessarily influence a nation's real GDP. Note that this implication hinges on the hypothesis of rational expectations and on the extent to which workers can adjust their wage bargains. Although most economists believe that the rational expectations hypothesis is reasonable, in many nations the process by which wages are determined may not, as we noted earlier, permit speedy wage adjustments. Nevertheless, to the extent that workers can bargain for higher wages in anticipation of higher prices stemming from expansionary policy actions, the real effects of those policies are likely to be limited.

Another key implication, it turns out, is that one result of well-intentioned policymaking can be persistent inflation, such as the consistently positive rates of inflation many nations of the world have experienced since the middle of the twentieth century. Let's look at why this is so.

Discretion, Credibility, and Inflation

Figure 14–16 displays consumer price inflation rates for selected nations in various regions of the world since the mid-1980s. We could have selected a number of other nations to include in the figure, but in all countries that we otherwise might have chosen, we also would have depicted positive consumer price inflation rates in nearly every single year. Why is this true, given that governments and central banks commonly express a desire to eliminate inflation?

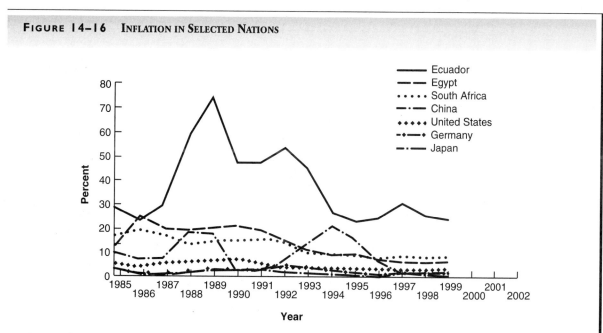

FIGURE 14–16   INFLATION IN SELECTED NATIONS

Since the mid-1980s, consumer price inflation rates in the United States, Germany, and Japan have been well below those in most other nations. Nevertheless, all nations typically have experienced positive inflation in nearly every year.

SOURCE: *World Economic Outlook,* International Monetary Fund (various issues; IMF and author estimates for 1998 and 1999).

FIGURE 14–17 **THE INFLATION BIAS OF DISCRETIONARY POLICYMAKING**

If the current equilibrium for the economy is point *A*, and if the policymaker's goals are to raise output toward the capacity output level *y** but to keep inflation low, then the policymaker's temptation is to split the difference between these conflicting objectives by inducing a rise in aggregate demand, to point *B*. But if workers realize that the policymaker has an incentive to permit prices to rise, then they will bargain for higher contract wages, thereby raising labor costs for businesses and shifting the aggregate supply schedule leftward. This means that if the policymaker ignores the temptation to induce a rise in aggregate demand, the result will be higher prices and lower real output at point *D*. To avoid this, the policymaker must raise aggregate demand as workers expect. The final equilibrium in the absence of policymaker credibility not to increase inflation, therefore, is at point *C*, with unchanged real output but a higher price level. The increase in the price level caused by a movement from point *A* to point *C* is an *inflation bias* resulting from discretionary policymaking.

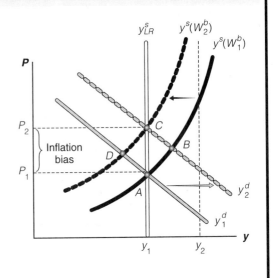

The Inflation Bias of Discretionary Economic Policymaking

A possible answer, it turns out, follows from our analysis of the determination of wages, employment, and output under rational expectations. To understand why, consider Figure 14–17. In the figure, we suppose that, given an initial base wage level W_1^b, the short-run aggregate supply schedule, $y^s(W_1^b)$ slopes upward. In the long run, when wages are able to adjust equiproportionately with price changes, the aggregate supply schedule is y_{LR}^s, which is vertical at the long-run equilibrium output level denoted y_1.

The aggregate demand schedule y_1^d crosses the short-run and long-run aggregate supply schedules at point *A*, determining the equilibrium price level P_1. Consequently, point *A* depicts a situation in which the short-run equilibrium and the long-run equilibrium coincide. The workers and firms have negotiated a contract wage that happens to match the nominal wage that arises if wages are completely flexible to changes in the aggregate price level.

In addition, Figure 14–17 displays a *target* output level, denoted y_T, that policymakers would like to achieve. We assume that this target level of output is the **capacity output level,** or the real GDP that firms could produce if labor and other factors of production were employed to their utmost. Actual output can never exceed the capacity output level, because the assessment of taxes on workers' incomes induces workers to supply fewer labor services than they otherwise would have desired. Thus, in the presence of income taxes firms are able to produce less real output than they otherwise would have planned to pro-

CAPACITY OUTPUT LEVEL
The level of real GDP that could be produced if all factors of production were fully employed.

duce. In addition, government regulations can reduce real output relative to the capacity output level that could be attained in the absence of regulations.

We shall assume that another objective of economic policymakers is to keep inflation as low as possible. Nevertheless, a policymaker's primary means of increasing output in the short run is through policy actions that move the aggregate demand schedule upward along the short-run aggregate supply schedule. This means that policymakers face a short-run trade-off between the goals of higher equilibrium output and minimum inflation. To see this, note that an increase in aggregate demand from point A in Figure 14–17 causes a rightward movement along the short-run aggregate supply schedule, causing real output to rise toward the target y_T. But a rise in aggregate demand also induces an increase in the price level, thereby generating higher inflation. Thus, remaining at the current equilibrium point A is more desirable from the standpoint of the policymaker's inflation objective.

It follows that a policymaker who cares about both the output and inflation goals tends to raise aggregate demand somewhat from point A, such as from y_1^d to y_2^d. This raises real output at the cost of additional inflation. The amount that the policymaker is willing to expand aggregate demand depends on the weight that the policymaker places on its output objective relative to its aim to keep inflation as low as possible. The policymaker's intended short-run equilibrium outcome at point B, therefore, represents a compromise outcome for the policymaker in light of this balancing of the policymaker's output and inflation goals.

If workers recognize the policymaker's goals, however, they will not let the point B outcome occur. The reason is that at point B, the price level is higher than workers and firms anticipated when determining the base wage W_1^b. Hence, the purchasing power of wages, or real wages, that workers had intended to earn is lower at point B than they would desire. Point B, therefore, is inconsistent with the wage strategy of workers.

Instead, workers recognize at the time that they negotiate their wages that the policymaker has an incentive to increase aggregate demand from y_1^d to y_2^d. They react by increasing their price expectation and negotiating a higher base wage, W_2^b, thereby inducing a leftward shift in the aggregate supply schedule, from $y^s(W_1^b)$ to $y^s(W_2^b)$. This yields point C in Figure 14–17. At point C, workers maintain the desired purchasing power of their wages, and the policymaker follows through on the aim to raise aggregate demand in an effort to increase output while holding down inflation. Thus, in contrast to point B, point C *is* a possible equilibrium point. At point C, however, the policymaker ultimately fails to increase real output, which remains equal to y_1.

Why doesn't the policymaker recognize that point B is unattainable when workers can respond by adjusting their wages and leave aggregate demand at the position y_1^d? The reason is that if workers fail to believe that the policymaker can follow through on such a commitment, then they will still raise their price expectation and negotiate an increase in their base wage. This wage increase causes the aggregate supply schedule to shift from $y^s(W_1^b)$ to $y^s(W_2^b)$.

Consequently, if the policymaker does follow through with a commitment to leave aggregate demand at y_1^d, point D results. Point D, however, is entirely inconsistent with the policymaker's aims. At this point, after all, inflation occurs and real output falls even *further* below the capacity output target y^*, to the level y_3. Therefore, point D is not a feasible equilibrium point.

Note, however, that *if* workers *can* believe a policymaker's commitment to keep the aggregate demand schedule at y_1^d, then point A is maintained as the final equilibrium point. In this special circumstance of a *credible* commitment to a zero-inflation policy, the policymaker accepts its inability to raise real output toward the capacity level. There is no inflation.

The Problem of Policy Credibility   We conclude that points A and C in Figure 14–17 are the two possible equilibrium points arising from the interaction between the policymaker's setting of aggregate demand and the determination of nominal wages by workers and firms. Point A results from commitment to a monetary policy rule, and so it denotes a *commitment equilibrium*. In contrast, point C follows from the inability or unwillingness by workers to believe that a policymaker renounces its ability to act in a discretionary manner by honoring such a commitment. Point C, in other words, is a point of *discretionary equilibrium*. Hence, these two points constitute the alternative outcomes that result from following a policy rule or pursuing discretionary policymaking.

Clearly, **policy credibility,** or the believability of the policymaker's willingness and ability to stick to a policy commitment, is the key determinant of which equilibrium point arises. Such credibility is difficult to achieve in the example illustrated in Figure 14–17, because of the **time inconsistency problem** that exists in the example. This problem is that although honoring a policy commitment yields zero inflation at point A in Figure 14–17, such an action is inconsistent with the aims of the policymaker, which has the ability to alter its policies at any time. In our example, after workers have committed to a base wage, the policymaker can expand aggregate demand, which benefits the policymaker but not workers (point B). This induces workers to bargain for an increase in their base wage, thereby forcing even a policymaker who might otherwise prefer to honor a commitment to zero inflation to raise aggregate demand in an effort to prevent a fall in real output (point D).

The result of the time inconsistency problem and the lack of policy credibility in our example is a higher price level at point C as compared with point A. Economists refer to the difference between the resulting price level P_2 at point C and the initial price level P_1 at point A as the **inflation bias** of discretionary economic policymaking. This is a bias toward inflation that stems from the ability of a policymaker to determine its policies in a discretionary manner in the presence of a time inconsistency problem and in the absence of policy credibility.

Making Economic Policies Credible   There are three types of economic policymaking that can stimulate aggregate demand and that thereby are subject to the time inconsistency problem illustrated in Figure 14–17: monetary pol-

POLICY CREDIBILITY
The believability of a policymaker's commitment to a stated intention.

TIME INCONSISTENCY PROBLEM
A situation in which a policymaker can better attain its objectives by violating a prior policy stance.

INFLATION BIAS Tendency for an economy to experience persistent inflation as a result of the time inconsistency problem and the lack of policy credibility.

icy, fiscal policy, and exchange rate policy. The same basic time inconsistency problem arises in all three areas of policymaking. This is that a policymaker may gain from short-run expansions of aggregate demand after workers negotiate their nominal wages.

How can economic policymakers gain sufficient credibility to honor commitments to noninflationary policies? It turns out that there are several possible mechanisms for reducing or even eliminating the inflation bias that can arise from discretionary policymaking.

Constitutional Limitations on Monetary Policy   One approach, which has been advocated by a number of observers, such as Milton Friedman of the Hoover Institution at Stanford University, would be for nations to adopt firm legal prohibitions against discretionary policymaking. In Germany, for instance, the nation's constitution requires the Bundesbank, Germany's central bank, to pursue a policy of price stability. The German constitution also limits the ability of the German government to interfere with the Bundesbank's policies. This makes a Bundesbank's commitment to low-inflation policies much more credible than it would be otherwise.

Establishing a Reputation   In the absence of constitutional limitations, a policymaker might gain credibility by establishing and maintaining a reputation as an "inflation hawk." To see how a policymaker might do this, reconsider Figure 14–17 on page 484. Recall that if a policymaker honors a commitment not to raise aggregate demand in pursuit of short-term output gains but is not believed by workers and firms, then the result is higher inflation and reduced output, as depicted in Figure 14–17 by a movement from point *A* to point *D*. If the policymaker cares only about the current real output level and inflation rate, it never desires for point *D* to occur. If the central bank wishes to establish a future reputation as an inflation hawk, however, then it might be willing to let output fall to point *D* in the figure. From that time onward, the policymaker's promises not to raise aggregate demand in pursuit of short-term output gains might then be credible.

Appointing a "Conservative," Independent Policymaker   The theory of the discretionary inflation bias implies that a key factor influencing the size of the inflation bias is how much a policymaker dislikes inflation relative to how much the policymaker desires to try to raise real output toward its capacity level. Thus, appointing a **conservative policymaker,** or an individual who dislikes inflation more than the average citizen, may be one means of reducing the size of the inflation bias.

Most proposals for the appointment of conservative policymakers as a possible way to limit the discretionary inflation bias have focused on central banks. One reason is that in most nations the officials who head such institutions are, indeed, appointed by elected leaders. Another reason is that central banks can be powerful policymaking institutions under either floating or fixed exchange rates. On the one hand, in a system of flexible exchange rates, expansionary monetary policies have the potential to be highly inflationary. On the

ON THE WEB

Learn more about the Bundesbank's structure at: **http://www.bundesbank. de/index_e.html**

CONSERVATIVE POLICYMAKER A central bank official who dislikes inflation more than an average citizen in society and who thereby is less willing to induce discretionary increases in the quantity of money in an effort to achieve short-run increases in real output.

other hand, even in a system of fixed exchange rates, central banks may have considerable input into decisions to devalue a nation's currency. Thus, the credibility of a commitment to an exchange rate target intended to be consistent with low inflation may depend in large part on the credibility of a nation's central bank.

Recently a number of economists, and notably Carl Walsh of the University of California at Santa Cruz, have proposed the use of **central banker contracts,** or legally binding agreements between governments and appointed central bank officials. Under such contracts, central bank officials would be punished, or perhaps rewarded, depending on the nation's inflation performance. One real-world example of a central banker contract has been in effect in New Zealand since 1989. Under the New Zealand central banking arrangement, consistent departures from price stability that clearly stem from aggregate demand expansions leads to dismissal of the head of the central bank.

The point of central banker contracts is to make central bank officials more *accountable.* Nevertheless, adopting central banker contracts does not preclude granting central bank officials considerable *independence* to conduct the monetary or exchange rate policies that they feel would be needed to keep inflation low. In fact, a number of economists contend that central bank independence may be a key element in a successful low-inflation policy. They argue that establishing a reputation as an inflation hawk is difficult for a central bank official who is constrained by political pressures to achieve other objectives as well, such as a low unemployment rate or a high growth rate for real output. Thus, these economists argue that governments should make central banks *politically independent* by insulating them from such political pressures. Furthermore, they argue, accountability for a country's inflation performance is an unfair burden to place on central bank officials if governments fail to grant these officials *economic independence,* or the power to determine their own budget or to provide direct financial support for government policy initiatives. From this perspective, a fully independent central bank would be both politically and economically independent.

To support their contention about the potential desirability of central bank independence, advocates of this approach point to evidence such as that depicted in panels (*a*) and (*b*) of Figure 14–18. Each panel plots an index measure of central bank overall political and economic independence along the horizontal axis. Panel (*a*) plots average annual inflation rates between the mid-1950s and the late 1980s along the vertical axis and illustrates that there has been an *inverse relationship* between central bank independence and average inflation. Hence, nations with more independent central banks, such as Germany, Switzerland, and the United States, typically experience lower average inflation.

Panel (*b*) of Figure 14–18 plots the variance of inflation along the vertical axis and indicates that there also has been an inverse relationship between central bank independence and inflation variability. That is, nations with more independent central banks tend to experience less inflation volatility.

CENTRAL BANKER CONTRACT
A legally binding agreement between a government and a central banking official that holds the official responsible for a nation's inflation performance.

ON THE WEB
Visit the Reserve Bank of New Zealand at:
http://www.rbnz.govt.nz

FIGURE 14-18 CENTRAL BANK INDEPENDENCE, AVERAGE INFLATION, AND INFLATION VARIABILITY

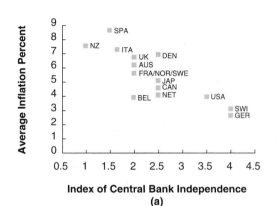

Index of Central Bank Independence
(a)

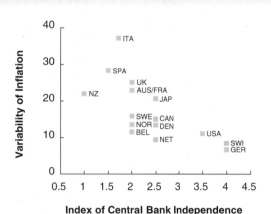

Index of Central Bank Independence
(b)

Key:

AUS:	Austria	NET:	Netherlands
BEL:	Belgium	NZ:	New Zealand
CAN:	Canada	NOR:	Norway
DEN:	Denmark	SPA:	Spain
FRA:	France	SWE:	Sweden
GER:	Germany	SWI:	Switzerland
ITA:	Italy	UK:	United Kingdom
JAP:	Japan	US:	United States

As panel (*a*) shows, nations with more independent central banks, such as Germany, Switzerland, and the United States, have lower inflation rates as compared with countries with less independent central banks. Panel (*b*) indicates that nations with more independent central banks also have experienced less inflation variability.

SOURCE: From "Central Bank Independence and Macroeconomic Performance" by Alberto Alesina and Lawrence Summers, in *Journal of Money, Credit, and Banking*, Vol. 25, No. 2, May 1993 is reprinted by permission. Copyright © 1993 by the Ohio State University Press. All rights reserved.

Together, panels (*a*) and (*b*) therefore indicate that greater central bank independence tends to yield more stable inflation rates, as well as reduced average inflation.

This evidence supporting the theoretical arguments favoring more independent central banks has induced a number of countries, such as France, Japan, Mexico, Pakistan, and the United Kingdom, to grant significantly greater political and economic independence to their central banks. In addition, the evidence, plus the low-inflation experience of Germany under its highly independent Bundesbank, led European nations to agree that if a European central bank ultimately is established, the central bank will have considerable independence from national governments.

FUNDAMENTAL ISSUE #6

Why does the rational expectations hypothesis indicate that economic policies may have limited real output effects and that the credibility of policymakers is important? The rational expectations hypothesis is that people use all available information and their understanding of how the economy functions to predict the price level. Hence, if workers make rational price level forecasts when negotiating their nominal wages, they will bargain for higher nominal wages when they correctly anticipate that policymakers plan to enact policies to expand real output. Such wage increases would induce firms to reduce employment and output, which would offset the intended effects of the policy actions. Thus, if workers recognize that policymakers have an incentive to try to expand real output, workers will respond by negotiating wage increases that push up the price level, spurring inflation. Only if policymakers can credibly commit to low-inflation policies would workers agree to suppress wage increases, thereby limiting inflation.

CHAPTER SUMMARY

1. **The Aggregate Demand Schedule:** This schedule displays all combinations of real income and the price level that maintain *IS–LM* equilibrium. Thus, at any point along an aggregate demand schedule, real income equals aggregate desired expenditures at the same time that the quantity of real money balances supplied equals the quantity of real money balances demanded.

2. **The Factors that Determine the Extent to which Changes in the Quantity of Money Can Influence Aggregate Demand in an Open Economy:** The key factors influencing how an increase in the amount of money in circulation may affect aggregate demand are the system of exchange rates and the extent of capital mobility. An unsterilized increase in the quantity of money does not influence aggregate demand under fixed exchange rates. In contrast, an increase in the money stock does push up aggregate demand if exchange rates float, and greater capital mobility adds to the amount by which aggregate demand rises.

3. **The Factors that Determine the Extent to which Fiscal Policy Actions Can Influence Aggregate Demand in an Open Economy:** The effects of an increase in government spending on aggregate demand depend on the exchange rate system that is in place and on the degree of capital mobility. Under fixed exchange rates, an increase in government spending causes aggregate demand to increase, and greater

capital mobility enlarges this effect. Under floating exchange rates, the aggregate demand effects of higher government expenditures are less significant, and greater capital mobility mutes them even further.

4. **The Aggregate Supply Schedule:** This schedule depicts all combinations of real output and the price level that reflect the production capabilities of all firms in the economy and the aggregate level of employment of labor in light of the process by nominal wages are determined. The aggregate supply schedule is vertical if wages adjust equiproportionately to changes in the price level, which can occur only if contracts specify full wage indexation or if sufficient time passes to permit such a complete wage adjustment, then the aggregate supply schedule is vertical. To the extent that nominal wages are less flexible, however, the aggregate supply schedule exhibits a more shallow, upward slope.

5. **A Nation's Price Level and Volume of Real Output, and the Effect of Economic Policies on Inflation and Real Output:** The intersection of the aggregate demand and aggregate supply schedules determines the equilibrium price level and real output level. At the point where these schedules cross, all workers and firms are willing and able to produce the amount of real output that yields a real income level equal to aggregate desired expenditures and money market equilibrium at the prevailing price level. If exchange rates float, then monetary policy actions are the primary means by which aggregate demand, the price level, and real output might be influenced by economic policymaking. Under fixed exchange rates, fiscal policy actions or currency devaluations are economic policy actions that have the greatest effects on aggregate demand, the price level, and real output.

6. **Why the Rational Expectations Hypothesis Indicates that Economic Policies May Have Limited Real Output Effects and that the Credibility of Policymakers Is Important:** According to the rational expectations hypothesis, individuals use all the information they have, plus their knowledge of how the economy functions, when they forecast the price level. Hence, workers who make rational price level forecasts when negotiating their nominal wages will bargain for wage increases if they correctly anticipate expansionary monetary, fiscal, or exchange rate policies intended to raise real output. The resulting rise in the overall wage level would induce firms to reduce employment and output, thereby offsetting the policy actions. Hence, if workers recognize that policymakers desire to raise real output, workers will bargain for inflationary wage increases. The key means by which policymakers might limit inflation would be by credibly committing to low-inflation policies.

QUESTIONS AND PROBLEMS

1. True or false? "In today's world with floating exchange rates and nearly perfect capital mobility among industrialized nations, the individual monetary policy actions of central banks are becoming irrelevant to their nations' inflation performances." Explain.

2. In anticipation of the eventual adoption of a common currency, a number of European nations have been moving toward a system of irrevocably fixed exchange rates. To qualify for entry into this system of fixed exchange rates,

however, nations must restrain their fiscal policies in clearly defined ways. Explain why such fiscal policy restraints might make sense if one key goal of European countries is to limit inflation.

3. Use an aggregate demand–aggregate supply diagram to explain why, in a system of fixed exchange rates, a currency devaluation typically results in domestic inflation. If workers' expectations are rational and if workers are able to renegotiate wage adjustments rapidly, under what circumstances would a devaluation induce an increase in real output? Under what circumstances would a devaluation fail to generate a rise in real output? Explain your reasoning.

4. Suppose that workers in a country gain clout in the wage bargaining process and are able to raise their base wages. If no other events occur, what would happen to the nation's price level and to its real GDP? Use an aggregate demand–aggregate supply diagram to explain your answer.

5. Suppose that workers in a small open economy with a fixed exchange rate realize that their nation's central bank and government wish to increase real GDP by 7 percent during the year leading up to an election, in the hope that higher employment would garner more votes for current leaders. Workers realize that 10 percent inflation would be required to yield this desired increase in real GDP. At present the nation has no constraints on the ability of its central bank and government to change its current exchange rate targets, and there is no central bank or governmental concern about high inflation. According to the basic theory of discretionary policymaking discussed in this chapter, would you predict that the central bank and government will devalue the nation's currency? If so, and if workers can bargain for wage changes, would you predict a rise in inflation and in real GDP for this nation? Justify your answers.

ON-LINE APPLICATION

If the aggregate supply schedule slopes upward, then a rise in the price level should induce an increase in a nation's real output. It follows that higher inflation should be associated with higher employment, or equivalently, with lower unemployment rates. This application allows you to take a direct look at unemployment and inflation data to judge for yourself whether or not the two variables appear to be related in the United States.

Internet URL: http://stats.bls.gov:80/

Title: U.S. Bureau of Labor Statistics: Economy at a Glance

Navigation: Begin at the home page of the U.S. Bureau of Labor Statistics (**http://stats.bls.gov**).

Application: Perform the indicated operations, and answer the following questions:

1. Click on *Economy at a Glance.* Then scan down to *Prices,* and click on *Consumer Price Index.* Take a look at the solid line showing inflation in the graph box. How much has the inflation varied in recent years? Compare this with previous years, especially the mid-1970s to the mid-1980s.

2. Back up to *Economy at a Glance,* and now click on *Unemployment Rate.* Take a look at the graph box. During what recent years was the unemployment rate approaching its peak value? Do you note any appearance of an inverse relationship between the unemployment rate and the inflation rate (part 1 above)?

REFERENCES AND RECOMMENDED READINGS

Agenor, Pierre-Richard. "The Labor Market and Economic Adjustment." *International Monetary Fund Staff Papers,* 43 (June 1996): 261–335.

Barro, Robert J. *Macroeconomic Policy.* Cambridge, Mass.: Harvard University Press, 1990.

Bryson, Jay, Chih-huan Chen, and David VanHoose. "Implications of Economic Interdependence for Endogenous Wage Indexation Decisions." *Scandinavian Journal of Economics,* 100 (1998): Forthcoming.

Calmfors, Lars, and John Driffill. "Bargaining Structure, Corporatism, and Macroeconomic Performance." *Economic Policy,* 3 (1988): 14–61.

Cukierman, Alex. *Central Bank Strategy, Credibility, and Independence.* Cambridge, Mass.: MIT Press, 1992.

Jadresic, Esteban. "Wage Indexation and the Cost of Disinflation." *International Monetary Fund Staff Papers,* 43 (December 1996): 796–825.

McCallum, Bennett T. *International Monetary Economics.* Oxford: Oxford University Press, 1996.

Pollard, Patricia. "Central Bank Independence and Economic Performance." Federal Reserve Bank of St. Louis *Review,* 75 (4) (July/August 1993): 21–36.

Sheffrin, Steven. *The Making of Economic Policy: History, Theory, Politics.* Cambridge: Blackwell, 1991.

Waller, Christopher. "Performance Contracts for Central Bankers." Federal Reserve Bank of St. Louis *Review,* 77 (5) (September/October 1995): 3–14.

Walsh, Carl, "Optimal Contracts for Central Bankers. *American Economic Review,* 85 (1) (March 1995): 150–167.

This conclusion does not necessarily mean that there are no circumstances under which central banks can influence aggregate demand in a system of fixed exchange rates. As we shall discuss shortly, central banks may choose to vary their exchange rate objectives as a means of bringing about shifts in the aggregate demand schedule.

Monetary Policy and Aggregate Demand in an Open Economy with a Floating Exchange Rate As you learned in Chapter 13, in a system in which exchange rates float, balance-of-payments deficits or surpluses lead to market exchange rate adjustments instead of foreign exchange market interventions by a nation's central bank. Panels (*a*), (*b*), and (*c*) of Figure 14–4 display the implications of an expansionary monetary policy action for aggregate demand in a system of floating exchange rates with low, high, and perfect capital mobility. Again, each panel displays pairs of diagrams depicting *IS–LM–BP* equilibrium positions and diagrams showing the corresponding aggregate demand schedules.

First consider panel (*a*), in which the steep slope of the *BP* schedule reflects the assumption of low capital mobility. An increase in the quantity of money in circulation from M_1 to a larger quantity M_2 causes the *LM* schedule to shift downward and to the right in diagram (*a*1), leading to a movement from point *A* to point *B* and a decline in the equilibrium nominal interest rate from R_1 toward R_2 and a rise in equilibrium real income from y_1 toward y_2.

Because capital mobility is low in diagram (*a*1), the fall in the equilibrium interest rate causes a relatively small capital outflow. Nevertheless, the increase in real income stimulates increased import spending, which leads to a balance-of-payments deficit at point *B*. As a result, there is downward pressure on the value of the nation's currency, leading to a domestic currency depreciation. Thus, the exchange rises from an initial value, denoted as S_1, to a higher value, S_2.

This currency depreciation reduces the effective price of the nation's exports while increasing the effective price of imports. Consequently, net export spending rises, causing an increase in aggregate autonomous expenditures and a rightward shift in the *IS* schedule in diagram (*a*1), from $IS(S_1)$ to $IS(S_2)$. Likewise, the domestic currency depreciation causes the *BP* schedule to shift downward and to the right, from $BP(S_1)$ to $BP(S_2)$, to maintain balance-of-payments equilibrium as the interest rate rises and real income increases. At point *C*, there is balance-of-payments equilibrium, and there is no further upward pressure on the exchange rate. At this final equilibrium point, the equilibrium interest rate is equal to R_2, and the equilibrium real income level is equal to y_2.

Thus, at the current price level P_1, there is a higher corresponding level of real income, y_2, that is consistent with *IS–LM* equilibrium. It follows that in diagram (*a*2), there is a rightward shift in the aggregate demand schedule, from $y^d(M_1)$ to $y^d(M_2)$. In contrast to the case of a fixed exchange rate, an expansionary monetary policy action raises aggregate demand under a floating exchange rate.

15

POLICY COORDINATION, MONETARY UNION, AND TARGET ZONES

FUNDAMENTAL ISSUES

1. What is structural interdependence, and how can it lead nations to cooperate or to coordinate their policies?

2. What are the potential benefits of international policy coordination?

3. What are the potential drawbacks of international policy coordination?

4. Could nations gain from adopting a common currency?

5. What is an exchange rate target zone?

Within the first decade of the twenty-first century, all nations of the European Union (EU) intend to be part of a European Monetary Union in which all would share the same currency, dubbed the "euro." A broader goal of EU nations is greater fiscal and even political union. Nevertheless, two questions remain open as the January 1, 1999, date for initial work on establishing the monetary union is set to begin. One is, which nations will have the greatest say in determining the union's overall economic policies? Germany, the United Kingdom, and France have more than 53 percent of the population of the proposed monetary union, but these countries together possess fewer than 35 percent of the votes in the EU's Council of Ministers and fewer than 44 percent of the seats in the EU Parliament. Some citizens of those nations already have begun to question whether monetary and fiscal policy decisions for the proposed monetary union will equally reflect the preferences of the "average" citizen of Europe.

Another question that the EU must struggle to answer is, who pays for the EU's official activities? Again, some in Europe already complain of possible inequities. For example, residents of Germany and the Netherlands naturally question why they are net contributors of funds that finance EU governance and policymaking, even though citizens of Denmark, in which per capita incomes are somewhat higher, have been net recipients of funds from the EU.

How can nations find a way to work toward common goals? Until the twentieth century, it was taken for granted that each individual nation should pursue its own citizens' interests. The German poet and statesman Johann von Goethe (1749–1832) summed up this perspective on the role of a nation in 1824: "Nothing is good for a nation but that which arises from its own core and its own general wants, without apish imitation of another." At the same time, however, there have always been those who have argued that nations should work together. In 1913, before the world had been wracked by two great wars, U.S. President Woodrow Wilson said, "Our interests are those of the open door—a door of friendship and mutual advantage."

Should countries seek self-reliance and the attainment of narrow national interests, or should they work together toward common goals? Political philosophers have most often posed this question, but in recent years it increasingly has occupied the attention of economists. In this chapter, we shall consider whether nations should determine their economic policies individually or jointly. We also shall discuss recent efforts by some nations, such as those in Western Europe, to develop unified approaches to policymaking.

INTERNATIONAL INTERDEPENDENCE

There is only one reason that nations might contemplate the joint determination of their economic policy actions. This is that international transactions in goods, services, and financial assets connect them. As a result, they may share common interests.

Structural Interdependence and International Policy Externalities

Economists are known to disagree about some issues. One general area of agreement, however, concerns the increasing openness of the world's economies. Economists widely concur that national economies are increasingly interconnected.

Structural Interdependence and Its Consequences In today's world, in which countries' citizens trade significant amounts of goods and services and exchange sizable volumes of financial instruments across national boundaries, national economies are **structurally interdependent.** This means nations' economic systems—their markets for goods and services, financial markets, and payment systems—are interlinked.

STRUCTURAL INTERDEPENDENCE The interconnectedness of countries' markets for goods and services, financial markets, and payment systems, which causes events in one nation to have effects on the economy of another nation.

An important consequence of structural interdependence is that events that benefit or harm the interests of one country may also have a bearing on the interests of citizens of another nation. This means that collective actions that citizens of a nation undertake in their own interest may spill over to influence the welfare of other countries' residents. Economists refer to such spillover effects as **externalities.** These are benefits or costs experienced by one individual or group as a result of actions by another individual or group in a separate location or market.

EXTERNALITY A benefit or cost felt by one individual or group stemming from actions by another individual or group in another location or market.

Externalities may be either *negative* or *positive.* A negative externality arises when market transactions among one set of individuals harm others. A commonly cited negative externality is pollution, in which the act of producing a good that benefits one group of firms and consumers fouls the air or water, thereby reducing the well being of others. Likewise, a negative *international externality* may arise if the actions of a body of individuals in one nation adversely affect economic performance of another nation. It is also possible that the collective actions of one nation's residents may improve the economic performance in another country. This constitutes a positive international externality.

International Policy Externalities A nation's political system typically charges individual leaders, groups of representatives or delegates, or government agencies with conducting economic policies on behalf of the nation's citizens. As we have discussed in the preceding chapters, such policies can alter the choices of private residents and businesses, thereby influencing a country's overall economic performance.

INTERNATIONAL POLICY EXTERNALITY A benefit or cost for one nation's economy owing to a policy action undertaken in another nation.

If national economies are structurally interdependent, then **international policy externalities,** or benefits or costs of policy effects that spill over onto other nations, may result. For instance, as the two-country models in prior chapters illustrated, *locomotive effects* or *beggar-thy-neighbor effects* can occur when a policy action in one nation affects the economic performance of other nations. If a locomotive effect arises, then a policy-induced increase in real income in one country also engenders a rise in real income in another country. Hence, the locomotive effect is an example of a positive international policy externality. In contrast, the beggar-thy-neighbor effect, which arises if a policy action raises real income at home at the expense of reduced real income abroad, constitutes a negative international policy externality.

STRATEGIC POLICYMAKING The formulation of planned policy actions in light of the structural linkages among nations and the manner in which other countries' policymakers may conduct their own policies.

National policymakers recognize that their policy actions may affect other countries. They also realize that decisions by foreign policymakers may influence economic performance at home. This gives policymakers an incentive to engage in **strategic policymaking,** meaning that they develop a plan for achieving objectives for their own nation, taking into account the extent to which their nation is structurally linked to others and courses of action that other nations' policymakers may pursue. Recognition that positive and negative externalities may result from policies that policymakers undertake also may induce them to band together to minimize the negative consequences of their individual policy choices and to enhance the positive spillovers that might result.

Accounting for Interdependence: International Policy Cooperation and Coordination

There are two ways that nations might try to work together to achieve their economic performance objectives.

INTERNATIONAL POLICY COOPERATION The adoption of institutions and procedures by which national policymakers can inform each other about their objectives, policy strategies, and national economic data.

International Policy Cooperation The first of these is through **international policy cooperation.** This refers to the formal establishment of institutions and processes through which national policymakers can collaborate on their national goals, provide information about specific approaches they intend to follow in implementing policies, and share information and data about their countries' economic performances.

An example of an institutional arrangement that facilitates international policy cooperation is the *Group of Seven (G7)*. As we discussed in Chapter 3, this is a collection of seven nations—Canada, France, Germany, Italy, Japan, the United Kingdom, and the United States—whose chief economic policy officials meet on a regular basis. At these meetings, G7 officials discuss their broad policy objectives and plans, as well as more specific economic issues of concern to the member nations.

BANK FOR INTERNATIONAL SETTLEMENTS (BIS) An institution based in Basle, Switzerland, which serves as an international loan trustee, as an agent for central banks, and a center of economic cooperation among the Group of Ten nations.

Another example is the **Bank for International Settlements (BIS).** This institution, which is based in Basle, Switzerland, functions as a trustee for various international loan agreements and serves as an agent in miscellaneous foreign exchange markets for many of the world's central banks. In 1930, private U.S. banks, including Citibank and J. P. Morgan, participated with governments of the Group of Ten (G10) nations in developing the BIS. Indeed, many private banks continue to own shares in the BIS. Its original task was to supervise the settlement of financial claims among European nations that related to terms of the World War I Armistice. After World War II, the BIS became a central agent for clearing payments among nations participating in the European Recovery Program designed to rebuild the economies of countries emerging from the ravages of that war. Ultimately the BIS developed into a clearing house for information of central banks of the G10 plus the Bank of Switzerland, the Swiss central bank. Economic staff members of the BIS organize periodic briefings for top G10 central banking officials and coordinate conferences for staff economists of policy-making agencies of the G10 nations.

INTERNATIONAL POLICY COORDINATION The joint determination of economic policies within a group of nations for the intended benefit of the group as a whole.

International Policy Coordination The BIS facilitated one instance of **international policy coordination,** which refers to the joint determination of national economic policies for the mutual benefit of a group of countries. In 1988, central banks and other banking regulators of the G10 nations adopted the *Basle Agreement,* which, as discussed in Chapter 7, established common risk-based bank capital adequacy standards—minimum levels of owner backing of banks' assets, adjusted for the riskiness of those assets—for private banking institutions incorporated within those countries.

By coordinating their banking policies, the G10 nations sought to address the international policy externalities that naturally can arise from the widespread competitive interactions of their countries' banks. For instance, if only one of the G10 countries had adopted tough capital standards for its banking system, its banks would have been placed at a competitive disadvantage in international financial markets, because its banks would have needed to back their assets with larger volumes of private capital. Likewise, if one nation had failed to adopt the Basle standards, its nations' banks could have grabbed larger shares of lending around the world. Coordination of the imposition of capital requirements ensured that neither of these policy externalities arose.

Proponents of international policy coordination argue that nations around the world could gain considerably from broad-based policy coordination. Rather than just coordinating their policies from time to time, as in the 1988 Basle Agreement on bank capital standards, these observers contend, nations should make policy coordination a day-to-day process. Indeed, many argue that countries could reap considerable gains from coordinating *all* their economic policies, including those aimed at broad output and inflation objectives.

FUNDAMENTAL ISSUE #1

What is structural interdependence, and how can it lead nations to cooperate or to coordinate their policies? When national economies are linked together, then they are structurally interdependent. As a result, policy actions in one country can have spillover effects, or international policy externalities, that influence economic performance in other nations. International policy externalities are said to be positive if they improve other countries' economic performances. They are negative if they worsen those nations' prospects. To enhance the potential for positive policy externalities, or to reduce the likelihood of negative externalities, nations may choose to cooperate by sharing information about economic data and policy objectives. They also may choose to coordinate their policymaking by determining policy actions that are in their joint interest.

PERFECT CAPITAL MOBILITY REVISITED:
CAN INTERNATIONAL POLICY COORDINATION PAY?

In Chapters 12 and 13, we contemplated the implications of policy actions for the economic performances of two nations that were completely open to cross-border capital flows, under the assumption that the nations' price levels were unaffected by policy actions. To consider how international policy coordination might be beneficial for two nations, let's again assume that capital is completely mobile across the nations' borders. In addition, suppose that the rate of exchange of the two nations' currencies floats freely in the foreign exchange market. Now, however, let's be more realistic by contemplating a flexible price level in both countries.

The Aggregate Demand Effects of National Monetary Policies

As we discussed in Chapter 14, if the domestic central bank increases the nominal quantity of domestic money in circulation, then, as shown in panel (a) of Figure 15–1, at the current price level P_1 there is a rise in the quantity of real money balances, from an initial level M_1/P_1 to a higher level M_2/P_1. The result is a rightward shift in the domestic LM schedule, from $LM(M_1/P_1)$ to

FIGURE 15–1   AGGREGATE DEMAND EFFECTS OF A DOMESTIC MONETARY EXPANSION IN A TWO-COUNTRY MODEL
WITH PERFECT CAPITAL MOBILITY AND A FLOATING EXCHANGE RATE

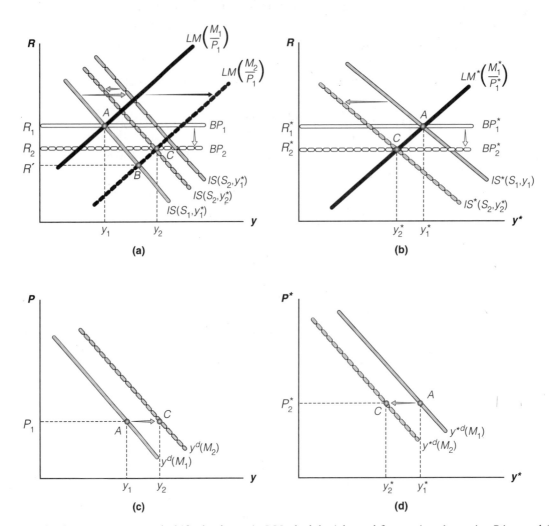

A rise in the domestic money stock shifts the domestic *LM* schedule rightward from point *A* to point *B* in panel (*a*). The resulting fall in the domestic interest rate induces capital to flow from the domestic country to the foreign country, causing the equilibrium exchange rate to rise from S_1 to S_2. This domestic currency depreciation causes the domestic *IS* schedule to shift rightward in panel (*a*) and, assuming that the net effect on the domestic trade balance of the domestic currency depreciation and rise in foreign real income is negative, it causes the foreign *IS* schedule to shift leftward in panel (*b*). The rise in foreign real income then causes the domestic *IS* schedule to shift leftward somewhat. In panels (*a*) and (*b*) points *C* are the final equilibrium points, which indicates that aggregate demand rises in the domestic country, as shown in panel (*c*), while aggregate demand falls in the foreign country, as shown in panel (*d*).

$LM(M_2/P_1)$. This causes the domestic interest rate to fall from its initial equilibrium value of R_1 at point A toward a lower value of R' at point B, below the BP schedule, denoted $BP(S_1)$, that corresponds to the initial equilibrium exchange rate. Under our maintained assumption of perfect capital mobility, this decrease in the domestic interest rate induces a movement of financial resources from the domestic country to the foreign country. Thus, there is an increase in the domestic demand for foreign currency and a reduction in the foreign demand for domestic currency. Consequently, the value of the domestic currency depreciates relative to the foreign currency, so the equilibrium exchange rate rises from its initial value of S_1 to a higher level, S_2.

Because the domestic currency depreciation reduces domestic imports and increases domestic exports, at the initial level of foreign real income, y_1^*, the domestic IS schedule shifts to the right in panel (a) of Figure 15–1, from $IS(S_1, y_1^*)$ to $IS(S_2, y_1^*)$. In the foreign country, by way of contrast, the appreciation of the foreign currency increases foreign imports and reduces foreign exports. We assume that this direct negative effect on the foreign trade balance is greater than the positive effect stemming from the offsetting rise in foreign exports generated by the rise in domestic real income, so that the foreign IS schedule shifts to the left on net in panel (b), from $IS^*(S_1, y_1)$ to $IS^*(S_2, y_2)$. The net decline in foreign real income causes foreign import spending to decline somewhat, so that domestic exports decline, inducing the domestic IS schedule to shift back to the left somewhat, from $IS(S_1, y_1^*)$ to $IS(S_2, y_1^*)$. At the final equilibrium points C in both panels, the equilibrium domestic nominal interest rate converges to an equality with the equilibrium foreign interest rate, with $R_2 = R_2^*$, as the BP schedules for both nations shift downward.

On the one hand, at the equilibrium point C in panel (a), the equilibrium level of domestic real income, y_2, is greater than its initial equilibrium value, y_1. As panel (c) indicates, this implies a rightward shift in the domestic aggregate demand schedule, from $y^d(M_1)$ to $y^d(M_2)$. Hence, as we saw in Chapter 14 for the case of a small open economy, an increase in the domestic money stock raises domestic aggregate demand.

On the other hand, at point C in panel (b), equilibrium foreign real income, y_2^*, is less than its initial level, y_1^*. As shown in panel (d), this is true at the current foreign price level, denoted P_1^*. Hence, as you learned in Chapter 13, under a floating exchange rate and perfect capital mobility, a domestic monetary expansion typically has a beggar-thy-neighbor effect on the foreign country. As panel (d) indicates, the rise in the quantity of domestic money in circulation, because of the response of the exchange rate, shifts the foreign aggregate demand schedule leftward, from $y^{*d}(M_1)$ to $y^{*d}(M_2)$. Thus, an increase in the domestic money stock *reduces* foreign aggregate demand and thereby constitutes a negative international policy externality for the foreign country.

A foreign monetary expansion also constitutes a negative international policy externality from the perspective of the domestic country. It causes the foreign LM^* schedule to shift to the right and then induces a rightward shift of the foreign IS^* schedule as the foreign currency's value depreciates and a leftward shift of the domestic *IS* schedule as the domestic currency's value appreciates. This generates declines in equilibrium nominal interest rates in both nations, a rise in equilibrium foreign real income, and a decline in equilibrium domestic real income.

Conflicting Monetary Policies and the Potential Role of Policy Coordination

The preceding discussion indicates that in a two-country setting with a floating exchange rate and perfect capital mobility, there is a natural *conflict* in monetary policymaking. Figure 15–2 illustrates such a policy conflict. In panel (*a*), we suppose that the domestic central bank desires to bring about a short-run increase in equilibrium domestic output, from y_1 to a target output level denoted y_T. To accomplish this objective, the domestic central bank must increase the quantity of domestic money in circulation from an initial value, M_1, to a higher level, M_2. Given the current level of the foreign money stock, M_1^*, this action causes the domestic aggregate demand schedule to shift rightward, from $y^d(M_1, M_1^*)$ to $y^d(M_2, M_1^*)$. Holding all else constant, equilibrium domestic real output then rises from y_1 at point *A* to y_T at point *B*.

FIGURE 15–2 AN EXAMPLE OF A TWO-COUNTRY MONETARY POLICY CONFLICT

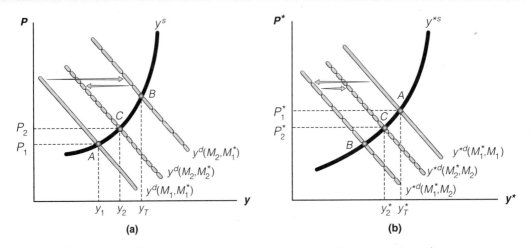

In panel (*a*), the domestic central bank increases the domestic money stock to try to raise real output to a target level, y_T, at point *B*. The resulting foreign currency appreciation causes the foreign aggregate demand schedule to shift leftward, pushing foreign output below the foreign central bank's target output level, y_T^*, at point *B* in panel (*b*). This induces the foreign central bank to increase the foreign money stock, yielding a final equilibrium at point *C* in panel (*b*), and causing the domestic aggregate demand schedule to shift back to the left in panel (*a*) to a final equilibrium at point *C*. Thus, on net, the final equilibrium output levels in the two countries can end up well below desired levels.

As we discussed earlier, however, this domestic monetary policy action causes the foreign aggregate demand schedule to shift leftward, from $y^{*d}(M_1^*, M_1)$ to $y^{*d}(M_1^*, M_2)$. In an effort to offset this resulting decline in foreign real output from the foreign central bank's initial target real output level y_T^*, which we assume it initially had achieved, the foreign central bank must raise the foreign money stock toward a level such as M_2^*. As shown in panel (*b*) of Figure 15–2, this foreign action shifts the foreign aggregate demand schedule to right from $y^{*d}(M_1^*, M_2)$ to a position such as that shown by $y^{*d}(M_2^*, M_2)$. Thus, we suppose that the foreign central bank's response is insufficient to completely offset the negative effect of the domestic monetary expansion. In this instance, equilibrium foreign output declines somewhat in the short run, to y_2^* at point *C*.

In the domestic country, the rise in the foreign money stock causes the domestic aggregate demand schedule to shift back to the left in panel (*a*), from $y^d(M_2, M_2^*)$ to $y^d(M_2, M_2^*)$. As a result, the net short-run effect is a net increase of domestic real income only to the level denoted y_2 at point *C*.

Thus, if the two central banks pursue their real income goals *independently*, pursuing the monetary policies that are only in the best interest of their own countries, they tend to work at cross-purposes. An expansionary policy action by one central bank tends to be offset by an expansionary policy action by the other central bank. As a result, it is possible, as shown in panels (*a*) and (*b*) of Figure 15–2, that both countries could end up in situations in which their real output levels are well below desired levels.

A Potential Gain from Policy Coordination

In principle, it might be possible for the two central banks to reduce the negative consequences of the policy conflict that they face in our previous example. The domestic central bank could do this by recognizing that any monetary expansion it initiates tends to reduce aggregate demand and equilibrium real output in the foreign country. At the same time, the foreign central bank could recognize that real output in the foreign country must fall somewhat below the foreign output target level to allow for domestic real output to be closer to its target level.

We illustrate the possible benefits of policy coordination in Figure 15–3. We consider the same initial situation as in Figure 15–2, in which the domestic country's initial equilibrium output level, y_1, is below the target level, y_T, but the foreign country's initial equilibrium output level is equal to the target level, y_T^*. If both central banks take their common interests into account and coordinate their policy efforts, then the domestic central bank recognizes that trying to raise real output to the target level y_T would generate a significant decline in foreign aggregate demand. Consequently, it will not attempt to raise real income all the way to the target level. Instead, it increases the domestic money stock by a smaller amount than it would if it were to act independently, from the initial quantity M_1 to a somewhat higher amount denoted M_2'. This action initially shifts the domestic aggregate demand

FIGURE 15–3 **AN ILLUSTRATION OF THE POTENTIAL BENEFITS OF INTERNATIONAL MONETARY POLICY COORDINATION**

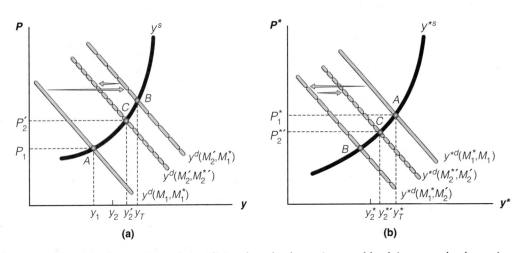

If two nation's central banks coordinate their policies, then the domestic central bank increases the domestic money stock by a smaller amount than it would have if it had acted independently, thereby inducing movement from point A to point B in panel (a). In response to the smaller decline in foreign real output shown by the movement from point A to point B in panel (b), the foreign central bank responds by increasing in the foreign money stock by a smaller amount than it would have under independent policymaking. Hence, foreign real output falls only slightly below the foreign output target, to $y_2^{*'}$ at point C in panel (b), which is above than the level y_2^* that would have arisen without coordination. The moderate increase in the foreign money stock causes a slight reduction in domestic aggregate demand. Hence, domestic output falls somewhat below the target level, to y_2' at point C in panel (a), which is closer to the domestic output target, as compared with the output level y_2 that would have arisen in the absence of coordination.

schedule from $y^d(M_1, M_1^*)$ to $y^d(M_2', M_1^*)$, causing a movement from point A to point B in panel (a).

With coordinated monetary policies, the foreign central bank likewise takes into account the effects of its policies on the domestic country. Therefore, when the mild domestic monetary policy expansion results in a reduction in foreign aggregate demand in panel (b) of Figure 15–3, from $y^{*d}(M_1^*, M_1)$ to $y^{*d}(M_1^*, M_2')$, the foreign central bank responds with a more moderate increase in the foreign money stock, as compared with the case of independent policymaking that we considered in Figure 15–2. This causes a moderate rise in foreign aggregate demand, from $y^{*d}(M_1^*, M_2')$ to $y^{*d}(M_2^{*'}, M_2')$. As a result, equilibrium foreign real output falls only slightly below the foreign output target, to $y_2^{*'}$ at point C. Although the foreign country's output thereby is somewhat less than the target level, this equilibrium foreign output level under coordinated policymaking nonetheless is greater than y_2^*, which is the output level that Figure 15–2 indicated would otherwise arise in the absence of coordination.

In the domestic country, the moderate increase in the foreign money stock causes a slight reduction in domestic aggregate demand in panel (a) of Figure 15–3, from $y^d(M_2', M_1^*)$ to $y^d(M_2', M_2^{*\prime})$. Consequently, on net, equilibrium domestic output still falls somewhat below the target level, to y_2' at point C. Nevertheless, it is closer to the domestic output target under coordinated policymaking than it would have been in the absence of coordination. With independent policymaking, as determined in Figure 15–2, domestic output would have been at the lower level, y_2.

Essentially, under coordinated policymaking the two nations' central banks partially sacrifice their own nations' individual interests for the common good of both nations. As a result, both nations are, in our example, better off than they would have been if their central banks were unwilling to make this sacrifice.

THE PROS AND CONS OF INTERNATIONAL POLICY COORDINATION

The previous example is a concrete illustration of the fact that nations potentially can benefit from working together to aim toward their national economic goals. There are several general arguments in favor of international policy coordination, however. In addition, there are some strong reasons to question whether policy coordination is always beneficial.

Potential Benefits of International Policy Coordination

Proponents of international policy coordination typically propose three broad rationales. The example depicted in Figures 15–2 and 15–3 illustrates the first of these, which is that coordination of policies can take into account and potentially minimize policy externalities. The second justification for coordination is that if national policymakers work together, they may be able to achieve a larger number of goals with their available policy instruments than they would achieve by acting alone. Finally, proponents of coordinated policymaking argue that coordination permits national policymakers to present a "united front" in the face of home political pressures that could push them toward pursuing mutually inconsistent and, therefore, ultimately harmful policies.

Internalizing International Policy Externalities   The act of coordinating policies for the mutual benefit of a group of countries effectively requires the nations' policymakers to behave as if their countries were a single entity. Thus, international policy coordination *internalizes* the externalities that individually formulated national policies would tend to produce. Imagine, for instance, what would happen if each of the fifty states of the United States were to make their policy decisions without regard to their effects on the other states. By coordinating the entire nation's policies through a federal government, the citizens of the fifty states minimize the potential for negative policy spillovers that would result from noncoordinated policymaking. In addition, to the extent that the federal system established by the U.S. Constitution promotes such an outcome, U.S. citizens gain from positive spillovers that their federal government can internalize to all the states via coordination of the states' collective actions.

This essentially is why policy coordination can pay in the example depicted in Figures 15–2 and 15–3 on pages 502 and 504. Internalizing the spillovers resulting from monetary policy actions permitted the nations' central banks to keep equilibrium output levels as close to target levels as possible. Likewise, in the real-world example of the Basle Agreement on bank capital regulation, recognizing the potential for negative competitive consequences for national banking systems may have permitted G10 nations to avoid those adverse outcomes.

Getting the Most Out of Limited Sets of Policy Instruments   It also is possible that international coordination can permit national policymakers to achieve a larger number of goals with the limited policy instruments they possess. As a simple example, suppose that two nations' central banks each have the same two goals: to achieve an increase in equilibrium domestic output and to minimize exchange rate variability. Each, therefore, has an incentive to increase their money stocks. But if the central banks increase their money stocks at different rates, then the rate of exchange between their currencies must vary. To prevent volatility of the exchange rate while achieving their common goal of raising national output levels, the central banks can coordinate their actions.

This is an intentionally simplified example, but it illustrates the basic point. If national policymakers have few policy instruments but related goals, then by working together to determine the appropriate settings of their policy instruments, they potentially could come closer to achieving their multiple objectives. Coordination thereby might be mutually beneficial.

Gaining Support from Abroad   The third rationale for international policy coordination is that policymakers in various countries might gain additional strength to withstand domestic political pressures by banding together with other policymakers. When faced with internal pressures to enact policies that might provide short-term gains at the expense of long-term social costs, policymakers could use their commitment to international coordination agreements as a justification for holding the line against such actions.

For example, suppose that an Italian government facing a difficult election were to call upon the Bank of Italy to engage in inflationary policies intended to spur the Italian economy during the months before the election. If the Bank of Italy could argue that such a policy would violate an accord to coordinate its policies with other central banks, thereby damaging Italy's credibility with those central banks and more broadly in world financial markets, then the Bank of Italy might be able to withstand the government's pressures.

ON THE WEB
Learn more about the Bank of Italy at:
http://www.bancaditalia.it/

FUNDAMENTAL ISSUE #2

What are the potential benefits of international policy coordination? The most significant gain that might arise from policy coordination is the internalization of international policy externalities, meaning that working together toward joint goals could permit national policymakers to minimize the ill effects of negative externalities or improve the prospect for benefits of positive externalities. It also is possible that policy coordination might increase the number of policy instruments that could be aimed at policymakers' objectives. In addition, establishing formal policy coordination agreements or institutions could assist a policymaker's efforts to resist domestic political pressures to enact short-sighted policies with potentially harmful long-term effects.

Some Potential Drawbacks of International Policy Coordination

In our example depicted in Figures 15–2 and 15–3, both nations unambiguously gained from policy coordination. Our example, however, was designed to illustrate a circumstance in which coordination *might* pay. International policy coordination might make two nations better off in certain circumstances, but it need not always be the best course for nations to follow.

There are several possible drawbacks associated with international policy coordination. For one thing, for coordination to work, countries must be willing and able to sacrifice at least a portion of their own interests. In addition, national policymakers must trust in the willingness and ability of their counterparts in other nations to make such sacrifices. Finally, well-intentioned efforts to coordinate policies might have negative consequences, such as higher average inflation rates.

How Much Should a Nation Sacrifice? Ultimately, what defines any nation is its *sovereignty,* or the supremacy of its citizens' own control of the resources within their country's geographic borders. If international policy coordination is to achieve benefits for a nation, its citizens and leaders must be amenable to giving up some degree of sovereignty. They must be willing to pursue *international* objectives along with purely domestic goals.

For instance, suppose that on January 1, 2004, a group of nations were to agree that their relative currency values must be fixed beginning March 1 of that year. At the end of February, however, one of the nations determines that it could gain by devaluing its currency relative to the currencies of the other countries in the group. Nevertheless, to abide by the policy coordination agreement, the nation's leaders would have to sacrifice the nation's discretion to pursue its own self-interest by devaluing its currency.

Can Other Countries Be Trusted? This last example illustrates a fundamental problem with international policy coordination, which is that there typically are incentives for countries that enter into coordination agreements to cheat. To see why this is so, consider Figure 15–4. Each cell in the figure gives hypothetical values, in "welfare units," of the citizens of two countries, denoted *A* and *B,* when their countries do or do not coordinate their policies. In the upper-left-hand cell of Figure 15–4, we see that if country *A* and country *B* conduct independent, noncoordinated policies, each derives a welfare level of 50 units. In contrast, if both nations coordinate their policymaking, then the lower-right-hand cell indicates that they both attain welfare levels of 75 units. Thus, policy coordination is beneficial for both countries.

Nevertheless, the potential for each country to gain from cheating could still result in a failure to coordinate policies. Country *A*'s policymakers know that country *A*'s welfare can be raised to 100 units if country *A* fails to follow through on a coordination agreement with country *B* while country *B*'s policymakers continue to honor the agreement. Consequently, there is an incentive for the policymakers in country *A* to renege on the deal to achieve higher national welfare. As a result, as indicated in the upper-right-hand cell of Figure 15–4, country *B*'s welfare declines to 25 units. Hence, country *A* gains, but only at country *B*'s expense. At the same time, country *B*'s policymakers face the same temptation to cheat and pursue a beggar-thy-neighbor policy, as the lower-left-hand cell of the figure shows.

Clearly, in this example the combined welfare of both nations' citizens is highest, at 150 units, if policymakers in the two nations follow through and coordinate their policies. Yet each nation has an incentive to renege in favor

FIGURE 15–4 **HYPOTHETICAL WELFARE LEVELS FOR TWO NATIONS**

If policymakers in two nations fail to coordinate their policies, then their combined welfare is 100 units. If both work together to coordinate policy actions, however, their total welfare is 150 units. The difficulty is that if either nation "cheats" and fails to coordinate as promised, it can raise its own welfare to 100 units while generating a 25-unit decline in the other nation's welfare.

	Country B does not coordinate	Country B coordinates
Country A does not coordinate	Country A welfare = 50 / Country B welfare = 50 / Total welfare = 100	Country A welfare = 100 / Country B welfare = 25 / Total welfare = 125
Country A coordinates	Country A welfare = 25 / Country B welfare = 100 / Total welfare = 125	Country A welfare = 75 / Country B welfare = 75 / Total welfare = 150

of a beggar-thy-neighbor policy that yields a lower welfare level of 125 units. If *both* countries cheat simultaneously, however, then total welfare is at its lowest, at 100 units. Nevertheless, each individual country might think that it is better off than it would be if it were to stick with the agreement only to be cheated by the other nation's policymakers.

This example illustrates a key problem of international policy coordination. Agreements to coordinate national policies can work only if all participants trust each other. Hence, each nation's commitment to an international policy coordination arrangement must be *credible* to other participating nations. In the absence of such credibility, each nation would recognize that it is worse off by agreeing to coordinate and exposing its citizens to the adverse effects caused by other nations' cheating.

Putting Faith in Other Nations' Policymakers The potential for deception and cheating is not the only factor that can cause individual nations to lose from agreeing to coordinate their policies with those of other countries. Another problem that a nation encounters when it sacrifices some sovereignty in hopes of reaping gains from coordination is the possibility that other nations' policymakers may lack competence to pursue the best common policy. That is, to be willing to cede some of its policymaking sovereignty to another country, a nation must be confident in two things. The nation must have confidence that policymakers in the other country will honor the coordination agreement. The nation also must believe that the other nation's policymakers have the ability to do their jobs effectively.

There is also the possibility that policymakers of coordinating nations may have conflicting outlooks on the appropriate policies for all nations to pursue jointly, even if the policymakers otherwise trust themselves to honor their agreements and to competently implement policy actions. Such conflicts may arise because of different policymaker preferences concerning, say, how much relative weight to place on real output versus inflation objectives. Alternatively, policymakers might not agree about the best way to implement a coordination agreement. For example, if Germany and the United Kingdom were to agree to coordinate their policies, but the Bundesbank's economic staff believed strongly in targeting money growth rates while the Bank of England's economic staff believed just as strongly in targeting nominal interest rates, then such a technical argument concerning policy implementation might still cause a coordination agreement to break down.

Could "Successful" Coordination Actually Be Counterproductive? Finally, even if nations agree to coordinate, stick to their agreement, and determine their policies taking joint welfare into account, there is still the possibility that in the end their citizens could be worse off. Economists have identified a key circumstance under which this could happen.

Discretionary Monetary Policies and Inflation without Coordination This circumstance in which successful policy coordination actually may reduce welfare was first pointed out by Kenneth Rogoff of Princeton University.

FIGURE 15–5 **DISCRETIONARY INFLATION BIASES WITH NONCOORDINATED MONETARY POLICIES**

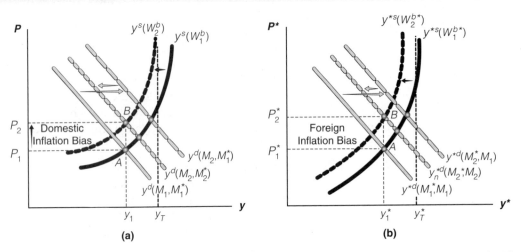

If policymakers in two countries seek to push their nations' output levels toward target levels given y_T and y_T^* but also dislike inflation, then they have an incentive to increase their stocks of money and raise aggregate demand somewhat at the cost of some inflation. An increase in the money stock in either nation, however, tends to depress aggregate demand in the other nation. In the end, noncoordinated monetary policies thereby result in aggregate demand schedules located at the positions given by $y_n^d(M_2, M_2^*)$ in panel (*a*) and $y_n^{d*}(M_2^*, M_2)$ in panel (*b*). Consequently, noncoordinated policymaking leads to policy externalities that reduce the extent to which the two policymakers are able to expand aggregate demand in their nations, which reduces the inflation biases that result from negotiation of higher base wages, W_2^b and W_2^{b*}, by workers and firms in the two countries.

Figure 15–5 illustrates Rogoff's basic argument. Panel (*a*) depicts an initial aggregate demand–aggregate supply equilibrium at point *A* for the domestic economy in the two-country, floating-exchange-rate, perfect-capital-mobility setting that we considered earlier in this chapter. At point *A*, the initial domestic price level is P_1, and the initial real output level, which we assume is equal to the long-run equilibrium output level, is y_1. As in Chapter 14, we assume that this output level is lower than it otherwise would be if there were no income taxes or government regulations that act to push real output below a socially desired output level equal to y_T. Panel (*b*) shows an analogous situation faced in the foreign economy, in which the initial equilibrium price level is equal to P_1^*, and the initial equilibrium output level is equal to y_1^*, which is below a desired output level that is equal to y_T^*.

In both panels, the positions of the nations' short-run aggregate supply schedules depend on the overall base level of nominal wages, initially given by W_1^b and W_1^{b*}. As we discussed in Chapter 14, workers and firms within the two countries establish these base wages in light of their price level expectations. The positions of the aggregate demand schedules depend on both nation's money stocks, which initially equal M_1 and M_1^*. As noted earlier in this chapter, with a floating exchange rate and perfect capital mobility, a rise in the domestic money stock typically increases domestic aggregate demand while depressing foreign aggregate demand. Likewise, an increase in the foreign money stock typically raises foreign aggregate demand while reducing domestic aggregate demand.

If policymakers desire to try to push real output toward the target levels y_T and y_T^* but simultaneously dislike inflation, then typically they have an incentive to raise aggregate demand in the hope of a short-run output expansion but at the cost of some inflation. Thus, the domestic central bank has an incentive to increase the domestic money stock to try to place the domestic aggregate demand schedule in a position such as the dashed schedule labeled $y^d(M_2, M_1^*)$ in panel (*a*). At the same time, the foreign central bank has an incentive to increase the foreign money stock to shift the foreign aggregate demand schedule rightward to a location such as that given by the dashed schedule denoted $y^{d*}(M_2^*, M_1)$ in panel (*b*).

As we discussed earlier, however, an increase in the domestic money stock results in a domestic currency depreciation that causes aggregate demand to decline in the foreign country. Thus, the domestic monetary expansion depresses somewhat the extent to which foreign aggregate demand increases. Consequently, on net the final position of the foreign aggregate demand schedule is at the somewhat lower level, denoted as $y_n^{d*}(M_2^*, M_2)$ in panel (*b*), where the subscript n indicates that monetary policies are *noncoordinated*. Likewise, an expansionary monetary policy action by the foreign central bank generates foreign currency depreciation that reduces domestic exports, causing the final position of the domestic aggregate demand schedule to be in a location such as that given by $y_n^d(M_2, M_2^*)$ in panel (*a*). Thus, noncoordinated policymaking in both nations leads to policy externalities that generate smaller aggregate demand changes than the countries' central banks have incentives to try to achieve.

As in Chapter 14, suppose that workers in both nations negotiate their base wages in light of their rational expectations of the price levels determined in part by the monetary policy actions of their nation's central banks. If workers recognize that their central banks have an incentive to increase their money stocks, then they negotiate higher base wages, W_2^b and W_2^{b*}. This causes the aggregate supply schedules in both countries to shift leftward. As a result, in panel (*a*), equilibrium real output in the domestic nation remains at its long-run level of y_1 at the final equilibrium point B, but the domestic price level rises to P_2. Thus, discretionary monetary policy by the domestic central bank generates a domestic inflation bias. In like manner, in panel (*b*), equilibrium foreign real output remains at y_1^*, but there is a foreign inflation bias owing to the higher foreign price level P_2^*.

Discretionary Monetary Policies and Inflation with Coordination

Now let's consider what happens if both central banks coordinate their discretionary policy choices, by *working together* to maintain a fixed exchange rate between their

FIGURE 15–6   **DISCRETIONARY INFLATION BIASES WITH COORDINATED MONETARY POLICIES**

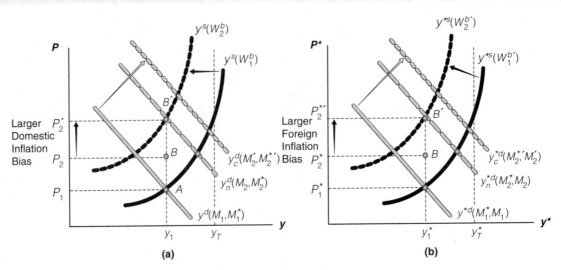

If two central banks with an incentive to expand their money stocks to raise output toward target levels work together to keep the exchange rate from changing, then they can push out their nations' aggregate demand by greater amounts, to $y_c^d(M_2', M_2^{*'})$ and $y_c^{d*}(M_2^{*'}, M_2')$, as compared with the aggregate demand levels that they could achieve without policy coordination, $y_n^d(M_2, M_2^*)$ and $y_n^{d*}(M_2^*, M_2)$. As a result, with coordinated policymaking both nations experience larger inflation biases resulting from adoption of discretionary policies by their central banks.

nations' currencies. To see how coordination can alter the inflation biases that the countries experience as a result of discretionary policymaking, consider Figure 15–6. Again, both central banks have an incentive to expand aggregate demand in their countries by raising their money stocks. Thus, the domestic central bank seeks to shift the domestic aggregate demand schedule rightward to the position given by $y^d(M_2, M_1^*)$ in panel (a). At the same time, the foreign central bank has an incentive to increase the foreign money stock to shift the foreign aggregate demand schedule to shift rightward to $y^{d*}(M_2^*, M_1)$ in panel (b).

As you saw in Figure 15–5, in the *absence* of coordinated monetary policies, exchange rate adjustments cause the aggregate demand schedules in both nations to shift back to the left somewhat, to positions labeled $y_n^d(M_2, M_2^*)$ and $y_n^{d*}(M_2^*, M_2)$. But if both countries coordinate their policies to keep the exchange rate from changing, then they eliminate spillover effects that exchange rate adjustments have on their imports and exports. This keeps the domestic monetary expansion from causing a contraction in foreign aggregate demand. It also prevents the foreign monetary expansion from inducing a decline in domestic aggregate demand. Hence, with coordinated policymaking, the final positions of the nation's aggregate demand schedules, denoted $y_c^d(M_2', M_2^{*'})$ and $y_c^{d*}(M_2^{*'}, M_2')$, correspond to the locations that each central bank desire to achieve.

Again, however, if workers in the two countries negotiate their base wages in light of their understanding that the central banks have the incentive to increase their money stocks, then they negotiate higher base wages W_2^b and W_2^{b*}. As a result, the aggregate supply schedules in both nations again shift leftward, and the final equilibrium points are points B' in panels (*a*) and (*b*) of Figure 15–6. Thus, in panel (*a*) the equilibrium domestic price level rises to P_2' with monetary policy coordination, and in panel (*b*) the equilibrium foreign price level increases to $P_2^{*\prime}$. If the central banks had not coordinated their policies, however, the ultimate equilibrium points would have been those from Figure 15–5, which are points B at the price levels given by P_2 and P_2^*. Therefore, Rogoff's conclusion is that coordination of discretionary monetary policies tends to lead to a larger inflation bias in each country.

The reason that the discretionary inflation bias is greater for both countries is that policy coordination that pegs the exchange rate eliminates the policy externalities that otherwise would restrain the increases in aggregate demand caused by discretionary monetary expansions. As a result, aggregate demand in each nation rises by a greater amount following a central bank increase in the money stock. The result is higher average inflation than each country would have experienced if its central banks had not coordinated their policies.

This does not mean that policy coordination is *necessarily* harmful. As we noted earlier, limiting international policy externalities can reduce policy conflicts and thereby help to stabilize equilibrium real output levels in interdependent nations. Nevertheless, Rogoff's argument illustrates a potential cost of the coordination of discretionary monetary policies: Such policies can lead to higher average inflation in the countries whose central banks coordinate their policies.

FUNDAMENTAL ISSUE #3

What are the potential drawbacks of international policy coordination? One difficulty with entering into policy coordination agreements is that nations must give up at least some measure of national sovereignty to implement such agreements. In addition, they must trust each other both to pursue promised policy actions and to do so in a competent manner. Yet there typically will be an incentive for one nation to cheat on a policy coordination agreement, in the pursuit of gains at another country's expense, and there is always the possibility that one nation's policymakers will fail to pursue policies that another nation believes to be appropriate. Finally, international policy coordination can, if policymakers' credibility levels are low within their own countries, lead to higher average inflation rates.

THE ECONOMICS OF MONETARY UNIONS

As we have discussed, if a nation chooses to enter into a international policy coordination arrangement, it must give up at least some degree of national sovereignty. Would there be any gain from taking another step and giving up its own currency in favor of a currency common to it and others in a coalition of policy-coordinating nations? That is, should a nation join a formal **monetary union,** or a grouping of nation–states that agree to use a single currency? To contemplate this issue, we must consider the theory of *optimal currency areas.*

MONETARY UNION A set of countries that choose to use a common currency.

Optimal Currency Areas

In 1991, nations of the European Union negotiated a treaty in the Netherlands city of Maastricht. Among other things, the Maastrict Treaty calls for establishment of a European Central Bank that would, beginning in 2002, issue a single European currency, the *euro.* Although many European government officials and citizens have hailed the treaty as a triumph of coordination and unity in the region, a number of economists have questioned whether European countries truly will benefit from these monetary provisions of the agreement. These nay-sayers have based their arguments on an economic theory developed more than thirty years ago by Robert Mundell of Columbia University. This is the **theory of optimal currency areas,** which is an analytical approach to determining the extent of a geographic area whose residents would be better off by fixing their exchange rates or even by using a common currency.

THEORY OF OPTIMAL CURRENCY AREAS A means of determining the size of a geographic area within which residents' welfare is greater if their governments fix exchange rates or adopt a common currency.

Each day, financial newspapers such as the *Wall Street Journal* or the *Financial Times* publish listings of exchange rates for more than fifty national currencies. These are not complete exchange rate listings, however, because these newspapers list only the currencies with large trading volumes in the foreign exchange markets.

Why are there so many different national currencies? Why is it that residents of all fifty states of the United States use the same currency, even though states such as California and New York have higher volumes of GDP than most nations of the world? Would the nations of the European Union actually benefit from following the example of the fifty U.S. states? The theory of optimal currency areas seeks to address these issues.

How Separate Currencies and a Floating Exchange Rate Can Be Beneficial
To understand the essential features of the theory of optimal currency areas, let's consider two hypothetical regions. People in one region, which we shall call region *A,* specialize in producing low-cholesterol foods. Residents of the other region, denoted region *B,* manufacture textiles. In both regions, wages and prices are sticky in the short run. Initially, both regions experience balanced trade.

Suppose that residents of one region are unable to move to the other region in pursuit of employment in the other region's industry. One possible reason for this state of affairs could be that there are language or cultural barriers that effectively prohibit employment in the other regions' firms. Another reason could be that one or both of the regions might have established restrictions that prevent region A residents who are employed in low-cholesterol food production from moving to region B to make clothing, and vice versa.

Nevertheless, let's suppose that residents of both regions face no restrictions on their ability to purchase the goods produced in both regions. Finally, let's suppose that each region has its own currency. The exchange rate for these currencies could either float in the foreign exchange market, or regional policymakers could fix the exchange rate.

Consider now what happens if residents of both regions were to lose their interest in keeping up with the most recent fads in clothing styles, thereby reducing the demand for the textiles produced in region B. At the same time, suppose that both regions' residents also become more health conscious, so that the demand for region A's low-cholesterol foods increases. As a result, country A begins to run a trade surplus, and its output and employment increases. In contrast, country B begins to experience a trade deficit, and its output and employment decline.

If the rate of exchange between the regions' currencies is fixed, then the assumed short-run stickiness of wage and prices causes unemployment to persist for some time in region B following the changes in consumers' tastes. In the long run, of course, the price of the low-cholesterol foods manufactured in region A increases, and the price of the textiles made in region B declines, leading to an ultimate rebalancing of trade between the two regions. Until this long-run adjustment occurs, however, region B can experience a significant unemployment problem.

If the exchange rate is flexible, however, then the trade surplus in region A and trade deficit in region B induce a rapid depreciation in the value of region B's currency relative to the currency of region A. This causes an immediate fall in the effective price of region B's textile goods as perceived by residents of region A and a speedy rise in the effective price of region A's low-cholesterol foods faced by residents of region B. As a result, trade between the two nations is balanced much more rapidly with a floating exchange rate, and region B's unemployment problem is much more short-lived.

This example illustrates a situation in which two regions benefit from using separate currencies whose relative values adjust freely in the foreign exchange market. Fixing the rate of exchange between the currencies, or taking the further step of adopting a single currency, eliminates the exchange rate's role as a mechanism for short-run adjustment to changes in relative demands for the regions' goods. This exposes the regions to the potential for chronic payments imbalances and unemployment problems.

Certainly, with separate currencies and a market-determined exchange rate, residents of both nations face foreign exchange risks arising from exchange rate movements and costs of converting one currency to another when they wish to purchase another region's goods. Nonetheless, adopting individual currencies and a floating exchange rate protects the regions from unemployment dangers that arise from language, cultural, or legal barriers to worker migration.

When Could Using a Single Currency Pay Off?   Now suppose that the conditions that have led to past constraints on worker migration break down. As a result, residents of region *A* can move freely to region *B* to work, and vice versa. Let's further suppose that shortly following this development, there once again is a rise in the demand for region *A*'s low-cholesterol foods and a decline in the demand for region *B*'s textile products.

The immediate results, again, are a trade surplus, higher output, and higher employment in region *A* and a trade deficit, lower output, and lower employment in region *B*. As a result, some residents of region *B* find themselves without work. Now, however, these unemployed region *B* residents can migrate—or perhaps even commute—to newly available jobs in region *A*. Thus, region *B* unemployment is at worst a temporary phenomenon. Indeed, unemployment for both regions together is minimized in the face of such changes in the relative demands for their products.

In this example, there is no reason that the rates of exchange between the two regions cannot be fixed, thereby permitting residents of both regions to avoid foreign exchange risks. Indeed, economists would conclude that the two regions together constitute an **optimal currency area,** or a geographical area within which fixed exchange rates may be maintained without slowing regional adjustments to changing regional circumstances. Furthermore, within such an optimal currency area, separate regions find it beneficial to adopt a *common currency* if the cost of converting currencies for regional trade exceeds any perceived gain from having separate currencies. If, for example, the residents of regions *A* and *B* continue to perceive sizable benefits from using separate currencies even though no barriers otherwise separate their regions, then they might wish to continue to incur currency conversion costs that arise when they trade goods. But if currency conversion costs are sufficiently large relative to the potential benefits of maintaining separate regional currencies, then the residents of the two regions that constitute an optimal currency area may gain, on net, from adopting a single, common currency.

OPTIMAL CURRENCY AREA
A geographic area within which labor is sufficiently mobile to permit speedy adjustments to payments imbalances and regional unemployment, so that exchange rates can be fixed and a common currency can be adopted.

Rationales for Separate Currencies

What benefits might residents of two regions with few or no barriers to worker mobility perceive as sufficiently large to justify maintaining separate currencies? One possible answer might be that residents of either region might regard the loss of their own region's currency as a sacrifice of sovereignty. If a region were a nation-state with its own cultural history that its residents associated in part with the region's currency—for instance, Britain with its pound sterling that evokes memories of a former empire or Germany with its deutsche mark that symbolizes the nation's commitment to low inflation—then convincing residents to give up their currency could prove difficult.

Lack of Fiscal Integration   Nationalism is not the only factor that might dissuade a country from joining others in using a single currency. Nations' governments maintain their own budgets with their own sources of revenues and distributions of expenditures. The key source of any government's revenues is taxes. As we discussed in Chapter 8, one type of taxation is *seigniorage,* or central bank profits earned from producing money whose market value exceeds its cost of production. Seigniorage typically is a relatively small portion of any nation's tax revenues. Nevertheless, in some nations it is a more important share of tax revenues than it is for others, meaning that such nations might have to undertake the politically painful task of increasing other taxes if they were to lose seigniorage following adoption of a common currency. Thus, these nations might value having a separate currency more than others.

For instance, in our hypothetical example of regions A and B, suppose that the two regions together were to constitute an optimal currency area. In principle, therefore, the two regions could maintain a fixed exchange rate without experiencing long-term trade imbalances or unemployment. Nonetheless, if the government of region A were to depend to a much larger extent upon seigniorage as a revenue source, then region A might be unwilling to agree to adopt a common currency. As a result, the two regions might keep their exchange rate fixed yet continue to use separate currencies.

Removal of Currency Competition   Another potential justification for retaining separate currencies is the potential for welfare gains stemming from *currency competition.* This idea was first put forward by the economist Frederick Hayek. He argued that a central bank may be hesitant to place too much currency in circulation if it recognizes that so doing reduces the exchange value of its nation's currency relative to those of other nations, thereby inducing people to prefer to hold less of its currency. Thus, fear of "lost business" to competing currencies issued by other central banks could lead a country's central bank to hold back on inflationary money growth.

Hayek argued that having many national currencies effectively in competition with each other could be advantageous to the residents of all nations. As a result, they could lose out if governments were to band together and adopt a common currency. Such a move reduces the extent of currency competition and can thereby remove an important check on inflation in regions that might adopt a common currency.

Is Europe an Optimal Currency Area?   Under the terms of the Maastricht Treaty on European Union (EU), qualifying members of the fifteen-nation EU are to begin using a common currency by the year 1999. The treaty requires a country wishing to join the proposed European Monetary Union (EMU) to have a government budget deficit no larger than 3 percent of its GDP, total government debt no greater than 60 percent of its GDP, an inflation rate no higher than one and a half percentage points higher than the average of the three best-performing EMU member nations, and long-term interest rates no higher than two points above the same benchmark (see "Policy Notebook: Meeting the Maastricht Treaty Requirements—All Smoke and Mirrors?").

POLICY NOTEBOOK

Meeting the Maastricht Treaty Requirements—
All Smoke and Mirrors?

Figure 15–7 shows the positions of European Union nations in their efforts to achieve the Maastricht Treaty debt and deficit constraints. As you can see, many nations now satisfy the Treaty's fiscal policy requirements. The progress toward meeting these requirements has been rapid. As late as 1996, only Luxembourg had met the Maastricht standards for government debts and deficits relative to GDP.

Was this a result of fiscal discipline? Or was it really the result of fiscal gimmickry? The best answers to these questions are probably yes and yes. Certainly, the governments of European nations embarked on a significant and politically painful belt-tightening effort during the 1990s. As Figure 15–7 indicates, however, the goal of most national governments appears to have been to *just meet* the Maastricht fiscal standards. To make the grade, some governments played fast and loose with their fiscal accounting. For example, in 1997 France counted one-time transfers of cash to the government due to company privatizations as an infusing of revenues that technically reduced the French government's deficit.

Likewise, Spain used one-time receipts of funds from privatization to offset losses on other state-run enterprises, thereby masking longer-term deficit problems that otherwise would have appeared greater on the eve of the proposed monetary union. In perhaps the ultimate accounting gimmick, Italy's government instituted a "euro tax" to raise its tax receipts and reduce its deficit in the near term. The government promised, however, to return part of the proceeds from the special tax in future years—presumably *after* Italy had technically satisfied the Maastricht fiscal limits and had been admitted into the European Monetary Union.

FOR CRITICAL ANALYSIS:

According to basic economic theory, people typically do the best that they can subject to constraints that they face. Thus, economic theory indicates that constraints typically are "binding," meaning that people operate along the constraints that they face. Does Figure 15–7 provide support for the theory?

ON THE WEB
Learn more about the Bank of Spain at:
http://www.bde.es/

Some nations, such as France and Italy, have expressed steadfast dedication to the goal of EMU, but others, such as Germany and the United Kingdom, have been more hesitant. There are a number of reasons for their hesitancy. Undoubtedly, one area of concern in the United Kingdom is the loss of the pound sterling and its historical role as a symbol of British sovereignty. Many German citizens fear that giving up the deutsche mark likewise could lead to a loss of real savings accumulated during their lifetimes.

Another reason that doubters often give for questioning the wisdom of a speedy movement to EMU, however, is uncertainty about whether the EU nations actually constitute an optimal currency area. Research by Barry Eichengreen of the University of California at Berkeley has compared measures of

FIGURE 15-7   **EUROPEAN UNION NATIONS' GOVERNMENT DEBTS AND BUDGET DEFICITS AS PERCENTAGES OF GDP**

Most European Union nations that meet the government budgetary criteria for admission into the European Monetary Union do so only by a narrow margin.

SOURCE: Data from European Commission.

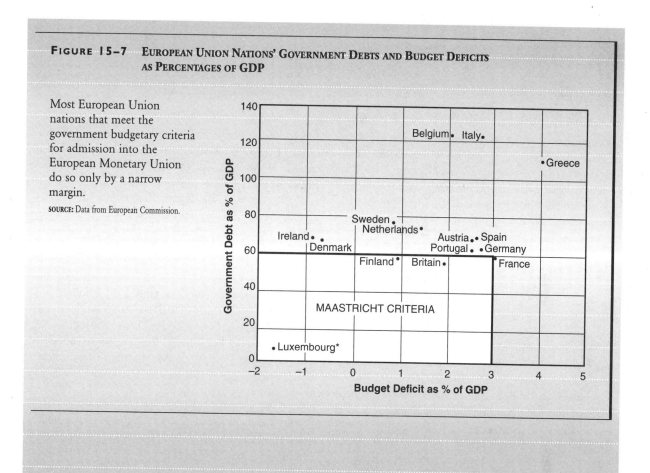

labor mobility in Western Europe with those of other countries with single currencies, such as the United States and Canada. His evidence indicates that labor is much less mobile in Western Europe, implying that this portion of the world really is not an especially strong candidate for an optimal currency area (see "Policy Notebook: European Asymmetries and Monetary Union").

Nevertheless, most Western European nations continue to express their desire for a common currency. Skeptics may question the economic wisdom of this goal, but pursuit of the goal remains a political reality throughout most of the region. This period in history promises a fascinating real-world experiment in which several nations may implement a common currency even though they fail to satisfy the classic criteria for an optimal currency area.

ON THE WEB

Take a look at the most recent data on European Union nations at:

http://www.europa.eu.int

POLICY NOTEBOOK
European Asymmetries and Monetary Union

According to the theory of optimal currency areas, key factors influencing the desirability of establishing a single currency for a group of geographical regions are the extent to which the regions are subjected to *asymmetric shocks*—variations in aggregate conditions that have different effects on the regions—and the degree to which labor is mobile among the regions. Figure 15–8 shows estimates of the relative degree of *economic divergence,* which is a measure of the extent to which regions experience asymmetric shocks, and of relative labor mobility for three sets of regions of the world: a narrow group of Germany and a small set of other closely aligned economies of the European Union (denoted "EU Core"), the entire set of European Union nations (denoted "EU 15"), and the United States. Note that even though the extent of economic divergence is not too much higher within U.S. states as compared with the fifteen nations of the entire European Union, U.S. labor mobility is much greater. Hence, the United States lies to the right of the 45-degree line in the figure, meaning that it tends to exhibit sufficient labor mobility to compen-

sate for the asymmetric effects of varying economic conditions that its states experience. In contrast, the fifteen nations of the European Union lie to the left of the 45-degree line. This indicates that labor mobility is low enough relative to the degree of economic divergence among the fifteen countries that this grouping of regions may not be a good candidate for a single currency.

Labor mobility is not much greater in the "core" group of European nations whose economies are closely aligned with Germany's economy. Nevertheless, the extent of economic divergence among these countries is much lower in comparison with the European Union as a whole. As a result, the "EU core" lies to the right of the 45-degree line, indicating that this smaller set of countries might be a stronger candidate for monetary union.

FOR CRITICAL ANALYSIS:
Which should come first in Europe: full economic integration or monetary union? Does the answer to this question depend on how one defines "Europe"?

ON THE WEB
Visit the European Central Bank (ECB) at:
http://www.ecb.int.

FUNDAMENTAL ISSUE #4

Could nations gain from adopting a common currency?

Countries qualify as an optimal currency area, or a geographic area in which movements of workers among regions alleviate unemployment and payments imbalances without the need for exchange rate adjustment, if labor is highly mobile across national boundaries. In such an environment, nations could save their residents from incurring foreign exchange risks and currency

FIGURE 15–8   ECONOMIC DIVERGENCE AND LABOR MOBILITY FOR EUROPE AND THE UNITED STATES

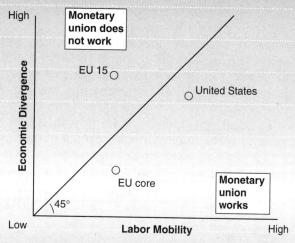

This figure depicts estimates of "economic divergence"–the extent to which regions experience asymmetric shocks–and of relative labor mobility for three regions: a narrow group of Germany and a small set of other closely aligned economies of the European Union ("EU Core"), all fifteen European Union nations ("EU 15"), and the United States. Although the degree of economic divergence is not too much higher within U.S. states as compared with the fifteen nations of the entire European Union ("EU 15"), U.S. labor mobility is sufficiently high to more than compensate for the asymmetric effects of varying economic conditions that U.S. states experience. In contrast, the fifteen nations of the European Union lie to the left of the 45-degree line, meaning that labor mobility is sufficiently low relative to the degree of economic divergence that this full set of countries may not benefit from adopting a single currency.

SOURCE: Data from Jose Vinals and Juan Jimeno, "Monetary Union and European Unemployment," in *CEPR Discussion Paper No. 1485,* October 1996.

conversion costs by joining a monetary union with a common currency. Nevertheless, even countries within an optimal currency area may resist joining a monetary union if their residents are sufficiently averse to giving up sovereignty, if their national governments would lose seigniorage revenues that they could not recoup via other sources of taxation, or if countries fear that the loss of currency competition could remove restraints on inflationary policymaking.

SPLITTING THE DIFFERENCE: EXCHANGE-RATE TARGET ZONES

In Chapters 12, 13, and 14, you learned that open economies face advantages and disadvantages when contemplating either a system of floating exchange rates or a system of fixed exchange rates. In this chapter, you have seen that failure to coordinate monetary policies can, with floating exchange rates, expose interdependent economies to negative policy externalities that might be at least partially offset via international policy coordination. Yet, coordinating their policies to fix the exchange rate can push up their average inflation rates.

In recent years some economists, such as Paul Krugman of Stanford University, have questioned whether nations of the world must really make a stark choice between fixed or floating exchange rates. They have proposed an approach that seeks a middle ground between these extremes. In a sense, this approach "splits the difference" by limiting exchange rate volatility while still permitting some variation in countries' currency values.

Target Zones

How can central banks limit exchange rate movements but allow the exchange rate to vary, nonetheless? Figure 15–9 illustrates one possible answer, which is the establishment of an exchange rate **target zone,** or a range within which central banks permit exchange rates to vary.

TARGET ZONE A range of permitted exchange rate variation between upper and lower exchange rate bands that a central bank defends by selling or purchasing foreign exchange reserves.

Establishing a Target Zone In Figure 15–9, there are upper and lower *bands,* or limits, for permissible values of the exchange rate, S. The upper band is denoted S_U and the lower band is denoted S_L. In a target zone system, a nation's central bank (or perhaps a group of central banks, such as those agreeing to participate in the European Monetary System) establishes specific values for these exchange rate bands. The central bank commits itself to intervening in the foreign exchange markets to ensure that its nation's currency value will not rise above the upper band or fall below the lower band. For instance, if the exchange rate approaches the upper band S_U, then the central bank must sell foreign exchange reserves in sufficient quantities to prevent additional depreciation of its nation's currency. In contrast, if the exchange rate approaches the lower band S_L, then the central bank must purchase sufficient amounts of foreign exchange reserves to halt any further currency appreciation.

Between the upper and lower bands, the central bank does not intervene in the foreign exchange markets. Thus, the exchange rate floats freely within the target zone. Because it does not move outside the zone, however, the scope for exchange rate variability is limited by the size of the upper and lower bands. On the one hand, if the values of S_U and S_L are very small, then the target zone essentially amounts to a fixed exchange rate system. On the other hand, if the central bank establishes a very large range between S_U and S_L, then the target zone looks much like a floating exchange rate arrangement.

FIGURE 15-9   AN EXCHANGE RATE TARGET ZONE

A target zone is a range within which a central bank permits the exchange rates to vary. If the exchange rate approaches the upper band S_U, then the central bank sells foreign exchange reserves in sufficient quantities to prevent additional depreciation of its nation's currency. In contrast, if the exchange rate approaches the lower band S_L, then the central bank purchases sufficient amounts of foreign exchange reserves to stem any further currency appreciation. Between the upper and lower bands, however, the central bank does not intervene in the foreign exchange market.

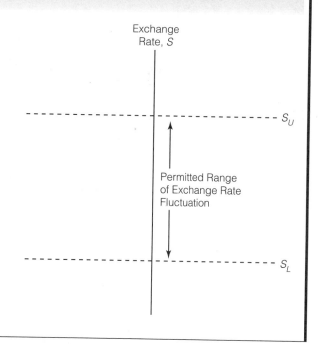

The Behavior of the Exchange Rate Inside the Target Zone   How will the exchange rate vary inside the target zone? To address this question, consider Figure 15–10. The upward-sloping dashed line shows how the exchange rate might vary in response to changes in factors that determine its value in a system of floating exchange rates, assuming for simplicity that there is a linear relationship between the exchange rate and these factors. As you learned in Chapter 13, with a floating exchange rate, variations in the quantity of money at home and abroad are important factors influencing a country's currency value.

It is tempting to envision that the exchange rate should vary along the dashed line in a target zone system, with the central bank intervening as soon as the exchange rate reaches either the upper or lower band of the target zone, at points *A* or *B*. Under this view, a target zone system truly amounts to a floating exchange rate within the zone, with a fixed exchange rate "limit" at the top and bottom of the zone.

In fact, it is unlikely that the exchange rate will vary along the dashed line. The reason is that speculators in the foreign exchange market alter their demand for the nation's currency if they anticipate a central bank intervention near either band of the zone. For example, if the exchange rate rises toward the upper band S_U in Figure 15–10, then foreign exchange market speculators anticipate that central bank foreign exchange reserve sales will take place to

Figure 15–10 **The Behavior of the Exchange Rate within a Target Zone**

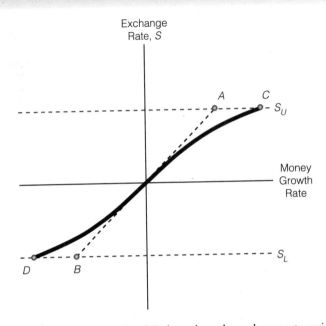

The upward-sloping dashed line between points A and B shows how the exchange rate varies in response to changes in the domestic money growth. An oversimplified view of how the exchange rate might vary inside a target zone is that it floats along this dashed line within the target zone, with fixed exchange rate limits at the top and bottom of the zone. In fact, however, speculators in the foreign exchange market alter their demands for the nation's currency if they anticipate a central bank intervention near either band of the zone. Hence, the equilibrium exchange rate in a target zone actually should lie below the dashed line as the exchange rate approached the upper band of the zone, with the central bank obliged to intervene by selling foreign exchange reserves only at an extreme limiting point beyond point A, such as point C. Likewise, the exchange rate should lie above the dashed line as the exchange rate approaches the lower band of the zone, inducing actual central bank interventions only at a point such as D, farther to the left from point B. As a result, the equilibrium exchange rate should lie along a smooth, S-shaped curve.

prevent the exchange rate from rising above S_U. Consequently, in this situation speculators expect that it is more likely that the exchange rate will decline in the future. They respond to this anticipation by increasing their current demand for the nation's currency, in the hope of earning future profits by selling the currency when the exchange rate declines and its value appreciates. The resulting current rise in the demand for the nation's currency, however, results in a current appreciation. Hence, foreign exchange market speculation depresses the exchange rate somewhat relative to its value under a true float.

This reasoning implies that the dashed line in Figure 15–10 cannot depict the actual values of the exchange rate in a target zone system. The exchange rate does not truly "float" freely within the target zone. Instead, the equilibrium exchange rate in a target zone should lie below the dashed line as the exchange rate approaches the upper band of the zone. Only at an extreme limiting point beyond point *A,* such as point *C,* is the central bank ultimately obliged to intervene by selling foreign exchange reserves. In contrast, if the exchange rate declines toward the lower band, S_L, speculators demand less of the nation's currency, which tends to push the equilibrium exchange rate upward. Hence, the equilibrium exchange rate should lie above the dashed line as the exchange rate approaches the lower band of the zone, inducing actual central bank interventions only at a point such as *D,* farther to the left from point *B.*

Thus, holding other factors unchanged, the equilibrium exchange rate in a target zone system should lie along a smooth curve such as the S-shaped curve displayed in Figure 15–10. As factors determining the exchange rate change, the exchange rate then should vary along this curve. Because this curve is more shallow than the dashed line that applies if the exchange rate truly floats between the bands, it follows that the establishment of a target zone does more than place absolute limits on exchange rate fluctuations. A target zone also should lead to less exchange rate variability *between* the bands. This is one of the potential benefits of adopting a target zone system, if one of a nation's objectives is to reduce foreign exchange risks and to prevent variations in economic performance arising from exchange rate volatility.

Does the Target Zone Model Fit the Facts?

The reasoning behind the S-curve model of the exchange rate under a target zone seems inescapable. This led a number of economists to spend much of the early 1990s developing theoretical extensions of Krugman's initial reasoning. They determined how a number of economic variables should behave in a target zone environment, including short- and long-term interest rates, the price level, and the balance of payments—all under the assumption that the S-curve reasoning should fit facts.

Real-World Evidence Nevertheless, a number of economists also began searching for evidence supporting this reasoning. In what Lars Svensson of Stockholm University has called "an excellent example of 'the great tragedy of Science—the slaying of a beautiful hypothesis by an ugly fact' (T. H. Huxley)"– these economists almost uniformly found little evidence of an S-curve relationship between exchange rates in real-world examples of target-zone-type arrangements, such as the Bretton Woods system and the European Monetary System.

The basic S-curve model failed the test of empirical relevance along a number of dimensions. For instance, one essential prediction of the model is the S-curve shape. In fact, economists have been able to find few historical cases in which movements in any nation's exchange rate traced out such a relationship. Indeed, there is little evidence of any long-lasting deterministic relationship between the exchange rate and factors that theory otherwise predicts should affect it. Furthermore, additional predictions about how variables such as interest rates and the price level should behave also receive very little support from real-world data.

Salvaging the Target Zone Theory Today, most economists agree that the basic S-curve model of target zones cannot be salvaged without taking into account two key factors. One is *imperfect policy credibility.* Any system that entails policy commitments to fix or otherwise limit movements in exchange rates generally is not fully credible. There always tends to be some doubt in the minds of foreign exchange market traders about whether or not a central bank will stand by an announced intention to defend an exchange rate target—or a zone limiting the range of movement of the exchange rate. As Krugman himself pointed out when he proposed the basic S-curve model, if there is a probability that central banks may fail to intervene as the exchange rate approaches an announced band, then the S-curve model has to be modified to account for that. The result is a lower likelihood of an S-shaped relationship between the exchange rate and factors that determine its value, such as money growth rates.

In addition, central banks may not intervene in foreign exchange market only at the bands of a target zone. They also may conduct **intra-marginal interventions,** or foreign exchange market interventions designed to move exchange rates to desired levels *within* a target zone. It turns out that if central banks conduct intra-marginal interventions, as many of them have done and continue to do, then the basic reasoning of the target zone model is still correct, but it is less likely that there is a fixed S-shaped relationship between the equilibrium exchange rate and its essential determinants.

This has led economists to modify the basic target zone framework to account for these two factors. For example, Michael Klein of Tufts University and Karen Lewis of the University of Pennsylvania developed a target zone model that allows for the possibility that people alter their beliefs about the true target zone bands that central banks are willing and able to defend based on their observations of actual central bank interventions. Klein and Lewis applied their amended target zone model to actual experience during a period of coordinated interventions by the German Bundesbank, Bank of Japan, and Federal Reserve between February and October of 1987. They found evidence that even though these central banks made strong efforts to make their policies credible by coordinating their foreign exchange market interventions and signaling their intentions, traders' perceptions of the intended target zone varied greatly during that eight-month interval.

This and other studies appear to indicate that the target zone model may be a useful explanation of exchange rate behavior within the bands of a target zone as long as the model accounts for imperfect credibility and intra-marginal interventions. Economists continue to explore how target zones have functioned in the past and may yet function in the future.

INTRA-MARGINAL INTERVENTIONS Central bank purchases or sales of foreign exchange reserves at exchange rate levels within a target zone.

FUNDAMENTAL ISSUE #5

What is an exchange rate target zone? An exchange rate target zone is a region between upper and lower exchange rate bands that central banks announce are upper and lower limits for exchange rate movements. In the case of a credible target zone, a country's central bank precommits itself to selling foreign exchange reserves to keep the nation's exchange rate at or below the upper band of the zone and to buying foreign exchange reserves to keep the nation's exchange rate at or above the lower band of the zone. The basic theory of exchange rate determination in a target zone indicates that the exchange rate should lie on an S-shaped curve. Real-world experience, however, indicates that imperfect policy credibility and intra-marginal interventions require modification of this basic target zone model.

CHAPTER SUMMARY

1. **Structural Interdependence and International Policy Cooperation or Coordination:** National economies are said to be structurally interdependent if one country's economy responds to events affecting the performance of another. In such situations, international policy externalities can exist, meaning that policy actions in one country can have spillover effects on the economies of other nations. Positive international policy externalities exert beneficial spillover effects on other nations' economic performances, whereas negative international policy externalities contribute to a worsening of those nations' economic performances. To enhance positive externalities or mitigate negative externalities, nations may decide to establish institutional structures for sharing data or for collaborating on national goals. They also may decide to coordinate their policies by determining policy actions that are best for their common good.

2. **The Potential Benefits of International Policy Coordination:** The most important potential gain that policy coordination might achieve is the internalization of international policy externalities. That is, joint determination of policy actions could allow policymakers to minimize negative externalities or to enhance positive externalities. Policy coordination might also enlarge the number of policy instruments that policymakers could aim at their collective goals. Finally, by joining a formal international policy coordination arrangement, a national policymaker may have more success in resisting domestic political pressures to engage in policy actions that have near-term benefits but potentially negative long-term effects.

3. **The Potential Drawbacks of International Policy Coordination:** One way in which a nation loses by entering into a policy coordination arrangement is that its policymakers sacrifice at least part of their national sovereignty. Furthermore, there must be mutual faith that nations will not cheat on a policy coordination agreement at the expense of other countries and that otherwise well-meaning policymakers in other nations will not pursue counterproductive policies. Another potential pitfall of international policy coordination is that it can, if policymakers' credibility levels are low among residents of their own nations, lead to the adoption of more inflationary policies.

4. **The Possibility that Nations Could Gain from Adopting a Common Currency:** Nations lie inside an optimal currency area if there is sufficient mobility of workers across national boundaries to alleviate unemployment and payments imbalances without the need for exchange rate adjustment. Countries in an optimal currency area could, in principle, eliminate foreign exchange risks and currency conversion costs faced by their residents if they were to form a monetary union with a common currency. Nonetheless, nations within an optimal currency area may choose to forgo using a common currency if their citizens resist giving up national sovereignty, if their governments have to sacrifice seigniorage revenues that they could not replace through other types of taxation, or if countries' residents are sufficiently concerned that the loss of currency competition among central banks may remove restraints on their willingness to pursue inflationary policies.

5. **Exchange Rate Target Zones:** An exchange rate target zone is a region between upper and lower exchange rate bands, or upper and lower limits within which central banks seek to restrain exchange rate variations. If a target zone policy is credible, then a nation's central bank can precommit to a policy of selling foreign exchange reserves to keep the nation's exchange rate at or below the upper band of the zone and purchasing foreign exchange reserves to keep the nation's exchange rate at or above the lower band of the zone. According to the basic target zone theory of exchange rate determination, the exchange rate should lie on an S-shaped curve. Actual evidence from periods in which target zone policies have been pursued, however, implies that imperfect policy credibility and intramarginal interventions must be taken into account for the target zone model to fit the facts.

QUESTIONS AND PROBLEMS

1. Suppose that two nations were to establish a central clearing house for interbank payments that cross their borders. In addition, the staffs of their central banks work together to develop rules and regulations for this clearing house, and they jointly fund and operate an agency charged with regulating this institution. Would this best be termed an example of policy cooperation or of policy coordination? Explain your reasoning.

2. A domestic government enacts a significant cut in taxes intended to spur its domestic industries. In addition, however, the tax cut gives foreign-owned firms

an incentive to relocate their offices and production facilities within domestic borders. The tax cut also has been carefully crafted to avoid spurring increased imports by domestic citizens. Would these effects of this domestic policy action be an example of a positive or negative international policy externality? Explain.

3. Workers who speak a common language and share a common culture are completely mobile within a region that encompasses three small economies that engage in large volumes of international trade and have floating exchange rates. Residents in each country must incur sizable costs each time they convert their home currency into a foreign currency, and they face significant foreign exchange risks. Is this region a potential candidate for monetary union? Justify your answer.

4. As noted in this chapter, there is not strong evidence that the nations of Western Europe constitute an optimal currency area in the conventional sense. Yet many of these countries continue to express interest in a common currency. Can you think of any other arguments that leaders of these nations might give to support their goal of European Monetary Union? Explain.

5. Suppose that a nation's central bank announces that it intends to intervene in foreign exchange markets to defend upper and lower limits on its nation's exchange rate. Yet foreign exchange market traders learn that the central bank has no foreign exchange reserves to use in such interventions. Would you expect the exchange rate to lie on the S-curve predicted by the basic target zone model? If so, why? If not, how do you think that the schedule for the exchange rate on the target-zone diagram would be shaped? Explain.

ON-LINE APPLICATION

Member nations of the European Union continue to try to work out a framework for adopting a single currency. This application acquaints you with issues concerning monetary policy in the EU and in the proposed European Monetary Union.

Internet URL:
http://www.cliffordchance.com/library/publications/emu_legal/section1.html

Title: Road to a Single Currency

Navigation: Begin at **http://cliffordchance.com,** the address for the home page of Clifford Chance, an international law firm. Click on *Library*, and then click on *Guide to Publications*. Next, click on *Legal Publications*. Under Europe, click on *European Monetary Union: The Legal Framework*, and then click on *Road to a Single Currency*.

Application: Read the article, and answer the following questions:

1. What is the difference between the European Monetary System and the European Monetary Union?

2. How will the value of the new currency, the euro, initially be set? What institution will have responsibility for determining its value thereafter?

REFERENCES AND RECOMMENDED READINGS

Branson, William H., Jacob A. Frenkel, and Morris Goldstein (ed.). *International Policy Coordination and Exchange Rate Fluctuations.* Chicago: University of Chicago Press, 1990.

Bryson, Jay, Henrik Jensen, and David VanHoose. "Rules, Discretion, and International Monetary and Fiscal Policy Coordination." *Open Economies Review,* 4 (1993): 117–132.

Canzoneri, Matthew B., Vittorio Grilli, and Paul R. Masson (ed.). *Establishing a Central Bank: Issues in Europe and Lessons from the U.S.* Cambridge: Cambridge University Press, 1992.

Canzoneri, Matthew B., and Dale W. Henderson. *Monetary Policy Coordination in Interdependent Economies: A Game Theoretic Approach.* Cambridge, Mass.: MIT Press, 1991.

DeGrauwe, Paul. *The Economics of Monetary Integration.* Oxford: Oxford University Press, 2nd Edition, 1997.

von Furstenberg, George M. and Joseph P. Daniels. *Economic Summit Declarations 1975–1989: Examining the Written Record of International Cooperation.* Princeton Studies in International Finance, Princeton, NJ: Princeton University, International Finance Section, February 1992.

Kenen, Peter. *Exchange Rates and Policy Coordination.* Ann Arbor: University of Michigan Press, 1989.

Klein, Michael and Karen Lewis. "Learning About Intervention Target Zones." *Journal of International Economics,* 35 (1993): 275–295.

Krugman, Paul, and Marcus Miller (ed.). *Exchange Rate Targets and Currency Bands.* Cambridge: Cambridge University Press, 1992.

McKibbin, Warwick, and Jeffrey D. Sachs. *Global Linkages: Macroeconomic Interdependence and Cooperation in the World Economy.* Washington, D.C.: Brookings Institution, 1991.

Mundell, Robert. "A Theory of Optimal Currency Areas." *American Economic Review,* 51 (1961): 657–665.

Niehans. *International Monetary Economics.* Baltimore: Johns Hopkins University Press, 1984.

Rogoff, Kenneth. "Can International Monetary Policy Coordination Be Counterproductive?" *Journal of International Economics,* 18 (May 1985): 199–217.

Svensson, Lars. "An Interpretation of Recent Research on Exchange Rate Target Zones." *Journal of Economic Perspectives,* 6 (1992): 119–144.

GLOSSARY

ABSORPTION A nation's total expenditures on final goods and services net of exports.

ABSORPTION APPROACH A theory of balance-of-payments and exchange-rate determination that emphasizes the role of a nation's expenditures, or absorption, and income. According to the absorption approach, if a nation's real income exceeds the amount of goods and services that it absorbs, then the nation will run a current account surplus. If a nation's real income is less than the amount of goods and services it absorbs, then the nation will run a current account deficit.

ABSORPTION INSTRUMENT A government's ability to increase or decrease a nation's absorption by changing its own purchases of domestic output or by influencing consumption and investment expenditures.

ADVERSE SELECTION The potential for those who issue financial instruments to intend to use borrowed funds to undertake unworthy, high-risk investment projects.

AGGREGATE DEMAND SCHEDULE Combinations of real income and the price level that maintain an *IS–LM* equilibrium and thereby ensure that real income is equal to aggregate desired expenditures and that the market for real money balances is in equilibrium.

AGGREGATE EXPENDITURES SCHEDULE A schedule depicting total desired expenditures by households, firms, and the government at each and every level of real national income.

AGGREGATE NET AUTONOMOUS EXPENDITURES The total amount of autonomous consumption, autonomous investment, autonomous government spending, and autonomous export spending, which are assumed to be independent of the level of national income.

AGGREGATE SUPPLY SCHEDULE A schedule depicting volumes of real output produced by all workers and firms at each possible price level.

AMERICAN OPTION An option in which the holder may buy or sell a security any time before or including the date at which the contract expires.

ANNOUNCEMENT EFFECT A change in private market interest rates or exchange rates that results from an anticipation of near-term changes in market conditions signaled by a central bank policy action.

ASSIGNMENT PROBLEM The problem of determining whether the central bank or the finance ministry should assume responsibility for achieving a nation's domestic or international policy objectives.

ASYMMETRIC INFORMATION Possession of information by one

party in a financial transaction that is not available to the other party.

AUTOMATED CLEARING HOUSE (ACH) A computer-based payments facility that interchanges credits and debits electronically.

AUTOMATED TELLER MACHINE (ATM) NETWORKS Bank-operated computer terminals that individuals can use to perform operations such as cash withdrawals.

AUTONOMOUS CONSUMPTION The amount of household consumption spending on domestically produced goods and services that is independent of the level of real income.

AUTONOMOUS EXPENDITURES MULTIPLIER A measure of the size of the multiple effect on equilibrium real income caused by a change in aggregate autonomous expenditures, which is equal to $1/(MPS + MPIM) = 1/(1 - MPC)$.

AUTONOMOUS INVESTMENT Desired investment that is independent of the level of real income.

BALANCE OF PAYMENTS SYSTEM A system of accounts that measures transactions of goods, services, income, and financial assets between domestic residents, businesses, and governments and the rest of the world during a specific time period.

BANK FOR INTERNATIONAL SETTLEMENTS (BIS) An institution based in Basle, Switzerland, which serves as an international loan trustee, as an agent for central banks, and a center of economic cooperation among the Group of Ten nations.

BASE YEAR A reference year for price-level comparisons, which is a year in which nominal GDP is equal to real GDP, so that the GDP deflator's value is equal to one.

BASIS POINT One hundredth of one percent.

BEGGAR-THY-NEIGHBOR EFFECT A policy action in a nation that benefits that nation's economy but that worsens economic performance in another nation.

BID–ASK MARGIN The difference between the *ask price,* or price at which a currency is offered for sale, and the *bid price,* or price offered for the purchase of the currency, expressed as a percent of the *ask price.*

BID–ASK SPREAD The difference between the *bid price,* or price offered for the purchase of a currency, and the *ask price,* or price at which the currency is offered for sale.

BOOK-ENTRY SECURITY SYSTEMS Computer systems that the Federal Reserve uses to maintain records of sales of treasury securities and interest and principal payments.

BORROWED RESERVES Reserves that central banks supply directly to private banks in the form of advances.

BP SCHEDULE A set of real income–nominal interest rate combinations that are consistent with a balance-of-payments equilibrium in which the current account balance and capital account balance sum to zero.

BUSINESS CYCLES Periods of fluctuation in real GDP around its natural level.

CALL OPTION An option contract giving the owner the right to purchase a financial instrument at a specific price.

CAMBRIDGE EQUATION A theory of the demand for money developed by economists at Cambridge University. The Cambridge equation postulates that the quantity of money demanded is a fraction of nominal income.

CAPACITY OUTPUT LEVEL The level of real GDP that could be produced if all factors of production were fully employed.

CAPITAL ACCOUNT A tabulation of the flows of financial assets between domestic private residents and foreign private residents.

CAPITAL CONTROLS Legal restrictions on the ability of a nation's residents to hold and exchange assets denominated in foreign currencies.

CAPITAL GAIN A rise in the value of a financial instrument at the time it is sold, as compared with its market value at the time it was purchased.

CAPITAL LOSS A decline in the market value of a financial instrument at the time it is sold, as compared with its market value at the time it was purchased.

CAPITAL MOBILITY The extent to which financial resources can flow across a nation's borders.

CAPITAL REQUIREMENTS Minimum equity capital standards that national regulatory agencies impose on banks.

CENTRAL BANKER CONTRACT A legally binding agreement between a government and a central banking official that holds the official responsible for a nation's inflation performance.

CLEARING HOUSE INTERBANK PAYMENTS SYSTEM (CHIPS) A privately owned and operated large-value wire transfer system linking about 120 U.S. banks, which allows them to transmit large payments relating primarily to foreign exchange and Eurocurrency transactions.

COMPOSITE CURRENCY A currency unit in which the value is expressed as a weighted average of a selected basket of currencies.

CONSERVATIVE POLICYMAKER A central bank official who dislikes inflation more than an average citizen in society and who thereby is less willing to induce discretionary increases in the quantity of money in an effort to achieve short-run increases in real output.

CONSUMER PRICE INDEX (CPI) A weighted sum of prices of goods and services that the government determines a typical consumer purchases each year.

CONVERTIBILITY The ability to freely exchange a currency for a reserve commodity or reserve currency.

CORE CAPITAL Defined by the Basel capital standards as shareholders' equity plus retained earnings.

COUNTRY RISK The possibility of losses on holdings of financial instruments issued in another nation because of political uncertainty within that nation.

COUPON RETURN A fixed interest return that a bond yields each year.

COVERED EXPOSURE A foreign exchange risk that has been completely eliminated with a hedging instrument.

COVERED INTEREST PARITY A condition relating interest differentials to the forward premium or discount.

CRAWLING PEG An exchange rate arrangement in which a country pegs its currency to the currency of another nation, but allows the parity value to change at regular time intervals.

CREDIT ENTRY A positive entry in the balance of payments that records a transaction resulting in a payment from abroad to a domestic resident.

CREDIT RISK The risk of loss that could take place if one party to an exchange were to fail to abide by terms under which both parties originally had agreed to make the exchange.

CROSS RATE A bilateral exchange rate calculated from two other bilateral exchange rates.

CROWDING OUT EFFECT A decline in real private investment spending induced by a rise in the demand for money and the equilibrium nominal interest rate caused by a rise in equilibrium real income that follows an expansionary fiscal policy action.

CURRENCY BASKET PEG An exchange rate arrangement in which a country pegs its currency to the weighted average value of a basket or selected number of currencies.

CURRENCY BOARD OR INDEPENDENT CURRENCY AUTHORITY An independent monetary agency that substitutes for a central bank. The currency board pegs the value of the domestic currency, and changes in the foreign reserve holdings of the currency board determine the level of the domestic money stock.

CURRENCY FUTURE An agreement to deliver to another a standardized quantity of a specific nation's currency at a designated future date.

CURRENCY OPTION A contract granting the right to buy or sell a given amount of a nation's currency at a certain price within a specific period of time.

CURRENCY SWAP An exchange of payment flows denominated in different currencies.

CURRENT ACCOUNT Measures the flow of goods, services, income, and transfers or gifts between domestic residents, businesses, and governments and the rest of the world.

CURRENT YIELD The coupon return on a bond divided by the bond's market price.

CYCLICAL UNEMPLOYMENT The fraction of a nation's labor force composed of individuals who have lost employment owing to business-cycle fluctuations.

DAYLIGHT OVERDRAFTS Bank overdrawals of reserve deposit accounts at Federal Reserve banks, which take place when they wire funds in excess of their balances in those accounts.

DEBIT ENTRY A negative entry in the balance of payments that records a transaction resulting in a payment abroad by a domestic resident.

DEFAULT RISK The possibility that an individual or business that issues a financial instrument may be unable to meet its obligations to repay the principal or to make interest payments.

DERIVATIVE CREDIT RISKS Risks stemming from the potential default by a party in a derivative contract or from unexpected changes in credit exposure because of changes in the market yields of instruments on which derivative yields depend.

DERIVATIVE MARKET RISKS Risks arising from unanticipated changes in derivatives market liquidity or payments-system failures.

DERIVATIVE OPERATING RISKS Risks owing to a lack of adequate management controls or from managerial inexperience with derivative securities.

DERIVATIVE SECURITY A financial instrument in which the return depends on the returns of other financial instruments.

DEVALUE A situation in which a nation with a pegged exchange rate arrangement changes the pegged, or parity, value of its currency so that it takes a *greater* number of domestic currency units to purchase one unit of the foreign currency to which the nation's currency value is pegged.

DIRECT FOREIGN INVESTMENT The acquisition of foreign financial assets that results in an ownership share in the foreign entity of 10 percent or greater.

DISCOUNT RATE The interest rate that the Federal Reserve charges on discount window loans that it extends to depository institutions.

DISCOUNTED PRESENT VALUE The value today of a payment to be received at a future date.

DOLLAR-STANDARD EXCHANGE RATE SYSTEM An exchange rate arrangement in which a country pegs its currency to the U.S. dollar and freely exchanges the domestic currency for the dollar at the pegged rate.

DOMESTIC CREDIT Total domestic securities and loans held as assets by a central bank.

DURATION A measure of the average time during which all payments of principal and interest on a financial instrument are made.

ECONOMIC EFFICIENCY The allocation of scarce resources at minimum cost.

ECONOMIC EXPOSURE The risk that changes in exchange values might alter a firm's present value of future income streams.

ECONOMIES OF SCALE Cost savings from pooling funds for centralized management.

EFFECTIVE EXCHANGE RATE A measure of the weighted-average value of a currency relative to a selected group of currencies.

ELASTICITIES APPROACH An approach that emphasizes changes in the prices of goods and services as the main determinant of a nation's balance of payments and the exchange value of its currency.

EQUITIES Ownership shares that might or might not pay the holder a dividend, whose values rise and fall with savers' perceived value of the issuing enterprise.

EUROBONDS Long-term debt instruments denominated in a currency other than that of the country in which the instrument is issued.

EUROCOMMERCIAL PAPER Unsecured short-term debt instrument issued in a currency other than that of the country in which the instrument is issued.

EUROCURRENCY A bank deposit denominated in a currency other than that of the nation in which the bank deposit is located.

EUROCURRENCY MARKET A market for the borrowing and lending of Eurocurrency deposits.

EURONOTES Short- and medium-term debt instruments issued in a currency other than that of the country in which the instrument is issued.

EUROPEAN CURRENCY UNIT (ECU) A composite currency of twelve of the participating countries of the European Union.

EUROPEAN OPTION An option in which the holder may buy or sell a financial instrument only on the day that the contract expires.

EXCESS RESERVES Cash assets that banks hold as a contingency against a need for liquidity.

EXCHANGE RATE ARRANGEMENT OR EXCHANGE RATE SYSTEM A set of rules that determine the international value of a currency.

EXCHANGE RATE BAND A range of exchange values, with an upper and lower limit within which the exchange value of the domestic currency can fluctuate.

EXCHANGE RATE INSTABILITY A situation in which a currency depreciation increases the difference between the quantity of foreign exchange supplied and the quantity of foreign exchange demanded instead of reducing the difference.

EXERCISE PRICE The price at which the holder of an option has the right to buy or sell a financial instrument; also known as the strike price.

EXPECTATIONS THEORY A theory of the term structure of interest rates that views bonds with differing maturities as perfect substitutes, causing their yields to differ solely because traders anticipated that short-term interest rates will rise or fall.

EXPENDITURE-SWITCHING INSTRUMENT A government's ability to alter, or switch, expenditures among imports and exports by enacting policies that change their relative prices.

EXTERNALITY A benefit or cost felt by one individual or group stemming from actions by another individual or group in another location or market.

FEDWIRE A large-value wire transfer system operated by the Federal Reserve that is open to all banking institutions that legally must maintain required cash reserves with the Fed.

FINANCIAL INTERMEDIATION Indirect finance through the services of financial institutions that channel funds from savers to those who ultimately make capital investments.

FINANCIAL TRADING SYSTEMS Institutional mechanisms linking traders of financial instruments.

FISCAL AGENT A term describing a central bank's role as an agent of its government's finance ministry or treasury department, in which the central bank issues, services, and redeems debts on the government's behalf.

FISHER EQUATION A condition that defines the real interest rate as the nominal interest rate less the expected rate of inflation.

FLEXIBLE EXCHANGE RATE SYSTEM An exchange rate arrangement whereby a nation allows market forces to determine the international value of its currency.

FOREIGN EXCHANGE MARKET EFFICIENCY When the spot and forward exchange rates reflect, and adjust quickly to, new and relevant information.

FOREIGN EXCHANGE RISK The risk that the value of a future receipt or obligation will change due to a change in foreign exchange rates.

45-DEGREE LINE A line that cuts in half the 90-degree angle of the coordinate axes on a diagram relating real income to aggregate desired expenditures and that provides a potential set of equilibrium points at which real income equals aggregate desired expenditures.

FORWARD EXCHANGE MARKET A market for contracts that ensure the future delivery of a foreign currency at a specified exchange rate.

FORWARD PREMIUM OR DISCOUNT The difference between the forward exchange rate and the spot exchange rate, expressed as a percentage of the spot exchange rate.

FRICTIONAL UNEMPLOYMENT The fraction of a nation's labor force composed of people who are temporarily out of work.

FUTURES CONTRACT An agreement to deliver to another a given amount of a standardized commodity or financial instrument at a designated future date.

FUTURES OPTIONS Options to buy or sell futures contracts.

GDP PRICE DEFLATOR A measure of the overall price level; equal to nominal gross domestic product divided by real gross domestic product.

GROSS DOMESTIC PRODUCT (GDP) The market value of all final goods and services produced within a nation's borders during a given period.

GROUP OF FIVE (G5) The nations of France, Germany, Japan, the United Kingdom, and the United States.

GROUP OF SEVEN (G7) The G5 plus Canada and Italy.

GROUP OF TEN (G10) Belgium, Canada, France, Germany, Italy, Japan, the Netherlands, Sweden, the United Kingdom, and the United States.

HEDGE A financial strategy that reduces the risk of capital losses arising from interest rate risks or currency risks.

HEDGING The act of offsetting or eliminating risk exposure.

HERSTATT RISK Liquidity, credit, and systemic risks across international borders.

INCOME IDENTITY A truism that states that real income is allocated among real household consumption, real household saving, real net taxes, and real imports.

INFLATION BIAS Tendency for an economy to experience persistent inflation as a result of the time inconsistency problem and the lack of policy credibility.

INSIDER INFORMATION Information that is available to inside directors and officers of a corporation but that generally is unavailable to the general public or to depository institutions that lend to the corporation.

INSOLVENCY A situation in which the value of a bank's assets falls below the value of its liabilities.

INSTITUTIONAL INVESTORS Institutions, such as insurance companies, investment companies, and pension funds, that manage funds on the behalf of designated groups of individuals.

INTERBANK FUNDS MARKETS Markets for large-denomination interbank loans and one-day to one-week maturities.

INTEREST-RATE FORWARD CONTRACT Contracts committing the issuer to sell a financial instrument at a given interest rate as of a specific date.

INTEREST RATE FUTURES Contracts to buy or sell a standardized denomination of a specific financial instrument at a given price at a certain date in the future.

INTEREST RATE RISK The possibility that the market value of a financial instrument will change as interest rates vary.

INTEREST-RATE SWAP A contractual exchange of one set of interest payments for another.

INTERNATIONAL CAPITAL MARKETS Markets for cross-border exchange of financial instruments that have maturities of one year or more.

INTERNATIONAL FINANCIAL DIVERSIFICATION Holding financial instruments issued in various countries to spread portfolio risks.

INTERNATIONAL MONETARY FUND A supranational organization whose major responsibility is to lend reserves to member nations experiencing a shortage.

INTERNATIONAL MONEY MARKETS
Markets for cross-border exchange of
financial instruments with maturities
of less than one year.

INTERNATIONAL POLICY COOPERATION
The adoption of institutions and
procedures by which national
policymakers can inform each other
about their objectives, policy
strategies, and national economic
data.

INTERNATIONAL POLICY COORDINATION
The joint determination of economic
policies within a group of nations for
the intended benefit of the group as a
whole.

INTERNATIONAL POLICY EXTERNALITY
A benefit or cost for one nation's
economy owing to a policy action
undertaken in another nation.

INTRA-MARGINAL INTERVENTIONS
Central bank purchases or sales of
foreign exchange reserves at exchange
rate levels within a target zone.

IS SCHEDULE A set of possible
combinations of real income and
the nominal interest rate that are
necessary to maintain the
income–expenditure equilibrium,
$y = c + i + g + x$ for a given level
of aggregate net autonomous
expenditures.

IS–LM EQUILIBRIUM A single point
shared in common by the *IS* and *LM*
schedules, at which the economy
simultaneously attains both an
income–expenditure equilibrium and
equilibrium in the money market.

JAMAICA ACCORDS A meeting of the
member nations of the IMF,
occurring in January 1976, amending
the constitution of the IMF to allow,
among other things, each member
nation to determine its own exchange
rate arrangement.

J-CURVE EFFECT A phenomenon in
which a depreciation of the domestic
currency causes a nation's balance of
payments to worsen before it improves.

**LARGE-VALUE WIRE TRANSFER
SYSTEMS** Payments systems such as
Fedwire and CHIPS that permit the
electronic transmission of large
volumes of funds.

**LAW OF DIMINISHING MARGINAL
RETURNS** The fact that the additional
output produced by an additional
unit of labor ultimately falls as firms
employ more units of labor.

LEANING AGAINST THE WIND Central
bank interventions to halt or reverse
the current trend in the market
exchange value of its nation's currency.

LEANING WITH THE WIND Central
bank interventions to support or
speed along the current trend in the
market exchange value of its nation's
currency.

LENDER OF LAST RESORT A central
banking function in which the central
bank stands willing to lend to any
temporarily illiquid but otherwise
solvent banking institution to prevent
its illiquid position from leading to a
general loss of confidence in that
institution.

LIQUIDITY EFFECT A reduction in the
equilibrium nominal interest rate
stemming from an increase in the
nominal quantity of money in
circulation.

LIQUIDITY RISK The risk of loss that
may occur if a payment is not
received when due.

LM SCHEDULE A set of combinations
of real income and the nominal
interest rate that maintains money
market equilibrium.

LOCOMOTIVE EFFECT A stimulus to
real income growth in one nation
due to an increase in real income
in another country.

LOMBARD RATE The specific name
given to the interest rate on central
bank advances that German and Swiss
central banks set above current market
interest rates.

LONG POSITION An obligation to
purchase a financial instrument at a
given price and at a specific time.

LOUVRE ACCORD A meeting of the
central bankers and finance ministers
of the G7 nations, less Italy, that took
place in February 1987. The
participants announced that the
exchange value of the dollar had
fallen to a level consistent with
"economic fundamentals" and that
central banks would intervene in the
foreign exchange market only to
ensure stability of exchange rates.

MANAGED OR DIRTY FLOAT An
exchange rate arrangement in which
a nation allows the international
value of its currency to be primarily
determined by market forces, but
intervenes from time to time to
stabilize its currency.

MARGINAL PRODUCT OF LABOR The
additional quantity of output that
firms can produce by employing
another unit of labor.

**MARGINAL PROPENSITY TO CONSUME
(MPC)** The additional consumption
resulting from an increase in disposable
income; a change in consumption
spending divided by a corresponding
change in disposable income; the slope
of the consumption function.

**MARGINAL PROPENSITY TO IMPORT
(MPIM)** The additional import
expenditures stemming from an
increase in disposable income; a

change in import spending divided by a corresponding change in disposable income; the slope of the import function.

MARGINAL PROPENSITY TO SAVE (*MPS*) The additional saving caused by an increase in disposable income; a change in saving divided by a corresponding change in disposable income; the slope of the saving function.

MARKET STRUCTURES The organization of the loan and deposit markets in which bank rivals compete.

MARSHALL–LERNER CONDITION A necessary condition for exchange rate stability, in which the sum of the elasticity of import demand and the elasticity of export supply must exceed unity.

MERCANTILISM A view that a primary determinant of a nation's wealth is its inflows of payments resulting from international trade and commerce, so that a nation can gain by enacting policies that spur exports while limiting imports.

MONETARY APPROACH Relates changes in a nation's balance of payments and the exchange value of its currency to differences between the quantity of money demanded and the quantity of money supplied.

MONETARY BASE Central bank holdings of domestic securities and loans plus foreign exchange reserves, or the sum of currency and bank reserves.

MONETARY ORDER A set of laws and regulations that establishes the framework within which individuals conduct and settle transactions.

MONETARY POLICY AUTONOMY The capability of a central bank to engage in monetary policy actions independent of the actions of other central banks.

MONETARY UNION A set of countries that choose to use a common currency.

MONEY MULTIPLIER The number by which a reserve measure is multiplied to obtain the total money stock of an economy.

MORAL HAZARD The possibility that a borrower might engage in more risky behavior after receiving the funds from a lender.

MULTIPLIER EFFECT The ratio of a change in the equilibrium real income to an increase in autonomous net aggregate expenditures. When the aggregate expenditure schedule shifts vertically, the equilibrium level of national income changes by a multiple of the amount of the shift, and the *IS* schedule shifts by this magnitude.

NATURAL GROSS DOMESTIC PRODUCT A level of real GDP that lies on a nation's long-run growth path.

NATURAL RATE OF UNEMPLOYMENT The sum of the rates of frictional and structural unemployment, or the unemployment rate that would arise if a nation's economy were always on its long-run growth path.

NET CREDITOR A nation whose total claims on foreigners exceed the total claims of foreigners on the nation.

NET DEBTOR A nation whose total claims on foreigners are less than the total claims of foreigners on the nation.

NETTING The process of combining separate risk exposures that a firm faces in its foreign-currency-denominated payments and receipts into a single net risk exposure.

NOMINAL EXCHANGE RATE A bilateral exchange rate that is unadjusted for changes in the two nations' price levels.

NOMINAL GROSS DOMESTIC PRODUCT The current market value of all final goods and services produced by a nation during a given period with no adjustment for prices.

NOMINAL YIELD The coupon return on a bond divided by the bond's face value.

NONBORROWED RESERVES Reserves that central banks supply to private banks through open-market operations rather than via advances.

NORMAL PROFIT A profit level just sufficient to compensate bank owners for holding equity shares in banks rather than other enterprises.

OFF-BALANCE-SHEET BANKING Bank activities that earn income without expanding the assets and liabilities that they report on their balance sheets.

OFFICIAL SETTLEMENTS BALANCE A balance of payments account that tabulates transactions of reserve assets by official government agencies.

OPEN-MARKET OPERATIONS Central bank purchases or sales of government or private securities.

OPERATING PROCEDURE A central bank guideline for conducting monetary policy over an interval spanning several weeks or months.

OPTIMAL CURRENCY AREA
A geographic area within which labor is sufficiently mobile to permit speedy adjustments to payments imbalances and regional unemployment so that exchange rates can be fixed and a common currency can be adopted.

OPTION A financial contract giving the owner the right to buy or sell an underlying financial instrument at a certain price within a specific period of time.

OVERVALUED CURRENCY A currency in which the current market-determined value is higher than the value predicted by an economic theory or model.

PASS-THROUGH EFFECT The effect of a currency depreciation that results in higher domestic prices of imported goods and services.

PAYMENT SYSTEM A term that broadly refers to the set of mechanisms by which consumers, businesses, governments, and financial institutions make payments.

PEGGED EXCHANGE RATE SYSTEM
An exchange rate arrangement in which a country pegs the international value of the domestic currency to the currency of another nation.

PENALTY RATE The general term for any interest rate on central bank advances that is set above prevailing market interest rates.

PER-CAPITA GROSS DOMESTIC PRODUCT The total value of final goods and services produced within a country during a given year divided by the number of people residing in the country.

PERPETUITY A bond with an infinite term to maturity.

PLAZA AGREEMENT A meeting of the central bankers and finance ministers of the G5 nations that took place at the Plaza Hotel in New York in September 1985. The participants announced that the exchange value of the dollar was too strong and that the nations would coordinate their intervention actions in order to drive down the value of the dollar.

POINT-OF-SALE (POS) NETWORKS
Systems in which people make payments for retail purchases via direct deductions from their deposit accounts at banks.

POLICY CREDIBILITY The believability of a policymaker's commitment to a stated intention.

POLICY INSTRUMENTS A financial variable that central banks can control in an effort to attain its policy objectives.

PORTFOLIO APPROACH Relates changes in a nation's balance of payments and the exchange value of its currency to the quantities demanded and supplied of domestic money, domestic securities, and foreign securities.

PORTFOLIO BALANCE EFFECT An exchange rate adjustment resulting from changes in government or central bank holdings of foreign-currency-denominated financial instruments that influences the equilibrium prices of the instruments.

PORTFOLIO DIVERSIFICATION Holding financial instruments with different characteristics so as to spread risks across the entire set of instruments.

PORTFOLIO INVESTMENT The acquisition of foreign financial assets that results in less than a 10 percent ownership share in the entity.

PORTFOLIO MOTIVE Modern term for Keynes's essential argument for a speculative motive for holding money, in which people hold both money and bonds and adjust their holdings of both components of financial wealth based on their anticipations concerning interest rate movements.

PRECAUTIONARY MOTIVE The motive to hold money for use in unplanned exchanges.

PREFERRED HABITAT THEORY
A theory of the term structure of interest rates that views bonds as imperfectly substitutable, so that yields on longer-term bonds must be greater than those on shorter-term bonds even if short-term interest rates are not expected to rise or fall.

PRICE ELASTICITY OF DEMAND
A measure of the proportional change of the quantity demanded to a proportional change in price.

PRICE ELASTICITY OF SUPPLY
A measure of the proportional change of the quantity supplied of a good, service, or financial instrument to a proportional change in its price.

PRINCIPAL The amount of credit extended when one makes a loan or purchases a bond.

PRODUCER PRICE INDEX (PPI) A weighted average of the prices of goods and services that the government determines a typical business purchases from other businesses during a given period.

PRODUCT IDENTITY A truism that states that real national product is the sum of real household consumption, real realized investment, real government spending, and real export spending.

PRODUCTION FUNCTION The relationship between the quantities of factors of production employed by firms and their output of goods and services using the current technology.

PURCHASING POWER PARITY A condition that states that if international arbitrage is unhindered, the price of a good or service in one nation should be the same as the exchange-rate-adjusted price of the same good or service in another nation.

PUT OPTION An option contract giving the owner the right to sell a financial instrument at a specific price.

RATIONAL EXPECTATIONS HYPOTHESIS The hypothesis that people form expectations using all available past and current information, plus their understanding of how the economy operates.

REAL CONSUMPTION The real amount of spending by households on domestically produced goods and services.

REAL DISPOSABLE INCOME A household's real after-tax income.

REAL EXCHANGE RATE A bilateral exchange rate that has been adjusted for price changes that occurred in the two nations.

REAL EXPORTS Real value of goods and services produced by domestic firms and exported to other countries.

REAL GROSS DOMESTIC PRODUCT A price-adjusted measure of aggregate output, or nominal GDP divided by the GDP price deflator.

REAL HOUSEHOLD SAVING The amount of income that households save through financial markets.

REAL IMPORTS The real flow of spending by households for the purchase of goods and services from firms in other countries.

REAL INTEREST PARITY A condition that postulates that in equilibrium the real rate of interest on similar financial instruments of two nations is equal.

REAL INTEREST RATE The nominal interest rate less the rate of price inflation expected to prevail over the maturity period of the financial instrument.

REAL MONEY BALANCES The price-level-adjusted value of the nominal quantity of money, defined as the nominal money stock divided by the price level.

REAL NET TAXES The amount of real taxes paid to the government by households, net of transfer payments.

REAL REALIZED INVESTMENT SPENDING Actual real firm expenditures in the product markets.

REALIGNMENT A change in an official exchange rate target.

REGULATORY ARBITRAGE The act of attempting to avoid banking regulations established within one's home country by moving banking offices and funds to nations with less stringent regulations.

REINVESTMENT RISK The possibility that available yields on short-term financial instruments may decline, so that holdings of longer-term instruments might be preferable.

RESERVE CURRENCY The currency commonly used to settle international debts and to express the exchange value of other nations' currencies.

RESERVE REQUIREMENTS Central bank regulations requiring private banks to hold specified fractions of transactions and term deposits either as vault cash or as funds on deposit at the central bank.

REVALUE A situation in which a nation with a pegged exchange rate arrangement changes the pegged, or parity, value of its currency so that it takes a *smaller* number of domestic currency units to purchase one unit of the foreign currency to which the nation's currency value is pegged.

RISK-ADJUSTED ASSETS A weighted average of bank assets that regulators compute to account for risk differences across assets.

RISK-BASED CAPITAL REQUIREMENTS Regulatory capital standards that account for different risk factors that distinguish banks' assets.

RISK PREMIUM The amount by which one instrument's yield exceeds another because it is riskier and less liquid.

RISK STRUCTURE OF INTEREST RATES The relationship among yields on financial instruments that have the same maturity but differ because of variations in default risk, liquidity, and tax rates.

SEGMENTED MARKETS THEORY A theory of the term structure of interest rates that views bonds with differing maturities as nonsubstitutable, so that their yields differ because they are determined in separate markets.

SEIGNIORAGE Central bank profits resulting from the value of a flow increase in a country's money stock over and above the cost of money production.

SHORT POSITION An obligation to sell a financial instrument at a given price and at a specific time.

SPATIAL ARBITRAGE The act of profiting from exchange rate differences that prevail in different markets.

SPECIAL DRAWING RIGHT (SDR) A composite currency of the International Monetary Fund in which the value is based on a weighted average value of the currencies of five member nations.

SPOT MARKET A market for contracts requiring the immediate sale or purchase of an asset.

STERILIZATION A central bank policy of altering domestic credit in an equal and opposite direction relative to any variation in foreign exchange reserves so as to prevent the monetary base from changing.

STOCK INDEX FUTURE Promises of future delivery of a portfolio of stocks represented by a stock price index.

STOCK OPTIONS Options to buy or sell firm equity shares.

STRATEGIC POLICYMAKING The formulation of planned policy actions in light of the structural linkages among nations and the manner in which other countries' policymakers may conduct their own policies.

STRUCTURAL INTERDEPENDENCE The interconnectedness of countries' markets for goods and services, financial markets, and payment systems, which causes events in one nation to have effects on the economy of another nation.

STRUCTURAL UNEMPLOYMENT The fraction of a nation's labor force composed of people who would like to be employed but who do not possess skills and other characteristics required to obtain jobs.

SUBSIDY RATE An interest rate on central bank advances that is set below other market interest rates.

SUPPLEMENTARY CAPITAL A measure that many national banking regulators use to calculate required capital, which includes certain preferred stock and most subordinated debt.

SWAP A contract entailing an exchange of payment flows between two parties.

SYSTEMIC RISK The risk that some payment intermediaries may not be able to meet the terms of payment agreements because of failures by other institutions to settle transactions that otherwise are not related.

TARGET ZONE A range of permitted exchange rate variation between upper and lower exchange rate bands that a central bank defends by selling or purchasing foreign exchange reserves.

TERM PREMIUM An amount by which the yield on a long-term bond must exceed the yield on a short-term bond to make individuals willing to hold either bond if they expect short-term bond yields to remain unchanged.

TERM STRUCTURE OF INTEREST RATES The relationship among yields on financial instruments with identical risk, liquidity, and tax characteristics but differing terms to maturity.

THEORY OF OPTIMAL CURRENCY AREAS A means of determining the size of a geographic area within which residents' welfare is greater if their governments fix exchange rates or adopt a common currency.

TIME INCONSISTENCY PROBLEM A situation in which a policymaker can better attain its objectives by violating a prior policy stance.

TOTAL CAPITAL Under the Basel bank capital standards, this is the sum of core capital and supplementary capital.

TRANSACTION EXPOSURE The risk that the cost of a transaction, or the proceeds from a transaction, in terms of the domestic currency, may change due to changes in exchange rates.

TRANSACTIONS MOTIVE The motive to hold money for use in planned exchanges.

TRANSFER PAYMENTS Governmentally managed income redistributions.

TRANSLATION EXPOSURE Foreign exchange risk that results from the conversion of the value of a firm's foreign-currency-denominated assets and liabilities into a common currency value.

TRIANGULAR ARBITRAGE Three transactions undertaken in three different markets and/or in three different currencies in order to profit from differences in prices.

UNCOVERED INTEREST PARITY A condition relating interest differentials to an expected change in the spot exchange rate of the domestic currency.

UNDERVALUED CURRENCY A currency in which the current market-determined value is lower than that predicted by an economic theory or model.

UNEMPLOYMENT RATE The percentage of a nation's labor force that is unemployed.

UNIVERSAL BANKING Banking environment under which depository institutions face few if any restrictions on their authority to offer full ranges of financial services and to own equity shares in corporations.

VALUE OF THE MARGINAL PRODUCT OF LABOR The price of output times the marginal product of labor.

VEHICLE CURRENCY A currency that individuals and businesses most often use to conduct international transactions.

WEALTH IDENTITY Shows the types of assets that constitute the household's total stock of wealth.

WORLD INDEX FUND A portfolio of globally issued financial instruments with yields that historically have moved in offsetting directions.

YIELD CURVE A chart giving the relationship among yields on bonds that differ only in their terms to maturity.

YIELD TO MATURITY The rate of return on a bond if it is held until it matures, which reflects the market price of the bond, the bond's coupon return, and any capital gain from holding the bond to maturity.

ZERO COUPON BONDS Bonds that pay lump-sum amounts at maturity.

INDEX

A

absorption approach, 297–302
   and current account balance,
      298–99
   economic expansion and
      contraction, 299–300
   policy instruments in, 300–301
absorption instrument, 301
ACH. *See* automated clearing house
adverse selection, 199
aggregate demand, 448–62, 478,
   499–502
aggregate expenditures schedule,
   348–49
aggregate net autonomous
   expenditures, 349
aggregate supply, 463–76
agriculture, 4
air pollution, 10
Alexander, Sidney, 300
Altunbas, Yener, 201
American options, 159
announcement effect, 251–52, 272
anti-inflationary monetary policy,
   81, 82, 264
Apollo space program, 335–36
appreciation of currency, 39–40
arbitrage, 53–54
   and purchasing power parity,
      62–63
   See also foreign exchange arbitrage
Argentina, 206
artificial currency units. *See* composite
   currencies
Asian interest rates, 122
ask price, 42
assignment problem of central banks,
   265–67

astronauts, 335–36
asymmetric information, 197–98
asymmetric shocks, 520
ATM networks. *See* automated teller
   machine (ATM) networks
automated clearing house (ACH),
   217–18
automated financial trading, 214–16
   See also electronic trading
automated teller machine (ATM)
   networks, 218
automatic clearing networks, 215
autonomous consumption, 343
autonomous dissaving, 341
autonomous expenditure volatility,
   435–37
autonomous expenditures
   multiplier, 354
autonomous import spending, 341
autonomous investment, 350

B

balance of payments, 17–29
   capital account, 20–21, 29–31
   current account, 19–20, 29
   deficits and surpluses in, 22–25
   equilibrium in, 23, 365–66
   examples of, 25–27
   and the exchange rate, 289–92
   merchandise trade, 23
   and money stock, 317
   official settlements balance, 22
   overall, 23
balance-of-payments position, 368–69
Banca d'Italia, 244, 257
banco (merchant's bench), 214
bank bailouts, 209

Bank of Canada, 251, 253
   See also Canada
bank capital requirements, 208–13
Bank of China, 209
   See also China
Bank of England, 77, 82, 208,
   228, 235
   history of, 237, 248
   interest rates of, 251
   on the WWW, 208, 265
   See also British Empire; British
      pounds; United Kingdom
Bank of France, 228, 409
   See also France
Bank for International Settlements
   (BIS), 99, 208, 497–98
   Annual Report, 125, 179
   and reserve requirements, 255
Bank of Japan, 250, 251
   balance sheet of, 238, 239, 240
   interventions by, 526
   NET system, 219
   and open-market operations, 253
   See also Japan
Bank of Lithuania, 95, 96
   See also Lithuania
Bank of Mexico, 91
   See also Mexican peso; Mexico
bank reserves
   demand for, 257–59
   equilibrium rates, 259–61
   and the monetary base in central
      banks, 256–57
bank robberies, 196
bank runs, 249
Bank of Thailand, 35–36, 122
   See also Thailand
Bank of the United States, 235–36
   See also Federal Reserve System

543